Electronic Services:
Concepts, Methodologies, Tools and Applications

Information Resources Management Association
USA

Volume II

INFORMATION SCIENCE REFERENCE

Hershey • New York

Director of Editorial Content:	Kristin Klinger
Director of Book Publications:	Julia Mosemann
Acquisitions Editor:	Lindsay Johnston
Development Editor:	David DeRicco
Publishing Assistant:	Michael Brehm
Typesetters:	Michael Brehm, Devvin Earnest, Keith Glazewski, Myla Harty, Christopher Hrobak, Ricardo Mendoza, Greg Snader, Jamie Snavely, Sean Woznicki, Deanna Zombro
Production Editor:	Jamie Snavely
Cover Design:	Lisa Tosheff
Printed at:	Yurchak Printing Inc.

Published in the United States of America by
Information Science Reference (an imprint of IGI Global)
701 E. Chocolate Avenue
Hershey PA 17033
Tel: 717-533-8845
Fax: 717-533-8661
E-mail: cust@igi-global.com
Web site: http://www.igi-global.com/reference

and in the United Kingdom by
Information Science Reference (an imprint of IGI Global)
3 Henrietta Street
Covent Garden
London WC2E 8LU
Tel: 44 20 7240 0856
Fax: 44 20 7379 0609
Web site: http://www.eurospanbookstore.com

Library of Congress Cataloging-in-Publication Data

Electronic services : concepts, methodologies, tools and applications /
Information Resources Management Association, editor. p. cm.
  Includes bibliographical references and index.
  Summary: "This multiple volume set is an all-inclusive research collection covering the latest studies on the consumption, delivery and availability of e-services"--Provided by publisher.
  ISBN 978-1-61520-967-5 (hbk.) -- ISBN 978-1-61520-968-2 (ebook) 1. Web
services. 2. Information networks. 3. Service-oriented architecture (Computer science) 4. Information technology--Management. I. Information Resources Management Association.
  TK5105.88813.E44 2010
  658.8'72--dc22
                        2010016049

British Cataloguing in Publication Data
A Cataloguing in Publication record for this book is available from the British Library.

All work contributed to this book set is original material. The views expressed in this book are those of the authors, but not necessarily of the publisher.

Additional Research Collections found in the
"Contemporary Research in Information Science and Technology"
Book Series

Data Mining and Warehousing: Concepts, Methodologies, Tools, and Applications
John Wang, Montclair University, USA • 6-volume set • ISBN 978-1-60566-056-1

Electronic Business: Concepts, Methodologies, Tools, and Applications
In Lee, Western Illinois University • 4-volume set • ISBN 978-1-59904-943-4

Electronic Commerce: Concepts, Methodologies, Tools, and Applications
S. Ann Becker, Florida Institute of Technology, USA • 4-volume set • ISBN 978-1-59904-943-4

Electronic Government: Concepts, Methodologies, Tools, and Applications
Ari-Veikko Anttiroiko, University of Tampere, Finland • 6-volume set • ISBN 978-1-59904-947-2

Knowledge Management: Concepts, Methodologies, Tools, and Applications
Murray E. Jennex, San Diego State University, USA • 6-volume set • ISBN 978-1-59904-933-5

Information Communication Technologies: Concepts, Methodologies, Tools, and Applications
Craig Van Slyke, University of Central Florida, USA • 6-volume set • ISBN 978-1-59904-949-6

Intelligent Information Technologies: Concepts, Methodologies, Tools, and Applications
Vijayan Sugumaran, Oakland University, USA • 4-volume set • ISBN 978-1-59904-941-0

Information Security and Ethics: Concepts, Methodologies, Tools, and Applications
Hamid Nemati, The University of North Carolina at Greensboro, USA • 6-volume set • ISBN 978-1-59904-937-3

Medical Informatics: Concepts, Methodologies, Tools, and Applications
Joseph Tan, Wayne State University, USA • 4-volume set • ISBN 978-1-60566-050-9

Mobile Computing: Concepts, Methodologies, Tools, and Applications
David Taniar, Monash University, Australia • 6-volume set • ISBN 978-1-60566-054-7

Multimedia Technologies: Concepts, Methodologies, Tools, and Applications
Syed Mahbubur Rahman, Minnesota State University, Mankato, USA • 3-volume set • ISBN 978-1-60566-054-7

Virtual Technologies: Concepts, Methodologies, Tools, and Applications
Jerzy Kisielnicki, Warsaw University, Poland • 3-volume set • ISBN 978-1-59904-955-7

Free institution-wide online access with the purchase of a print collection!

INFORMATION SCIENCE REFERENCE
Hershey · New York
Order online at www.igi-global.com or call 717-533-8845 ext.100
Mon–Fri 8:30am–5:00 pm (est) or fax 24 hours a day 717-533-7115

List of Contributors

Contents

Volume 1

Section I. Fundamental Concepts and Theories

This section serves as the foundation for this exhaustive reference tool by addressing crucial theories essential to the understanding of electronic services. Chapters found within these pages provide an excellent framework in which to position electronic services within the field of information science and technology. Individual contributions provide overviews of the history of electronic services, difficulties of assessing the value of web services, and the evolution, evaluation, and adoption of electronic services for business-to-business commerce. Within this introductory section, the reader can learn and choose from a compendium of expert research on the elemental theories underscoring electronic services.

Section II. Development and Design Methodologies

This section provides in-depth coverage of conceptual architectures, frameworks and methodologies related to the design and implementation of electronic services. Throughout these contributions, research fundamentals in the discipline are presented and discussed. From broad examinations to specific discussions on particular frameworks and infrastructures, the research found within this section spans the discipline while also offering detailed, specific discussions. Basic designs, as well as abstract developments, are explained within these chapters, and frameworks for designing successful web service portals, ensuring accessibility and usability, and providing electronic banking systems are included.

Section III. Tools and Technologies

This section presents extensive coverage of the technology that informs and impacts information resources management. These chapters provide an in-depth analysis of the use and development of innumerable devices and tools, while also providing insight into new and upcoming technologies, theories, and instruments that will soon be commonplace. Within these rigorously researched chapters, readers are presented with examples of the tools that facilitate and support the emergence and advancement of information resources management. In addition, the successful implementation and resulting impact of these various tools and technologies are discussed within this collection of chapters.

Volume II

Section IV. Utilization and Application

This section introduces and discusses the utilization and application of electronic services around the world. These particular selections highlight, among other topics, electronic services in countries including Thailand, Greece, Denmark and Jordan; e-banking solutions; and electronic education and student support services. Contributions included in this section provide excellent coverage of the impact of information resources management on the fabric of our present-day global village.

Section V. Organizational and Social Implications

This section includes a wide range of research pertaining to the social and organizational impact of electronic service. Chapters included in this section analyze the enablers and inhibitors of Internet technology adoption, discuss consumer attitudes towards different electronic services, consider the challenges of consumer trust and electronic services, and demonstrate the positive impact of early user involvement and participation on electronic self-services. The inquiries and methods presented in this section offer insight into the implications of electronic services at both a personal and organizational level, while also emphasizing potential areas of study within the discipline.

Section VI. Managerial Impact

This section presents contemporary coverage of the managerial implications of information resources management. Particular contributions address knowledge and skills required by IT professionals in Internet-based firms, architecture to align e-recruiting and retention processes, and protocols commonly used to implement negotiation in e-markets and electronic contracts. The managerial research provided in this section allows administrators, practitioners, and researchers to gain a better sense of how electronic services can inform their practices and behavior.

Section VII. Critical Issues

This section addresses conceptual and theoretical issues related to the field of electronic services, which include issues related to self-services, online financial activities and the security of web-based services. Within these chapters, the reader is presented with analysis of the most current and relevant conceptual inquires within this growing field of study. Particular chapters address effectiveness of self-service systems and consumer behavior when using those systems, methods to valuing a company's intellectual capital, electronic services in the library virtualization process, and security issues. Overall, contributions within this section ask unique, often theoretical questions related to the study of information resources management and, more often than not, conclude that solutions are both numerous and contradictory.

Section VIII. Emerging Trends

This section highlights research potential within the field of electronic services while exploring uncharted areas of study for the advancement of the discipline. Chapters within this section highlight new trends in sponsored strategic search, e-therapy, and meta-enterprise information systems. These contributions, which conclude this exhaustive, multi-volume set, provide emerging trends and suggestions for future research within this rapidly expanding discipline.

Preface

Electronic services have exploded in both population and popularity within the last decade. The establishment of the dot-com era in the late 90's first introduced electronic services to the common consumer, at the same time leading many companies to begin offering electronic services to end-users. In spite of the 'bursting' of the dot-com bubble in the early years of the 21st century, electronic services continue to remain an integral part of the modern information technology landscape. From academic web portals and online banking to web mining and online knowledge sharing, this constantly-evolving array of electronic services is critical to the success of modern businesses, academic communities, and consumers.

With the constant changes in the landscape of electronic services, it is a challenge for researchers, practitioners, and experts to take in the volume of innovative advances and up-to-the-moment research in this diverse field. Information Science Reference is pleased to offer a three-volume reference collection on this rapidly growing discipline, in order to empower students, researchers, academicians, and practitioners with a wide-ranging understanding of the most critical areas within this field of study. This collection provides the most comprehensive, in-depth, and recent coverage of all issues related to the development of cutting-edge electronic services, as well as a single reference source on all conceptual, methodological, technical and managerial issues, and the opportunities, future challenges and emerging trends related to the development, application, and implications of electronic services.

This collection entitled, **"Electronic Services: Concepts, Methodologies, Tools and Applications"** is organized in eight (8) distinct sections, providing the most wide-ranging coverage of topics such as: 1) Fundamental Concepts and Theories; 2) Development and Design Methodologies; 3) Tools and Technologies; 4) Utilization and Application; 5) Organizational and Social Implications; 6) Managerial Impact; 7) Critical Issues; and 8) Emerging Trends. The following provides a summary of what is covered in each section of this multi-volume reference collection:

Section 1, *Fundamental Concepts and Theories*, serves as a foundation for this extensive reference tool by addressing crucial theories essential to the understanding of information resources management. Chapters such as "E-Services: Characteristics, Scope and Conceptual Strengths" by Ada Scupola, Anders Henten and Hanne Westh Nicolajsen, and "Services, E-Services, and Nonservices" by Anders Henten give an overview of electronic services while examining the provision and development of electronic services at the conceptual level. "Web Services, Service-Oriented Computing, and Service-Oriented Architecture: Separating Hype from Reality" by John Erickson and Keng Siau sheds some light on the definition of service-oriented architecture and the difficulties of assessing the value of web services. Additional selections, including "The Evolution of B2B E-Services from First Generation E-Commerce Solutions to Multichannel Architectures" by Christine Legner, and "Electronic Marketplace Support for B2B Business Transactions" by Norm Archer focus on the evolution, evaluation, and adoption of electronic services for business-to-business commerce. These and several other foundational chapters provide a wealth of expert research on the elemental concepts and ideas surrounding electronic services.

Section 2, ***Development and Design Methodologies***, presents in-depth coverage of the conceptual design and architecture of electronic services, focusing on aspects including portal design, service design, and service delivery. Design concerns are the focus of such chapters as "Building Portal Applications" by Jana Polgar and Tony Polgar, and "Creating Successful Portals with a Design Framework" by Joe Lamantia. "The Evolving Portfolio of Business-to-Business E-Services: Service and Channel Innovation" by by Christine Legner explains why a well-designed business-to-business architecture is required to cope with the growing number of electronic services and the complexity of serving multiple electronic channels, offering solutions for how to do so. M. Ángeles Moraga, Julio Córdoba, Coral Calero, and Cristina Cachero's "A General View of Quality Models for Web Portals and a Particularization to E-Banking Domain" presents and compares several portal quality models, with a particular focus on models adapted for e-banking situations. With contributions from leading international researchers, this section offers copious developmental approaches and design methodologies for electronic services.

Section 3, ***Tools and Technologies***, presents extensive coverage of the various tools and technologies used in the development and implementation of electronic services. This comprehensive section includes such chapters as "Towards a Design Process for Integrating Product Recommendation Services in E-Markets," by Nikos Manouselis and Constantina Costopoulou, and "Web Mining for Public E-Services Personalization" by P. Markellou and A. Panayiotaki, which describe various techniques and models for providing more personalized services in online environments. "Improving M-Commerce Services Effectiveness with the Use of User-Centric Content Delivery" by Panagiotis Germanakos, Nikos Tsianos, Zacharias Lekkas, Constantinos Mourlas, and George Samaras presents tools to adapt to the challenges and constraints caused by the mobility in the business sector. Finally, electronic services and technologies for students' use are discussed in "21st Century E-Student Services" by Gary R. Langer. In all, this section provides coverage of a variety of tools and technologies that inform and enhance modern electronic services.

Section 4, ***Utilization and Application***, describes how electronic services have been utilized and offers insight on important lessons for their continued use and evolution. Including chapters such as "Web Services in Distributed Information Systems: Availability, Performance and Composition" by Xia Zhao, Tao Wang, Enjie Liu, and Gordon J. Clapworthy, and "Evolution of Online Financial Trading Systems: E-Service Innovations in the Brokerage Sector" by Alexander Yap and Wonhi Synn, this section investigates numerous methodologies that have been proposed and enacted in electronic services, as well as their results. As this section continues, a number of case studies in the use of electronic services are presented from multiple industries across the world, in selections such as "E-Banking Diffusion in the Jordanian Banking Services Sector: An Empirical Analysis of Key Factors" by Ali Alawneh and Ezz Hattab, "E-Services in Danish Research Libraries: Issues and Challenges at Roskilde University Library" by Ada Scupola, and "Business Process Change in E-Government Projects: The Case of the Irish Land Registry" by Aileen Kennedy, Joseph P. Coughlan and Carol Kelleher. Contributions found in this section provide comprehensive coverage of the practicality and current use of electronic services.

Section 5, ***Organizational and Social Implications***, includes chapters discussing the organizational and social impact of electronic services. "Factors Relating to the Adoption of Internet Technology by the Omani Banking Industry" by Salim Al-Hajri and Arthur Tatnall presents a discussion of the enablers and the inhibitors of Internet technology adoption in Oman, and "Early User Involvement and Participation in Employee Self-Service Application Deployment: Theory and Evidence from Four Dutch Governmental Cases" by Gerwin Koopman and Ronald Batenburg demonstrates that the deployment success of electronic self-services is positively related to the extent of early user involvement and participation. This section continues with issues in consumer trust and electronic services, covered in chapters such as "Culture and Consumer Trust in Online Businesses" by Robert Greenberg, Bernard Wong-On-Wing, and Gladie Lui, and "Building Consumer Trust for Internet E-Commerce" by George Yee. The section concludes with several chapters remarking upon consumer attitudes towards different electronic services, in selections such as Jesus Enrique Portillo Pizana's "Measuring Consumer Attitudes Towards Self-Service Technologies." Overall, these chapters present a detailed investigation of the complex relationship between individuals, organizations and electronic services.

Section 6, ***Managerial Impact***, presents focused coverage of electronic services as it relates to improvements and considerations in the workplace. "Competence of Information Technology Professionals in Internet-Based Ventures" by Tobias Kollmann and Matthias Häsel articulates the knowledge and skills required by IT professionals in young Internet-based firms in order to find suitable partners and align e-business strategy and information technology. "Contract Negotiation in E-Marketplaces: A Model Based on Dependency Relations" by Larbi Esmahi and "E-Contracting Challenges" by Lai Xu and Paul de Vrieze presents an overview and examples of protocols commonly used to implement negotiation in e-markets and electronic contracts. In all, the chapters in this section offer specific perspectives on how managerial perspectives and developments in electronic services inform each other to create more meaningful user experiences.

Section 7, ***Critical Issues***, addresses vital issues related to electronic services, which include self-services, online financial activities and the security of web-based services. Chapters such as "Effectiveness of Web Services: Mobile Agents Approach in E-Commerce System" by Kamel Karoui and Fakher Ben Ftima, and "Self-Service Systems: Investigating the Perceived Importance of Various Quality Dimensions" by Calin Gurau focus on the effectiveness of self-service systems and consumer behavior when using those systems. Later selections, such as "A Survey of Attacks in the Web Services World" by Meiko Jensen and Nils Gruschka , "Security Threats in Web-Powered Databases and Web Portals" by Theodoros Evdoridis and Theodoros Tzouramanis, and "An Approach for Intentional Modeling of Web Services Security Risk Assessment" by C. Misra Subhas, Kumar Vinod, and Kumar Uma address security by looking at tools, resources and patterns in attacks. This section also asks unique questions about ways to valuing a company's intellectual capital, electronic services in the library virtualization process, and online journalistic services.

The concluding section of this authoritative reference tool, ***Emerging Trends***, highlights areas for future research within the field of electronic services, while exploring new avenues for the advancement of the discipline. Beginning this section is "Sponsored Search as a Strategic E-Service" by Roumen Vragov. This selection discusses the potential of sponsored searching, while evaluating the extent to which consumers and advertisers can rely on sponsored search as an effective strategic infomediary. Emerging *electronic therapeutic systems are* presented in "The Digital Divide and the Emerging Virtual Therapeutic System" by Christine H. Barthold and John G.McNutt, and "E-Therapy" by Catarina I. Reis, Carla S. Freire, and Josep M. Monguet. These chapters explore systems of online health and mental healthcare, both formal and informal, and discuss their effectiveness. These and several other emerging trends and suggestions for future research can be found within the final section of this exhaustive multi-volume set. Although the primary organization of the contents in this multi-volume work is based on its eight sections, offering a progression of coverage of the important concepts, methodologies, technologies, applications, social issues, and emerging trends, the reader can also identify specific contents by utilizing the extensive indexing system listed at the end of each volume. Furthermore to ensure that the scholar, researcher and educator have access to the entire contents of this multi volume set as well as additional coverage that could not be included in the print version of this publication, the publisher will provide unlimited multi-user electronic access to the online aggregated database of this collection for the life of the edition, free of charge when a library purchases a print copy. This aggregated database provides far more contents than what can be included in the print version in addition to continual updates. This unlimited access, coupled with the continuous updates to the database ensures that the most current research is accessible to knowledge seekers.

As a comprehensive collection of research on the latest findings related to using technology to providing various services, *Electronic Services: Concepts, Methodologies, Tools and Applications*, provides researchers, administrators and all audiences with a complete understanding of the development of applications and concepts in electronic services. Given the vast number of issues concerning usage, failure, success, policies, strategies, and applications of electronic services in organizations, *Electronic Services: Concepts, Methodologies, Tools and Applications*, addresses the demand for a resource that encompasses the most pertinent research in electronic services development, deployment, and impact.

Chapter 3.13
SLA Monitoring of Presence-Enable Services:
A New Approach Using Data Envelopment Analysis (DEA)

Tapati Bandopadhyay
ICFAI Business School, India

Pradeep Kumar
ICFAI Business School, India

ABSTRACT

The concept of presence was initially associated with an instant messaging service, allowing an end user to recognize the presence of a peer online to send or receive messages. Now the technology has grown up to include various services like monitoring performance of any type of end user device, and services are accessible from anywhere, any time. The need for enhanced value remains the driving force behind these services, for example, Voice over Internet Protocol (VoIP) services, which is drawing tremendous research interest in services performance evaluation, measurement, benchmarking, and monitoring. Monitoring service level parameters happens to be one of the most interesting application-oriented research issues because various service consumers at the customer companies/end users' level are finding it very difficult to design and monitor an effective SLA (Service Level Agreement) with the presence-enabled service providers. This chapter focuses on to these specific issues and presents a new approach of SLA monitoring through Data Envelopment Analysis (DEA). This extreme point approach actually can work much better in the context of SLA monitoring than general central-tendency-based statistical tools, a fact which has been corroborated by similar application examples of DEA presented in this chapter and has therefore it acts as the primary motivation to propose this new approach. Towards this end, this chapter first builds up the context of presence-enabled services (Day, Rosenburg, & Sugano, 2000), its SLA and SLA parameters, and the monitoring requirements. Then it explains the basics of DEA and its application in various other engineering and services context.

Ultimately, a DEA application framework for monitoring an SLA of presence-enabled services is proposed which can serve as a clear guideline for the customers of presence-enabled services, not only for SLA monitoring but also at various other stages of implementing presence-enabled services frameworks. This approach exploits the definitive suitability of the application of DEA methods to presence-enabled service monitoring problems, and can be easily implemented by the industry practitioners.

INTRODUCTION

Presence-Enabled Services

Presence technology allows end users and network elements to know the status and availability of other end users in order to improve communications efficiency. Today, presence has expanded to include monitoring the registration and the busy or idle status of any type of end user device, including wireless phones, VoIP clients, traditional POTS phones, push-to-talk clients, multimedia clients, and more. In addition, the concept of presence has been extended to include various other dimensions. For example: Availability: It allows an end user to explicitly share their availability to communicate with their colleagues (Gurbani, Faynberg, Lu, Brusilovsky, Gato, & Unmehopta, 2003). Typical availability states include out of office, in a meeting with a client, in a conference call, on vacation, and so forth. An end user can provide this information, or it can be inferred from the end user's online calendar. Other dimensions include Location: geographical location of an end user's device. Wireless networks can triangulate signal strength measurements to provide the location of wireless handsets and PDAs. Instant messaging clients is another dimension where the concept of location was extended to laptop-based, instant messaging clients, or IP softphones that might connect to wireline access networks

at work, home, or remote locations (Sun, 2002). Presence server and presence policies are important dimensions which determine the ability of the end user to control access to their presence and location information, using the presence server in conjunction with their presence policy. The presence server, in accordance with the end user's policy, provides the presence and location information to various presence applications.

By collecting and disseminating presence information (status of end user devices, availability of the individual, and location), the most effective and appropriate means of communicating to a person or a device can be identified. Network applications (for example, find me/follow me service) can use presence information to efficiently and appropriately route or block incoming communication requests (Roach, 2002).

Presence-Enabled Services Architecture

Presence service architecture (Day, Rosenberg, & Sugano, 2000) includes a wide variety of end user communication clients, integration of multiple real-time communication services into an integrated communications suite, and new end user services that can be developed for spanning and combining wireline telephony, wireless telephony, messaging services, and so forth. Types of information and protocol elements include presence information from a wide variety of end user clients and network elements that can be accessed through a central presence server, plus standard presence protocols and standard event packages that allows presence-enabled services to be developed separately from the end user clients and presence server vendors. These all support the basic requirement of seamlessly integrating or enhancing existing services through the inclusion of presence information.

Presence-enabled services may be classified broadly as:

- **Information sharing services:** These help to determine the most appropriate means of contacting another end user/device. For example, if end users do not have their instant messaging client active, their colleagues might send an e-mail. In more complex scenarios, the presence server can collect and forward presence information across a variety of end user devices. Another instance may be where an employee may have multiple presence clients such as a wireless phone, a VoIP soft-client, an instant messaging client, and so forth, and the most appropriate means to contact him/her can be found given the nature of the communication, priority, time schedules, and work/availability status.
- **Service-enabling:** Presence information allows service providers to automatically re-route high priority incoming communication sessions.

Various Types of Presence-Enabled Services

Examples of presence-enabled services include: call services like Presence-Enabled Call Pick Up, which is a wire-line call pick-up service that allows multiple employees/groups or remote workers to answer each others' phones, and Presence-Enabled Call Distribution, which is a centralized call distribution system that subscribes to the presence and availability status of the devices across multiple switching systems and PBXs. Consequently, devices can be geographically distributed and served by a multiple switching system or PBXs, or they can be served by a combination of PBXs and switching systems. This includes devices served by wireless switching systems.

Then there are facilities like Presence-Enabled Conferencing where existing conference services can be augmented to provide presence information to all participants, and Presence-Enabled Find Me/Follow Me Service where the application server queries the presence status of the wireless phone before forwarding the call and routes it to the appropriate communication device accordingly. Other services include Presence-Sensitive Voice Mail Greeting service to automatically switch between multiple prerecorded messages. Location-based services cater to requirements regarding information like Location Information to simplify the interaction if the agent or IVR system knew the location of the calling party, Location-Based Call Routing where incoming calls are forwarded to the nearest, idle wireless phone or VoIP soft-client, and Location Proximity Alerting.

Implementation of Presence-Enabled Services

The key network/service delivery elements (Day, Rosenberg, & Sugano, 2000) for providing presence-enabled service are as follows.

From Figure 1, the following basic service elements can be identified from the viewpoint of a customer company for setting up the SLA performance parameters:

1. Presence user agents
2. Presence network agents
   a. IP MS (IP multimedia subsystems)
   b. MSC (Mobile switching centers)
   c. IMSA (Instant messaging service agents)

In the next section, we discuss SLA and the SLA components of presence-enabled services.

MAIN THRUST OF THE CHAPTER

Service Level Agreement (SLA) For Presence-Enabled Services

Typical SLAs identify and define the service offering itself, plus the supported products, evaluation criteria, and QoS (Quality of Service) that customers should expect. It includes the re-

707

Figure 1. A basic presence-enabled services framework (Based on RFC 2778, IETF, Feb., 2000) (Day, Rosenberg, & Sugano, 2000)

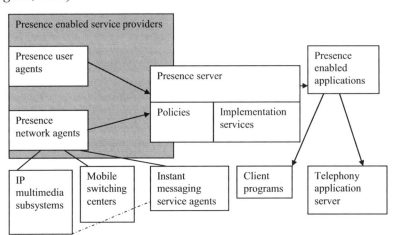

sponsibilities of an IT services provider (such as an ISP or ASP), reflects the rights of the service provider's users, and also includes the penalties assessed when the service provider violates any element of the SLA.

SLAs are the key to ensuring consistent QoS, performance, and uptime in business-critical computing environments, and they complement other contractual agreements that cover a variety of details, including corrective actions, penalties and incentives, dispute-resolution procedures, nonconformance, acceptable service violations, reporting policies, and rules for terminating a contract. These contracts generally fit under what some analysts call Service Level Management (SLM), which provides managing and service contract capabilities. Four areas that require detailed SLAs are the network itself, hosting services, applications, and customer care, including help desk services. Each area contains its own set of elements, metrics, typical industry ranges, and criteria for calculating these metrics. For instance, the network SLA would include details on bandwidth, performance, and QoS. Well-designed SLAs also detail the nature and types

of tools required for users and service providers to monitor and manage them.

Some enterprises accept a "best effort" delivery standard for the service providers (which are best suited for the approach elaborated in this chapter using DEA for such SLA monitoring), while others demand that their providers offer service with specific guarantees for application availability on a customer-by-customer basis (in these cases, traditional statistical approaches still work).

The SLA parameter value-range varies accordingly to the type of services; for example, real-time applications such as presence-enabled technologies such as Voice over IP (VoIP) or interactive media cannot operate effectively at a loss rate of 5% which is acceptable for typical Web browsing (Gurbani, Faynberg, Lu, Brusilovsky, Gato, & Unmehopta, 2003). Data latency, as with data loss, is another critical parameter in VoIP and multimedia environments where delays must not impact end-user performance; real-time interactive applications require response times of 100 milliseconds (ms) or less.

SLA Parameters for Presence-Enabled Services

Considering the parameters that a network SLA should include, and the typical elements of presence-enabled services, SLA parameters for presence-enabled services will include service hours and availability, downtime and so forth, customer support levels, throughputs, responsiveness, restrictions, functionalities, multi-platform communication domains support (synchronous/asynchronous), multiple device support, multiple protocol support, data loss acceptability, data security, real-time application suitability, and many other characteristics depending upon the specific implementation scenario of the presence-enabled service.

DEA APPROACH FOR THE SLA MONITORING OF PRESENCE-ENABLED SERVICES

Basic Introduction to DEA (Data Envelopment Analysis)

DEA or Data Envelopment Analysis is commonly used to evaluate the relative efficiency of a number of producers/providers of any goods/services. A typical statistical approach is characterized as a central tendency approach, and it evaluates producers relative to an average producer. In contrast, DEA is an extreme point method and compares each producer with only the "best" producers. A producer is usually referred to as a decision-making unit or DMU. The DEA approach is essentially to find a set of criteria weights which present each entity in the best possible light.

A fundamental assumption behind an extreme point method is that if a given producer, A, is capable of producing Y(A) units of output with X(A) inputs, then other producers should also be able to do the same if they were to operate efficiently. Similarly, if producer B is capable of

producing Y(B) units of output with X(B) inputs, then other producers should also be capable of the same production schedule. Producers A, B, and others can then be combined to form a composite producer with composite inputs and composite outputs. Since this composite producer may not necessarily exist, it is typically called a virtual producer.

The analysis primarily focuses on finding the "best" virtual producer for each real producer. If the virtual producer is better than the original producer by either making more output with the same input or making the same output with less input, then the original producer is *inefficient*. The procedure of finding the best virtual producer can be formulated as a linear program. Analyzing the efficiency of *n* producers is then a set of *n* linear programming problems.

DEA has got some features which make it an interesting and effective tool for comparing various decision-making units in a real-life situation. For example, in the DEA method, multiple input/output models are handled, where no assumption of a functional form relating inputs to outputs is a must. DMUs are directly compared against a peer or combination of peers. Inputs and outputs can have very different units. These features make DEA an effective option for estimating "relative" efficiency of a DMU; it converges very slowly to "absolute" efficiency or "theoretical maximum". The limitation is that since DEA is a non-parametric technique, statistical hypothesis tests are difficult and are the focus of ongoing research.

Examples of DEA Applications in Various Engineering and Services Sectors

DEA applications have generally focused on evaluation of alternative design configurations, performance improvement interventions, assessment of process/system performance and benchmarking. Example application domains range from design evaluation of turbofan jet engines

(Bulla, Cooper, Wilson, & Park, 2000), circuit-board manufacturing processes (Triantis, 2003), to process improvement intervention (Hoopes, Triantis, & Partangel, 2000) with a need for the input/output variables of the empirical function to effectively represent the underlying processes (Sun, 2002); example applications of DEA in this context had been well-documented by Hoopes and Triantis (2001).

The key application issues have been, for example, how well-established engineering design methodologies, such as design of experiments (DOE), could effectively interface with the DEA methodology; how to explore these methodological interfaces (Kabnurkar, 2001), and how to continue to pursue innovative engineering DEA applications.

One DEA modeling approach: The network model has been proposed to measure and improve disaggregated process performance, by *open the input/output transformation box* (Cooper, Park, & Yu, 2001). This application of DEA is useful where efficiency performance of the specific production stages (represented by nodes) (Cooper, Park, & Yu, 2001) or modules are evaluated, for example, the basic service elements of presence-enabled services architecture (Day, Rosenberg, & Sugano, 2000). Goal Programming and Data Envelopment Analysis (GODEA) (Triantis, 2003) provided another application domain for DEA with an approach that combined conflicting objectives of efficiency, effectiveness, and equity in resource allocation for service organizations, for example, banks or financial services institutions.

Consequently, Data Envelopment Analysis (DEA) has been a popular technique for bank efficiency studies; however, DEA requires that units operate in consistent "cultures" to produce fair and comparable results .DEA has been appropriately applied to measure performance in the service sector, as a means of measuring performance and possibly as a monitoring tool for use in the longer term. In software processes also, DEA has been well applied. Data Envelopment Analysis (DEA) methods are ideal for measuring the efficiency of software production processes. DEA methods have proven to be very valuable, in practice, as a management tool appropriate for both planning and control activities, and as new tools for forecasting and trade-off analysis.

Another most interesting application of DEA has been in the context of dynamical systems, be it historical, causal or closed (Vaneman & Triantis, 2003), which exhibit a high degree of correlation between the variables at the initial time *t0* with the variables at the final time *t*. Here, DEA techniques have been defined and developed as the dynamic data envelopment analysis (DDEA) by adding the element of time to the DEA model. This application of DEA can be directly connected to the real-time data handling aspects of SLA monitoring of services like VoIP, and so forth.

Characteristics of Problems Suitable for DEA Applications

The basic strength of DEA as a tool or method, as is apparent from the basic introduction, is that DEA generates an efficiency frontier by defining a "best producer" which does not necessarily have to be real, and is most often virtual, that is, combinations of the most desirable values across all real producers making the best virtual producer profile which gets reflected in the efficiency frontier. Consequently, problems which can be better solved by DEA other than statistical/operations research approaches have some typical characteristics which actually can be directly mapped onto DEA characteristics; for example:

- Problems with multiple inputs and outputs with different units of measurement;
- Unstructured, not well-defined problems where no or minimally-stable functional forms are available or can be assumed to relate inputs to outputs;
- Problems dealing with similar level payer comparisons;

- Problem domains which have no/minimal/extremely dynamic or changing/evolving benchmarking standards (extreme point techniques can actually be useful to derive the benchmarks in such situations);
- Problems/systems where "relative" efficiency is more important than "absolute" efficiency; and
- Problem domains where the parameters are not clearly defined so it cannot be modeled around parameters as is possible with many traditional operations research techniques.

DEA Model Orientation Options

An input-oriented measure quantifies the input reduction which is necessary to become efficient holding the outputs constant. Symmetrically, an output-oriented measure quantifies the necessary output expansion holding the inputs constant. A non-oriented measure quantifies necessary improvements when both inputs and outputs can be improved simultaneously. In applications, the choice of a certain measure mostly depends on three criteria:

- the "primal" interpretation, that is, the meaning of the efficiency score with respect to input and output quantities;
- the "dual" interpretation, that is, the meaning of the efficiency score with respect to input and output prices; and
- the axiomatic properties of the efficiency measure (e.g., monotonicity, units invariance, indication of efficiency, continuity).

Most of the measures are similar with respect to these criteria. T denotes the technology and (X^k, Y^k) denotes the input output data of the DMU under evaluation.

Distance

- **Radial**: This measure (Debreu-Farrell-measure) indicates the necessary improvements when all relevant factors are improved by the same factor equi-proportionally. This can also be thought of as the "radial part" of the CCR (Charnes, Cooper, & Rhodes, 1978) / BCC (Banker, Charnes, & Cooper, 1984) measure.

non-oriented: $\max\{\theta \mid ((1-\theta)X^k, (1+\theta)Y^k) \in T\}$
input: $\min\{\theta \mid (\theta X^k, Y^k) \in T\}$
output: $\max\{\varphi \mid (X^k, \varphi Y^k) \in T\}$

- **Additive**: This measure quantifies the maximal sum of absolute improvements (input reduction/output increase measured in "slacks"). It has a price interpretation (as the difference between actual and maximal profit) and indicates Koopmans efficiency, but it is not invariant with respect to units of measurement.

non-oriented: $\max\{\sum_i s_i + \sum_j t_j \mid (X^k - s, Y^k + t) \in T, (s, t) >= 0\}$
input: $\max\{\sum_i s_i \mid (X^k - s, Y^k) \in T, s >= 0\}$
output: $\max\{\sum_j t_j \mid (X^k, Y^k + t) \in T, t >= 0\}$

- **maxAverage:** This measure (F̈arel-Lovell or Russell or SBM (School-Based Management) measure) quantifies the maximal average of relative improvements (input reduction/output increase measured in percentages of the current level). It has no straightforward price interpretation, but it is both an indicator for Koopmans efficiency (for positive data) and units invariant.
- **minAverage**: This measure quantifies the minimal average of relative improvements which is necessary to become weakly efficient. Weak efficiency means there does

not exist a point in the technology set which is better in every input and output. For a weakly efficient point, an arbitrary small improvement suffices to become Koopmans-efficient, whence the minAverage measure also quantifies the infimum average of improvements which is necessary to become Koopmans efficient. It has neither a straightforward price interpretation nor is it an indicator for Koopmans efficiency, but it is units invariant.

Which model option will be applicable to which parameter depends primarily upon the following:

1. the purpose of analysis, for example, for benchmarking, the output-oriented model will be suited, whereas for cost monitoring, the input-oriented cost minimization model can be more applicable; and
2. the availability of criterion data, for example, if there is no coinciding point in the data spectrum where both input and output are getting better (a very likely scenario with conflicting objective criteria as is the case of SLA parameters, e.g., QoS vs. cost), then the minAverage model can be chosen.

Presence-Enabled Services SLA and DEA: Applicability

Problems with presence-enabled services are typically different from traditional engineering context in various aspects. For example, they have multi-platform, non-standardized communication domains. For monitoring these services thereof, we need an approach to efficiently, and even more desirably, automatically handle real-time service-oriented performance data. Other problems related to these sets of services are the facts that they are still non-stabilized, ever-evolving, or developing procedures and policies, which is the reason why there is a lack of benchmarking data availability for the SLA parameters themselves. The basic op-

erational elements will therefore include efficient and, preferably, automated recording, processing, and monitoring SLA data elements.

THE DEA APPLICATION FRAMEWORK FOR MONITORING THE SLA PARAMETERS OF PRESENCE-ENABLED SERVICES

In the following section, we are presenting a simple algorithm to implement the DEA approach for automated monitoring of the SLA parameters in a generic implementation scenario of presence-enabled services. Consequently, we have taken the following assumptions:

1. In this implementation scenario, we are concerned primarily with getting the best possible efficiency from the service providers with the minimum possible cost, which is reflected in the first consideration of the algorithm.
2. This being a generic and simplified scenario, we have not specified the variables in designing the DEA input/output variables formulation. The variables will have to be defined in the specific implementation contexts of presence-enabled services. As we have seen in the previous sections, there are various types of presence-enabled services, each of which need a set of inputs, some of which are common and some which are unique to their specific implementation requirements. And consequently, the output requirements also vary. For example, location information service performance requirements will primarily be the real-time accuracy of the data, whereas for call services, the availability of QoS parameters will be the most important output variables for monitoring and control. So, depending on the implementation-specific requirements, the input-output variables can be defined.

Using these assumptions, now we can formulate the algorithm.

In this algorithm, the number of suppliers/providers (called as **Decision-Making Units or DMUs** in context of DEA) of presence-enabled services about which adequate SLA parameter values/historical data is available = n. Number of output decision variables Y = SLA parameter values + cost = s. Number of input variables X i.e. SLA parameter values = r. Weights on input variables = w_j and Weights on output variables = v_i

The Algorithm

- **Step 1:** Minimum cost/maximum efficiency ratio-wise best producer: Basic LP form -:

$$MINe_0^{'} = \frac{\sum_{j=1}^{r} v_i x_{i0}}{\sum_{j=1}^{s} w_j y_{j0}}$$

  $e_0^{'}$ reflects the reciprocal measure of input minimization model.
- **Step 2:** Calculate $e_0^{'}$ for all DMUs.
- **Step 3:** Choose the DMU with minimum value-set (as we are calculating the reciprocal measure) of the parameters. This can be represented as the best virtual producer.
- **Step 4:** Calculate the SLA parameter value-variances for each parameter from this best virtual producer against each real producer. The value-variances can be calculated in real-time automatically and can be identified during the monitoring process.
- **Step 5:** Invoke the appropriate SLA management action consequently when required.

The implementation framework as described in the algorithm above, for monitoring presence-enabled services SLAs with DEA is shown in Figure 2.

Figure 2 does not show the SLA parameters exclusively emanating from each service delivery unit/element because in that case the Figure will become very complex and hence not highly readable and practically applicable. Moreover, the algorithm, being generic, will have to be qualified with implementation-specific variables which will in turn depend on the types of service delivery units/elements involved to produce a particular type of presence-enabled service. Also, many parameters will emanate from more than one service element so there exists an m:n relationship between the SLA parameters and service delivery elements, which actually makes it a best-suited application for DEA.

Implementing the Framework

Explanation on how to implement the framework as shown in Figure 2 is given below, with the help of two example cases on two SLA parameters. We have used the EMS software in these examples. Efficiency Measurement System (EMS) is software for Windows 9x/NT which computes Data Envelopment Analysis (DEA) efficiency measures. EMS uses the LP Solver DLL BPMPD 2.11 for the computation of the scores. It is an interior point solver.

Preparing the Input Output Data

The first and probably most difficult step in an efficiency evaluation is to decide which input and output data should be included. EMS accepts data in MS Excel or in text format. Additionally to "standard" inputs and outputs, EMS can also handle "nondiscretionary" inputs and outputs (i.e., data which are not controlled by the DMUs).

The size of analysis is limited by the memory of the machine used. There is theoretically no limitation of the number of DMUs, inputs, and outputs in EMS. Although the code is not optimized for large-scale data, EMS has successfully solved problems with over 5,000 DMUs and about 40 inputs and outputs.

When EMS computes an efficiency score (which is a distance to the efficient frontier), it does not alter the values of non-discretionary data,

Figure 2. Role of DEA in monitoring of SLAs of presence-enabled services

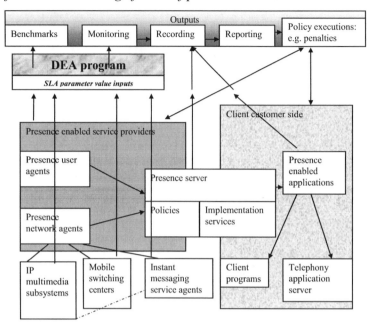

that is, the distance will only be computed in the directions of the "normal" (discretionary) inputs and outputs while the non-discretionary are fixed.

Weights restrictions can be specified in the form $W(p, q) >= 0$, where p is the vector of input weights and q is the vector of output weights (or shadow prices). Both "Cone Ratio" constraints and "Assurance Region" constraints can be incorporated.

Example Case I

Suppose we have three input parameters for SLA monitoring, for example, cost, bandwidth, and availability, and two outputs, for example, throughput and reliability, and we want to have the restriction $p1 > p2$ then the corresponding row in the weights restriction matrix W is (1;–1; 0; 0; 0). If we incorporate bounds on the marginal rates of substitutions like $0.5 <= q1 / q2 <= 5$, then it can be transformed into two constraints, $q1 - 0.5q2 >= 0$ and $-q1 + 5q2 >= 0$, yielding the rows (0;

0; 0; 1;–0.5) and (0; 0; 0;–1; 5) in the matrix W. Thus in this example one has W =

1	−1	0	0	0
0	0	0	1	−0.5
0	0	0	−1	5

This form of input can be now loaded onto the specific DEA model to be chosen in the next few steps. Input-output data can be loaded by pressing Ctrl+O (Menu File ! Load data). Ctrl+M (Menu DEA ! Run model) will display a dialog where the model can be specified.

- returns to Scale,
- convex and nonconvex envelopment, and
- constant, variable, no increasing or no decreasing returns to scale.

Example Case II: Choosing an Efficiency Measure and Super-Efficiency

An efficiency measure quantifies, in one way or another, a "distance" to the efficient frontier of the technology, that is, the service delivery mechanism in this context. EMS allows computation of various distances in input-, output-, and non-oriented versions. Detailed discussions on orientation are in the previous section.

Super-Efficiency

If we choose a radial distance, then EMS allows us to compute so-called "super-efficiency" scores by checking the box. For inefficient DMUs, the super-efficiency score coincides with the standard score. For efficient DMUs, a score is computed which indicates the maximal radial change which is feasible such that the DMU remains efficient. Formally, it is defined like the standard score, but the DMU under evaluation is excluded from the constraints (i.e., the definition of the technology set).

So, if we want to find out the actually-available best producer based on the SLA parameters values they had promised to deliver and they actually deliver, then we can choose the super-efficiency model. If we choose the super-efficiency model, then in the results table a big score may appear. This means that the DMU remains efficient under arbitrary large increased inputs (input-oriented) or decreased outputs (output-oriented), respectively.

We can specify selections of DMUs which should be computed (Evaluation) and which should be used for building the envelopment (Technology), for example, producers of world-standard services but which are not available as options. This allows us to compute producer efficiency, that is, for each DMU selected in Evaluation, a score is computed.

If computations are finished, EMS will display the results in a table. The window caption tells which model was computed, that is, whether with constant returns to scale, radial distance, input

orientation, or weights restrictions with restriction matrix. The result table contains:

- **DMU name:** An additional {X} indicates that this DMU was excluded from building the technology as specified in Technology. A DMU name without score indicates that this DMU built the technology but was not evaluated as specified in Evaluation.
- **Benchmarks:**
  ○ **for inefficient DMU:** the reference DMUs with corresponding intensities (the "lambdas") in brackets;
  ○ **for efficient DMU:** the number of inefficient DMUs which have chosen the DMU as Benchmark, slacks {S} or factors {F}. Depending of the chosen distance, for radial and additive measures the slacks are displayed;
- For the minAverage and maxAverage measures the factors are displayed. In addition, for the minAverage measure, slacks are displayed for those inputs and outputs with factors = 1 (or 0 for non-oriented measure); and
- For Nonconvex (FDH) models, instead of the weights for each DMU, the number of dominated and dominating DMUs and lists of these DMUs are displayed.

From the results table, the benchmark values for the input parameters (if input-oriented model is chosen) or the output parameters (if output-oriented model is chosen) are chosen and this set of values can now be used for variance analysis with the actual parameter values delivered during the SLA monitoring process.

The two examples show how DEA can be used for SLA monitoring and benchmarking based on:

1. how the parameter values can be input as constraints into the system; and
2. how a benchmark can be obtained, using the EMS software as the example tool.

Implementing the framework as shown in Figure 2 can be done using other LP-supporting tools with further programming extension abilities to develop the DEA models.

CONCLUSION

The primary contribution of this chapter has been into the exploration of applicability of DEA as a new approach to benchmark, assess, and monitor SLAs and the service providers for presence-enabled services. It serves this purpose finally with two simple and specific examples addressing two basic application issues of DEA models, that is, the input and the model selection process.

The concept that has been developed and explained in this chapter can be extended further:

- to incorporate the SLA parameters values being generated/monitored from each of the service delivery elements;
- to incorporate other aspects of DEA models to suit specific company needs; for example, in this chapter, the example is primarily concerned with the virtual best producer with minimum cost/maximum efficiency ratio. But a company for which cost is not a critical factor but efficiency is, can go for a different DEA model; based on other parameters too; and
- to incorporate the tools for implementing the DEA programs that can also be integrated into the framework as shown in Figure 2.

The potential of application of this concept is even more significant in the current context where presence-enabled services like VoIP are emerging as the primary services in ITeS based on which many businesses/organizations are evolving and progressing. This will also enable industrial practitioners who are actively involved in designing and managing service level agreements. This is seen as a very crucial component of the overall business processes of many organizations of today which are showing a proliferating trend towards outsourcing basic support/infra-structural services, the need emanating primarily from these organizations' priorities to focus on developing core competencies to gain and retain sustainable competitive advantage. Being the backbone of the basic process-running and services required by these organizations, the support/infra-structural services like presence-enabled services quite often determine the quality of services that are produced as part of these organizations' core competencies. Consequently, the effective and efficient benchmarking, monitoring, and controlling of these services becomes crucial for organizational success. Therefore, not only from an academic or research point of view, but also from the hard-core industry practitioners' view, it is a crucial challenge for managing the service level agreements with various service producers/providers, a challenge which needs to be addressed with innovative, new ideas and approaches aiming towards a cost-effective, sustainable method which utilizes IT resources optimally for managing SLAs. This chapter suggests one such method, and opens up possibilities of using various other methods and approaches for handling the challenges of service-level management.

REFERENCES

Banker, R. D., Charnes, A., & Cooper, W.W. (1984), Some models for estimating technical and scale inefficiencies in data envelopment analysis. *Management Science, 30*(9), 1078-1092.

Bulla, S., Cooper, W. W., Wilson, D., & Park, K. S. (2000). Evaluating efficiencies of turbofan jet engines: A data envelopment analysis approach. *Journal of Propulsion and Power, 16*(3), 431-439.

Charnes, A., Cooper, W., & Rhodes, E. (1978), Measuring the efficiency of decision making units, *European Journal of Operational Research*, *2*(6), 429-444

Cooper, W. W., Park, K. S., & Yu, G. (2001). An illustrative application of IDEA (Imprecise Data Envelopment Analysis) to a Korean mobile telecommunication company. *Operations Research, 49*(6), 807-820.

Day, M., Rosenberg, J., & Sugano, H. (2000). *A Model for Presence and Instant Messaging* (RFC 2778). Internet Engineering Task Force.

Gurbani, V. K., Faynberg I., Lu H. L., Brusilovsky A., Gato J., & Unmehopta, M. (2003). *The SPIRITS (Services in PSTN Requesting Internet Services) Protocol*, Internet Engineering Task Force, RFC 3910.

Hoopes, B., & Triantis, K. (2001). Efficiency performance, control charts, and process improvement: Complementary measurement and evaluation. *IEEE Transactions on Engineering Management, 48*(2), 239-253.

Hoopes, B., Triantis, K., & Partangel, N. (2000). The relationship between process and manufacturing plant performance: A goal programming approach. *International Journal of Operations and Quantitative Management, 6*(4), 287-310.

Kabnurkar, A. (2001). *Math modeling for data envelopment analysis with fuzzy restrictions on weights.* M.S. thesis, Virginia Tech, Department of Industrial and Systems Engineering, Falls Church, VA.

Kao, C., & Liu, S. T. (2000). Fuzzy efficiency measures in data envelopment analysis. *Fuzzy Sets and Systems, 113*(3), 427-437.

Roach, A. B. (2002). *Session Initiation Protocol (SIP)—Specific Event Notification* (RFC 3265), Internet Engineering Task Force.

Rosenberg, J. (2003). A Presence Event Package for the Session Initiation Protocol (SIP), Internet Engineering Task Force.

Sun, S. (2002). Assessing computer numerical control machines using data envelopment analysis. *International Journal of Production Research, 40*(9), 2011-2039.

Triantis, K. (2003). Engineering applications of DEA: Issues and opportunities. In W. W. Cooper, L. M. Seiford, & J. Zhu (Eds.), *Handbook of DEA* (pp. 401-442). Kluwer Publishers.

Vaneman, W., & Triantis, K. (2003). The dynamic production axioms and system dynamics behaviors: The foundation for future integration. *Journal of Productivity Analysis, 19*(1), 93-113.

This work was previously published in Architecture of Reliable Web Applications Software, edited by M. Radaideh; H. Al-Ameed, pp. 307-322, copyright 2007 by IGI Publishing (an imprint of IGI Global).

Chapter 3.14
Towards a Design Process for Integrating Product Recommendation Services in E-Markets

Nikos Manouselis
Agricultural University of Athens, Greece

Constantina Costopoulou
Agricultural University of Athens, Greece

ABSTRACT

Online recommendation services (widely known as recommender systems) can support potential buyers by providing product recommendations that match their preferences. When integrated into e-markets, recommendation services may offer important added value. They can help online buyers to save time and make informed purchase decisions, as well as e-market operators to respond to buyer product queries in a more efficient manner, thus attracting more potential buyers. On the other hand, the variety of intelligent recommendation techniques that may be used to support such services can often prove complex and costly to implement. Toward this direction, this chapter proposes a design process for deploying intelligent recommendation services in existing e-markets, in order to reduce the complexity of such kinds of software development. To demonstrate the applicability of this approach, the proposed process is applied for the integration of a wine recommendation service in a Greek e-market with agricultural products.

INTRODUCTION

The rapid adoption of e-commerce practices and technologies has led to the development of numerous e-markets that offer a wide variety of products and services to the online buyers. From the buyers' perspective, this can lead to an often overwhelming amount of product information related to the purchase process. To facilitate searching, comparing, and selecting products in the context of e-markets, different types of integrated services or systems have been proposed. A particular class of such systems are the recommender systems, which facilitate the decision-making process of online buyers by providing recommendations about products matching their preferences (Schafer, Konstan, & Riedl, 2001). Recommender systems were originally defined as using the opinions of a community of users, to help individuals in that community to identify more effectively the content of interest from a potentially overwhelming set of choices (Resnick & Varian, 1997). Nowadays, the term has acquired a broader connotation, describing any system that produces individualized recommendations as output, or has the effect of guiding the user in a personalized way to interesting or useful items, in a large space of possible options (Burke, 2002).

Recommender systems use different types of techniques in order to provide personalised recommendations. According to Burke (2002), these techniques can be categorised as a content-based recommendation, collaborative recommendation, demographic recommendation, utility-based recommendation, as well as knowledge-based recommendation. Most of these techniques engage artificial intelligence (AI) methods in order to recommend products that best match each individual user's needs. For instance, recommender systems have previously engaged techniques, such as:

- decision tree induction and association rules mining, in order to identify users with similar interests and to extract rules that reflect their buying behavior (Changchien & Lu, 2001; Kim, Lee, Shaw, Chang, & Nelson, 2001; Cho, Kim, & Kim, 2002; Wang, Chuang, Hsu, & Keh, 2004);
- statistical methods, such as the calculation of user-to-user and item-to-item ratings' correlation, in order to create neighbourhoods of like-minded users (Herlocker, Konstan, & Riedl, 2002; Deshpande & Karypis, 2004; Miller, Konstan, & Riedl, 2004);

- classification methods, such as clustering algorithms and neural networks, to categorise users with similar preferences (Lee, Jun, Lee, & Kim, 2005; Martin-Guerrero et al., 2006; Lihua, Lu, Jing, & Zongyong, 2005); and
- taxonomy- and ontology-based approaches for representing user preferences and product spaces (Middleton, Shadbolt, & Roure, 2004; Hung, 2005).

This has led to a rich variety of AI-based approaches, which can be integrated in recommender systems.

On the other hand, surveys of online e-commerce systems (e.g., Holzmueller & Schluechter, 2002) reveal that most of the existing commercial e-market applications do not include a product recommendation service (i.e., a recommender system for products), or do not engage some intelligent technique to produce their product recommendations. This observation can be partially explained if we consider the inherent complexity of designing intelligent recommendation services, as well as the deployment and evaluation costs of such services. For instance, in the e-commerce domain there are several proposals of product recommendation algorithms (such as the ones proposed by Kim, Cho, Kim, Kim, & Suh, 2002; Cheung, Kwok, Law, & Tsui, 2003; Kim, Yum, Song, & Kim, 2005; Li, Lu, & Xuefeng, 2005) or stand-alone product recommendation systems (such as the approaches of Yen & Kong, 2002; Lee, 2004; Hung, 2005). Nevertheless, these are developed on a case-by-case basis, and include no guidelines related to how an intelligent product recommendation service can be designed, tested, and integrated into an existing e-market. Very few studies in the recommendation literature have addressed such issues (Stolze, 2002; Richard & Tchounikine, 2004). This can be an obstacle for e-market designers and developers, since the deployment of such services can often prove complex and confusing to them.

The aim of this chapter is to propose an efficient design process for deploying intelligent product recommendation services in existing e-markets. For this purpose, a set of design steps is suggested, based on a series of preliminary stages (Manouselis & Costopoulou, 2005) and an iterative software development approach, the rational unified process (RUP) (Boggs & Boggs, 2002). Then, these design steps are followed for integrating a wine recommendation service in an existing e-market. The remainder of this chapter is structured as follows. First, we give an overview of the preliminary stages and the process workflows of the RUP approach and identify a generic design process for integrating recommendation services in e-markets. Then, we demonstrate the application of the proposed design process in an already operating Greek e-market with agricultural products. Finally, we present the conclusions of this study and identify some future trends in this domain.

A DESIGN PROCESS FOR E-MARKET RECOMMENDATION SERVICES

The Preliminary Stages

The value of product recommendation is mainly focused on saving time, responding to buyer product's queries quickly, making informed purchase decisions, and consequently attracting more potential buyers. As mentioned, although numerous product recommendation implementations have been proposed, they are mostly developed on a case-by-case basis. So far, there has been not any proposal for an overall process of integrating recommendation services in e-markets. An attempt has been made to address this issue by Manouselis and Costopoulou (2005), providing a preliminary set of design stages. These stages are briefly described as follows:

1. **Identification of actors and supported tasks.** This is responsible for the identification of the involved actors and the tasks to be supported in an existing e-market. The outcome of this stage is a formal specification of actors and their tasks, using the Unified Modeling Language (UML).

2. **Definition of recommendation items.** This is responsible for the identification of the product characteristics (attributes). The outcome is a formal specification of the recommended products' database, using entity-relationship (ER) diagrams.

3. **Development of recommendation algorithm.** This is responsible for the development of an algorithm that will be used to provide the recommendations. A number of candidate algorithm variations can also be developed, in accordance to related mathematical models (Herlocker et al., 2002). The outcomes of this stage are: (i) a flowchart of the recommendation algorithm, and (ii) the algorithm variations (optional).

4. **Rapid prototyping.** This is responsible for the implementation of the recommendation service components that take into account the architectural, functional, and technical requirements of the examined e-market. These components may refer to the recommended products' database, the recommendation algorithm or different algorithm variations, as well as the user interfaces. The outcome of this stage is a recommendation service prototype.

5. **Pilot evaluation.** This is responsible for performing an initial evaluation of the service prototype, either by using simulated or real data. As a result, design choices can be finalized. If any fine tuning is required, we can go back to the development of recommendation algorithm stage. The outcome of this stage is the final version of the recommendation service to be integrated in the e-market under study.

Although these stages can serve as a design approach for integrating product recommendation services in e-markets, they have not been supported with a set of systematic design and analysis tools (such as the UML ones), nor do they correspond to the stages of a systematic software development process. For this purpose, this chapter has further refined them.

The Rational Unified Process Approach

Software development involves a number of steps to be carried out, so that a software system is properly modeled, analysed, designed, specified, and implemented. UML is the de-facto software industry standard modeling language for visualizing, specifying, constructing, and documenting the elements of systems, in general, and software systems, in particular (Booch, Rumbaugh, & Jacobson, 1998). It provides a rich set of graphical artifacts to help in the elicitation and top-down refinement of software systems from requirements capture to the deployment of software components (Saleh, 2002). In UML, a system is described using different levels of abstraction and considering various views (i.e., business view, use case view, design and process view, implementation view). Each view is realized using different UML modeling tools (diagrams), such as use case diagrams, activity diagrams, sequence diagrams, collaboration diagrams, statechart diagrams, class diagrams, component diagrams, and deployment diagrams (Saleh, 2002).

UML is largely process-independent, meaning that it can be used with a number of software development processes. One of the most popular systematic approaches is the rational unified process (RUP) approach, a design and development process that is especially well suited to UML (Booch et al., 1998; Boggs & Boggs, 2002). The RUP development starts with six process workflows (i.e., business modeling, requirements or system use case modeling, analysis and design,

implementation, test, and deployment) that adopt the various UML views, and continues with three more process workflows (i.e., configuration management, project management, and environment). The first six process workflows, which are directly related to the design and deployment of a system, are:

- **Business modeling** that describes the structure and dynamics of the business activities around the system. It results in business use case diagrams, activity diagrams, and analysis-level class diagrams with business entities.
- **Requirements or system use case modeling** that describes user requirements using use case diagrams. It results in identifying actors, use cases, and use case diagrams.
- **Analysis and design** that describes the structural and architectural aspects of the system. Analysis results in describing the flow of events in use cases by developing analysis-level sequence or collaboration diagrams. Design results in developing design-level sequence or collaboration diagrams, design-level class diagrams, statechart diagrams, component diagrams, and a deployment diagram.
- **Implementation** that takes into account the above UML diagrams in order to develop software components and integrate them in an initial version of the software system.
- **Test** that describes testing cases, procedures, and defect-tracking metrics.
- **Deployment** that covers the final system delivery and configuration.

The Proposed Design Process

The preliminary stages and the RUP process workflows have been studied in order to identify parts where the two approaches complement each other, as well as where they are overlapping. This led to the merging of the two approaches into a set of seven design steps aiming to facilitate the integration of a product recommendation service in an existing e-market. In Figure 1, the design process is presented following a waterfall model, where all design steps are also linked to the expected results of each step. These steps can be detailed as follows:

I. **Business modeling.** This step concentrates on the business activities that will be generally supported by the system (referred to here as the e-market business). It concerns the identification of business actors (anyone or anything that is external to the e-market business but interacts with it), business workers (roles within the e-market business), and business use cases (a group of related workflows within the e-market business that provide value to the business actors). The outcome of this step is a business use case diagram, which illustrates business use cases, business actors, and business workers for business activities, as well as the interactions between them. Activity diagrams can also be used to model the workflow through a particular business use case.

II. **System modeling.** This step specifies the scope of the system, using use cases and actors. Use cases include anything that is inside the system, whereas actors include anything that is external, interacting with the system. The outcome of this step is a system use case diagram, which provides an overview of the identified actors and use cases, as well as the associations between them.

III. **Definition of recommendation items.** This step concerns the identification and modeling of the products to be recommended and their recommendation-relevant characteristics. Similarly (if required), the characteristics that will be stored to the

Figure 1. Design process of product recommendation service

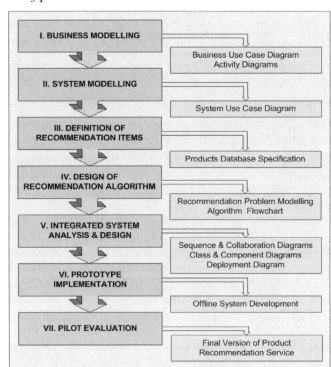

buyers' profiles are also defined. This step is closely coupled with the enhancement of the databases of the e-market. Therefore, the outcome of this step is expected to be in the form of an ER diagram, which is generally used to describe the static aspects of databases.

IV. **Design of recommendation algorithm.** This step deals with the formulation of the recommendation problem, based on the supported use cases as defined in the business use case diagram, and the definition of the recommendation items during the previous step. Thus, we define the algorithm that will be used by the recommendation service in order to produce the recommendation. The outcome of this step is a model of the recommendation problem (e.g., in the form of a function synthesizing the various parameters) and a flowchart of the produced algorithm.

V. **Integrated system analysis and design.** This step involves the analysis and design of the e-market system, introducing new use cases, as well as sub-systems and software components required to implement them. At this point, each new use case of the e-market has to be supported by the appropriate (new or existing) sub-systems. During the e-market system analysis, the interactions between the involved actors and the e-market sub-systems are illustrated using sequence diagrams (for each new use case). Moreover, during the e-market design, a number of class diagrams have to be developed, representing the information that e-market sub-systems hold and exchange, by displaying the classes in a system. Additionally, there have to be developed one or more component diagrams, which will illustrate the components in the e-market system (the physical modules of software code) and the dependencies between them. Finally, another result of e-market design is

a deployment diagram, which is concerned with the physical deployment of the system, the network layout, and the location of components in the network. This diagram illustrates all nodes of the e-market system network, the connections between them, and the processes that will run on each one.

VI. **Prototype implementation.** This step concerns the implementation of the recommendation service components, such as the recommended products' database, the recommendation algorithm or different algorithm variations, and the user interfaces. The outcome of this step is a service prototype, usually as a standalone off-line system module.

VII. **Pilot evaluation.** This step is related to performing an initial evaluation of the service prototype, using either simulated or real data. The appropriate variation of the recommendation algorithm is selected, and the user interface design and functionalities are finalized. If any fine tuning is required, we can go back to Step III. The outcome of this step is the final version of the product recommendation service, ready to be integrated into the e-market system.

A CASE STUDY

In this section, the proposed design process is applied in a real case study. It refers to the integration of a wine recommendation service in a Greek e-market that offers agricultural products (*www.greekproducts.com*). This e-market provides access, among others, to a product catalog of Greek wines. The wines offered come from various producers and areas, and often have totally different characteristics. This e-market is an established one, which does not include a recommendation service so far. A potential buyer can browse categories of wines classified according to characteristics such as the variety name and price range. The results of browsing provide the user with a list of matching wines. In the following, the proposed design steps for integrating a wine recommendation service in this e-market are applied. All UML diagrams have been produced using the Rational Rose modeling tool.

I. Business Modeling

From the buyer's perspective, the e-market business refers to an e-market that facilitates online users in finding appropriate products according to their needs. Thus, the business actors of the e-market under study that will take advantage of the e-market business are the following:

- **Buyer**, who is interested in finding Greek agricultural products in the e-market and is expected to be a consumer or a business entity (retailer, manufacturer, agent/broker, distributor, wholesaler etc.).
- **Seller**, who is offering Greek agricultural products to interested buyers through the e-market and is expected to be a producer, processor, or cooperative/association of producers.

Furthermore, the business workers of the e-market are the following:

- **Transaction processor**, who is responsible for receiving orders, processing them, and taking necessary actions for timely product delivery.
- **Relationships manager**, who is responsible for establishing contact with new business actors (either buyers or sellers).
- **Content provider**, who is responsible for the collection, authoring, and publication of the information in the e-market. This actor is responsible for collecting, publishing, and updating information about available products and about participating sellers.

Moreover, he or she is responsible for all other kinds of content published in the e-market such as news, newsletter, sector studies, and health information.

The business use case diagram of the e-market under study provides an overview of the e-market business context and the way that the involved business actors are engaged (Figure 2). Marked in this diagram is the "Search product" business use case, which will be further analysed in this chapter, since it is the one mainly affected by the integration of the wine recommendation service. The workflow of each business use case can be further analysed in detail using activity diagrams.

II. System Modeling

Since our focus is on the integration of a wine recommendation service, use case modeling is engaged to demonstrate how new use cases can be introduced in the e-market system. For the "Search product" business use case, only the Buyer business actor, the Relationships manager business worker, and the Content provider business worker participate. All of them are involved in a number of system use cases related to the "Search product" business use case, which are:

- **Publish product** concerns the description of a product characteristics and the submission of this description to the e-market.
- **Update product** concerns the modification of some characteristics of a product.
- **Delete product** concerns the request for deletion of a product description from the e-market.
- **View product category** concerns viewing a category of a particular type of products in the e-market.
- **Browse** concerns browsing product categories and viewing lists of products in each category.

Figure 2. Business use case diagram of the case study e-market

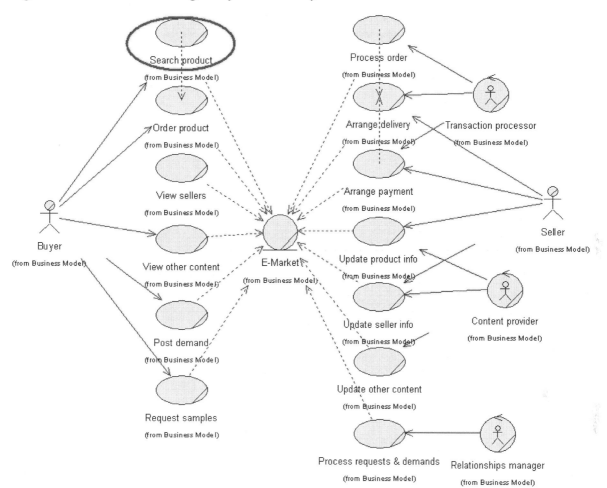

- **View product** concerns viewing the characteristics of a product, as stored in the e-market.

In order to integrate the wine recommendation service in the e-market, the following new use cases have to be added:

- **Make user profile** concerns submitting a registration request to the e-market so that a user profile is created.
- **Approve user profile** concerns checking and approving (or not) a user registration request.

- **Login** concerns the logging in to the e-market process. It aims to allow only registered users to evaluate products and receive recommendations.
- **Evaluate product** concerns the submission of an evaluation (rating) of a product offered by the e-market.
- **Recommend** concerns the request for a recommendation of appropriate products, using already available product evaluations, so that a ranked list of recommended products is presented to the customer.

Figure 3 illustrates the use case diagram that is related to the "Search product" business use case. Marked in this diagram are the additional e-market system use cases required for the wine recommendation service.

III. Definition of Recommendation Items

The products candidate for recommendation in our case study are wines. In the e-market under study, wines are described using characteristics such as a unique ID, their name, their producer, a short description, and their price. The proposed wine recommendation service aims to follow the rationale of the Amazon recommendation service, which collects ratings of products from buyers who have tried them in order to help new buyers decide what to purchase.

In our case study, a more complex recommendation algorithm is engaged, based on multi-attribute utility theory (MAUT) (Keeney, 1992). It will produce wine recommendations based on multi-attribute subjective evaluations. This is the reason why a number of criteria that can affect buyers' choice have to be introduced. For the needs of this case study, eight criteria have been adopted from related literature (Baourakis, Matsatsinis, & Siskos, 1996), forming a set $\{g_1,\ldots,g_8\}$ of criteria for wine evaluation (namely odor, quality, company image, packaging, authenticity, environmental influence, and price advertisement). According to Roy (1996), each criterion g_i $(i=1,\ldots,8)$ is a non-decreasing real valued function,

Figure 3. Use case diagram related to "Search product" business use case

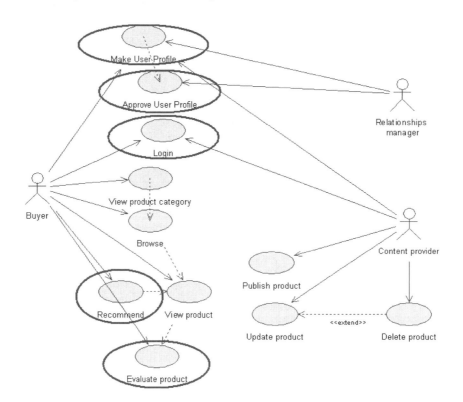

exhaustive, and non-redundant. We engage MAUT to represent the preference of the buyers upon the multiple criteria. Therefore, the total utility U of a wine a is defined as an additive value function of the following form:

$$U(a) = \sum_{i=1}^{8} w_i g_i(a) \qquad (1)$$

where $g_i(a)$ is the evaluation value of product a on criterion g_i, and w_i is a weight indicating the importance of criterion g_i for a particular buyer, with:

$$\sum_{i=1}^{8} w_i = 1 \qquad (2)$$

The MAUT modeling affects the design of the recommendation service, since both the wine evaluations and the evaluator's importance weights have to be stored. This leads to the design of an appropriate database component to store wine evaluations. This component is specified using an ER diagram (Figure 4). A database component

storing the buyer evaluations of wines upon these criteria is added to the system.

IV. Design of Recommendation Algorithm

In order to calculate the utility of a candidate product (wine) for a buyer who initiates the recommendation service, the following recommendation algorithm is considered: let m buyers to have provided evaluations for a particular product a. Now, the utility of the particular product a for each one of the buyers can be calculated. In the case where only one (m=1) evaluation exists, the utility for this buyer is given by formula 1. In the case where more than one (m>1) evaluations exist, the utilities U^k (k=1,…,m) for these buyers are calculated using formula 3:

$$a \rightarrow \begin{cases} U^1 = \sum_{i=1}^{8} w_i^1 g_i^1(a) \\ \quad \dots \\ U^m = \sum_{i=1}^{8} w_i^{z_j} g_i^{z_j}(a) \end{cases} \qquad (3)$$

Figure 4. An ER diagram of the wine evaluations database

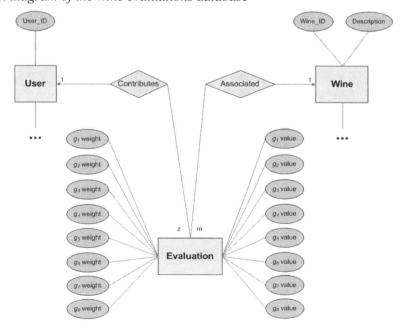

In order to predict the preferences of a new buyer in regards to the product a, the algorithm takes as input the utilities of the previous buyers, and produces as outcome the predicted utility U^{buyer}. A flowchart of this algorithm is depicted in Figure 5. Different formulas can be used for calculating U^{buyer}, leading to different variations of the algorithm that can be compared for performance.

V. Integrated System Analysis & Design

In the studied e-market system, use cases are supported by a set of sub-systems. The following e-market sub-systems are identified:

- **Interface sub-system**, responsible for the interaction with the users, passing information to and from the users to the e-market.

Figure 5. The recommendation algorithm flow

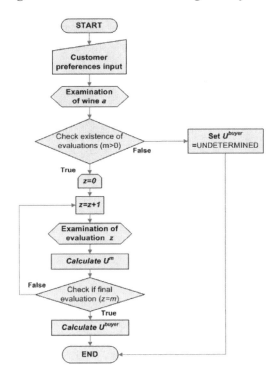

- **Search sub-system**, responsible for transforming user search interactions to queries that are understandable from e-market, as well as for returning the results to the interface sub-system.
- **Repository sub-system**, responsible for storing the descriptions and evaluations of products, providing data to the e-market interface according to the users' requests.

Sequence diagrams have been produced for each new use case. For brevity reasons, only the sequence diagram for the "Evaluate product" use case is presented (Figure 6). Moreover, for the e-market design, class diagrams have also been produced for the new use cases. Figure 8 presents the component diagram for the "Evaluate product" use case. More specifically, the user is authenticated and logs into the system, using the appropriate component user authentication (after the user information is checked in the users database). Then, the eight components that collect both the importance weight and the evaluation upon each criterion are appropriately storing them in the product evaluation database. Finally, Figure 9 presents the deployment diagram of the studied e-market system. At the server side, a MySQL server is the database server of the e-market that manages the e-market databases. At the same machine, an Apache Web server has been also installed, together with CGI scripting capabilities. On the client side, the user can view the e-market though a Web browser.

VI. Prototype Implementation

In this step, the prototype off-line version of the recommendation service has been implemented. Figure 10 provides an example of the wine recommendation user interface design. It demonstrates how on a regular screenshot of the e-market under study, a recommendation hint will appear next to a specific wine when the list of 'Search' results is presented to a buyer. The total suitability of a

Figure 6. Sequence diagram for "Evaluate product" use case

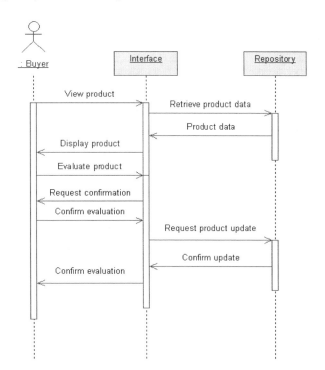

wine for the buyer is scaled to a value from *1* to *5* and represented as a number of stars (a visual cue often used in such systems).

Figure 11 illustrates the way the wine recommendation service prototype can be integrated with the existing e-market architecture. In this figure, a layered view of the e-market with five levels of abstraction is presented: data storage, data management, supporting services, market services, and user interfaces. Each of these layers contains a number of e-market components, which have been enriched by the introduction of the additional system components (highlighted in Figure 11). For instance, the market services level included the "publish new wine," "browse wine list," and "view wine details" services. By integrating the recommendation service, an "evaluate wine" service has been added at this layer. Similarly, the "wine recommendation algorithm" has been added to the supporting services level, and the "wine evaluations" to the data storage level. The

new components of the studied e-market layered architecture have been implemented according to the results of the proposed design steps.

VII. Pilot Evaluation

This step deals with the selection of the appropriate variation of the wine recommendation algorithm. Simulated data about existing wines and their evaluations have been created and stored in the e-market system databases. More specifically, the wines' database has been populated with the descriptions of 10 wines $\{a_1, .., a_{10}\}$. It was assumed that a group of simulated buyers had previously provided evaluations for all 10 wines. Results comparing the recommendations of the algorithm variations to the actual preferences of buyers have been produced. The pilot evaluation results indicated which variation seems to be more suitable for the wine recommendation service of the examined e-market (Manouselis & Costopou-

Figure 7. Class diagram for the "Evaluate product" use case (holds for all products, as well as for the wine case study)

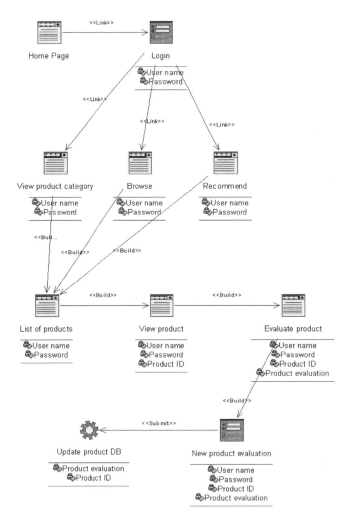

lou, 2005). The integration of the proposed wine recommendation service in the e-market system has not yet taken place. The public deployment of this service in the e-market will be fully operative after the final decision of the e-market owners.

CONCLUSION

Recommender systems can offer important added value when integrated into e-markets. They can support potential buyers during the information gathering phase by providing product recommendations that match their preferences. However, the majority of the existing e-markets are not providing advanced recommendation services, although such services may offer a competitive advantage to an e-market. Some reasons might be the inherent complexity of intelligent recommendation services, as well as their deployment and evaluation costs. Currently, recommendation services are developed on a case-by-case basis, and to our knowledge there are no guidelines for integrating product recommendation services in e-markets.

Figure 8. Component diagram corresponding for "Evaluating product" use case (depicts only the components for only the wine case study, for other products additional ones will have to be included according to their evaluation criteria)

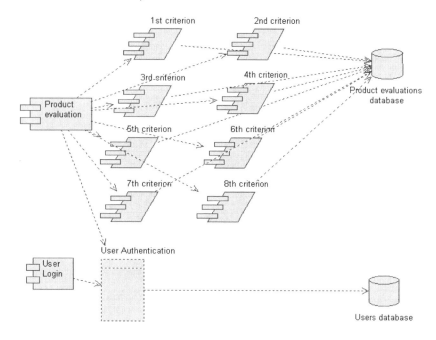

Figure 9. Deployment diagram of e-market

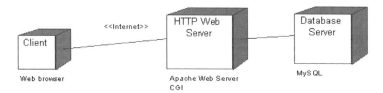

To this direction, it is worth it to identify a framework for an efficient design process that will reduce the complexity of this kind of deployment. In particular, it is important to provide e-market designers with guidelines on how to efficiently design, develop, evaluate, and integrate recommendation services in existing e-markets. Thus, this chapter presented a design process for integrating intelligent product recommendation services in e-markets. This process is applied to a real e-market offering Greek agricultural products, for the deployment of a recommendation service of a particular type of products (i.e., wine). Similar services can be developed for other types of products. This work may be useful to two groups: academics/researchers studying product recommendation services for e-commerce applications; and e-market system designers and implementers considering the integration of product recommendation services in e-markets. Our next steps include the application of the proposed design process in other e-markets.

Future trends in the design and integration of intelligent recommendation services in e-markets include more focus on the aspects of evaluating different AI-based recommendation techniques, in order to choose the most appropriate one for

Figure 10. Interface design for wine recommendation results

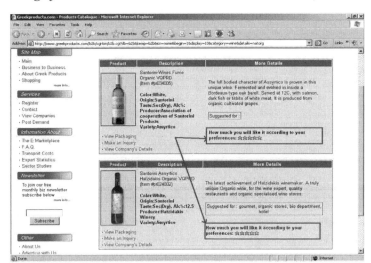

Figure 11. Wine recommendation integrated into layered e-market architecture

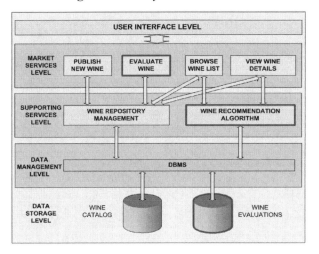

deploying in a particular market context. This type of evaluation mainly includes two aspects:

- The evaluation of the different ways recommendations can be presented and explained to the buyers of the e-markets (small-scaled pilot experiments can help e-market designers to decide, for example, the appropriate interface design, as discussed by Herlocker, Konstan, & Riedl, 2000).
- The evaluation of various intelligent techniques for the recommendation algorithms so that the one providing higher accuracy and

coverage results can be selected (simulation experiments can facilitate this design choice decisions, as discussed by Herlocker et al., 2002).

REFERENCES

Baourakis, G., Matsatsinis, N. F., & Siskos, Y. (1996). Agricultural product development using multidimensional and multicriteria analyses: The case of wine. *European Journal of Operational Research, 94*(2), 321-334.

Boggs, W., & Boggs, M. (2002). *Mastering UML with Rational Rose.* Alameda, CA: SYBEX Inc.

Booch, G., Rumbaugh, J., & Jacobson, I. (1998). *The Unified Modelling Language user guide.* Boston: Addison Wesley.

Burke, R. (2002). Hybrid recommender systems: Survey and experiments. *User Modelling and User-Adapted Interaction, 12,* 331-370.

Changchien, S. W., & Lu, T.-C. (2001). Mining association rules procedure to support on-line recommendation by customers and products fragmentation. *Expert Systems with Applications, 20,* 325-335.

Cheung, K.-W., Kwok, J. T., Law, M. H., & Tsui, K.-C. (2003). Mining customer product ratings for personalized marketing. *Decision Support Systems, 35,* 231-243.

Cho, Y. H., Kim, J. K., & Kim, S. H. (2002). A personalised recommender system based on Web usage mining and decision tree induction. *Expert System with Applications, 23,* 329-342.

Deshpande, M., & Karypis, G. (2004). Item-based Top-N recommendation algorithms. *ACM Transactions on Information Systems, 22*(1), 143-177.

Herlocker, J., Konstan, J. A., & Riedl, J. (2000). *Explaining collaborative filtering recommendations.* Paper presented at the 2000 Conference on Computer Supported Cooperative Work.

Herlocker, J., Konstan, J. A., & Riedl, J. (2002). An empirical analysis of design choices in neighborhood-based collaborative filtering algorithms. *Information Retrieval, 5,* 287-310.

Herlocker, J. L., Konstan, J. A., Terveen, L. G., & Riedl, J. T. (2004). Evaluating collaborative filtering recommender systems. *ACM Transactions on Information Systems, 22*(1), 5-53.

Holzmueller, H. H., & Schluechter J. (2002). Delphi study about the future of B2B marketplaces in Germany. *Electronic Commerce Research & Applications, 1,* 2-19.

Hung, L. (2005). A personalized recommendation system based on product taxonomy for one-to-one marketing online. *Expert Systems with Applications, 29*(2), 383-392.

Keeney, R. L. (1992). *Value-focusedtThinking: A path to creative decision making.* Cambridge, MA: Harvard University Press.

Kim, J. K., Cho, Y. H., Kim, W. J., Kim, J. R., & Suh, J. H. (2002). A personalized recommendation procedure for Internet shopping support. *Electronic Commerce Research and Applications, 1,* 301-313.

Kim, J.W., Lee, B. H., Shaw, M. J., Chang, H.-L., & Nelson, M. (2001). Application of decision-tree induction techniques to personalized advertisements on Internet storefronts. *International Journal of Electronic Commerce, 5*(3), 45-62.

Kim, Y. S., Yum, B.-J., Song, J., & Kim, S. M. (2005). Development of a recommender system based on navigational and behavioral patterns of customers in e-commerce sites. *Expert Systems with Applications, 28*(2), 381-393.

Lee, J.-S., Jun, C.-H., Lee, J., & Kim, S. (2005). Classification-based collaborative filtering using market basket data. *Expert Systems with Applications, 29,* 700-704.

Lee, W.-P. (2004) Towards agent-based decision making in the electronic marketplace: Interactive recommendation and automated negotiation. *Expert Systems with Applications, 27*(4), 665-679.

Li, Y., Lu, L., & Xuefeng, L. (2005). A hybrid collaborative filtering method for multiple-interests and multiple-content recommendation in E-Commerce. *Expert Systems with Applications, 28,* 67-77.

Lihua, W., Lu, L., Jing, L., & Zongyong, L. (2005). Modeling multiple interests by an improved GCS approach. *Expert Systems with Applications, 29*, 757-767.

Manouselis, N., Costopoulou, C. (2005). *Designing Recommendation Services for e-Markets* (Tech. Rep.) Athens, Greece: Agricultural University of Athens, Informatics Laboratory.

Martin-Guerrero, J. D., Palomares, A., Balaguer-Ballester, E., Soria-Olivas, E., Gomez-Sanchis, J., & Soriano-Asensi, A. (in press). Studying the feasibility of a recommender in a citizen Web portal based on user modeling and clustering algorithms. *Expert Systems with Applications, 30*, 299-312.

Middleton, S. E., Shadbolt, N. R., & Roure, D. C. (2004). Ontological user profiling in recommender systems. *ACM Transactions on Information Systems, 22*(1), 54-88.

Miller, B. N., Konstan, J. A., & Riedl, J. (2004). PocketLens: Toward a personal recommender system. *ACM Transactions on Information Systems, 22*(3), 437-476.

Resnick, P., & Varian, H. R. (1997). Recommender systems. *Communications of the ACM, 40*(3), 56-58.

Richard, B., & Tchounikine, P. (2004). Enhancing the adaptivity of an existing Website with an epiphyte recommender system. *New Review of Hypermedia and Multimedia, 10*(1), 31-52.

Roy, B. (1996). *Multicriteria methodology for decision aiding.* Dordrecht, The Netherlands: Kluwer Academic Publishers.

Saleh, K. (2002). Documenting electronic commerce systems and software using the unified modelling language. *Information and Software Technology, 44*, 303-311.

Schafer, J. B., Konstan, J., & Riedl, J. (2001). E-commerce recommendation applications. *Data Mining and Knowledge Discovery, 5*, 115-153.

Stolze, M. (2002). Domain-oriented recommender applications: A framework for intimate recommending. In F. Ricci & B. Smith (Eds.), *Proceedings of the Adaptive Hypermedia Workshop on Recommendation and Personalization in eCommerce* (pp. 24-131). Computer Science Technical Report, Malaga: University of Malaga.

Wang, Y.-F., Chuang, Y.-L., Hsu, M.-H., & Keh, H.-C. (2004). A personalized recommender system for the cosmetic business. *Expert Systems with Applications, 26*, 427-434.

Yen, B. P.-C., & Kong, R. C. W. (2002). Personalization of information access for electronic catalogs on the Web. *Electronic Commerce Research and Applications, 1*, 20-40.

This work was previously published in Artificial Intelligence and Integrated Intelligent Information Systems: Emerging Technologies and Applications, edited by X. Zha, pp. 398-417, copyright 2007 by IGI Publishing (an imprint of IGI Global).

Chapter 3.15
Improving M-Commerce Services Effectiveness with the Use of User-Centric Content Delivery

Panagiotis Germanakos
National & Kapodistrian University of Athens, Greece

Nikos Tsianos
National & Kapodistrian University of Athens, Greece

Zacharias Lekkas
National & Kapodistrian University of Athens, Greece

Constantinos Mourlas
National & Kapodistrian University of Athens, Greece

George Samaras
University of Cyprus, Cyprus

ABSTRACT

Advances in wireless communications and information technology have made the Mobile Web a reality. The Mobile Web is the response to the need for anytime, anywhere access to information and services. Many wireless applications have already been deployed and are available to customers via their mobile phones and wirelessly-connected PDAs. However, as communications and other IT usage becomes an integral part of many people's lives and the available products and services become more varied and capable, users expect to be able to personalize a service to meet their individual needs and preferences. The involved sectors have to meet these challenges by reengineering their front-end and back-end office. This article will examine the interaction requirements regarding a friendlier, personalized and more effective multi-channel services environment. It will present the mobility challenges and constraints implemented into the business sector, investigating the current m-commerce situation and the extended user characteristics presenting a high level user-centric m-commerce architecture.

INTRODUCTION

The Internet revolution has brought about a new wave of conducting business and proved to be an important marketing tool for all sorts of business fields that found this new means as convenient as it is creative. With the emergence of wireless and mobile technologies, new communication platforms and devices, apart from PC-based Internet access, are now emerging, making the delivery of services available through a variety of multi-channel mediums without loosing their integrity or quality of their content (Germanakos et al., 2005a). Inevitably, this increases user requirements, which are now focused upon an *"anytime, anywhere and anyhow"* basis. Moreover, the explosive growth in the size and use of the World Wide Web as well as the complicated nature of most Web structures may lead in orientation difficulties, as users often lose sight of the goal of their inquiry, look for stimulating rather than informative material, or even use the navigational features unwisely. To alleviate such navigational difficulties, researchers have put huge amounts of effort to identify the peculiarities of each user group and design methodologies and systems that could deliver an adapted and personalized Web content. Challenges therefore range not only on adapting to the heterogeneous user needs and user environment issues, such as current location and time (Panayiotou, & Samaras, 2004), but also on a number of other considerations with respect to multi-channel delivery of the applications concerning multimedia, services, entertainment, commerce, and so forth. That is why, when the next big thing in technological gadgets, the mobile phone flooded the market, offering cheap SMS services using the GSM technology and enabling the extremely successful i-Mode and mobile Internet, various business institutions felt they couldn't stay away from this new rising opportunity.

Relevant channel and distribution strategies are critical for future advancement of m-commerce services to achieve accessible, customer-focused and responsive services. Following the growing user demands and requirements as well as the rapid development of the technological advancements and infrastructure capabilities, the development of m-commerce services should not only focus on making the service available on the Internet, but also examine the different delivery platforms. Indisputably, this is the vision of an interoperable, transparent and secure continent whereby multi-channel service delivery integration is considered fundamental.

This article emphasizes the proliferation of m-commerce services delivery starting with a reference to multi-channel delivery characteristics of user-centric services and the investigation of the m-commerce status and dimensions in various application areas (market fields). The adaptation and personalization considerations with regards to new user requirements and demands is also analyzed emphasizing the significance and peculiarities of user profiling for providing a more personalized m-commerce services result. It further presents a high level architecture for personalizing m-commerce services, introducing a comprehensive user profiling that incorporates intrinsic user characteristics such as user perceptual preferences (visual, cognitive and emotional processing parameters), on top of the "traditional" ones (such as name, age, education, etc.).

SERVICE REQUIREMENTS AND DELIVERY

To struggle against the amplification of the digital divide and therefore to think 'user interaction' whatever the age, income, education, experience, and the social condition of the citizen. (Europe's Information Society, 2004)

The specific theme above reveals exactly the need for user-centric m-government services development and personalized content delivery. In many ways, the new technology provides greater opportunities for access. However, there are important problems in determining precisely what users want and need, and how to provide Web-based services content in a user-friendly and effective way. User needs are always conditioned by what they already get, or imagine they can get. A channel can change the user perception of an m-government application: when users have a free choice between different channels to access an application, they will choose the channel that realizes the highest relative value for them. However, separate development of different channels for a single service (multi-channel delivery) can lead to inconsistencies such as different data formats or interfaces. To overcome the drawbacks of multiple-channel content delivery, the different channels should be integrated and coordinated.

Since successful m-government service delivery depends on a vast range of parameters, there is not a single formula to fit all situations. However, there have been reported particular steps (IDA, 2004) that could guide a provider throughout the channel selection process. Moreover, it should be mentioned that the suitability and usefulness of channels depends on a range of factors, out of which technology is only one element. Additional features that could affect the service channels assessment could be: directness, accessibility and inclusion, speed, security and privacy and availability. To realize their potential value though, channels need also to be properly implemented and operated.

The design and implementation complexity is rising significantly with the many channels and their varying capabilities and limitations. Network issues include low bandwidth, unreliable connectivity, lack of processing power, limited interface of wireless devices and user mobility. On the other hand, mobile devices issues include small size, limited processing power, limited memory and storage space, small screens, high latency, and restricted data entry (Germanakos et al., 2005a).

AN OVERVIEW OF M-COMMERCE/ M-MARKETING THEORETICAL FRAMEWORK

It is generally agreed that m-commerce is the use of mobile or handheld devices for communication and commerce transactions without any formal conceptualization of the term currently in existence, due to the continuous technological evolution. Therefore, there is no clear, inclusive and broad definition of all the aspects it might include (Balasubramanian et al., 2002).

What needs to be taken into account is what m-commerce means for an organisation belonging to a specific market field and which definition is more close to the needs of these institutions. Therefore, Easton's (2002) approach could be more descriptive, simple and close to what these organisations need to know about the m-commerce term. Easton claims that: (a) m-commerce is the purchase of a product or a service through wireless devices; (b) there is a number of physical limitations to the above devices indicating to the end-user that it is more convenient to sign up to mobile services by using the traditional interface of the PCs; and (c) the models used by the organisations in the case of m-commerce are more close to "click and mortar" paradigm. For example, in a theatre context the users will receive information about the performance and the box office contact details through mobile commerce and then they will purchase the ticket at the box office, or payment of the ticket will be done wirelessly with various methods, but still the transaction will be fulfilled when the purchaser attends the performance at the theatre.

Furthermore, what someone should be interested in is not the mobile Internet itself, "the representation of the physical world" in the wireless devices, but rather the mobile marketplace in which different kinds of transactions take place: communication services and wireless purchase. The mobile marketplace covers three dimensions (see *Figure 1*): personalisation according to local

737

Figure 1. M-marketplace dimensions

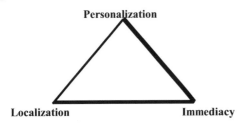

position of the holder and the relevance of information to his preferences, localization through the local based services, and immediacy (Lindgren, Jedbratt, & Svebsson, 2002).

As literature indicates, mobile phones are a communication medium that keeps people connected at any place, wherever they go and any time. Therefore, it is accounted as the most effective tool of direct marketing, while wireless marketing involves reaching and servicing customers and developing relationships with them through premium services (Bayne, 2002). Towse & Elgew (2003) describe marketing as "the process whereby the organisation's goals for its products and services are strategically developed and implemented to meet carefully reached price, product, place and promotion preferences of targeted customer groups." In this mentioned marketing mix (5Ps: product, place, promotion, price and, for arts organisations, people) it is clear that the mobile phone sets a new spectrum of marketing applications.

The infrastructures to support great financial transaction through mobile devices are still under development and consequently the mobile phone is used more closely to marketing applications. Therefore, the greater part of analysis in this article mainly concerns the modern m-marketing services era and dedicates a narrower part to the transactional nature of the medium. However, m-marketing is included by definition in the term of "m-commerce," and in the article the terms are used according to each case.

Under the term "m-marketing," two main methods are analyzed: push and pull marketing.

Pull marketing method involves the consumers pulling what interests them toward themselves, either the product or information itself. Here the messages are sent instantly after a personal request of the recipient. In the case of push marketing method the marketer sends—or better—pushes the message to the consumers, but in this case the message is sent massively to the subscribers of such service. Another term that is under the umbrella of push marketing is "location-based services" (LBS) or "mobile location services" (MLS). These are "applications that utilize information related to the geographical position of their users in order to provide value-added services to them" (Giaglis et al., 2003).

Mobile Related Technological Aspects

The present technologies used in telecommunication are GSM (générale système mobile/global system for mobile communications), WAP (wireless application protocol), and GPRS (general packet radio service), which, accompanied by the third generation mobile devices (3G), offer to the end-user a broad variety of capabilities. Mobiles can hardly replace computers due to device limitations such as the screen and the low memory. Even processing capabilities were quite low in the beginning of the 3G development. The first services offered were mostly data services like text alerts for news and entertainment. These alerts are closely related to the wider used form of communication, text messages or else SMS. Text messages are enriched in the later version of the 3G devices with graphics, videos or picture launched as the MMS (multimedia message services) services (Paavilainen, 2002). The services that are slowly launched in the telecommunication markets are the location-based services, which are closely related to the global positioning system (GPS), cell identification and Bluetooth. With these technologies each mobile is detected according to its exact location (Giaglis et al., 2003). With Bluetooth it will be easier to receive text alerts customized to the geographical location, for example, information about the nearest theatre, or receive a promotion alert when the user is near to a theatre house.

The Role of New Media in Modern Society

It would be inadequate to examine the use of mobile commerce and marketing by the vari-

ous business institutions without presenting the general context of the modern era and what has led to the decision of following this innovative technology. Subsequent to the suggestions that technologies should not be seen without being connected to other processes and factors that set the frameworks, we present an overview to the social and economic tendencies that lead to the spread of m-commerce (Hesmondhalgh, 2002).

Table 1. Challenges of marketing in digital era

Frameworks	Trends
Globalisation	1. global market
	2. global brands, i.e., Tate
	3. Global organizations, i.e., Guggenheim
Society	1. cash rich, time poor → materialistic hedonism
	2. increased leisure time, "the hurried leisure class"
	3. increased technology ownership (mobile, PCs, PDAs)
	4. Individualism
Technology	1. digitalistion of cultural products and data compression, i.e., musical pieces in Mp3 formats, films in DVD
	2. Internet → development of peer-to-peer transactions, e-commerce
	3. rise of Internet → growth of commerce
	4. Information, easy access o data
Virtualisation of digital channels	1. development of new channels, i.e., mobile phones and virtualization of products/services
Virtualisation of payments	1. plastic cards with magnetic stripe/ chip & pin (debit, credit, loyalty cards)
	2. Smart cards
	3. electronic cash/ electronic wallet
	4. Micropayments
Media trends	1. from mass messages to individual
	2. From generic to specific
	3. from print to electronic
	4. from passive to interactive
	5. from plenty of time to fastest way of communication
	6. 24 hours a day/ 7 days a week, global presence
Law	1. Issues of privacy and security
	2. Data Protection Act
	3. Intellectual Property issues
	4. fraud

The use of mobile is not just a technological trend that needs to be followed. Practice has shown that society accepts technological developments not just for the sake of fashion but when they offer an advanced solution to the needs of each era. The social and economical index change continuously and the market itself decides which technology will spread and survive. The next step is the high penetration of video phones with high resolution screens or i-mode services whose music portals and ringtone downloads have created havoc to the networking marketplace. Therefore, it is the market that allows ideas and technological visions to become part of the everyday consuming life (Knell, 2003). In *Table 1* that follows, we refer to the main issues rising in the modern digital era (Hesmondhalgh, 2002; O'Connor, 2001; Postma, 1999).

Taking into account all these factors, the business institution has to face a number of challenges in modern life. As consumers live in a multimedia and cross-cultural environment, they demand combinations of forms and new delivery methods, the marketers should keep in mind that they have to satisfy these needs in order to keep their audiences close to their institution.

EVALUATING M-COMMERCE IN RELATION TO VARIOUS MARKET FIELDS

It is quite clear so far that the literature offered on the subject of m-commerce is quite narrow and even sometimes inadequate. In the past five years there were a number of managerial handbooks analyzing the new mobile era either for commerce or marketing. The initial stimuli derived from the book of Turban et al. (2002) where the authors dedicate the last chapter to mobile commerce as a natural evolution of e-commerce through a new portable medium. The m-commerce is perceived as a follower of e-commerce (Easton, 2002) as long as mobile Internet is developed and so the

consumers are able to use portable devices to purchase items. Mobile phone is seen by many authors as the physical transformation of the Internet and the leader of the new media (Stafford et al., 2004; Candace, 2005).

Paavilainen (2002) introduces the mobile Internet as the alternative of desktop Internet. Mobile advertising, text alerts and mobile commerce models are described through different case studies from the commercial sector. Mobile entertainment, that is, ringtones, downloads and text alerts, is rich with cases from music and film industries, as sector journals like the New Media Age show. Although someone would think that this marketing trend would hardly expand in other forms of the business institutions, like culture, there is a release by the DigiCULT (2004) scheme that proves the opposite. Mobile devices applying location-based services (LBS) can be integrated in a museum or gallery exhibition giving the option to be another communication channel after the audio guides and the information kiosks. Moreover, scenarios like booking tickets through mobile, receiving text alerts for the latest exhibition or information how to get to an art gallery are becoming more obvious examples in the cultural sectors. The referred applications are included according to Mahatanankoon et al. (2005) in two modes of m-commerce: (i) the content delivery mode and (ii) the transaction mode.

Mobile Marketing

As part of the new strategies, the use of the mobile as a marketing and communication tool plays mainly an important role. With the introduction of text messaging boom marketers were totally influenced and seized the SMS as a new advertising chance. Haig (2002) describes the history of SMS and introduces various applications of mobile devices in marketing like the text alerts. With the introduction of the third generation mobile phones (3G) the capabilities of the devices to support image, sounds and movie clips grow, increasing the number of applications. Marketers find themselves holding a powerful interactive and totally personal marketing tool. However, there are still a great number of barriers which limit the widespread of the medium and its success according to Scharl et al. (2005), and they have to do either with the technological features of the devices, the transmission process or customer behaviour itself.

Customer Behaviour

Kleijnen et al. (2004) used the Technology Acceptance Model (TAM) to examine a number of factors that influence the quicker penetration of mobile technologies in the market in order to explain this trend of text messaging. Factors like cost of the devices and services, the value they offer to the end-user as well as the easiness of use are important in order to make special mobile services apart from voice mail more acceptable. Moreover, Brumer & Kumar (2005) also introduced the influential factors of utility, convenience and fun, which are the most interesting point, for example, for an arts organisation. An innovative and entertaining way of advertising, promotion or ticket booking could be critical in order to catch the customers' attention and make them act. This last factor mainly influences the mobile advertisements (m-advertisement), toward which the attitude of consumers is more positive

than toward traditional advertising, as Tsang et al. (2004) claim. What influences the attitudes of the end-users apart from the entertaining way of presentation is the content of the provided advertising services and its amount of information.

A key concept that should be looked into is the limitation of the irritation caused by interfering and unwanted messages. Therefore, it is important for organisation using the mobile services to ask for permission to deliver them to customer. Permission marketing is the term that should be closely related to any action of direct marketing.

Permission Marketing and Trust

Godin's book "Permission Marketing" (2002) is the most common reference in the literature under the subject of mobile marketing (Kavassalis et al., 2003) and there is no critical point suggested by other authors toward what it claims. The introduction of permission in marketing tactics, especially in direct promotions, comes in contraposition to the traditional way of advertising—interruptive marketing, as explained later.

Additionally, trust, security and privacy are the emerging issues for m-commerce. The fear of manipulation of personal data is the main limit in the consumer's shift to positive attitude. Good sources of information about privacy policies are the independent protecting bodies set to protect the end-users [for example, the Data Protection

Figure 2. An m-commerce personalization architecture

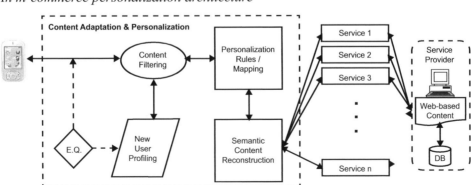

Act of 1998 is followed by the majority of the cases and the organisations show great respect to its lines, the Wireless Location Industry Association (WLIA) declares an adopted privacy policy by its members and so did the Mobile Marketing Association (MMA) with a relative declaration]. It must also be said though, that in cases of transactions through mobile phones, the risk of hacking is lower than that of the Internet due to the evolving technologies and the use of high standard encryption.

Effectiveness

How could effectiveness be defined in a very unstable context? This is the main question underlying this subject. It is quite difficult to find research on the effectiveness of the new medium due to the very recent introduction of mobile commerce in the market. The given difficulty still rises given the peculiarities of the various market fields. More specifically, for an arts organisation, for example, it is even more difficult to define effectiveness, as this can be meant under totally different aspects depending on what aims each cultural institution has set. Drucker (1995) and Heman & Renz (1999) also briefly referred to the effectiveness in non-profit organisations.

The factors that can make mobile an effective new media for organizations were examined in depth. A good attempt to measure the wireless marketing results by introducing the Mobile Return of Investment (ROI) was also made by Bayne (2002) and that is a useful guide for any organisation which wishes to monitor its investment on this new technology. Moreover, Kavassalis et al. (2003) introduced more indicators of effectiveness in their empirical studies, while Frolick & Chen (2004) assess the mobile commerce applications.

The majority of the research converges to the same conclusion. No matter what the effects of the mobile practices are, which in each case can be totally different, what is important is the benefit

that someone can gain by being the first in the market for using this new technology.

PRINCIPLE DRIVERS OF AN M-COMMERCE OPEN SERVICE INFRASTRUCTURE

The deployment of a m-commerce open service platform that could be shared by networked private and public institutions could be a promising approach with further insights on maintaining wireless service provision sustainability in a long-term perspective. Wireless technology is about extending the availability of an e-commerce infrastructure to mobile and wireless channels. It becomes more fully developed and, as bandwidth increases with the availability of "always on" connectivity, next generation applications and entirely new practices will arise different from those delivered over existing static networks (Caldow, 2001).

The large array of new communication technology opportunities and the rapid emergence and change of standards, as well as the variety of mobile channels, offer different technical capabilities for sustainable architectures and technology frameworks in order to meet critical requirements like broadband, interoperability, scalability, transparency, personalization, privacy and security (Germanakos et al., 2005a).

Extended User Requirements and the Personalization Problem

The user population is not homogeneous, nor should be treated as such. To be able to deliver quality services, m-commerce systems should be tailored to the needs of individual users providing them with personalized and adapted information based on their perceptions, reactions, and demands. Therefore, a serious analysis of user requirements has to be undertaken, documented and examined taking into consideration their multi-application to the various delivery channels and devices. Some of the user (customer) requirements and arguments anticipated could be clearly distinguished into (Germanakos et al., 2005c): (a) general user service requirements (flexibility: anyhow, anytime, anywhere; accessibility; quality; and security), and (b) requirements for a friendly and effective user interaction (information acquisition; system controllability; navigation; versatility; errors handling; and personalization).

Although one-to-one Web-based service provision may be a functionality of the distant future, user segmentation is a very valuable step in the right direction. User segmentation means that the user population is subdivided into more or less homogeneous, mutually exclusive subsets of users who share common user profile characteristics. The subdivisions could be based on: demographic characteristics (i.e., age, gender, urban or rural-based, region); socio-economic characteristics (i.e., income, class, sector, channel access); psychographic characteristics (i.e., lifestyle, values, sensitivity to new trends); individual physical and psychological characteristics (i.e., disabilities, attitude, loyalty).

The issue of personalization is a complex one with many aspects and viewpoints that need to be analyzed and resolved. Some of these issues become even more complicated once viewed from a moving user's perspective; in other words, when constraints of mobile channels and devices are involved. Such issues include, but are not limited to: what content to present to the user, how to show the content to the user, how to ensure the user's privacy, how to create a global personalization scheme. As clearly viewed, user characteristics and needs, determining user segmentation and thus provision of the adjustable information delivery, differ according to the circumstances and they change over time (Panayiotou & Samaras, 2004).

User Profiling Characteristics: A More Comprehensive Approach

One of the key technical issues in developing personalization applications is the problem of how to construct accurate and comprehensive profiles of individual users and how these can be used to identify a user and describe the user behaviour, especially if they are moving (Adomavicious & Tuzhilin, 1999). According to the Merriam-Webster Dictionary, the term profile means "a representation of something in outline." User profile can be thought of as being a set of data representing the significant features of the user, like preferences, characteristics, and activities, derived from a set of keywords that are compared against information items.

User profiling can either be *static*, when it contains information that rarely or never changes (e.g., demographic information), or *dynamic*, when the data change frequently. Such information is obtained either *explicitly*, using online registration forms and questionnaires resulting in static user profiles, or *implicitly*, by recording the navigational behaviour and/or the preferences of each user. In the case of implicit acquisition of user data, each user can either be regarded as a member of group and take up an aggregate user profile or be addressed individually and take up an individual user profile. The data used for constructing a user profile could be distinguished into: (a) the data model, which could be classified into the demographic model (which describes who the user is), and the transactional model (which describes what the user does); and (b) the profile model, which could be further classified into the factual profile (containing specific facts about the user derived from transactional data, including the demographic data), and the behavioural profile (modeling the behaviour of the user using conjunctive rules, such as association or classification rules). The use of rules in profiles provides an intuitive, declarative and modular way to describe user behaviour (Adomavicious & Tuzhilin, 1999)). Additionally, in the case of a mobile user, by user needs it is implied both the thematic preferences (i.e., the traditional notion of profile) as well as the characteristics of their personal device called "device profile." Therefore, here, adaptive personalization is concerned with the negotiation of user requirements and device abilities. As Web developers regard personalization as the best way to filter out unnecessary or irrelevant information for their users, some argue on issues like it may restrict the extent and the variety of information users receive, that people often do not have well-defined preferences, they need to answer detailed questions to personalize their Web pages, that the recommendation process is a black box for end-users and so on (Wang & Lin, 2002).

But, could the user profiling be considered complete incorporating only these dimensions? Do the designers and developers of m-commerce applications take into consideration the real users' preferences in order to provide them with really personalized Web-based service content? Many times this is not the case. How can a user profiling be considered complete, and the preferences derived optimized, if it does not contain parameters related to the user perceptual preference characteristics? We could define *user perceptual preference characteristics* as all the critical factors that influence the visual, mental and emotional processes liable of manipulating the new information received and building upon prior knowledge that is different for each user or user group. These characteristics, which have been primarily discussed in Germanakos et al. (2006), determine the visual attention, cognitive and emotional processing taking place throughout the whole process of accepting an object of perception (stimulus) until the comprehensive response to it (Germanakos et al., 2005c). The proposed comprehensive user profiling could be considered as the main raw content filtering module of an m-commerce personalization architecture. To our knowledge, nowadays, there is not research that

moves towards the consideration of user profiling incorporating optimized parameters taken from these research areas in combination.

AN OVERVIEW OF M-COMMERCE PERSONALIZATION ARCHITECTURE

Based on the above-mentioned considerations, an m-commerce personalization architecture is overviewed trying to convey the essence and the peculiarities encapsulated. The current system, depicted in *Figure 2*, is composed of a number of interrelated components, as detailed below:

Entry Point

It is the user access interface of the system. It accepts multi-device (enables the attachment of various devices on the infrastructure, such as mobile phones, PDAs, desktop devices, etc.) identifying the characteristics of the device and the preferences as well as the location of the user (personalization/location-based) and multi-channel (due to the variety of multi-channel delivery, for example, over the Web, telephone, interactive kiosks and so on, this module will identify the different characteristics of the channels) requests. It is directly communicating with the "content filtering" component exchanging multi-purpose data.

Content Filtering

This component is considered the main link of the "entry point" with the "'new' user profiling" and the "personalization rules/mapping" components of the architecture. It actually transmits the data accumulated both directions and it makes the filtering of the content, according to the personalization processing characteristics, delivering the adapted and personalized service. The whole processing varies from security, authentication, user segmentation, service content identification, "new" user profiling characteristics and so forth.

"New" User Profiling

This is the main component of the architecture and it is called "'new' user profiling" component. At this component all the requests are processed. It is responsible for the custom tailoring of information to be delivered to the users, taking into consideration their habits and preferences, as well as, for mobile users mostly, their location ("location-based") and time ("time-based") of access (Panayiotou & Samaras, 2006). It also keeps the user logs and retrieves data according to user login to the system. This component accepts requests from the "entry point" component and, after the necessary processing and further communication with the "content filtering" component, either sends information back or communicates with the next component ("personalization rules/mapping") accordingly. This component is comprised of the following two elements:

The "Traditional" User Profile

It contains all the information related to the user necessary for the Web personalization processing. It is composed of two elements: the (a) user characteristics (the so-called "traditional" charac-

teristics of a user: knowledge, goals, background, experience, preferences, activities, etc.), and (b) the device/channel characteristics (contains characteristics referring to the device or channel the user is using and contains information like: bandwidth, size, connectivity, power processing, interface and data entry, memory and storage space, battery lifetime, etc. These characteristics are mostly referred to mobile users and are considered important for the formulation of a more integrated user profile, since it determines the technical aspects of it). Both elements are completing the user profiling from the user's point of view.

User Perceptual Preference Characteristics

This is the new component/dimension of the user profiling. It contains all the visual attention, cognitive and emotional processing parameters that completes the user preferences and fulfils the user profile. User perceptual preference characteristics could be described as a continuous mental processing starting with the perception of an object in the user's attentional visual field and going through a number of cognitive, learning and

Figure 3. User perceptual preference characteristics—three-dimensional approach

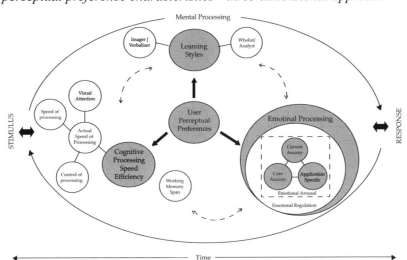

emotional processes giving the actual response to that stimulus, as depicted in *Figure 3*. These characteristics have been primarily discussed in Germanakos et al. (2006) and Germanakos et al. (2005a).

As can be observed, its primary parameters formulate a three-dimensional approach to the problem.

The first dimension investigates the visual and cognitive processing speed efficiency of the user, the second his/her learning style, while the third captures his/her emotional processing during the interaction process with the information space. All the above dimensions have specific characteristics and implications into the information space based on which the personalization rules in the "personalization rules/mapping" component will be constructed. Suggestively, we present in *Figure 4* the data implications diagram of the learning styles chosen.

For a better understanding of the three dimensions' implications and their relation with the information space a diagram that presents a high level correlation of these implications with selected tags of the information space (a code used in Web languages to define a format change or hypertext link) is depicted in *Figure 5*. These tags (images, text, information quantity, links – learner control, navigation support, additional navigation support, and aesthetics) have gone through an extensive optimization representing group of data affected after the mapping with the implications.

The particular mapping is based on specific rules created, liable for the combination of these tags and the variation of their value in order to better filter the raw content and deliver the most personalized Web-based result to the user. As it can be observed from the diagram, each dimension has primary (solid line) and secondary (dashed line) implications on the information space altering dynamically the weight of the tags.

Figure 4. Riding's learning styles characteristics and implications

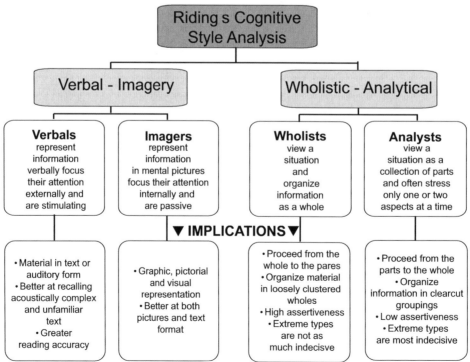

Figure 5. Data: Implications correlation diagram

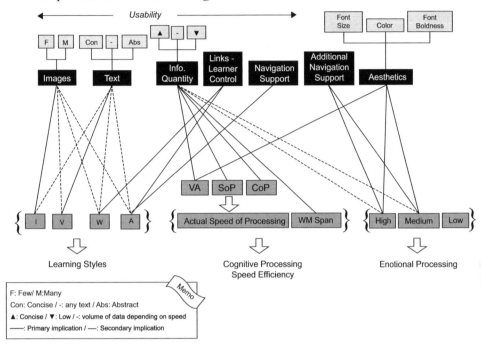

Therefore, we include in the learning styles dimension Riding's Cognitive Style Analysis, which applies in a greater number of information distribution circumstances, since it deals rather with cognitive than learning style. Henceforth, for example, the number of images (few or many) to be displayed has a primary implication on imagers, while text (more concise or abstract) has a secondary implication. An analyst may affect primarily the links – learner control and navigation support tag, which in turn is secondary affected by high and medium emotional processing, while might secondary affect the number of images or kind of text to be displayed, consequently. Actual speed of processing parameters (visual attention, speed of processing, and control of processing), as well as working memory span, is primarily affecting information quantity. Eventually, emotional processing is primarily affecting additional navigation support and aesthetics, as visual attention does, while secondary affects information quantity.

A practical example of the Data – Implications Correlation Diagram could be as follows:

a user might be identified that is: Verbalizer (V) – Wholist (W) with regards to the learning style, has an actual cognitive processing speed efficiency of 1000 msec, and a fair working memory span (weighting 5/7), with regards to his/her cognitive processing speed efficiency, and (s)he has a high emotional processing. The tags affected, according to the rules created and the Data – Implications Correlation Diagram, for this particular instance are the: images (few images displayed), text (any text could be delivered), information quantity (less info since his/her cognitive speed is moderate), links – learner control (less learner control because (s)he is Wholist), additional navigation support (significant because (s)he has high emotional processing), and high aesthetics (to give more structured and well defined information, with more colors, larger fonts, more bold text, since (s)he has high emotional processing).

At this point it should be mentioned that in case of internal correlation conflicts primary implications take over secondary ones. Additionally, since emotional processing is the most dynamic parameter compared to the others, any changes occurring at any given time are directly affecting the yielded value of the adaptation and personalization rules and henceforth the format of the content delivered.

Personalization Rules/Mapping

At this component all the calculations such as the user categorization and mapping, content reconstruction and content adaptation takes place. In order for the current component to run properly, Web-based semantic services content is conveyed in the form of metadata from the "semantic content reconstruction" component. Once the provided content is adjusted based on the developed rules to the user characteristics it returns the corresponding adapted and personalized result to the "content filtering" component.

Semantic Content Reconstruction

This component is based on metadata and it is responsible for describing the content (data) available from the "service provider" (service 1, service 2, …service n). In this way a common understanding of the data, that is, semantic interoperability, openness, is achieved. The data manipulated by the system is described using metadata that comprises all needed information to unambiguously describe each piece of data and collections of data. This provides semantic interoperability and a human-friendly description of data. This component is also directly related to the "personalization content reconstruction" component providing the altered Web-based metadata service content. It is consisted of two elements:

- Perceptual provider characteristics: It identifies the provider characteristics assigned to the Web-based services content. They are involving all these perceptual elements that

the provider has been based for the design of the content.

- Semantic content properties: This element performs the identification and metadata description of Web-based services content based on predetermined ontologies. It is implemented in a transparent manner removing data duplication and the problem of data consistency.

Service Provider

This is the last component of the architecture and is directly connected to the "semantic content reconstruction" component. It contains transition mechanisms and the databases of Web-based services content as supplied by the provider without being through any further manipulation or alteration.

CONCLUSION

Indisputably, by implementing mobile commerce and mobile marketing a business institution attains a leading image of an organisation close to the technological trends and the needs of modern audiences. It differentiates itself in an era when each institution competes for a share of market and a share of heart not only through its work but also its marketing tactics. The healthy image of an innovative and avant-garde organisation can only work for the benefit of its long-term viability. It is hard to predict what the future will bring. Surely there will be an increasing number of organisations adopting the mobile services. However, the future is nearer than generally estimated while the circumstances rapidly change. There can be futuristic scenarios which one day might become reality, but what is of more importance is always to know what the end-users finally need. The various institutions need to keep close and open to any kind of evolvement, not only to technological developments but also to how their audiences respond to them.

On these grounds, this article made a reference to the m-commerce content delivery investigating multi-channel delivery characteristics of user-centric m-commerce services and the adaptation and personalization considerations with regards to new user requirements and demands. It analyzed the current situation of m-commerce services, ranging from theoretical considerations to technological parameters, and it underpinned the significance of the user profiling, introducing the comprehensive user profiling that incorporates intrinsic user characteristics such as user perceptual preferences. It has finally presented an overviewed m-commerce personalization architecture that considers cognitive learning styles as its main personalization filter, in an attempt to provide the user with the most personalized m-commerce content result.

REFERENCES

Adomavicious, G., & Tuzhilin, A. (1999). User profiling in personalization applications through rule discovery and validation. In *Proceedings of the ACM Fifth International Conference on Data Mining and Knowledge Discovery (KDD'99)* (pp. 377-381).

Balasubramanian, S., Peterson, R.A., & Jarvnpaa, S.L. (2002). Exploring the implications of m-commerce for markets and marketing. *Journal of the Academy of Marketing Science, 30*(4), 348-361.

Bayne, K.M. (2002). *Marketing without wires.* Wiley.

Caldow, J. (2001). *E-gov goes wireless: From Palm to shining Palm.* Institute of Electronic Government, IBM Corporation.

Candace, D.P. (2005). *E-commerce and m-commerce technologies.* IRM Press.

Drucker, P.F. (1995). *Managing the non-profit organisation: Practices and principles.* Butterworth-Heinemann.

Easton, J. (2002). *Going wireless: Transform your business with mobile technology.* Harper Business.

Europe's Information Society. (2004a). *User interaction.* Retrieved from http://europa.eu.int/information_society

Frolick, M.N., Chen, L.-D. (2004, Spring). Assessing m-commerce opportunities. *Information Systems Management,* pp. 53 -61.

Germanakos, P., Tsianos, N., Lekkas, Z., Mourlas, C., & Samaras, G. (2006). Capturing essential intrinsic user behaviour values for the design of comprehensive Web-based personalized environments. *Computers in Human Behavior Journal,* Special Issue on Integration of Human Factors in Networked Computing. (accepted)

Germanakos, P., Samaras, G., & Christodoulou, E. (2005a). Multi-channel delivery of services—the road from eGovernment to mGovernment: Further technological challenges and implications. In *Proceedings of the First European Conference on Mobile Government* (Euro mGov 2005) (pp. 210-220).

Germanakos, P., Tsianos, N., Mourlas, C., & Samaras, G. (2005b). New fundamental profiling characteristics for designing adaptive Web-based educational systems. In *Proceeding of the IADIS International Conference on Cognition and Exploratory Learning in Digital Age (CELDA2005)* (pp. 10-17).

Germanakos, P., Mourlas, C., & Samaras, G. (2005c). Considering the new user requirements for apt mobile Internet services delivery. In *Proceedings of the IADIS International Conference on WWW/Internet 2005* (pp. 148-152).

Giaglis, G.M., Kourouthanassis, P., & Tsamakos, A. (2003). Towards a classification framework for mobile location services. In B.E. Mennecke & T.J. Strader (Eds.), *Mobile Commerce: Technology, Theory, and Applications*. Hershey, PA: Idea Group Publishing. Retrieved from http://www.eltrun.gr/papers/mBook-classification.pdf..

Haig, M. (2002). *Mobile marketing: The message revolution*. Kogan Page.

Heman, R.D., & Renz, D.O. (1999). Theses on nonprofit organisational effectiveness. *Nonprofit and Voluntary Sector Quarterly*, *28*(2), 107-126.

Hesmondhalgh, D. (2002). *The cultural industries*. SAGE.

Interchange of Data Between Administrations. (2004). *Multi-channel delivery of eGovernment services*. Retrieved from http://europa.eu.int/idabc/.

Kleijnen, M., Wetzels, M., & de Ruyter, K (2004). Consumer acceptance of wireless finance. *Journal of Financial Services Marketing, 8*(3), 206-217.

Knell, S. (2003). The shape of things to come: Museums in the technological landscape. *Museum and Society*, *1*(3), 132-146.

Mahatanankoon, P., Wen, J.H., & Lim, B. (2005). Consumer-based m-commerce: Exploring consumer perception of mobile applications. *Computer Standards and Interfaces*, *27*, 347-357.

O'Connor, J., & Galvin, E. (2001). *Marketing in the digital age*. Prentice Hall.

Panayiotou, C., & Samaras, G. (2006). Mobile user personalization with dynamic profiles: Time and activity. In *Proceedings of On the Move to Meaningful Internet Systems 2006: OTM 2006 Workshops* (PerSys 2006). Part II (pp. 1295-1304).

Panayiotou, C., & Samaras, G. (2004). mPERSONA: Personalized portals for the wireless user: An agent approach. *Mobile Networks and Applications (MONET), Special Issue on Mobile and Pervasive Commerce*, *9*(6).

Paavilainen, J. (2002). *Mobile business strategies: Understanding the technologies and opportunities*. Wireless Press.

Postma, P. (1999). *The new marketing era: Marketing to the imagination in a technology-driven world*. McGraw-Hill.

Stafford, M.R., & Faber, R.J. (2004). *Advertising, promotion and new media*. M.E. Sharpe.

Towse, R. (Ed.). (2003). *A handbook of cultural economics*. Elgew Edward.

Tsang, M.M., Ho, S.-C., & Liang, T.-P, (2004). Consumer attitudes toward mobile advertising: An empirical study. *International Journal of Electronic Commerce*, *8*(3), 65-78.

Turban, E., King, D., Lee, J., Warkentin, M., Chung, H.M. (2002). *Electronic commerce 2002: A managerial perspective*. Prentice Hall.

Wang, J., & Lin, J. (2003). Are personalization systems really personal? – Effects of conformity in reducing information overload. In *Proceedings of the 36th Hawaii International Conference on Systems Sciences* (HICSS'03) (p. 222c). IEEE Computer Society.

This work was previously published in E-Commerce Trends for Organizational Advancement: New Applications and Methods, edited by M. Khosrow-Pour, pp. 151-166, copyright 2010 by IGI Publishing (an imprint of IGI Global).

Chapter 3.16
Web Mining for Public E-Services Personalization

Penelope Markellou
University of Patras, Greece

Angeliki Panayiotaki
University of Patras, Greece

Athanasios Tsakalidis
University of Patras, Greece

INTRODUCTION

Over the last decade, we have witnessed an explosive growth in the information available on the Web. Today, Web browsers provide easy access to myriad sources of text and multimedia data. Search engines index more than a billion pages and finding the desired information is not an easy task. This profusion of resources has prompted the need for developing automatic mining techniques on Web, thereby giving rise to the term "Web mining" (Pal, Talwar, & Mitra, 2002).

Web mining is the application of data mining techniques on the Web for discovering useful patterns and can be divided into three basic categories: Web content mining, Web structure mining, and Web usage mining. Web content mining includes techniques for assisting users in locating Web documents (i.e., pages) that meet certain criteria, while Web structure mining relates to discover-

ing information based on the Web site structure data (the data depicting the Web site map). Web usage mining focuses on analyzing Web access logs and other sources of information regarding user interactions within the Web site in order to capture, understand and model their behavioral patterns and profiles and thereby improve their experience with the Web site.

As citizens requirements and needs change continuously, traditional information searching, and fulfillment of various tasks result to the loss of valuable time spent in identifying the responsible actor (public authority) and waiting in queues. At the same time, the percentage of users who acquaint with the Internet has been remarkably increased (Internet World Stats, 2005). These two facts motivate many governmental organizations to proceed with the provision of e-services via their Web sites. The ease and speed with which business transactions can be carried out over the Web has been a key driving force in the rapid growth and popularity of e-government, e-commerce, and e-business applications.

In this framework, the Web is emerging as the appropriate environment for business transactions and user-organization interactions. However, since it is a large collection of semi-structured and structured information sources, Web users often suffer from information overload. Personalization is considered as a popular solution in order to alleviate this problem and to customize the Web environment to users (Eirinaki & Vazirgiannis, 2003). Web personalization can be described, as any action that makes the Web experience of a user personalized to his or her needs and wishes. Principal elements of Web personalization include modeling of Web objects (pages) and subjects (users), categorization of objects and subjects, matching between and across objects and/or subjects, and determination of the set of actions to be recommended for personalization.

In the remainder of this article, we present the way an e-government application can deploy Web mining techniques in order to support intelligent and personalized interactions with citizens. Specifically, we describe the tasks that typically comprise this process, illustrate the future trends, and discuss the open issues in the field.

BACKGROUND

The close relation between Web mining and Web personalization has become the stimulus for significant research work in the area (Borges & Levene, 1999; Cooley, 2000; Kosala & Blockeel, 2000; Madria, Bhowmick, Ng, & Lim, 1999). Web mining is a complete process and involves specific primary data mining tasks, namely data collection, data reprocessing, pattern discovery, and knowledge post-processing. Therefore, Web mining can be viewed as consisting of the following four tasks (Etzioni, 1996):

- **Information Retrieval—IR (Resource Discovery):** It deals with automatic retrieval of all relevant documents, while at the same time ensuring that the non relevant ones are fetched as few as possible. The IR process mainly deals with document representation, indexing, and searching. The process of retrieving the data that is either online or offline from the text sources available on the Web such as electronic newsletters, newsgroups, text contents of HTML documents obtained by removing HTML tags, and also the manual selection of Web resources. Here are also included text resources that originally were not accessible from the Web but are accessible now, such as online texts made for search purposes only, text databases, and so forth.

- **Information Extraction—IE (Selection and Pre-Processing):** Once the documents have been retrieved in the IR process, the challenge is to automatically extract knowledge and other required information without human interaction. IE is the task of identifying specific fragments of a single document that constitute its core semantic content and transforming them into useful information. These transformations could be either a kind of pre-processing such as removing stop words, stemming, etc. or a pre-processing aimed at obtaining the desired representation such as finding phrases in the training corpus, transforming the presentation to relational or first-order logic form, and so forth.

- **Generalization (Pattern Recognition and Machine Learning):** Discover general patterns at individual Web sites or across multiple sites. Machine learning or data mining techniques are used for the generalization. Most of the machine learning systems, deployed on the Web, learn more about the user's interest than the Web itself.

- **Analysis (Validation and Interpretation):** A data driven problem, which presumes that there is sufficient data available, so that potentially useful information can be extracted and analyzed. Humans also play an important role in the information or knowledge discovery process on the Web, since the Web is an interactive medium. This is especially important for validation and/ or interpretation but under Etzioni's view (1996) of Web mining, "manual" (interactive, query triggered) knowledge discovery is excluded and thus the focus is placed on automatic data-triggered knowledge discovery.

Web mining refers to the overall process of discovering potentially useful and previously unknown information, knowledge, and patterns from Web data. In this sense, it implicitly covers the standard process of knowledge discovery in databases (KDD) and can be considered as a KDD extension applied to the Web (Markellos, Markellou, Rigou, & Sirmakessis, 2004a). Specifically, Web mining can be categorized into three areas of interest based on which part of the Web is mined:

- **Web Content Mining**: Focuses on the discovery/retrieval of useful information from Web contents/data/documents. Web content data consist of unstructured data (free texts), semi-structured data (HTML documents) and more structured data (data in tables, DB generated HTML pages)
- **Web Structure Mining:** Focuses on the structure of the hyperlinks within the Web as a whole (inter-document) with the purpose of discovering its underlying link structure. Web structure data consist of the Web site structure itself
- **Web Usage Mining**: Mines the secondary data derived from Web surfers' sessions or behaviors and focuses on techniques that

could predict user behavior while the user interacts with the Web (Cooley, 2000). Web usage data can be server access logs, proxy server logs, browser logs, user profiles, registration data, user sessions or transactions, cookies, user queries, bookmark data, mouse clicks and scrolls, and any other data as the result of interactions

Recently, Web usage mining (Srivastava, Cooley, Deshpande, & Tan, 2000) has been proposed as an underlying approach for Web personalization (Mobasher, Cooley, & Srivastava, 2000). The goal of Web usage mining is to capture and model the behavioral patterns and profiles of users interacting with a Web site. The discovered patterns are usually represented as collections of pages or items that are frequently accessed by groups of users with common needs or interests. Such patterns can be used to better understand behavioral characteristics of visitors or user segments, improve the organization and structure of the site, and create a personalized experience for visitors by providing dynamic recommendations. In particular, techniques such as clustering, association rule mining, and navigational pattern mining that rely on online pattern discovery from user transactions can be used to improve the scalability of collaborative filtering when dealing with clickstream and e-government data.

WEB MINING TECHNIQUES IN E-PUBLIC SERVICES

For the implementation and successful operation of e-government, the proper design, which will be the basis in order to receive a series of strategic, administrative, and operational benefits, is necessary. The application of e-government in the public domain can be gradually performed in fourteen (14) levels (Markellou, Panayiotaki, & Tsakalidis, 2003). This allows the unobstructed flow of information from/to the public sector and gives the possibility not only to the citizens but also to the enterprises (private sector) to acquire better access in the services that state provides. One of these levels is the upgrade of portal with applications adjusted to every user, where Web mining techniques may be applied to improve access to information through the provided e-services (Markellou et al., 2004a; Markellou, Rigou, & Sirmakessis, 2004b).

Specifically, the deployment of Web mining in the e-government domain relates to the analysis of citizen behavior and the production of adequate adaptations. For example, given a specific citizen, the presentation of required information from an e-government portal can be tailored to meet individual needs and preferences by providing personal recommendations on topics relative to those already visited. This process is typically based on a solid user model, which holds up-to-date information on dynamically changing citizen behavior. This enables on-the-fly portal content assembly, addressing exactly what the citizen needs to know without wasting time on topics the user is already proficient or not interested in. The flowchart of this procedure is shortly illustrated

in Figure 1. E-government application constructs users' profiles integrating various sources of data, pre-processes the data and applies Web mining techniques to provide the users with personalized Web experiences.

In order to personalize an e-government site, the system should be able to distinguish between different users or groups of users. This process is called user profiling and its objective is to create an information base that contains the preferences, characteristics, and activities of the users. In the Web domain, user profiling has been developed significantly, since Internet technologies provide easier means of collecting data about the users of a Web site, which in the case of e-government sites are citizens that must be satisfied by the provided services. A user profile can be either static, when the information it contains is never or rarely altered (e.g., demographic information), or dynamic when the user profile's data change frequently. Such information is obtained either explicitly (e.g., preferences, background, etc.) using online registration forms and question-naires, or implicitly, by recording the navigational behavior and other users' actions from server logs,

Figure 1. Application of Web mining techniques in e-government domain

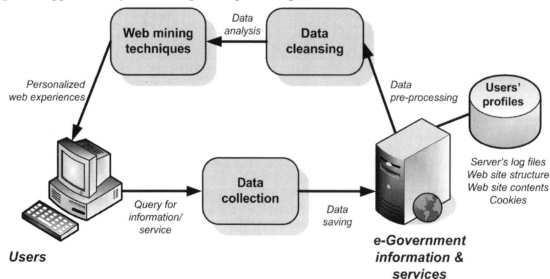

cookies, and so forth. User profiling is extremely useful to G2C (government-to-consumer) and G2B (government-to-business) applications. For example, a public authority, such as a Ministry of Finance and Economy, can customize its information/services concerning chemical and customs procedures to the relevant actors that import chemical goods. Using this aspect, the actors are facilitated in completing the necessary procedures without getting lost in the "maze" of information provided through a multi-field covering e-government Web site.

Another technique that can be used is the one of clustering. Page clustering identifies groups of pages that seem to be conceptually related according to the users' perception. User clustering results in groups of users that seem to behave similarly when navigating through a Web site. Such knowledge can be used in e-government in order to perform public services segmentation.

Classification technique can be applied after clustering in order to assign a new user to the defined groups. It uses features with high discriminative ability for defining the various profiles, for example, the profile of an active citizen may include the following values: Sex=male, 34<=Age<=40, Job=worker, Education= basic, MaritalStatus=marital, NumberOfChildren=4, and so forth. This knowledge can be used in applying personalization to e-government services and better supporting the needs of the users providing the right information, to the right people, at the right time.

For discovering relations between different types of available information in an e-government environment association rules can be applied. This technique may identify correlations between pages/users/services or other types of items, not directly connected and reveal previously unknown associations between groups of such items with specific similarities. The form of an association rule can be "65% of citizens that their MaritalStatus=marital search e-government portal for information about LifeEpisodes=having a

baby" or "40% of the citizens who accessed help desk asked about online filling-in of tax returns and VAT." For example, the last rule may indicate that this information is not easily accessible or explanatory enough and requires redesign tasks from the portal technical group.

An extension of the previous technique comprises the sequential pattern discovery that can be used for revealing patterns of co-occurrence, which incorporates the notion of time. For example a pattern may be a Web page or a set of pages accessed immediately after another set of pages: "55% of new businesses who apply for a certain certificate will use the certificate within 15 days" or "Given the transactions of a citizens who has not apply for any information/services during the last 3 months, find all citizens with a similar behavior."

Finally, as search engines often appear as a helpful tool at e-government, personalized Web search systems may be used to enhance their functionality. In order to incorporate user preferences into search engines, three major approaches are proposed (Shahabi & Chen, 2003):

- **Personalized Page Importance:** Modern search engines employ the importance scores of pages for ranking the search results, as well as traditional text matching techniques.
- **Query Refinement:** A process composed of three steps: obtaining user profiles from user, query modification and refinement.
- **Personalized Metasearch Systems:** Metasearch systems could improve the retrieval rate by merging various ranked results from multiple search engines into one final ranked list.

FUTURE TRENDS

On the road to enhance an e-government application and treat each user individually, personalization plays a central role. The benefits for both public authorities and citizens are significant when it really works. However, several issues still remain unclear. First of all, determining and delivering personalization is a data intensive task and requires numerous processing steps. This usually causes intolerably long response times, which in turn may lead to site abandonment. To avoid this constrain, parts of the process can be executed offline or special algorithms and structures can be used to guarantee fast online operation.

Another challenge is to ensure personalization accuracy. It is true that unsuccessful recommendations can slow down the process, confuse, and disorientate users. It is preferable not to deliver any recommendations than deliver a set of useless or harmful ones. Apart from that, personalization should be delivered in the appropriate way (avoiding user intrusion and loss of concentration) and not deprive users control over the whole process. Moreover, as e-government sites are dynamic environments, issues concerning the content or structure updating e.g. newly added topics, pages, services, etc. can be taken into consideration.

Last but not least, privacy violation during the user profiling process should be encountered (Volokh, 2000). Many users are reluctant to giving away personal information either implicitly as mentioned before, or explicitly, being hesitant to visit Web sites that use cookies (if they are aware of their existence) or avoiding to disclose personal data in registration forms. In both cases, the user loses anonymity and is aware that all of his actions will be recorded and used, often without his consent. Additionally, even if a user has agreed to supply personal information to a site, through cookie technology such information can be exchanged between sites, resulting to its disclosure without his permission. Although the new technologies and products for protecting user's privacy on computers and networks are becoming increasingly popular, none can guarantee absolutely secure communications. Electronic privacy issues in the foreseeable future

will become highly crucial and intense (Markellos et al., 2004b).

CONCLUSION

Governments enhance their attempt to offer efficient, advanced and modern services to their users (citizens and businesses) based on information and communication technologies and especially the Web. The remarkable acceptance of this powerful tool has changed the way of conducting various activities and offers citizens, businesses and public authorities limitless options and opportunities. However, the emerging problem to deal with is the way an e-government can provide its users with the right information and service according to their specific needs and preferences. To this direction, Web mining and personalization are used for supporting tailored Web experiences.

These techniques appear as the most promising for the future, since they help to establish one-to-one relationships between users and governments, improve the performance of provided information and services, increase users' satisfaction and promote e-loyalty. On the other hand, governments take advantage of them, as long as they save costs (e.g., transactions, communication, task management, etc.), improve response times, automate various processes, provide alternative channels of cooperation and communication, and upgrade and modern their profile and image.

Many research and commercial approaches, initiatives and tools are available, based on Web site structure and contents, user's navigation, behavior and transaction history, server log files, and so forth. However, personalization requires rich data in order to provide successful output. This is not always feasible, since many users are often negative towards the idea of being stereotyped. Moreover, individuals' privacy has been put in jeopardy by the tasks of recording their activities and saving the appropriate data into their profiles. Summarizing, governments should work hard in the direction of providing the legal framework for ensuring the protection of users' privacy and also eliminating the possibility of misuse their personal information.

REFERENCES

Borges, J., & Levene, M. (1999, August 15). Data mining of user navigation patterns. Proceedings of the WEBKDD'99 Workshop on Web Usage Analysis and User Profiling, San Diego, CA (pp. 31-36).

Cooley, R. (2000). Web usage mining: Discovery and application of interesting patterns from Web data. PhD Thesis, Department of Computer Science, University of Minnesota.

Eirinaki, M., & Vazirgiannis, M. (2003). Web mining for Web personalization. ACM Transactions on Internet Technology, 3(1), 1-27.

Etzioni, O. (1996). The world wide Web: Quagmire or Gold Mine. Communications of ACM, 39(11), 65-68.

Internet World Stats. (2005). Internet Usage Statistics—The Big Picture. World Internet Users and Population Stats. Retrieved June 25, 2005, from http://www.internetworldstats.com/stats.htm

Kosala, R., & Blockeel, H. (2000). Web mining research: A survey. SIGKDD Explorations: Newsletter of the Special Interest Group (SIG) on Knowledge Discovery & Data Mining, ACM, 2(1), 1-15.

Madria, S. K., Bhowmick, S. S., Ng, W. K., & Lim, E. P. (1999, August 30-September 1). Research issues in Web data mining. Proceedings of Data Warehousing and Knowledge Discovery, Florence, Italy (pp. 303-312).

Markellos, K., Markellou, P., Rigou, M., & Sirmakessis, S. (2004a). Web mining: Past, present, and future. In S. Sirmakessis (Ed.), Text mining and applications (pp. 25-35). Berlin; Heidelberg, Germany: Springer Verlag.

Markellos, K., Markellou, P., Rigou, M., Sirmakessis, S., & Tsakalidis, A. (2004b, April 14-16). Web personalization and the privacy concern. Proceedings of the 7th ETHICOMP International Conference on the Social and Ethical Impacts of Information and Communication Technologies, Challenges for the Citizen of the Information Society, Syros, Greece.

Markellou, P., Panayiotaki, A., & Tsakalidis, A. (2003, June 3-6). E-government and applications levels: Technology at citizen service. Proceedings of IADIS International Conference, E-Society, Lisbon, Portugal (pp. 849-854).

Markellou, P., Rigou, M., & Sirmakessis, S. (2004a). Mining for Web personalization. In A. Scime (Ed.), Web mining: Applications and techniques (pp. 27-48). Idea Group Publishing.

Markellou, P., Rigou, M., & Sirmakessis, S. (2004b). Web personalization for e-marketing intelligence. In S. Krishnamurthy (Ed.), Contemporary research in e-marketing: Volume 1 (pp. 232-250). Idea Group Publishing.

Mobasher, B., Cooley, R., & Srivastava, J. (2000). Automatic personalization based on Web usage mining. Communications of the ACM, 43(8), 142-151.

Pal, S. K., Talwar, V., & Mitra, P. (2002). Web mining in soft computing framework: Relevance, state of the art and future directions. IEEE Transactions on Neural Networks, 13(5), 1163-1177.

Shahabi, C., & Chen, Y. S. (2003, September 22-24). Web information personalization: Challenges and approaches. Proceedings of Databases in Networked Information Systems: The 3rd International Workshop, Japan (pp. 5-15).

Srivastava, J., Cooley, R., Deshpande, M., & Tan, P. N. (2000). Web usage mining: Discovery and applications of usage patterns from Web data. SIGKDD Explorations: Newsletter of the Special Interest Group (SIG) on Knowledge Discovery & Data Mining, ACM, 1(2), 12-23.

Volokh, E. (2000). Personalization and privacy. Communications of the ACM, 43(8), 84-88.

KEY TERMS AND DEFINITIONS

Clickstream: It is a record of a user's activity on the Internet, including every Web site and every page of every Web site that the user visits, how long the user was on a page or site, in what order the pages were visited, any newsgroups that the user participates in and even the e-mail addresses of mail that the user sends and receives. Both ISPs and individual Web sites are capable of tracking a user's clickstream.

Cookie: The data sent by a Web server to a Web client, stored locally by the client and sent back to the server on subsequent requests. In other words, a cookie is simply an HTTP header that consists of a text-only string, which is inserted into the memory of a browser. It is used to uniquely identify a user during Web interactions within a site and contains data parameters that allow the remote HTML server to keep a record of the user identity, and what actions she/he takes at the remote Web site.

Data Mining: The application of specific algorithms for extracting patterns (models) from data.

Knowledge Discovery in Databases (KDD): The nontrivial process of identifying valid, novel, potentially useful, and ultimately understandable patterns in data.

Server Log: Web servers maintain log files listing every request made to the server. With log file analysis tools, it's possible to get a good idea of where visitors are coming from, how often they return, and how they navigate through a site. Using cookies enables Webmasters to log even more detailed information about how individual users are accessing a site.

Web Mining: The discovery and analysis of useful information from the Web.

Web Personalization: It is the process of customizing a Web site to the needs of specific users, taking advantage of the knowledge acquired from the analysis of the user's navigational behavior (usage data) in correlation with other information collected in the Web context, namely structure, content and user profile data. Due to the explosive growth of the Web, the domain of Web personalization has gained great momentum both in the research and the commercial area.

Web Usage Mining: The application of data mining techniques to Web clickstream data in order to extract usage patterns.

Chapter 3.17
Location–Based Services

Ali R. Hurson
The Pennsylvania State University, USA

Xing Gao
The Pennsylvania State University, USA

INTRODUCTION

The past decade has seen advances in wireless network technologies and an explosive growth in the diversity of portable computing devices such as laptop computers, handheld personal computers, personal digital assistants (PDAs), and smart phones with Internet access. Wireless networking technologies and portable devices enable users to access information in an "anytime, anywhere" fashion. For example, a mobile user (MU) on the highway may query local weather, traffic information, nearby gas stations, next rest areas, or restaurants within 10 miles. Such new demands introduce a new type of services, *location-based services* (LBS), where certain location constraints (e.g., the user's current location) are used in the service provision.

The idea of queries with location constraints is originally introduced by Imielinski and Badrinath (1992), in which mobile users are likely to query information relating to their current positions, leading to the need for LBS. Such services are also termed as location dependent information services (LDIS)

in Lee, Lee, Xu, and Zheng (2002). LBS system is the context sensitive systems in a mobile computing environment that consider the user's location as a significant and dynamic factor affecting the information and services delivered to the users. The major LBS applications include:

- Destination guides with maps, driving directions, and real time prompt
- Location-based traffic and weather alerts
- Wireless advertising and electronic coupons to nearby mobile devices
- Movie, theatre and restaurant location and booking
- Store locating applications helping users to find the desired services
- Telematics-based roadside assistance (e.g., OnStar from General Motors)
- Personal content and messaging (Live Chat with friends)
- Mobile Yellow Pages provide local information
- Information Services (News, Stocks, Sports)

DOI: 10.4018/978-1-60566-026-4.ch391

- E911: (Wireless carriers provide wireless callers' numbers and locations.)

Generally, LBS services can be classified into three general categories: telematics LBS, Internet LBS, and wireless LBS (Telc).

Telematics LBS is the integration of wireless communications, vehicle monitoring systems, and location devices. Telematics LBS applications include automated vehicle location, fleet tracking, online navigation, and emergency assistance. For example, a trucking company can track all their fleet, proactively warn about traffic ahead, and estimate the arrival time. Commercial LBS providers are beginning to offer important management applications that help direct vehicle fleets and ensure optimal usage of key assets. Telematics LBS is a multibillion dollar service industry and is currently the largest segment of the LBS market (Telc).

Internet LBS provide Internet users the services relevant to their specified locations. Because they use a user-specified location instead of the user's current location, no positioning technology is required. For example, one can find turn-by-turn driving direction from one location to another and search for tour information about the destination. These services are targeting applications with stationary users, relatively powerful computers, and reliable network connections. As a result, Internet LBS support sophisticated services, such as local business searching and comparison, trip planning, online virtual tours, and so forth.

Wireless LBS deliver location relevant content to cell phones, PDAs, and other wireless devices. Equipped with automated positioning technologies, MUs can query local weather, nearby traffic information, and local businesses close to them. For example, a user can search neighboring post office or coffer shop from the PDA. The wireless LBS market is currently in a nascent stage, but it will potentially become the largest segment of the LBS market. The deployment of third generation (3G) mobile network, which support handsets that are both mobile and location sensitive, will lead to more wireless LBS subscribers and more useful LBS applications.

This article focuses on the discussion on wireless LBS system, and the term LBS refers to wireless LBS in the rest of this article. It compares LBS and traditional database system, introduces existing LBS systems, and reviews the related research works. Next, it describes a representative LBS system model and explains the functionality of the LBS system. It introduces the major components, their roles, and interactions. The discussion also covers issues related to mobile devices, positioning technologies, spatial databases, location aware queries, and so forth. In particular, this article will provide a detailed review on location dependent query processing and caching. Issues such as query processing algorithms, validity region, and query result caching are discussed. Then, it foresees the new service demands, emerging applications, and trends in future LBS systems. Finally, the article provides a summary on the above discussion and concludes this article.

BACKGROUND

Compared to traditional database (DB) services, new characteristics of LBS lead to significant differences between LBS databases and traditional databases. A database in LBS is a *spatial database* (SDBS) (Guting, 1994), which is capable of representing, querying, and manipulating spatial data (such as point, line, and region) to efficiently process queries with spatial restrictions and support applications such as the *geographical information system* (GIS). An SDBS is required to handle continuously changing data, locations of moving objects, and provide location aware services to mobile users. LBS also face other research challenges (Jensen et al., 2001) in order to support the following features: nonstandard dimension hierarchies in database; imprecision and varying precision; movement constraints and transportation networks; multiresolution objects and maps in data modeling; spatial data mining on vehicle movement; and continuous location change in query processing techniques. Interested readers are referred to Jensen et al. (2001) for more details.

LBS have introduced two types of queries with location constraints. The ***location aware query*** (LAQ) is the query with certain location constraints (Seydim, Dunham, & Kumar, 2001). As a special type of LAQ, the ***location dependent query*** (LDQ) (Barbara, 1999) is the query whose result depends on querying location, that is, the mobile user's current location. For example, "Phone numbers of all McDonald's in New York City" is an LAQ, while "Phone number of the nearest McDonald's" is an LDQ. LDQ is one of the core functions of LBS. Two common types of LDQs are the ***nearest neighbor*** (NN) query, that retrieves the qualifying database object closest to the querying position, and the ***window query*** that retrieves all satisfying database objects within an axis-parallel rectangle centered at the querying position.

LDQ processing and result caching have new characteristics not observed in traditional database systems. An LDQ may have different results in different region called ***validity region***

(VR). LDQs can be answered by the cached result of the same LDQ, if the MU remains within the cached result's VR. There are several algorithms for the DB server to determine the VR for NN and window query result sets (Zheng, Lee, & Lee, 2004; Zheng & Lee, 2001). To improve the performance, in certain applications, the limited validity region for LDQ result sets needs also be considered in LDQ caching. The following section describes the LBS system model and important research issues including positioning technology, LDQ processing, and LDQ caching.

LBS SYSTEM

LBS System Model

A typical LBS system consists of four components (Steiniger, Neun, & Edwardes, 2006) as shown in Figure 1:

- **Mobile devices:** LBS users request services and receive data using mobile devices, which can be personal digital assistants (PDA), mobile phones, laptops, and vehicle-mounted devices.

Figure 1. LBS system components

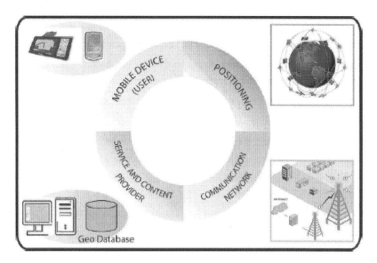

- **Communication network:** The communication network can be a wireless cellular network, wireless LAN, or other type of wireless network. It transfers the users' data and service requests to the service provider and forwards the requested information back to the users.
- **Positioning component:** User's location is an essential part of the LDQ, and it can be a symbolic entity (e.g., a street address) entered by the user or a geometric entity (e.g., the latitude and longitude coordinates) automatically acquired using positioning mechanisms. The user position can be obtained either by using the mobile communication network or by using the devices equipped with Global Positioning System (GPS). Further possibilities to determine the indoor position are active badges and radio beacons.
- **Service and content provider:** The service provider offers a number of different services to the user and is responsible for the service request processing. The requested data is usually stored and maintained at separated databases.

Positioning, Querying, and Caching Issues

- **Positioning technologies:** LBS require user's location, which can be input by the user manually or acquired by the device or network automatically. A user can input his/her street address or natural area code, which represents a location using alphanumeric characters code that is shorter than the latitude/longitude equivalent. Alternatively, one acquires a user's location via device-based techniques and network-based techniques. The premium example of device-based techniques is the GPS and the Assisted GPS (A-GPS). GPS is the worldwide satellite-based radio

navigation system consisting of 24 satellites launched by the U.S. Department of Defense. The mobile device equipped with a GPS receiver locates itself by comparing signals from four satellites. A GPS system has a high accuracy, ranging from 5 to 30 meters. In A-GPS, the mobile network or a third party service provider can assist the mobile device to achieve a very high accuracy, between 1 to 10 meters. A similar system is the GLObal NAvigation Satellite System (GLONASS) system comprised of 24 satellites launched by Russia. In 2005, the European Union launched its Galileo navigating system, which consists of 30 satellites and has a higher accuracy than GPS.

Due to the cost and power constraints of a GPS receiver, most handsets in cellular network are not equipped with GPS receivers, and network-based techniques are widely used in cellular networks to locate wireless subscribers. The commonly used network-based positioning techniques include Cell ID, angle of arrival (AOA), time of arrival (TOA), time difference of arrival (TDOA), and enhanced observed time difference (EOTD). Cell-ID, the simplest location approach in cellular networks, uses the serving base station (BS) to approximate the user's location. The accuracy is low and potential deviation depends on the radius of service cell, which is normally between 200 and 3000 meters. Other techniques use triangulation technology: finding the user's location by measuring at least three different signals between the user and fixed servers. Using AOA, the position can be determined if the user's signal is received by at least three BSs with additional electronics to detect the compass direction from which the signal arrives. The BSs send this compass data (i.e., angles) to a mobile switch to calculate the geographical location of the MU with the accuracy in the range of 100 to 200 meters. If the user's signal is received by at least three BSs with a synchronized atomic clock, TOA can compare the user's signal to compute the user's geographical location. The accuracy is between 100 and 200 meters. Zeimpekis, Giaglis, and Lekakos (2003) provides an in-depth analysis and evaluation of the commonly used indoor and outdoor wireless positioning technologies.

- **LDQ processing:** The two most common types of LDQs are nearest neighbor (NN) queries and window queries that have been intensively studied in the literature. A more general form of NN query *is* k-NN query that returns the k nearest neighbors to the querying location. The k-NN queries can be classified into six major categories: simple k-NN queries, approximate k-NN queries, reverse k-NN queries, constrained k-NN queries, k-join queries, and continuous k-NN queries. The most representative algorithm for NN query processing is a branch-and-bound R-tree traversal algorithm (Roussopoulos, Kelley, & Vincent, 1995). The algorithm searches R-tree in a depth first manner, starting from the root node. It records the nearest neighbor found so far and the distance. This algorithm skips the nodes if the distance to node is farther than the shortest distance found so far. For the k-NN query processing, the procedure is similar expect maintaining k nearest neighbor and their distances to the querying location.

Window query retrieves all objects in an axis-parallel rectangle. This characteristic makes R-tree very attractive in efficient window query processing. A typical algorithm answers the window query in R-tree. The algorithm first retrieves the root node and compares the entries of its children nodes with the querying window. Nonintersecting entries will not contain qualifying points, and are therefore skipped. The searching algorithm recur-

sively retrieves those entries intersecting with the querying window. When it reaches the leaf level, it will return the qualifying data object(s), if any.

- **LDQ caching:** Validity region is the essential information for LDQ caching schemes. Much research has been done in algorithms to generate LDQ result VR; and there are several algorithms for the DB server to determine the VR for an NN query result. Zheng and Lee (2001) built a static *Voronoi diagram* (VD) to index the objects in SDBS by partitioning the plane into Voronoi cells (VC), one for each object. The VC is a convex polygon that consists of the points closer to the object in this VC than to any other objects. As a result, VD is the most suitable mechanism to find the NN and the corresponding VR: the object in the same VC with the querying locations is the NN result, and the VC is the corresponding nearest neighbor validity region (NNVR). It is, however, expensive to maintain VD due to DB updates, and it is also inapplicable for the k nearest neighbor (k-NN) query when k is unknown. Even when k is known, an order-k VD is very expensive in terms of computational and storage overhead (Zhang, Zhu, Papadias, Tao, & Lee, 2003). Consequently, Zhang et al. (2003) introduced algorithms to calculate NNVRs during run time that avoids the large storage overhead at the expense of extra computing overhead.

A window VR is therefore the region within which the result set remains unchanged. The Minkowski region (MR) is introduced to examine the VR of a window query result set, which may contain zero, one, or multiple results. The MR of an object is an axis-parallel rectangle identical to the query window whose geometric center is the corresponding object. If the querying position is within the MR of an object a, then object a will be a result. Otherwise, object *a* is not in the window query result set. Thus, the VR of a window query result set is the area that is within the MRs of all result objects, and outside the MRs of all other objects.

LDQ caching has attracted much research attention. Ren and Dunham (2000) proposed a semantic caching scheme for location dependent results. An incoming query is decomposed into two disjointed parts: a probe query that can be answered by the cached data and a remainder query that has to be answered by the DB server. This scheme reduces the network traffic, allows query resolution during the disconnection, and in some cases allows partial query resolution. Zheng, Xu, and Lee (2002) presented algorithms for cache invalidation and cache replacement strategies that takes the validity of information into account. Zheng, Lee, and Lee (2004) presented a semantic NN caching scheme and addressed mobile user's intercell roam issues. The aforementioned caching schemes rely on DB servers to provide VRs for the LDQ results. Considering that DB servers may not always provide VRs for LDQ results due to the computation and storage overhead, Gao and Hurson (2005) and Gao, Sustersic, and Hurson (2006) suggested an LDQ proxy caching scheme where the proxy can calculate the estimated validity regions (EVR) for the LDQ result based on the querying history and the cache contents.

FUTURE TRENDS

In the next few years, LBS growth will continue with the following trends (Desiniotis, Markoulidakis, & Gaillet, 2006):

- **Market value:** Several reports published around 2000 claimed that LBS would become the most promising "killer applications," with billions of revenue in a few years. Unfortunately, those predictions were not met. A recent Juniper Research report estimates the total available market for mobile LBS will reach $8.5 billion by end of 2010 (Juniper, 2005) considering the fast growth of markets in Asia Pacific region.
- **Mobile devices:** The mobile devices will have more functions, better connection, and improved usability.
- **Vehicle navigation devices:** One major pushing power for the growth of LBS market is the increasing popularity of portable navigation devices such Garmin and Tom-Tom. These devices will be less expensive and equipped with more functions such as music player, hands-free phone kit, a Web browser, and so forth.
- **Improved accuracy:** Accuracy and compatibility of LBS are going to be critical competitive factors for carriers to compete for customers in the future. Most LBS carries currently using GPS system will move toward A-GPS that offers greater accuracy levels.

The research topics in LBS system will continue in LDQ query processing and caching. At the same time, more attention might be given to emerging topics or concerns. Vehicular users desire to exchange information between neighboring vehicles; thus, short range communication protocols need to be proposed for various applications. Security is always a concern and deserves continuous study in the future LBS system. LBS system tends to collect users' information and statistics to improve system performance, which raises the research topics on user privacy.

CONCLUSION

LBS have attracted much attention from both researcher and service providers in the past a few years. This article reviewed different types LBS services and described its system components. It also discusses several important research issues and the future trend of LBS.

REFERENCES

Barbara, D. (1999). Mobile computing and databases—a survey. *Knowledge and Data Engineering*, 108-117.

Desiniotis, C., Markoulidakis, J. G., & Gaillet, J.-F. (2006). Mobile LBS market. In *Proceedings of the LIAISON-ISHTAR Workshop*.

Gao, X., & Hurson, A. R. (2005). Location dependent query proxy. In *Proceedings of the ACM Symposium of Applied Computing*, (pp. 1020-1024).

Gao, X., Sustersic, J., & Hurson, A. R. (2006). Window query processing with adaptive proxy cache. *Mobile Data Management*.

Guting, R. (1994). An introduction to spatial database systems. *Very Large Databases Journal*, 3(4), 357–399. doi:10.1007/BF01231602

Imielinski, T., & Badrinath, B. (1992). Querying in highly mobile distributed environments. In *Proceedings of the Very Large Databases Conference*, (pp. 41-52).

Jensen, C. S., Friis-Christensen, A., Pedersen, T. B., Pfoser, D., Saltenis, S., & Tryfona, N. (2001). Location-based services—a database perspective. In *Proceedings of the Scandinavian Research Conference on Geographical Information Science*, (pp. 59-68).

Juniper Research. (2005). Mobile location based services: Information services, tracking, navigation, community & entertainment.

Lee, D. L., Lee, W.-C., Xu, J., & Zheng, B. (2002). Data management in location-dependent information services: Challenges and issues. *IEEE Pervasive Computing / IEEE Computer Society [and] IEEE Communications Society*, 1, 65–72. doi:10.1109/MPRV.2002.1037724

Ren, Q., & Dunham, M. (2000). Using semantic caching to manage location dependent data in mobile computing. *MobiCom*, 210-221.

Roussopoulos, N., Kelley, S., & Vincent, F. (1995). Nearest neighbor queries. *Management of Data*, 71-79.

Seydim, A., Dunham, M., & Kumar, V. (2001). Location dependent query processing. *MobiDE*, 47-53.

Steiniger, S., Neun, M., & Edwardes, A. (2006). *Foundations of location based services*. CartouCHe project lecture notes. Retrieved December 12, 2007, from www.geo.unizh.ch/publications/cartouche/lbs_lecturenotes_steinigeretal2006.pdf

Telc. Retrieved December 12, 2007, from http://www.telcontar.com/company/marketplace.html

Zeimpekis, V., Giaglis, G., & Lekakos, G. (2003). A taxonomy of indoor and outdoor positioning techniques for mobile location services. *SIGECOM Exchanges*, 19-27.

Zhang, J., Zhu, M., Papadias, D., Tao, Y., & Lee, D. (2003). Location-based spatial queries. *Management of Data*, 443-454.

Zheng, B., & Lee, D. (2001). Semantic caching in location-dependent query processing. In *Proceedings of the Symposium on Spatial and Temporal Databases*, (pp. 97-116).

Zheng, B., Lee, W.C., & Lee, D. (2004). On semantic caching and query scheduling for mobile nearest neighbor search. *Wireless Networks Journal, 10*(6).

Zheng, B., Xu, J., & Lee, D. (2002). Cache invalidation and replacement strategies for location-dependent data in mobile environments. *Transaction on Computers . Special Issue on Database Management and Mobile Computing, 51*(10), 1141–1153.

KEY TERMS AND DEFINITIONS

Geographic Information Systems: A computer system designed for storing, manipulating, analyzing, and displaying data in a geographic context.

Location Aware Query: is the query with certain location constraints.

Location-Based Services: Personalized services based on certain location constraints, normally the user's current location.

Location Dependent Query: The query whose result depends on the users' current location.

Nearest Neighbor: A query that returns the nearest objects to the user.

Spatial Database: A database system that offers spatial data types in its data model and query language and supports spatial data types in its implementation.

Validity Region: A regions where a location dependent query result remains valid.

Window Query: A query that returns all satisfying database objects within an axis-parallel rectangle centered at the querying position.

This work was previously published in the Encyclopedia of Information Science and Technology, Second Edition, edited by M. Khosrow-Pour, pp. 2456-2461, copyright 2009 by IGI Publishing (an imprint of IGI Global).

Chapter 3.18
Database Support for M–Commerce and L–Commerce

Hong Va Leong
The Hong Kong Polytechnic University, Hong Kong

INTRODUCTION

M-commerce (mobile commerce) applications have evolved out of e-commerce (electronic commerce) applications, riding on recent advancement in wireless communication technologies. Exploiting the most unique aspect inherent in m-commerce, namely, the mobility of customers, l-commerce (location-dependent m-commerce) applications have played an increasingly important role in the class of m-commerce applications. All e-commerce, m-commerce, and l-commerce applications rely on the provision of information retrieval and processing capability. L-commerce applications further dictate the maintenance of customer and service location information. Various database systems are deployed as the information source and repository for these applications, backed by efficient indexing mechanisms, both on regular data and location-specific data.

Bean (2003) gave a good report on supporting Web-based e-commerce with XML, which could be easily extended to m-commerce. An m-commerce framework, based on JINI/XML and a workflow engine, was defined by Shih and Shim (2002). Customers can receive m-commerce services through the use of mobile devices such as pocket PCs, PDAs, or even smart phones. These mobile devices together with their users are often modeled as mobile clients. There are three types of entities central to m-commerce and l-commerce applications: mobile device, wireless communication, and database. In this article, we focus our discussion on mobile-client enabled database servers, often referred to as mobile databases. Mobile databases maintain information for the underlying m-commerce and l-commerce applications in which mobile devices serve as the hardware platform interfacing with customers, connected through wireless communication.

Location is a special kind of composite data ranging from a single point, a line, a poly-line, to a shape defining an area or a building. In general, locations are modeled as spatial objects. The location of a static point of interest, such as a shop, is maintained in a database supporting spatial features and operations, often a spatial database (Güting,

DOI: 10.4018/978-1-60566-026-4.ch154

1994). The location of a moving object, like a mobile customer, needs to be maintained in a moving object database (Wolfson, Sistla, Xu, Zhou, & Chamberlain, 1999), a database that supports efficient retrieval and update of object locations. To enable l-commerce, both spatial databases and moving object databases need to support location-specific query processing from mobile clients and location updates they generated.

The two major types of data access requirements for a mobile database are data dissemination and dedicated data access. Data dissemination is preferred, since it can serve a large client population in utilizing the high bandwidth downlink channel to broadcast information of common interest, such as stock quotations, traffic conditions, or special events. On the other hand, dedicated data access is conveyed through uplink channels with limited bandwidth. To disseminate database items effectively, the selected set of hot database items can be scheduled as a broadcast disk (Acharya, Alonso, Franklin, & Zdonik, 1995). Proper indexes can be built to facilitate access to broadcast database items (Imielinski & Badrinath, 1994). Redundancy can be included in data (Leong & Si, 1995) and index (Tan & Ooi, 1998) to combat the unreliability of wireless communication.

For dedicated data access, queries and updates to databases are transmitted from the client to the server. L-commerce services involve processing of location-dependent queries (Madria, Bhargava, Pitoura, & Kumar, 2000). The high frequency of updates to the location of moving objects calls for special indexing technique. The call-to-mobility ratio serves as a good indicator on the tradeoff of indexing mechanisms. The moving object databases should enable efficient execution of queries such as k-nearest neighbor, reversed nearest neighbor (Benetis, Jensen, Karĉiauskas, & Ŝaltenis, 2006), and nearest surrounder search (Lee, Lee, & Leong, 2006). In addition, they should support continuous queries (Prabhakar, Xia, Kalashnikov, Aref, & Hambrusch, 2002), such as continuous k-nearest neighbor, being executed continuously

and returning location-dependent results (Lee, Leong, Zhou, & Si, 2005). Reversing the role of query and data, it is equally important to process data streams effectively (Babu & Widom, 2001) such as incoming sensor data streams (Mokbel, Xiong, Hammad, & Aref, 2005) for traffic monitoring in navigational applications.

A related and interesting research problem is the location privacy of a mobile client. For instance, the application server should not be able to deduce the exact location of Alice, when she raises a query to look for a nearest restaurant on the State Street. Yet, the information returned to Alice should enable her to determine the nearest restaurant. Location cloaking technique (Gedik & Liu, 2005) and location anonymizer (Mokbel, Chow, & Aref, 2006) would be used to ensure a form of k-anonymity, such that Alice is indistinguishable from other k-1 clients around the State Street.

BACKGROUND

The three fundamental elements for m-commerce applications, namely, mobile device, wireless communication, and database support can be considered orthogonal. First, the variety of mobile devices differs vastly in computational power, ease of programming, interoperability of operating environments, and support for auxiliary devices. Some mobile clients are based on high-end laptops, while others are based on low-end PDAs or cellular phones. Second, wireless communication offers varying bandwidth and reliability, based on low-bandwidth and unreliable GSM connections, medium-bandwidth GPRS/EDGE and Bluetooth connections, or high-bandwidth 802.11g and WCDMA/CDMA2000 connections. Third, the database may be as primitive as a file system or simple relational database like MS Access, or as complex as the high performance Oracle with transactional and spatial data support. Transactions ensure a sequence of database operations to be executed consistently. This leads to a "cube"-like taxonomy as shown in Figure 1. The support of l-commerce requires a new location maintenance module at the database. However, for most practical applications involving the location of moving objects, transactional access is not required on the location, owing to the inherent imprecise nature of the changing location over time.

In Figure 1, the taxonomy for m-commerce and l-commerce support is displayed. Planes LP and HP represent the low computing power equipment and high computing power equipment respectively, whereas planes LB and HB reflect the availability of low and high communication bandwidth. With the availability of transactions in the TXN plane, this gives rise to eight different regions.

Region zero represents the support of standard file or simple database access from PDA connecting through low-speed modem or phone. Processing is basically performed at the server, since it is too expensive for clients to support complex mechanism. To reduce bandwidth consumption, information distillation/extraction (Cowie & Lehnert, 1996) may be performed to reduce the amount of information transmitted. Simple client/server data access paradigm suffices. Region one assumes an improved wireless network, with

large scale WCDMA/CDMA2000 (3G) or small scale 802.11g (WiFi). Recent 802.16 (WiMAX) development and deployment lead to improved bandwidth in medium scale mobile environment. As a result, data access is more effective and conventional client/server data processing techniques can be adopted in a rather straightforward manner.

Region two corresponds to a mobile client with higher computational power. Information transmitted can be transcoded to reduce the bandwidth consumption. Interactive and intelligent mechanisms such as multi-resolution browsing (Leong & Si, 2005) can be employed. Database items are cached to combat the low communication bandwidth, unreliable communication, and frequent disconnection. Research work addressing this issue was pioneered by the Coda file system in 1992 (Satyanarayanan, 2002), in which files are cached by clients and updates made during client disconnection are reintegrated upon reconnection. Caching in an object-oriented database was studied by Chan, Leong, Si, and Wong (1999). Configurations in region three allow easy access to data from server. With ample bandwidth and processing power, prefetching of database items allows the preparation for potential network disconnection (Jing, Helal, & Elmagarmid, 1999). Numerous research works on mobile data access have been

Figure 1. Taxonomy on m-commerce and l-commerce support

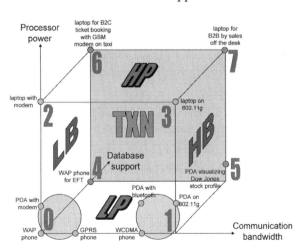

conducted with respect to regions two and three.

Plane TXN represents the transactional equivalence of the four regions. Regions four and five involve the use of PDAs or phones to access databases in a transactional manner. Owing to the low device capability, the only effective mechanism is to execute the transaction at the server. Clients only implement the user interface, supplying the required data and displaying the result sets. Information distillation could be needed for the low bandwidth configurations in region four. The use of a proxy server helps to simplify the client/server design, since the proxy will be responsible for contacting different parties involved in the transaction. Finally, for regions six and seven, there are a lot more research potentials, since the client is more powerful in executing more complex algorithms. For instance, it would be appropriate to implement on the client a variant of the optimistic concurrency control protocol (Bernstein, Hadzilacos, & Goodman, 1987) for region six and two phase locking with lock caching (Franklin, Carey, & Livny, 1997) for region seven configurations.

In practical m-commerce applications, clients are moving around. This results in l-commerce applications, involving location-dependent queries (Madria et al., 2000). The configuration and taxonomy remain similar, except for better database support need. Research and application focus should be on the low communication bandwidth, as well as on client mobility. This corresponds to plane LB. Under such configurations, a large client population communicates with database servers over wireless communication channels (Alonso & Korth, 1993). A geographical information system component enables location-dependent queries to be resolved through geo-referencing (Choy, Kwan, & Leong, 2000). Moving object databases can keep track of the whereabout of clients (Wolfson et al., 1999) effectively.

STRONG DATABASE SUPPORT

M-commerce and l-commerce applications involve access to one or more databases, often being accessed concurrently by multiple clients. Location management is an element inherent in l-commerce. Efficient operations through moving object databases should be provided (Wolfson et. al., 1999). Transactions are executed to ensure the database consistency despite concurrent access. The correctness criterion of serializability on concurrent transactions can be enforced through concurrency control protocols. Concurrency control protocols in a client/server or a mobile environment can be classified according to their nature (Franklin et al., 1997; Jing et al., 1999). In m-commerce and l-commerce applications, simultaneous access to multiple databases, which are administered by different organizations, is a norm rather than an exception. One should provide consistent accesses to those multiple databases with a transaction-like behavior, known as global serializability (Breitbart, Garcia-Molina, & Silberschatz, 1992). The distributed activity accessing the multiple databases is called a global transaction. Tesch and Wäsch (1997) presented an implementation of global transactions on the ODMG-compliant multidatabase systems. Creating such a multidatabase system could involve a lot of coordination efforts, both at the system level and the enterprise managerial level. The execution cost of the global transactions, in terms of concurrency control and atomic commitment, can be high. Thus, global transactions have not been widely adopted, despite their usefulness and convenience. Rather, multiple subtransactions were commonly executed on individual databases without enforcing global serializability.

In a mobile environment, it is appropriate to relax the overly restrictive serializability correctness criteria. It is often acceptable for a mobile client not to see the updates made by concurrently executing mobile clients, in exchange for a faster execution and a higher probability of committing its transaction. This is particularly true about the location of a moving object, which is inherently imprecise. Recency and freshness of location value is considered more important. Isolated-only transactions (Satyanarayanan, 2002) were proposed to reduce the impact of client disconnection. N-ignorance (Krishnakumar & Bernstein, 1994), bounded inconsistency (Wong, Agrawal, & Mak, 1997), and update consistency (Shanmugasundaram, Nithrakashyap, Sivasankaran, & Ramamritham, 1999) were some of the common weaker forms of correctness criteria. In these approaches, they try to ignore some of the operations in a transaction or allow them to be executed out-of-order in some controlled manner.

Transaction processing throughput in a mobile environment can be improved by utilizing the broadcast bandwidth effectively. The database can be broadcast and transactions can be processed against the database items broadcast. This is very useful for read-only transactions (Pitoura & Chrysanthis, 1999) simply by tuning for a consistent set of database items over the broadcast. To enable update transaction processing, the hybrid protocol by Mok, Leong, & Si (1999) ensures serializability by performing validation for update transactions, and utilizing the uplink channel to request for additional database items not available over the broadcast. Consistency across database items is ensured through the use of timestamps. In update consistency (Shanmugasundaram et al., 1999), a mobile client is only required to see updates made at server consistent with the values it reads, without having to follow the same serialization order as those observed by other mobile clients; it can be enforced by the cycle-based algorithm.

With the embracement of the Internet computing paradigm, more and more enterprises are willing to publicize their databases as part of their drive toward B2B or B2C E-commerce. Under most cases, these databases can be accessed from outside the enterprise via a Web interface. The ability to access consistent information using global transactions becomes more practical

and manageable. Although updates to databases are normally restricted across departments or enterprises, more and more databases become enabled for the execution of read-only transactions by external parties, through the provision of Web-services (Hoang, Kawamura, & Hasegawa, 2004). Weakly consistent global transactions could be executed based on a sequence of Web-service requests. Furthermore, the presence of a high proportion of read-only transactions even renders the concurrency control for global transactions far more efficient.

Under certain B2B setting, it would be advantageous to automate the workflow process across enterprises (Vonk & Grefen, 2003). It is important to ensure the transactional execution of a low level workflow process, albeit the more relaxed consistency requirement on higher level process. Naturally, the overall process can be modeled as a nested transaction, which is destined to be long-lived that global serializability could be too restrictive in delivering good performance. Instead, the adoption of special transactions to roll back unintended effects is more appropriate (Tesch & Wäsch, 1997). With respect to the B2C setting, mobile clients would normally only initiate local transactions or simple global transactions spanning across a small number of databases, rather than a long-lived workflow process. The limitation of communication bandwidth and occasional network disconnection implies a longer transaction execution cycle.

FUTURE TRENDS

Owing to the complexity of global transaction processing and the resource limitations of mobile clients, it is sensible to migrate the coordination effort to the proxy server and the Web server, thereby relieving the mobile clients from the complex processing. This is especially true in the context of regions four and five. As a result, there would be the decoupling of the transaction processing mechanism from the application logic, with basic transactional support at the proxy. The application logic can further be delivered conveniently through the adoption of mobile agents (Yau, Leong, & Si, 2003), preferably intelligent agents that can make sensible decision on behalf of the client, only reporting back the outcome and obtaining confirmation from the client. For instance, mobile agents can act on behalf of the client for event-driven transactions like stock selling transactions or auctioning. Support for global transactions can be provided primarily on the wired network through the agent.

Web services allow the bundling of higher level or more complex operations on the databases to be invoked by clients (Hoang et al., 2004), simplifying the need to ensure local serializability of transactions on a particular database. For regions six and seven configurations, more complicated control can be established at the clients, whose higher computing power can also be dedicated to filter for information more effectively, with reference to its local cache, and to provide value-added operations on the data. One could leverage on the computing power of these mobile clients for m-commerce and l-commerce, by engaging in the popular paradigm of peer-to-peer computing (Avancha, D'Souza, Perich, Joshi, & Yesha, 2003) and pervasive cooperative computing. For instance, group-based location reporting exploiting peer-to-peer computing power is effective in reducing the update cost for changing client locations (Lam, Leong, & Chan, 2007).

The location of a client in l-commerce is a piece of sensitive information that deserves protection. There is an increasing concern on the privacy issue of mobile clients, in the context of location-dependent service (Mokbel et. al., 2006) and data mining (Verykios et al., 2004). A server is able to deduce the movement and even spending pattern of a client. Privacy should be protected and the quality of service should not be undermined excessively. This is a highly challenging task to strike a good balance. Finally, effective visual-

ization of the result set and navigation through the result sequence to decide on the next step is important, since low-end mobile devices are normally equipped with a relatively small display, a constraint that is only mitigated at a much slower pace than advancement in network bandwidth and processing power.

CONCLUSION

Database support is an important and fundamental issue in m-commerce and l-commerce applications. With respect to the vast difference in the power and capacity of mobile devices, the varying wireless communication bandwidth, and the new dimension of client mobility and network disconnection, adjustments need to be made to render appropriate database support to these applications. In this article, we gave a generic classification along the three major characteristics for m-commerce and l-commerce environments. The different issues on database support were surveyed and discussed. In the future, there should be a division of research efforts, in providing effective transactional support at the server or proxy through agents or Web services, while leveraging on the capability of the peer clients in information organization and presentation. There is also a serious quest for better value-added computing support and solutions, including data-intensive stream processing and client privacy preservation.

REFERENCES

Acharya, S., Alonso, R., Franklin, M., & Zdonik, S. (1995). Broadcast disks: Data management for asymmetric communication environments. In *Proceedings of ACM SIGMOD International Conference on Management of Data* (pp. 199-210). ACM.

Alonso, R., & Korth, H. (1993). Database system issues in nomadic computing. In *Proceedings of ACM SIGMOD International Conference on Management of Data* (pp. 388-392). ACM.

Avancha, S., D'Souza, P., Perich, F., Joshi, A., & Yesha, Y. (2003). P2P m-commerce in pervasive environments. *ACM SIGecom Exchanges, 3*(4), 1–9. doi:10.1145/844351.844353

Babu, S., & Widom, J. (2001). Continuous queries over data streams. *SIGMOD Record, 30*(3), 109–120. doi:10.1145/603867.603884

Bean, J. (2003). Engineering global e-commerce sites: A guide to data capture, content, and transactions. Morgan Kaufmann Publishers.

Benetis, R., Jensen, S., Karĉiauskas, G., & Ŝaltenis, S. (2006). Nearest and reverse nearest neighbor queries for moving objects. *The VLDB Journal, 15*(3), 229–249. doi:10.1007/s00778-005-0166-4

Bernstein, P. A., Hadzilacos, V., & Goodman, N. (1987). Concurrency control and recovery in database systems. Reading, MA: Addison-Wesley.

Breitbart, Y., Garcia-Molina, H., & Silberschatz, A. (1992). Overview of multidatabase transaction management. *The VLDB Journal, 1*(2), 181–239. doi:10.1007/BF01231700

Chan, B. Y. L., Leong, H. V., Si, A., & Wong, K. F. (1999). MODEC: A multi-granularity mobile object-oriented database caching mechanism, prototype, and performance. *Journal of Distributed and Parallel Databases, 7*(3), 343–372. doi:10.1023/A:1008738928499

Choy, M., Kwan, M., & Leong, H. V. (2000). Distributed database design for mobile geographical applications. *Journal of Database Management, 11*(1), 3–15.

Cowie, J., & Lehnert, W. (1996). Information extraction. *Communications of the ACM, 39*(1), 80–91. doi:10.1145/234173.234209

Franklin, M. J., Carey, M. J., & Livny, M. (1997). Transactional client-server cache consistency: Alternatives and performance. *ACM Transactions on Database Systems, 22*(3), 315–363. doi:10.1145/261124.261125

Gedik, B., & Liu, L. (2005). A customizable k-anonymity model for protecting location privacy. In *Proceedings of International Conference on Distributed Computing Systems* (pp. 620-629). IEEE.

Güting, R. H. (1994). An introduction to spatial database systems. *The VLDB Journal, 3*(4), 357–399. doi:10.1007/BF01231602

Hoang, P. H., Kawamura, T., & Hasegawa, T. (2004). Web service gateway—A step forward to e-business. In *Proceedings of IEEE International Conference on Web Services* (pp. 648-655). IEEE.

Imielinski, T., & Badrinath, B. R. (1994). Mobile wireless computing: Challenges in data management. *Communications of the ACM, 37*(10), 18–28. doi:10.1145/194313.194317

Jing, J., Helal, A. S., & Elmagarmid, A. (1999). Client-server computing in mobile environments. *ACM Computing Surveys, 31*(2), 117–157. doi:10.1145/319806.319814

Krishnakumar, N., & Bernstein, A. J. (1994). Bounded ignorance: A technique for increasing concurrency in a replicated system. *ACM Transactions on Database Systems, 19*(4), 586–625. doi:10.1145/195664.195670

Lam, G. H. K., Leong, H. V., & Chan, S. C. F. (2007). Group-based location reporting with peer-to-peer clients. In L. T. Yang, & M. K. Denko *Handbook on Mobile Ad Hoc and Pervasive Communications*. American Scientific Publishers.

Lee, K. C. K., Lee, W. C., & Leong, H. V. (2006). Nearest surrounder queries. In *Proceedings of International Conference on Data Engineering* (pp. 85-94). IEEE.

Lee, K. C. K., Leong, H. V., Zhou, J., & Si, A. (2005). An efficient algorithm for predictive continuous nearest neighbor query processing and result maintenance. In *Proceedings of International Conference on Mobile Data Management* (pp. 178-182). IEEE.

Leong, H. V., & Si, A. (1995). Data broadcasting strategies over multiple unreliable wireless channels. In *Proceedings of International Conference on Information and Knowledge Management* (pp. 96-104). ACM.

Leong, H. V., & Si, A. (2005). Multi-resolution information transmission in mobile environments. *Mobile Information Systems: An International Journal, 1*(1), 25–40.

Madria, S. K., Bhargava, B. K., Pitoura, E., & Kumar, V. (2000). Data organization issues for location-dependent queries in mobile computing. In *Proceedings of International Conference on Database Systems for Advanced Applications* (pp. 142-156). Springer-Verlag.

Mok, E., Leong, H. V., & Si, A. (1999). Transaction processing in an asymmetric mobile environment. In *Proceedings of International Conference on Mobile Data Access* (pp. 71-81). Springer-Verlag.

Mokbel, M. F., Chow, C., & Aref, W. G. (2006). The new casper: Query processing for location services without compromising privacy. In *Proceedings of International Conference on Very Large Data Bases* (pp. 763-774).

Mokbel, M. F., Xiong, X., Hammad, M. A., & Aref, W. G. (2005). Continuous query processing of spatio-temporal data streams in PLACE. *GeoInformatica, 9*(4), 343–365. doi:10.1007/s10707-005-4576-7

Pitoura, E., & Chrysanthis, P. K. (1999). Scalable processing of read-only transactions in broadcast push. In *Proceedings of International Conference on Distributed Computing Systems* (pp. 432-439). IEEE.

Prabhakar, S., Xia, Y., Kalashnikov, D. V., Aref, W. G., & Hambrusch, S. E. (2002). Query indexing and velocity constrained indexing: Scalable techniques for continuous queries on moving objects. *IEEE Transactions on Computers, 51*(10), 1124–1140. doi:10.1109/TC.2002.1039840

Satyanarayanan, M. (2002). The evolution of coda. *ACM Transactions on Computer Systems, 20*(2), 85–124. doi:10.1145/507052.507053

Shanmugasundaram, J., Nithrakashyap, A., Sivasankaran, R., & Ramamritham, K. (1999). Efficient concurrency control for broadcast environments. In *Proceedings of ACM SIGMOD International Conference on Management of Data* (pp. 85-96).

Shih, G., & Shim, S. S. Y. (2002). A service management framework for m-commerce applications. *Mobile Networks and Applications, 7*(3), 199–212. doi:10.1023/A:1014574628967

Tan, K. L., & Ooi, B. C. (1998). On selective tuning in unreliable wireless channels. [Elsevier.]. *Data & Knowledge Engineering, 28*(2), 209–231. doi:10.1016/S0169-023X(98)00018-4

Tesch, T., & Wäsch, J. (1997). Global nested transaction management for ODMG-compliant multi-database systems. In *Proceedings of International Conference on Information and Knowledge Management* (pp. 67-74). ACM.

Verykios, V. S., Bertino, E., Fovino, I. N., Provenza, L. P., Saygin, Y., & Theodoridis, Y. (2004). State-of-the-art in privacy preserving data mining. *SIGMOD Record*, *33*(1), 50–57. doi:10.1145/974121.974131

Vonk, J., & Grefen, P. (2003). Cross-organizational transaction support for e-services in virtual enterprises. *Journal of Distributed and Parallel Databases*, *14*(2), 137–172. doi:10.1023/A:1024884626434

Wolfson, O., Sistla, A. P., Xu, B., Zhou, J., & Chamberlain, S. (1999). DOMINO: Databases for moving objects tracking. In *Proceedings of ACM SIGMOD International Conference on Management of Data* (pp. 547-549). ACM.

Wong, M. H., Agrawal, D., & Mak, H. K. (1997). Bounded inconsistency for type-specific concurrency control. *Journal of Distributed and Parallel Databases*, *5*(1), 31–75. doi:10.1023/A:1008622921917

Yau, S. M. T., Leong, H. V., & Si, A. (2003). Distributed agent environment: Application and performance. *Information Sciences Journal*, *154*(1-2), 5–21. doi:10.1016/S0020-0255(03)00003-3

KEY TERMS AND DEFINITIONS

Continuous Query: A continuous query is a query, which is re-evaluated continuously. For example, the query "give me the most updated temperature" will return different readings depending on the current moment. Some continuous queries are also location-dependent. For instance, the query "show me the nearest gas station" will continually execute a location-dependent query. Advanced query processing technique is needed, in conjunction with moving object databases.

Geographical Information System: A geographical information system is an information system that stores and manipulates data for geographical entities such as streets, road junctions, railway, land-use, or even terrain. The data is associated with the location of the entities to allow fast geo-referencing.

Location-Dependent Query: A location-dependent query is a query whose results depend on the current location of the query issuer. For example, the query "which is the nearest gas station?" will return different gas stations depending on the current location of a driver.

Mobile Database: A mobile database is a database accessible to mobile clients. There are appropriate mechanisms to take into account of the limitation of the wireless bandwidth, the use of downlink broadcast channel, and the effect of client mobility.

Moving Object Database: A moving object database is a database that maintains efficiently the location information about moving objects, with proper indexing on the object location.

Serializability/Global Serializability: Serializability is the generally accepted correctness criterion for concurrent execution of transactions. The concurrent execution should produce the same effect and lead to the same database state as one possible sequential execution of the same set of transactions. Global serializability is the correctness criterion for concurrent execution of global transactions over many database systems. It is a stronger correctness criterion than serializability.

Spatial Database: A spatial database is a database that maintains spatial data, including the topology and relationship between points, lines and shapes, and supports spatial operations and queries, such as the area of a shape, the distance between two entities, whether a shape is covered by or next to another.

Transaction/Global Transaction: A transaction is a sequence of operations on a database that should appear as if it were executed non-interfered, even in the presence of other concurrent transactions. A transaction should satisfy the ACID properties, namely, atomicity, consistency, isolation, and durability. A global transaction is a distributed transaction that is executed on two or more database systems.

This work was previously published in the Encyclopedia of Information Science and Technology, Second Edition, edited by M. Khosrow-Pour, pp. 967-973, copyright 2010 by IGI Publishing (an imprint of IGI Global).

Chapter 3.19
A Data Quality Model for Web Portals

Angélica Caro
University of Bio Bio, Chile

Coral Calero
University of Castilla-La Mancha, Spain

Mario Piattini
University of Castilla-La Mancha, Spain

ABSTRACT

Web portals are Internet-based applications that provide a big amount of data. The data consumer who uses the data given by these applications needs to assess data quality. Due to the relevance of data quality on the Web together with the fact that DQ needs to be assessed within the context in which data are generated, data quality models specific to this context are necessary. In this chapter, we will introduce a model for data quality in Web portals (PDQM). PDQM has been built upon the foundation of three key aspects: (1) a set of Web data quality attributes identified in the literature in this area, (2) data quality expectations of data consumers on the Internet, and (3) the functionalities that a Web portal may offer its users.

DOI: 10.4018/978-1-59904-847-5.ch008

INTRODUCTION

In recent years, Web portals have risen in popularity as a way of aggregating, organizing, and presenting content in a highly uniform, customizable, and personalized way. In simplest terms, a portal is a Web site that provides content and application functionality in a way that is both useful and meaningful to the end user (Secrist 2003).

In general, Web portals provide users with access to different data sources (providers) (Mahdavi, Shepherd, Benatallah, 2004), as well as to online information and information-related services (Yang, Cai, Zhou, & Zhou, 2004). Moreover, they create a working environment where users can easily navigate in order to find the information they specifically need to quickly perform their operational or strategic tasks and make decisions (Collins, 2001). So, users or data consumers aimed at using the data offered by these applications need to ensure that these data are appropriate for the use they need, being fundamental to assess the quality of data.

Data and information quality (DQ hereafter) is often defined as "fitness for use," that is, the ability of a data collection to meet user requirements (Strong, Lee, & Wang 1997; Cappiello, Francalanci, & Pernici, 2004). This definition suggests the relativity of this concept because data considered appropriate for a specific use may not be appropriate for another. Even more, this definition involves understanding DQ from the user's point of view and, consequently, understanding that the quality of data cannot be assessed independently of the people who use data (Wang & Strong, 1996).

Due to the relevance of DQ on the Web together with the fact that DQ needs to be assessed within the context of its generations (Knight & Burn, 2005), in the last years the research community started studying the subject of DQ in the Web context (Gertz, Ozsu, Sattke, & Sattler, 2004). However, despite the sizeable body of literature available on DQ and the different domains studied on the Web, we have found no works on DQ that address the particular context of Web portals. Likewise, except for a few works in the DQ area, such as (Wang & Strong, 1996; Burgess, Fiddian, & Gray, 2004; Cappiello et al., 2004), most of the contributions target quality from the data producers' or data custodians' perspective and not from the data consumers' perspective (Burgess, et al., 2004). The last perspective differs from the two others in two important aspects: (1) data consumers have no control over the quality of available data and (2) the aim of consumers is to find data that match their personal needs, rather than provide data that meet the needs of others.

So, consequently to this situation, the aim of our research work is the creation of a Data Quality Model for Web Portals (PDQM). The objective of this chapter is to present the definition of PDQM. This model is focused on the data consumer's perspective and as key pieces in its

definition we have taken: (1) a set of Web DQ attributes identified in the literature, (2) the DQ expectations of data consumers on the Internet described by Redman (Redman, 2000) and (3) the functionalities that a portal Web may offer its users (Collins, 2001).

BACKGROUND

Data Quality and the Web

Research on DQ began in the context of information systems (Strong et al., 1997; Lee, 2002) and it has been extended to contexts such as cooperative systems, data warehouses or e-commerce, among others. Due to the particular characteristics of Web applications and their differences from the traditional information systems, the research community started to deal with the subject of DQ on the Web (Gertz et al., 2004). In fact, the particular nature of the Internet has forced to pay attention to a series of particular issues of this context that can affect or influence the quality of data. We have summarized some of them in Table 1.

In the last years, based on the previous Web issues and others, frameworks and models to deal with DQ in different domains in the Web context have been proposed. Among them we can highlight those shown in Table 2.

Concerning Table 2, we can make two important observations. First, the frameworks proposed tackle different domains on the Web. This reasserts the idea that DQ needs to be assessed within the context of the data source (Knight & Burn, 2005). Second, for Web portals we have not found specific DQ frameworks.

During the past decade, an increasing number of organizations have established Web portals to complement, substitute, or widen existing services to their clients. In general, portals provide users with access to different data sources (providers) (Mahdavi, et al., 2004), as well as to online information and information-related services (Yang et al., 2004).

Table 1. Particular issues of Web context that can affect DQ

Issues	Description	Authors
Data Quality from the User's Perspective	It implies that DQ cannot be assessed independently of the people who use data.	(Strong, et al., 1997; Cappiello et al., 2004; Gertz et al., 2004; Knight & Burn, 2005)
Demand for realtime services	Web applications interact with different external data sources whose workload is not known. This situation can drastically influence response times, affecting DQ in aspects such as opportunity or updatedness.	(Amirijoo, Hansson, & Son, 2003).
Development of electronic commerce	DQ is essential to achieve the development of e-commerce on the Web as well as to win customer's trust.	(Lim & Chin, 2000; Davydov, 2001; Haider & Koronios, 2003).
Dynamism on the Web	The dynamism with which data, applications and sources change can affect DQ.	(Pernici & Scannapieco, 2002; Gertz et al., 2004)
Integration of structured and non-structured data	The use of nonstructure data (e-mails, work documents, manuals, etc.) and their integration with structured data is an important challenge because both of them contain knowledge of great value for organizations.	(Finkelstein & Aiken, 1999)
Integration of data from different sources	The access to diverse data sources that probably do not have the same level of DQ can damage the DQ of the product of this integration that is given to users.	(Naumann & Rolker, 2000; Zhu & Buchmann, 2002; Angeles & MacKinnon, 2004; Gertz et al., 2004; Winkler, 2004)
Need to understand data and their quality	A common language that facilitates communication between people, systems and programs is essential and to be able to evaluate DQ, it is necessary to understand data and the criteria used for determining their quality.	(Finkelstein & Aiken, 1999; Gertz et al. 2004)
Typical problems of a Web page	Un-updated information, publication of inconsistent information, obsolete links and so on.	(Eppler & Muenzenmayer 2002).
Users' Loyalty	This involves the need of an appropriate management of the data of each user or type of user, data fitness for users, and the permanent data output that keeps the interest and loyalty of users.	(Davydov, 2001)

Table 2. Summary of Web DQ frameworks in the literature

Author	Domain	Framework structure
(Katerattanakul & Siau, 1999)	Personal Web sites	4 categories and 7 constructors
(Naumann & Rolker, 2000)	Data integration	3 classes and 22 quality criterion
(Aboelmeged, 2000)	e-commerce	7 stages to modeling DQ problems
(Katerattanakul & Siau, 2001)	e-commerce	4 categories associated with 3 categories of data user requirements.
(Pernici & Scannapieco, 2002)	Web information systems (data evolution)	4 categories, 7 activities of DQ design and architecture to DQ management.
(Fugini, Mecella et al., 2002)	e-service cooperative	8 dimensions
(Graefe, 2003)	Decision making	8 dimensions and 12 aspects related to (providers/consumers)
(Eppler, Algesheimer, & Dimpfel, 2003)	Web sites	4 dimensions and 16 attributes
(Gertz et al., 2004)	DQ on the Web	5 dimensions
(Moustakis, Litos et al., 2004)	Web sites	5 categories and 10 sub-categories
(Melkas, 2004)	Organizational networks	6 stages to DQ analysis with several dimensions associated with each of them
(Bouzeghoub & Peralta, 2004)	Data integration	2 factors and 4 metrics
(Yang et al., 2004)	Web information portals	2 dimensions within the global model

In the same way, the amount of people that access these applications grows every day. They use them from business to education and entertainment. In each case, people need to make operations related to data and they need that these data are appropriate for the use they need. For example, if the purpose is to obtain the cinema billboard to find out the movie's schedule, users will hope to receive the appropriate data to plan what movie to watch and at what time, and all this performed in accord with their plans. So, they need data to be valid, correct, believable, accessible, and so forth. That is, they need data with quality.

Nowadays, DQ is a critical factor of success for Web applications (Schaupp, Fan, & Belanger, 2006). Web portals owners need to know the DQ needs of data consumers as a way to ensure their loyalty. Data consumers aimed at using the data offered by these applications need to ensure that the obtained data are appropriate for the use they need.

The challenge of our research is to develop a DQ model for Web portals that meets these needs. So, the first step to achieve this objective is to define, in a theoretical way, a model that supports the DQ perspective of data consumers and identifies a set of DQ attributes that allow the assessment of DQ in Web portals. The next

section will describe the process developed to obtain this model.

DEFINING A DQ MODEL

To produce the PDQM model we defined the process shown in Figure 1. This process is divided into two parts. The first one, presented in this chapter, consists of the theoretical definition of PDQM and the second one, now in progress, consists of the preparation of PDQM to be used in evaluation processes.

The first part is composed by four phases. During the first phase, we have recompiled Web DQ attributes from the literature, which we believe should be applicable to Web portals. In the second phase we have built a matrix for the classification of the attributes obtained in the previous phase. This matrix reflects two basic aspects considered in our model: the data consumer's perspective and the basic functionalities which a data consumer uses to interact with a Web portal. In the third phase we have used the obtained matrix to analyse the applicability of each Web DQ attribute in a Web portal. The fourth phase (not essential), corresponds to the validation of the selected set of DQ attributes. The theoretical model generated

Figure 1. Development process of PDQM

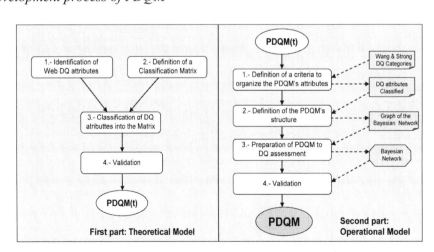

in this part will be used as an input for the second part into the general process. In next subsections we will describe each phase developed to define our model.

Foundations of PDQM

PDQM is a data quality model for Web portals focused on the data consumer's perspective. For the theoretical definition we have considered three key elements:

- **Data consumer's point of view:** When data management is conceptualized as a production process (Strong et al., 1997), we can identify three important roles in this process: (1) data producers (who generate data), (2) data custodians (who provide and manage resources for processing and storing data), and (3) data consumers (who access and use data for their tasks). The data consumer's perspective differs from the data producer's and the data custodian's perspectives in two important aspects (Burgess et al., 2004):
- Data consumers have no control over the quality of available data.
- The aim of consumers is to find data that match their personal needs, rather than provide data that meet the needs of others.

In other words, data consumers expect to find in a Web portal, or by means of it, the data that "meet their requirements." So, to consider the data consumer's perspective in our model we have used the DQ expectations of the data consumer on the Internet, proposed in (Redman, 2000). These expectations are organized into six categories: privacy, content, quality of values, presentation, improvement, and commitment:

- **Web Data Quality Attributes:** As shown in Table 2, different DQ models have been proposed in the literature for different

domains in the Web context. With the idea of taking advantage of work already carried out in this context we have decided to study these works and consider their application to the specific domain of Web portals. Specifically, our intention is to identify Web DQ attributes that can be used in our model.

- **Web portal functionalities:** Web portals present basic software functionalities to data consumers deploying their tasks. Under our perspective, consumers judge data by using application functionalities. So, we used the Web portal software functions that Collins proposes (Collins, 2001) considering them as basic in our model. These functions are as follows: Data Points and Integration, Taxonomy, Search Capabilities, Help Features, Content Management, Process and Action, Collaboration and Communication, Personalization, Presentation, Administration, and Security. Behind these functions, the Web portal encapsulates the producer-custodian role.

Once having defined these aspects, we carry out the first part of the development process to generate PDQM. In the next subsections we will explain each phase.

Phase 1. Identification of Web Data Quality Attributes

The first phase in the development of our model consisted of a systematic review of the relevant literature (Kitchenham, 2004). With this task we aimed at identifying DQ attributes which had been proposed for different domains in the Web context (Web sites (Katerattanakul & Siau, 1999; Eppler et al., 2003; Moustakis et al., 2004), data integration (Naumann & Rolker, 2000; Bouzeghoub & Peralta, 2004), e-commerce (Katerattanakul & Siau, 2001), Web information portals (Yang et al., 2004), cooperative e-services (Fugini et al.,

2002), decision making (Graefe, 2003), organizational networks (Melkas, 2004) and DQ on the Web (Gertz et al., 2004)). The idea was to take advantage of work already carried out in the Web context and apply it to Web portals.

In this review we studied 55 works, published between 1995 and 2004. From the studied work we selected the projects in which DQ attributes applicable to the Web context were proposed. Thus, we obtained a total of 100 Web DQ attributes. Our objective was to reduce this number, having also detected certain synonymous among the attributes identified. Those attributes were combined including the ones which had similar name and meaning, obtaining a final set of 41 attributes. Figure 2shows these attributes, pointing out for each attribute the work where they were put forward, as well as the total number of pieces of work where they can be found referred to. In addition, the symbols ⊆ and ⊊ were used to represent how they were combined (⊆ indicates the same name and meaning and ⊊ marks the fact that only the meaning is the same).

From this set of DQ attributes we will determine which of them can be applicable to the Web portal context.

Phase 2. Definition of a Classification Matrix

In the second phase we defined a matrix which would allow us to perform a preliminary analysis of how applicable the previously identified attributes were to the domain of Web portals. The matrix was defined basing on the relationship that exists between: (1) The functionalities of a Web portal (Collins, 2001): data points and integration, taxonomy, search capabilities, help features, content management, processes and actions, communication and collaboration, personalization, presentation, administration and security; and (2) The data quality expectations of Internet data consumers as stated in (Redman, 2000): privacy, content, quality of values, presentation, improvement, and commitment.

In this matrix we carried out an analysis of which expectations were applicable to each of the different functionalities that a portal offers to a data consumer. This is represented in Figure 3 with a "√" mark.

The description of each one of these relationships (functionality, expectation) is shown in Appendix A.

Figure 2. Web data quality attributes 1-41

Author	Year	Accessibility	Accuracy	Amount of data	Applicability	Attractiveness	Availability	Believability	Completeness	Concise Representation	Consistent Representation	Cost Effectiveness	Customer Support	Currency	Documentation	Duplicates	Ease of operation	Expiration	Flexibility	Granularity	Interactive	Internal Consistency	Interpretability	Latency	Maintainable	Novelty	Objectivity	Ontology	Organization	Price	Relevancy	Reliability	Reputation	Response time	Security	Specialization	Source's Information	Timeliness	Traceability	Understand ability	Validity	Value-added	Number of Attributes
Nauman and Rolker	2000		x	x			x	x	x	x	x		x		x							x	x			x	x	x	x	x	x	x							x	⊗	x		x	22
Katerattanakul and Siau	1999, 2001	x	⊗			x																				x														x		⊗		6
Eppler	2001	x	x		x				x	⊗	⊗			x			⊗				x	⊗			x									⊗	x			x	x	⊗			16
Fugini et al	2002		⊗		x			⊗	x													x									⊗						⊗		x				8
Pernici and Scannapieco	2002		x						x									x													⊗												4
Graefe	2003	⊗					⊗	x														x			x						⊗										⊗	⊗	8
Bouzeghoub and Peralta	2004													x																								x					2
Gertz	2004								x					x	x					x							x																5
Melkas	2004	x	x	⊗			x	x	x	x	x				x	x					x				x						x		x	⊗	x			x	x	⊗		x	20
Moustakis	2004				⊗		⊗																								⊗									x			4
Yang et al.	2004		x				⊗	x						x																	⊗												5
Number of references		4	7	2	3	1	1	6	7	3	3	1	1	4	1	1	2	1	1	1	1	2	3	1	1	1	2	1	1	1	6	2	2	3	4	1	1	5	3	4	1	3	

Figure 3. Matrix for the classification of attributes of Web data quality

	Data Points and Integration	Taxonomy	Search Capabilities	Help Features	Content Management	Process and Action	Collaboration and Communication	Personalization	Presentation	Administration	Security	Category of Data Consumer Expectations
					√	√	√	√		√	√	Privacy
	√	√		√	√	√			√			Content
	√		√		√	√		√	√		√	Quality of Values
	√	√	√	√	√	√	√		√	√	√	Presentation
	√	√	√		√	√			√			Improvement
			√	√	√							Commitment

Phase 3. Classification of Data Quality Attributes into the Matrix

The third phase of the development process of the PDQM model (see Figure 1), consisted of classifying the Web data quality attributes (shown in section 2) into each one of the relationships (functionality, expectation) established in the classification matrix created in phase 2 (and presented in the previous subsection). In Figure 4, we will set out a summary of the attributes applicable to each portal functionality.

As it can be seen in Figure 4, there are some DQ attributes which were not classified into the matrix. This is basically due to the fact that they could no be assessed by data consumers, for example, ontology and latency.

As a result of this phase we obtained a set of 34 DQ attributes that can be used to assess DQ in a Web portal (see Appendix B).

Figure 4. Data quality attributes for functionality

Functionalities	Accessibility	Accuracy	Amount of data	Applicability	Attractiveness	Availability	Believability	Completeness	Concise Representation	Consistent Representation	Cost effectiveness	Customer support	Currency	Documentation	Duplicates	Ease of operation	Expiration	Flexibility	Granularity	Interactive	Internal consistency	Interpretability	Latency	Maintainable	Novelty	Objectivity	Ontology	Organization	Price	Relevancy	Reliability	Reputation	Response time	Security	Specialization	Source's information	Timeliness	Traceability	Understand ability	Validity	Value-added	Total of Attributes
Data Points and Integration	✓	✓	✓			✓		✓	✓			✓	✓				✓								✓					✓	✓							✓	✓	✓		15
Taxonomy	✓		✓			✓		✓				✓				✓														✓	✓							✓	✓	✓		11
Search Capabilities	✓		✓			✓	✓	✓	✓			✓	✓			✓									✓					✓	✓								✓	✓		13
Help Features	✓		✓					✓				✓				✓										✓													✓	✓		8
Content Management	✓		✓	✓		✓	✓	✓	✓			✓	✓	✓	✓	✓						✓			✓	✓		✓		✓	✓	✓		✓	✓	✓		✓	✓	✓	✓	24
Process and Action	✓	✓	✓	✓		✓	✓	✓	✓			✓				✓	✓					✓			✓					✓	✓	✓		✓	✓			✓	✓	✓		21
Collaboration and Communication						✓			✓							✓						✓			✓									✓					✓			6
Personalization		✓						✓					✓			✓																						✓	✓	✓		7
Presentation			✓		✓		✓		✓			✓	✓			✓	✓	✓				✓								✓	✓				✓			✓	✓	✓		15
Administration			✓					✓	✓							✓																		✓					✓			6
Security	✓	✓	✓					✓	✓							✓						✓												✓					✓	✓		10
Number of References	7	4	9	2	1	3	6	5	9	1	0	8	5	1	1	8	4	1	0	0	0	5	0	0	3	2	0	1	0	7	7	2	0	5	3	1	0	7	11	8	1	

Phase 4. Validation

The fourth phase consisted of the validation of the set of DQ attributes selected. The method selected for this validation was the development of a survey. In this survey, users of Web portals were asked about the importance they gave to the DQ attributes considered in PDQM.

As a starting point, we performed a partial survey to validate the DQ attributes assigned to the data points and integration functionality. The questionnaire contained four questions. The aim of the first two questions (open questions) was to obtain from the respondents the attributes they considered important for the functionality under study. The results showed that the most mentioned attributes were: accessibility, accuracy, understandability, currency, consistent representation, and relevance (all considered in our model for the functionality under study), organization, source's information, and response time (all considered in our model but not for this functionality).

In the third question (also open question) we showed all the attributes considered in our model for the functionality and we asked data consumers for other attributes that they consider necessary. As a result, the most-proposed attributes were Attractiveness with 22%, Security with 12%, and source's information, response time and easy of operation with 10%. All of them were considered in our model but not classified within this functionality.

Finally, in the fourth question (close question), the participants had to assign a degree of importance between levels 1 and 7 (1 not important and 7 very important) to each attribute. The attributes that had at least 70% of preferences (adding the percentages of level 6 and 7) will be considered as important for data consumers. Among the 15 attributes assigned to this functionality, 10 of them appeared to be relevant (with more of a 70% of preferences) for the subjects. This result showed a coincidence with the subjects of at least 66%, for the asked functionality.

Considering this experience and the results obtained from this partial validation of PDQM, we decided to develop a new survey to validate the complete model. The purpose of this new survey was to collect ratings of the importance of each one of the 34 DQ attributes of PDQM. The survey questionnaire was composed of 34 questions, one for each DQ attribute. Each question was measured by using a 5-point Lickert scale where 1 means "Not Important" and 5 "Very Important."

We used a sample of student subjects (convenience sampling) for our survey. A group of 70 Master students in the final-year (fifth) of Computer Science was enrolled (from a software engineering class). The total effective sample was 54, or 77% of the subjects that had initially been enrolled.

We decided that DQ attributes that had a mean of 3 or more (considering the choices "moderately important," "important," and "very important") would be kept in the PDQM. All the others are rejected. Regarding the results of the survey, 33 DQ attributes obtained a mean of 3 or more (97%). These 33 attributes made up the new version of PDQM. The DQ attribute Source's Information was eliminated because their mean was 2.56 (see in Table 3 the row marked).

Table 3 shows the retained DQ attributes list and descriptive statistics about them. A detailed description of the validation process can be found in Caro et al. (2007).

FUTURE WORK

As a result of our work, so far, we have defined a theoretical DQ model for Web portals. Our future work will be centred in the development of the second part of the development process of PDQM, that is, we will convert PDQM into an operational model. This means that we need to define a structure where we can organize DQ attributes and associate measures and criteria for them.

Table 3. Final set of DQ attributes of PDQM

Attribute	Mean	Min	Max	Attribute	Mean	Min	Max
Attractiveness	4.06	2	5	Interactivity	3.19	1	5
Accessibility	4.52	3	5	Interpretability	3.87	2	5
Accuracy	4.28	2	5	Novelty	3.67	2	5
Amount of Data	3.96	2	5	Objectivity	3.50	1	5
Applicability	4.00	2	5	Organization	3.94	2	5
Availability	4.60	3	5	Relevancy	4.09	2	5
Believability	4.15	2	5	Reliability	4.15	2	5
Completeness	3.85	2	5	Reputation	3.46	2	5
Concise Representation	3.63	2	5	Response Time	4.30	2	5
Consistent Representation	3.63	2	5	Security	4.22	2	5
Currency	4.54	3	5	Source's Information	2.56	1	5
Customer Support	3.54	1	5	Specialization	3.61	2	5
Documentation	3.31	1	5	Timeliness	4.06	2	5
Duplicates	3.00	1	5	Traceability	3.63	1	5
Ease of Operation	3.72	2	5	Understandability	4.02	2	5
Expiration	3.28	1	5	Validity	3.57	1	5
Flexibility	3.26	2	5	Value added	3.98	1	5

Considering the uncertainty inherent in quality perception, we have decided to use a probabilistic approach (Bayesian network and Fuzzy logic) to structure, refine, and represent the 33 DQ attributes. The construction of a BN for a particular quality model can be carried out in two stages (Malak, Sahraoui, Badri, & Badri, 2006). At the first one, the graph structure is built. This graphical approach is essential in order to establish the appropriate relationships among DQ attributes and it provides us with a generic structure for our model. At the second stage it is necessary to define the node probability tables for each node of the graph. This stage must be developed according to the evaluation context (Shankar & Watts, 2003).

After the generation of the structure of PDQM and its preparation for DQ evaluation in a specific context, the validation process will be conducted. This validation will be used for the adjustment of our model with the judgments of data consumers for a specific context.

One of the advantages of our framework will be its flexibility. Indeed, the idea is to develop a global framework that can be adapted for both the goal and the context of evaluation. From the goal's perspective, the user can choose the sub-network that evaluates the characteristics he or she is interested in. From the context's point of view, the parameters (probabilities) can be changed to consider the specific context of the evaluated portal. This operation can be performed by using available historical data from the organization.

CONCLUSION

Web portals are applications that have been positioned like information sources or means of accessing information over the last decade. On the other hand, those who need to use information from these portals must be sure; somehow, that this information is suitable for the use they wish.

In other words, they really need to assess the level of the quality of the obtained data.

In the literature, there are no specific proposals for data quality models for Web portals. In this chapter we have presented the first part of the development of a Data Quality Model for Web portals (PDQM) that considers the consumers' point of view. This model has been built upon three fundamental aspects: a set of Web data quality attributes found in the relevant literature, data quality expectations of data consumers on the Internet, and the functionalities which a Web portal may offer its users.

The main contribution of this work is the identification, based on the data consumer's perspective, of a set of 33 DQ attributes that can be used for DQ evaluation in Web portals. This work has generated a theoretical model that will be used to generate an operational model that could be used in different contexts and processes of DQ evaluation in Web portals.

ACKNOWLEDGMENT

This research is part of the following projects: CALIPSO (TIN20005-24055-E) supported by the Ministerio de Educación y Ciencia (Spain), DIMENSIONS (PBC-05-012-1) supported by FEDER, and by the "Consejería de Educación y Ciencia, Junta de Comunidades de Castilla-La Mancha" (Spain), and COMPETISOFT (506AC0287), financed by CYTED.

REFERENCES

Aboelmeged, M. (2000). A soft system perspective on information quality in electronic commerce. In *Proceedings of the Fifth Conference on Information Quality,* (pp. 318-319).

Amirijoo, M., Hansson, J., & Son, S. (2003). Specification and management of QoS in imprecise real-time databases. In *Proceedings of the Seventh International Database Engineering and Applications Symposium,* (pp. 192-201).

Angeles, P., & MacKinnon, L. (2004). Detection and resolution of data inconsistencies, and data integration using data quality criteria. *QUATIC, 2004,* 87–93.

Bouzeghoub, M., & Peralta, V. (2004). A framework for analysis of data freshness. In *Proceedings of the International Workshop on Information Quality in Information Systems, (IQIS2004),* ACM, Paris, France, (pp. 59-67).

Burgess, M., Fiddian, N., & Gray, W. (2004). Quality measures and the information consumer. In *Proceedings of the Ninth International Conference on Information Quality,* (pp. 373-388).

Cappiello, C., Francalanci, C., & Pernici, B. (2004). Data quality assessment from the user's perspective. In *Proceedings of the International Workshop on Information Quality in Information Systems, (IQIS2004),* ACM, Paris, France, (pp. 68-73).

Caro, A., Calero, C., Caballero, I., & Piattini, M. (2007). (to appear). A Proposal for a set of attributes relevant for Web portal data quality . *Software Quality Journal.*

Collins, H. (2001). Corporate portal definition and features. AMACOM.

Davydov, M. (2001). Corporate portals and e-business integration. McGraw-Hill.

Eppler, M., Algesheimer, R., & Dimpfel, M. (2003). Quality criteria of content-driven Web sites and their influence on customer satisfaction and loyalty: An empirical test of an information quality framework. In *Proceedings of the Eighth International Conference on Information Quality,* (pp. 108-120).

Eppler, M., & Muenzenmayer, P. (2002). Measuring information quality in the Web context: A survey of state-of-the-art instruments and an application methodology. In *Proceedings of the Seventh International Conference on Information Quality,* (pp. 187-196).

Finkelstein, C., & Aiken, P. (1999). XML and corporate portals. Wilshire Conferences.

Fugini, M., Mecella, M., Plebani, P., Pernici, B., & Scannapieco, M. (2002). *Data quality in cooperative Web information systems*.

Gertz, M., Ozsu, T., Saake, G., & Sattler, K.-U. (2004). Report on the Dagstuhl Seminar "Data Quality on the Web". *SIGMOD Record, 33*(1), 127–132. doi:10.1145/974121.974144

Graefe, G. (2003). Incredible information on the Internet: Biased information provision and a lack of credibility as a cause of insufficient information quality. In *Proceedings of the Eighth International Conference on Information Quality,* (pp. 133-146).

Haider, A., & Koronios, A. (2003). Authenticity of information in cyberspace: IQ in the Internet, Web, and e-business. In *Proceedings of the Eighth International Conference on Information Quality,* (pp. 121-132).

Katerattanakul, P., & Siau, K. (1999). Measuring information quality of Web sites: Development of an instrument. In *Proceedings of the 20th International Conference on Information System,* (pp. 279-285).

Katerattanakul, P., & Siau, K. (2001). Information quality in Internet commerce design. In M. Piattini & C. Calero, & M. Genero (Ed.), Information and database quality. Kluwer Academic Publishers.

Kitchenham, B. (2004). *Procedures for performing systematic reviews*.

Knight, S. A., & Burn, J. M. (2005). Developing a framework for assessing information quality on the World Wide Web. *Informing Science Journal, 8*, 159–172.

Lee, Y. (2002). "AIMQ: A methodology for information quality assessment." Information and Management. Elsevier Science, 133-146.

Lim, O., & Chin, K. (2000). An investigation of factors associated with customer satisfaction in Australian Internet bookshop Web sites. In *Proceedings of the 3rd Western Australian Workshop on Information Systems Research,* Autralia.

Mahdavi, M., Shepherd, J., & Benatallah, B. (2004). A collaborative approach for caching dynamic data in portal applications. In *Proceedings of the Fifteenth Conference on Australian Database,* (pp. 181-188).

Malak, G., Sahraoui, H., Badri, L., & Badri, M. (2006). Modeling Web-based applications quality: A probabilistic approach. In *Proceedings of the 7th International Conference on Web Information Systems Engineering,* Wuhan, China, (pp. 398-404). Springer LNCS.

Melkas, H. (2004). Analyzing information quality in virtual service networks with qualitative interview data. In *Proceedings of the Ninth International Conference on Information Quality,* (pp. 74-88).

Moustakis, V., Litos, C., Dalivigas, A., & Tsironis, L. (2004). Web site quality assesment criteria. In *Proceedings of the Ninth International Conference on Information Quality,* (pp. 59-73).

Naumann, F., & Rolker, C. (2000). Assesment methods for information quality criteria. In *Proceedings of the Fifth International Conference on Information Quality,* (pp. 148-162).

Pernici, B., & Scannapieco, M. (2002). Data quality in Web information systems. In *Proceedings of the 21st International Conference on Conceptual Modeling,* (pp. 397-413).

Redman, T. (2000). Data quality: The field guide. Boston: Digital Press.

Schaupp, C., Fan, W., & Belanger, F. (2006). Determining success for different Web site goals. In *Proceedings of the 39th Hawaii International Conference on Systems Science (HICSS-39 2006)* (p. 107.2). Kauai, HI. USA: IEEE Computer Society.

Secrist, M. (2003). Portalise It! Dev2Dev.

Shankar, G., & Watts, S. (2003). A relevant, believable approach for data quality assessment. In *Proceedings of the Eighth International Conference on Information Quality (IQ2003),* (pp. 178-189).

Strong, D., Lee, Y., & Wang, R. (1997). Data quality in context. *Communications of the ACM, 40*(5), 103–110. doi:10.1145/253769.253804

Wang, R., & Strong, D. (1996). Beyond accuracy: What data quality means to data consumers. *Journal of Management Information Systems; Armonk; Spring, 12*(4), 5-33.

Winkler, W. (2004). Methods for evaluating and creating data quality. *Information Systems, 29*(7), 531–550. doi:10.1016/j.is.2003.12.003

Yang, Z., Cai, S., Zhou, Z., & Zhou, N. (2004). Development and validation of an instrument to measure user perceived service quality of information presenting Web portals. *Information and Management. Elsevier Science, 42,* 575–589. doi:10.1016/S0378-7206(04)00073-4

Zhu, Y., & Buchmann, A. (2002). Evaluating and selecting Web sources as external information resources of a data warehouse. In *Proceedings of the 3rd International Conference on Web Information Systems Engineering,* (pp. 149-160).

KEY TERMS

Data Quality: Data has quality when it has "fitness for use," that is, when it meets user requirements.

Data Consumer: Person who uses data for a specific purpose and can be affected by its quality.

Data Quality Attribute: Characteristics or properties of data that are relevant in a specific context.

Data Quality Model: A defined set of relevant attributes and relationships between them, which provides a framework for specifying data quality requirements and evaluating data quality.

Evaluation: The activity of assessing the quality of a system or the data it contains.

Portal Functionalities: Basic software functions in Web portals that are used for users to interact with a Web portal.

Web Portals: Internet-based applications that enable access to different sources (providers) through a single interface which provides personalization, single sign on, content aggregation from different sources and which hosts the presentation layer of Information Systems.

APPENDIX A
Table 4.

Functionality	Categories of DQ Expectations of Data Consumers on Internet					
	Privacy	Content	Quality of Values	Presentation	Improvement	Commitment
Data Points and Integration. They provide the ability to access information from a wide range of internal and external data sources and display the resulting information at the single point-of-access desktop.		Data Consumers need a description of portal areas covered, use of published data, etc.	Data consumers should expect the result of searches to be correct, up-to-date and complete	Formats, language, and other aspects are very important for easy interpretation	Users want to participate with their opinions in the portal improvements and know what the results of applying them are	
Taxonomy. It provides information context (including the organization-specific categories that reflect and support the organization's business).		Data consumers need a description of what data are published and how they should be used, as well as easy-to-understand definitions of every important term, etc.		Formats and language in the taxonomy are very important for easy interpretation; users should expect to find instructions when reading data	Users should expect to convey their comments on data in the taxonomy and know what the result of improvements are	
Search Capabilities. This provides several services for Web portal users and needs to support searches across the company, the WWW, and into search engine catalogs and indexes.			Data consumers should expect the result of searches to be correct, up-to-date and complete	Formats and language are important for consumers, both for searching and for easy interpretation of results	Consumers should expect to convey their comments on data in the taxonomy and be aware of the result of improvements	
Help Features. These provide help when using a Web portal.				Formats, language, and other aspects are very important for easy interpretation of help texts		Consumers should be able to ask and obtain answers to any question regarding the proper use or meaning of data, update schedules, etc., easily.

Content Management. This function supports content creation, authorization, and inclusion in (or exclusion from) Web portal collections.	A privacy policy for all consumers to manage, access sources and guarantee Web portals data should exist	Consumers need a description of data collections	A consumer should expect all data values to be correct, up-to-date and complete	Formats and language should be appropriate for easy interpretation	Consumers should expect to convey their comments on contents and their management and be aware of the result of improvements	Consumers should be able to ask any question regarding the proper use or meaning of data, etc
Process and Action. This function enables Web portal users to initiate and participate in a business process of a portal owner.	Data consumer should expect that there is a privacy policy to manage the data about the business in a portal	Consumers should expect to find descriptions about the data published for this function, their uses, etc.	All data associated with this function must be correct, up-to-date and complete	Formats and other aspects are very important in order to interpret data	Consumers should expect to convey their comments on contents and their management and know the results of improvements	Consumer should be able to ask and obtain an answer to any question
Collaboration and Communication. This function facilitates discussion, locating innovative ideas, and recognizing resourceful solutions.	Consumers should expect that there is a privacy policy for all consumers that participate in activities of this function					A consumer should be able to ask and have any question answered regarding the proper use or meaning of data for this function.
Personalization. This is a critical component in creating a working environment that is organized and configured specifically for each user.	Consumers should expect privacy and security regarding their personalized data, profile, etc.		Data about the user's profile should be correct and up-to-date			
Presentation. It provides the web portal user with both the knowledge desktop and the visual experience that encapsulate all of the portal's functionality.		The presentation of a Web portal should include data about areas covered, appropriate and inappropriate uses, definitions, etc.	Data of this function should be correct, up-to-date and complete.	Formats, language, and other aspects are very important for the easy interpretation and appropriate use of data.	Consumers should expect to convey their comments on contents and their management	
Administration. This function provides a service for deploying maintenance activities or tasks associated with the Web portal system.	Data consumers need security for data about the portal administration		Data about tasks or activities of administration should be correct and complete			

Security. It provides a description of the levels of access that each user is allowed for each application and software function included in the Web portal.	Consumers need a privacy policy regarding the data of the levels of access.		Data about the levels of access should be correct and up-to-date	Data about security should be in a format and language for easy interpretation		

APPENDIX B

Table 5.

	Attribute	Definition
1	Accessibility	The extent to which the Web portal provides enough navigation mechanisms so that visitors can reach their desired data faster and easier.
2	Accuracy	The extent to which data are correct, reliable, and certificated as free of error.
3	Amount of Data	The extent to which the quantity or volume of data delivered by the portal is appropriate
4	Applicability	The extent to which data are specific, useful and easy applicable for the target community.
5	Attractiveness	The extent to which the Web portal is attractive for their visitors.
6	Availability	The extent to which data are available by means the portal.
7	Believability	The extent to which data and their source are accepted as correct.
8	Completeness	The extent to which data, provides for a Web portal, are of sufficient breadth, depth, and scope for the task at hand.
9	Concise Representation	The extent to which data are compactly represented without superfluous or not related elements
10	Consistent Representation	The extent to which data are always presented in the same format, compatible with previous data and consistent with other sources.
11	Customer Support	The extent to which the Web portal provides on-line support by means text, e-mail, telephone, etc.
12	Documentation	Amount and usefulness of documents with meta information.
13	Duplicates	The extent to which data delivered for the portal contains duplicates.
14	Ease of Operation	The extent to which data are easily managed and manipulate (i.e., updated, moved, aggregated, etc.)
15	Expiration	The extent to which the date until which data remain current is known
16	Flexibility	The extent to which data are expandable, adaptable, and easily applied to other needs.
17	Interactivity	The extent to which the way which data are accessed or retrieved can be adapted to one's personal preferences through interactive elements.
18	Interpretability	The extent to which data are in language and units appropriate for the consumer capability.
19	Novelty	The extent to which data obtained from the portal influence the knowledge and the new decisions.
20	Objectivity	The extent to which data are unbiased and impartial.
21	Organization	The organization, visual settings or typographical features (colour, text, font, images, etc.) and the consistent combinations of these various components.
22	Relevancy	The extent to which data are applicable and helpful for users' needs.
23	Reliability	The extent to which users can trust the data and their source.
24	Reputation	The extent to which data are trusted or highly regarded in terms of their source or content.
25	Response Time	Amount of time until complete response reaches the user.
26	Security	Degree to which information is passed privately from user to information source and back.

27	Specialization	Specificity of data contained and delivered for a Web portal
28	Source's Information	The extent to which information about the author/owner of Web portal is delivered to the data consumers
29	Timeliness	The availability of data on time, that is, within the time constrains specified by the destination organization
30	Traceability	The extent to which data are well-documented, verifiable, and easily attributed to a source.
31	Understandability	The extent to which data are clear, without ambiguity, and easily comprehensible
32	Currency	The extent to which the Web portal provides not obsolete data.
33	Validity	The extent to which users can judge and comprehend data delivered by the portal.
34	Value added	The extent to which data are beneficial and provide advantages from their use.

Chapter 3.20
User Facing Web Services in Portals

Jana Polgar
NextDigital, Australia

ABSTRACT

In SOA framework, Portal applications aggregate and render information from multiple sources in easily consumable format to the end users. Web services seem to dominate the integration efforts in SOA. Traditional data-oriented web services require portlet applications to provide specific presentation logic and the communication interface for each web service. This approach is not well suited to dynamic SOA based integration of business processes and content. WSRP 2.0 aim at solving the problem and providing the framework for easy aggregation of presentation services. Is not practical to publish portlets locally if the organisation wishes to publish their portlets as web services to allow their business partners using these services in their portals. UDDI extension for WSRP enables the discovery and access to user facing web services while eliminating the need to design local user facing portlets. Most
importantly, the remote portlets can be updated by the web service providers from their own servers.

VISION FOR USER-FACING PORTLETS

Web services introduced the means for integrating and sharing business processes via the Internet. WSRP (WSRP specification version 1 (2003)) goal is to extend the integration further by providing framework for sharing web service presentation components. WSRP specification formulated a standard protocol which enables all content and application providers to create web services, generate their presentation faces as HTML fragments and offer them to the consumers to be plugged into their local portals.

Portals and portlets (JSR 168 (2005)) provide specific presentation logic to aggregate data from multiple sources which could be legacy systems,

Enterprise Information Systems (EIS), local or remote web services, or EIS with exposed web service interfaces. The first draft of JSR 286 (JSR 286 (2008) brings new features to the Java portlets capabilities introduced by WSRP 2.0 (WSRP Specification version 2.0 (2008)). JSR 286 new features include:

- Interportlet communication: coordination between portlets and allow building composite applications based on portlet components;
- Shared render parameters enable to specify which render parameters they can share with other portlets;
- Resource serving feature enables portlets to serve resources within the portlet context;
- Frameworks for better support for JSF and Struts
- Alignment with WSRP 2.0
- Better user experience using AJAX patterns
- Portlet filters to selectively define the portlets which can transform the content of portlet requests and responses on the fly.

The WSRP specification is intended for presentation-oriented web services, user-facing web services that can be easily integrated with portals. They let businesses provide content or applications without requiring any manual content or application-specific adaptation by portal presentation logic. It is envisaged that in the near future portals will easily aggregate WSRP services without any programming effort. The only effort required is the actual deployment of remote portlets in the local portal server (Hepper, S and Hesmer, S. (2003)). We are not taking into account the effort needed for the "implementation", that is the design of the portal page which is needed in any case.

The WSRP specification (WSRP specification version 1 (2003) and WSRP 2.0 are the effort of the working group at OASIS (http://www.oasis-open.org/committees/wsrp). It aims to provide a set of options for aggregating user-facing web

services (remote portlets) from multiple remote web services within one portal application. WSRP standard has been conceived for implementing simple services. The developer of the portlet provides the markup fragments to display web service data. The current version allows for more complex services that require consumer registration, support complex user interaction, and operate on transient and persistent state maintained by the service provider. Before looking at the functionality of WSRP, note that what WSRP refers to as a portlet is the combination of a portlet implementation and any configuration data that supports the implementation. WSRP 2.0 (WSRP Specification version 2.0 (2008) is closely aligned with the JSR 286 thus providing the framework for publishing JSR 286 portlets as web services.

WSRP AND WSRP RELATED STANDARDS

WSRP defines the notion of valid fragments of markup based on the existing markup languages such as HTML, (X)HTML, VoiceXML, cHTML, etc (Figure 1). For markup languages that support CSS (Cascading Style Sheet) style definitions, WSRP also defines a set of standard CSS class names to allow portlets to generate markup using styles that are provided by WSRP compliant portals such that the markup assumes the look and feel of the consuming portal.

WSRP is fully integrated with the context of the web services standards stack. It uses WSDL additional elements to formally describe the WSRP service interfaces and requires that at least SOAP binding be available for invocations of WSRP services. WSRP also defines the roles of web service *producers* and *consumers*. Both *producers* and *consumers* use a standard protocol to provide and consume web services for user facing portlets. The WSRP specification requires that every *producer* implement two required

Figure 1. WSRP related standards

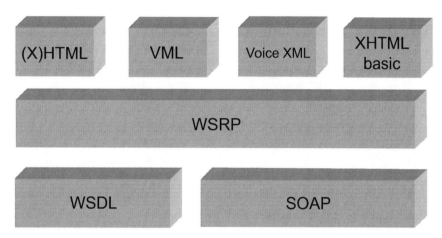

interfaces, and allows optional implementation of two others:

1. **Service Description Interface (required):** This interface allows a WSRP *producer* to advertise services and its capabilities to consumers. A WSRP *consumer* can use this interface to query a *producer* to discover what user-facing services the *producer* offers.
2. **Markup Interface (required):** This interface allows a *consumer* to interact with a remotely running portlet supplied by the *producer*.
3. **Registration Interface (optional):** This interface serves as a mechanism for opening a dialogue between the *producer* and *consumer* so that they can exchange information about each others' technical capabilities.
4. **Portlet Management Interface (optional):** This interface gives the *consumer* control over the life cycle methods of the remote portlet.

URL generation concept: To support user interaction, all the URLs embedded in the markup fragment returned by the remote *producer* service must point back to the *consumer* application.

Therefore, the *consumer* needs to send a URL template as part of the invocation of the `get-Markup()` method. For example, the consumer may send the URL template with two variables: `navigationState` and `sessionID:`.

```
http://neptune.monash.edu.au/myApp?ns={navi
    gationState}&si={sessionID}
```

The *producer* responsibility is to generate a markup fragment in which all the interaction URLs must point back to the *consumer*. The *producer* generates a link pointing to the URL replacing the template variables `navigationState` and `sessionID` with concrete values:

```
http://neptune.monash.edu.au/
    myApp?ns=page2&si=4AHH55A
```

Alternatively, the predetermined pattern allows the *producer* to create URLs that is compliant with this pattern. The *consumer* then parses the markup and rewrites variable parts of URL to point back to the application.

ROLE OF PRODUCERS AND CONSUMERS

WSRP is a protocol in which the interaction always occurs between two web applications or web services. The *consumer* application acts as a client to another application called *producer*. The *producer* provides end-user-facing (also called presentation services) web services in the form of remote portlets. These remote portlets are aggregated into the *consumer's* portal page in the same way as local portlets.

Let's start with comparing WSRP with a web services application. The web based application *consumer* uses HTTP, SOAP and browsers to interact with remote servers hosting web services. In response they receive web service raw **data** needed to create the markup (typically HTML or HTML form). The input data are posted by submitting the form via a browser.

HTTP protocol is also utilized with WSRP. *Consumers* can be seen as intermediaries that communicate with the WSRP *producers*. *Consumers* gather and aggregate the **markup** delivered by local as well as remote portlets created by the *producers* into a portal page. This portal page is then delivered over SOAP and HTTP to the client machine (PC or a workstation). The *consumer* is responsible for most of the interactions with the remote systems, ensuring user privacy and meeting the security concerns with regard to the processing information flow.

In a sense of additional capabilities, today's *consumers* of WSRP are more sophisticated than simple web service clients:

1. *Consumer* aggregates multiple interface components (local and remote portlets) into a single page. In addition, features like personalization, customization and security are also available for remote portlets;
2. The aggregation into a single page is not straightforward since it involves applying *consumer*-specific page layouts, style and skins to meet the end-user requirements. Therefore, the *consumer* must have knowledge of "presenting" related features in remote portlets to apply customization and rendering.
3. The *consumer* can aggregate content produced by portlets running on remote machines that use different programming environments, like J2EE and .NET.
4. *Consumers* are able to deal with remotely managed sessions and persistent states of WSRP web services.

The *producer* is responsible for publishing the service and portlet capabilities descriptions in some directory e.g. UDDI. It allows the *consumer* to find the service and integrate it into portal. The purpose of the portlet capabilities description is to inform the *consumer* about features each portlet offers. *Producer's* major responsibilities are listed below:

5. *Producers* are capable of hosting portlets (they can be thought of as portlet containers). Portlets generate markup and process interactions with that markup;
6. *Producers* render markup fragments which contains web service data.;
7. *Producers* process user interaction requests; and
8. *Producers* provide interfaces for self description, and portlet management.

The *consumer* can optionally *register* with the *producer*. The *producer* is responsible for specifying whether the registration is required. Typical registration contains two types of data: *capabilities* (for example, window states and modes the *producer's* remote portlets support), and *registration properties* (required data prescribed in the service description). Upon successful registration, the *consumer* receives a unique registration handle. This handle allows all portlets to be scoped to fit to the local portal. Optionally, the *consumer* may provide the credentials to the *producer*.

Portlet management is an optional interface implemented by the *producer*. It allows the *consumer* to manage the lifecycle of portlets exposed in the service description. These exposed portlets can be cloned and customized at the *consumer* portal. Note that the original portlets exposed in the service description cannot be modified.

Important points to note is that WSRP based web services are synchronous and UI-oriented. *Consumers* can invoke the web service in the usual way and interact with the service UI. The typical browser-server interaction protocol is then translated into protocol suitable for *consumers* of user facing web services. A typical processing would consist of the following steps:

- The web service interfaces exposed by the *producer* to the *consumer* are described using Web Services Description Language (WSDL). WSDL is the mandatory interface between the client and service that enables the client to bind to the service and use it;
- Optionally, *consumers* can be registered in a *producer's* portal;
- Portal detects the remote portlet on its page and sends getMarkup() message to the *producer*. The markup interface supports end user interaction and it is another mandatory interface in WSRP;
- In response it receives a HTML fragment from the *producer;*
- Portal (*consumer*) aggregates the fragment into the portal page; and
- Optional functionality is the use of the portlet management. The portlet management defines operations (API) for cloning, customizing and deleting portlets.

The actual interaction between WSRP *consumers* and *producers* is more complex. We assume that the user can dynamically add a portlet to the portal page. In response, the portal invokes the WSRP remote service. This action specifies a new portlet instance that allocates a corresponding portlet instance on the portal side. When a user wants to view this portlet, the portal obtains the WSRP markup that defines the fragment to be displayed. The returned markup contains portlet action links and/or a portlet session identifier. When the user clicks on the link (*Click-on-Action*), a request goes from the browser to the portal. The portal maps the request into the invocation of the WSRP service. The capability to maintain the session identity is provided through the parameters that are passed, such as the session ID. This allows the WSRP service to look up the previous session details. When the user does not want to access the WSRP service any more, the session is closed, the portlet is removed, and its instance is destroyed.

WSRP PROCESSING SCENARIOS

The goal of WSRP is to make implementation of remote web services and access to the remote content easy. WSRP service scenarios come in several flavours ranging from simple view to complex interactions and configurations. Please note that our examples are based on IBM's WebSphere 5.1 Portal server. Some of the operations could be implemented differently on IBM Websphere 6.1 Portal or on other vendors' platforms. There are typically three different situations to deal with remote portlets: simple case of just processing view portlet, user interaction and dealing with the state information, and handling of configuration and customization.

REGISTRATION PROCESS

We have to start with two steps which have to be performed in all scenarios at the *consumer* portal:

Registering with the producer portal allows the *producer* to be known to the consumer and make available the list of WSRP services that could be consumed by the consumer portal. There are possible situations:

- Consumer has *online* access to the *producer*. In this scenario it is possible to use the XML configuration interface to configure new *producer* and remote web services. If in-band registration is supported in the producer, the consumer can register through the WSRP registration port type (register() call).
  a. If in-band registration is not supported by the producer, the consumer administrator must manually obtain the registration handle from the *producer*'s administrator.
  b. If the registration is required by the *producer*, it is necessary to implement a registration validation process for informing the producer whether a registration data from the consumer are valid.
- If the *consumer* works *offline* with regard to the *producer,* only the XML configuration interface can be used to create a *producer.*

Consuming the WSRP service allows you to integrate WSRP services from registered *producers* into the *consumer* portal and interact with them as they were local portlets.

WSRP 2.0 provides additional APIs relevant to the portlet lifetime: set|RegistrationLifetime and getRegistrationLifetime which allow the management of the registration.

SIMPLE VIEW PORTLET

In our simple View portlet example, we assume that the web service requires only to be viewed by the end-user. Portlet has to be rendered and no interaction or forms are implemented.

Based on our description of available APIs, we need only getMarkup() operation to be implemented (Figure 2). This operation returns WSRP markup fragment which is then aggregated in the portal page.

Figure 2. Simple view portlet

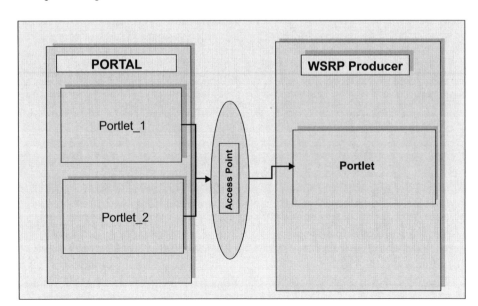

INTERACTIVE SERVICE WITH TRANSIENT CONVERSATIONAL STATE

In this scenario, we need the WSRP implementation to support user interaction and maintain the conversational state of the application. Similarly to servlets (Servlets Specification 2.4 (2004)), the WSRP protocol operates over stateless HTTP. In order to generate correct responses, the application must be stateful and maintain its state. The state may span across several request/response cycles. The WSRP protocol distinguishes between two states: transient and persistent (Figure 3). Navigational state is used when *producer* requires generation of markup for the portlet, several times during its conversation with the *consumer*. This state locally encapsulates required data needed to keep track of the conversation about the current state of the portlet. It means that the *producer* does not hold the transient state locally and the user can store or bookmark the URL using the navigational state. The state is stored with the URL only and both *page refresh* and *bookmarked pages* generate the output the end user expects. The session state is maintained using sessionID which is generated when the portlet initializes the session for a particular end-user. During the interaction the sessionID is moved between the *producer* and *consumer*.

The persistent state survives the conversation and will cease to exist only when either *consumer* or *producer* are discarded. The persistent state is the property exposed by the *producer* via the portlet management interface. In the case of registration (Consumer Registration), the registration state is maintained with the help of the registrationHandle generated during the consumer registration. WSRP protocol allows the consumer to customize the portlet and keep its state using portletHandle.

As an example we use again the University course offerings service that provides an overview of subjects offered in different semesters and allows users to click on the course offerings to navigate to the individual subjects and then on a "back-link" navigate back to the course offerings. Such a service should maintain conversational state within a *WSRP Session* to always display the correct view for a particular user and return a session ID for an internally managed session in each response of the getMarkup() operation (Figure 4). The markup returned may also contain links that will trigger invocations of the performBlockingInteraction() operation. This operation allows the portlet to perform logical operations updating state that could be shared with other portlets at the *producer*.

INTERACTIVE SERVICE CONTAINING PERSISTENT DATA

Let us consider a remote service that maintains configuration data that can be associated with individual portlets available from the *producer*. An example for such a service is a tutorial allocation service that allows individual users to define their own personal schedules for tutorials. This situation requires the implementation of configuration data and ability to retain application persistent state for the end user.

Since customization of portlets is not available in WSRP protocol, the *consumers* create new portlets using clonePortlet (Figure 5), specifying an existing portlet – either a producer offered portlet or one previously cloned by the consumer. The new portlet will be initialized with the same configuration data as the existing portlet. New portlets can also be cloned during the processing of a performBlockingInteraction() method. This is enabled when the *consumer* sets a flag preventing the user to customize the configuration data of the supplied portlet. The clone operation returns a portlet with updated configuration data and the customization is allowed. The portlet implementation can also make an attempt to update

Figure 3. WSRP states

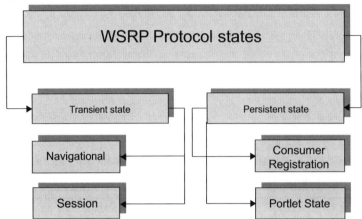

its configuration. This attempt typically results in the *producer* cloning the configuration data and applying the update to the cloned configuration. In either of these cases, the consumer obtains a handle (portletHandle) for referring to the new portlet when calling the *producer*.

When a portlet is no longer needed, it can be discarded by calling destroyPortlets(), passing the portlet handle. At this point, all persistent data can be discarded as well.

INTERACTIVE SERVICE CONTAINING CONFIGURATION DATA AND MAINTAINING SESSION

The *producer* may need to use both configuration data and transient session state to satisfy the application requirements. Several remote sessions may be associated with a portlet at any given time. For example, many remote sessions to the same portlet may exist for a *consumer* that is a

Figure 4. Conversational interactive services

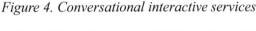

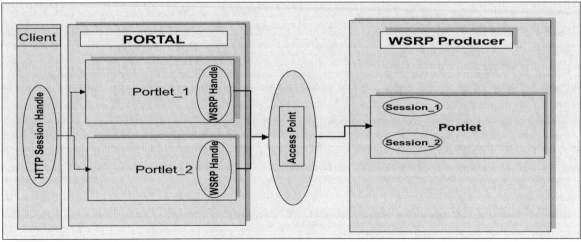

Figure 5. Interactive service with configuration data

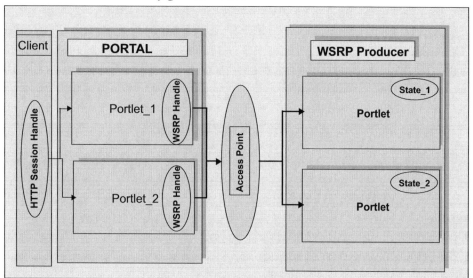

portal with shared pages referencing the portlet and being used concurrently by multiple end users (Figure 6).

A typical information flow pattern starts with the end-user adding the remote portlet to a page. This is done for example by portal administrators via administration interface or XML configuration interface. The portlet invokes `clonePortlet()` operation on the remote service specifying an existing portlet and optionally including pre-configuration data. In return it obtains a new portlet handle (`portletHandle`) that it stores together with a newly created portlet instance on the portal database. The reason for cloning is that the original portlets exposed in the service description cannot be customized.

Figure 6. Interactive service with configuration data and session maintenance

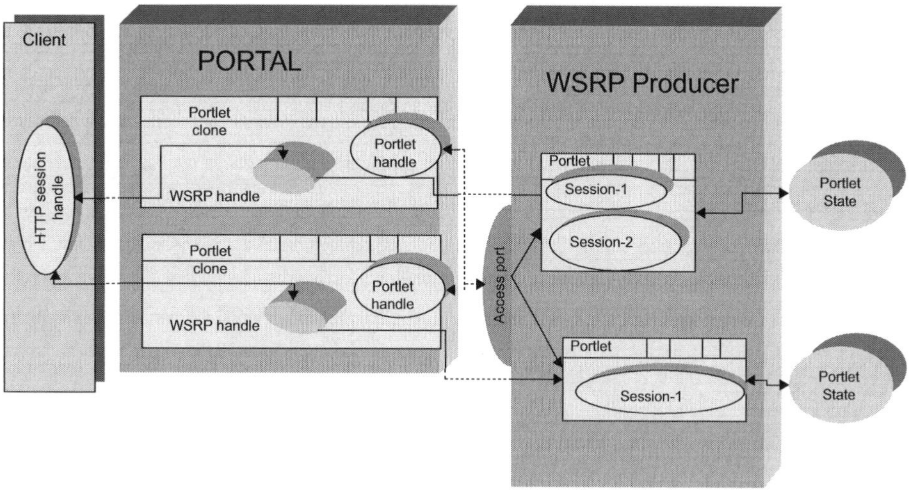

In the view mode, the portal determines the portlet handle (`portletHandle`) and uses it to make a call to the `getMarkup()` operation of the remote service. The operation returns the HTML fragment to be aggregated and displayed in the page within a `doView()` operation.. The response may contain action links, and could include a session handle (`sessionID`) if the portlet wants to maintain the conversation state. The portal typically needs to rewrite any action links to point to the *consumer* site and must store any returned session handle in a manner that allows it to be used on subsequent requests.

When the user clicks on an action link in the markup, a HTTP request is sent from the browser to the portal. The portal processes the request and maps it to an invocation of the `perform-BlockingInteraction()` operation of the remote service and passes the `sessionID` which allows the remote service to look up the associated session state. In the `performBlockingInteraction()` invocation, the remote service typically changes the state. When the `performBlockingInteraction()` operation returns, the portal refreshes the page. This results in an invocation of `getMarkup()` on all the portlets on the page and starts a new user-interaction cycle.

When an end user is finished with a portlet instance and discards it from a portal page, the portal recovers the handle of the portlet which is no longer needed and invokes `destroyPortlets()` on the remote service. The remote service discards the portlet and is free to release any resources associated with this portlet.

RESTFUL WEB SERVICES

Data oriented web services are characterised by their complexity. Their development involves implementing various infrastructural components (WSDL, SOAP). Web services solution has to invest in creating a robust Web service infrastructure model. From the development point of view, it becomes increasingly complex to design

and learn the technology. Presentation oriented services such as WSRP based services provide relief from the complexity of the infrastructure. The newly introduced features from JSR 286 provide sufficient flexibility in terms of inter-portlet communication and event processing, AJAX use, and resource serving capability. The presentation logic embedded in the remote portlet takes care of the easy rendering.

The new wave in web services are the RESTful Web services characterised by a simple XML-over-HTTP transmission. The RESTful services encapsulate data in a simple XML form and transport it over HTTP the same way as a Web page request. It takes full advantage of the REST architecture style which is related to a Web resource. In turn, this Web resource is a representation identified by a Uniform Resource Indicator (URI). The resource can be any persistent entity, and queries or updates the resource are applied through the URI and therefore influence a state change in its representation. In REST, a user to invoke operations on a Web resource using HTTP request methods in a Web service style. REST is closely associated with HTTP and leverages all HTTP features, such as methods, headers, and types.

ROLE OF UDDI IN WEB SERVICES

Portlets (JSR 168 (2005)) provide user interface to data delivered from web services. Before we explain the remote portlet publishing and discovery process in UDDI, we need to refresh the concept of publishing and discovering the web services in UDDI (Hugo Haas, P. L. H., Jean-Jacques Moreau, David Orchard, Jeffrey Schlimmer, Sanjiva Weerawarana (2004)). Web services expose their interfaces by registering in UDDI (UDDI Specifications (2005)). The web service consumer must find the service, bind to it and invoke the service. The basic mechanism

Figure 7. Publish-Find-Bind Mechanism in UDDI

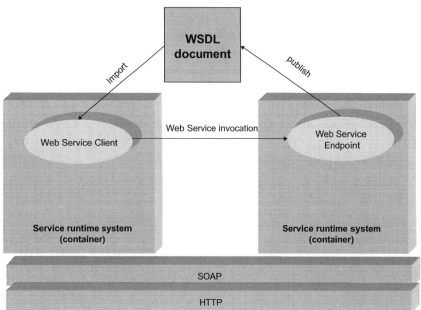

for publishing and discovering data – oriented Web services is in Figure 7.

Regardless of whether the web service will be accessible to a single enterprise or to other companies (public access), the details about the service (its interface, parameters, location, etc.) must be made available to *consumers*. This is accomplished with a WSDL description of the Web service and a Web service directory where the details of the Web service are published (refer to Web Services Description Language (WSDL)). There are three steps which have to be performed in order to discover and use a web service published in the UDDI:

Publishing web service (step 1): In order to be accessible to interested parties, the web service is published in a Registry or web service directory. There are several choices regarding where to publish a web service:

1. If the web service is intended for the general public then a well-known registry is recommended. Consequently the WSDL description together with any XML schemas referenced by this description is made public.

2. The web service intended for enterprise use over an intranet should be published in a corporate registry only. No public access from the outside of the firewall is required.

3. Finally, providing all clients are dedicated partners in business, and there is an existing agreement on usage of this service, the web service can be published on a well-known location on the company server - with proper security access protection. Such a server would be placed on the public side of the company firewall but it would allow limited access, similar to a B2B Web server.

4. Web services directories are made up of a repository and the taxonomies (classification of registered entities for easier search) associated with them. There are no restrictions on publishing the web service in multiple registries, or in multiple categories.

Discovery of web service (step 2): Registry implementations can differ but there are some common steps, outlined below, that the client must perform before it can discover and bind (step 3) to the service:

1. The client must determine how to access the web service's methods, such as determining the service method parameters, return values, and so forth. This is referred to as *discovering the service definition interface.*
2. The client must locate the actual web service (find its address). This is referred to as *discovering the service implementation.*

Bind to the web service and invoke it (step 3): The client must be able to bind to the service's specific location. The following types of binding may occur:

1. Static binding during client development or at the deployment time.
2. Dynamic binding (at runtime).

From the client point of view, the binding type and time play important roles in possible scenarios relevant to the client's usage of the web service. The following situations are typical:

1. A web service (WSDL and XML schemas) is published in well-known locations. The developers of the application that use the service know the service, its location, and the interface. The client (which is a process running on a host) can bypass the registry and use the service interfaces directly. Alternatively, the client knows the location and can statically bind to the service at the deployment time.
2. The web service expects its clients to be able to easily find the interface at build time. These clients are often generic clients. Such clients can dynamically find the specific implementation at runtime using the registry. Dynamic runtime binding is required.

Development of web service clients requires some rules to be applied and design decisions to be made regarding which binding type is more ap-

propriate for the given situation (static or dynamic binding). Three possible cases are discussed:

1. *Discovering the service interface definition*: If we are dealing with a known service interface, and the service implementation is known (no registry is required), the actual binding should be static.
2. *Discovering the service implementation*: In this case, static binding is also appropriate because we know the interface. We need to discover the service implementation only at build time.
3. The client does not know the service interface and needs to discover the service interface dynamically at build time. The service implementation is *discovered dynamically at runtime*. This type of invocation is called Dynamic Invocation Interface (DII). In this case, the binding must be dynamic.

Each WSDL description of the service published in UDDI must contain the following six elements: definitions, types, message, portType, binding, and service. The main elements of the UDDI data model are listed below (Figure 2):

- `businessEntity` represents the physical company which registered the services with UDDI;
- `businessService` represents a specific service offered by a company;
- `bindingTemplate` contains instructions for service invocation;
- publisherAssertion structure allows businesses to publish relationships between businessEntities within the company; and
- `tModel` is a structure similar to a database table. It contains the following information about an entity: the name, description, URL, and the unique key.

The relationships between the description and actual registered structures are outlined

Figure 8. UDDI model composition

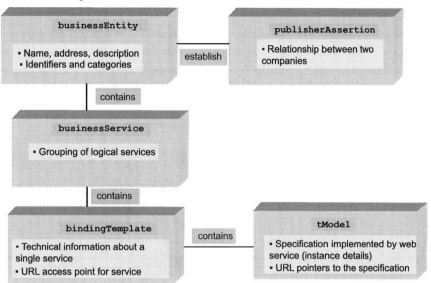

in Figure 9. The `portType` is represented by a UDDI structure called `tModel`. This `tModel` is categorized using unified *Category System* and the WSDL `EntityType` structure. The relevant *Category System* is known as WSDL `portType` `tModel` category and distinguishes it from other types of `tModels` with which the service might be associated.

A WSDL binding is also represented by a `tModel` structure. This is the binding `tModel` structure. This kind of categorization uses the same *Category System* as the `portType` tModel, but with a different key value to differentiate a binding tModel from a portType tModel.

The WSDL may represent a web service interface for an existing service. However, there

Figure 9. Mapping from WSDL to UDDI

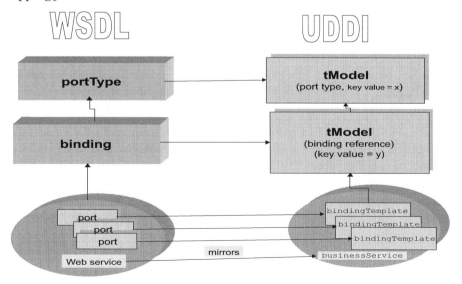

Figure 10. Publishing and locating remote portlets with the UDDI

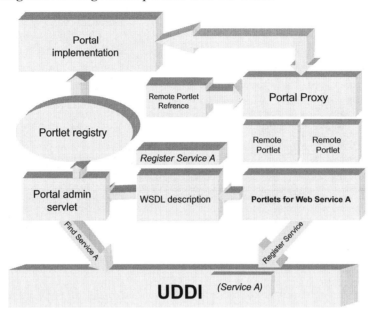

may be an existing UDDI `businessService` that is suitable, and WSDL information can be just added to that existing service. If there is no suitable existing service found in the UDDI registry, a new `businessService` must be created. Finally, the WSDL binding port is represented by UDDI `bindingTemplate`. A WSDL service may contain multiple ports. These ports are exactly mirrored by the containment relationship in a UDDI `businessService` and its `bindingTemplates`.

REGISTERING WSRP SERVICES AS REMOTE PORTLETS IN UDDI

WSRP *producer* is considered as a web service on its own, exposing multiple `Bindings` and `PortTypes`. It is described through the WSRP WSDL services description and some additional portlet types. Portlets are not fully fledged services, they are only HTML fragments. Therefore, they do not expose `PortType`, `binding` template and access points. The portlet is exposed by its *producer* and

consumer interacts indirectly with remote portlets using the *producer's* infrastructure. The remote portlet is addressed by a `portletHandle` defined within the *producer's* scope.

Figure 4 shows an example how a portal finds and integrates a remote portlet published in the UDDI. Content or application providers (known as WSRP *producers*) implement their service as WSRP service and publish it in a globally accessible directory. *Producer's* WSDL description provides the necessary information about remote service actual end-points. The directory lets the *consumers* easily find the required service. Directory entries, published in WSDL format, briefly describe the WSRP components and offer access to details about the services. The portal administrator uses the portal's published functions to create remote portlet web service entries in the portal local registry. Furthermore, the portlet proxy binds to the WSRP component through SOAP, and the remote portlet invocation (RPI) protocol ensures the proper interaction between both parties. Typical discovery and binding steps are summarized below:

- A provider offers a set of portlets and makes them available by setting up a WSRP *producer* and exposing them as remote portlets. These portlets are then made available to other businesses by publishing them in a UDDI registry. The provider may perform the publishing task either through a custom built user interface or through the interface provided by a UDDI Server.
- End-user wants to add a portlet to his own portal. Using the tools provided by his portal (for example portal administrative interface or a custom-written XML interface[1]), he/she searches for remote portlets. After finding the suitable remote portlet, these portlets can be added to the portal pages. Alternatively, a portal administrator could search the UDDI registry for portlets and make them available to end-users by adding them to the portal's internal database.
- The user can now access the page containing newly added and running remote portlets. Behind the scenes, the portal is making a web service call to the remote *producer*, and the *producer* is returning a markup fragment with the required data for the portal to render on the portal page.

In order to provide necessary information about remote portlets, WSRP extended the definition of the bind namespace for `portTypes` and SOAP binding. The following extensions are defined (WSRP specification version 1 (2003). This WSDL defines the following `portTypes` (normative definitions):

- **WSRP_v1_Markup_PortType:** This is the port on which the Markup Interface can be accessed. All *producers* must expose this `portType`.
- **WSRP_v1_ServiceDescription_PortType:** This is the port on which the Service

Description Interface can be accessed. All *producers* must expose this `portType`.
- **WSRP_v1_Registration_PortType:** This is the port on which the Registration Interface can be accessed. Only *producers* supporting in-band registration of *consumers* need expose this `portType`.
- **WSRP_v1_PortletManagement_PortType:** This is the port on which the Management Interface can be accessed. *Producers* supporting the portlet management interface expose this `portType`. If this `portType` is not exposed, the portlets of the service cannot be configured by consumer*s*.

SOAP bindings for these portTypes are listed below:

1. **WSRP_v1_Markup_Binding_SOAP:** All *producers* must expose a port with this binding for the `WSRP_v1_Markup_PortType` (the `Markup portType`).
2. **WSRP_v1_ServiceDescription_Binding_SOAP:** All *producers* must expose a port with this binding for the `WSRP_v1_ServiceDescription_PortType` (`ServiceDescription portType`).
3. **WSRP_v1_Registration_Binding_SOAP:** *Producers* supporting the `Registration portType` must expose a port with this binding for the `WSRP_v1_Registration_PortType`.
4. **WSRP_v1_PortletManagement_Binding_SOAP:** *Producers* supporting the `PortletManagement portType` must expose a port with this binding for the `WSRP_v1_PortletManagement_PortType`.

Web service is typically represented by several remote portlets and relevant WSDL description (Figure 11) which contains pointers to all required and optional WSRP portlet interfaces (e.g. registration interface, service description, etc.) in the form of a `portType`.

Figure 11. WSDL definition for WSRP example

```
<?xml version="1.0" encoding="UTF-8"?>
<wsdl:definitions xmlns:urn="urn:oasis:names:tc:wsrp:v1:bind"
    xmlns:wsdl="http://schemas.xmlsoap.org/wsdl/"
    targetNamespace="urn:myproducer:wsdl">
 <wsdl:import namespace="urn:oasis:names:tc:wsrp:v1:bind"
    location="http://www.oasis-open.org/committees/wsrp/
      specifications/version1/wsrp_v1_bindings.wsdl"/>
 <wsdl:service name="WSRPService">
   <wsdl:port name="WSRPBaseService"
     binding="urn:WSRP_v1_Markup_Binding_SOAP">
     <soap:address xmlns:soap="http://schemas.xmlsoap.org/wsdl/soap/"
     location="http://myproducer.com:9098/portal/producer"/>
 </wsdl:port>
 <wsdl:port name="WSRPServiceDescriptionService"
     binding="urn:WSRP_v1_ServiceDescription_Binding_SOAP">
     <soap:address xmlns:soap="http://schemas.xmlsoap.org/wsdl/soap/"
     location="http://myproducer.com:9098/portal/producer"/>
 </wsdl:port>
 <wsdl:port name="WSRPRegistrationService"
   binding="urn:WSRP_v1_Registration_Binding_SOAP">
     <soap:address xmlns:soap="http://schemas.xmlsoap.org/wsdl/soap/"
       location="http://myproducer.com:9098/portal/producer"/>
 </wsdl:port>
 <wsdl:port name="WSRPPortletManagementService"
   binding="urn:WSRP_v1_PortletManagement_Binding_SOAP">
     <soap:address xmlns:soap="http://schemas.xmlsoap.org/wsdl/soap/"
     location="http://myproducer.com:9098/portal/producer"/>
   </wsdl:port>
 </wsdl:service>
</wsdl:definitions>
```

In essence, WSRP *producers* are web services. They expose `PortTypes` and `bindings` which the *consumers* can use to access and interact with. It means that the process of publishing a *producer* corresponds to publishing a web services together with associated portlet metadata. Besides the `portletHandle`, the `Portlet Title` and textual description, all further portlet metadata are missing in the UDDI. These remaining metadata must be retrieved from the respective ports (`Service-Description portType` or `PortletManagement portType`).

Presentation oriented service has been developed to ease the burden of complexity of data oriented services. Specifically, to eliminate the need of developing the presentation logic at the consumer site. It is still using SOAP as main transport feature. There is still need to take into account the binding to service markup and service description.

SUMMARY AND CRITICAL LOOK AT WSRP

WSRP can be used to create powerful portal services from originally non-portal-centric applications. WSRP provides easy access to remote web services and their user-facing representations. Web services offer a mechanism to create remotely accessible and platform independent services. Portlet standard - JSR 168 - complements this mechanism by defining a common platform and APIs for developing user interfaces in the form of portlets. WSRP enables reuse of these portlets. Only one generic proxy is required to establish the connection. The WSRP could be used to facilitate the development of an entire network of presentation-oriented web services. It would allow the portal users easily discover and use any number of remote services. There is no need to develop custom adapters, build client interfaces, and spend time locally deploying the customized portlets.

WSRP 1.0 is lacking any standard for transaction handling, there are some problems associated with security, reliability, and load balancing[2]. Furthermore, the response time could be unpredictably long. The portal pages are aggregated from multiple *producers* and portal must wait until all fragments are ready for rendering. Any remote service may slow down the entire portal.

WSRP 2.0 is fully aligned with the portlet specification 286 and contains all additional features announced with JSR 286. Therefore, it supports building composite applications using coordination means. The event and public parameters support loose coupled event paradigm. Similar as JSR 286 it also allows for additional AJAX use cases utilizing resource serving through the portlet. The capability of setting HTTP headers and cookies, filters, request dispatching provides a framework for better integration with servlets.

Using WSRP and UDDI extension for remote portlets, makes the end-user completely shielded from the technical details of WSRP. In contrast to the standard use of data-oriented web services, any changes to web service structure are implemented within the remote portlet and the *consumer* is not affected by these changes.

UDDI version 1.1 allows the *producers* to describe its presence together with each of the services it offers. The most important feature planned for higher versions of UDDI specification (specifically version 2 and higher) is the provision of cross portlet communication. Portlets should be able to broadcast their event information to other portlets spread across multiple *producers* if necessary. This feature allows other portlets to tailor their generated content according to broadcasted events. This feature is being well supported by the WSRP 2 which enables the inter portlet communication on the consumer site.

So far, there is seemingly no need to publish remaining portlet metadata. However, we envisage that the concept of semantic web and web service matchmaking as outlined in R. Akkiraju, R. Goodwin, Prashant Doshi, Sascha Roeder (2003) will require better annotation of available remote portlets functionalities to be published in a public registry. In such case, searching for portlets defining certain metadata values in UDDI will become the necessity.

Comparing WSRP and RESTful Web service, the latter does not provide any presentation logic. However, RESTfull web services rely on standard HTTP protocol, utilizing the power of the resource URI to maintain the resource state. WSRP uses classic web service infrastructure (WSDL, UDDI and SOAP), which still requires the negotiation of various contracts between the provider and consumer. The burden of the implementation is leveraged by the presentation logic being provided by the producer.

With data oriented services, the portlet displaying web service's raw data arriving from a `UDDI businessService` structure (web service) reflects the infrastructure of the web service and needs to bind to the service. This is an undesirably tight coupling of user interface and service raw data which often cause problems to the *consumer* in time of any changes to web service raw data. This problem is typically resolved by the *producer* providing relevant libraries.

REFERENCES

JSR 168 (2005). Portlet Specification, http://www.jcp.org/en/jsr/detail?id=168

Servlets Specification 2.4 (2004). http://www.jcp.org/aboutJava/communityprocess/final/jsr154, last accessed November, 2005

JSR 286 (2008). Portlet Specification, http://jcp.org/en/jsr/detail?id=286

Danny Coward, Y. (2003). JSR-000154 Java™ Servlet 2.4 Specification (Final Release). Sun Microsystems Inc. http://www.jcp.org/aboutJava/communityprocess/final/jsr154/

Hepper, S and Hesmer, S. (2003). Introducing the Portlet Specification, JavaWorld, last accessed 2005, http://www-106.ibm.com/developerworks/websphere/library/techarticles/0312_hepper/hepper.html

Web Services Description Language (WSDL): An Intuitive View. developers.sun.com. http://java.sun.com/dev/evangcentral/totallytech/wsdl.html

WSRP specification version 1 (2003). Web Services for Remote Portlets, OASIS. http://www.oasis-open.org/committees/download.php/3343/oasis-200304-wsrp-specification-1.0.pdf. Last accessed 2005

WSRP Specification version 2.0 (2008). http://docs.oasis-open.org/wsrp/v2/wsrp-2.0-spec-os-01.html#_Toc04

Web Services Description Language (WSDL): An Intuitive View. developers.sun.com. http://java.sun.com/dev/evangcentral/totallytech/wsdl.html

R. Akkiraju, R. Goodwin, Prashant Doshi, Sascha Roeder (2003). A Method for Semantically Enhancing the Service Discovery Capabilities of UDDI. *In the Proceedings of IJCAI Information Integration on the Web Workshop*, Acapulco, Mexico, August 2003. www.isi.edu/info-agents/workshops/ijcai03/papers/Akkiraju-SemanticUDDI-IJCA%202003.pdf

Hugo Haas, P. L. H., Jean-Jacques Moreau, David Orchard, Jeffrey Schlimmer, Sanjiva Weerawarana (2004). Web Services Description Language (WSDL) Version 2.0 Part 3: Bindings. W3C. http://www.w3.org/TR/2004/WD-wsdl20-bindings-20040803

UDDI Specifications (2005). Universal Description, Discovery and Integration v2 and v3. http://www.uddi.org/specification.html, last accessed November, 2005

WSRP specification version 1 (2003). Web Services for Remote Portlets, OASIS. http://www.oasis-open.org/committees/download.php/3343/oasis-200304-wsrp-specification-1.0.pdf. Last accessed 2005.

ENDNOTE

[1] In IBM WebSphere Portal 5.1, this activity is supported via the configuration portlets or XML configuration interface

KEY TERMS AND DEFINITION

Portlet: A Web application that displays some content in a portlet window. A portlet is developed, deployed, managed and displayed independently of all other portlets. Portlets may have multiple states and view modes. They also can communicate with other portlets by sending messages.

Portal: A Web application which contains and runs the portlet environment, such as Application Server(s), and portlet deployment characteristics.

Web Services: A set of standards that define programmatic interfaces for application-to-application communication over a network

Web Services for Remote Portlets: Presentation oriented Web services.

This work was previously published in the International Journal of Web Portals, Volume 1, Issue 2, edited by J.Polgar, and G. Adamson pp. 44-66, copyright 2009 by IGI Publishing (an imprint of IGI Global).

Chapter 3.21
Containers and Connectors as Elements in a Portal Design Framework

Joe Lamantia
MediaCatalyst B.V., The Netherlands

ABSTRACT

This article defines the standardized elements used in the building blocks portal design framework in detail, as the second in a series of articles on a Portal Design Framework. This article explains the (simple) rules and relationships for combining Containers and Connectors into portal structures. This article shares best practices, examples, and guidelines for effectively using the building blocks framework during portal design efforts.

OVERVIEW OF THE CONTAINER BLOCKS

The building block system includes seven types of Containers, beginning with the Tile at the lowest level of the stacking hierarchy, and increasing (conceptual) size and complexity to include a collection of interconnected Dashboards or Portals, called a Dashboard or Portal Suite. From smallest to largest, the Container blocks are:

- Tile
- Tile Group
- View
- Page
- Section
- Dashboard or Portal
- Dashboard or Portal Suite

Like musicians in a band, the different kinds of Container blocks in the system play different roles in the overall effort to construct dashboards or portals. The smaller (lower in the stacking hierarchy) blocks - Tiles, Tile Groups, and Views—enable the display of content, and support users' interactions with content. Sections, Dashboards or Portals, and Dashboard or Portal Suites—the larger blocks, that are higher in the stacking hierarchy—enable the navigation, organization, and management of collections of content. Pages straddle the middle of the size continuum; they are the largest block whose role is primarily to provide a framework for display of and interaction with dashboard or portal content, and the smallest Container which plays an important navigational / organization role in the system.

The Connectors (described later in this article) 'hold things together'; thereby creating navigation paths amongst destinations, establishing a tangible architecture or structure, providing referential cues for orientation with the environment, and allowing movement into and out of the environment. The different kinds of Containers work in concert with Connectors to enable the creation of scalable, navigable, and easily maintainable information architectures that support high-quality user experiences.

Each Container definition includes:

- Mandatory components
- Optional components
- Stacking size
- Detailed description
- Example rendering (for illustrative purposes only)
- Rendering description

Tile

- *Mandatory Components: Tile Header, Tile Body*
- *Optional Components: Tile Footer*
- *Stacking Size: 1*

Description

Tiles are the fundamental building block of the dashboard or portal framework. Tiles locate content and functionality within the coherent information and navigation structure of the dashboard or portal environment. Tiles clearly identify the sources and broader contexts of the information or tools they contain (very important in situations where terminology is ambiguous, conflicting or overlapping, or when differing data sources provide differing values for the same metrics), and offer consistent access to onvenience functionality such as printing and emailing the Tile contents for use outside the dashboard.

Tiles consist of two required components—a Tile Header and Tile Body—and one optional component—the Tile Footer. Tiles may include multiple Control Bars (note: adding multiple Control Bars can quickly increase development complexity and lower usability levels). The Tile Header contains a mandatory Title, optional Subtitle, mandatory source indicator identifying the origins of the content, and may include buttons or links for Convenience Functionality (described in detail in a subsequent part of this series).

The mandatory Tile Body can contain nearly any form of content. Tiles commonly contain text, charts, tables, interactive maps, scrolling news feeds, RSS consoles, video, slideshows, syndicated XML structured documents, links to documents and resources, and complex transactional functionality. Of course, this is only a small subset of the tremendous diversity of Tile-delivered content available in the rapidly growing libraries of widgets published for Apple's OSX desktop, Yahoo's widget platform, Google Gadgets, web desktops such as NetVibes, and the many social networking platforms including FaceBook and MySpace. In the end, the range of content that can appear within a Tile is limited only by imagination and ingenuity.

The optional Tile Footer is a structurally consistent location for contextual links, pointers to related destinations and content. The Tile Footer commonly offers links to additional resources or source data in another format (tab delimited, .pdf, etc.), links to other Tiles, Pages or areas of the Dashboard that provide related content or functionality, links to other applications and environments offering comprehensive functionality or information out of scope for the Tile, etc.

The sizes and internal layouts of individual Tiles will vary depending upon several factors including, but not limited to their content, priority vs. neighboring Tiles or other building blocks, and expectations for reuse. It is good practice to define a grid for screen layouts that prescribes standard sizes for Tiles and all screen elements, and match the sizes and internal layouts of Tiles to this reference grid.

Here are a few guidelines on information design and interaction design standards within Tiles:

- Each chart, table, or text block within a Tile needs an accurate title or label
- Charts may have a footer area that offers additional data values, a key or legend for the items shown in the chart, links to additional resources, or source data in another format
- Tiles that contain long lists, large tables, or other large objects may scroll, depending on the interaction and design standards and capabilities of the dashboard or portal platform
- Tables in Tiles often allow users to change sorting order or open and hide columns
- Charts summarizing large amounts data can offer interactions or drill-down behaviors allowing users to navigate deep data sets

Many of these interaction behaviors and design best practices are now offered as standard functionality - making them 'free' or 'low-cost' in design and development terms - by leading business intelligence and portal platform vendors. Additionally, these capabilities are also becoming standard in many general purpose presentation frameworks, including RUBY and AJAX libraries, and the various for-purchase (Adobe AIR, Flex, Laszlo Webtop, etc.) and open-source development toolkits.

Stacking Note: Tiles stacked inside larger building blocks retain their individual Tile Header, Tile Body, and any optional components. (See Figure 1)

Example Rendering

{tile_structure_2.ai}

Rendering Description

This wire frame style illustration shows the structure of a Tile with an attached Control Bar. The Tile Header offers several types of convenience functionality (print, email, and pdf export of the Tile). The Control Bar offers a single selector. The Tile Body contains a chart and table, each with a title and footer or key. The Tile Footer contains four links, to a mixed set of destinations either within or outside the portal.

TILE GROUP

- *Mandatory Components: Tile Group Header, Tile Group Body*
- *Optional Components: Tile Group Footer*
- *Stacking Size: 2*

Description

A Tile Group typically combines two or more Tiles together—likely from different sources or perspectives—into a larger unit of information or functionality that allows the combination of resources to answer more complicated questions, or achieve more complicated tasks. A Tile Group might answer the question, "How are my daily sales vs. my competitor's daily sales?" by presenting a Daily Sales Tile and a Competitor Sales Tile next to one another, under the combined title 'Daily Sales vs. Competitor Sales'.

Tile Groups consist of two required components—a Tile Group Header and Tile Group Body—and may include an optional Tile Group Footer. Tile Groups may include multiple Control Bars (note: adding multiple Control Bars can quickly increase development complexity and lower usability levels). The Tile Group Header contains a mandatory Title, optional Subtitle, man-

Figure 1. Tile components and structure

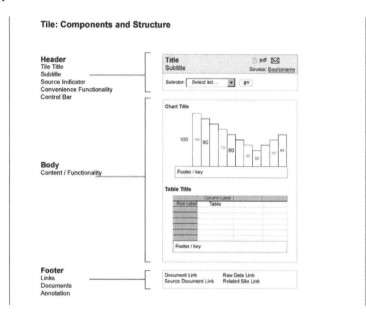

datory content source indicator, and may include buttons or links for Convenience functionality.

In the scenario above, the two stacked Tiles likely present information that comes from different data sources (perhaps one internal, and one licensed from a third party market metrics service), and it's likely that the Tiles were created by different organizations that used the Building Blocks system to coordinate user experience design and development efforts that rely on a common enterprise portal or platform foundation. The consumers of the individual Tiles are likely affiliated with separate business units or operating groups, and may not need or be aware of the other Tiles, or the Tile Group. The consumers of the Tile Group could easily be part of a third element of the organization – or perhaps they are affiliated with the originating groups for the separate tiles, but share a common management perspective or performance incentive that requires a comparative presentation of the source information.

Stacking Note: Tile Groups stacked inside larger building blocks retain their individual Tile Group Header, Tile Group Body, Tile Group Footer, and any optional components.

Design Note: While Container defintions require the presence of some components to maintain the structural integrity of the Buildng Blocks system (Tiles always have a Tile Header, etc.), they do not mandate constant visibility or display of all the structurally required components. Excess chrome is the enemy of a good user experience at all levels of structure, and should be avoided. Many existing interaction patterns, control mechanisms and design principles can help eliminate excess chrome, and minimize the presence of chrome in general to that which is necessary for a high quality user experience, without increasing the effort or cost of relying on the Building Blocks. (See Figure 2)

Example Rendering

{tilegroup_structure_2.ai}

Rendering Description

This wire frame illustration shows the structure of a Tile Group with an attached Control Bar. The Tile Group Header offers several types of convenience functionality (print, email, and pdf

Figure 2. Tile group components and structure

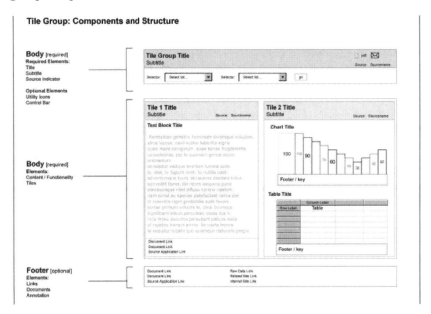

export of the Tile as rendered). The single Control Bar offers two selectors. The Tile Group Body contains two stacked Tiles; one Tile offers text, the other contains the combination of a chart and table seen previously. Note that both stacked Tiles retain their individual Tile Headers and Tile Footers. In this rendering, neither stacked Tile offers convenience functionality, though it is possible for stacked Tiles to offer convenience functionality.

VIEW

- Mandatory Components: View Header, View Body
- *Optional Components: View Footer*
- *Stacking Size: 3*

Description

Views consist of two required components—a View Header and View Body—and may include an optional View Footer. Views may include multiple Control Bars (note: adding multiple Control Bars can quickly increase development complexity and lower usability levels). The View Header contains a mandatory Title, optional Subtitle, mandatory source indicator, and may include icons for accessing standard convenience functionality.

A View typically combines Tiles and Tile Groups together to present a comprehensive set of information resources that address a single perspective within an area of interest. In common use, Views allow Dashboard or Portal users to see the most logical subsets of all available Tiles related to one aspect of an area of interest. For example, many Tiles might provide information about a single product—too many to appear on one Page—but the Customer View of a product presents only those Tiles that show information about a single Product in relation to major Customers. Another defined View could offer marketing information for that same product, and a third might allow executives to check inventory levels for the product at various storage facilities.

Views stacked inside larger building blocks retain their individual View Header, View Body, View Footer, and any optional components. (See Figure 3)

Example Rendering

{views_structure_2.ai}

Rendering Description

This wire frame shows the structure of a View with an attached Control Bar. The View Header offers several types of convenience functionality (print, email, and pdf export of the View as a single unit). The Control Bar offers two selectors. The View Body contains two stacked Tile Groups, one Tile offering text, the other offering the combination of a chart and table seen previously. The stacked Tile Groups retain their individual Tile Group Headers, but do not include Tile Group Footers. In this rendering, neither stacked Tile Group offers convenience functionality, though it is possible for stacked Tiles to offer convenience functionality. The View Footer contains links to a variety of documents, applications, and destination sites.

PAGE

- *Mandatory Components: None*
- *Optional Components: Page Header, Page Footer*
- *Stacking Size: 4*

Description

It's best to talk about Pages in two senses; specifically as Containers from the Building Block system, and generally as destinations for users navigating dashboard or portal environments. In the first sense, as part of the hierarchy of building blocks in the dashboard or portal system, Pages are simply a larger kind of Container without mandatory components. They are governed by the same principles of portability, openness, independence, etc. as the other blocks, which means individual Pages may not be visible to some types of users, depending on security restrictions, and could consist of a mix of smaller building blocks and elements of free-form content. One possible al-

Figure 3. View components and structure

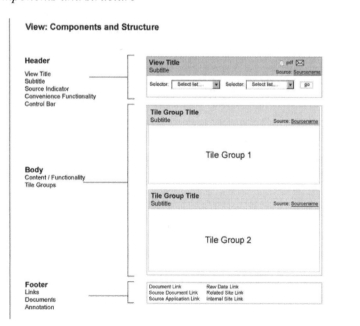

ternate name considered for Pages was 'nodes,' to emphasize the distinction between their building block system role and their browser navigational role, but that felt too abstract.

In the second sense, Pages take on their traditional role as presentation canvases for content and functionality, linked together by navigation mechanisms: they serve as the single-screen units of display and interaction familiar from the Web paradigm. In this role, Pages become the delivery vehicle for combinations of Containers and Connectors that allow users to work with content, and move through the dashboard or portal environment. Pages typically combine collections of Tiles, Tile Groups, and Views with a set of accompanying Connectors (Section Connectors, Page Connectors, Crosswalk Connectors, Geography Selectors, and Utility Navigation) to create a navigable user experience. Pages – following the principle of Openness – may include free-form content or navigation mechanisms. Common examples of free-form content include search functionality, global navigation, links to intranets and extranets,

feedback forms for requesting new features, and branding elements.

A Page can consist of a single Tile, or only free-form content, may or may not have a Page Header or Page Footer managed as building blocks assets, and might not be connected to or accessible from other areas of the Dashboard or Portal. For example, a Page dedicated to account administration functions might only be visible to members of the user group Administrators, who themselves cannot see other areas of the Dashboard or Portal, and thus would not require navigation connections to other Pages in the Dashboard or Portal. (See Figure 4)

Example Rendering

{page_structure_2.ai}

Rendering Description

This wire frame shows the structure of a Page that mixes free-form content with building block content. The free-form elements appear in the form of a stock ticker, market summary, and a staff

Figure 4. Page components and structure

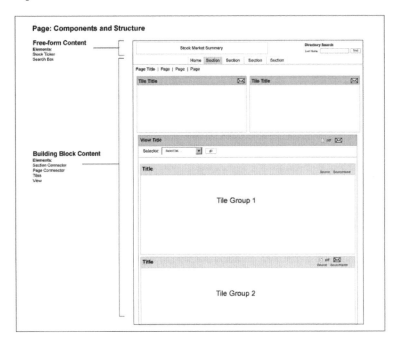

directory search box. Branding elements such as logos identifying the individual dashboard often appear as free-form content. These free-form content elements could also appear as a formally defined Page Header building block, managed as an asset in a library of reusable Tiles.

The building block content includes a navigation cluster made of a Section Connector and a Page Connector, two stacked Tiles, and a View that contains two stacked Tile Groups (Tiles not shown). On this Page, the two independent Tiles and the View are stacked at the same level within the containing Page. The layout of this Page places the Tiles above the View to ensure they remain visible without scrolling, but this layout is not necessary by the rules of the building block system. The individual Tiles on this Page do not include either Control Bars or Footers. The View includes a Control Bar with two selectors. None of the blocks offers Convenience Functionality, though of course this is possible across all levels of the stacking hierarchy, and is commonly available for the Page itself.

SECTION

- *Mandatory Components: 1 Page*
- *Optional Components: NA*
- *Stacking Size: 5*

Description

The Section is primarily an organizational building block, but it does have a mandatory component of at least a single Page. Sections typically consist of collections of Pages related to a core conceptual element of the information architecture or mental model for the Dashboard or Portal. It is not uncommon to see broadly defined Sections such as "Products", "Customers", "Supply Chain", or "Sales". Deep or complex Sections offering a considerable number of Pages or a large amount of content commonly include summary style Pages that condense or introduce the full contents of the

Section in an overview. Shallow sections offering few Pages often do not require a summary style Page. (See Figure 5)

Example Rendering

{section_products.eps}

Rendering Description

This site map style rendering shows a Section, titled Products, which contains five Pages that offer a variety of content related to the two types of Products produced and sold by a fictional company. The Section begins with a summary Page titled Products Overview. The four additional Pages are titled Branded Products, Product Focus, Co-Branded Products, and Co-brand Product Focus. The five pages contain a mixture of stacked Tiles, Tile Groups, and Views. The summary Page, titled Products Overview (P.3), offers the following: two stacked Tiles, Daily Sales (T.1) and Top 10 Products by Volume (T.12); and a stacked View, titled Products Sales Briefing (V.3).

By personal preference, only the blocks stacked at the level of the Page – level 3 – are individually identified on this map-style rendering; the Views and Tile Groups would obviously include further Tiles stacked within. I use this rendering convention to cut down on visual clutter in maps of large dashboards or portals. For your own renderings, feel free to itemize every stacked block at every level on the Page, or even list the dashboard or portal contents in simple outline fashion without pictures. Each stacked block in the rendering is identified by its Title, and a unique ID code or label, to allow synchronization with a master list of building blocks available across all dashboards. The numbered lines indicate that each Page includes a standard Page Connector, offering navigation between all the numbered Pages in the Section.

Figure 5. Example section

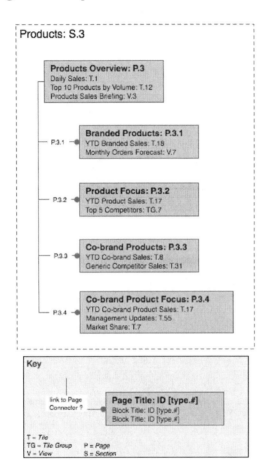

DASHBOARD OR PORTAL

- *Mandatory Components: 1 Section*
- *Optional Components: N/A*
- *Stacking Size: 6*

Description

The Dashboard or Portal is the largest single unit of meaning possible to assemble from stacked building blocks. A Dashboard or Portal must consist of at least one Section (itself made of at least a single Page). Dashboards or Portals typically consist of several connected Sections, assembled from connected Pages that contain a variety of stacked building blocks, combined with a smaller number of stand-alone Pages dedicated to utility functionality or administration. Most

Dashboards or Portals rely on a variety of Connectors to link assembled building blocks into a cohesive and navigable whole. A Dashboard or Portal's information architecture often aligns with a single mental model, or a small set of closely overlapping mental models, though this obviously depends on the needs and goals of the expected users.

To most users of internal tools situated withing an enterprise, a Dashboard or Portal is the total set of Sections, Pages and other stacked building blocks their security and access privileges permit them to see and use when they visit a URL or some other user experience destination (note: for web-delivered Dashboards or Portals, it is common practice to create a URL and expose this address via an intranet or other internal gateway). Since each user has an individually determined and potentially different set of security and access rights to each possible Section, Tile, View, and Page, each user will likely see a different combination of Dashboard or Portal content that is tailored to his or her own needs.

In this way, individual Dashboards or Portals often draw from a pool of defined Tiles and blocks which:

- Serve a group of executives running a large organizational unit within an enterprise, such as Marketing, Manufacturing, or Information Technology
- Provide a class of information resources giving insight across an enterprise, such as inventory monitoring, sales forecasting, financial reporting, quality control assessment
- Offer functionality in support of specific roles that entail responsibilities across the enterprise, such as regional directors, account managers, or human resources directors

I recommend labeling or branding these kinds of internally focused Dashboards or Portals clearly, to help communicate their contents and purpose to users and administrators who will likely have to work with many different tools and environments, and may easily suffer disorientation as a result. A simple title such as "Corporate Finance and Accounting Dashboard" can help distinguish one Dashboard or Portal in a Suite from another for busy users. I also recommend creating a log-in or destination page that orients users and confirms they are accessing the correct Dashboard or Portal to meet their needs.

In more public and social settings, the patterns of architecture, usage, and design at this level of size and complexity naturally differ.

Design Note: Depending on the depth and complexity of the assets offered within any one Dashboard or Portal, it may make sense to create a separate Home Page that introduces the structure and contents of the Dashboard, and offers unique content. Home Pages in this style commonly provide trend charts with roll-ups of more granular metrics, score-card style visualizations that communicate status for major areas of interest, alerts that require business attention, and high-level summarizations of the more extensive information available deeper inside. (See Figure 6)

Example Rendering

{dashboard.eps}

Rendering Description

This sitemap style rendering shows a medium-sized Dashboard or Portal designed to meet the information and business functionality needs of a large enterprise with multiple operating units and business lines. In this context, the Dashboard provides cross-unit summaries of many important metrics for senior managers, and could even provide them business functionality to alter business processes, change supply chain structures, or revise finance and resource allocations.

This Dashboard or Portal consists of a dedicated Home Page, and five major sections: Marketing, Finance, Products, Supply Chain,

and Administration. The first four sections – S.1 through S.4 – are linked via a Section Connector, offering direct navigation between these Sections. Each of these Sections includes a summary style Page. The Administration Section is not linked and navigable via the Section Connector: access to this Section would come via another path, generally direct URL entry or at the Dashboard or Portal log-in prompt (not shown). Within the major sections, all Pages are linked and navigable via Page Connectors.

DASHBOARD OR PORTAL SUITE

- *Mandatory Components: Dashboards*
- *Optional Components: N/A*
- *Stacking Size: 7*

Description

A Dashboard or Portal Suite consists of a group of stacked (though at this high level of structure, the construct is more akin to a collection of interlinks rather than hierarchically arranged) Dashboards or Portals sharing integrated content and common infrastructure. Stacking Dashboards or Portals as a Suite allows design and support teams to organize and manage distinct but related Dashboards or Portals as a single unit, and can help users by giving them quick and direct access to the collection of interconnected Dashboards or Portals. These Suites generally serve a diverse population of users who draw on a variety of business intelligence resources or other functionality to execute job functions at a variety of levels within the enterprise. The goals or purposes of the Dashboards or Portals in a Suite may vary dramatically; hence their individual content offerings will also vary dramatically. Users whose business needs or functions require them to work with single Dashboards or Portals in a Suite may not realize the commonalities underlying the various individual Dashboards or Portals they use. Users whose needs span multiple Dashboards or

Figure 6. Example dashboard or portal

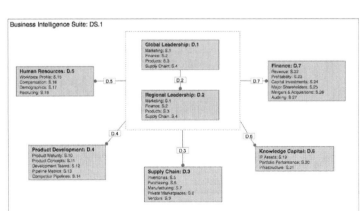

Portals in a Suite typically rely on a Dashboard or Portal Connector to move from one Dashboard or Portal to another within the Suite.

From an enterprise level architectural or IT administrative viewpoint, the Dashboard or Portal Suite can become the connection point to other enterprise level systems, such as metadata registries and repositories, ERP and SCM applications, enterprise data stores, security and authentication platforms, intranets, extranets, etc. The Dashboard or Portal Suite is also a useful unit for enterprise level perspectives including IT portfolio management, business process man-agement, strategic information management, and knowledge management. (See Figure 7)

Example Rendering

{dashboard_suite.eps}

Rendering Description

This sitemap style rendering shows an enterprise level Dashboard Suite made up of seven individual Dashboards that share assets. Five of the seven provide depth of content in major domains of a global enterprise: Supply Chain, Human Resources, Product Development, Knowledge Capital, and Finance. Each of these domain Dashboards has

Figure 7. Example dashboard suite

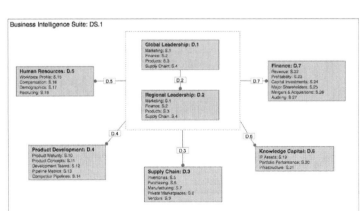

a distinct internal structure, with the individual Sections identified on this map.

The remaining two Dashboards—Global Leadership and Regional Leadership—aggregate assets for presentation to the different levels of executive leadership within the enterprise. Within this scheme, the information architecture of the two leadership Dashboards is closely parallel, but the scope of the assets shown in each would differ; users of the Regional Leadership Dashboard would have a view of Finance assets for their individual regions, and not globally, as in the Global Leadership Dashboard.

In this Suite, The five domain Dashboards are linked to the two Leadership Dashboard via a Dashboard Connector, meaning that each of these is navigable from the Leadership Dashboards. The Regional Leadership Dashboard is also linked to the Global Leadership Dashboard via another Dashboard Connector. Whether these Connectors allow two-way access is dependent on the individual access rights of the various Dashboard users. The Dashboard Connector here ensures that the members of the respective leadership teams can literally see what their colleagues see when discussing a course of action.

OVERVIEW OF THE CONNECTOR BLOCKS

The building block system includes several types of Connectors that make it possible for designers and architects to link the different areas of a Dashboard together via a consistent, easily understandable navigation model. The system also ensures the resulting information architecture can grow in response to changing needs and content. There's no special stacking hierarchy for the Connectors. However, they do have an official stacking size (most are size 3) in order to keep Dashboards constructed with the building blocks internally consistent.

The defined Connectors are:

- Control Bar
- Section Connector
- Page Connector
- Dashboard Connector
- Crosswalk Connector
- Contextual Crosswalk Connector
- Utility Navigation
- Geography Selector

Control Bars allow access to deeper collections of similar blocks, such as Tile Groups and Tiles offering narrowly focused content. Section, Page, and Dashboard Connectors offer hierarchically driven navigation paths between larger Containers. Crosswalk Connectors and Contextual Crosswalks extend the capabilities of the default Building Blocks navigation model to include links that express context-driven associative relationships between Containers, regardless of their location within the Dashboard or Portal structure. Combinations of Connectors provide the familiar patterns of paths from a user's current location to higher or broader levels of the Dashboard, links to items at the same level, links to contextually related items at all levels, etc.

CONNECTOR DEFINITIONS

Each Connector definition includes:

- Mandatory components
- Optional components
- Stacking size
- Detailed description
- Example rendering (for illustrative purposes only)
- Rendering description

CONTROL BAR DEFINITION

- *Mandatory components: Controls for manipulating Container content*

- *Optional components: None*
- *Stacking size: special – can be attached to Tiles, Tile Groups, or Views*

Control Bar Description

A Control Bar increases the amount of content offered by a Tile, Tile Group, or View by giving users the ability to change the content displayed within the block. Designers attach a Control Bar to a block to increase the effective depth (or scope) of the block's content. Control Bars allow dashboard designers to increase the depth of a new or existing Container block without increasing the on-screen size of the block or creating a large number of very similar blocks.

One common way of using Control Bars is to allow users to perform repeated tasks on one object that is a member of a group of similar objects. For example, a Tile that allows users to approve or reject purchase orders for one operating unit could be augmented with the addition of a Control Bar. The Control Bar will expand the scope of purchase order approval functionality by allowing the user to choose one or more operating units from a list of all available operating units. The approval functionality itself should appear and remain within the Tile, though the scope may expand with successive revisions of the Tile.

Another common use for Control Bars is to provide tools for choosing different combinations of data parameters for display within a block, such as selecting a single item for focus (or rendering of available data) from a list of many other items of the same type, shifting the start or end dates for a time period, changing a measurement unit or referencing an axis for comparison.

The controls—buttons, sliders, actuators, etc.—in a Control Bar are often rendered as standard form elements such as radio buttons or select lists, or hyperlinks. They could just as easily appear as custom scripted elements, applets, or AJAX / RIA delivered sliders. The types and styles of controls presented should be driven by the guidelines of good user experience design. And perhaps your budget!

A primary benefit of Control Bars is to reduce the total number of blocks necessary for a dashboard—though they do increase the complexity of individual blocks—thereby lowering overall development costs and saving valuable screen real estate. For example, consider a single product that is part of a family of fifteen related products: placing a Control Bar on a Tile that shows the inventory for one of those products allows users to change between displaying the same kind of inventory data for any product in the family, instead of simultaneously displaying fifteen separate Tiles with the same inventory data for all the different products in the family. Control Bars also work well when users need to compare metrics, items, or groups of metrics or items, in a side-by side fashion.

Control Bars attached to stacked blocks retain their functionality. Stacking Containers with attached Control Bars can lead to complex possible permutations of scope and depth for block content. Explore the potential combinations and permutations carefully, especially in regards to security and access rights. Control Bars should not replace functionality already located within a block, or serve as a means of combining wildly different sorts of content together into a single block that is incoherent or inconsistent. I recommend limiting the use of Control Bars to one per Container. (See Figure 8)

Example Rendering

{Control_bar.ai}

Rendering Description

This rendering shows a Tile with attached Control Bar that allows users to shift the focus of the Tile to any of a list of fifteen individual products, chosen via the select list shown. When the user chooses a product, the contents of the Tile refresh to show weekly inventory data for the new product, as well as a reference table and associated documents and links for the same new product.

Figure 8. Example control bar

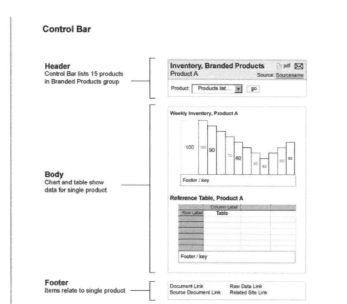

PAGE CONNECTOR DEFINITION

- *Mandatory components: links to all Pages in the parent Section*
- *Optional components: None*
- *Stacking size: 3*

PAGE CONNECTOR DESCRIPTION

The Page Connector links all the Pages stacked within a single Section of the Dashboard. The Page Connector typically appears on every Page within a Dashboard, though this is not required. As users navigate from Section to Section, the links in the Page Connector change to reflect the different Pages stacked in each Section. Of course, placing a Page Connector on any Page does not preclude creating other groups of links to other Pages located throughout the Dashboard. The Building Blocks are an open system—architects and designers should introduce additional (Free Form, within the view of the blocks) navigation models and mechanisms into the experience as needed. (See Figure 9)

Example Rendering

{page_connector.eps}

Rendering Description

This rendering shows the navigation links to Pages appearing in a Page Connector for a Section titled Products, which contains a Section summary page and four other Pages.

SECTION CONNECTOR DEFINITION

- *Mandatory components: links to all Sections in the Dashboard*
- *Optional components: link to Dashboard Home Page*
- *Stacking size: 3*

SECTION CONNECTOR DESCRIPTION

The Section Connector is a high level Connector that provides a link to each Section making up the Dashboard. The Section Connector typically appears on every Page within the Dashboard,

Figure 9. Example page connector

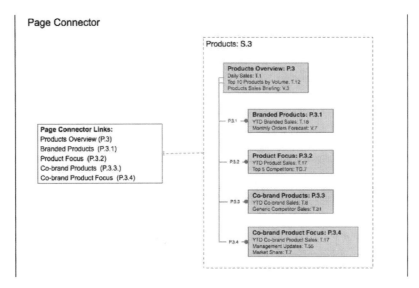

though this is not required. The Section Selector is akin to the ubiquitous global navigation element familiar from many web sites, though its actual content when displayed to a user will vary based on security settings or access rights. The links in the Section Connector should take users either to the Section Summary Page for that Section or to the chosen default Page within the Section. Include a link to any Dashboard Home Page in the Section Connector, especially if it offers unique content not available elsewhere in the dashboard. (See Figure 10)

Example Rendering

{section_connector.eps}

Rendering Description

This rendering shows the navigation links to Section summary Pages appearing in a Section Connector for a Dashboard that includes a Home Page and five Sections. Four of the Sections are navigable via the Section Connector, the remaining fifth Section—S.5 Administration—is dedicated to administrative uses, and is not navigable or linked via the Section Connector.

DASHBOARD CONNECTOR DEFINITION

- Mandatory components: links to each Dashboard in a Dashboard Suite
- *Optional components: NA*
- *Stacking size: 3*

Dashboard Connector Description

The Dashboard Connector allows users with access to two or more Dashboards within a Dashboard Suite to move quickly and directly amongst all the Dashboards they may access, without passing through multiple log-in or authentication interfaces. Dashboard Connectors typically appear on every Page of a Dashboard, though this is not required. The individual links in a Dashboard Connector often point to the Homepage for each listed Dashboard. A less-common linking behavior for Dashboard Connectors is to connect to the last visited Page in each linked Dashboard or to a default Page of the users choosing that is stored as a personalization preference. For administrators and maintenance staff, Dashboard Connectors can offer the same quick and direct access to the separate administrative areas of each Dashboard in a Suite. (See Figure 11)

Figure 10. Example section connector

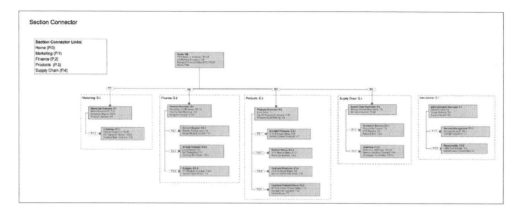

Example Rendering

{dashboard_connector.eps}

Rendering Description

This rendering shows the Dashboard links appearing in the Dashboard Connector for the Business Intelligence Suite described above.

CROSSWALK CONNECTOR DEFINITION

- *Mandatory components: recurring item (link origin), destination building block*
- *Optional components: None*
- *Stacking size: None*

CROSSWALK CONNECTOR DESCRIPTION

A Crosswalk Connector is a direct navigation path between individual building blocks, regardless of origin and destination locations in the Dashboard structure. Crosswalk Connectors provide a hub and spoke style path from many locations to a single destination, rather than a uniquely occurring link between two blocks. Crosswalks often take the form of a recurring name, term, or object that consistently links to another single building block offering content related to the linked item.

Common examples of Crosswalk Connectors include:

- Product names linked to a summary Page or View of the identified product
- Topic terms linked to a news aggregator or RSS aggregator block that shows recent items related to that topic
- Competitor names linked to a profile snapshot or market intelligence block
- Market or product family names linked to sales performance blocks
- Colleague names linked to profile information blocks showing their role, responsibilities, and direct reports (See Figure 12)

Example Rendering

{crosswalk_connector.eps}

Rendering Description

This rendering shows all the appearances of a Crosswalk Connector that links the instances of a product name to a destination Page in the Products Section (S.3) titled "Product Focus" (S.3.2), in this case a Page offering detailed information and tools related to a single product.

Figure 11. Example dashboard connector

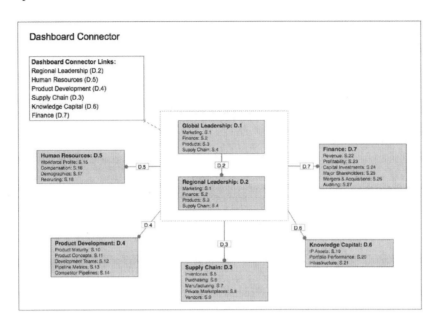

CONTEXTUAL CROSSWALK DEFINITION

- *Mandatory components: linked term (recurring item), origin contexts associative relationship, destination building blocks*
- *Optional components: None*
- *Stacking size: None*

Contextual Crosswalk Description

Contextual Crosswalks allow dashboard architects to create a direct link between blocks that is sensitive to context, instead of simply point to point. Contextual Crosswalks typically link a recurring item, such as a product name, to a destination block that varies based on the location of the originating link within the Dashboard's information architecture. With a Contextual Crosswalk, the destination block of each occurrence of the product name is determined by the location or context of the link within the Dashboard structure; that is, by relying on the users' current location to offer insight into the things they are most interested in seeing.

For example, each occurrence of a product name throughout a Dashboard could link either to a block offering inventory information for that product, or to a block offering sales information for competing products. When the product name is located in the Supply Chain section of the Dashboard, it would connect to the inventory block: when the product name is located in the Sales section, the link would connect to the competitor sales block.

Contextual Crosswalks are useful when Dashboards offer a substantial amount of content that addresses several different facets or aspects of an important and recurring topic, term or item. Contextual Crosswalks often appear in the form of a Page showing Views for an item, both of which are chosen via Control Bar to give users ready access to the other available collections of blocks matching the other origin contexts.

Keeping the broader principles of the Building Blocks in mind, it's perfectly logical for Contextual Crosswalks to link from one of several Dashboards or Portals within a Dashboard Suite to another destination Dashboard.

Figure 12. Example crosswalk connector

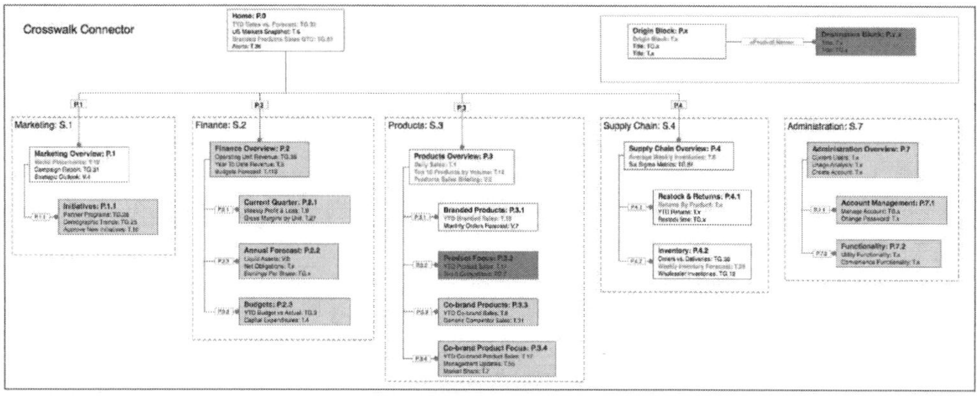

While Contextual Crosswalks can express any kind of associative relationship, in practice, it's best to define a limited set of types of Contextual Crosswalk in advance and apply them consistently across the Dashboard or Portal Suite. We know well that complex navigation models increase the work required for designers, developers, users and administrators. Prescribing the available set of Crosswalk Connectors (Contextual and standard) in advance will make it much easier to maintain consistent and easily understood navigation models. (See Figure 13)

Example Rendering

{contextual_crosswalk.eps}

Rendering Description

This rendering shows the navigation paths for a Contextual Crosswalk that links from a number of different origin contexts (or locations) to one of a number of similar destinations within the Products Section of a medium-size Dashboard. The legend on the map identifies the origin contexts and destinations for the Contextual Crosswalk, as well as the linked term: a Product Name. In this case, the Contextual Crosswalk directly links product names in six possible origin contexts (Marketing, Finance, Supply Chain, etc.) with six matching

briefings that provide detailed information on the status of a that same product. Those briefings appear as Views available from the Branded Product Focus Page (which contains the Marketing, Supply Chain, and Competitors briefings) or the Co-brand Product Focus Page (which contains the Customers, Regulatory, and Auditing briefings). After clicking the linked product name in the Supply Chain Section, a user navigates to the Branded Product Focus Page (P.3.2), which presents them with the Supply Chain Briefing (V.3.2.2).

UTILITY NAVIGATION DEFINITION

- *Mandatory components: links to Dashboard Utility Functionality*
- *Optional components: None*
- *Stacking size: 3*

Utility Navigation Description

This Connector gives users consistent access to the most important utility functions and features for a Dashboard or Portal, gathering ubiquitous links to these necessary tools into a single building block. Utility Navigation should include links to any Utility Function that must be accessible from most or all Dashboard Sections or Pages.

Utility Navigation is typically considered to have a stacking size of 3, meaning it is placed at

Figure 13. Example contextual crosswalk

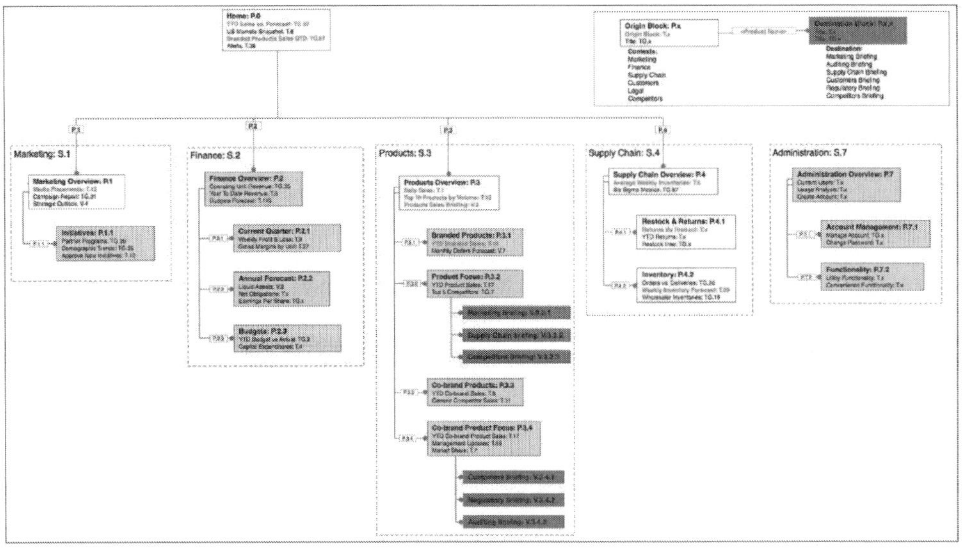

the Page level of the stacking hierarchy and not within individual Tiles, Tile Groups or Views. This approach is common practice in design settings and enterprise environments where standardized functionality is often supplied by or closely connected to externally defined services supplied via SOA – situations where some sort of dependency links the Dashboard or Portal to another system or environment. (See Figure 14)

Example Rendering

{utility_navigation.jpg}

{ltd_utilitybar.tif}

Rendering Description

This Utility Navigation component uses icons to provide links to eight distinct Utility Functions, an enterprise directory, a news feed aggregator, managed documents (Resources), a calendar, enterprise search, KPI driven alerts, prioritized staff updates and personalization settings. As you review the illustrations and examples of Utility Navigation and the other Connectors, keep in mind that no rule from the Building Blocks system

requires Utility Navigation to appear onscreen collected together in a single location (though good conceptual and practical reasons for doing so often apply). Likewise, the design decision about how to provide access and use – via icons, text, or other features – should be driven by the particulars of your project and user needs. (See Figure 15)

GEOGRAPHY SELECTOR DEFINITION

- *Mandatory components: controls or links for shifting the geographic context of a Container*
- *Optional components: None*
- *Stacking size: special – can be attached to Tiles, Tile Groups, Views, or Pages,*

GEOGRAPHY SELECTOR DESCRIPTION

The Geography Selector allows designers and architects to decouple the information architecture of a Dashboard from the shifting organizational structures based on geography that many enter-

Figure 14. Example utility navigation

prises rely on to understand the fundamentals of their activities. The Geography Selector presents users with controls or links allowing them to change the geographic reference point of a Container, while maintaining the structure of that Container. In the same way that Control Bars increase the depth of a Tile, Tile Group, or View, a Geography Selector increases the scope or depth of a Container while reducing the number of additional Containers to manage. For example, a Geography Selector might allow users the ability to change the focus of a sales activity chart located in a Tile from one US state to another.

Large enterprises often operate in or with reference to multiple states (or provinces, departments, etc.), regions, countries or even continents. These geographic concepts or schemes frequently differ from unit to unit within an enterprise. They often change dramatically from year to year to suit external environmental changes or internal reorganizations. Just as aligning a site map to an organization chart creates a brittle structure subject to disruption during reorganization, tying a Dashboard's information architecture to an

enterprise's current geographic scheme is a recipe for frustration.

Some Geography Selectors allows users to choose from a single set of geographic units, such as states or counties, with respect to the parameters determining the data shown for a defined set of KPI's (fixed Containers, variable scope for their content). Other Geography Selectors allow users to traverse a hierarchy of geographic units, with respect to the parameters determining the data shown for a defined set of KPI's (fixed Containers, variable scope for their content). It's possible to attach Geography Selectors to Containers with Control Bars. In these cases, the Geography Selector typically drives the Container contents before the Control Bar. (See Figure 16)

Example Rendering

{geography_selector.ai}

Rendering Description

This rendering shows a Tile Group with attached Geography Selector and Control Bar. The geographic scheme represented is hierarchical, spanning three tiers, beginning with State, moving to district and concluding with territory. Of course, many businesses use non-hierarchical geographic schemes, irregular schemes, or a combination of these options; in these cases the structure and quality of the underlying data, functionality and business logic may require creative solutions to the problems spawned by unusual intersections of the various choices.

CONCLUSION

This set of Connectors provides the minimum tools necessary for the assembly of coherent Dashboards across a wide variety of circumstances. I encourage you to refine this starting set, or create additional types of Connectors to meet new challenges.

Figure 15. Recalling the example business intelligence dashboard designed with the Building Blocks system from Part 1, this illustration shows a Dashboard Page which includes several of the Connectors

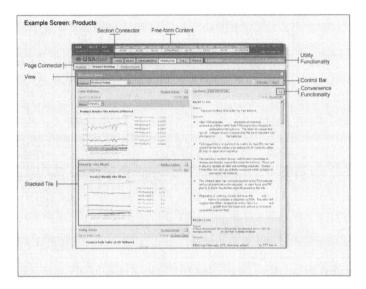

When combined in a fashion that meets the specific needs and context of a tile-based design effort, the Containers and Connectors can strike a good balance between cost, flexibility, and customization in terms of the user experience, systems and technology efforts and business perspective.

With proper assembly, using the stacking hierarchy and the small set of required elements, portal designers can create a consistent and scalable structure that supports a high quality user experience, lowers development costs and establishes a basis for sharing of resources across the enterprise.

Figure 16. Example geography selector

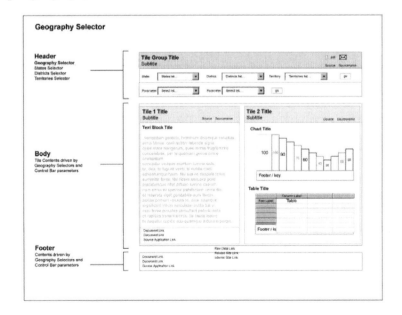

The next paper of this series will describe a common set of utility and convenience functionality often used to extend the reach and relevance of portal content to other contexts of use, making practical suggestions for following the principles of Openness, Independence and Portability underlying the Building Block system.

This work was previously published in the International Journal of Web Portals, Volume 2, Issue 1, edited by J.Polgar pp. 58-81, copyright 2010 by IGI Publishing (an imprint of IGI Global).

Chapter 3.22
A Simple and Secure Credit Card–Based Payment System

Chi Po Cheong
University of Macau, China

INTRODUCTION

Credit card is the most popular payment method used in Internet shopping. The idea of credit card payment is to buy first and pay later. The cardholder can pay at the end of the statement cycle or they can pay interest on the outstanding balance. Therefore, there are many credit card-based electronic payment systems (EPSs) that have been developed to facilitate the purchase of goods and services over the Internet such as CyberCash (VeriSign), iKP (Bellare, Garary, Hauser, et al, 1995), SET (Visa and MasterCard, 1997), CCT (Li & Zhange, 2004), and so forth. Usually a credit card-based EPS involves five parties: cardholder, merchant, acquirer bank, issuer bank, and financial institution.

Internet is an open system and the communication path between each other is insecure. All communications are potentially open for an eavesdropper to read and modify as they pass between the communicating endpoints. Therefore, the payment information transmitted between the cardholder and the merchant through Internet is dangerous without

a secure path. SSL (Zeus Technology, 2000) is a good example to secure the communication channel. Besides the issue of insecure communication, there are a number of factors that each participant must consider. For example, merchant concerns about whether the credit card or the cardholder is genuine. There is no way to know the consumer is a genuine cardholder. As a result, the merchant is incurring the increase in losses due to cardholder disputes and frauds. On the other hand, cardholders are worried about the theft of the privacy or sensitive information such as the credit card number. They don't want any unauthorized usage of their credit cards and any modification to the transaction amount by a third party. These security issues have deterred many potential consumers from purchasing online.

Existing credit card-based EPSs solve the problems in many different ways. Some of them use cryptography mechanisms to protect private information. However, they are very complicated, expensive, and tedious (Xianhau, Yuen, Ling, & Lim, 2001). Some EPSs use the Certificate Authority (CA) model to fulfill the authentication, integrity, and nonrepudiation security schemes. However, each participant requires a digital certificate during

DOI: 10.4018/978-1-60566-014-1.ch175

the payment cycle. These certificates are issued by independent CAs but the implementation and maintenance cost of this model is very high. In addition, the validation steps of Certificate-based systems are very time-consuming processes. It requires access to an online certificate server during the payment process. Moreover, the certificate revocation list is a major disadvantage of the PKI-based certification model (The Internet Engineering Task Force). The cardholder's certificate also includes some private information such as the cardholder's name. The requirement of a cardholder's certificate means software such as e-Wallet is required to be installed on the cardholder's computer. It is the barrier for the cardholder to use Certificate-based payment systems. To solve this problem, Visa Company has developed a new payment system called Verified by Visa (VbV) (http:www/visa-asia.com/ap/sea/merchants/productstech/vbv_implementvbv.shtml). However, sensitive information such as credit card number is still passed to the merchant. Therefore, the cardholder is not protected by the system.

Evaluation Factors

A successful credit card-based EPS should be simple, secure, and easy to use and has low deployment and maintenance cost. A set of evaluation criteria is described by Sahut (2005). Security is one of the important factors in identifying a good EPS. However, factors such as cost, convenience, ease of use, and so forth, must be also considered when designing a new EPS.

The new EPS must have a balance between security and convenience, especially on the cardholder side. This article proposes a new payment system called simple and secure credit card-based payment system (SSCCPS) which is a "cryptography free" and "certificate free" system.

Traditional Credit Card Payment Systems

Most credit card-based EPSs do not utilize on the traditional credit card payment infrastructure. Many credit card-based EPSs have been designed and developed but most of them, such as SET, have been poorly received by consumers. The main problem is that lots of requirements must be fulfilled by all participants, especially the cardholder. However, the complex or technical requirements to the cardholder will prevent the successful implementation of the system in the marketplace. For example, during the authentication process, the cardholder has to use a smart card reader, which is to be installed at home. In addition, software such as e-wallet and e-certificate has to be installed in the cardholder's computer. All the requirements act as barriers to the adoption of credit card-based EPSs. The objective of this article is to design a simple and secure credit card payment system which utilizes the existing infrastructure and minimizes the complex mechanism.

Traditional Payment Flow

The payment flow of the traditional transaction is shown in the Figure 1, and consists of five participants, including Issuer Bank, Acquirer Bank, Consumer, Merchant, and financial institution. The cardholder gives the credit card to the merchant cashier. The cashier swipes the credit card through an electric draft capture (EDC) or point of sale (POS) equipment and keys in the transaction amount. The EDC/POS dials a stored telephone number to call a gateway and sends the captured data to the acquirer bank. The acquirer bank constructs an ISO 8583 (Financial Transaction Card Orginated Messages) authorization request message and sends it to the issuer bank through tradition financial network. The issuer bank extracts the information from the authorization request message such as primary account number, expiration date, currency code, merchant type, transaction date time, and so forth, and goes through the local validation policies. The issuer bank constructs the authorization response message and sends it to the acquirer bank either approved or declined. The acquire bank forwards the response code to the merchant to complete the transaction.

There are many different types of financial messages defined in ISO 8583. Each type of message is composed of different data fields. The values in each data field may be redefined by individual credit card companies. Table 1 shows the typical message types and Table 2 shows data fields used in traditional credit card payment system.

Table 1. Typical message types

Message Number	Description
0100	Authorization request
0110	Authorization request response
0120	Authorization advice
0130	Authorization advice response
0400	Acquirer reversal request
0410	Acquirer reversal request response

Table 2. Typical data fields

ISO Bit Num	Field Name	Length
2	Primary account number (PAN) (e.g., credit card number)	19
4	Amount, transaction	12
7	Transmission data and time	10
11	System trace audit number	6
12	Time, local transaction	6
13	Date, local transaction	4
14	Date, expiration	4
18	Merchant type	4
32	Acquiring institution identification code	11
38	Authorization identification response	6
39	Response code	2
42	Card acceptor identification code (e.g., merchant number)	15

Trust Relationships

A well-defined trust relationship is based on the existing established physical relationship. For example, the relationship between the cardholder and the issuer bank is gradually building up since the credit card was issued. The proposed system is based on the trust relationships among the participants described as follows.

Existing Trust Relationships

- **Cardholder and issuer bank:** The cardholder trusts the issuer bank as it issues the card. The cardholder applies the credit card in his or her favorable bank and is normally a customer of the bank for a long time. Therefore, the relationship has been built. During the online payment process, any online electronic message from the issuer bank is trusted by the cardholder, which is based on the physical relationship.
- **Merchant and acquirer bank:** The merchant bank is usually called the acquirer bank because it acquires payment records, such as payment charge slips from the merchant. To provide the online payment in the Internet, the merchant must register in the acquirer bank before starting the business. In the online credit card-based EPS, the same relationship has been built between merchant and acquirer bank. The difference is that the merchant receives the response from the Internet and not from the electric draft capture (EDC).
- **The financial institution and the member bank:** The financial intuition is a large data center acting as a gateway between the acquirer bank and the issuer bank, such as Visa and MasterCard Company. When the issuer or acquirer banks carry out the credit card business, they have to apply to the financial institution for the network. Then each participant bank or member bank will

be assigned a unique bank identification number (BIN). As a result, both the acquirer bank and the issuer bank have built the trusted relationship when they registered in the financial institution.

Transitive Trust Relationships

- **Acquirer bank and issuer bank:** The relationship between issuer bank and acquirer bank is interrelated with financial institution. They must become a member bank in the financial institution before running the credit card business. The acquirer and issuer bank must accept and follow the rules or policies of the financial institution. The financial institution not only supports but also monitors the individual member bank. Therefore, each member bank has built a trusted relationship.

- **The cardholder and merchant:** The cardholder and the merchant can extend the trust relationship based on the two way trust relationship between their actors.

SIMPLE AND SECURE CREDIT CARD-BASED PAYMENT SYSTEM (SSCCPS)

The proposed payment system uses mobile phone as an authentication device. Figure 2 (International Telecommunication Union) shows the growth of mobile phone users between 1990 and 2005 compared with the fixed lines. The total number of mobile phone subscribers in the world was estimated at 2.14 billion in 2005. Around 80% of the world's population have mobile phone coverage as of 2006, and that is expected to increase to 90% by the year 2010. As the number of mobile phone users increase rapidly, it will support the adoption of SSCCPS.

The simple and secure credit card-based payment system (SSCCPS) aims to improve the confidence and simplify the payment process for the cardholder and the merchant over open networks. It can reduce disputes and fraudulent activities related to the use of credit cards. SSCCPS uses the bank identification number (BIN) provided by participating issuers and issuer customer number (ICN) to authenticate the cardholder. The cardholder sends the merchant information with the

Figure 2. Mobile telephones growing faster than fixed lines (source ITU [11])

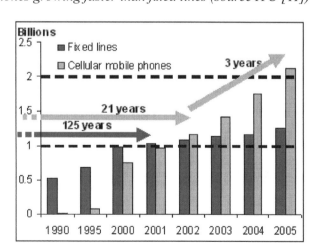

use of mobile phone to the issuer bank, which will authenticate the merchant. The cardholder inputs the issuer preapproval number (IPAN) in the merchant Web site for the final confirmation. Therefore, the confidence of the consumer can be gained. In SSCCPS, no software is required and there isn't any complex cryptographic mechanism between cardholder and merchant.

Payment Cycle of SSCCPS

The basic cycle of SSCCPS is shown in Figure 3 and the details are as follows:

1. A cardholder selects the desired items and clicks the checkout button in the merchant online shop. The merchant requests the cardholder to fill in nonsensitive information including issuer identification number (IIN), issuer customer number (ICN), and other billing information such as delivery address, telephone number, and so forth. The cardholders then wait for the issuer preapproved number (IPAN) and merchant signature (MS) from the issuer bank before going to Step 8.

2. The cardholder's order request is sent to the merchant. The merchant will send a verification request message to the acquirer bank. The verification request message includes merchant number and merchant trace number and the information of the cardholder.

3. The acquirer bank receives the verification request message from the merchant. It will modify the message and forward it to the issuer bank through the traditional financial network.

4. The issuer bank will verify the verification request message from the acquirer bank. The issuer bank checks the validity of the issuer customer number, the adequacy of the credit line and other authorization rules or policies. After the check, a verification message will then be sent to the merchant.

5. If it is a valid transaction, the issuer sends the transaction summary, that is, IPAN and MS, to the cardholder's mobile phone through short message service (SMS).

6. The merchant receives a verification message from the issuer through the acquirer. If it is a valid response, the merchant follows the payment step; otherwise it rejects the transaction.

Figure 3. The payment flow of the SSCCPS

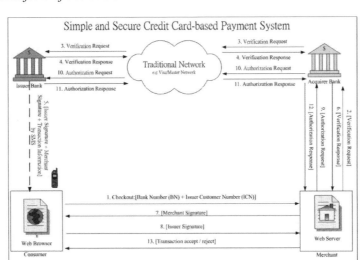

7. For a valid transaction, the merchant prompts the cardholder to input the IPAN and also displays the transaction details and MS at the same time. The IPAN is provided by the issuer bank through SMS to the cardholder's mobile phone in Step 5.

8. The cardholder inputs the IPAN after verifying the MS and transaction summary and then sends the IPAN to the merchant by clicking the confirm button.

9. The merchant will send an authorization request message to the acquire bank with some data added into the traditional message such as IPAN.

10. The acquire bank receives the authorization request message from the merchant and will forward it to the issuer bank.

11. When the issuer bank receives the authorization request from the acquirer bank, it will obtain the IPAN from the authorization request and compares it with the IPAN sent to the cardholder. If they are identical, it will accept the transaction; otherwise, it will reject it. The issuer bank then sends an authorization response back to acquirer bank either approved or declined.

12. When the acquirer bank receives the authorization response message, it will send the authorization response message (either approved or declined) to the merchant.

13. Based on the response code, the merchant sends an approved or declined response to the cardholder.

Security Schemes in SSCCPS

Four basic security schemes are used to evaluate the proposed system including authentication, confidentially, integrity, and nonrepudiation.

- **Cardholder authentication:** The merchant can determine a genuine cardholder by the use of IPAN. The IPAN is a unique number generated by the issuer bank and is used only once in the transaction. The issuer bank sends the IPAN to the cardholder's mobile phone by using SMS. Only the genuine cardholder will receive the SMS because the mobile phone number was registered to the bank. The cardholder submits IPAN to the merchant. The merchant will then send an authorization request message with IPAN. The issuer bank compares the value of IPAN when it receives the authorization request message. Only the genuine cardholder knows the IPAN. If they are identical, the consumer is a genuine cardholder. In SSCCPS, the merchant does not need to authenticate the cardholder. The authentication process is done by the issuer bank.

- **Merchant authentication:** In SSCCPS, the merchant authentication process is unimportant during the payment process. The purpose for authenticating the merchant is for the cardholder to ensure that sensitive information is sent to a genuine merchant. In most of the credit card-based payment systems, the merchant authentication is performed by the use of the merchant certificate in the beginning of the payment process. However, in the SSCCPS, no sensitive information such as credit number is sent to the merchant directly. The authentication process is performed during the verification process. The merchant generates a merchant signature during the verification process. The merchant signature is divided in two parts: the merchant number and the merchant trace number. The merchant number is a unique identification number issued by the acquirer bank during the merchant registration. The merchant trace number is a one-time used number generated by the merchant to identify each transaction. During the payment process, the merchant Web site pops up a window showing the merchant signature and requesting the cardholder to submit IPAN. Then the issuer bank receives the merchant signature from the verification request message. After passing the verification process, the issuer sends the merchant signature, issuer preapproved number (IPAN) and transaction summary to the cardholder's mobile phone through SMS. The cardholder will compare two merchant signatures. If they are identical, the merchant is a genuine merchant.

- **Confidentiality:** Most existing credit card-based EPSs only ensure a secure communication path between the cardholder and the merchant or use encryption mechanisms to encrypt the financial data. Financial information will eventually be sent to the merchant side regardless of whether the merchant is honest or not. In SSCCPS, no sensitive information is sent to the merchant. The merchant only knows the issuer customer number (ICN), which is not sensitive financial information. Cardholders are willing to use SSCCPS because it hides their privacy information.

- **Integrity:** Data integrity ensures that the message or transaction cannot be altered from its source. Many existing payment systems are using digital signature mechanism to assure integrity. In SSCCPS, data integrity is done by the cardholder. The issuer bank sends the transaction summary such as transaction date, time, amount, and so forth, to the cardholder's mobile phone. The cardholder can check the transaction summary such as transaction amount. If the data matches the original, the cardholder submits the IPAN through the merchant Web site.

- **Nonrepudiation:** Nonrepudiation is a way to guarantee that the cardholder and merchant cannot deny the transaction in later.

It is usually provided through public key cryptography by digital signing. SSCCPS uses mobile phone as a nonrepudiation mechanism instead of the public key infrastructure. Only the mobile phone owner can receive IPAN and the transaction summary. No one can abuse or read the message from the cardholder's mobile phone. SSCCPS assumes that only the genuine cardholder can receive the IPAN during the payment process. If the merchant can obtain an authorization request message with a valid IPAN, it means that the cardholder has agreed and cannot deny the transaction.

CONCLUSION

Most existing credit card-based EPSs are complex and expensive. And the payment systems using cryptography or certificate authorities are much more expensive. Using SSCCPS, cardholders can protect their sensitive information from merchants. During the payment cycle, the merchant doesn't know the actual credit card information and obtains the issuer customer number (ICN) only. In addition, it does not require any software such as e-wallet and cardholder's certificate. Therefore, it is convenient for any cardholder to use SSCCPS. It is a true "cryptography free" and "certificate free" payment system. Furthermore, it fully utilizes the traditional payment infrastructure without increasing the deployment and maintenance cost. With SSCCPS, the cardholder will gain more confidence in online shopping. Hence, it not only improves the security of online payment but also simplifies the process. In conclusion, SSCCPS will benefit all parties involved, as disputes and fraudulent activities will be reduced.

REFERENCES

Bellare, M., Garary, J.A., Hauser, R., Herzberg, A., Krawczyk, H., Steinerm, M. et al. (1995, July 12). *iKP: A family of secure electronic payment protocols.*

Financial Transaction Card Originated Messages. *Interchange message specifications—Part 1: Message, data elements and code values.*

International Telecommunication Union ITU/UNCTAD. World Information Society Report 2006, and ITU World Telecommunication Indicators Database. ISO 8583-1:2003. *Financial transaction card originated messages—Interchange message specifications—Part 1: message, data elements and code values.*

Li, Y., & Zhange, X. (2004). A security-enhanced one-time payment scheme for credit card. In *Proceedings of the 14th International Workshop on Research Issues on Data Engineering: Web Services for E-commerce and E-government Applications (RIDE'04).* IEEE. Retrieved April 26, 2007, from http://www.visa-asia.com/ap/sea/merchants/productstech/vbv_implementvbv.shtml

The Internet Engineering Task Force. *Internet X.509 Public Key Infrastructure Certificate and Certificate Revocation List (CRL) Profile.* www.ietf.org/rfc/rfc3280.txt

Visa and MasterCard. (1997). *SET Secure Electronic Transaction Specification Book 1: Business Description.*

Xianhua, X., Yuen, S. S., Ling, G., & Lim, T. C. (2001). Virtual card payment protocol and risk analysis using performance scoring. In *Proceedings of the 15th International Parallel and Distributed Processing Symposium (IPDPS'01)* (pp. 10018a). IEEE.

Zeus Technology. (2000, June 16). SSL: Theory and practice.

KEY TERMS AND DEFINITIONS

Acquirer: An acquirer is an organization or a bank that collects authorization requests and sales slips from merchant. It directly connects to the merchant's POS/EDC in the traditional payment system.

Authentication: It is a method to identify cardholder and merchant before payment. Authentication is the mechanism in which the system will identify the cardholder or merchant, "Is that really you?"

Certificate Revocation: The certificate can be revoked by the Certificate Authority (CA) before their scheduled expiration date. There are different revocation reasons defined in RFC 3280. A revoked certificate will be added to the Certificate Revocation List (CRL) and it should not be used by other system.

Digital Certificates: It is issued by a Certification Authority (CA). It contains the owner name, expiration date and the owner's public key and is to verify who are sending the message.

Encryption: It is the process to encrypt the message and make it unreadable without special knowledge. Encryption is to protect the public communication network such as Internet.

E-Wallet: It is also known as a digital wallet and likes a physical wallet used in the electronic payment system. It provides the security and encryption for the personal information.

Financial Institution (Card Brand): A large data center that provides the financial services and network between acquirer bank and issuer bank.

Identification: Identification is a mechanism by which the system asks the user, "Who are you?" user identifies himself or herself to the system by a user name or user number in the computer system.

Integrity: Data integrity ensures that the transaction is unchanged from its source and has not been accidentally or maliciously altered.

Issuer: A issuer is an organization or a bank which issues credit card to cardholder. It provides the authorization services to acquirer.

Merchant: An organization or an individual accepts credit card payment by selling product or service.

Nonrepudiation: A strong and substantial evidence is available to the sender of message that the message has been delivered, and to the receipt.

Short Message Service (SMS): The service is available on mobile phones, which permits the sending or receiving of short messages. SMS messages are two-way alphanumeric paging messages up to 160 characters that can be sent to and from mobile phone.

This work was previously published in the Encyclopedia of Multimedia Technology and Networking, Second Edition, edited by M. Pagani, pp. 1299-1306, copyright 2009 by IGI Publishing (an imprint of IGI Global).

Chapter 3.23
Self–Service Systems:
Quality Dimensions and Users' Profiles

Călin Gurău
Montpellier Business School, France

ABSTRACT

The evolution of information technology applications has changed the landscape of the service industry, offering the possibility of customer empowerment through self-service applications. Considering the main three streams of research already applied in the study of self-services, this chapter investigates customers' perceptions about eight dimensions that characterise the quality of the self-service experience. On the other hand, the study attempts to analyse the influence of the self-service users' profile (gender, Internet usage experience, and online self-service usage experience), and to provide specific insights about the needs and wants of various categories of customers.

INTRODUCTION

In the last 15 years, the evolution of information technology applications has changed the landscape of the service industry. The implementation of self-service technology has created new service channels and procedures. Nowadays, clients can

DOI: 10.4018/978-1-60566-064-6.ch004

conduct bank transactions through automated teller machines (ATM) or on the Internet (online banking), make reservations or purchase tickets through online kiosks, check-in automated hotels, or use self-scanning systems in retail stores (Bobbitt & Dabholkar, 2001). The integration of self-service technology with Internet applications has increased even more the convenience of information-rich services; the customers can now access the service from their homes or offices, 24 hours a day, without geographical limitations.

On the other hand, the introduction of effective **self-service systems** allows companies to automate the repetitive elements of services, concentrating their resources and personnel on more personalised aspects of the company–customer relationship, and thus providing more added-value to their clients. However, the implementation of this strategy requires more than the introduction of self-service applications. These **self-service systems** need to be tied-in with employee-related policies and procedures. These internal procedures must insure that the customer can rely on virtual assistance when using a self-service interface and that can feel comfortable in a range of transactions without human intervention (Kotler, Armstrong, Saunders, & Wong, 2002).

Copyright © 2010, IGI Global. Copying or distributing in print or electronic forms without written permission of IGI Global is prohibited.

The production and consumption of services have specific characteristics that permit **customer empowerment** but, on the other hand, create challenges related with customer satisfaction and with customer's perception regarding service quality. By comparison with products, the services are (Zeithaml, Bitner, & Gremler, 2002a):

1. **Intangible:** Services cannot be seen, tasted, felt, heard, or smelled. This makes evaluating service quality very difficult and potential consumers look for visible indicators of quality.
2. **Inseparable:** Services are produced and consumed at the same time and cannot be separated from their providers. Provider and client must interact for the service to occur and therefore both parties become part of the service provided.
3. **Variable:** As consumer and producer are both part of the service, the quality of services may vary greatly depending on who provides them and when, where, and how they are provided. Marketers must therefore take steps towards achieving quality control amongst their service providers.
4. **Perishable:** Services must be consumed as they are provided and cannot be stored for later use. This becomes a problem if demand fluctuates and service opportunities are missed. Marketers must develop strategies to either keep demand constant or provide the equivalent supply of service to match the fluctuating demand.
5. **No transfer of ownership:** Services cannot be owned by the user. Marketers therefore should develop strategies to enable consumers to recall the quality of service they received.

The introduction of online self-services has changed the way in which companies relate to their customers. This new technology eliminates firm's personnel from the service interface, replacing it with software applications that can be accessed through real-time Internet connection. On the other hand, the **self-service system** gives additional responsibilities to the customer, who will initiate, generate, and consume the service interacting directly with software applications. However, this additional responsibility is not necessarily perceived as negative by the involved customers. In fact, many studies have shown that customers, and especially online service users, enjoy having a greater degree of control over the service they require. The self-service systems might permit a better customisation of the online service, resulting in improved satisfaction for the user.

On the other hand, the lack of a direct relationship with an employee might represent a disadvantage for customers that prefer direct human interactions. The dialogue with an employee might add a personal quality to the service provided, and can provide quick and flexible solutions when things do not go as planned. All these factors, together with the propensity of customers to adopt a new technology, can significantly influence the adoption and frequency of use of a specific online self-service.

The purpose of this exploratory study is to identify the quality dimensions that influence customers' perceptions about online self-service systems. On the other hand, considering that these perceptions can vary from one customer to another, the research attempts to identify the sociodemographic characteristics that influence the perception of online self-service quality dimensions and their practical use, creating the basis of a general customer profiling. After a brief but comprehensive presentation of the streams of research that are relevant for the study of self-service systems, the chapter presents the research objectives of this research project, as well as the methodology applied to collect primary and secondary data. These results obtained from data analysis are then presented and discussed in direct relation with the defined research objectives. The chapter ends with a summary of the main findings and with propositions for future research.

ONLINE CUSTOMER SELF-SERVICE: PREVIOUS RESEARCH

Customer empowerment through self-service technology is a new but fertile field of studies. Previous research on this topic can be categorised into three main streams:

a.   the **innovation diffusion theory** – although many self-services offered online were previously provided into the physical environment, the application of self-service technology can be considered an innovation;

b.   **consumer readiness** to adopt the online self-service technology; and

c.   **e-service quality** and customer satisfaction, which studies the self-service dimensions that are considered essential for online service quality.

Considered from an empirical point of view, these research streams complement each other well; the diffusion theory considers customers' perceptions about the characteristics of online self-services before and during the trial phase, the consumer readiness framework analyses the personal capacities of online users, and, finally, the e-service quality-customer satisfaction theory emphasises customers perceptions during and after the interaction with self-service systems.

The innovation diffusion theory was formulated by Rogers (1962) and applied in a large number of projects (Gerrard & Cunningham, 2003). Rogers (1995) defined five main characteristics of innovations that influence their adoption rate by the population:

•   Relative advantage represents the additional benefit offered by the innovation in comparison with the existing offer on the market. The research conducted on the adoption of banking self-services identified as sources of relative advantage economic benefits (Black, Lockett, Wiklofer,

& Ennew, 2001; Loudon & Delle Bitta, 1993; Polatoglu, & Ekin, 2001), convenience (Black et al., 2001; Loudon & Delle Bitta, 1993; Polatoglu, & Ekin, 2001), performance (Polatoglu, & Ekin, 2001), and independence, eliminating the need to rely on others (Black et al., 2001).

•   Compatibility is the consistency of the innovation with existing values, past experiences, and needs of the potential adopters. For example, familiarity with the Internet and online applications was identified as an essential factor for customers' willingness to adopt online self-service technologies (Black et al., 2001).

•   Complexity – the level of difficulty of the innovation will influence its speed of adoption. In the case of online self-service technology, this dimension can be related either with the simplicity and/or friendliness of the Web interface or with the user's level of capability (Black et al., 2001; Hewer & Howcroft, 1999; Polatoglu, & Ekin, 2001; Rotchanakitumnuai & Speece, 2003).

•   Trialability is the capacity to interact with the innovation. Trialability is essential to transmit firsthand information about self-service applications and facilitate consumers' learning about the use of the new technology (Hewer & Howcroft, 1999).

•   Observability is the degree of innovation visibility within the society at large, or in a social/professional group. This dimension is not always applicable to characterise the adoption of online self-services, because in most cases the interaction between the customer and the online applications is not visible to other users (Black et al., 2001; Gerrard & Cunningham, 2003). However, the organisation that attempts to introduce a new self-service on the Internet may increase its observability by actively promoting and demonstrating the use of this service.

Another determinant of customer's readiness to adopt innovations is the perceived level of risk (Holak, 1988; Labay & Kinnear, 1981; Lockett & Littler, 1997; Ostlund, 1974). Many studies have outlined that the online environment is considered more risky than the physical market (Pavlou, Liang, & Xue, 2007). This perception can represent an important deterrent for the adoption of self-services, especially when the online process implies a transaction—buying a flight ticket, or an online transmission of confidential information—online banking operations.

Consumer readiness to embrace the self-service technology is explained in the academic literature by three main variables:

1. **Role clarity:** Since traditionally the services were produced through the interaction between a customer and a specialised employee, the adoption of self-service technology requires customer empowerment and a modified consumer behaviour. Role ambiguity for staff or customers can create important problems for the introduction of new services (Easingwood, 1986), and limits the capacity of consumer to participate in the co-production of services (Larsson & Bowen, 1989). Meuter, Bitner, Ostrom, and Brown (2005) have also investigated the relationship between **role clarity** and self-service system trial.

2. **Motivation:** Intrinsic and extrinsic **motivation** were identified as essential factors for the successful introduction of online self-service technology (Barczak, Ellen, & Pilling, 1997). Some customers welcome a higher degree of empowerment, because they find the participation in the co-production of services intrinsically attractive (Bateson, 1985; Dadholkar, 1996; Rogers, 1995; Schneider & Bowen, 1995). On the other hand, the customers might be motivated by specific extrinsic advantages, such as price discounts, time saving, or convenience (Dadholkar, 1996; Schneider & Bowen, 1995).

3. **Ability:** The online environment in general and the self-service system in particular may require specific personal skills. A complex or unfriendly Web site interface can transmit to the customer the fear that she/he will not have the **ability** to interact with the system, and therefore prevent her/him to engage in a proactive behaviour (Jayanti & Burns, 1998; Meuter et al., 2005).

The theories of **e-service quality** are based on the traditional **SERVQUAL** model (Parasuraman, Berry, & Zeithaml, 1988). This model is based on extensive research conducted by Parasuraman, Zeithaml, and Berry (1985) and Parasuraman et al. (1988) who initially identified ten determinants of service quality: tangibles, reliability, responsiveness, competency, courtesy, communication, credibility, security, access, and understanding the customer. These dimensions were later reduced to five features, using factor analysis: tangibles, reliability, responsiveness, assurance, and empathy.

The specific characteristics of the Internet have required a significant adaptation of these quality dimensions to online services. Zeithaml, Parasuraman, and Malhotra (2001) and Zeithaml et al. (2002b) have identified a series of **e-service quality** dimensions: reliability, responsibility, access, flexibility, ease of navigation, efficiency, assurance/trust, security, price knowledge, site aesthetics, and customisation/personalisation, developing on their basis the e-**SERVQUAL** model. Yang et al. (2003) have investigated the quality of e-retailing services, identifying three additional dimensions: convenience, continuous improvement, and collaboration. Another study of Jun and Cai (2001) in the context of Internet banking services has found six main dimensions of online systems quality: content, accuracy, ease of use, timeliness, aesthetics, and security.

A model, developed by Curran and Meuter (2005), explains how customers decide whether to use a self-service technology. They identified four elements that can be used as predictors of attitudes toward self-service systems: ease of use, usefulness, need of interaction, and risk. The study demonstrates that self-service systems should be useful and easy to handle, but also that these dimensions are not enough to insure customer satisfaction. Analysing **self-service systems** such as ATMs and phone banking, the authors conclude that there is room for improvement in the design and functionality of this service technology.

Bateson (1985) explored the factors that determine a customer to choose a do-it-yourself option (including self-service alternatives), or the traditional service delivery system. The findings indicated that time (consuming time), control (control over the received service), effort (the effort made to access the service), and dependence (depending or not on another person) are the most important elements that influence the decision to use a specific service system. The customers that preferred the self-service option emphasised that time and control represent essential factors for their choice. The importance of personal control was confirmed by Meuter, Ostrom, Roundtree, and Bitner (2000) and Meuter, Ostrom, Bitner, and Roundtree (2003) that demonstrated that many perceived benefits of the self-service technology can be linked with this dimension.

A study conducted by Lee and Allaway (2002) attempted to verify if the manipulation of personal control over a new self-service technology leads to predictable changes in the way consumers perceived the risk associated with this technology. An additional objective was to verify if the specific dimensions of personal control (predictability, controllability, and outcome desirability) contribute equally to variations in perceived risk, perceived value, and adoption intention. The results showed that an increased sense of control over the self-service technology reduces perceived risk, heightens perceived value, and stimulated the intention to adopt and use self-service technology. This study also stated that marketers should evaluate six issues in relation to their self-service system: (a) whether the Web site is easy to understand for new customers, (b) whether the potential adopters are able to predict the benefits before using the service, (c) whether the customers can adapt the service to their personal preferences, (d) whether the customers can change their usage level/involvement with the system, (e) how desirable the benefits are of using the self-service technology from the customers perspective, and (f) if potential adopters have enough knowledge and skills to successfully self-service systems.

According to the Boston Consulting Group, there are three important issues that a company must take into account when implementing an online **self-service system**. The online site must be like a professional off-line salesperson: (a) it should inspire trust and provide solutions to consumer's problems; (b) must be entertaining, and (c) should create a community of interest, by allowing customers to actively interact with the site.

Despite these projects focused on self-service technology, this topic still has many unknown elements. Expressing this problem, Gournaris and Dimitriadis (2003) stated that few academic efforts have been devoted to the identification of the criteria used by customers to assess a Web's portal quality. This study attempts to fill in this knowledge gap, investigating the quality dimensions used by customers to shape their perception about online self-service systems.

RESEARCH METHODOLOGY

Considering the existing research in the area of online self-service systems, the following research objectives have been defined for this study:

- To define the quality dimensions that may influence consumers' perceptions of online self-service systems.

- To evaluate the importance of these quality dimensions for online self-service users.
- To investigate the way in which personal characteristics of users influence their perception about the quality dimensions of online self-service systems.

The research was only focused on the self-service systems that involve online transactions and payments, such as travel booking, online retailing, or online insurance, which involve a certain level of risk.

In order to answer these research objectives, both secondary and primary data have been collected and analysed. In the first stage of the research process, a series of academic and professional articles dealing with the subject of self-service systems and with the quality dimensions of online services have been accessed and consulted, in order to identify the specific quality dimensions that influence the perception of online customers. On the basis of this secondary research (Bateson, 1985; Curran & Meuter, 2005, Lee & Allaway, 2002; Meuter et al., 2000, 2003; Parasuraman et al., 1985, 1988; Zeithaml et al., 2001, 2002b), the following dimensions have been identified:

- **Perceived level of security:** The level of risk perceived by a customer using an online self-service system.
- **Flexibility:** The possibility of the client to change options during his/her with the self-service system without restarting the whole process.
- **Personalisation:** The possibility to adapt the self-service systems with personal options, depending on the country, the way information is displayed, personal preferences, and so forth.
- **Information about pricing conditions and fees:** The clarity and completeness of the information provided by the self-service Web site regarding the pricing conditions and fees of the service transaction.

- **Tools for problem solving:** The self-service Web sites provide specific information/solutions to the users that encounter problems during the service transaction.
- **Web page design:** The attractiveness and logic of the self-service Web page interface.
- **Personal contact:** The possibility to contact an employee who can help in problem situations.
- **Trial/demo before using the actual service:** The self-service Web site provides a trial/demonstration of the client interaction with the self-service system, helping him/her to understand the functioning of the online self-service system, without concluding a real transaction.

The definitions of these eight quality dimensions have been refined through face-to-face interviews with 15 online self-service users and their validity was also verified through the answers obtained to the main questionnaire survey. In the second stage of the research project, a questionnaire was applied to 250 respondents contacted in the Internet area of London and Edinburgh airports. From these, 228 respondents have answered all the questions, providing usable data. The questionnaire contained two main parts: a first one asking for information about the personal profile of the respondent (gender, age, education level, profession, frequency of using the Internet, frequency of using self-service systems), and the second part in which the respondent was asked to evaluate the importance of the eight quality dimensions, using a 5-item Likert scale (very low importance, low importance, medium importance, high importance, very high importance). Another two open-ended questions have been included at the end of the questionnaire, asking the respondents to indicate specific problems they encountered during their interaction with online self-service systems, and to provide any other comments related to this topic. The collected data was analysed using the SPSS software.

GENERAL DEMOGRAPHICS

52.2% of respondents were males and 47.8% females. In terms of age, 18% were between 18 and 25 years old, 56.1% were between 26 and 35 years, and 25.9% between 36 and 50 years old. 46.5% of respondents had a high-school education level, and 24.5% were university graduates. The professions of respondents were very diverse, 18.8% being students, 21.5% working as administrative staff, and 6.6% having a managerial function. 5.3% declared themselves profession entrepreneurs or self employed.

97 respondents (42.5%) indicated a high frequency of Internet usage (every day), 65 respondents (28.5%) could be defined as medium frequency users (3 to 5 times a week), while the remaining 66 (29%) were low frequency users (1–2 times a week). The large majority of respondents are using regularly online **self-service systems** (159 respondents, 69.7%), which means that they access online self-service applications more than three times a week, while the (69 respondents, 30.7%) rest are using these systems only occasionally (1–2 times a week).

THE IMPORTANCE OF QUALITY DIMENSIONS

The data presented in Table 1 indicate the level of importance of the eight quality dimensions considered in this study, as well as the standard deviation of the received answers.

The security of the **self-service system** was considered by respondents as the most important quality dimension. This result is logical considering the subject of this study—self-services permitting online transactions, and therefore transmission of personal data and money transfers. The capacity of the Web site to provide clear and complete information about the products/services offered, the transaction and the procedure of money transfer is also considered very important, with a mean value of 4.64.

The respondents also show a specific concern in relation with crises situations and the tools for problem solving—level of importance of 4.24. They also prefer to deal with flexible self-service system, which permit them to change their options during the transaction, without restarting the whole process—level of importance of 4.1.

Personalisation, Web page design, and the personal contact have very similar levels of importance, with medium to high importance levels, and finally, the existence of a trial/demo application was considered as the less important quality dimension, with a level of only 2.68. This result can be partially explained by the fact that many respondents were experienced users of online self-service systems, for which the trail/demo application has lost its utility. On the other hand, this low level of interest for demonstrations can be the consequence of users' tendency to use repeatedly sites that they already know. These two explanations were confirmed by the answers provided by some respondents to the open-ended questions. They indicated that they are already very familiar with these Web sites, and with the general procedural logic of **self-service systems**, and therefore, they do not consider the trial/demo application as important for them. However, they emphasised that such facility can be very useful

Table 1. The medium importance of the quality dimensions of online self-service systems

Quality dimension	Level of importance	Standard deviation
Security	4.8	0.402
Flexibility	4.1	0.55
Personalisation	3.74	1.002
Information	4.64	0.48
Tools for problem solving	4.24	0.484
Web page design	3.6	0.831
Personal contact	3.58	1.078
Trial/demo	2.68	0.942

when accessing a new self-service system, because it can significantly reduce the perceived risk of the transaction and accelerate the learning process.

The standard deviation of the answers provided by respondents for personal contact, Web site personalisation, and the availability of a trial/demo application is quite high, which might indicate the existence of various clusters of users with different preferences. These elements are explored in more detail in the following section.

THE INFLUENCE OF CUSTOMER'S PROFILE ON THE IMPORTANCE OF QUALITY DIMENSIONS

The gender of respondents seems to have a very little influence on the perceived importance of the online self-service quality dimensions (see Table 2). It is easy to see that the differences are insignificant, as they are also very close to the general values presented in Table 1.

The frequency of Internet usage has a significant influence on the perceived importance of a few quality dimensions (see Table 3). The lower the online expertise of respondents is, the higher is the importance associated to security, information, Web page design, the existence of a

trial/demo application, and especially, to the possibility to contact a person for additional advice. The impersonal nature of the Internet interaction can create a perception of high risk to the less experienced Internet users, who feel the need to be helped and supported by a customer service employee. On the other hand, the frequency of the Internet usage seems to have little influence on the need for personalisation, or for problem solving tools.

The trend is reversed for the perceived importance of flexibility and personalisation. These results can be explained by the specific demand of experienced Internet users for highly customised online interfaces and services. In their case, the difference between two sites offering the same service can be made by the level of personalisation and flexibility embedded in the Web interface.

The data presented in Table 4 show the differences between regular and occasional users in the way they perceive the importance of various quality dimensions. The level of importance associated with some dimensions is significantly influenced by the expertise of the respondent. The occasional users are much more concerned than the regular users regarding the level of information presented on the Web site (4.97 in comparison with

Table 2. The influence of gender on the perceived importance of quality dimensions

Gender/quality dimension	Males	Females
Security	4.78	4.82
Flexibility	4.11	4.09
Personalisation	3.71	3.77
Information	4.65	4.64
Tools for problem solving	4.24	4.23
Web page design	3.59	3.61
Personal contact	3.56	3.6
Trial/demo	2.7	2.66

Table 3. The influence of the online expertise of respondents on the perceived importance of quality dimensions

Frequency of Internet usage/ quality dimension	High frequency	Medium frequency	Low frequency
Security	4.75	4.77	4.89
Flexibility	4.18	4.14	3.95
Personalisation	3.8	3.71	3.68
Information	4.58	4.57	4.82
Tools for problem solving	4.27	4.22	4.21
Web page design	3.53	3.6	3.71
Personal contact	2.84	3.54	4.71
Trial/demo	2.42	2.89	2.85

4.5), the Web page design (3.93 in comparison with 3.46), the availability of a personal contact (3.78 in comparison with 3.49), and the level of security implemented by the service Web site (4.99 in comparison with 4.72). The highest difference in the perceived importance is found in relation with the trial/demo application, occasional users evaluating this dimension at 3.48, while regular users rank it as a low to medium importance (2.33).

The logical explanation of these differences is the higher level of risk perceived by the occasional users in relation with online **self-service systems**, because of their reduced transactional experience. In this situation, they are trying to find and apply strategies for risk reduction, which include elements provided by the online **self-service system**, such as the information provided by the Web site, the Web site design, the trial/demo application, and the possibility to contact an employee for additional information.

On the other hand, it is interesting to note that the differences between the two groups of users are much smaller in relation with the flexibility of the **self-service system**, and the available tools for problem solving. Unfortunately, it is difficult to explain these differences with the available data. Further qualitative research may develop a detailed profile of consumers' behaviour during their interactions with online **self-service systems**.

CONCLUDING REMARKS

The findings of this exploratory study demonstrate that the importance associated with various quality dimensions that characterised the online self-service systems is variable. This variation is introduced by the specific elements that define consumers' profile, and which influence their perceptions and online behaviour.

The gender seems to have a very small influence on the perceived importance of these quality dimensions, which means that this variable cannot be effectively used for segmenting and targeting the population of users. On the other hand, both the frequency of Internet usage and the respondents' expertise in using online self-service systems produce significant differences in the perception of quality dimensions. As a rule, the less experienced users feel more insecure in their interaction with **online self-service systems**, looking for specific elements that can support and reassure them: increased transaction security, more information, the possibility to contact a customer support service, or to use before the real transaction a trial/demo application. The companies implementing **online self-service systems** should take into account these specific requests and provide additional customer support in the first stages of the interaction. Although this strategy is difficult to apply, since the same site is accessed by customers with various levels of expertise, a possible solution is to increase the flexibility of the Web interface, and to permit an increased customisation of the service offer, that can be defined by every online user in direct relation with his/her needs, preferences, and level of expertise. This can increase significantly the level of control perceived by the customers, which, according to other authors, represents an important determinant of consumer satisfaction (Lee & Allaway, 2002; Meuter et al., 2000).

Table 4. The influence of the online self-service expertise of respondents on the perceived importance of quality dimensions

Frequency of online self-service usage/quality dimension	Regular users	Occasional users
Security	4.72	4.99
Flexibility	4.07	4.17
Personalisation	3.72	3.78
Information	4.5	4.97
Tools for problem solving	4.21	4.29
Web page design	3.46	3.93
Personal contact	3.49	3.78
Trial/demo	2.33	3.48

The findings of this study can be useful both for academics and for professionals. On one hand, the results can be used to refine the existing framework of analysis regarding online self-service systems. However, the statistical analysis of quantitative data is not enough to provide an in-depth understanding of consumers' perceptions and use of online self-service systems. This analytical approach has to be complemented with qualitative studies, in which individual case studies can be developed to illustrate the specific interaction between individuals and self-service systems.

On the other hand, these results can provide for companies important insights into the way in which the quality of online **self-service systems** is evaluated by various categories of customers, and the measure in which this evaluation will influence the user choice and behaviour. These elements are essential in the online environment, where any minor problem can encourage the customer to search for another service provider. The specific characteristics of the Internet empower the customer, who can easily search, using specialised software applications, other similar firms with more effective self-service systems.

This study has a number of limitations determined by the applied research methodology. The sample of self-service users is quite small, and the collected data had mainly a quantitative nature. The complexity of users' interactions with online **self-service systems** can hardly be fully explained through a statistical analysis of quantitative data. Future research projects should complement this approach with qualitative studies of online consumer behaviour, investigating at the same time strategic process applied by companies for the design and implementation of effective online self-service systems.

REFERENCES

Barczac, G., Ellen, P. S., & Pilling, B. K. (1997). Developing typologies of consumer motives for use of technologically based banking services. *Journal of Business Research*, *38*(2), 131–139. doi:10.1016/S0148-2963(96)00032-X

Bateson, J. (1985). Self-service consumer: An exploratory study. *Journal of Retailing*, *61*(3), 49–76.

Black, N. J., Lockett, A., Wiklofer, H., & Ennew, C. (2001). The adoption of Internet financial services: A qualitative study. *International Journal of Retail & Distribution Management*, *29*(8), 390–398. doi:10.1108/09590550110397033

Bobbitt, L. M., & Dadholkar, P. A. (2001). Integrating attitudinal theories to understand and predict use of technology-based self-service. *International Journal of Service Industry Management*, *12*(5), 423–450. doi:10.1108/EUM0000000006092

Curran, J., & Meuter, M. (2005). Self-service technology adoption: Comparing three technologies. *Journal of Services Marketing*, *19*(2), 103–113. doi:10.1108/08876040510591411

Dabholkar, P. A. (1996). Consumer evaluations of new technology-based self-service options: An investigation of alternative models of service quality. *International Journal of Research in Marketing*, *13*(1), 29–51. doi:10.1016/0167-8116(95)00027-5

Easingwood, C. J. (1986). New product development for service companies. *Journal of Product Innovation Management*, *3*(4), 264–275. doi:10.1016/0737-6782(86)90005-6

Gerrad, P., & Cunningham, J. B. (2003). The diffusion of Internet banking among Singapore consumers. *International Journal of Bank Marketing, 21*(1), 16–28. doi:10.1108/02652320310457776

Gournaris, S., & Dimitriadis, S. (2003). Assessing service quality on the Web: Evidence from business-to-consumer portals. *Journal of Services Marketing, 17*(5), 529–548. doi:10.1108/08876040310486302

Hewer, P., & Howcroft, B. (1999). Consumers distribution channel adoption and usage in the financial services industry: A review of existing approaches. *Journal of Financial Services Marketing, 3*(4), 344–358.

Holak, S. L. (1988). Determinants of innovative durable adoption: An empirical study with implications for early product screening. *Journal of Product Innovation Management, 5*(1), 50–69. doi:10.1016/0737-6782(88)90032-X

Jayanti, R. K., & Burns, A. C. (1998). The antecedents of preventative health care behavior: An empirical study. *Journal of the Academy of Marketing Science, 26*(1), 6–15. doi:10.1177/0092070398261002

Jun, M., & Cai, S. (2001). The key determinants of Internet banking service quality: A content analysis. *International Journal of Bank Marketing, 19*(7), 276–291. doi:10.1108/02652320110409825

Kotler, P., Armstrong, G., Saunders, J., & Wong, V. (2002). Introduction to marketing (2nd ed.). London: Pearsons Education, S.A.

Labay, D. G., & Kinnear, T. C. (1981). Exploring the consumer decision process in the adoption of solar energy systems. *The Journal of Consumer Research, 8*(3), 271–278. doi:10.1086/208865

Larsson, R., & Bowen, D. E. (1989). Organization and customer: Managing design and coordination of services. *Academy of Management Review, 14*(2), 213–233. doi:10.2307/258417

Lee, J., & Allaway, A. (2002). Effects of personal control on adoption of self-service technology innovations. *Journal of Services Marketing, 16*(6), 553–572. doi:10.1108/08876040210443418

Lockett, A., & Littler, D. (1997). The adoption of direct banking services. *Journal of Marketing Management, 13*, 791–811.

Loudon, D. L., & Della Bitta, A. J. (1993). Consumer behaviour: Concepts and applications (4th ed.). New York: McGraw-Hill.

Meuter, M., Ostrom, A., Roundtree, R., & Bitner, M. (2000). Self-service technologies: Understanding customer satisfaction with technology-based service encounters. *Journal of Marketing, 64*(3), 50–64. doi:10.1509/jmkg.64.3.50.18024

Meuter, M. L., Bitner, M. J., Ostrom, A. L., & Brown, S. W. (2005). Choosing among alternative service delivery modes: An investigation of customer trial of self-service technologies. *Journal of Marketing, 69*(2), 61–83. doi:10.1509/jmkg.69.2.61.60759

Meuter, M. L., Ostrom, A. L., Bitner, M. J., & Roundtree, R. I. (2003). The influence of technology anxiety on consumer use and experience with self-service technologies. *Journal of Business Research, 56*(11), 899–906. doi:10.1016/S0148-2963(01)00276-4

Ostlund, L. E. (1974). Perceived innovation attributes as predictors of innovativeness. *The Journal of Consumer Research, 1*(2), 23–29. doi:10.1086/208587

Parasuraman, A., Berry, L. L., & Zeithaml, V. A. (1988). Servqual: A multiple-item scales for measuring consumer perceptions of service quality. *Journal of Retailing, 64*(1), 12–40.

Parasuraman, A., Zeithaml, V. A., & Berry, L. L. (1985). A conceptual model of service quality and its implications for future research. *Journal of Marketing, 49*(4), 41–50. doi:10.2307/1251430

Pavlou, P. A., Liang, H., & Xue, Y. (2007). Understanding and mitigating uncertainty in online exchange relationships: A principal-agent perspective. *MIS Quarterly*, *31*(1), 105–136.

Polatoglu, V. N., & Ekin, S. (2001). An empirical investigation of the Turkish consumers' acceptance of Internet banking services. *International Journal of Bank Marketing*, *19*(4), 156–165. doi:10.1108/02652320110392527

Rogers, E. M. (1962). The diffusion of innovations. New York: The Free Press.

Rogers, E. M. (1995). The diffusion of innovations (4th ed.). New York: The Free Press.

Rotchanakitumnuai, S., & Speece, M. (2003). Barriers to Internet banking adoption: A qualitative stud among corporate customers in Thailand. *International Journal of Bank Marketing*, *21*(6/7), 312–323. doi:10.1108/02652320310498465

Schneider, B., & Bowen, D. E. (1995). Winning the service game. Boston: Harvard Business School Press.

Zeithaml, V. A., Bitner, M. J., & Gremler, D. D. (2002a). Services marketing (3rd ed.). New York: McGraw-Hill.

Zeithaml, V. A., Parasuraman, A., & Malhotra, A. (2001). *A conceptual framework for understanding e-service quality: Implications for future research and managerial practice* (MSI Working Paper Series No. 00-115, pp. 1-49). Cambridge, MA: MSI.

Zeithaml, V. A., Parasuraman, A., & Malhotra, A. (2002b). Service quality delivery through Web sites: A critical review of extant knowledge. *Journal of the Academy of Marketing Science*, *30*(4), 362–375. doi:10.1177/009207002236911

Chapter 3.24
21st Century E–Student Services

Gary R. Langer
Minnesota State Colleges and Universities, USA

STUDENT SERVICES IN THE DIGITAL AGE

Developments in information technology and distance learning are revolutionizing the way post-secondary education is organized and delivered in the United States and the world. Higher education is undergoing a fundamental transformation. How higher education transforms in the early years of the 21st century will set the context for the extent to which higher education as an institution will continue to serve as the primary deliverer of educational content, certificates, and degrees. A critical element in this knowledge transfer is the depth and breadth of online student services support. This article will explore the design and development of such services in the Minnesota State Colleges and Universities System[1] (www.mnscu.edu).

In this Knowledge Age, citizens can learn every day—anytime and anywhere. In addition to a growing student population that is not only becoming older and increasingly diverse, there is a rapid rise of a digital generation (Tapscott, 1998) that expects and demands that this learning be interactive, collaborative, distributed, and lifelong. To meet the changing needs of students and the changing nature of work and careers in the 21st century (Howell, 2003), colleges and universities need to develop and design not only appropriate emerging curriculum, but also on-demand interaction and online services (Kassop, 2003). It is not only the distance education or technology-savvy students who expect, need, and use such services, but also commuter and dormitory students. It is not about distance, but the amount of technology involved, where the learning starts, and how services are structured. Some of the characteristics of these new, digital learners are:

- Older than "average" undergraduate
- Place bound
- Broad set of responsibilities/roles
- Working in a career field
- Limited time to devote to studies
- Emerging multi-mode student
- Technology savvy
- Accustomed to service on demand

DOI: 10.4018/978-1-60566-198-8.ch319

- Expect choice and convenience
- Become the 'hardy' learner of the future (Milliron, 2001)

Online student services connect students to the institution, to the faculty, and to other students on their schedule and needs. But are all students the same, with the same needs?

Learner Segments

There is more than one learner type. Through research conducted for the Minnesota State Colleges and Universities, seven different learner segments have been identified (PricewaterhouseCoopers, 2001).

1. Corporate Learners—individuals employed in a corporate setting and seeking education to advance their careers
2. Professional Enhancement Learners—individuals seeking to advance or shift their careers
3. Degree Completion Learners—individuals seeking to complete a degree, typically older students also employed full time
4. Life Fulfillment Learners—individuals interested in education for its own sake
5. College Experience Learners—typically the traditional 18- to 24-year-old residential college student
6. Remediation and Test Preparation Learners—individuals interested in learning as a prerequisite for an examination or entrance to an educational program
7. Pre-College (K-12) Learners—individuals interested in taking post-secondary work prior to completion of high school (Figure 1)

Online, interactive services will need to be provided to each segment in an individualized and content-specific way. Current portal developments (St. Sauver, 2004) provide the customization and personal content and services all learners in this digital age expect.

A higher education e-learning system must leverage the best content created and establish a seamless gateway so that learners can access the content from any number of entry points. In the digital age, with e-learners taking control of their learning process, these relationships are simply indispensable. As these "hardy" e-learners (Milliron, 2001) control and manage more of their own information and knowledge, educational institutions must help learners do so actively and responsibly.

Figure 1. Seven learner segments

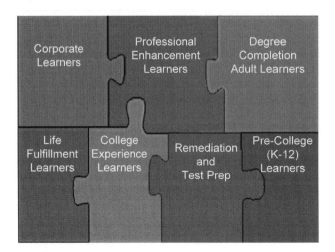

Learners need easy access to career and education information and decision-making tools through gateways or portals in order to create their seamless pathway to lifelong learning and occupational success. Critical to this process is the development of an electronic mentoring system. Since learners today are digital, they will be presenting their accomplishments, résumé, and competencies in digital formats within the context of electronic portfolios (Educause, 2004). The examination of 21st Century E-Student Services at the Minnesota State Colleges and Universities will feature online information and tools that provide access and interaction.

INFORMATION RESOURCES, TOOLS, AND REPOSITORIES

To navigate their lifelong education journey, digital learners need to have access to: a) career and education information, b) decision-making assessments and tools, and c) a personal, electronic repository or portfolio. The portfolio provides an electronic locker for relevant information and other personal documentation, such as journals, goals statements, résumés, academic history, and course/work projects, and forms the basis of an e-mentoring environment.

Career and Education Information Resources

ISEEK (www.iseek.org) is a portal in Minnesota for seamless access to career and education information. ISEEK is an acronym for Internet System for Education and Employment Knowledge and is managed through a collaboration[2] that is unique in the country. The site provides information on exploring careers (descriptions, labor market information, skill requirements, career planning process, etc.), planning your education (finding a school, program, area of study or course, admission and financial aid information, and steps to higher education), and finding a job (job application steps, search job postings, salary search, information on state and local businesses, information on job loss and transition, etc.). In addition, there is an employer section with resources to find employees and employer services, such as immigration or unemployment tax issues. There is also an interactive training fulfillment center that electronically connects counselors with other counselors, as well as employers with training providers to fulfill requested needs.

Through ISEEK, a user does not have to search different Web sites to find information, but can go to one place to learn about a career, view a video about that career, and find skill requirements and schools offering that training, along with typical salaries. By sharing information that typically is maintained in silos by the different data custodians, students from middle school through lifelong learners have a user-friendly system in which to research and find appropriate career and education information.

While ISEEK provides just Minnesota information, there is a Web site that provides national information. CareerOneStop (www.careeronestop.org) is a U.S. Department of Labor-sponsored site that provides a wealth of career and labor information at the national level as well as direct links to state-based data. The site also provides links to schools and programs throughout the country.

Many states have gateways so learners can easily find educational programs and courses that meet their needs. Such sites provide an easy way for a variety of learner types to find relevant information. For example, a student in high school might want to find an online post-secondary class because his or her high school does not offer many advanced classes, or a corporate employee may want a specific course or two for advancement, or a student may want to locate a campus that provides the major he or she is seeking.

Through iSeek Solutions (see above), Minnesota has established the Minnesota Virtual University (www.MnVU.org) to aggregate and promote online opportunities from almost all post-secondary institutions in the state.

The Minnesota State Colleges and Universities has created Minnesota Online (www.Minnesota Online.org) to showcase over 70 programs with 1,200 credit and non-credit courses. This allows a learner to take courses from a large, diverse system and combine them into a degree program.

With students taking courses when, where, and how they want, transfer is becoming an increasing issue. Minnesota has developed a powerful site, Minnesota Transfer (www.MnTransfer.org), to provide information for high school and college students and advisors and educators. There is information on transfer policies and procedures, course equivalencies, articulation agreements, and the network of transfer specialists. With the addition of CAS (see below), a more interactive system is now available for determining course transfer.

With library information becoming increasingly digital, online services are available through MnLINK (www.MnLINK.org). MnLINK provides an electronic gateway to library resources throughout the state at local public and regional libraries, K-12 libraries, public and private higher education academic libraries, and state agency libraries. Learners can locate resources at any of these sites and either access them directly or request an inter-library loan. This enables users in any part of the state to take advantage of the vast resources available collectively by all these participating library systems. Minitex (www. minitex.org) is another collaborative that leverages the buying power of a variety of library systems to efficiently purchase electronic databases.

Decision-Making Assessments and Tools

The 21st century learner needs more than just access to resources to locate information. Interactive assessments and tools can provide immediate feedback on choices, planning, and future directions.

Learners need to know where they have been and what they need to do in the future to achieve their goals. They also need to benchmark themselves against various requirements, such as degree program, skills, interest, and so forth. ISEEK and CareerOneStop contain many skill and interest inventories that can help a learner to determine if he or she is planning in the right direction. Online distance learning assessments—such as "Is distance learning for me?"[3]—are good indicators for success in Internet-based courses.

In higher education, degree audit systems are automated advising tools that not only can provide information about which courses and requirements have been completed, but what still needs to be done in order to successfully graduate. DARS (Degree Audit Reporting System of Miami University of Ohio) is a widely used system for quick, easy, and consistent interpretation of educational policies and procedures. Through Web-based degree audits, students are empowered with information and planning guides that previously were totally paper-and-pencil based and prone to misinterpretation. With DARS, students and advisors can immediately determine future courses to take and whether other requirements are met, such as minimum grade point average or residency requirements. DARS can also enable a student to do "what if" scenarios—"What if I want to change my major or change schools?"

There is now a higher level Web-based system, most often at a state level, that ties together campus-based degree audit information. CAS (Course Applicability System, also produced by Miami University of Ohio) aggregates campuses degree requirements and transfer articulation tables. Students create a list of completed courses and then can determine how these transfer to various institutions and what they need to complete that degree program. CAS can be found at www. transfer.org and has been implemented in several states including Arizona, Minnesota, Ohio, and Wisconsin.

In Fiscal Year 2003, the Minnesota State Colleges and Universities had over 5,000 students attending more than one of their institutions, and more than 100 were attending three or more institutions simultaneously. The CAS tool can greatly assist users in finding similar courses that will work in the student's home institution. This enables them to stay on track and graduate earlier. CAS is also useful for the student who attends a residential campus during the year, but returns home for the summer because CAS can list required courses from two institutions at one time. This permits the student to learn and earn while home for the summer.

Electronic Portfolio

So far, we have looked at information resource sites and tools that can assist in planning and decision making, but what should a learner do with all this data? Where can it be stored in some meaningful, organized repository (NLII, 2003)? The latest killer application is the electronic portfolio. Through such a digital repository, the learner can store demographic information, academic history, personal objectives, assessments, résumés, course and work projects, extracurricular activities, and other electronic files, including text, audio, video, and hyperlinks.

The eFolioMinnesota system is unique in that it is user controlled, rather than institution controlled, and available free to all Minnesota residents. The vision is to have a lifelong eFolio account so that K-12 students can begin their career and educational planning, continue to use this repository through middle school and high school, then continue through their two- or four-year degree and into their work life. Workers change careers many times through their lives and also continue with advanced training and education. With eFolio, they can maintain a record of their achievements.

With eFolioMinnesota, a user can maintain a site that is public, private, or password protected.

This enables the user to share specific data in his or her eFolio with an advisor (academic record or extra curricular activities), with a prospective employer (tailored résumé with work samples), or other students (collaborative class project). More information can be found in this book and at www.efoliomn.com. There is a national Electronic Portfolio Virtual Community of Practice (Educause, 2004) that provides a resource on standards and examples.

ELECTRONIC STUDENT SERVICES

In developing the new model for student services, the Minnesota State Colleges and Universities reviewed best practices for e-services and followed the seminal *Guide to Developing Online Student Services* by the Western Cooperative for Educational Telecommunications (WCET, 2000), as well as standards put forth by the accrediting bodies and other groups, such as the National Academic Advising Association. A highly effective collaboration between the Office of the Chancellor and the colleges and universities resulted in the agreement of sharing e-services campus and system responsibilities. Web-based, interactive services have focused on these key student areas:

- Information for Prospective Students
- Admissions
- Financial Aid
- Registration
- Orientation Services
- Academic Advising
- Technical Support
- Career Services
- Library Services
- Services for Students with Disabilities
- Personal Counseling
- Instructional Support and Tutoring
- Bookstore
- Services to Promote a Sense of Community

The old silos of isolated staff, and information with a hallmark of lack of communication and bureaucracy, must make way for new services for students (Shea, 2003). This will require a new delivery model that focuses on integrated systems, organizations, and processes; cross-functional teams; anytime and anyplace service; consistent information; and integrated and common interfaces.

Colleges and universities today have integrated student records systems that enable transactions to synchronize with other aspects of the business function, making it possible, for example, for prospective student demographic data to be loaded into the admissions module upon receipt of an application or for financial aid to be notified immediately if a student drops a class. The Integrated Student Records System (ISRS) is a system developed by the Minnesota State Colleges and Universities. Most of the ISRS processes have been designed for use in an in-person model, that is, a student at a window with a clerk on the other side. Now these services are being redesigned to provide anytime, online access. Oblinger (2003) finds that adult learners bring customer service expectations to education, and they want the ability to conduct their collegiate transactions in a manner similar to Capella.edu or Amazon.com. Through a system-wide Seamless Project, students will have the capability of enrolling in courses anywhere in the system, as well as receive services from those campuses. This departure from a place-bound paradigm to the virtual campus presents new opportunities for serving students, encouraging cooperation, reducing duplication, and leveraging resources.

In the evolution of Web services, there are four distinct generations of organization of information as shown in Table 1 (Burnett, 2003).

By offering Generation IV services, the student can truly have decision-making guides, personalized recommendations, proactive communications, enhanced community, and other individualized services. While it may take time for some colleges to get to this level, it is this stage of sophistication that students will expect and upon which they may make their enrollment decision.

Another view of interactivity has been presented by Hanna (2003) as represented in Figure 2. His Modes of Teaching and Learning Interactions can be adapted to student services to indicate the continuum of information and interactions from static (similar to Generation I above) to dynamic (Generation IV).

Student services Web sites may contain some or all of these generations or interactivity at one time. Through a Web audit tool developed in collaboration with WCET (*http://wcet.info/consulting/audit.asp*), campuses can determine current generation level. Through incremental approaches, they can then design and develop their Web strategy so that it can be elevated to Generation IV.

E-Mentor

A higher education e-learning system must leverage the best content created and establish a seamless gateway so that learners can access the content from any number of entry points. In the digital age, with e-learners taking control of their

Table 1. Four generations of organization of information for the Web

Generation I Institutional View What - Content Silos/departments Institutional Perspective Text	Generation II Customer View Information is Grouped by Interest Who then What - Content in Context Institutional Perspective Text
Generation III Web Portal My Home Page My Interest and My Perspective My Transactions Integration of My information	Generation IV High Touch & High Tech Text Interaction Decision Criteria How - guided step-by-step Experiences Relationships Advising

Figure 2. A model of interactivity

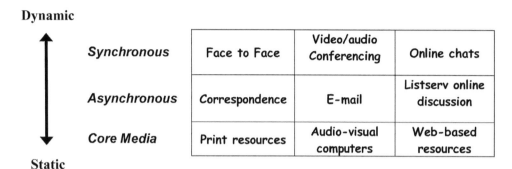

Dynamic

Synchronous	Face to Face	Video/audio Conferencing	Online chats
Asynchronous	Correspondence	E-mail	Listserv online discussion
Core Media	Print resources	Audio-visual computers	Web-based resources

Static

learning process, these relationships are simply indispensable. As e-learners control and manage more of their own information and knowledge, educational institutions must help learners do so actively and responsibly. As e-learners become more responsible knowledge and learning managers, the e-mentor is an indispensable agent providing the crucial relationship link between the learner and the institution. The e-mentor system consists of online e-services and other supportive systems.

Potentially, every learner can be connected with an e-mentor for the purpose of meeting lifelong learning needs. Currently an e-mentor is defined as an individual at an institution(s) who is designated to guide a learner in achieving his or her education or training goals. The e-mentor should be available online via the learning portal. The e-mentor will coordinate and work with the campus-based advisors, counselors, and faculty, as well as staff at workforce centers and other offices that can further the e-learner's education and training opportunities. The e-mentor then helps to identify the gap between what the learner knows and needs to know; in addition, the mentor identifies the educational resources available and those needed from a variety of entities to meet the learning need. The e-mentor helps the learner identify the delivery mode (face-to-face, online synchronous, online asynchronous), critical content, and e-learning resources that will best meet the learning need by:

- locating e-learning resources that directly meet the learner needs;
- identifying learning gaps, and locating resources and e-faculty who can help;
- developing a personal learning plan (eFolio);
- setting up an ongoing assessment and achievement plan (progress monitoring); and
- helping the learner become a responsible and active manager of his or her information and knowledge.

As e-learners become more responsible knowledge and learning managers, the e-mentor is an indispensable agent providing the crucial relationship link between the learner and the institution. The Minnesota State Colleges and Universities are in the process of establishing an e-service call center that will be the basis of an e-mentor system that includes online services and tools, including the eFolio.

CONCLUSION

The 21st century learner will have exciting opportunities never before available. Online access and highly interactive tools will aid in information gathering and decision making. Web portals that provide interactive and personalized resources will provide learners the services they need anytime, anywhere. The result will be more effective student services that assist the learner in achieving their academic and career goals.

REFERENCES

NLII Annual Review. (2003). Electronic portfolio: The digital me. *The New Academy,* 28-29.

Burnett, D. (2003, November). *Four generations. WCET Webcast.* Retrieved from http://www.wcet. info/events/Webcast/Darlene_Webcast_Nov20. pdf

Educause. (2004). *Electronic portfolio virtual community of practice.* Retrieved from http:// www.educause.edu/vcop/e_port.asp

Hanna, D. E. (2003). Building a leadership vision: Eleven strategic challenges for higher education. *EDUCAUSE Review,* (July/August): 25–34.

Howell, S. L., Williams, P. B., & Lindsay, N. K. (2003). Thirty-two trends affecting distance education: An informed foundation for strategic planning. *Online Journal of Distance Learning Administration, 6*(3), 1–17.

Kassop, M. (2003). Ten ways online education matches, or surpasses, face-to-face learning. *Technology Source,* (May/June).

Milliron, M. (2001). Touching students in the digital age: The move toward learner relationship management (CRM). *Learning Abstracts, 4*(1).

Oblinger, D. (2003). Boomers, gen-Xers & millennials: Understanding the new students. *EDUCAUSE Review,* (July/August): 37–47.

PricewaterhouseCoopers. (2001). E-Learning market analysis final report: Prepared for the Minnesota State Colleges and Universities. Internal Executive Summary Report (p. 8).

Shea, P. (2003, October). Reinventing student services in a new learning environment with few resources. *Proceedings of the WICHE Policy Forum: Weathering the Perfect Storm.* Salt Lake City, UT.

St. Sauver, J. (2004). Why are portalized university home pages rare? *Syllabus, 17*(8), 21–24.

Tapscott, D. (1998). Growing up digital. New York: McGraw-Hill.

WCET (Western Cooperative for Educational Telecommunications). (2000). *Guide to developing online student services.* Retrieved from http://www.wcet.info/resources/publications/ guide1003/guide.pdf

KEY TERMS AND DEFINITIONS

CareerOneStop: This is the federal Department of Labor's Web-based gateway to job listings, résumés, and career information nationwide.

CAS: The Course Applicability System is a Web-based planning tool for academic programs and transfer. Developed and licensed by Miami University of Ohio.

DARS: The Degree Audit Reporting System for electronic advising through a match of degree requirements with a student's completed courses that includes transfer articulation of course equivalencies. Developed and licensed by Miami University of Ohio.

eFolio: This is a term that is an abbreviation for an electronic portfolio; it is part of the brand name for the system developed by Avenet, LCC, and the Minnesota State Colleges and Universities: eFolioMinnesota.

E-Learners: These are students who take advantage of learning that is usually Internet-based learning, but could be any electronically enhanced learning; e-learners are technology savvy, motivated, and self-directed.

E-Mentor: A term for an online guide, system, or person that provides information, resources, assistance, and direction for learners.

ISEEK: An acronym for the Internet System for Education and Employment Knowledge system, a comprehensive online tool of information and resources on careers, jobs, education programs, and providers; developed by a collaboration of Minnesota agencies and institutions.

Learner Segments: The different populations of students that utilize post-secondary education and training opportunities for their own unique needs. Seven segments were identified for the Minnesota State Colleges and Universities system by research by PricewaterhouseCoopers.

MnLINK: MnLINK is the Minnesota Library Information Network, a statewide virtual library that electronically links major Minnesota libraries.

MnTransfer: This is a Web-based system that provides transfer information, articulation agreements, transfer specialist contacts, and course equivalency tables for Minnesota institutions.

ENDNOTES

[1] The Minnesota State Colleges and Universities are strategically positioned to provide a national forum for the education in the digital age. Leading the country with a unique administrative merger, the 32-institution system offers the full continuum of educational opportunities from technical to community college to university and graduate education.

[2] ISEEK is operated collaboratively through a unique Joint Powers Agreement called iSeek Solutions by these organizations: Department of Administration (Office of Technology), Department of Education, Department of Employment and Economic Development, Governor's Workforce Development Council, Higher Education Services Office, Minnesota Private College Council, Minnesota State Colleges and Universities, and University of Minnesota.

[3] MnVU uses an adaptation of a questionnaire developed by the Extended Learning Institute of Northern Virginia Community College; see www.mnvu.org/mnvu/5102.jsp.

This work was previously published in the Encyclopedia of Distance Learning, Second Edition, edited by P. Rogers; G. Berg; J. Boettcher; C. Howard; L. Justice; K. Schenk, pp. 2160-2167, copyright 2009 by IGI Publishing (an imprint of IGI Global).

Section IV
Utilization and Application

This section introduces and discusses the utilization and application of electronic services around the world. These particular selections highlight, among other topics, electronic services in countries including Thailand, Greece, Denmark and Jordan; e-banking solutions; and electronic education and student support services. Contributions included in this section provide excellent coverage of the impact of information resources management on the fabric of our present-day global village.

Chapter 4.1
The Measurement of Electronic Service Quality:
Improvements and Application

Grégory Bressolles
BEM–Bordeaux Management School, France

Jacques Nantel
HEC Montréal, Canada

ABSTRACT

Several measurement scales have been designed by both practitioners and researchers to evaluate perceptions of electronic service Quality. This chapter tests three of the main academically developed scales: Sitequal (Yoo & Donthu, 2001), Webqual 4 (Barnes & Vidgen, 2003) and EtailQ (Wolfinbarger & Gilly, 2003) and compares them against the scale ensuing from our research: NetQual (Bressolles, 2006). Based on 204 evaluations of consumers that participated in a laboratory experiment involving two Canadian Websites in travel and online insurance, NetQual best fits the data and offers the highest explanatory power. Then the impact of nature of task and success or failure to complete the task on the evaluation process of electronic service quality and attitude toward the site is examined and discussed on over 700 respondents that navigated on six different Websites.

DOI: 10.4018/978-1-60566-910-6.ch019

INTRODUCTION

A relatively recent form of commerce, electronic commerce is increasingly becoming routine. Despite recent years' turbulence, electronic commerce is on the rise in Canadian commercial landscape. Representing a sales volume of $4.7 billion, about 1.3% of Canadian retail sales, e-commerce is becoming an indispensable tool for retailers Statistics. In total, 67% of Canadian households use the Internet (eMarketer 2005). While only 18.4% of consumers that use the Internet claim to purchase products on the Web, 56% of Web users report using this medium to obtain product information before purchasing it at a brick-and-mortar store. The systematic increase of Internet integration in consumers' decision making processes has created a strong impetus for retailers to go online. In 2005, 34% of Canadian retailers had a Website and 11.4% sold products on the Web. The proportions at finance and insurance sectors were 43% and 8%, respectively, compared with 51% and 14% for that of arts and culture. While both transactional and informational commercial activity on the Web is growing, studies did not find sites directed at consumers to always meet expectations.

A study by the e-tailing group[1] found that only 3% of consumers who visit a site to complete a purchase; more than 47% of consumers abandon their order before checking out (cart abandonment). Partly explained by Internet anonymity, such statistics could be also explained by the fact that many sites do not meet consumers' needs or poorly tailor their decision-making processes. One could argue that having an online presence and posting low prices seemed to be sufficient to succeed; neither of these conditions, however, does guarantee service quality. Inevitably, certain quality issues have appeared, such as the inability to carry out online transaction, non-compliance with delivery time, undelivered products, unanswered emails, and inaccessible or inadequate information. As at a brick-and-mortar store, the service quality of a commercial Website plays a vital role in its survival. Internet sales have particular characteristics that differentiate them from traditional sales. For these reasons, measurement instruments have been developed by practitioners and researchers to evaluate service quality in e-commerce.

While literature on service quality includes articles that compare various scales across different contexts such as health, arts, professional services, and retail stores, it do not offer any study that offer a comparison of Web-oriented scales. Results observed in tangible situations, where interpersonal contact is a key, can not be taken for granted in a virtual context (Bitner, Brown & Meuter, 2000; Dabholkar, 2000; Parasuraman & Grewal 2000). For instance, Parasuraman & Grewal (2000) posit that online and offline environments are sufficiently different to justify the development of scales specifically dedicated to the measurement of electronic service quality. Even when the same product or service was purchased, online and offline environments present different shopping experiences. Consequently, such measurement instruments of service quality became a necessity.

This article starts by defining the concept of electronic service quality, and compares it with the traditional one. Given the abundance of measures of electronic service quality put forth by practitioners and researchers, we then selected to test three of the main academically developed scales: Sitequal (Yoo & Donthu, 2001), Webqual 4 (Barnes & Vidgen, 2003) and EtailQ (Wolfinbarger & Gilly, 2003) and to compare them against the scale ensuing from our research, NetQual (Bressolles, 2006). Based on 204 evaluations of consumers who participated in a laboratory experiment that involved two Canadian Websites (travel and online insurance), we intend to determine the most relevant scale in terms of content, parsimony and explanatory power in an e-commerce context. Then we explore the impact of task nature and success or failure to complete a specific task on the electronic service quality evaluation. The link between electronic service quality and attitude toward site is studied. Discussion of limitations and future research avenues conclude the paper.

THEORETICAL BACKGROUND OF ELECTRONIC SERVICE QUALITY

Definition, Similarities and Differences with Traditional Service Quality

Whereas dimensions, variables, and other aspects of traditional service quality have received extensive study over the past two decades, the study of electronic service quality is a relatively new domain. While traditional service quality was defined as an overall evaluation or an attitude relative to the superiority of the service (Parasuraman, Zeithaml & Berry, 1988), electronic service quality were considered as "the extent to which a Web site facilitates efficient and effective shopping, purchasing, and delivery of products and services." (Zeithaml, Parasuraman & Malhotra, 2002, p.363). This transactional quality entails the evaluation of the pre- and post-service experience. Based on the last definition, we can draw a parallel with traditional service quality to elucidate the similarities and differences between these two concepts.

One of the most important and arguably one of the most evident differences between traditional service quality and electronic service quality is the replacement of interpersonal interaction with human-machine interaction. This distinction raises many questions concerning the types of dimensions that can or must be considered when assessing service quality in the e-commerce context. Online commerce specific characteristics render direct application of service quality dimensions developed in other environments inappropriate; at best, these dimensions fail to capture all of the subtleties of the evaluation of service quality of commercial Websites. The classic dimensions of traditional service quality are tangible elements, reliability, reactivity, assurance and empathy of service provider (Parasuraman, Zeithaml & Berry, 1988).

To date, no consensus exists regarding electronic service quality dimensions. Although largely anecdotal, dimensions proposed recur fairly systematically as security/privacy, Website design, ease of use, reliability and the quality of the information contained in the site. Moreover, positive feelings such as warmth and attachment expressed for traditional services are not present in the perception of electronic service quality; whereas negative feelings such as anger, irritation, and frustration are apparently less intense or noticeable on the Internet than that expressed during problems encountered with traditional services (Parasuraman, Zeithaml & Malhotra, 2002). On the other hand, if classic evaluations of traditional service quality were based on measuring the gap between expectations and perceptions, it is difficult to apply such a model to the electronic service

quality measurement where respondents find it hard to formulate their expectations. Therefore, a direct measure of the perceptions of electronic service quality after delivering the service seems practical.

Methods of Measuring Electronic Service Quality

As offline, there are different methods to measure a Website quality (Cunliffe 2000); however, methods could be grouped under two broad categories:

- **Behavioural measures**. Behaviour measures focus on the measurement of commercial activity of the site; that is number of clicks, number of unique visitors or conversion rate of new visitors (Totty, 2003) and analysis of log files (Lynch & Ariely, 2000; Johnson *et al.*, 2004). Albeit useful, the previous measures do not capture consumer's cognitive and attitudinal evaluations of the site and are limited to analyzing apparent behaviors on the Internet.
- **Attitudinal measures**. These are based often on traditional measurement scales that evaluate consumers' perceptions or reflect these perceptions by soliciting expert opinions; nonetheless, attitudinal measures developed to date have some limitations. First, they do not evince the structure of perceived electronic service quality dimensions; for example, Madu & Madu (2002) listed multiple characteristics of a Website without specifying relations between these characteristics. Moreover, the measures examine the performance of Websites in general rather online commerce sites in particular (e.g. Hoffman & Novak, 1996). Hence there might be a lack of generalizability to purchasing behaviours on commercial Websites because these measures neglect attributes related to purchasing such

as order placing, financial security, respect for privacy, payment modes, delivery, etc. Finally, psychometric properties have not been consistently established and verified, particularly the one- or multi-dimensional nature of measures used. Two approaches fall into this category. The first is generally based on expert evaluations or interstitial surveys and is more common among practitioners. The second is more grounded in psychometric theory and, therefore, more prevalent among scholars.

Measurement of Electronic Service Quality by Practitioners

Practitioners have adopted various approaches to measure quality or efficacy of commercial Websites. Approaches ranges between questioning consumers after completing the purchase (bizrate.com, directpanel.com) and evaluating sites by professional experts (gomez.com). Despite the diversity of approaches applied, none of the initiatives taken alone does encompass the entire online transaction, from information search to order placing, problems with delivery and after-sale service. While they help forming the picture of important attributes of online shopping, neither practitioners' studies aid at constructs conceptualization nor they validate or check reliability of the utilized measures. To fill this gap and to better understand what consumers want during the online purchasing experience, scholars of marketing and computer science have both attempted to develop valid instruments to measure electronic service quality.

Measurement of Electronic Service Quality by Scholars

Four of the principal studies that examine the measurement of perceptions of electronic service quality reported in the academic literature have been retained for this study to determine which scale is best suited to measuring the perceptions of electronic service quality and to study the impact of scale dimensions on attitude toward the site assessment.

- **Webqual** (Barnes & Vidgen, 2003). This scale was developed based on an iterative process involving application in diverse domains such as online bookstores and auction sites. The authors identified three dimensions (a) usability of the site refers to pragmatic elements such as the way the consumer perceives and interacts with the site. Associated with the site design, these qualities include appearance, ease of navigation and image projected, (b) quality of information refers to quality of content offered on the site defined as precise pertinent information that users consider well formatted, and (c) quality of interaction refers to the quality of service interaction the users receive on the site; this includes elements of trust and empathy or more precisely information and transaction security, product delivery, personalization and communication with service provider. Webqual did not consider the entire online purchasing process because "all questions can be completed without having performed the full purchasing process" (Barnes & Vidgen, 2003, p.124). While this approach provides insight into users' perceptions, it does not take into account all aspects of the online service life cycle - navigation, selection, ordering, payment, delivery, and customer service. Therefore, Webqual can not be said to measure all the perceptions of electronic service quality because some service experience aspects are neglected. The use of students in the study to evaluate perceptions of electronic service quality is also questionable. While students might be considered frequent users of the Internet and books buyers, it would be more adequate to examine a sample of clients that have had several service experiences at the site concerned.

- **eTailQ** (Wolfinbarger & Gilly, 2003). The methodology behind this scale construction is online and offline focus groups, along with a classification task and an online survey of a panel of consumers. It includes four factors (a) site design that includes navigation, search for information, product selection, order process, and personalization, (b) customer service including online assistance, response to customers' emails, ease of returning items, empathy, and reactivity, (c) reliability/respect for commitments refers to adequate description, presentation, and delivery of products or services ordered at the promised quality level, and (d) security/privacy reflected by security of payments and confidentiality of personal data. The sample used at the study was not random, but rather comprised regular online purchasers; therefore it is deemed poorly representative of the overall population of cyber-consumers. In addition, evaluations obtained do not pertain to particular one or two sites, but rather to general evaluations of electronic service quality perceptions.
- **Sitequal** (Yoo & Donthu, 2001): The final version of this scale has nine items reflecting 4 dimensions (a) ease of use and capacity to obtain information, (b) design and creativity of site with multimedia content and colors, (c) speed of the order process and reactivity to consumers' requests, and (d) security of financial and personal information. The authors focused exclusively on the elements of Website experience and did not empirically verify results on a sample of cyber-users; they also used a sample of students where each student navigated three different sites.

- **NetQual** (Bressolles, 2006). The final scale tested in this study includes 18 items (see Appendix I for a list of items) distributed along 5 dimensions (a) quality and quantity of information available, (b) ease of site use, (c) design or aesthetic aspect of the site, (d) reliability or respect for commitment, (e) security/privacy of personal and financial data. The dimensions retained refer to the functional characteristics of both the site and transaction. Following a series of semi-structured interviews, the scale was developed and refined on a sample of over 1,200 online consumers who were customers of five commercial Websites representing different online sales sectors - travel, insurance, digital products and energy.

A fifth scale, the *E .S. Qual* proposed by Parasuraman et al. (2005) initially considered in this study, was not retained for further analysis. Unlike other scales, the *E .S. Qual* does not focus on the quality of the site *per se* but rather on quality of the e-services inherent in navigation, such as logistics, possibility to speak with someone, etc... Because present article proposes an optimal way to measure the quality of a Website, we decided to limit analyses to major scales proposed to measure consumers' evaluations of Websites. While scales identified above exhibit similarities in content or dimensions, each has distinctive features (table 1).

METHOD

A series of studies was conducted in concert with six Canadian companies that each has an e- commerce site. The studies were conducted on over 700 consumers between the months of July 2004 and May 2005. The companies evaluated were (a) Destina.ca, a travel site owned by Air Canada, (b) ING/Bélair Direct, a well-known Canadian

Table 1. Summary of the principal measurement scales for electronic service quality

Scale	Author	Number of items	Dimensions	Dependent variables	Sample
Sitequal	Yoo and Donthu (2001)	9	- Ease of use - Aesthetic design - Processing speed - Security	- Attitude toward site - Site loyalty - Site equity - Purchase intention - Site revisit intention - Site quality	94 students who visit and interact with 3 sales Websites online
Webqual (4)	Barnes and Vidgen (2003)	22	- Usability - Information - Interaction	-	380 questionnaires on three online bookshop Websites evaluations by students
eTailQ	Wolfinbarger and Gilly (2003)	14	- Website design - Fulfillment/reliability - Security/Privacy - Customer service	- Satisfaction - Attitude toward site - Loyalty intentions - Global quality	Online survey of 1013 customer members of a panel
NetQual	Bressolles (2006)	18	- Information - Ease of use - Reliability/fulfillment - Site design - Security/privacy	- Overall quality - Satisfaction - Attitude toward site	855 customers of 2 commercial Websites (travel and electronic goods)
e-S-Qual **e-RecS-Qual**	Parasuraman, Zeithaml and Malhotra (2005)	22 11	- Efficiency - Fulfillment - System availability - Privacy - Responsiveness - Compensation - Contact	- Perceived value - Loyalty intentions	Respondents who have carried out at least 3 online purchases over the previous 3 months on amazon.com (650 people) or wal-mart.com (253 people)

in automobile insurance, (c) Hydro-Québec, the largest Canadian energy provider and exporter, (d) Radio-Canada, the Website of the Canadian French-speaking official public television station, (e) the National Archives of Canada, and (f) Revenu Québec, the official Website of information, services, and applications that help promote compliance with Quebec province tax and regulations in Canada.

The same procedure was used for each of the sites studied. In each case, over 100 consumers were recruited via a hyperlink placed on the site. This procedure was mainly intended to recruit actual consumers that have at least minimal experience with both the Web and the site in question. Consumer who showed an interest in our research program by registering and providing their contact information were then invited to participate at a laboratory navigation session. At this session, each participant was to perform an individual task with an average duration of one hour. Participants were offered $50 for their participation in the study. During navigation and throughout the experiment, participants were told to verbalize out loud every thought that go through their minds, regarding difficulties encountered, surprising aspects of site, or a simple description of what they are doing. Known as protocol analysis, this approach is grounded in the work of Simon (1956) and Ericsson & Simon (1993) and proved to be very useful for Website analysis (Senecal, Gharbi & Nantel, 2002; Benbunan-Fich, 2001; Li & Biocca, 2001). In each of the four studies, i.e. one study for each scale, the experiment was supervised by a project manager. Data were collected in four of the following distinct steps.

Step 1: Warm-Up Task

After the welcome and a brief description of the assigned tasks, participants were invited to go to a general portal in order to read their horoscope. They were then asked to consult the movie listings on the site to find a film. This task was very important to enable the participants get familiar with navigation and with the method, i.e. verbalizing aloud thoughts and actions. The warm-up task ended when the participants finished the tasks, i.e. reading the horoscope and selecting a film on the site.

Step 2: Experimental Task

Each participant was informed of the task that they were to perform. Table 2 shows the required task that corresponds to the Website studied. Although the task was prescribed, participants were told of their ability to interrupt the navigation at any time, for any reason. Ongoing concurrent verbalization was, however, a requirement throughout the navigation process. For each task, navigation data were recorded in video and sound sequence, i.e. AVI format, using CAMTASIA software.

Step 3: The Questionnaire

After completing navigation, participants were asked to complete an online evaluation questionnaire that included items from the four electronic

Table 2. A listing of each site's experimental task

Site	Task
Destina	Reservation and purchase of a trip for the holiday period
ING direct	Purchase of an automobile insurance policy
Hydro-Québec	Enrolling for direct payment mode
Radio Canada	Finding information on the site
National Archives	
Revenu Québec	

service quality scales under study. The questionnaire responses were saved and updated online. The questionnaire, comprising seven point Likert-type scaling, was intended to measure participants' site perceptions, i.e. electronic service quality, attitude toward site, etc....The questionnaire also included a series of sociodemographic-oriented questions.

Step 4: The Interview

In the final step, participants were interviewed for ten minutes by the project manager with regard to completion of the experimental task and general site evaluation. This semi-structured interview consisted of three sections: (a) completion of the task, (b) general site evaluation, and (c) a series of specific questions regarding the appearance of the site under study. The interview was recorded in audio format using MP3 recording software.

RESULTS

A Comparison of Four Electronic Service Quality Measurement Scales

To determine which of the four scales selected (Webqual 4, Sitequal, EtailQ and NetQual) best reflects electronic service quality perceptions, the data gathered by the online questionnaire from 204 consumers that visited the two first partner sites of the study, travel and online insurance, were analyzed. Scales were compared to determine reliability, quality of fit and explanatory power. To verify reliability for each dimensions of scales compared, Cronbach's alpha coefficients and Jöreskog's Rhô were calculated. Table 3 summarizes findings with regard to both of the previous measures for each scale.

All coefficients obtained satisfy the criteria that Nunnally (1978) recommended for confirmatory research, over .80 for established or over .70 for new measures. The internal reliability of the

Table 3. Internal reliability of measures, Cronbach's alpha and Rhô coefficients

Webqual	α	ρ	Sitequal	α	ρ	EtailQ	α	ρ	NetQual	α	ρ
Usability	.93	.93	Ease of use	.94	.94	Website design	.83	.81	Information	.93	.92
Information	.93	.93	Aesthetic design	.79	.86	Customer service	.80	.80	Ease of use	.95	.95
Interaction	.81	.81	Processing Speed	.63	.64	Fulfilment/ reliability	.77	.70	Site design	.90	.90
			Security	.85	.85	Security/ Privacy	.89	.87	Security/ Privacy	.86	.85

dimensions for each scale is thus verified. The only dimension with a low reliability coefficient was Sitequal's "Processing speed" (Yoo & Donthu, 2001). This is probably the case because the previous scale dimension is composed of only two items with relatively low correlation, i.e. 0.46.

Confirmatory factor analysis (C.F.A.) using EQS 6 software (Bentler & Wu, 2002) were performed on each of the four scales to check fit with collected data and to determine the scale that best fit the data. Appendix 2 presents the C.F.A. results for the four scales tested. The 'Reliability' dimension of the NetQual scale, which refers to the precision and speed of delivery and after-sale service quality, was not taken into account because this dimension was not applicable to the experiment nature, specifically for the information task. Main fit indices, i.e. absolute, incremental, and parsimony, were calculated to verify the quality of measures fit and are provided in Table 4. The indices GFI, AGFI of Joreskog, NFI and NNFI of Bentler and Bonnet, and CFI of Bentler should be close to 0.95 and greater if possible. As for

the RMSEA of Steiger, it is recommended that a score less than 0.05 be obtained to be acceptable (Hu and Bentler 1998). Appendix 3 presents the definition of the different fit indices retained for comparing the four scales.

While the four scales fit the data well, NetQual could be said to present the best fit index. Specifically, its RMSEA was the lowest (.084). The parsimony indices of NetQual are also lower than those of the other three scales; one should notice that this scale contains 18 items distributed along four dimensions. The other indices, the absolute and the incremental, are higher than those of the other scales, particularly Webqual and EtailQ. However, direct comparison of indices among the four scales is not indicative because scales do not use the same model, i.e. they are not nested models; the conclusion one can draw is that given the commonly accepted criteria, NetQual could be said to best fits the data.

To verify the superiority of NetQual over the three other scales, the means of the R^2 coefficients, based on standardized solution, were calculated.

Table 4. Fit indices of each of the four scales

	Parsimony indices		Absolute indices			Incremental indices	
	AIC	Chi² / df	RMSEA	GFI	AGFI	NFI	NNFI
Sitequal	9,66	51,66 / 21 = 2,46	.085 [.056; .114]	.94	.87	.95	.94
Webqual	15,98	531,38 / 186 = 2,85	.096 [.086; .105]	.75	.69	.83	.87
EtailQ	93,50	235,50 / 71= 3,32	.113 [.103; .123]	.85	.78	.86	.87
NetQual	36,19	175,68/72= 2,44	.084 [.07; .09]	.90	.90	.93	.94

Table 5. Explanatory power of each scale

Mean of R^2			
Sitequal	Webqual	EtailQ	NetQual
.67	.58	.57	**.73**

The mean provides an indication of the explanatory power of the scale and is identical to the R^2 coefficient of the regression multiple determination. Results are presented in Table 5.

Based on these results, we can conclude that NetQual is superior to the three other scales considered, Webqual 4, Sitequal, and EtailQ, in predicting electronic service quality perceptions because it best fits the data and posses the highest explanatory power. To further assess the qualities of NetQual, we want to try to determine whether the nature of the task performed by a consumer, i.e. transactional versus informational, has any impact on site evaluation. In addition, the potential of NetQual to predict the overall site performance (Chen & Wells, 1999) was evaluated.

Impact of Nature of the Task on the Evaluation Process of Electronic Service Quality and Attitude toward the Site

In order to determine the impact of the nature of the task on the evaluation process of electronic service quality and attitude toward the site, over 700 respondents on six Websites completed an online questionnaire after performing a specific task (see table 2). The questionnaire measures electronic service quality using the NetQual scale and attitude toward the site (Chen & Wells 1999). According to Chen & Wells (1999), attitude toward the site (ATS) could be considered to represent the predisposition of Internet users to respond favourably or unfavourable to a Website during a situation of particular exposure. This global measure of site evaluation includes measures concerning the capacity of the site to create a relationship with the consumer, intention to revisit the site, satisfaction with service, comfort with navigation, and the judgement about the fact that surfing the site is a good way to spend time. Although the measure of attitude toward the site is reliable, Chen & Wells (1999) conceded that it cannot supply a complete picture of consumers' judgements related to their online purchasing experience.

Second order confirmatory factor analysis was performed on a global sample of 704 observations on 6 sites to determine the fit of the model. The conditions to create a second order factor for electronic service quality were met. First, theoretical foundations are with favour to this decision, given that electronic service quality is a multidimensional construct. Second, first order dimensions are sufficiently correlated to justify the creation of a second order factor that would demonstrate construct convergent validity (Chin, 1998). Based on first order factor analysis, correlation between dimensions varies from 0.30 to 0.57. Third, to prove the importance of each dimension in the second order construct, when the second order factor is created, regression coefficients with each of the dimensions should be high. According to Hair et al. (1998), these regression coefficients should be greater than 0.50. In our case, regression coefficients varied from 0.587 for the 'security/privacy' dimension to 0.881 for the 'information' dimension. Table 6 demonstrates that fit indices of model are satisfactory.

The contribution of electronic service quality to the different dimensions, and its impact on attitude toward the site, were then further measured by differentiating the sites on which Internet users had to perform a transactional task, i.e. Destina, ING, and Hydro-Quebec, or an informational task, i.e. National Archives, Radio Canada, and Revenu Québec. We posit that the nature of the task, whether transactional or informational, influences the evaluation process of electronic service quality. To test this hypothesis, multi-group confirmatory factor analysis was performed. Both the results and the fit of the global model presented in Table 7 were found satisfactory.

Table 6. Fit of the model for the global sample

χ^2	GFI	AGFI	RMSEA [interval] (90%)	SRMR	NFI	NNFI	CFI	χ^2/df	AIC (AICo)
630,44	.90	.90	.56 [.045; .062]	.060	.91	.92	.93	630,44/146 = 4,3	338,44 (6595,72)

Table 7. Fit indices of a second order multi-group model

χ^2	GFI	AGFI	RMSEA [interval] (90%)	SRMR	NFI	NNFI	CFI	χ^2/df	AIC (AICo)
824,47	.90	.90	.061 [.056; .066]	.075	.90	.91	.94	824,47/292 = 2,82	240,47 (6257,93)

Before extending the analysis, we determined whether any variations observed between the two sub-samples, transactional versus informational task, were statistically significant. To achieve this, a χ^2 test was performed between a model where the parameters are constrained to be equal between the two groups and a model where the parameters are freed. This test was significant at the .00 level (χ^2 constrained - χ^2 free = 843.61 – 824.47 = 19.14 [df = 298 – 292 = 6]). This result confirms that any differences between the two sub-samples are statistically significant and not simply due to chance.

Several results can be inferred from Table 8. First, it appears that regardless of the nature of the task, i.e. transactional versus informational, the impact of service quality on attitude toward the site is relatively strong (factor contribution > 0.90). Moreover, the global model has good predictive power (mean R^2 > 0.65 for the two sub-samples). NetQual therefore seems to be a good measure to predict perceptions of electronic service quality and their impact on attitude toward the site. Lastly, NetQual four dimensions (Information, Ease of use, Design and Security/Privacy) contribute, in varying degrees according to nature of task, to the formation of second order judgement of electronic service quality. The 'Reliability' dimension of the NetQual scale, which refers to the precision and speed of delivery and after-sale service quality, was not included in this analysis because this dimension was not applicable to the experiment nature, specifically the information task.

The weight of each of NetQual dimensions can be further clarified according to nature of task performed on the site. Consumers that performed a transactional task on the site (57%) placed more importance on the quality and quantity of information presented (factor contribution of the 'Information' dimension is 0.809), along with the design of the Website (0.734) and the security of personal and financial data (0.635). The transactional nature of

Table 8. Factor contributions of NetQual dimensions and their impact on attitude toward the site by type of task

	NetQual → Information	NetQual → Ease of use	NetQual → Design	NetQual → Security/ Privacy	NetQual → ATS	mean R^2
Transactional task	.809	.716	.734	.635	.987	.716
Informational task	.730	.831	.487	.398	.959	.652

the task users were asked to perform, along with the intangible orientation of the goods sold on the site (trips, insurance and electricity) might explain the relative importance of pervious dimensions. Inversely, for users that were asked to perform an informational task (43%), ease of use appeared to be the most important dimension (0.831). ease of navigation and information on the site are apparently prerequisites for task completion.

The evaluation process of electronic service quality varies according to the type of task performed on the site. Internet users that consult a site to find information place greater importance on ease of use of the site, whereas consumers that want to perform a transaction focus on information presented, both textual and visual, along with the security aspect of the purchase.

Impact of Completion of the Task on Attitude toward the Site and the Evaluation Process of Electronic Service Quality

To extend this analysis, we studied the impact of the respondent's ability to successfully complete the specified task on the evaluation process of the service quality of the site. We postulate that individuals that failed to complete the task will evaluate service quality more poorly than participants that successfully completed the task. To achieve this, a confirmatory multi-group factor analysis was performed for over 400 respondents that navigated four of the six sites previously studied; Responses concerning the Radio-Canada and National Archives sites were disregarded because the percentages of successful completion of task were very high and would result in a bias

to the analysis. To determine whether any variations observed between the two sub-samples, i.e. success or failure, are statistically significant, a χ^2 test was performed between a model at which parameters were constrained to be equal between the two groups and a model at which the parameters were freed. Test result was significant at .00 (χ^2 constrained - χ^2 free = 773.23 – 754.75 = 18.48 [df = 297 – 292 = 5]), showing that any differences observed between the two sub-samples are statistically significant and not simply due to chance. The fit indices of the global model were satisfactory and are included in Table 9.

The contributions of electronic service quality to different dimensions, along with service quality impact on attitude toward site when the task was completed or not are illustrated in Table 10. These contributions do not seem to vary sharply between individuals that completed the designated task (49%) and those that did not (51%). Regardless of the outcome of navigation, electronic service quality had a strong positive impact on attitude toward the site. In descending order of importance, dimensions in evaluation of electronic service quality are: information, ease of use, design, security/privacy, and whether the individual had completed the task. This result is not surprising and it affirms the structural stability of the NetQual scale.

Even though scale structure is stable regardless of whether the task was completed or not, a significant difference exist in dimensions' mean scores between individuals that successfully completed the task and those that did not. Individuals that completed the task tend to evaluate the site more positively (mean = 4.888) than individuals that did not successfully complete the task (mean =

Table 9. Fit indices of the second order multi-group model

χ^2	GFI	AGFI	RMSEA [interval] (90%)	SRMR	NFI	NNFI	CFI	χ^2/df	AIC (AICo)
754,75	.89	.89	.060 [.054; .065]	.067	.90	.91	.93	754,75/292 = 2,58	170,75 (5694,78)

Table 10. Factor contributions of NetQual dimensions and their impact on attitude toward the site according to whether the task was completed

	NetQual → Information	NetQual → Ease of use	NetQual → Design	NetQual → Security/ Privacy	NetQual → ATS	mean R^2
Success	.739	.765	.675	.498	.990	0.696
Failure	.801	.763	.710	.595	.971	0.704

4.391). This difference is significant at the .00 level (t = 4.723). This applies to each scale dimensions. Table 11 summarizes the results test of equality of means for each NetQual' scale dimensions. Notably, the differences in means were higher for the "Information" (mean $_{success}$ -mean $_{failure}$ = .837) and "Security/Privacy" (mean $_{success}$ - mean $_{failure}$ = .728) dimensions, suggesting an important role for information and security/privacy on task completion.

CONCLUSION, LIMITS AND RESEARCH AVENUES

This article provides an empirical test for four academically developed scales that measure electronic service quality: Sitequal (Yoo & Donthu, 2001), Webqual 4 (Barnes & Vidgen, 2003) EtailQ (Wolfinbarger & Gilly, 2003), and NetQual (Bressolles, 2006). The results educe the relative superiority of the scale developed as part of our research, NetQual, over the other three scales considered at measuring perceptions of electronic service quality. NetQual best fits the data and exhibits the strongest

explanatory power; in addition, the scale has an apparent positive, significant impact on attitude toward site, regardless of the nature of the task performed, i.e. transactional versus informational, or task outcome, i.e. success or failure.

Results demonstrate that the contributions of service quality to different dimensions vary according to the type of task performed on the site. Individuals that performed a transactional task considered information presented on the site, i.e. textual and visual, along with the security/privacy aspect of the transaction to be of particular importance; on the other hand, individuals that completed an informational task placed more importance on site ease of use.

Regarding the impact of task completion on electronic service quality evaluation, success or failure to complete a task has no real impact on NetQual structure; contributions of service quality to each dimension were similar in both situations. Nevertheless, significant difference existed regarding evaluation. Respondents that did not successfully complete the task evaluate each dimension of service quality more poorly than those who successfully completed the task. Re-

Table 11. t-test of equality of means for dimensions of electronic service quality according to whether the task was completed

Dimension	Success	Failure	t-Student	Sig.
Information	5,475 (n = 234)	4,638 (n = 252)	6,412	.000
Ease of use	4,424 (n = 244)	4,155 (n = 258)	1,990	.000
Design	4,650 (n = 243)	4,189 (n = 257)	3,871	.000
Security/Privacy	5,470 (n = 222)	4,742 (n = 242)	5,318	.000
NetQual	4,888 (n = 218)	4,391 (n = 240)	4,723	.000

spondents' inability to complete the task, therefore, could be said to manifest itself in overall evaluation of site quality by affecting each dimension.

This study has a number of limitations that represent research avenues. To validate results, research should replicate findings on various commercial Websites, particularly e-commerce sites. Notably sites considered in this research exclusively offer services, i.e. travel, insurance, electricity, information, etc... The 'reliability' dimension of the scale which pertains to precision, speed of delivery, and after-sale service among other elements was thus removed. In addition, investigating the quality of electronic service in different cultural consumption contexts (Tsikriktsis 2002) is an interesting research area. Research should attempt to understand the impact of nature of task performed on the site, and its success or failure outcome on electronic service quality evaluation.

Rigorous attention must be paid to the nomological validity of the concept of service quality delivered by commercial Websites. This implies attentive examination of both antecedents and consequences of service quality. Antecedents of electronic service quality refer to concrete elements such as specific characteristics of design, possibility of ordering in a limited number of clicks, logos, and other signs of reassurance among other factors. Consumer perceptions of these attributes shape evaluation of service quality on a site. However, the consequences of electronic service quality have not been adequately studied and conceptualized. Such consequences would probably include both intentions, i.e. to revisit the site, to repurchase, along with actual behaviour, i.e. positive word-of-mouth, purchase volume, etc. (Yoo & Donthu 2001; Swinder *et al.* 2002). While this study demonstrates the impact of electronic service quality on attitude toward site and nuances this impact according to the type of task performed and completion of the task, electronic service quality could be better conceptualized by examining its links with other concepts such as

satisfaction after purchase, perceived value, perceived control, and perceived convenience.

In addition, the study of electronic service quality evaluation suggests specific dimensions or attributes of a Website, i.e. ease of use and security, to pose particular influence on consumer decision making. Nonetheless, no published work was found to explore the influence of individual or situational characteristics on electronic service quality. Consideration of these variables may explain context variations in the importance of electronic service quality dimensions. Taking into account socio-economic, motivational and attitudinal criteria such as age, income, innovativeness, impulsiveness, propensity to seek variety, risk aversion, attitude toward advertising and direct marketing, and involvement with IT seem pertinent and necessary for the study of online purchasing (Donthu & Garcia, 1999) and perceived quality of this purchase.

Expectations of Internet users that adopt utilitarian navigational behaviour seem to differ from those users engaged in experiential hedonic behaviour (Hoffman & Novak, 1996). Visitors with goal-directed behaviour, i.e. cognitive, extrinsic motivation, usually visit sites to find specific information about a product/service, solve a particular problem, or purchase a certain product; whereas visitors engaged in hedonic navigational behaviour want to be entertained and would seek an intrinsically gratifying experience. Hoffman & Novak (1996) conclude that "the optimal design of a Website differs according to whether the behaviour is goal-directed or experiential" (p.62). Considering the orientation, utilitarian or hedonic, of the Internet user's navigation behaviour, therefore, might provide more insight into differences of the importance placed on the dimensions of perceived quality evaluation of an online purchase. On the other hand, studying the role of consumer's familiarity with the Internet and expertise at online shopping is inadequate to date (Szymanski & Hise, 2000). Extant research, notably Novak, Hoffman & Yung (2000), considers the level of user expertise as an important factor in studying online behaviour and differentiates between search and navigation habits of experts and novices. User familiarity with the Internet and expertise in online commerce are elements that might modify the importance placed on different dimensions of electronic service quality.

From a managerial standpoint, and similar to the case of traditional service quality in Parasuraman, Zeithaml & Berry (1988), the NetQual scale of electronic service quality would be useful for managers and decision makers such as Webmasters designing and upgrading commercial Websites and would help managers evaluate and monitor changes in perceptions of service quality of retail and service sites. The scale can also be used to set performance objectives in terms of electronic service quality. In addition, online merchants can use the scale to perform a competitive analysis of their sector and highlight main strengths and weakness of site in terms of electronic service quality compared with competitors. Measures of site efficiency such as the analysis of log files, visit-purchase conversion rate, and rate of retention can be determined and analyzed. The scale can then be used to refine analysis of reasons for success or failure of a particular site in terms of electronic service quality. Further studies of these themes are therefore necessary.

REFERENCES

Barnes, S. J., & Vidgen, R. T. (2003). An Integrative Approach to the Assessment of E-Commerce Quality. *Journal of Electronic Commerce Research*, *3*(3), 114–127.

Benbunan-Fich, R. (2001). Using Protocol Analysis to Evaluate the Usability of a Commercial Web Site. *Information & Management*, *39*, 151–163. doi:10.1016/S0378-7206(01)00085-4

Bentler, P. M., & Wu, E. J. C. (2002). *EQS 6 for Windows User's Guide*. Encino, CA: Multivariate Software, Inc.

Bitner, M. J., Brown, S. W., & Meuter, M. L. (2000). Technology Infusion in Service Encounters. *Journal of the Academy of Marketing Science*, *28*(1), 138–149. doi:10.1177/0092070300281013

Bressolles, G. (2006). La qualité de service électronique: NetQual. Proposition d'une échelle de mesure appliquée aux sites marchands et effets modérateurs [Electronic service quality: NetQual – Proposition of a measurement scale to commercial Websites and moderating effects]. *Recherche et Applications en Marketing*, *21*(3), 19–45.

Chen, Q., & Wells, W. D. (1999). Attitude Toward the Site. *Journal of Advertising Research*, *39*(5), 27–37.

Chin, W. W. (1998). Issues and opinion on structural equation modelling. *MIS Quarterly*, (March): 7–16.

Cunliffe, D. (2000). Developing Usable Web Sites - A Review and Model. *Internet Research*, *10*, 295–308. doi:10.1108/10662240010342577

Dabholkar, P. A. (2000). Technology in Service Delivery: Implications for Self-Service and Service Support. In Swartz T.A. and Iacobucci D. (Eds.), *Handbook of Services Marketing* (pp. 103-110). New York: Sage.

Donthu, N., & Garcia, A. (1999). The Internet Shopper. *Journal of Advertising Research*, *39*(3), 52–58.

eMarketer (2005). North-America on Line: Demographics and Usage.

Ericsson, K. A., & Simon, H. A. (1993). *Protocol Analysis: Verbal reports as data* (2nd ed.). Cambridge, MA: MIT Press.

Hair, J. F., Anderson, R. E., Tatham, R. L., & Black, W. C. (1998). *Multivariate Data Analysis with Readings* (5th ed.). Upper Saddle River, NJ: Prentice-Hall.

Hoffman, D. L., & Novak, T. P. (1996). Marketing in Hypermedia Computer-Mediated Environment: Conceptual Foundations. *Journal of Marketing, 60*, 50–68. doi:10.2307/1251841

Johnson, E. J., Moe, W. W., Fader, P. S., Bellman, S., & Lohse, G. L. (2004). On the Depth and Dynamics of Online Search Behaviour. *Management Science, 50*(3), 299–309. doi:10.1287/mnsc.1040.0194

Li, H., Daugherty, T., & Biocca, F. (2001). Characteristics of Virtual Experience in Electronic Commerce: A Protocol Analysis. *Journal of Interactive Marketing, 15*(3). doi:10.1002/dir.1013

Lynch, J. G., & Ariely, D. (2000). Wine Online: Search Cost and Competition on Price, Quality and Distribution. *Marketing Science, 19*(1), 83–103. doi:10.1287/mksc.19.1.83.15183

Madu, C. N., & Madu, A. A. (2002). Dimensions of E-quality. *International Journal of Quality & Reliability Management, 19*(3), 246–258. doi:10.1108/02656710210415668

Novak, T. P., Hoffman, D. L., & Yung, Y.-F. (2000). Measuring the Customer Experience in Online Environments: A Structural Modeling Approach. *Marketing Science, 19*(1), 22–42. doi:10.1287/mksc.19.1.22.15184

Nunnally, J. (1978). *Psychometric Theory* (2nd ed.). McGraw-Hill.

Parasuraman, A., & Grewal, D. (2000). The Impact of Technology on the Quality-Value-Loyalty Chain: A Research Agenda. *Journal of the Academy of Marketing Science, 28*(1), 168–174. doi:10.1177/0092070300281015

Parasuraman, A., Zeithaml, V. A., & Berry, L. L. (1988). SERVQUAL: A Multiple-Item Scale for Measuring Consumer Perceptions of Service Quality. *Journal of Retailing, 64*(1), 12–40.

Parasuraman, A., Zeithaml, V. A., & Malhotra, A. (2005). E-S-QUAL: A Multiple-Item Scale for Assessing Electronic Service Quality. *Journal of Service Research, 7*(3), 213–234. doi:10.1177/1094670504271156

Senecal, S., Gharbi, J.-E., & Nantel, J. (2002). The Influence of Flow on Hedonic and Utilitarian Shopping Values. In S. Broniarczyk & K. Nakamoto (Eds.), *Advances in Consumer Research*, 29.

Simon, H. A. (1956). Models of Thought. New Haven, CT: Yale University Press.

Swinder, J., Trocchia, P. J., & Gwinner, K. P. (2002). Consumer Perceptions of Internet Retail Service Quality. *International Journal of Service Industry Management, 13*(5), 412. doi:10.1108/09564230210447913

Szymanski, D., & Hise, R. T. (2000). e-Satisfaction: An Initial Examination. *Journal of Retailing, 76*(3), 309–322. doi:10.1016/S0022-4359(00)00035-X

Totty, M. (2003, June 16). E-Commerce (A Special Report): Selling Strategies - Business Solutions. *Wall Street Journal*, p. 4.

Tsikriktsis, N. (2002). Does Culture Influence Web Site Quality Expectations? An Empirical Study. *Journal of Service Research, 5*(2), 101–112. doi:10.1177/109467002237490

Wolfinbarger, M., & Gilly, M. C. (2003). eTailQ: Dimensionalizing, Measuring and Predicting Etail Quality. *Journal of Retailing, 79*(3), 183–198. doi:10.1016/S0022-4359(03)00034-4

Yoo, B., & Donthu, N. (2001). Developing a Scale to Measure the Perceived Quality of Internet Shopping Sites (SITEQUAL). *Quarterly Journal of Electronic Commerce, 2*(1), 31–47.

Zeithaml, V. A., Parasuraman, A., & Malhotra, A. (2002). Service Quality Delivery through Web Sites: A Critical Review of Extant Knowledge. *Journal of the Academy of Marketing Science, 30*(4), 362–375. doi:10.1177/009207002236911

APPENDIX 1

List of Items on the NetQual Scale (Bressolles, 2006)

Information:

Info1: This site provides relevant information
Info2: This site provides accurate information
Info3: This site provides in-depth information about the product(s) or service(s) proposed

Ease of Use:

Eoful: This site is easy to use
Eofu2: It is easy to search for information
Eofu3: This site is easy to navigate
Eofu4: The organization and layout of this site facilitate the search for information
Eofu5: The layout of this site is clear and simple

Site Design:

Design1: This site is colorful
Design2: This site is creative
Design3: This site has an attractive appearance

Reliability:

Relia1: The product or service is delivered by the time promised by the company
Relia2: You get what you ordered from this site
Relia3: You get your merchandise quickly when you order
Relia4: After-sale support on this site is excellent

Security/Privacy:

Secu1: I am confident in the security on this site
Secu2: I feel like my privacy is protected on this site
Secu3: I trust the web site administrators will not misuse my personal information

APPENDIX 2

C.F.A. Results for the Four Scales Tested (Figures 1, 2, 3, and 4)

Figure 1. Sitequal C.F.A.

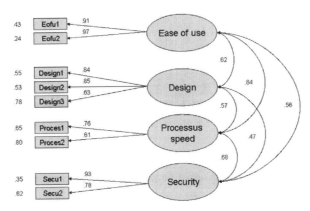

Figure 2. EtailQ C.F.A.

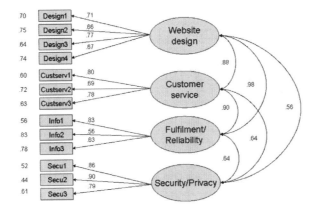

Figure 3. Webqual C.F.A

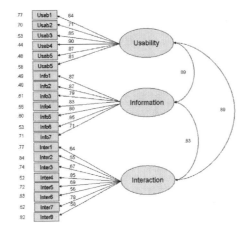

Figure 4. NetQual C.F.A

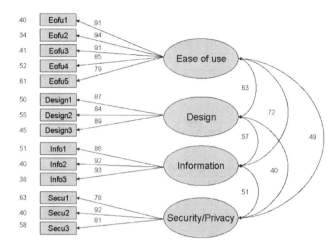

APPENDIX 3

Definition of the Different Fit Indices Retained for Comparing the Four Scales

Parsimony Indices

*   AIC (Akaike Information Criterion): take into account both the measure of fit and model complexity. AIC has become quite popular in SEM applications, particularly for purposes of examining competitions models.
*   Chi^2 / df: The Chi-square value represents a test statistic of the goodness of fit of the model, and it is used when testing the null hypothesis that the model fits the analysed covariance matrix perfectly. When the proposed model is fit to the data using a SEM program, the program will judge the obtained Chi-square value in relation to the model's degrees of freedom (df), and output associated is *p* value.

Absolute Indices

*   RMSEA (Root Mean Square Error of Approximation): take into account model complexity, as reflected in the degree of freedom. Some researchers have suggested that a value of the RMSEA of less than .05 is indicative of the model being a reasonable approximation to the data.
*   GFI (Goodness-of-Fit Index): measure the proportion of variance and covariance that the proposed model is able to explain (similar to R^2 in regression analysis).
*   AGFI (Adjusted Goodness-of-Fit Index): similar to the GFI but take into account the number of parameters.

Incremental Indices

- NFI (Normed Fit Index): is computed by relating the difference of the Chi-square value for the proposed model to the Chi-square value for the independent or null model.
- NNFI (Non Normed Fit Index): is a sample variant of the NFI that take into account the degrees of freedom of the proposed model (model complexity).

This work was previously published in Transforming E-Business Practices and Applications: Emerging Technologies and Concepts, edited by Lee, I., pp. 344-363, copyright 2010 by IGI Publishing (an imprint of IGI Global).

Chapter 4.2
Enabling Scalable Semantic Reasoning for Mobile Services

Luke Albert Steller
Monash University, Australia

Shonali Krishnaswamy
Monash University, Australia

Mohamed Methat Gaber
Monash University, Australia

ABSTRACT

With the emergence of high-end smart phones/PDAs there is a growing opportunity to enrich mobile/pervasive services with semantic reasoning. This article presents novel strategies for optimising semantic reasoning for realising semantic applications and services on mobile devices. We have developed the mTableaux algorithm which optimises the reasoning process to facilitate service selection. We present comparative experimental results which show that mTableaux improves the performance and scalability of semantic reasoning for mobile devices.

INTRODUCTION

The semantic web offers new opportunities to represent knowledge based on meaning rather than syntax. Semantically described knowledge can be used to infer new knowledge by reasoners in an automated fashion. Reasoners can be utilised in a broad range of semantic applications, for instance matching user requirements with specific information in search engines, matching match client needs with functional system components such as services for automated discovery and orchestration or even providing diagnosis of medical conditions. A significant drawback which prevents the large uptake and deployment of semantically described knowledge is the resource intensive nature of reasoning. Currently available semantic reasoners are suitable for deployment on high-end desktop or service based infrastructure. However, with the emergence of high-end smart phones / PDAs the mobile environment is increasingly information rich. For instance, information on devices may include sensor data, traffic conditions, user preferences or habits or capability descriptions of remotely invokable web services hosted on these devices. This information is can be highly useful to other users in the environment.

Thus, there is a need to describe this knowledge semantically and to support scalable reasoning for mobile semantic applications, especially in highly dynamic environments where high-end infrastructure is unsuitable or not available. Computing power is limited to that available on resource constrained devices and as shown in Figure 1, there is insufficient memory on these devices to complete reasoning tasks which require significant time and memory to complete.

Since mobile users are often on the move and in a highly dynamic situation, they generally require information quickly. Studies such as (Roto & Oulasvirta, 2005) have established that mobile users typically have a tolerance threshold of about 5 to 15 seconds in terms of response time, before their attention shifts elsewhere, depending on their environment. Therefore, there is a need for mobile reasoners which can meet the twin constraints of time and memory.

For example, consider the following mobile application scenario. A mobile user has just arrived in Sydney airport and wishes to search for food and other products. Sydney airport provides touch screen kiosk terminals which allow the user to search for stores (and other airport facilities) by category. The location of the store and facility is then displayed on a map as well as the location of the user (which is the fixed location of the kiosk), as illustrated in Figure 2. These kiosks are not very convenient as they are only located at fixed point locations, are limited in their search options and user request complexity and do not take user context into account. Additionally, they do not scale, as kiosks can only be used by one user at a time.

Alternatively, the increasing abundance of mobile devices such as PDAs and mobile phones as well as their increasing computational and communication capabilities provide new opportunities for on-board service discovery. Consider the case where the information kiosk is a directory/repository of services available in the airport which mobile users can connect to from their phone or PDA. The user can then access, search and use this information using their respective phones at their convenience.

There are two modes of service matching:

- centralised service matching which occurs on a server on behalf of the user and
- partially or completely decentralised approaches where matching occurs on the resource constrained device itself.

Under a centralised approach (see Figure 3) the kiosk (or a connected machine) is a high-end server which handles all service discovery requests on the mobile user's behalf. However, there are two major drawbacks with this approach. Firstly, although purchase of a server is relatively cheap, there are significant costs involved for this kind of service provision, including scalability to handle potentially thousands of requests, wireless network provision, maintenance costs, security considerations and quality of service issues. The significant costs would outweigh the limited benefit to a central authority such as the Sydney

Figure 1. Error showing that there was not enough memory to perform reasoning when attempting to run Pellet on a PDA (the reasoning task was the Printer inference check given in section 6.1).

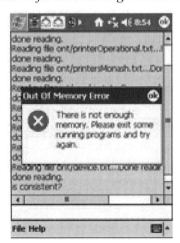

Figure 2. Sydney airport store finder kiosk. The store search screen is shown on the left, while the search result for an Internet café is on the right. The location of the Internet café is indicated by the computer icon in the bottom right side of the screen.

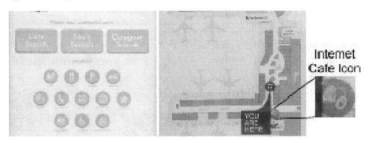

airport. In environments where there is no such central authority this infrastructure may not even be possible (eg a city center or decentralised precinct). Secondly, if users are faced with the choice of paying for wireless access to a service matcher or utilising existing kiosks such as those already at Sydney airport, they are likely to choose the kiosk since it is free (albeit limited in its service provision capability).

For this environment we advocate a partially decentralised approach (see Figure 4a) in which the kiosk is merely a directory or repository, to which users can sync with, to download service advertisements for the airport, using short range WiFi or Bluetooth. The ontology file provider could also be a provider accessed via the Internet or even shared using secondary storage such as an SD card downloaded previously at home or by another person. Service matching can then occur independently as needed, on the user's device itself. This solution would be inexpensive to deploy and to use as there are no overheads

for the service providing authority and there are no connectivity overheads for the user (eg they may simply use Bluetooth for once-off access to the service descriptions). In addition, this model would be better suited to provision of personalised selection by factoring in historical / user preference data.

There are also other application scenarios which demand on-device matching. For instance, a user may wish to discovery services which are hosted remotely by devices in a temporary mobile ad-hoc network (see Figure 4b) such scenarios include: students sharing data on a field trip (Chatti, Srirama, Kensche & Cao, 2006), emergency situations, traffic information sharing, etc. Alternatively, services may be installed or removed from a user's own device on a needs basis. Determining which services should be installed or removed requires comparing current or prospective services to the user's current needs on the device itself (see Figure 4c), for example Google[1] and Yahoo[2] already offer many mobile

Figure 3. Example: Centralised server-based matching provision

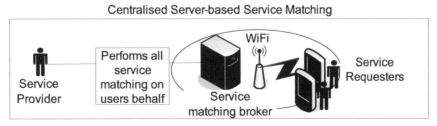

Figure 4. Three example configurations of on-device matching: (a) partial decentralisation where files are served centrally (by a WiFi/Bluetooth connected server or Internet provider) but matching occurs on-board the device, (b) on-device matching of remote services hosted on other mobile devices in a mobile ad-hoc network (c) on-device matching of services on the same device (local services only).

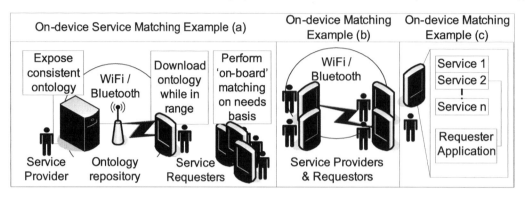

applications such as blogging, news, finance, sports, etc.

We have provided three examples demonstrating a growing number of situations where there is a clear need for approaches to enable mobile reasoning on resource constrained devices. The next question remains as to how the user will access these services from the mobile device and perform service discovery on the device. There are two main challenges here:

1. the mechanism to perform semantically-driven service selection on a mobile device in an efficient way;
2. the interface challenges of presenting this information to the user.

In order to facilitate the matching of user needs, context and requests with a set of potential services such as those outlined in the scenarios above, our focus is on the first key issue of enabling scalable service discovery mechanisms to operate on a mobile device. This approach requires new strategies to enable mobile reasoning on resource constrained devices, to perform matching of request to services. The Tableaux algorithm is well known and used by reasoners such as Pellet, RacerPro and FaCT++. Therefore this article

aims to enable these reasoners to perform mobile semantic reasoning. The key challenge is to enable semantic reasoning to function in a computationally cost-efficient and resource-aware manner on a mobile device.

In this article we present our mTableaux algorithm, which implements strategies to optimise description logic (DL) reasoning tasks so that relatively large reasoning tasks of several hundred individuals and classes can be scaled to small resource constrained devices. We present comparative evaluations of the performance of Pellet, RacerPro and FaCT++ semantic reasoners which demonstrate the significant improvement to response time achieved by our mTableaux algorithm. In order to gain efficiency, some strategies reduce completeness, in a controlled manner, so we also evaluate result accuracy using recall and precision. Finally, in our evaluation we present experimental evaluations that demonstrate the feasibility of the semantic service discovery to operate on a mobile device.

This article takes an important step forward in developing scalable semantic reasoning techniques which are useful for both mobile/pervasive and standard service selection algorithms. The remainder of the article is structured as follows. In section 2 we describe related work. In section

3 we present our discovery architecture, followed by a discussion of our optimisation and ranking strategies in section 4. In section 5 we formally define our strategies. Section 6 we provide an implementation and performance evaluations and in section 7 we conclude the article.

RELATED WORK IN PERVASIVE SERMANTIC SERVICE REASONING

The limitations of syntactic, string-based matching for web service discovery coupled with the emergence of the semantic web implies that next generation web services will be matched based on semantically equivalent meaning, even when they are described differently (Broens, 2004) and will include support for partial matching in the absence of an exact match. While current service discovery architectures such as Jini (Arnold, O'Sullivan, Scheifler, Waldo & Woolrath, 1999), UPnP (UPnP, 2007), Konark (Lee, Helal, Desai, Verma & Arslan, 2003), SLP (Guttman, 1999), Salutation (Miller & Pascoe, 2000) and SSDM (Issarny & Sailhan, 2005), UDDI (UDDI, 2009) and LDAP (Howes & Smith, 1995) use either interface or string based syntactic matching, there is a growing emergence of DAML-S/OWL-S semantic matchmakers. DReggie (Chakraborty, Perich, Avancha & Joshi, 2001) and CMU Matchmaker (Srinivasan, Paolucci & Sycara, 2005) are examples of such matchmakers which support approximate matching but they require a centralised high-end node to perform reasoning using Prolog and Racer, respectively. Similarly, LARKS (Sycara, Widoff, Klusch & Lu, 2002) which is designed to manage the trade-off between result accuracy and computation time, employs a centralised approach but defines its own language and reasoner. IRS-III (Cabral, Domingue, Galizia, Gugliotta, Tanasescu et al., 2006) is based on WSMX (WSMO, 2009) and utilises Lisp. DIANE (Küster, König-Ries & Klein, 2006) is designed

for ad-hoc service discovery and defines its own semantic language. It captures request preferences as fuzzy sets defining acceptable ranges. DIANE also supports dynamic attributes, which are realised at runtime. Anamika (Chakraborty, Joshi, Yesha & Finin, 2004) is an ad-hoc architecture which utilises an ontological approach for routing and discovery based on service type but does not perform complex reasoning or support context.

There are in addition, architectures developed specifically for the pervasive service discovery domain which are driven by context, such as MobiShare (Doulkeridis, Loutas & Vazirgiannis, 2005) which utilised RDF subclass relations for service type, with no reasoning, COSS (Broens, 2004) which utilises semi-OWL for service type, inputs and outputs with lattice structures for ranking Boolean context attributes, and CASE (Sycara et al., 2002) and Omnipresent (Almeida, Bapista, Silva, Campelo, Figueiredo et al., 2006) which utilise OWL with Jena (Jena, 2009) rules. However all of these architectures too, require the existence of a high-end central node.

This reliance on a high-end, centralised node for performing semantically driven pervasive service discovery can clearly be attributed to the fact that semantic reasoners used by these architectures (including Prolog, Lisp and Jess, as well as more newly available OWL reasoners such as FaCT++ (2008), RacerPro (2008) and KAON2 (2008)) are all resource intensive. These reasoners cannot be deployed onto small resource constrained devices in their current form, due to the twin constraints of memory and processing time.

Kleeman et. al. (Kleemann, 2006) have developed KRHyper, a novel first order logic (FOL) reasoner for deployment on resource constrained devices. In order to use DL with KRHyper it must be transformed into a set of disjunctive first order logic clauses. It implements the common DL optimisations of backjumping, semantic branching, Boolean constraint propagation, lazy unfolding and absorption as described in (Horrocks & Patel-Schneider, 1999). These optimisations are also implemented by widely used reasoners such as FaCT++ and Pellet. A performance evaluation shows that it performs first order reasoning quickly, solving 35% of satisfiable horn clauses, 29% of unsatisfiable clauses, 54%, non-horn satisfiable problems, 39% of non-horn unsatisfiable problems in 10 seconds. It does not utilise caching schemes which incur additional overhead and memory consumption for smaller tasks, but optimise larger tasks. Performance comparisons with RacerPro show that it performs better for small tasks and not as well for larger tasks. This FOL reasoner meets the goal of providing competitive performance results with a DL reasoner. However, it still exhausts all memory when the reasoning task becomes too large for a small device to handle and fails to provide any result.

Therefore, there is a need for an optimised semantic reasoner which performs better than currently available reasoners. This reasoner must also support adaptation to the environment, to reduce memory consumption of the processing required (which may reduce result accuracy) according to resource or time constraints. In the next section we outline our novel architecture to meet this need.

RESOURCE-AWARE AND COST-EFFICIENT PERVASIVE SERVICE DISCOVERY

Our pervasive service discovery architecture is illustrated in Figure 5. The modules in this diagram all reside on the user's device. The database of ontologies includes those collected from service repositories or kiosks or other sources, as described in section 1.

In this model, the mobile user submits a request to his or her device and discovery manager utilises the semantic reasoner to match the request with services from the database of collected ontologies.

The discovery manager takes available resources such as available memory, CPU usage, remaining battery life or remaining time (provided by the context manager), into consideration. It may load the entire ontology into memory in the beginning, or if memory is low it will load portions of ontology on demand. The adaptive discovery manager also may stop matching a particular request with a service after the service failed to match a particular request attribute or it may instruct the mTableaux reasoner to reduce the accuracy of its result when resources become low (eg low memory) or when the result is taking too long to process. The semantic reasoner module contains our mTableaux algorithm, which incorporates our optimised reasoning strategies. It also includes strategies to reduce result accuracy to meet resource constraints.

In summary, our architecture addresses two main goals. Firstly, it addresses the need for scalable reasoning on a mobile device by providing strategies to optimise the reasoning process. Secondly, when there are not enough resources or time remaining to complete a request, our architecture provides strategies to reduce the result's accuracy in order to utilise less resources and time. This article concentrates on providing a semantic reasoner that is able to operate in on a mobile device (mTableaux module) and discuss this in more detail in the next section. As a simple extension to this reasoner we also discuss adaptive accuracy reduction to reduce resource or time consumption where there are insufficient resources to complete a task in full.

MTABLEAUX: REASONING FOR PERVASIVE SERVICE DISCOVERY

In this section we discuss current Tableaux semantic reasoners and present mTableaux, our algorithm for enabling Tableaux reasoning on mobile devices.

Figure 5. Pervasive service discovery architecture

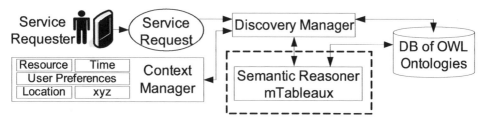

Semantic Reasoners

The effective employment of semantic languages requires the use of semantic reasoners such as Pellet (2003), FaCT++ (2008), RacerPro (2008) and KAON2 (2008). Most of these reasoners employ the widely used Tableaux (Horrocks & Sattler, 2005) algorithm. These reasoners are shown in Figure 6, which is a detailed version of the semantic reasoner and ontology database components from Figure 5 and illustrates the component parts required for OWL reasoning. Reasoners can be deployed on servers and interacted with via DL Implementation Group (DIG) interface specification which uses XML over HTTP. Alternatively, interaction may be facilitated directly using native APIs, which requires RDF/XML parsing functionality to load OWL files into the reasoner. Pellet utilises either Jena or OWL-API for interaction and RDF parsing.

Semantic OWL Reasoners contain a knowledge base K which encompasses terminological knowledge *TBox* and assertional knowledge *ABox*, such that $K = TBox \cup ABox$. *TBox* encompasses class definitions and expressions while *ABox* encompasses individual and literal assertions of class membership and relations. The knowledge base is stored as a set of triples $<C, R, O>$, where C is the set of classes, R is a set of roles and O is the set of object assertions. The object assertions are organised into a graph structure of the form $<O_1, R, O_2>$ where O_1 is an object connected to O_2 by role R. DL Tableaux reasoners such as Pellet, reduce all reasoning tasks to a consistency check.

Tableaux is a branching algorithm, in which disjunctions form combinations of branches in the tree. Inferred membership for an individual I to class type RQ implies $I \in RQ$, where $RQ \in TBox$ and $I \in ABox$. $I \in RQ$ is checked by adding $\neg RQ$ as a type for I, in an otherwise consistent ontology. If the assertion of $I{:}\neg RQ$ results in a clash for all branches dependant on $\neg RQ$ for I, then class membership $I \in RQ$ is proven.

Figure 7 presents an example containing individuals $d, e, f, g, h, i, j, k, n, m, o$ which are connected by roles Q, R, S, P and some individuals are asserted to be members of class types A, B, C, T. For instance, individual d is connected to f by role R and f is a member of class A. Assume we want to find the truth of $d \in RQ$ where $RQ = \exists P.(\geq 1P) \wedge \exists R.(A \wedge \exists R.(B \wedge C))$, using the Tableaux algorithm, $\neg RQ$ is first added asserted as

Figure 6. Semantic reasoner components

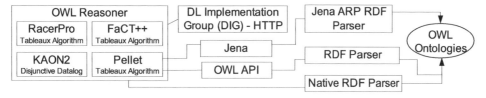

Figure 7. Example clash

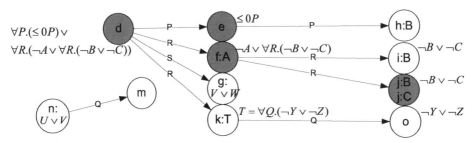

a type label to individual *d*, where $\neg RQ = \forall P.(\leq 0P) \vee \forall R.(\neg A \vee \forall R.(\neg B \vee \neg C))$. Tableaux applies the first element of the disjunction, a universal quantifier: $\forall P.(\leq 0P)$, which asserts the max cardinality rule $\leq 0P$ to node *e*, because *e* is a *P*-neighbour to individual *h*. *h* violates the max cardinality of 0 for *P* and creates a clash, because *e* has a *P*-neighbour *h*. All remaining disjunction elements and sub-elements also clash thereby proving *d*∈*RQ* as true.

The shaded nodes in Figure 7 indicate those which contribute to a clash. Application of any expansion rules to other nodes results in unnec-essary processing. The full Tableaux extract for the standard Tableaux method is listed in Box 1.

All elements of the negated request generate a clash, so $d \in RQ$ is proven to be true. Those disjunction branches and expansion rules which contributed to clashes proving $d \in RQ$ are bolded. The processing involved in applying all other rules did not contribute to the proof of $d \in RQ$.

mTableaux Strategies

The work in this article concentrates on optimi-sations for the Tableaux algorithm. As observed in section 4.1 (see Figure 7), Tableaux reasoners

Box 1.

```
Assert d: ∀P.(≤ 0P) ∨∀R.(¬A ∨ ∀R.(¬B ∨ ¬C)).
Apply Unfolding Rule k: ¬X ∨∀Q.(¬Y ∨¬Z)
Apply Universal Quantifier o: ¬Y ∨ ¬Z.
Apply Branch 1, Element (1/2) o:¬Y, no clash.
Apply Branch 2, Element (1/2) n:U, no clash.
Apply Branch 3, Element (1/2) i: ∀P.(≤ 0P)
    Apply Universal Quantifier j:≤ 0P
    Apply Max Rule j:≤ 0P, CLASH.
Apply Branch 3, Element (2/2) i: ∀R.(¬A ∨∀R.∀R.(¬B ∨ ¬C).
    Apply Universal Quantifier g:¬A ∨ ∀R.(¬B ∨ ¬C).
        Apply Branch 4 Element (1/2) g:¬A, CLASH.
        Apply Branch 4 Element (2/2) g: ∀R. (¬B ∨ ¬C).
            Apply Universal Quantifier l,j: ¬B ∨¬C.
            Apply Branch 6 Element (1/2) i:¬B, CLASH.
            Apply Branch 6 Element (2/2) i:¬C, no clash.
            Apply Branch 7 Element (1/2) j:¬B, CLASH.
            Apply Branch 7 Element (2/2) j:¬C, CLASH.
```

leave scope for optimisation by dropping rules which do not contribute to an inference check, or applying first the rules which are more likely to create a clash. In addition, since inference proofs relate only to a subset of the ontology, it is not necessary to load the entire ontology into memory. Minimising the processing time and memory consumption are the twin goals of our reasoning approach as this enables scalable deployment of reasoners to small/resource constrained devices. We provide an overview of our optimisations as follows.

Semantic reasoners initially check ontologies for overall consistency. Since this check need only occur once for each ontology, we assume this has already been performed on the kiosk (i.e., the location from which the ontology is downloaded) or by the service advertiser before the ontology is released for download. Alternatively, there may be a service that is able to provide consistent versions of ontologies. Our mTableaux algorithm provides strategies to for reducing processing time and memory consumption for inference checks of the form: $I \in RQ$ by providing strategies for:

- **optimisation:** by dropping and reordering tableaux expansion rules and
- **adaption:** to reduce result accuracy when resources become low and only load ontology subsets which are relevant to the inference task.

The optimisation strategies include: 1. selective application of consistency rules, 2. skipping disjunctions, 3. associate weights with disjunctions and other expansion rules (such as existential quantifiers and cardinality restrictions) and increasing the weight of those which are likely to lead to clashes if applied in order to apply these first, by 3a. searching for potential clashes from specific disjunctions and 3b. searching from a specific term. The first two strategies drop expansion rules (disjunctions, existential quantifiers and maximum cardinality

restrictions), therefore completeness cannot be guaranteed (soundness is in tact) because some clashes may not be found. The third optimisation alters the order in which expressions are applied, but does not skip any, thereby maintaining both completeness and soundness. We note, that most reasoners such as FaCT++ and RacerPro perform ontology realisation, in which all individuals are checked for inferred membership to every class type in the ontology. mTableaux does not require nor perform full ontology realisation, rather only specific individual I to class type RQ membership $I \in RQ$ is performed, where RQ is a user request and I denotes a set of potential service individuals to be checked.

In the first strategy (selective consistency), application of consistency rules to a subset of individuals only, reduces the reasoning task. This subset can be established using the universal quantifier construct of the form $\forall R.C = \{\forall b.(a, b) \in R \rightarrow b \in C\}$ (Baader, Calvanese, McGuinness, Nardi & Patel-Schneider, 2003), where R denotes a relation and C denotes a class concept. The quantifier implies that all object fillers of relation R, are of type C. Application of this rule adds role filler type C to all objects for the given role R, which can give rise to an inconsistency. Therefore, we define the subset as being limited to the original individual being checked for membership to a class, and all those individuals which branch from this individual as objects of roles specified in universal quantifiers.

The second optimisation (disjunction skipping), applies or skips disjunctions, according to whether they relate to the request type. A disjunction may be applied when one of its elements contains a type which can be derived from the request type. Derived types include elements of conjunctions/disjunctions and role fillers of universal quantifiers and their unfolded types.

For the third strategy, expressions are ordered by weight using a weighted queue. To establish weights for expansion rules (disjunctions, existential quantifiers and maximum cardinality restrictions) these expressions are ranked by recursively checking each element in a particular disjunction (rank by disjunction) or asserted term (rank by term) for a potential clash. If a pathway to a clash is found, the weighted value is increased for of all expressions which are involved in this path.

The adaptive strategies involve simple extensions to the optimisation strategies to avoid exhausting the available memory or time by providing a result to the user with a level of uncertainty, when resources become low. We describe our optimisation strategies in detail, in the next section, which the adaptive extensions are briefly discussed in future work (section 7).

MTABLEAUX ALGORITHM: OPTIMISATION AND RANKING STRATEGIES

In this section we formally describe the optimisation strategies listed in the previous section.

Selective Consistency

In the selective consistency strategy, Tableaux completion rules are only applied to a subset of individuals, rather than all those individuals in the ontology, let SC denote this set. Completion rules which are added as types to individual A are only applied if $A \in SC$.

For the membership inference check $I \in RQ$, before reasoning begins, SC is initially populated using the function *popuInds(IS)*, such that $SC = $ *popuInds({I})*. *popuInds(IS)* is a function which recursively calls *getInds(e, AV)* to select universally quantified r-neighbour individuals of e, and those neighbour's universally quantified r-neighbours, etc. *popuInds(IS)* is given by equation 1, where $e.AV$ denotes the set of universal quantifiers of the form $\forall R.C$ which have been added as type labels to an individual e.

$$popuInds(IS) = \bigcup_{e \in IS} popInds(getInds(e, e.AV)) \quad (1)$$

getInds(e, AV) is the function which returns the set of r-neighbours for the individual e, where the relation r is restricted by a universal quantifier of the form $\forall r.c$, which has been added as a type to the individual e. The function is given by equation 2, where OS is the set of objects in the triple $<e, r, OS>$ that contains e and r, and av must be a universal construct. A universal quantifier can be added to e by the unfolding of a concept already added to e or by application of another expansion rule.

$$getInds(e, AV) = \bigcup_{av \in AV} OS, < e, r, OS >, av \rightarrow \{\forall r.c\} \quad (2)$$

After reasoning has begun, new universal quantifiers may be added to an individual a which is in the set SC. If the new quantifier restrictions role R which is not yet restricted by another quantifier added to a, and a has R-neighbours, these neighbours need to be added to SC. Therefore, whenever a universal quantifier av_{new} is added an individual a in SC, R-neighbours are added to SC by a call to *getInds(e, AV)* such that $\{a.AV = a.AV + av_{new}\} \wedge \{SC = SC + addInds(a, \{av_{new}\})\}$ where $A \in SC$.

For example, for the inference check in section 4.1, $d \in RQ$, a call to *popuInds({d})* returns only $\{d\}$ because d does not yet contain any universal quantifies. Application of the first element of the disjunction RQ asserts $d: \forall P.(\leq 0P)$. A call to *getInds(d, d.AV)* returns $\{e\}$, because e is a P-neighbour of d and P was restricted in $\forall P.(\leq 0P)$, thus $SC = \{d, e\}$ therefore expansion rules for e can now be applied. Application of the second element in RQ asserts $d: \forall R.(\neg A \vee \forall R.(\neg B \vee \neg C))$ and a call to *getInds(d, d.AV_{new})* returns $\{f\}$ because f is an R-neighbour of d and R was restricted in $\forall R.(\neg A \vee \forall R.(\neg B \vee \neg C))$. Figure 8 illustrates that SC = $\{d, e, f, i, j, k, o\}$, therefore any

Figure 8. Selective consistency

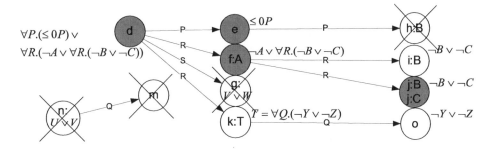

expansion rules relating to all other individuals *n, m, g* or *h* were not applied (shown as crossed out in Figure 8).

Disjunction Skipping

When a disjunction is encountered during the reasoning process, the disjunction skipping strategy determines whether this disjunction is applied to create a new branch or skipped. Let *D* denote a disjunction, of the form $D = \{d_1 \vee d_2 \vee ... \vee d_m\}$, where d_i is a disjunction element. Let *nn(e)* denote *e* in non-negated form. Non-negated form implies that a negated term is made positive such that $nn(e) = x$ if $e = \neg x$, or $nn(e) = x$ if $e = x$, where *x* is a class type name or logical expression. *D* is applied if at least one of its non-negated elements $nn(d_i)$ is contained within the set *DS*, such that $\exists_{d_i \in_D}(d_i) \in DS$. Let *DS* denote a set of class type names and logical expressions defined in the ontology.

For the membership inference check $I \in RQ$, *DS* is populated using the *popu(E)* function such that $DS = popu(\neg RQ)$, where $\neg RQ$ is the negated request type definition. We assume *RQ* was a conjunction, $\neg RQ$ is a disjunction *D*. *popu(E)*, given in expression 3, recursively collects terms which can be derived from elements in the set *E* of class terms or expressions.

$$popu(E) = \bigcup_{e \in E} nn(e) + pop(decomp(e)) \quad (3)$$

E may be a conjunction of the form $E = \{e_1 \wedge ... \wedge e_m\}$, a disjunction of the form $E = \{e_1 \vee ... \vee e_m\}$, or generic set $E = \{e_1 ,..., e_m\}$. Let *decomp(e)* denote the function which returns a empty or non-empty set, of terms and expressions which can be derived from *e*. *decomp(e)* is given in expression 4. Derived implies that where *e* is a universal or existential quantifier then *decomp(e)* returns a set containing the role filler for *e* or where *e* is a unary atomic term an empty or non-empty set is returned containing its expanded expressions, retrieved, using the *unfold(e)* function.

$$decomp(e) = \begin{cases} \{C\} & if \quad e = \forall R.C \vee e = \exists R.C, \\ unfold(e) & if \quad e^1 \end{cases} \quad (4)$$

For example for the type check in section 4.1, $d \in RQ$, $\neg RQ$ unfolds to $\forall P.(\leq 0P) \vee \forall R.(\neg A \vee \forall R.(\neg B \vee \neg C))$. Therefore, $DS = popu(\neg RQ) = \{RQ, \forall P.(\leq 0P) \vee \forall R.(\neg A \vee \forall R.(\neg B \vee \neg C)), \forall P.(\leq 0P), \leq 0P, \forall R.(\neg A \vee \forall R.(\neg B \vee \neg C)), \neg A \vee \forall R.(\neg B \vee \neg C), A, \forall R.(\neg B \vee \neg C), \neg B \vee \neg C, B, C\}$. As a result, the disjunctions $\{U \vee Y\}$ and $\{\neg Y \vee \neg Z\}$ are skipped because none of their non-negated elements are contained in *DS*, while all other disjunctions are applied, as illustrated in Figure 9.

Weighted Disjunctions and Terms

This strategy seeks to manage the order in which completion rules for disjunctions, existential quan-

Figure 9. Selective consistency

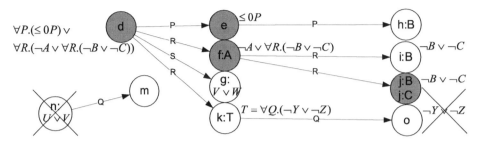

tifiers and maximum cardinality in the knowledge base are applied, such that the expressions which are most likely to contribute to a clash, are applied first. The order of application for all other expressions remains arbitrary. This strategy does not compromise completeness.

A weighted queue Q is used in two instances. A weighted disjunction queue Q^{disj} maintains the order in which disjunctions will be applied for a particular individual A. The order of existential quantifier and maximum cardinality rule application is maintained by the role restriction queue Q^{rest}. A queue Q contains pairs $<object(x), weight(x)>$ such that $object(x)$ is an object and $weight(x)$ is a positive integer representing the weight of $object(x)$ and multiple $object(x)$ can have the same $weight(x)$. $nweight(x)$ is a double value representing a normalised weight for $object(x)$ such that $0 \leq normalised(x) \leq 1$. Normalised values are calculated by dividing the current weight by the highest weight in the queue, given by $nweight(x) = weight(x)/\max_{x \in Q^{ind}}(weight(x))$. Queue objects $object(x)$ are given by the queue iterator in descending $nweight(x)$ order [1..0].

This strategy employs two different approaches: disjunction weighting and term weighting. Both approaches utilise the *ClashDetect(C, I, CP)* function which attempts to find a pathway from term C (asserted to individual I) to a potential clash and returns a set CP containing terms (disjunctions, existential quantifiers and maximum cardinality

expressions) if a clash pathway was found, or an empty set if no clash was found. All weight values $weight(x)$ of expressions x in the clash pathway are incremented, such that $increment_{x \in ClashDetect(C, I, CP)}(weight(x))$ and $increment(v) = v++$. Note, if a term forms a clash path, but is not yet asserted to the individual, its weight is maintained by the queue and used in the event that it is added as a type for the individual.

ClashDetect(I, C, CP) calls the function which handles each kind of expression passed to it. For instance, if C is a maximum cardinality restriction it calls *CheckMaxRestriction(I, mx, CP)*. *ClashDetect(I, C, CP)* pseudo code is given in Box 2. Each of the functions referred to in the above pseudo code, are described in Appendix A.

For example for the type check in section 4.1, $d \in RQ$, $\neg RQ$ unfolds to $\forall P.(\leq 0P) \vee \forall R.(\neg A \vee \forall R.(\neg B \vee \neg C))$. A clash pathway exists which includes: $\{d:\neg RQ, e:\leq 0P, f: \forall R.(\neg B \vee \neg C), j: \neg B \vee \neg C\}$. Therefore all the disjunctions and expressions involved in this path are incremented. The individuals involved are shaded in Figure 7, section 4.1. The queues are illustrated in Figure 10.

Now that we have detailed our optimisation strategies, we discuss our work in implementing the strategies in the next section. We also provide a performance evaluation comprising a comparison with current reasoners and performance on a resource-constrained device.

Box 2.

```
ClashDetect:
Inputs: Let I be an individual, Let C be a type, Let CP be a set of in-
dividuals and logic expressions involved in a clash.
Outputs: CP
Switch(C)
Case C is primitive, negation, nominal or literal value:
    Return CheckPrimitive(I, C, CP).
Case C is a disjunction:
    Return CheckDisjunction(I, C, CP).
Case C is a conjunction:
    Return CheckConjunction(I, C, CP).
Case C is a universal quantifier logic expression:
    Return CheckUniversalQuantifier(I, C, CP).
Case C is an existential quantifier logic expression:
    Return CheckExistentialQuantifier(I, C, CP).
Case C is a maximum role restriction logic expression:
    Return CheckMaxRestriction(I, C, CP).
```

IMPLEMENTATION AND PERFORMANCE EVALUATION

In this section we provide two case studies in order to evaluate our mTableaux algorithm to answer the following two main questions:

1. How does mTableaux perform when compared to other reasoners?
   a. Since mTableaux does not guarantee completeness for all strategies, how much does mTableaux impact on result accuracy reduced, as measured using recall and precision?

2. How does mTableaux scale in terms of meeting the twin constraints of processing time and memory usage on a mobile device?
   a. Does mTableaux enable successful completion of a reasoning task such that a result can be obtained on a resource constrained device (i. e., available memory was not exceeded)?

Figure 10. Example disjunction and role restriction queue

Q_{disj} *object(x)*	Q_{disj} *nweight(x)*	Q_{rest} *object(x)*	Q_{rest} *nweight(x)*
d: $\neg A \vee \forall R.(\neg B \vee \neg C)$.	1.0	e: $\leq 0P$.	1.0
j: $\neg B \vee \neg C$	1.0		
i: $\neg B \vee \neg C$.	0		
n: $U \vee V$.	0		
o: $\neg Y \vee \neg Z$.	0		

b. Does mTableaux significantly improve performance compared to normal execution of Tableaux with no optimisation strategies enabled?

c. Which mTableaux strategies or combination of strategies work best?

d. Do different strategies work better for different scenarios / reasoning tasks?

e. Do the optimisation strategies improve performance for positive as well as negative type checks?

We do this using two case studies as well as the Galen[3] ontology. Our two case studies are detailed in the next two subsections.

Case Study 1: Searching for a Printer

Bob is walking around at his university campus and wishes to locate laser printer-fax machine (to print some documents and send a fax). He issues a service request from his PDA for a listing of black and white, laser printers which support a wireless network protocol such as Bluetooth, WiFi or IrDA, a fax protocol and which have a dialup modem with a phone number. Equations 5-8 show Bob's request in Description Logic (DL) (Baader et al., 2003) form, while equation 9 presents a possible printer.

$$\text{PrinterRequest} \equiv \text{PhModem} \wedge \exists\text{hasColour.}\{\text{Black}\} \wedge \text{hasComm.}\{\text{Fax}\} \wedge \text{LaserPrinterOperational} \cap \text{WNet} \quad (5)$$

$$\text{PhModem} \equiv \exists\text{hasComm.}(\text{Modem} \wedge \geq 1 \text{ phNumber}) \quad (6)$$

$$\text{LaserPrinterOperational} \equiv \text{Printer} \wedge \exists\text{hasCartridge.}\{\text{Toner}\} \wedge \geq 1 \text{ hasOperationalContext} \quad (7)$$

$$\text{WNet} \equiv \exists\text{hasComm.}\{\text{BT}\} \wedge \exists\text{hasComm.}\{\text{WiFi}\} \wedge \exists\text{hasComm.}\{\text{IrDA}\} \quad (8)$$

$$\text{Printer(LaserPrinter1)},$$
$$\text{hasColour(LaserPrinter1, Black)},$$
$$\text{hasCartridge(LaserPrinter1, Toner)}, \text{hasComm(LaserPrinter1, BT)},$$
$$\text{hasComm(LaserPrinter1, Fax)}, \text{hasOperationalContext(LaserPrinter1, Ready)},$$
$$\text{Modem(Modem1)}, \text{hasComm(LaserPrinter1, Modem1)}, \text{phNumber (Modem1, "9903 9999")} \quad (9)$$

Note, these equations are simplified for illustrative purposes, the actual ontology used for this case study comprises 141 classes, 337 individuals and 126 roles. Equation 5 defines five attributes in the request, the first is unfolded into equation 6, specifying the printer must have a modem which has a phone number. The second attribute specifies a black and white requirement. The third attribute requires support for the fax protocol, and the fourth unfolds into equation 7, specifying a printer which has a toner cartridge and at least one operational context. The fifth unfolds into equation 8, which specified that one of the wireless protocols (Bluetooth, WiFi or IrDA) are supported. Equation 9 shows a DL fragment defining the LaserPrinter1 individual as meeting the service request. We also define an individual LaserPrinter2 as the same as equation 9, but without a phone number.

Case Study 2: Searching for a Movie Cinema

Bob is in a foreign city centre and has walked past several shops, short range ontology download points, and other people carrying devices with accumulated ontologies of their own. As such Bob collects a range of ontologically described service advertisements. He sits down in a park out of network range, and decides to find a movie cinema with a café attached which has a public phone and WiFi public Internet. He issues a request for a retail outlet which has at least 5 cinemas that each screen movies, has a section which sells coffee and tea, sells an Internet service which supports access using the WiFi protocol and sells a fixed phone service. We specify that an individual VillageCinemas matches the service request and GreaterUnionCinemas is the same as VillageCinemas except it provides Bluetooth Internet access rather than by WiFi, and therefore fails to match the request. The request specifies universal and existential quantifier and cardinality restrictions. The ontologies for this scenario contain 204 classes, 241 individuals and 93 roles.

Implementation

Our mTableaux strategies have been implemented as an extension to the Pellet 1.5 reasoner which supports OWL-DL with SHOIN expressivity. That is, mTableaux is implemented into the Pellet source tree. (Sirin, Parsia, Grau, Kalyanpur & Katz, 2007) discusses the implementation and design of Pellet. We chose Pellet because it is open source, allowing us to provide a proof of concept and compare performance with and without the strategies enabled. We selected Pellet over FaCT++ because it is written in Java, making it easily portable to small devices such as PDAs and mobile phones, while FaCT++ is written in C++. An addition, we are using Jena as the ontology repository used by Pellet to read the ontology. We implemented the optimisation strategies: selective consistency, skip disjunctions, and rank by disjunctions and terms, and we evaluate the impact these have on performance in the next sections. We intend to make the source code for the system available for download on completion of the project.

Comparison of mTableaux with Other Reasoners

In order to show how mTableaux compares to other widely used OWL semantic reasoners, we provide a performance comparison with FaCT++

1.1.11, RacerPro 1.9.2 beta and Pellet 1.5 without our optimisations. As stated in section 4.2, these reasoners perform an ontology "realisation" in which consistency checks are used to determine all the inferred class types for every individual in the ontology, $I_{[1, 2, .., n]} \in RQ_{[1, 2, .., m]}$, where n denotes the number of individuals in the ontology and m denotes the number of classes, resulting in $n.m$ possible individual and class combinations. Subsequent queries to the reasoner then draw from this pre-inferred data. Since an ontology realisation is unnecessary for service discovery in which specific service candidates are compared against single request class types, mTableaux does not perform an ontology realisation. Therefore, our performance evaluation presents two results for mTableaux one with full realisation and one where a subset of individuals are compared against a single user request class type such that $I_{[1, 2, .., n]} \in RQ$. The individuals represent discoverable services.

The evaluation was conducted on a Pentium Centrino 1.82GHz computer with 2GB memory with Java 1.5 (J2SE) allocated maximum of 500MB for each experiment. All times are presented are computed as the average of 10 independent runs. We performed our evaluation using both of the case studies described in section 6.1 and 6.2, as well as several publically available ontologies, including: Galen[iii], Tambis[4], Koala[5] and Teams[6]. Galen is a large ontology of medical terms with 2748 classes and 844 roles. Tambis, Koala and Teams ontologies have 183, 20 and 9 classes respectively. For each of our Printer and Product ontologies we checked 20 service candidates against the request printer and product user request, respectively. The Galen, Tambis, Koala and Teams ontologies did not contain individuals so we created a matching (positive) and non-matching (negative) individual for request each class type that we checked. The expected results for each ontology are illustrated in table 1.

Figure 11 presents the total time required to perform the 8 inference checks for the Galen

Table 1. Expected results for each ontology

Ontology	Request Class	Positive	Negative	Total
Printer	PrinterRequest	3	17	20
Product	ProductRequest	3	17	20
Galen	BacterialGramPositiveStainResult	1	1	2
	FailureOfCellUptakeOfBloodGlu-cose-DueToCellInsulinResistance	1	1	2
	AcutePulmonaryHeartDisease	1	1	2
	LocalAnaesthetic	1	1	2
Tambis	small-nuclear-rna	1	1	2
	peptidase	1	1	2
Koala	MaleStudentWith3Daughters	1	1	2
	KoalaWithPhD	1	1	2
Teams	MarriedPerson	1	1	2
	MixedTeam	1	1	2
Total		16	44	60

ontology and Figures 12 and 13 present the total time to check all 20 service individuals against the user request class for the product and printer case studies, respectively. The 4 inference checks for each of the Tambis, Koala and Teams ontologies are not graphed because they completed in under 1 second.

As illustrated in Figure 11, mTableaux significantly outperformed the other reasoners for the Galen ontology, requiring only 0.67 seconds to perform the 8 inference checks. mTableaux with realisation almost performed as well as FaCT++ and outperforms RacerPro. Pellet with no optimisations performed poorly, requiring more than 40

seconds to complete. Figure 12 and 13 show that RacerPro performed worst, followed by Pellet, for the Product and Printer ontologies. mTableaux is slower when a full realisation is performed, because this compares irrelevant individuals against the user request. FaCT++ performed slightly better than mTableaux for the Product ontology, which we attribute to its implementation in C++. We note that mTableaux with realisation and FaCT++ could not complete the printer ontology and did not provide a result.

These results show, that our optimisation strategies significantly improve the performance of Pellet. We also observed that for all evalua-

Figure 11. Reasoner comparison using galen ontology

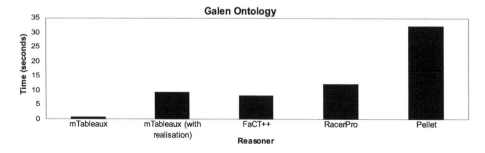

Figure 12. Product ontology reasoner comparison

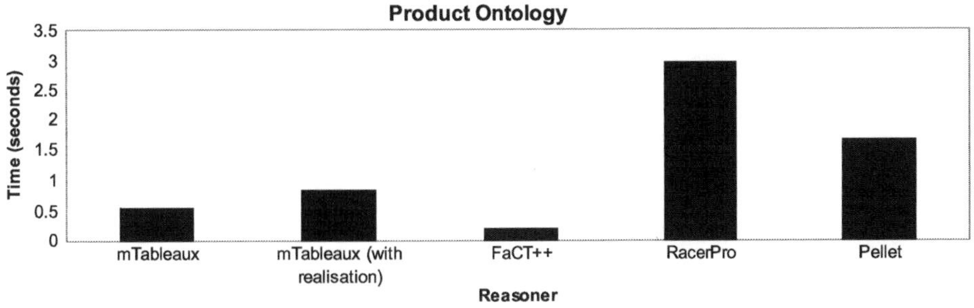

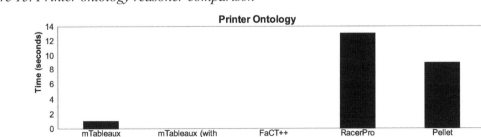

tions the number of branches applied when using mTableaux was less than half that of Pellet. We conclude that when the amount of available memory available is constrained as on a small device, the performance improvements resulting from mTableaux will be significantly enlarged.

Since some strategies to not guarantee completeness, we measure the accuracy of mTableaux compared to other reasoners using recall and precision metrics, as illustrated in equations 10 and 11, where x denotes the number of service individuals which were expected to match but also actually found to match by the reasoner to match, n denotes the total number of service individuals which were expected to match (including any not returned by the reasoner) and N denotes the total number of service individuals which the reasoner claims do indeed match. Note that an expected match implies that a true match can be deduced by a reasoner in which completeness holds.

$$\text{Recall} = x \,/\, n \qquad (10)$$

$$\text{Precision} = x \,/\, N \qquad (11)$$

The recall and precision results obtained by completing the matching detailed in table 1, are provided in table 2. For instance mTableaux returned all 16 of the service individuals which were expected to match. The results show that the actual results were as expected for all reasoners except that FaCT++ did not match the positive individual with the class type MaleStudentWith3Daughters in the Koala ontology, because FaCT++ does not match Boolean literal values which were present in the request class type. Therefore, although mTableaux does not guarantee completeness for the selective consistency (SC) and skip disjunction (SD) strategies, there was no degradation in result accuracy on the ontologies tests in our evaluation. We conclude in data sets representing realistic scenarios such as the ones we used, mTableaux

Figure 13. Printer ontology reasoner comparison

Table 2. Total actual results for each reasoner

Reasoner	Actual Positive	Actual Negative	Recall	Precision
mTableaux	16	44	16/16 = 1.0	16/16 = 1.0
Pellet	16	44	16/16 = 1.0	16/16 = 1.0
RacerPro	16	44	16/16 = 1.0	16/16 = 1.0
FaCT++	15	45	15/16 = 0.937	15/15 = 1.0

does not compromise result completeness as measured by recall and precision. In our tests, we checked to see whether ontology consistency was compromised by applying the negation of a specific class expression $\neg RQ$ to an individual I, in order to check whether the individual holds inferred membership to this expression $I \in RQ$. All applied expansion rules and disjunctions which led to clashes (causing an inconsistent ontology for all models) were the result of the negated expression $\neg RQ$ having been asserted. Since CS and SD strategies include or exclude individuals and disjunctions based on universal quantifies and expressions which result from the individual I and expression $\neg RQ$, respectively, there was no breach of completeness. Completeness may be compromised when the application of disjunctions, or expressions resulting from these disjunctions, do not relate to the expression RQ, which would result in a failure of mTableaux to prove a positive inference. In models of the knowledge base, parts of the ontology which do not relate to the class type RQ involved in the inference check may interact with each other to create clashes. It is in these cases where completeness is not guaranteed.

Since mTableaux outperformed all reasoners except for FaCT++ in some case while preserving completeness in our case studies, we now provide a performance evaluation to show how mTableaux performs on a small resource constrained device, in the next section. We also show which strategies work best together and the level of overhead incurred by using each optimisation.

mTableaux Performance on a Mobile Device

We performed an evaluation on a HP iPAQ hx2700 PDA, with Intel PXA270 624Mhz processor, 64MB RAM, running Windows Mobile 5.0 with Mysaifu Java J2SE Virtual Machine (JVM) (Mysaifu, 2009), allocated 15MB of memory. We executed the four type check combinations shown in table 1, to evaluate both case study requests against a matching/positive and non-matching/negative service individual, defined as individual A and B, respectively. We executed each of the 4 consistency checks outlined in table 3 with every combination of the 4 optimisation strategies enabled (16 times). Table 4 indicates which strategies were enabled for each of the 16 tests (organised

Table 3. Type membership checks

Case Study	Request	Individual		Expected Result
Case Study 1	Fax Laser Printer	A	#LaserPrinter1 (with phone number)	Match
		B	#LaserPrinter2 (no phone number)	No Match
Case Study 2	Movie Cinema	A	#MovieCinema2 (WiFi Internet)	Match
		B	#MovieCinema2(Bluetooth Internet)	No Match

Table 4. Optimisation tests

Test	a	b	c	d	e	f	g	h	i	j	k	l	m	n	o	p
Selective Consistency		×		×		×		×		×		×		×		×
Skip Disjunctions			×	×			×	×			×	×			×	×
Rank by Disjunction					×	×	×	×					×	×	×	×
Rank by Term									×	×	×	×	×	×	×	×

in bitwise order). Pellet with SHOIN expressivity was used for all tests. Test 16 represents normal execution of the Tableaux algorithm, with none of our optimisations strategies enabled. Successfully executed tests returned the expected result shown in table 3.

Figure 14 shows two graphs, which each show the consistency time to perform a type check for individual A and B against the request for the tests in table 3, using Pellet with SHOIN expressivity. The left and right graph present results for the printer and product case studies, respectively. Tests which did not complete due to insufficient available memory or which required more than 800 seconds to execute, omitted from the graph. In addition to consistency checking, an additional 35-40 seconds was required load the ontology into the reasoner (not shown on graph).

Test a, with no optimisations (standard Tableaux algorithm) failed to complete due to insufficient memory. The same occurred for many of the tests which are not shown on the graph. This demonstrates that our strategies reduce memory consumption, making reasoning feasible on resource constrained devices. We note that in all tests, the Java virtual machine (JVM) used all of the memory allocated to it. Since the graphs in Figure 14 are difficult to interpret, we re-ordered (see table 5) the tests in an attempt to arrange the fastest processing times at the front of the graph. We show the re-ordered results in the graph in Figure 15.

With optimisations enabled the best result for case study 1 and 2 was 18 and 35-70 seconds, respectively. This illustrates significant performance improvements in both scenarios.

When used in isolation, the selective consistency strategy proved to be the most effective in case study 2, while skip disjunctions was more effective in case study 1. Utilising both of these strategies together provided even better results,

Figure 14. processing time required to perform each test, for Selective Consistency (SC), Skip Disjunction (SD), Rank by Disjunction (RD) and Rank by Term (RT) strategies, showing total consistency time to perform an inferred membership check for matching individual A and non-matching individual B, for the Printer ontology (left) and Product ontology (right).

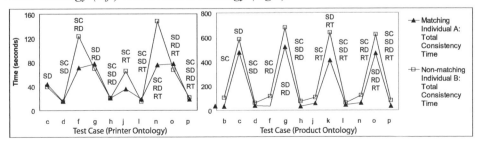

Table 5. Re-ordered Optimisation tests

Test #	1	2	3	4	5	6	7	8	9	10	11	12	13	14	15	16
Selective Consistency	×	×	×	×	×	×		×	×							
Skip Disjunctions	×	×	×	×			×			×	×	×				
Rank by Disjunction			×	×				×	×	×	×		×	×		
Rank by Term		×	×			×			×	×		×	×		×	

which suggests there is no advantage in selecting different strategies for different scenarios.

We found that the weighted strategies (rank by disjunctions and terms) did reduce the number of disjunction branches applied, by up to half in some cases, but this failed to significantly reduce the number of consistency rules applied overall. In addition, the ranking strategies did not improve performance when used in combination with the selective consistency and skip disjunction strategies. However, we observed that tests 13, 14, and 15, when matching individual A, in case study two, completed in 972, 982 and 983 seconds (not shown on graph), respectively, compared to 2139 seconds in test 16. This suggests that the rank disjunction and individual strategies improve performance but are far less effective than selective consistency or skip disjunction strategies. These ranking algorithms need to be improved in future work.

Due to the fact that our selective consistency and disjunction skipping strategies reduce the number of potential rules and disjunctions to be applied, they improve performance in all cases. However, the results also showed that the optimisations can be less effective in improving performance for non-matching individuals B than with matching individuals A, as shown in every test in case study 2 and some in case study 1. This is because the Tableaux algorithm continues applying branches and consistency rules until a clash is found. This will inherently result in more rules to apply for non-matching individuals which do not clash for all branches. This finding also motivates the need for a resource-aware strategy, in which branches below a certain threshold are not applied, where resources are low, to assume no-match with some uncertainty rating.

Figure 16 illustrates the overhead cost incurred in executing the optimisation strategies for each test in from table 5, and shows the level to which

Figure 15. Re-ordered processing time required to perform each test, for Selective Consistency (SC), Skip Disjunction (SD), Rank by Disjunction (RD) and Rank by Term (RT) strategies, showing total consistency time to perform an inferred membership check for matching individual A and non-matching individual, for the Printer ontology (left) and Product ontology (right).

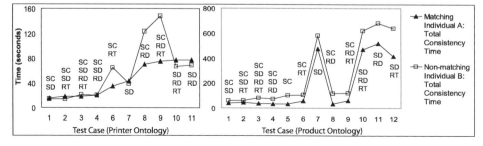

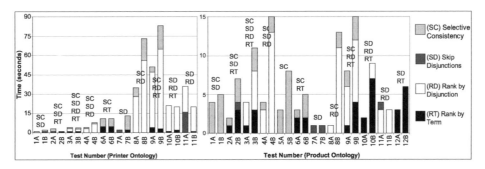

Figure 16. Optimisation overhead breakdown. Each test was conducted twice, once for matching individual A and once for the non-matching individual B, for each case study (left graph: Printer, right graph: Product). EG 1A indicates test 1, individual A (see table 3).

each strategy contributes to the total overhead for the test. Each test is completed twice, for both matching individual A and non-matching individual B. We observed that skip disjunctions resulted in little to no overhead in all cases. Overhead costs for selective consistency was similar for both case studies, usually remaining under 5 seconds and peaking to 18 in tests 8B and 9B (test 8 and 9 for individual B) in case study 1, indicating a greater number of individuals to add to the weighted queue. Case study 1 recorded higher rank disjunction overhead than case study 2, suggesting there were fewer disjunctions and clash paths in the ontologies of case study 2, to evaluate. Rank disjunction overhead was also significantly higher for tests 8 and 9 for both case studies due to the skip disjunction strategy being disabled. It was also higher when type checking individual B compared to A, due to the reasoner exhaustively branching on disjunctions where a clash is never found.

In summary, we have demonstrated that:

1. mTableaux outperforms reasoners such as RacerPro and Pellet, performs comparatively with FaCT++ when full realisation is performed and faster than FaCT++ when it is not,
2. mTableaux does not compromise completeness as measured by recall and precision when all clashes are the direct consequence of the inference check rather than other unre-

lated concepts in the ontology as in realistic data sets such as those in our evaluation,

3. mTableaux minimises memory consumption such that successful completion of reasoning tasks on resource limited devices is possible,
4. mTableaux significantly reduces processing time compared with normal Tableaux with no optimisations,
5. selective consistency and skip disjunction strategies work best together while rank by disjunction and term strategies provided no added performance benefit,
6. the selective consistency strategy was more effective in case study 2 while skip disjunctions was more effective in case study 1, and provided the best results for both scenarios when used together, and
7. mTableaux strategies improved performance for both positive and negative type checks, however overall performance for negative type checks in case study 2 was poorer, leaving scope for resource-aware reasoning in future work.

CONCLUSION AND FUTURE WORK

We have presented a novel strategy for improving the scalability of the Tableaux algorithm for mobile semantic reasoning. mTableaux was shown to significantly reduce processing time and minimize memory consumption of pervasive discovery reasoning tasks in two case studies, so that they can be completed on small resource constrained devices. It was also shown to outperform RacerPro and Pellet without reducing the quality of results returned in realistic datasets such as in our scenarios. It also performed comparatively with FaCT++ when a full realisation was undertaken and outperformed FaCT++ when a realisation was not. The mTableaux strategies achieve this by limiting the number of branches and expansion rules applied and by applying the most important branches first to avoid the need for full branch saturation.

However, despite these significant optimisations, it is still possible that large ontologies may still exhaust all available memory before completing the task or require excessive amounts of time. In order to cater for time and memory constraints in situations where ontology or request size is too large even with the optimisation strategies enabled we are implementing the adaptive strategies briefly mentioned in section 4.2 which take available memory and time into consideration:

- The adaptive request condition matching strategy has the goal of matching first, the most important conditions in the request as deemed by the user, at the request level. The user is asked to specify weights of importance to each request condition. The most important conditions are matched first. In the event that important conditions do not match the reasoner will not continue to attempt to match less important conditions, if a threshold is exceeded. The threshold is determined based on the amount of time and memory available, under the assumption that limited processing power is better spent attempting to match another potential service.
- Our adaptive expansion rule application strategy utilises the weighted expansion

rules from the weighted disjunctions and terms strategy in section 5.3. Similar to the strategy above, its goal is to stop the application of expansion rules which have a weight that falls below a certain threshold, except this occurs at the reasoner level. The threshold is increased when remaining time or memory becomes low.

- On-demand ontology loading has a goal of only loading of portions of the total ontology into the reasoner's memory. Reasoners such as Pellet, currently utilise an ontology parser and loader such as Jena (Jena, 2009) or OWL-API (WonderWeb, 2008) to load ontology files into memory. This data is then supplied in its entirety to the reasoner which creates classes, roles and individuals to represent all of this information as objects. Loading all of these parsed triples into the reasoner incurs significant initialisation costs and requires more processing time for lookup and retrieval during reasoning. In addition, if there is insufficient memory available to complete the reasoning task, the task fails even if most of the ontology data was irrelevant to the inference check. Unfder this on-demand loading strategy, rather than iterating all triples in the ontology to create objects in the reasoner, the reasoner instead queries the triples in order to create only the specific classes, roles or individuals which it requires during the reasoning process. That is if a URI of an individual is encountered by the Tableaux algorithm and no individual object is found within the reasoner to match the URI, it asks that the individual and the data associated with it is, be loaded into its knowledge base.

Our current work focuses on implementation and evaluation of these adaptive strategies to enhance the operation of mTableaux.

REFERENCES

Pellet. (2003). Retrieved from http://www.mind-swap.org/2003/pellet/.

FaCT++. (2008). Retrieved May 1, 2007, from http://owl.man.ac.uk/factplusplus/.

KAON2. (2008). Retrieved June 21, 2007, from http://kaon2.semanticweb.org.

RacerPro. (2008). Retrieved May 23, 2007, from http://www.racer-systems.com.

Almeida, D. R. d., Bapista, C. d. S., Silva, E. R. d., Campelo, C. E. C., Figueiredo, H. F. d., & Lacerda, Y. A. (2006). A Context-Aware System Based on Service-Oriented Architecture. In *20th International Conference on Advanced Information Networking and Applications(AINA'06)* (pp. 205-210). IEEE Computer Society.

Arnold, K., O'Sullivan, B., Scheifler, R. W., Waldo, J. & Woolrath, A. (1999). *The Jini Specification.* Addison-Wesley.

Baader, F., Calvanese, D., McGuinness, D. L., Nardi, D. & Patel-Schneider, P. F. (2003). *The Description Logic Handbook: Theory, Implementation, and Applications.* Cambridge University Press.

Broens, T. (2004). *Context-aware, Ontology based, Semantic Service Discovery.* Enschede, The Netherlands, University of Twente: 87.

Cabral, L., Domingue, J., Galizia, S., Gugliotta, A., Tanasescu, V., Pedrinaci, C. et al. (2006). IRS-III: A Broker for Semantic Web Services based Applications. In *5th International Semantic Web Conference (ISWC 2006)*, Athens, GA, USA.

Chakraborty, D., Joshi, A., Yesha, Y., & Finin, T. (2004). Towards Distributed Service Discovery in Pervasive Computing Environments. *IEEE Transactions on Mobile Computing.*

Chakraborty, D., Perich, F., Avancha, S. & Joshi, A. (2001). DReggie: Semantic Service Discovery for M-Commerce Applications. In *Workshop on Reliable and Secure Applications in Mobile Environment, In Conjunction with 20th Symposium on Reliable Distributed Systems (SRDS).*

Chatti, M. A., Srirama, S., Kensche, D., & Cao, Y. (2006). Mobile Web Services for Collaborative Learning. In *4th International Workshop on Wireless, Mobile and Ubiquitous Technology in Education* (pp. 129-133). IEEE.

Doulkeridis, C., Loutas, N., & Vazirgiannis, M. (2005). A *System Architecture for Context-Aware Service Discovery.*

Guttman, E. (1999). Service Location Protocol : Automatic Discovery of IP Network Services. *IEEE Internet Computing, 3*(4), 71-80.

Horrocks, I., & Patel-Schneider, P. F. (1999). Optimising Description Logic Subsumption. *Journal of Logic and Computation, 9*(3), 267-293.

Horrocks, I., & Sattler, U. (2005). A Tableaux Decision Procedure for SHOIQ. *19th International Conference on Artificial Intelligence (IJCAI 2005).*

Howes, T. A., & Smith, M. C. (1995). *A Scalable, Deployable Directory Service Framework for the Internet.* Technical report, Center for Information Technology Integration, Univerity of Michigan.

Issarny, V., & Sailhan, F. (2005). Scalable Service Discovery for MANET. *Third IEEE International Conference on Pervasive Computing and Communications (PerCom)*, Kauai Island, Hawaii.

Jena - HP Semantic Framework. (2009). from http://www.hpl.hp.com/semweb/.

Kleemann, T. (2006). Towards Mobile Reasoning. *International Workshop on Description Logics (DL2006)*, Windermere, Lake District, UK.

Küster, U., König-Ries, B., & Klein, M. (2006). Discovery and Mediation using DIANE Service Descriptions. *Second Semantic Web Service Challenge 2006 Workshop*, Budva, Montenegro.

Lee, C., Helal, A., Desai, N., Verma, V., & Arslan, B. (2003). Konark: A System and Protocols for Device Independent, Peer-to-Peer Discovery and Delivery of Mobile Services. *IEEE Transactions on Systems, Man and Cybernetics, 33*(6).

Miller, B. A., & Pascoe, R. A. (2000). Salutation Service Discovery in Pervasive Computing Environments. *IBM Pervasive Computing White Paper.*

Mysaifu, J.V.M. (2009). Retrieved from http://www2s.biglobe.ne.jp/~dat/java/project/jvm/index_en.html.

Roto, V., & Oulasvirta, A. (2005). Need for Non-Visual Feedback with Long Response Times in Mobile HCI. *International World Wide Web Conference Committee (IW3C2)*, Chiba, Japan.

Sirin, E., Parsia, B., Grau, B. C., Kalyanpur, A., & Katz, Y. (2007). Pellet: A Practical OWL-DL Reasoner. *Web Semantics: Science, Services and Agents on the World Wide Web, 5*(2).

Srinivasan, N., Paolucci, M., & Sycara, K. (2005). Semantic Web Service Discovery in the OWL-S IDE. *39th Hawaii International Conference on System Sciences*, Hawaii.

Sycara, K., Widoff, S., Klusch, M. & Lu, J. (2002). LARKS: Dynamic Matchmaking Among Heterogeneous Software Agents in Cyberspace. *Autonomous Agents and Multi-Agent Systems, 5*, 173-203.

Universal Description Discovery and Integration (UDDI). (2009). Retrieved from http://uddi.xml.org/.

Universal Plug and Play (UPnP). (2007). Retrieved March 12, 2007, from http://www.upnp.org.

OWL-API. (2008). Retrieved from http://owlapi.sourceforge.net/.

Web Service Modelling Ontology (WSMO) Working Group. (2009). Retrieved from http://www.wsmo.org/.

ENDNOTES

[1] http://www.google.com/mobile

[2] http://www.yahoo.com/mobile

[3] http://www.cs.man.ac.uk/~horrocks/OWL/Ontologies/galen.owl

[4] http://www.mindswap.org/ontologies/debugging/miniTambis.owl

[5] http://protege.stanford.edu/plugins/owl/owl-library/koala.owl

[6] http://www.mindswap.org/ontologies/team.owl

APPENDIX A

This section provides pseudo code detailing the functions referred to in section 5.3. Note that hasType(I, C) returns true if individual I has been assigned the class type C, and unfold(C) returns a set of all logic expressions and type names which type C is the equivalent of.

CheckPrimitive

```
Inputs: I, C, CP. Outputs: CP.
Let I denote an individual.
Let C denote a primitive class name or a literal value.
Let CP denote a set (clash path).
Let S denote a set S = {}.
If hasType(I, ¬C):
    CP ← I + CP.
    Return CP.
Else:
    S ← unfold(C).
    Foreach y_i in S:
        CP ← ClashDetect(I, y_i, CP).
        If CP ≠ null: Return CP.
    Return null.
```

CheckDisjunction

```
Inputs: I, D, CP. Outputs: CP.
Let I denote an individual.
Let D denote a disjunction.
Let CP denote a set (clash path).
Let S denote a set S = {}.
Let e denote a disjunct element in D where D = {e_1 ∨ e_2 ∨..∨e_n }.
For each e_i in D:
    S ← ClashDetect(I, e_i, CP).
    If S = null: Return null.
    Else: CP ← S + CP.
Return CP.
```

CheckConjunction

```
Inputs: I, C, CP. Outputs: CP.
Let I denote an individual.
Let C denote a conjunction.
Let CP denote a set (clash path).
Let S denote a set S = {}.
```

Let e denote a conjunct element in C where $C = \{e_1 \wedge e_2 \wedge \_ \wedge e_n\}$.

For each e_i in C:

    $S \leftarrow \text{ClashDetect}(I, e_i, CP)$.

    If $S \neq \text{null}$:

        $CP \leftarrow S + CP$.

        Return CP.

    Return null.

CheckUniversalQuantifier

Inputs: I, av, CP.

Outputs: CP.

Let I denote an individual.

Let CP denote a set (clash path).

Let av denote a universal restriction expression, let avR denote the role to which av applies to, let avC denote the role filler type defined in av for avR, such that $av = \forall avR.avC$.

Let o_i denote an avR-neighbour to I.

Let $O = \{o_1, o_2, o_n\}$.

Let denote a set $S = \{\}$.

For each o_i in O:

    $S \leftarrow \text{ClashDetect}(O_i, avC, CS)$.

    If $S \neq \text{null}$:

        $CP \leftarrow S + CP$.

        Return CP.

    Return null.

CheckExistentialQuantifier

Inputs: I, sv, CP. Outputs: CP.

Let I denote an individual.

Let CP denote a set (clash path).

Let sv denote an existential quantifier restriction, let svR denote the role to which sv applies to and let svC denote the role filler type for svR defined in sv such that $sv = \exists svR.svC$.

Let mx denote a maximum cardinality role restriction, let mxN denote the cardinality value defined in mx and let mxR denote the role to which mx applies to, such that $mx = (\leq mxR\ mxN)$.

Let o_i denote an svR-neighbour to I.

Let $O = \{o_1, o_2, o_n\}$, where $o_i \neq o_{i+1..n}$.

Let mx_i^{SVR} denote an mx which applies to the role svR.

Let $MX = \{mx_1^{SVR}, mx_2^{SVR}, mx_m^{SVR}\}$.

For each o_i in O:

    If (svR is a functional role) AND ($n \geq 1$ AND $\text{hasType}(o_i, \neg SVC)$):

        Return $CP + I + SV$.

    Else:

        For each mx_i^{SVR} in MX:

```
        If mxN_i ≤ n + 1 AND hasType(o_i, ¬SVC):
            Return CP + I + SV + MX.
```

CheckMaxRestriction

Inputs: I, mx, CP. Outputs: CP.

Let I denote an individual.

Let CP denote a set (clash path).

Let mx denote a maximum cardinality role restriction, let mxN denote the cardinality value defined in mx and let mxR denote the role to which mx applies to, such that mx=(≤ mxR mxN)

Let o_i denote an mxR-neighbour to I.

Let $O = \{o_1, o_2, o_n\}$, where $o_i \neq o_{i+1..n}$.

If $mxN < n$:

   Return $CP + I + mx$.

This work was previously published in the International Journal on Semantic Web & Information Systems, Volume 5, Issue 2, edited by A. Sheth, pp. 91-116, copyright 2009 by IGI Publishing (an imprint of IGI Global).

Chapter 4.3
Adding Value to SMEs in the Courier Industry by Adopting a Web-Based Service Delivery Model

Paul Darbyshire
Victoria University, Australia

ABSTRACT

The aim of this research is to design a framework for a Web system that is intended for linking small and medium transport companies with their customers. The unique aspects of the framework are two-fold. The framework utilizes Web services, which means that it can be applied to existing software and hardware environments. This reduces the need for specialized integration and development, the cost of which becomes a further barrier to SMEs in adding value to customers through existing systems. The framework is additionally designed to link both communities of SMEs and customers in a fledgling digital ecosystem arrangement. Such arrangements offer inherent added value to both types of participants.

INTRODUCTION

One of the great promises of the Internet is that it would help level the playing field somewhat for small to medium businesses by giving them access to market share and allowing them to compete more effectively with larger corporations. We know that technology does make small businesses more competitive and helps in reducing the exclusivity of markets once thought to be beyond their reach. However, the playing field will never be really level and "small businesses are seldom on the cutting edge when it comes to a new technology" (Campbell, 2004). These companies simply cannot afford to provide the value-added services offered by their larger counterparts.

The courier industry is a very good example of this. Small and medium size courier companies generally offer a broad range of services and can provide valuable local service and knowledge to their customers. Utilization of the Web for e-commerce by these companies gives a number of advantages for the logistics trade, such as new market penetration, targeted advertisement of new and existing services, increased quality of services, acceleration of information processing, and customers' feedback improvement. However, these companies are often overlooked in favor of the larger providers that can offer a more expensive but value-added service. Services such as tracking of shipment deliveries, immediate delivery notification, and other information including GPS information is expensive to provide but gives customers value-added services they are willing to pay for. Another barrier to adoption is the high demand placed on resources for a Web system's ability to integrate with existing systems. This in turn increases the cost of qualitative logistics for the Web-system development.

While small and medium businesses may not be on the cutting edge of technology, generally their smaller size gives them agility to more rapidly adopt technology solutions. It is possible for small and medium courier companies to overcome many of these barriers by integrating two relatively new paradigms in ICT (information and communication technology) to develop a new service delivery model in which to do business. The evolution of e-commerce-type systems has been relatively rapid given the short time since the development of the Web. One of the emerging trends evident with Web 2.0 tools is that of communities. In particular, communities of consumers and businesses (Lemphers, 2007) coming together in a digital environment dedicated to a particular service. Additionally, by basing the new model on Web-services technologies, we can decrease the burden on existing systems by allowing transport companies to seamlessly integrate Web services' functionality into their enterprise software applications. By bringing together many smaller to medium transport companies in this way, more value-added services can be implemented through

the technologies with the cost spread between more players.

The suggested new service delivery model provides integration between transport companies through Internet technologies such as XML, SOAP, UDDI, WSIL, and Web services. In this way the transport companies can receive more opportunities to attract customers and improve the quality of services and therefore increase their profits. The architecture for the selected business model of the Web-system design is based on thorough requirements analysis and research of contemporary Internet technologies. The core of the system uses J2EE that is cross-platform, multiuser, object-oriented, and scalable; thus, the framework may be applied to various software and hardware environments. The XML Web-services mechanism allows the framework to integrate with external Web systems. It uses UDDI for delivery agents to reach their customers and partners with information about their services. Service description information is stored in WSIL format, so it can be distributed to any location using an XML document. SOAP is used for the XML data exchange mechanism between delivery agents, customers, and external Web systems. It provides users with remote calls to the Web system's functionality.

The aim of this research is to develop a framework for a new service delivery model that assists small and medium transport companies at providing their services through the Internet. The proposed model is for an advanced logistics B2B solution that integrates multiple transport companies and provides them with a unified Web interface to extend their business over the Internet. In the remainder of this article, a brief literature review is given followed by the proposed developed framework for the target model. A costing for the development of the model is then given, followed by the conclusions and opportunities for further research.

BACKGROUND LITERATURE

The transport and courier industry has grown rapidly over the last few years. In 1977 in the United States, 3.2% of the value of all goods shipped were sent by parcel carriers or courier companies. In 1997 this percentage had climbed to 12.3%, with revenue to the courier industry being over US $38 Billion (Morlok, Nitzberg, & Balasubramaniam, 2000). Most of this trade (approximately 90% to 95%), is dominated by the four biggest carriers, with their growth rate during this period approximately 13.21%. This industry represents an important component of the US economy at over 10% of GDP. Figures for other developed countries are not so clear cut, but the World Trade Organization indicates an important industry worldwide with large revenues still dominated by four large players (WTO, 1998).

Recent trends which include the implementation of services such as parcel tracking, delivery notification, and customer tracking via Web systems have become possible through the development e-commerce systems, satellite tracking with Global Positioning Systems (GPS), and advances in customer support and information systems (Roy, 2001). While there are many smaller courier companies that make acceptable revenues it is particularly difficult for them to compete with the larger players in terms of these value-added services which the larger companies have introduced over the past decade. However, recent trends in business models and technologies do suggest a possible solution for the smaller players in this industry. As a result of the Web 2.0 technologies enabling further developments in e-commerce, many companies are taking advantage of network and relationship building software. This comes at a time when emerging social trends of networking seem to be dominating the Web among younger members of the Web community with sites such as Facebook, Friendster, Habbo, MySpace, and so on.

According to Chang and Uden (2007), SMEs will need to embrace the concept of digital ecosystems in order to remain competitive. "A digital ecosystem is a self-organising digital infrastructure aimed at creating a digital environment for networked organisations that supports the cooperation, the knowledge sharing, the development of open and adaptive technologies and evolutionary business models" (European Commission, 2004). Embracing such technologies becomes important for SMEs, particularly when competing with much larger players in a fixed market as is evident in the courier industry. These systems provide further opportunities and economic benefits through networking with other SME's, creating virtual enterprises and crowd sourcing. Indeed integrating with other SME's in such ecosystems will be necessary in the new digital business landscape where community is key (Lemphers, 2007).

In a study involving three on-demand service delivery models, Warkentin and Bajaj (2001) indicated that a key to success in this area would be in developing strong networks of cross-industry partners. They also propose a Web-based business model incorporating e-commerce systems, community networking, and content. There are many advantages to be gained in developing these cross-industry relationships and aligning goals across physical and virtual channels can create synergies and virtual organizations more effectively able to compete with larger market players (Steinfield, Adelaar, & Lai, 2002). Indeed, Chang, West, and Hadzic (2006) describe a digital ecosystem for a collaborative group of logistic enterprises to compete in a global environment. The digital ecosystem described provides many value-added benefits for the various logistics enterprises through the creation of partnerships and sharing of resources. However, the description of the ecosystem does not include the customer. By including the customer into such an ecosystem, we can create a truly horizontal e-marketplace and provide more value-added benefits to the customers.

Overview of Existing Systems

Transportation software is defined at the Web site of Chozam Inc. as software that gives business the ability to effectively manage trucking, barge traffic, and multimodel transport operations in an organized, logical fashion. Utilizing transportation software allows streamlining business while maintaining a customizable system that includes dispatch, sales, rating, payroll, accounting, and total logistics. Transportation software also gives the ability to connect with shippers, vendors and logistics organizations as well as manage vehicle maintenance (Chozam Inc., 2005).

In the Uniteds State and abroad there are a number of various software solutions for logistics business, which primarily can be broken down into software that supports various types of transport operations (order creation, miles calculation), and software that allows for better management of assets as they interact within the supply chain (supply chain management).

TMW Systems is the largest provider of enterprise management software for the trucking industry (Canada IT, 2006) and developer of trucking software for dispatch and transportation solutions (TMW Systems, 2005). TMW Systems offers two operations and dispatch software products that currently manage the transportation operations of over 500 common carriers and private fleets. The Framework for the TMW Systems suite is shown below in Figure 1. TMW Systems' customers gain efficiency by being able to better manage their assets as they interact within the supply chain. While TMW Systems seamlessly integrates and interfaces both software products with complementary software partners that are the best in the industry in their areas of specialization, such integration is not flexible enough due to the software demands placed on customers. The utilization of Web services can help provide a more flexible integration mechanism.

Manhattan Associates' Transportation Management solutions are able to automate, standardize, and optimize critical processes—streamlining, planning, and execution—and substantially reduce procurement time and associated transportation costs. The Transportation Management solutions can be leveraged on demand or as licensed solutions and offer comprehensive functionality covering the entire spectrum of processes related to a global intraenterprise transportation network (Manhattan Associates 2005). Modularity of Manhattan Associates' Transportation Management is very good architectural decision, but the system is also intended for one big transport company. It cannot be used by a number of small to medium

Figure 1. Three layers of the TMWSuite's framework (TMWSuite, 2005)

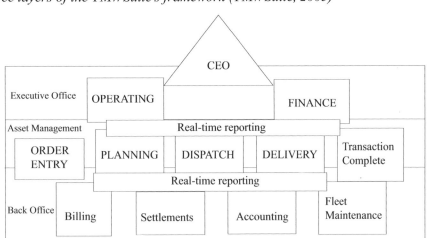

transport companies; also, it does not provide any external XML interfaces.

GT Nexus' unified software applications combine advanced supply chain modeling and event management capabilities with global transportation and trade document management to enable full control over the flow of inventory from order point to final delivery (GT Nexus, 2005). GT Nexus' strategy is to build a comprehensive logistics software solution, invest in the global infrastructure and service provider connections to support the solution, then deliver the whole thing as a service, over the Web, for a fraction of the cost, and none of the risk, of traditional supply chain software. Such strategy makes GT Nexus to be a service provider that is a comprehensive business scheme. The greatest advantage of this scheme is its ability to attract customers without big finance and with less risk for a customer.

While there are many other similar solutions in the marketplace, currently there is no transport software in the market that provides an electronic marketplace for small and medium transport companies. Some existing software systems provide very useful features, but not one of them offers budget e-logistics solution for orders taking and execution. Additionally, none of these provide user-friendly interfaces for customers' shipment tracking, pick-up, and drop-off as in DHL's Small Business Center. The value-added benefits available in these larger solution packages are available as a direct result of the cost of these existing systems. As a result, these systems are not a viable option to smaller SMEs.

Web-Services-Based Logistics

At present, one can choose appropriate tools and technologies from a wide range that is well presented in the printed literature and on the Internet. For a successful design and development of a Web-based communications framework for the transport industry a lot depends on the right choice of proper technology.

Web services provide a layer of abstraction above existing software systems, such as application servers, CORBA, .NET servers, and messaging and packaged applications. Web services work at a level of abstraction similar to the Internet and are capable of bridging any operating system, hardware platform, or programming language, just as the Web is. Unlike existing distributed systems, Web services are adapted to the Web. The default network protocol is HTTP. Most existing distributed computing technologies include the communication protocol as part of their scope. With Web services, the communication protocol is already there, in the far-flung, worldwide Web.

Cerami (2002) defined Web service as "any service that is available over the Internet, uses a standardized XML messaging system, and is not tied to any one operating system or programming language." Cerami names several alternatives for XML messaging, XML Remote Procedure Call (XML-RPC), SOAP, and HTTP GET/POST for pass of XML documents. He also advises that a Web service may have two additional properties: a Web service should be self-describing; a Web service should be discoverable (Cerami, 2002).

New applications become possible when everything is Web-service enabled. Web services are a trend which will facilitate Enterprise Reconstruction through Industry Deconstruction (Bieberstein et al., 2005). Once the world becomes Web-service enabled, all kinds of new business paradigms, discussion groups, interactive forums, and publishing models will emerge to take advantage of this new capability (Newcomer, 2002). However, this will entail a drastic rethink on Web based components for business applications. The Web-service architecture provides an interesting alternative for drastically decoupling presentation form content. For example, a site could consist of nothing but container pages that pass parameters to the real logic via SOAP or XML-RPC. This makes it easy to change presentation and also lets humans and computers "share" a single Web service (Cerami, 2002). However, while remote interfaces make the components distributable, it must be remembered that they have an overhead cost of remote communication, serialization, and network latency.

As Zhang and Chang (2002) wrote, in the last couple of years various on-line shipping tools have been developed for e-commerce application developers. They bring the example of the transportation industry; United Parcel Service of America (UPS) that provides several on-line XML Tools and HTML Tools (UPS On-line E-Commerce Tools, http://www.ec.ups.com/), and Federal Express (FedEx) that provides in-house Web tools (FedEx API, http://www.fedex.com/) for developers in order to facilitate the development of online shipping tools. But they have not seen a common service interface to allow users to easily hook up with existing tools. The developers of client applications usually are forced to construct by hand multiple requests for different back-end servers requiring a great deal of time and effort, although integration software vendors have been addressing this issue for years. Different shipping carriers might require distinctive implementations and could have proprietary platforms and their own constraints.

Sun *ONE Web Services Developer's Guide* (Sun, 2003) describes a Logistics sample application. Since the sample application follows a *session facade* design pattern to handle all business logic with *remote session beans*, these can be exposed as Web services. This adds another dimension of extending the architecture, so that different portions of the application can be accessed in multiple ways, with minimal coding. A well-layered architecture ensures code reuse.

MODEL FOR WEB-SERVICES ARCHITECTURE

The goal of the suggested service delivery model is to provide an Internet workplace for multiple transport companies that allow them to receive and fulfill orders, track shipments, notify customer about shipment delivery, send and receive payments, and obtain technical support in case of problems. The novelty of this model lies in the opportunities for transport companies to work together simultaneously and use the services of each other, through a common XML interface for instant messages between them. Also transport companies can use the services of external delivery agents, such as DHL, FedEx, and so on. The Framework also provides a customer interface for examination of transport companies and the services they provide.

The main user categories of the Web system are

- Delivery Agent: a transport company that uses the Web system's services to extend its business
- External Agent: a large transport company or insurance company that provides an interface for interaction with the Web system and is able to use its services
- Customer: a person or a company that requests delivery service(s)
- System Administrator: a main person responsible for proper functioning of the Web system; he or she must have access to every data and every interface in the system
- Helpdesk Engineer: a person responsible for proper functioning of the Web system; he or she has access to order data and database transactions and is able to solve common problems or give users help

The framework is a B2B model that provides transport companies, or delivery agents (*D*s), and their customers (*C*s) up-to-date information facilities via prevalent Internet technologies. The high-level Web system overview is shown in Figure 2.

Special performance requirements are suggested for the Web system; however, it obviously must be realized that any such system based on

Figure 2. High-level Web system overview

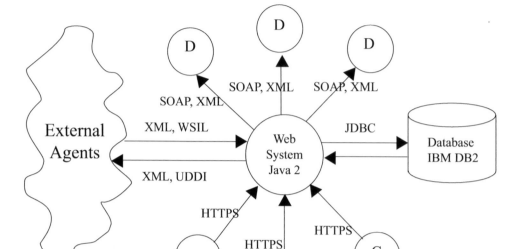

Internet delivery has no control over Internet performance. Notwithstanding, desirable qualities are that it must maintain a load of simultaneous work of multiple users and demonstrate high-speed response. The following performance indicators are suggested:

- Number of simultaneously working users—1000
- Account creation time—at most 0.5 second
- Order creation time—at most 1 second
- Sending off payment time—at most 0.5 second
- Sending off message time—at most 0.5 second
- Log-in time—at most, 0.1 second
- Show list of orders time—at most, 1 second
- Report creation time—at most, 3 seconds

The communications framework uses Web services for implementation of distributed computing. Targeted Web services offer productivity gains and cost reductions to logistics businesses that are integrated into the Web system. Web services can provide them with a common tool to interact with customers, contractors, and subcontractors in a seamless way.

Web services are an essential part of the new service delivery model's technical architecture, because they allow spreading the functionality of Web system's business model over enterprise applications for transport companies. The Web system's context involves the five types of users outlined previously, two of which (delivery agents and external agents) access Web system's functionality via Web services. This approach allows seamless integration of their enterprise applications with the projected Web system at the service level of the software application. The Web services mechanism includes the framework for a Web services data flow mechanism, business entities implementation and common alliance interface to allow users and businesses to easily hook up with existing tools.

Business Functionality

The Business model of the proposed framework for integration between multiple carrier services includes a description of the main actors of the system (omitted here for brevity), business logic, and use of technologies that help to implement the solution. At a high level, system functionality is represented by a set of modules and interfaces that provide the following features:

From the transport company (delivery agent) perspective:

- Enable delivery agents to place and edit their Web profile describing what services they offer, what locations, what price, and other specific conditions they have.
- Give delivery agents complete information about their orders, at what stage they are, in what location, and estimated time of delivery.
- Notify delivery agents about shipments delivery.
- Provide delivery agents with a variety of daily, weekly and monthly reports about their business transactions carried out via the Web system.
- Provide delivery agents with an interface to the services of other agents for the purpose of subcontracting work.
- Provide delivery agents with an interface to insurance companies for the purpose of shipment insurance.
- Provide delivery agents with an interface for solving technical problems.

From the customer perspective:

- Give customers complete information about the transport companies, services they offer, and any specific conditions related to their services.

- Help customers to make their choice of most efficient transport vendor, guided by given conditions.
- Allow customers to make order(s) using selected transport companies.
- Accept various kinds of payment.
- Give customers complete information about the state of their shipments.
- Notify customers about delivery of their shipments.
- Provide customers with an interface for solving technical problems.

From the Web-service perspective:

- Provide full information about a customer's order to external delivery agents.
- Provide information exchange between delivery agents.
- Secure interaction between delivery agents.
- Provide necessary information about subject of insurance to insurance company.
- Provide interaction between insurance company, delivery agents, and customers.
- Sends notification to indicated system administrator.

Application Architectural Design

The framework is developed around a layered architecture design implementing the model-view-controller (MVC) design pattern. The MVC model design pattern maps the traditional (input, processing, output) roles to controller, model, view components which exist in a relationship designed to decouple data access, business logic, and data presentation and user interaction. Thus, the design is based upon abstracting the application into distinct tiers:

- The presentation layer
- The Web layer
- The service layer

Table 1. Layered architecture

Layer	Responsibility	Tool/Technology
Browser	Client tool to access Web-service delivery system.	Internet Explorer, Netscape Navigator Mozilla, Opera, and Firefox
Presentation Layer	Allows users to send their requests to the Web system and presents their data in the appropriate format. Provides standard navigation elements.	HTML, JSP
Processing Layer	Separates presentation logic from presentation view, security, user-input validation, Charest filter, and redirection.	IBM Websphere, Application Server, Servlets
Service Layer	Provides communication with the external system & sends and receives XML messages.	SOAP, UDDI, WSIL, Web services
Business Layer	Responsible for implementing business logic.	EJB
Data Access Layer	Provides access to the database, implements connection pool, data serialization, constructs queries to retrieve data from the database.	JDBC, JNDI
Database Layer	Provides mechanism for storing all data used by the Web system in the form of tables, indexes, and views. Provides mechanism for data protection from unauthorized access, backup/recovery, and database integrity.	IBM DB2 Universal Database

Presentation logic is separated from the business logic in such a way that Servlets are used for control (controller), JSP pages for presentation (view), and EJBs are used to manage business components (model). A Servlet is a small, Java-based object that receives a request and generates a response based on that request. The layered architecture is presented in Table 1 and shows the application's logical layers. The name of each layer is shown in the first column, the second column describes what it is responsible for, and the third column lists tool(s) or technology that can be utilized at this level.

Figure 3 shows a pictorial representation of the model's layered architectural elements as described in Table 1. It is the Web services in the service layer that act as the interface between the various elements from the delivery and external agents.

The core of the framework is the service layer that provides the Web-services stack, which includes data representing computing commands, application programming interfaces (APIs), security levels, and data to be processed and transported over standard Internet transport mechanisms (HTTP, FTP). In other words, the standardized instruction sets of Web-services XML files hold the information necessary to invoke the application commands. Web services also represents a global standard for APIs accessible over the Internet. An API is an interface for letting a program communicate with another program. The following base protocols formed the initial specification for Web services:

- Simple Object Access Protocol (SOAP)—defines the runtime message that contains the service request and response. SOAP is independent of any particular transport and implementation technology.
- Web Services Description Language (WSDL)—describes a Web Service and the SOAP Message. It provides a programmatic way to describe what a service does, paving the way for automation.
- Universal Discovery, Description, Integration (UDDI)—UDDI is a cross industry

Figure 3. Layered architecture depiction

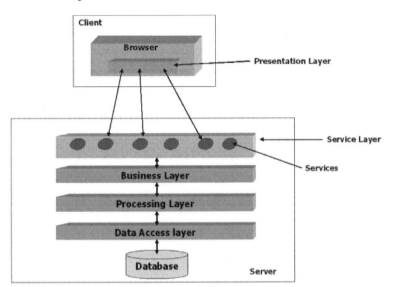

Figure 4. Web-services base protocols application

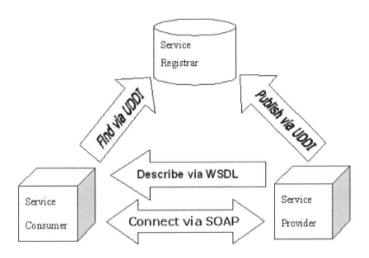

initiative to create a standard for service discovery together with a registry facility that facilitates the publishing and discovery processes.

The Application of these protocols for Web services is shown in Figure 4.

Data-Flow Mechanism

The data-flow mechanism is used by a basic architecture of Enterprise Java Bean (EJB)-based client/server Web system's application. The client side of an EJB architecture contains the EJB interfaces needed for invoking business-specific methods on an EJB as well as for managing handles to server-side objects, created by in-house developers for the transport companies. The server side of EJB architecture contains the instances of the actual EJB component implementation, as well as the container code that maps calls to and from clients and EJBs after appropriate service-management infrastructure logic has been executed. The data-flow mechanism of the framework is shown in the Figure 5.

The main components of the data-flow mechanism interact as follows:

- An EJB client application utilizes the Java Naming and Directory Interface (JNDI) to look up references to home interfaces and call home and remote Web-service interfaces to utilize all EJB-based functionality from the EJB implementation.

- The Web-services home interfaces provide operations for clients to create, remove, and find handles to Web-services remote interface objects. Underlying stubs marshal home interface requests and unmarshal home interface responses for the client.

- The Web-services remote interfaces provide the business-specific client interface methods defined for a particular EJB. Underlying stubs marshal remote interface requests and unmarshal remote interface responses for the client.

The EJB implementations are the actual EJB application components implemented by developers to provide any application-specific business method invocation, creation, removal, finding, activation, deactivation, database storage, and database loading logic. It uses the Java

Figure 5. The data-flow mechanism of the Web system

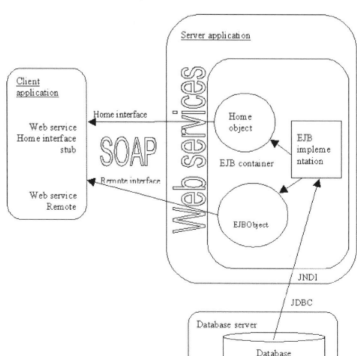

Naming and Directory Interface (JNDI) to get Java Database Connectivity (JDBC) connection from the connection pool and utilizes it for data retrieval. The EJB container manages the distributed communication skeletons used to marshal and unmarshal data sent to and from the client. Containers also may store EJB implementation instances in a pool and delegates to perform any service-management operations related to a particular EJB, before calls are delegated to the EJB implementation instance.

The database model, while not directly relevant to the article, is included in Appendix 1 for completeness.

WORKFLOW

To access system functionality through the Web services, a delivery agent (DA) must have implementation of the Web-services interface. So a DA's software should have a module that provides interaction between the DA's logistics software and projected Web-system's framework. The transport companies' software developers may easily create this module, because all interface methods must be described in the documentation for Web services.

The implementation module performs authorization and authentication for the DA, then the DA can select one of the following options: view own, new and operating orders, update order

Figure 6. Delivery agents complete work-flow model

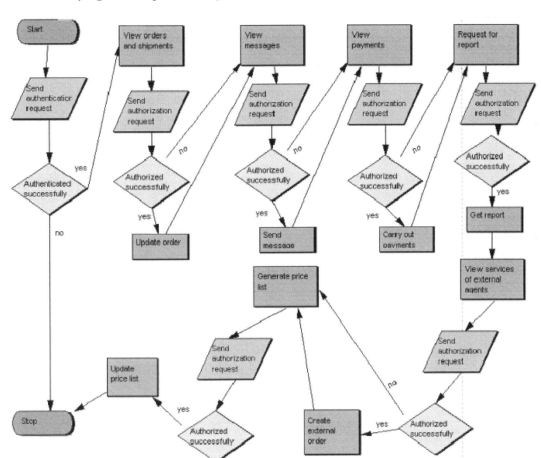

Figure 7. Work-flow diagram for delivery agent's activities through HTTPS protocol

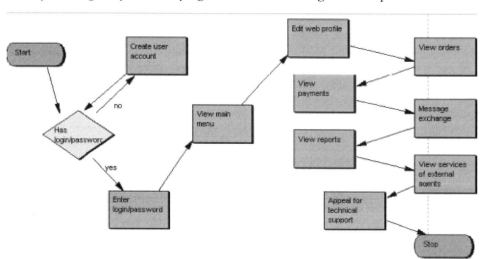

Figure 8. Work-flow diagram for customer's activities

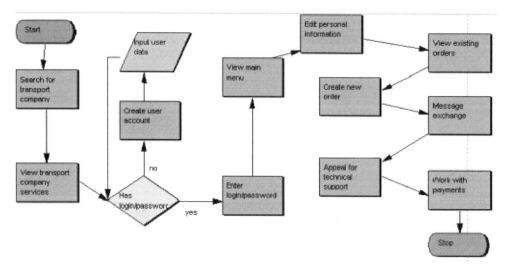

Figure 9. Work-flow diagram for external agent's activities

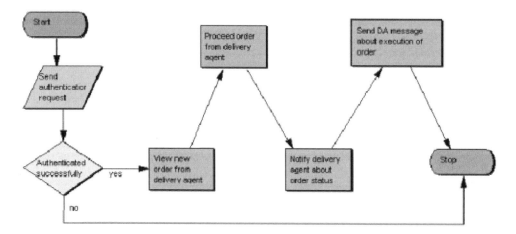

status, message exchange, work with payments, work with reports, use services of external agents, or update price list. The work-flow diagram for DA's activities through the Web service(s) is shown in Figure 6. The Web system's interface through the HTTPS protocol is used mainly for DA's registration and account configuration. However, a DA can also view some data of the Web system to facilitate fault finding. To start working via the HTTPS interface, a DA must be logged in to the system. The DA then gets to the main menu, where they select one of the following options: edit Web profile, view orders, view payments, message exchange, and view reports, view services of external agents, or appeal for technical support. The work-flow diagram for the DA's HTTPS activities is shown in Figure 7.

A customer can search for a delivery company and can view courier services without logging into the Web system. For other activities, a customer must register him- or herself in the Web system. To access personal functionality, a customer must be logged in to the system, to gain access to the main menu, where he or she can select one of the following options: edit personal information, create new orders, view existing orders, work with payments, message exchange, or appeal for technical support. The work-flow diagram for customer's activities is shown in Figure 8.

To gain access to the Web-system's functionality, an external agent (EA) must first be authenticated. The EA performs all activities from its own interface, so it uses only the functionality of the Web system, not the user interface. An EA can use one of the following options: get new order from delivery agent, precede order from delivery agent, notify delivery agent about order status, or send delivery agent message about execution of order. The work-flow diagram for the EA's activities is shown in Figure 9

FRAMEWORK DEVELOPMENT COSTING

Costs of the Web-system framework development project consist of

- Human resource costs
- Software costs
- Hardware costs
- Other costs

Human Resource Costs

Working out costs, especially human resources costs, can have very differing results from one location to the next. In the following tables, all values are in US dollars, based on a generic review of the monster.com job site. The results are shown in Table 2.

Software Costs

The software needed to be purchased for the Web-system framework development was considered. The staff will work on PCs using Windows XP Home Edition and Microsoft Office. Also, each project participant needs special software:

- Project manager and system architect use QSEE-SuperLite for modeling and analysis of system's architecture. QSEE-SuperLite is the superset of traditional CASE tools that supports modeling of computer systems, and it is freeware. Also, the project manager requires Microsoft Project for project planning.
- Software developers should use Eclipse IDE for code development. Eclipse is an open-source community whose projects are focused on providing an extensible development platform and application frameworks for building software. Eclipse provides extensible tools and frameworks that span the

Table 2. Human resources costs

Title	Skill Set	Salary (Month)	Period	Qty	Cost
Project Manager	Understands needs, identifies root causes of problems, and develops and implements creative and pragmatic solutions. Ability to create detailed functional and technical design specifications for software development efforts. Experience developing software tests for functional, stress, and regression testing that include manual, ad hoc, and automated testing elements.	$8,000	18 weeks	1	$32,000
System Architect	Software architecture leadership experience, including designing complex, multicomponent software systems. Experience establishing an enterprise framework for all phases of software development: requirements, design, development, testing, and delivery.	$8,000	18 weeks	1	$32,000
Software Developer	Familiarity with all aspects of the development life cycle. Minimum of 3 years software development experience. Working experience with SQL, XML, COM, MFC, Wi-Fi, USB, Windows XP. Strong communication and interpersonal skills. High-level problem-solving skills. Strong mathematical and mechanical background preferred. Ability to handle multiple tasks.	$5,000	9 weeks	4	$40,000
Software Consultant	Must be able to work independently and with a team. Experience in performing mass updates to mapping systems and maintaining high Quality Control standards. Able to anticipate users' needs and develop into documented solutions. Must have good interpersonal skills to work with customer.	$5,000	1 month	2	$10,000
Hardware Consultant	Cost estimations of hardware systems. Analysis of cost research data. Formulation of Cost Research. Modeling and simulation.	$4,000	18 weeks	1	$16,000
Test Engineer	Possesses general knowledge of QA systems and methodologies, use of debugging tools, knowledge of manual tests tools. Ability to write and implement test plans. Creates thorough technical/functional test plans/ scripts and performs QA testing of end-user application development.	$4,500	9 weeks	2	$18,000
Support Engineer	Strong communication skills. Strong computer hardware and software skills. Ability to find bottlenecks where problems can occur. Ability to fix common problems and to find a way how to fix complex problems. Strong customer service skills.	$4,000	18 weeks	1	$16,000
Total				12	$164,000

Table 3. Software usage

Project participant	Qty	Software
Project Manager	1	Windows XP Home Edition, QSEE-SuperLite, Microsoft Office, Microsoft Project
System Architect	1	Windows XP Home Edition, Microsoft Office, QSEE-SuperLite, Eclipse IDE, JUnit
Software Developer	4	Windows XP Home Edition, Microsoft Office, WebSphere Application Server for developers, Eclipse IDE, JUnit
Software Consultant	2	Windows XP Home Edition, Microsoft Office
Hardware Consultant	1	Windows XP Home Edition, Microsoft Office
Test Engineer	2	Windows XP Home Edition, Microsoft Office, JUnit
Support Engineer	1	Windows XP Home Edition, Microsoft Office

software development life cycle, including support for modeling, language development environments for Java, C/C++ and others, testing and performance, business intelligence, rich client applications, and embedded development. It is freeware.

- Test engineers and software developers use JUnit for testing. JUnit is a regression-testing framework written by Erich Gamma and Kent Beck. JUnit is open-source software, released under the Common Public License Version 1.0 and hosted on SourceForge.

The estimates of software used by each project participant are given in Table 3.

The Web platform and database software to be used will be IBM DB2 Universal Database and WebSphere Application Server. DB2 Universal Database is the first multimedia, Web-ready relational database management system that is strong enough to meet the demands of large corporations and flexible enough to serve small- and medium-sized businesses. It costs $475. WebSphere Application Server is the core Web-services J2EE 1.3-certified application server, optimized for ease of administration in a single-server deployment environment. It exists in two modifications; the server version costs $4,000 and the developers' version costs $750. The security software to be used will be Zone Alarm Pro 5.5; it costs $55 and has a free trial.

Therefore, calculations of software costs are shown in Table 4.

Hardware Costs

Most staff will work at desktop PCs, but the project manager and software consultants need laptops. Also, hardware for the Web server is needed: server, network hub, and firewall. Thus, calculations of hardware costs are given in Table 5.

Other Costs

Other costs of Web system development are Internet traffic; tea, coffee and meals for staff; and various unforeseen costs. It is estimated that other costs don't exceed $1,000. So, all costs of Web system development are presented in Table 6.

927

Table 4. Calculation of software costs

Title	Price	Quantity	Cost
Windows XP Home Edition	$50	12	$450
Microsoft Office	$350	12	$4,200
QSEE-SuperLite	freeware	2	$0
Microsoft Project	$510	1	$510
WebSphere Application Server for Developers	$750	4	$3,000
Eclipse IDE	freeware	4	$0
JUnit	freeware	7	$0
DB2 Universal Database	$475	1	$475
WebSphere Application Server	$4,000	1	$4,000
Zone Alarm Pro 5.5	$50	1	$50
Total			$12,685

Table 5. Calculation of hardware costs

Title	Price	Quantity	Cost
Desktop PC	$850	9	$7,650
Laptop	$1,500	3	$4,500
Database server	$5,000	1	$5,000
Web server	$5,000	1	$5,000
Total			$22,350

Table 6. All costs of Web system development

Title	Sum
Human resources costs	$164,000
Software costs	$12,635
Hardware costs	$22,350
Other costs	$1,000
Total	$199,985

ADDING VALUE

The previous sections have concentrated on the technical aspects of the framework, including the database design, the work flow, and costing. In this section we explore the added value benefits which result as a direct consequence from the architecture itself, and those which are made possible (or more feasible) from the architectural design. Of course, it must be recalled that the latter benefits, (those made more feasible by the architecture) are achievable without the architecture developed in this research. This can be seen in value-added benefits within existing systems discussed previously. However, such systems are beyond the reach of SMEs and the raison d'etre of the architecture developed in this research is to facilitate added-value benefits for this group of entities.

Added Value From Digital Ecosystem

The structure of the architecture provides a basic digital ecosystem within the transport industry domain. Many of the added-value benefits will flow from this architecture. Previous research has identified a *Virtuous Circle,* expected to arise from the use of digital ecosystems (Giorgetti & Louarn, 2004). This is highlighted in Figure 10, where the digital ecosystem makes viable new organizational and business models, which in turn encourage and require cooperation, which improves competitiveness and efficiencies, which leads to development that feeds back into the digital ecosystem.... This becomes the *virtuous circle.*

Figure 10. Virtuous circle (Giorgetti & Louarn, 2004)

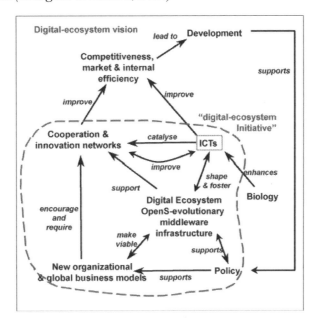

The architecture developed within this research is somewhat different as it additionally incorporates customers into the digital ecosystem as well as the SMEs. When we include the customer into the ecosystem, we are creating a more horizontal e-marketplace which should help in providing the customer with even further value-added benefits. Similar to the benefits described by Giorgetti and Louarn (2004), the architecture is designed to foster cooperation between the SMEs within the ecosystem, giving rise to synergies. The result of the synergies then flow to the customers as added value within the ecosystem. The flow of added value within the digital ecosystem is depicted in Figure 11.

Before discussing specific added value for the different entities, it is worth noting that one of the main aims of the architecture is to group many SMEs within the digital ecosystem. This allows the cost of development to be amortized over many SMEs. When we can amortize the expense amongst many players, it then becomes viable (from a group basis) to develop further technologies which in turn can add value to both

SMEs and customer. Some of these technologies such as parcel tracking, delivery notification and GPS information were initially discussed, but only as technologies viable for the large companies to implement. Alone, such technologies are beyond the reach of SMEs, but when participating in a digital ecosystem with many other others, their introduction now becomes viable. It was not in the intent of this research to build these technologies, but rather to develop and build the framework from which their development becomes viable for the stakeholders.

We can view the value-added benefits from two basic perspectives: that of the SME; that of the customer.

Added Value for SMEs

From Figure 11, we can see that the added value expected from the digital ecosystem arises from the cooperation between the SME and the synergies that then develop. Apart from the amortization of costs offsetting the cost of development for further added-value components discussed

Figure 11.Conceptual view of added-value flow within digital ecosystem

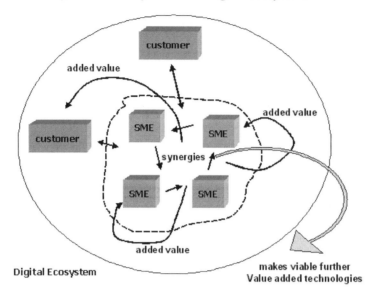

above, the cooperation should result in useful partnerships benefiting both SME and customers. SMEs can form alliances and utilize each others logistic chains and operation areas to provide a more holistic service to customers. The added value to SMEs is the ability to retain customers by being able to supply services even though those services might not be supplied by the SME directly. Each of the SMEs will have the ability to *farm out* services to participating partner SMEs when customers require services not directly supplied by the SME or when the SME is unable to supply the service due other reasons. The customers still interface with the initial point of contact, giving them the possibility of still retaining the customer for future transactions.

The partnerships formed will additionally support new organization and business models, helping the SMEs to compete more effectively in an increasingly global system. This can be accomplished due to architecture of the ecosystem allowing the SMEs to interface to external larger companies. These larger companies can act as a global extension to the smaller SME, again allowing the SME to remain the virtual carrier to the customer.

Added Value for Customers

Customers benefit from added-value services in a number of ways. The natural competition resulting from the participating cooperating SMEs in the digital ecosystem will encourage transparent competitive pricing for the customer. Additionally, the mirrored benefits to the customer from those of the SMEs will result in a wider range and availability of services. This should flow on from the SMEs utilizing the logistic chains and services of each other. This will also provide a one-stop point of access for many customers, far more desirable then sourcing different services from multiple vendors. The ability of SMEs to link to more global carriers also provides access to global based services through their SMEs.

Further value-added services such as parcel tracking, delivery notification etc, could possibly be made available to customers through the prospect of these services now being viable to implement. However, such services would not directly be available through the adoption of the initial basic ecosystem by the SMEs, but rather as a consequence of further development due to viability. Nevertheless, such services would be added-value services as a consequence of the architecture, not normally available through SMEs operating alone.

CONCLUSION

The infrastructure described within this project consists of many stakeholders (delivery agents, drivers, companies, and consumers), customers, information technology, corporate security, and application owners to resolve complex technical and process issues. Problems needed to be resolved by the new architecture include those of scalability, extensibility, security, management, interoperability, provisioning, and administration. This project demonstrates an infrastructure initiative that can be a catalyst to rethink the development process and create a more efficient organization domain to meet the demands of agile business strategy, delivering a secure, scalable, reliable, and extensible Web-services environment.

The project addresses organizational and project challenges by understanding the technology, issues, and dynamics of evaluating, selecting, and deploying new Web-service infrastructure components; overcoming the challenges of deploying the new technologies, products, and best practices used to integrate business processes across the disparate application platforms and organizational boundaries; and exploring the evaluation criteria used to select Web-services infrastructure components for the chosen enterprise.

This project provides a framework to simplify the integration process between multiple-carrier services and allows improved transport services for the smaller and medium-sized companies using Web services to automate dispatching and real-time customer services. The designed architecture can be adopted as a new service-delivery model that incorporates implementation of user and functionality requirements, business processes, design patterns, and making use of existing technologies to define an accomplished B2B e-logistics solution.

The decomposition of the business domain depicts the design strategy for service-oriented architecture and method, defining the roles for Transport Company's (delivery agent) clients, Web services, administrators, external agents, and helpdesk engineers. These are processes of the services-oriented modeling architecture that consists of the three general steps: identification, specification and realization of services, and components and flows

This Web-services model allows any user access through the use of XML tags for information exchange using the other three standards: SOAP, UDDI, and WSDL. The technical architecture is implemented using XML as a way of designing and documenting the architecture of services, showing their relationships, dependencies, and so on, and is also a structure by which the right delivery services, at the necessary application levels, is enforced.

It allows both consumer and provider not to be tied in to a particular service set and truly minimizes the impact of change to switch service providers. Thus, the projected Web system allows transport companies to seamlessly integrate Web-services' functionality into their enterprise software applications, such as supply chain management, enterprise resource planning, and others.

The total projected costs of project implementation can be questioned as to the affordability for a small- to medium-sized courier company. However, as the project is designed to implement a small digital ecosystem facilitating the development of cross-industry relationships, these initial costs can be amortized across many companies, thus reducing the overall cost per company and making affordable and available value-added services usually associated with larger companies.

Future Research

Web services have an overwhelming need for increased privacy and protection in the industry and research community. The consumer and the relevant transport companies require privacy and protection when using Web-services. The W3C published a document, *Web Services Architecture,* which describes privacy requirements for future research along with other relevant research areas into XML, Platform for Privacy Preferences Project, for future research of Web-services based applications.

Selective components of the architecture will most likely be replaced or enhanced in differing ways. Research into different techniques to lower long-term costs of management and a higher long-term value for all players in the enterprise is required. To be consistent with open standards for creating, describing, and accessing data, a commitment to new and improved standards will be adhered to, especially as the Web-services technology architecture is still young. Many technological advances by major players have still not created a clear or mature standard.

The main conception of the architecture is to enable the transport industry to interchange specialist services within their domain, offering an improved level of services to clients and sub-contracted companies. As well as technological advances, a consideration of social and economical changes has to be acknowledged when deciding on future project directions.

REFERENCES

Bieberstein, N., et al. (2005). *Service-oriented architecture compass: Business value, planning, and enterprise roadmap.* Englewood Cliffs, NJ: Prentice Hall.

Campbell, A. (2004). *Technology levels the playing field.* Retrieved January 2, 2008, from http://trendtracker.blogspot.com/2004/04/trend-technology-levels-playing-field.html

Canada IT. (2006). *TMW systems acquires Maddocks Systems Inc.* Retrieved September 2006 from http://www.canadait.com/cfm/index.cfm?It=106&Id=24394&Se=2&Lo=2

Cerami, E. (2002). *Web services essentials.* New York: O'Reilly.

Chang, E., West, M., & Hadzic, M., (2006, August). A digital ecosystem for extended logistics enterprises. In *Proceedings of the 11th International Workshop on Telework.* Fredericton, Canada:

Chang, V., & Uden, L. (2007, November). The three e's: E-learning, e-knowledge and e-ecosystems for SMEs. In Proceedings of the Eighth International We-B (Working for E-Business) Conference. Melbourne Australia:

Chozam Inc. (2005). *Technology information center.* Retrieved August 30, 2005, from http://www.chozamtech.com/software/industry/transportation/transportation_software.html

European Commission. (2004). *Digital business ecosystems.* Retrieved April 12, 2008, from http://www.digital-ecosystems.org/

Giorgetti, M., & Louarn, M. L. (2004). *Technologies for digital ecosystems—Supporting regional growth and innovation.* Retrieved February, 2007, from http://www.ve-forum.org/apps/pub.asp?Q=1270

GT Nexus. (2005). GT Nexus' Web site. Retrieved August 30, 2005, from http://www.gtnexus.com/en/delivery_model/

Lemphers, D. (2007, November). *Communitize–Doing business with ourselves!* Keynote address at the Eighth International We-B (Working for E-Business) Conference, Melbourne Australia.

Morlok, E., Nitzberg, B., & Balasubramaniam, K. (2000). *The parcel service industry in the US: Its Size and role in commerce* (Tech. Rep., University of Pennsylvania , School of Engineering and Applied Science, Systems Engineering Department). Available online from http://www.pti.psu.edu/mautc/docs/MA-III-0007.pdf

Newcomer, E. (2002). *Understanding Web services: XML, WSDL, SOAP, and UDDI.* Boston: Addison-Wesley Professional.

Nickerson, J., Hamilton, B., & Wada, T. (2001). Market position, resource profile, and governance: Linking Porter and Williamson in the context of international courier and small package services in Japan. *Strategic Management Journal, 22*(3), 251-273. Retrieved April 12, 2008, from http://cniss.wustl.edu/summerschool/nickersonpaper.pdf

Roy, J. (2001). Recent trends in logistics and the need for real-time decision tools in the trucking industry. In *Proceedings of the 34th Annual Hawaii International Conference* (p. 9). Retrieved April 12, 2008, from http://www.hicss.hawaii.edu/HICSS_34/PDFs/DTIST02.pdf

Steinfield, C., Adelaar, T., & Lai, Y. (2002). Integrating brick and mortar locations with e-commerce: Understanding synergy opportunities. In *Proceedings of the 35th Annual Hawaii International Conference on System Sciences (HICSS'02)* (Vol. 8, p. 216.2).

Sun. (2003). *Logistics sample application: Design.* Retrieved July 28, 2005, from http://docs.sun.com/source/817-1243-10/dvlpdsgn.html

TMWSuite Systems Inc. (2005). TMW Systems, Inc. Retrieved August 30, 2005, from http://www.tmwsystems.com/fileUploads/contentManager-Documents/TMWSuiteBrochureFINALNOPics%5B0%5D.pdf

Warkentin, M.,& Bajaj, A. (2001). The On-demand delivery services model for e-commerce. In A. Gangopadhay (Ed.), *Managing business with electronic commerce: Issues and trends.* Hershey, PA: Idea Group.

WTO. (1998, June 12). Postal *and courier services* (S/C/W/39). Retrieved April 12, 2008, from http://www.wto.org/english/tratop_e/serv_e/w39.doc

Zhang, L-J., & Chang, H. (2002*). E-logistics processes integration framework.* Retrieved July 28, 2005, from http://www.Webservicesarchitect.com/content/articles/zhang01print.asp

APPENDIX 1: DATABASE MODEL

The database model can be used as a design plan by the database developer(s) to implement the data model in a specified database management system. The Web system uses the following main tables:

- Delivery Agent
- Courier Service
- Location
- Customer
- Order
- Shipment
- Payment
- Document
- Price List
- History

These tables are organized as follows:

- Delivery Agent (DA) has a number of Courier Services, which it provides. One DA may be linked to many Courier Services. Also, Delivery Agent has a number of Locations, in which it provides its services. One DA may be linked to many Locations. Delivery Agent has a number of Orders, and Customers are linked to that Orders. Customers are not linked to the DA directly. One DA may be linked to many Orders. Delivery Agent is not linked to the Shipment and Payment directly. There may be a number of Documents that are linked to the DA. So, one DA may be linked to many Documents.
- Courier Service may be linked to Delivery Agent, but Courier Service may exist even if it is not linked to any Delivery Agent. Courier Service may be linked to a Location, but it is unnecessary. If a Courier Service is linked to a Location, it may also be linked to another Location, where it is also provided. Courier Service is linked to an Order, one Courier Service may be linked to many Orders. Courier Service is not linked to Customer, Shipment and Payment directly; they are linked through an Order. Courier Service absolutely is not linked to Document. Courier Service may be linked to Price List (Price List's structure will be discussed later).
- There is a reference of Locations in the Web system. Orders and Delivery Agents can refer to Locations.
- Customer has a number of Orders that he or she has made. One Customer may be linked to many Orders, but one Order must be linked to one and only one Customer. Customer is linked to Delivery Agents through Orders. Customer is linked to Payment directly. One Customer may be linked to many Payments, but one Payment must be linked to one and only one Customer. There may be a number of Documents that are linked to the Customer. So, one Customer may be linked to many Documents.
- Order is the most important table in the system. Order refers to one Delivery Agent, one Courier Service, two Locations, one Customer, one Shipment, and many Payments. Delivery Agent, Locations, and Customer may exist without Order. ER diagram for Order is shown in Figure 12. Delivery Agent and Payments are optional for Order.

- Shipment is a subject of Order. For reasons of database normalization, Shipment is separated from Order; one Order may include some Shipments. Every Shipment must be linked to a Customer.

- Payment is linked to an Order. For reasons of database normalization, Shipment is separated from Order; one Order may include some Shipments. Every Shipment must be linked to a Customer. Customer has a number of Payments that he or she has made. So one Customer may be linked to many Payments, but one Payment must be linked to one and only one Customer.

- Document is linked to Delivery Agent, Customer, Order, or Shipment. One Document may be linked to only one of the following: Delivery Agent, Customer, Order or Shipment, but Delivery Agents, Customers, Orders and Shipments may be linked to many Documents.

- Price List is linked to Delivery Agent. Every Delivery Agent has one Price List. Every Price List has a number of Courier Services. One Courier Service may be linked to many Price Lists.

- History is linked to Delivery Agents, Courier Services, Locations, Customers, Shipments, and Payments. Every History record refers to one Delivery Agent and one Customer necessarily. History can have links to Courier Service, Location, Order, Shipment, and Payment but they are optional.

- Authorization is a specific table. Authorization is linked to Delivery Agents and Customers. Logins and Passwords are stored in Authorization table.

The complete Database Model is shown below in Figure 12.

Figure 12.Complete database model for proposed architecture

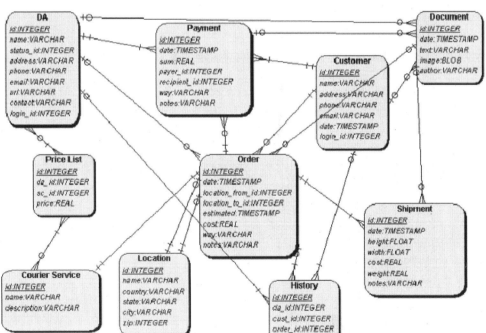

IBM DB2 Universal Database is the database management system recommended in this project. The database is accessed through the Java Database Connectivity (JDBC) driver. A connection pool is used, which contains a group of JDBC connections that are created when the connection pool is registered, usually when starting up the Web Server. The Web system borrows a connection from the connection pool, uses it, and then returns it to the connection pool by closing it. This DBMS is designed to work well is a Web-services environment. Data flow between the Web System Database and corresponding eLogistics applications uses a Web service in connection with the EJB-based architecture.

Security

The Delivery Agent and the Customer enter login and password in the corresponding electronic form at the main page to log into the Web system. The Web system then performs authentication; if it is successful, the user gets access to Web system's functionality. The System Administrator and the Helpdesk Engineer have their own service interface that is a thin client to the Web system's database. Using their corresponding Login ID and password at the main logon page of the Web system. The Web system performs authentication; and if successful, the secure user gets access to Web system's service functionality. The authentication is performed before every request from a secure user to the Web system. Interaction between authenticated users and the Web system is performed via Hyper-Text Transfer Protocol Secure (HTTPS). HTTPS is the secure version of HTTP, the communications protocol of the World Wide Web. HTTPS encrypts the session data using a version of the SSL (Secure Socket Layer) protocol. The level of protection depends on the correctness of the implementation by the Web browser and the server software and the actual cryptographic algorithms supported.

This work was previously published in E-Commerce Trends for Organizational Advancement: New Applications and Methods, edited by M. Khosrow-Pour, pp. 239-263, copyright 2010 by IGI Publishing (an imprint of IGI Global).

Chapter 4.4
Web Services in Distributed Information Systems:
Availability, Performance and Composition

Xia Zhao
University of Bedfordshire, UK

Tao Wang
University of Bedfordshire, UK

Enjie Liu
University of Bedfordshire, UK

Gordon J. Clapworthy
University of Bedfordshire, UK

ABSTRACT

Distributed information systems are growing rapidly in response to the improvement of computer hardware and software and this is matched by the evolution of the technologies involved. This article focuses mainly on Web Services technology and discusses related technical issues including availability, performance and composition. It also introduces Grid, agents and Semantic Web technologies that can work together with Web Services to serve different business goals.

INTRODUCTION

Distributed information systems are becoming more popular as a result of improvements in computer hardware and software, and there is a commensurate rise in the use of the associated technologies. Because of the increasing desire for business-to-business (B2B) communication and integration, technologies such as Service-Oriented Computing (SOC), Semantic Web, Grid, Agents/ Multi-agents, peer-to-peer, etc., are receiving a high level of interest nowadays.

As a part of distributed information systems, web information systems play an important role in the modern, ubiquitous Internet world and the applicability of Web Services as a particular implementation of SOC has been widely recognized for current B2B integration (e.g. e-commerce, e-government and e-healthcare).

However, building all aspects of Web Services comprehensively needs further improvement, for instance, Quality Of Service (QoS) has yet to be properly addressed. Likewise, the detection of service availability to achieve self-healing in the invocation process, service reuse, how best to define atomic services, and service composition are all issues that urgently require more research.

Meanwhile, it should be noted that Web Services play only a partial role in evolving distributed information systems. With the development of future computer hardware, software and business requirements, many other technologies will probably emerge that will serve particular business goals better. Therefore, much recent research has been focusing not only on individual technologies in distributed systems, but also on the possibility of combining currently available technologies to improve business outcomes.

In this article, we concentrate mainly on Web Services and technical issues associated with current Web Services standards, but we also give a brief overview of three other distributed technologies, namely Grid, agents and Semantic Web, which can work with Web Services. Thus, it concentrates initially on the background of services in distributed information systems, then it introduces Grid, agent and Semantic Web technologies. After that, the article discusses several technical aspects of Web Services in current distributed information systems, in particular, general Web Service availability and performance issues and the possibility of combining agent technology and Web Services to provide improved understanding of service availability. We then introduce JSON (Javascript Object Notation), which may provide an alternative to current approaches that

will deliver better Web Service Performance and discuss service composition, illustrating it with an implementation from the EU Living Human Digital Library (LHDL) project.

WEB SERVICES AND RELATED TECHNOLOGIES IN DISTRIBUTED INFORMATION SYSTEMS

Internet applications are developed and hosted by many different organizations, and customers from all over the world access them via the Internet from their desktops, or possibly from hand-held devices, such as a PDA or mobile phone. Originally, Internet applications referred to activities such as web browsing, FTP, and email. More recently, they have also included more advanced applications that are generally referred to as services. These mirror our real-world business activities in the cyber world.

Let us take a ticket-booking system as an example. The processes may include: the initial search for the right ticket, using criteria such as price, timing, etc; the actual booking, which will include some form of payment process which itself may involve authentication processes such as a credit check by the credit-card company; then various forms of after-sales service, such as notifications a few days before travel, etc. In the real world, all the services may be provided by different specialist companies and achieved by human interaction, using their knowledge and intelligence. In the cyber world, these actions are achieved by so-called software services. To avoid continually having to rebuild services, there has been a trend towards using "atomic" services as building blocks from which to construct more complex services.

In open distributed systems, independent components cooperate with each other in order to achieve a goal. Apart from SOC, Grid technology and agent technology are the most widely used technologies for developing distributed systems. In this article, the authors do not offer a syntactic classification of the technologies, but rather, discuss the problem from a developer's standpoint.

Web Services

Web Services are emerging as a promising technology for building distributed applications. A Web Service is a software system that is designed to support interoperable machine-to-machine interaction over a network. As one instantiation of Service-Oriented Architecture (SOA), they have the property of being loosely-coupled, open-standard, language- and platform-independent. "Loosely-coupled" implies that service providers can modify backend functions while retaining the same interface to clients; the core service functions are encapsulated and remain transparent to clients. "Open-standard" ensures the viability of collaboration and integration with other services. Language and platform independence enables services to be developed in any language and deployed on any platform.

Technical Issues in Web Services

The following lists some technical issues in Web Services, some of which will be the main focus of this article.

- **Defining and building atomic services:** An atomic service generally solves an individual, specific problem. The granularity of what are chosen as atomic services has to be defined carefully. If an atomic service is too complicated, it may not be easy to employ it in a variety of applications, so it becomes less useful. It may also mean that similar atomic services, differing only in a few subtle ways, may have to be created to cover the range of possible circumstances, which will result in a large library of atomic services being established.

On the other hand, if atomic services are kept very simple, then composing even fairly straightforward tasks requires the use of many atomic services, which makes their creation tedious and time consuming. There is no general guideline for identifying the appropriate level of granularity. One should definitely seek the opinion of domain experts on how to split tasks—the breakdown of a task into its components should correlate closely with the "internal" description that a user familiar with the domain would see as natural.

- **Cooperation between services:** By combining atomic services, one can create more complicated services. This should be a design goal for future Web Services development as it provides the possibility of using existing services to reduce development time and of providing greater transparency and efficiency for users.
- **Service availability and performance:** Service availability and performance are two factors in the Web Services QoS (Quality of Service) model. (Lee et al., 2003) categorized the Web Service QoS into 12 aspects: performance, reliability, scalability, robustness, exception handling, accuracy, integrity, accessibility, availability, interoperability and security. In general, a high-quality service implies that it is secure and has high availability, high throughput, rapid response, execution and transmission, and low round-trip delay.

Grid

The Grid concept (Foster & Kesselman, 1998; Foster, Kesselman & Tuecke, 2001) is encapsulated by 'coordinated resource sharing and problem solving in a dynamic, multi-institutional virtual organization'. IBM defines a Grid in a more commercial way as 'a standards-based application/resource-sharing architecture that makes it possible for heterogeneous systems and applications to share, compute and store resources transparently' (Clabby Analytics, 2004).

Grid has evolved through several phases. It began as a means of sharing computing resources; then, as an extension, data sharing was added, and some special devices such as scientific instruments and medical equipment were included. The marriage of the first generation of Grid with Web technology led to generic Grid services.

Later, the focus moved to knowledge sharing and led to collaboration between organizations while retaining the security requirements of each. The knowledge Grid facilitates data mining across the Internet and requires techniques for abstracting heterogeneous data, creating metadata, publishing, discovering and describing data in the Grid.

With the maturity of SOA and Web Services technologies, the Grid Community has begun to combine them and build a Grid infrastructure. The emergence of the Open Grid Services Architecture (OGSA) (http://www.globus.org/ogsa/) is an example that represents an evolution towards a Grid system architecture based on Web services concepts and technologies. OGSA is a community standard with multiple implementations. It provides a framework, and the users can define a wide range of interoperable, portable services.

Agents

Multi-agent systems evolved from a need for knowledge-aware, distributed, problem-solving mechanisms. According to Jennings (2001), agents have the following characteristics:

- **Problem solvers:** By clearly identifying problem-solving entities with well-defined boundaries and interfaces;
- **Proactive:** By being both reactive (able to respond in a timely fashion to changes in their environment) and proactive (able to opportunistically adopt goals and take the initiative);

- **Goal-oriented:** They are designed to fulfill a specific role;
- **Context-aware:** They are situated (embedded) in a particular environment over which they have partial control and absorbability, they receive inputs related to the state of their environment through sensors and they act on the environment through effectors;
- **Autonomous:** They have control over both their internal state and their own behavior.

Some toolkits, frameworks and libraries are based on agent technology. Some frameworks allow developers to define their own architecture and inter-relationships between the agents, for example, JADE (Java Agent Development Framework) (http://jade.tilab.com/) provides a communication architecture for the agents with good debugging functions. Camacho, Aler, Castro & Molina (2002) have compared some of these platforms.

Research into agents has focused on providing formal proofs to proof-of-concept demonstrators and provided only limited, pragmatic support in terms of systems, software and tools. In contrast, according to Payne (2008), research into Web Services has focused on the user community, resulting in pragmatic, bottom-up enabling technology that readily facilities the robust construction of service-oriented systems. Much of the focus of Web Services research has been on developing declarative descriptions that application developers can share and that their tools can use to construct and develop large-scale distributed software.

Foster, Jennings & Kesselman (2004) describe Grid and agents as 'brain meets brawn' –historically, the Grid community has focused on 'brawn' (the infrastructure and tools for sharing within dynamic and geographically distributed virtual organizations), while agents have been associated with 'brain' (the development of concepts, methodologies and algorithms for autonomous problem solvers). They share some common interests such as a robust infrastructure and autonomous and flexible behaviors and becoming mutually stronger when allied.

Semantic Web

One aim of introducing Web Services is to achieve machine-to-machine communication. With the basic Web Services technologies, this can be achieved at a certain level such as invocation between service requesters and service providers, but many other forms of communication, such as service discovery, service selection and service composition, cannot be accomplished efficiently and dynamically. With the development of Semantic Web technologies, such as ontologies, semantics can be used in conjunction with Web Services to offer better services.

Knowledge discovery is a key issue in distributed systems. Take service discovery in the Web Service world as an example—there may be many services that can solve a particular problem on the Internet, but how does one find them? Or, if someone has developed such a service, how can they let other people know about it? Further, as a customer, how can I tell which of the various available services is better than the others? These needs are very familiar to us in the real world and to resolve them, we read reviews, receive 'word of mouth' opinion, etc. The question is, how can we achieve this in the cyber world?

Web Services within the basic SOA concept can solve some of these problems. For example, service providers hide functionalities through service interfaces and publish machine-readable descriptions of their services in publicly accessible registries. Service consumers discover these services by querying the registry and bind to the selected services dynamically.

The Semantic Web has made further strides towards solving this problem. It is an evolution of the World Wide Web in which information is machine processable (rather than being only human oriented), thus permitting browsers or other software agents to find, share and combine information for us more easily.

Data and the relationships among the data are well understood by the machines that process them. This allows the machines to do more than simply display the requested web pages to the user; software will be able to analyze and process metadata—data about the data—to find the best pages to display to a particular user or to deliver to another machine.

Data that is generally hidden away in HTML files is often useful in some contexts, but not in others. The majority of data on the Web is in this form at the moment, which makes it difficult to use on a large scale, because there is no global system for publishing data in such a way that it can be easily processed by anyone.

The main problem with the use of standards for Web Service description (e.g. WSDL) and publishing (e.g. in this case, a semantic broker) is that the syntactic definitions used in these descriptions do not completely describe the capacity of a service and cannot be understood by software programs. It requires a human to interpret the meaning of inputs, outputs and applicable constraints as well as the context in which the services can be used.

Semantic Web Services (SWS) research aims to automate the development of Web-Service-based applications through Semantic Web technology. By providing formal representations based on ontologies, we can facilitate the machine interpretation of Web Service description. Thus, a business organization can view a Semantic Web Service as the basic mechanism for integrating data and processes across applications on the Web.

WEB SERVICE AVAILABILITY

The term *"availability"* indicates whether a service is ready to respond immediately to a request, or not (Erradi, Padmanabhuni &Varadharajan, 2006). This is useful for some busy and popular services within a system—for example, a consumer would like to use a fast service, but too many requests for the same service will cause a reduction in throughput and performance on the server. The current consensus seems to be, first, to try to ensure that all services are available, then try to improve the performance of the services.

From its definition, Web Services, the most popular middleware, consists of SOAP, WSDL and UDDI. The UDDI specification V3 (Adam, 2005) does not provide query APIs with associated QoS information. A typical process from a service consumer will be: consumer query in UDDI, construct the request and receive the response. All of these processes are encoded in XML. From within, Web Services can be considered as XML-message based, with the messages having 3 classifications: query, request and response.

Stateless and Context-Unaware Web Services

An atomic Web Service is used for specific tasks and can be seen as a stateless and context-unaware process. There are two states for a service, namely active and asleep. An available service has two requirements: it is ready immediately for a request, and a service consumer can receive the correct response within the necessary time. If a service cannot perform a specific task in the required time, it can be seen as unavailable.

Services providers register and publish a service as an interface, at which point the service is in the sleep state. It is activated only when it receives a request; after execution, the service will return to the sleep state. The service has no knowledge about its context—we call this *context-unaware*. The context includes factors that can affect the service QoS, such as network QoS, container throughput, hardware throughput and execution time.

Heavyweight ESB Framework for Service Availability

To increase service availability, services can be distributed to different service containers and then use a QoS meter to manage access control, request filtering and request scheduling. For example, Erradi, Padmanabhuni &Varadharajan (2006) suggest a Web-Services DiffServ Framework by adding a request classifier, request dispatcher and QoS manager. This kind of framework is a prototype of the Enterprise Service Bus (ESB) (Chappell, 2004—services are published as end-points, all requests are filtered and scheduled as the QoS requires.

ESB frameworks are generally characterized as 'heavyweight'—complex, centralized and difficult. Complex indicates that they are hard to configure or install. Furthermore, many additional libraries are required within the products. As a result, it is very easy to get exceptions because of version-control issues. Centralized implies that an ESB product tries to gather all functions such as routing, inter-change protocol, service monitoring, security, and so on—it is constructing a 'super' link between distributed objects. It is found that users generally have to receive training before they can use it effectively.

ESB frameworks improve the availability of atomic Web Service, but they do not solve the problems of stateless and context-unawareness. In another words, ESB frameworks have not addressed the root of the problem.

Lightweight and Context-Aware Agents for Availability

According to Payne (2008), many systems assume prior knowledge of the context and, hence, focus on a specific problem. For example, a service provider gives a fixed value to a service's execution time, but this value will obviously be different depending upon whether a single request or one hundred separate requests have just arrived. Moreover, when we consider the various factors contributing to possible network delay, the response time can vary substantially. If both the service provider and the service consumer use the fixed value without any dynamic environmental consideration, when many requests come simultaneously, service consumers may find that the service is not as available as expected.

As mentioned earlier, agents have a knowledge of context and the ability to monitor changes to the context—*"Agents are embedded in a particular environment over which they have partial control and observe-ability. They receive inputs related to the state of their environment through effectors"* (Payne, 2008, p12-14). This context-monitoring ability is also what the service needs.

Likewise, agents are autonomous as *"they have control both over their internal state and over their own behaviour"* (Payne, 2008. p12-14). As noted above, an atomic service performs a specific task by accepting a request and returning a response. If the throughput is fixed, more requests mean slow execution and the service will crash if the request exceeds the throughput. Providing a capacity for autonomy on a stateless service will be helpful for service execution. Moreover, agents have knowledge about new agents, which can be used to conduct requests to several services performing same function.

Suppose we map a service with an agent into a pair named Agent-ServiceX which has the characteristics of both the agent and the service. The Agent-ServiceX will be context-aware and autonomous and will have knowledge of other services. For instance, within the Jade agent platform, services can be used for specific tasks, service agents can be used as service monitors and directory agents can be used to filter and schedule requests. The agent system will not only perform a similar function to ESB frameworks but will also provide QoS information based on the changing context, rather than fixed values set up by the service providers.

WEB SERVICE PERFORMANCE

The term *"performance"* associated with a Web Service represents how quickly the service can be completed or how rapidly the user can obtain the result (Lee, Jeon, Lee, Jeong & Park, 2003).

For each individual service, let T_{total} be the time between the client sending the request with parameters and receiving a response with the result, so

$$T_{total} = T_{request} + T_{response} + T_{exec} + T_{serialization} + T_{RTD} \qquad (1)$$

where $T_{request}$ is the transmission time for the request, $T_{response}$ is the transmission time for the response, T_{exec} is the execution time for the service, $T_{serialization}$ is the serialization time for the service and T_{RTD} is the round-trip delay for the process. Serialization and deserialization are coupled; here, serialization time means the time for serialization and deserialization.

The transmission time for request and response can be calculated as:

$$T_{request} = \frac{L_{request}}{R} \; ; \; T_{response} = \frac{L_{response}}{R},$$

where $L_{request}$ is the length of the request message, $L_{response}$ is the length of the response message, and the R is the transmission rate.

Then, Equation 1 can be reformatted as:

$$T_{total} = \frac{L_{request}}{R} + \frac{L_{response}}{R} + T_{exec} + T_{serialization} + T_{RTD} \qquad (2)$$

so it is clear that the time of a service is effected by length of request, length of response, transmission rate, execution time, serialization time and round-trip delay.

Execution time is based on the software throughput and hardware configuration. Routing delay and transmission rate are decided by the network QoS. Execution time and network QoS are outside the consideration of this article. Suppose the transmission rate and round-trip delay are of fixed value, the time of a service is decided by the request and response length, the request and response delivery and serialization. In another words, the performance of a service is decided by the message length, serialization and message transmission.

FACTORS AFFECTING WEB SERVICE PERFORMANCE

In this section, we discuss three main factors that affect Web Service performance.

XML

XML is designed for data storage and transmission. It uses plaintext as tags, so platforms that can process plaintext can also process XML; in another words, XML can be used on any platform. This made it attractive for use in SOAP.

Reducing the volume of data to be transmitted will clearly reduce the transmission time. Unfortunately, plaintext formatted xml with repeated labels makes the file much bigger than the user may expect. The website of SoapUI (www.soapui. org), a leading tool for Web Service testing, shows that a SOAP request of "hello world" is almost 280 bytes, and the SOAP response would be 350 Bytes. Menasce (2002) shows that XML's way of representing data usually results in files of substantially greater size (on average, 400% larger) than representations of the same data in binary.

HTTP

HTTP (Hypertext Transfer Protocol) is used for SOAP as it will not be blocked by a firewall. Assuming that the transmission rate and round-trip delay are of fixed value, an efficient method for message delivery would be helpful. This efficiency has three requirements: once and exactly once delivery; message arrival in the right sequence; and message arrival in the exact form.

A single delivery can be used to ensure accurate response and no repeat request. If a response message exceeds the maximum segment size of the TCP protocol, a message is divided into several packages, and all the packets should arrive in the correct sequence and in the exact form.

HTTP uses the Best Effort QoS (Quality of Service) model, which means that it will perform a FIFS (First In First Service) policy to transform all data packets without filtering. Thus, packages sent by HTTP have no guarantee on the order of the arriving packets and no guarantee of packets being delivered to the destination. If there is no bandwidth available, the packets are simply discarded.

SOAP

SOAP (Simple Object Access Protocol) defines a set of serialization rules for encoding data in XML and all data is serialized as elements—all the data transmitted by SOAP are encoded in repeated tags.

From Equation 2, we know that, to reduce transmission time, serialization should try to use less time and decrease the length of the message. But SOAP goes the other way because SOAP defines a complex format for a message, with repeated element tags. It is time-consuming to encapsulate information into a SOAP envelope and retrieve information from a SOAP envelope. In effect, SOAP uses more bytes to express repeated tags which results in longer messages.

Possible Solution for Atomic Service Performance

Using JSON Instead of XML

According to RFC 4627 (Crockford, 2006), JSON (JavaScript Object Notation) is an open, text-based data-exchange format. Like XML, it is human-readable, platform independent and enjoys a wide availability of implementations (Aziz & Mitchell, 2007). Furthermore, it provides mechanisms for data serialization and deserialization.

In contrast to the document-oriented XML, JSON is data-oriented. Without repeated element tags, a message encoded with JSON will use fewer bytes than when encoded with XML and will thus be transmitted faster. The decrease in message length is a strong reason to adopt JSON for service communication protocol, because serialization and deserialization occur in both sides of the service consumer and the service container. JSON has its own method for data serialization and deserialization and, as far as we know, there are no documents comparing the serialization performance of JSON and SOAP. Thus, further investigations should be performed to obtain detailed information concerning possible performance improvements.

WEB SERVICE COMPOSITION

Individual services, which provide a single specific functionality, are referred to as atomic services. Traditionally, only atomic services are available, so complex functionality has to be achieved by a series of service invocations via service requesters, as shown in Figure 1.

However, if one is regularly performing the same complex task, continually having to invoke several services successively makes this approach time consuming and error prone. By use of service composition, the same task can be achieved by assembling existing atomic services, possibly from different service providers, into a composite service. For example, consider a travel booking scenario, which may include a series of tasks such as booking flights and trains, booking hotels and purchasing travel insurance. There may be various services for flight booking, accommodation booking and travel insurance purchase available from different service providers. A travel agent may offer a composite Web Service that integrates all of these services together to create customized functions—the composite service will handle all of the coordination among the atomic services involved. Thereafter, service requesters can directly invoke the new composite services without having to worry about the internal coordination changes, as shown in Figure 2.

Composition is an important aspect of Service-Oriented Architecture (SOA). The composite service usually performs functions including coordination, monitoring, conformance and Quality of Service (QoS) composition (Papazoglou, 2003).

- Coordination refers to the execution of the control and data flow of the component services and the output of the composition. A typical example is defining a workflow process and applying a workflow engine for the run-time execution of the whole process.
- Monitoring can be event based, which allows the composite service to publish the events subscribed from the component

Figure 1. Service request of a series of atomic services

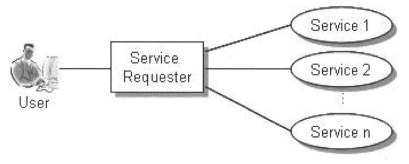

Figure 2. Service request with a composite service

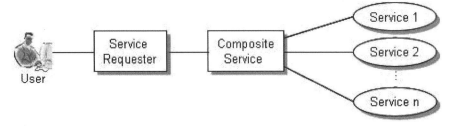

services; this may include filtering, correlating, and so on.

- Conformance ensures that the constraints among component services are properly imposed and that the integrity of the composite service is achieved by appropriate service parameter matching and data fusion.

- QoS Composition includes the overall cost, performance, privacy, security, scalability, reliability, etc., of the composite service.

Compared with traditional approaches, Web Service composition brings the following benefits.

Prompting reusability: The composite Web Service is built from existing autonomous Web Services, and since the composition is a new Web Service, it can itself be reused either directly or as part of a new composition.

Transparency: Assembling a commonly used flow of services into a single service by using composition can significantly reduce the complexity for requesters who wish to access an extended series of services on a regular basis.

Approaches to Web Service Composition

Currently, there are two major approaches for Web Service composition, namely Web Service choreography and Web Service orchestration.

Some groups also apply semantic technologies to enhance the composition process.

In this article, we mainly focus on the basic approaches of choreography and orchestration. The distinctive difference between these two methods is that orchestration describes a process flow between services that are controlled by a single party; whereas choreography refers to a more collaborative interaction between the parties involved and tracks the sequence of messages among them in which no single party truly owns the conversation (Peltz, 2003).

Orchestration

Service orchestration refers to a process in which one party acts as a coordinator in relation to other services. The coordinator may receive a message from one service and make decisions based on the messages such as changing the content of the data, then invoking another service. The orchestration model addresses the local internal communications among data and control flow. It is usually used within one organization, in which constraints on the services are not viewed globally. The orchestration process is also known as an *executable process* as it is intended to be executed by an orchestration engine.

The orchestration approach has been well recognized by industry. The Web Service Business Execution Language (WS-BPEL) (www.oasis-open.org/committees/wsbpel/), which is co-proposed by IBM, Microsoft, BEA, SUN and Oracle and standardized by OASIS, is the main workflow standard for Web Service orchestration. WS-BPEL is an executable language and most supporting development environments offer process execution engines.

Choreography

In service choreography, there is no coordinating party—all participants are treated equally in achieving the composition goal. It is a more decentralized form of processing which is based on rules known to each service. It captures interactions from a global perspective and does not present any internal communications among the participants that do not appear in the global interactions. Therefore, choreography is commonly used in the inter-organization environment.

Choreography addresses the agreements among the interaction participants. Although its interactions include both data and control flow of the communication, from the global point of view, it focuses more on the constitution of composition conformance.

Further into standards, the Web Service Choreography Definition Language (WS-CDL) (www. w3.org/TR/2004/WD-ws-cdl-10-20041217/), which is defined by the W3C, describes Web Service collaborations among cooperating participants. WS-CDL is the current *de facto* standard for Web Service choreography. It is based on meta-model and XML syntax and is non-executable.

Combining Choreography and Orchestration

As mentioned earlier, choreography and orchestration are two service composition approaches that concentrate on different perspectives of interaction, namely global and local. However, they are supposed to work together to form the complete service composition, and the standard language WS-CDL can also be used in conjunction with WS-BPEL. In fact, several research initiatives have already explored approaches to combining WS-CDL and WS-BPEL.

The TrustCoM project proposes an approach for automated derivation of the executable business process from choreographies in virtual organizations (Weber, Haller & Mulle, 2008). The approach is mainly based on an XML tree query. The CDL2BPEL algorithm is introduced, which consists of 5 main steps: a) reading a source document; b) generating an object tree for the source document; c) performing validation; d) performing transformation on the tree; e) serializing the resulting object trees to a set of documents in the target language. A Knowledge Base (KB) is introduced in CDL2BPEL; it stores CDL patterns and their respective BPEL replacements and is used to record the information gap between WS-CDL and WS-BPEL. This approach allows the re-use of the choreography patterns and achieves automated WS-CDL to WS-BPEL generation. However, it is simply based on the XML syntax transformation and no validations are mentioned on global constraints.

Mendling & Hafner (2007) implemented a proof-concept mapping between BPEL and WS-CDL for inter-organizational workflows. They adopted the concept of Model Driven Architecture (MDA). Mapping between WS-CDL and WS-BPEL is implemented in XSLT and can be supported in both directions. A wscdl2bpel.xslt is already implemented. The transformation algorithm is defined according to the WS-CDL XML tag elements. This approach achieves bilateral mapping between WS-BPEL and WS-CDL and offers tool support for automated generation of BPEL stubs. However, it does not provide validation on the BPEL stubs generated or formalization to handle complex workflows. As far as we know, the backward mapping, from WS-BPEL to WS-CDL, has not yet been implemented.

Since both WS-CDL and WS-BPEL can be represented in graphs using UML or similar technologies, another approach worth considering is to apply graph transformation theory to transform between WS-CDL and WS-BPEL. Triple Graph Grammar (TGG) (Königs, 2005) may provide a good method to achieve this. In TGG, models can be defined and transformed in either direction, which makes it possible to perform transformations from WS-CDL to WS-BPEL and back again. TGG can synchronize and maintain the correspondence of the two models, which helps to achieve composition conformance during transformation. In addition, TGG supports working incrementally, which would allow a complex transformation process to be completed step by step. However, further research has to be performed to evaluate this idea.

AN EXAMPLE: WEB SERVICE COMPOSTION AT ORCHESTRATION LEVEL

In this section, we describe, from the orchestration perspective, a proof-concept Web Service composition example that was implemented in the EU LHDL (Living Human Digital Library) project. In the context of this article, the details of the background of the project and the implementation of the atomic services used in composition are not important. However, more information can be found in Zhao, Liu, Clapworthy, Quadrani, Testi & Viceconti (2008) and Zhao, Liu & Clapworthy (2008).

Instead of simply giving the end users the existing WS-BPEL designers, we implemented a web-based tool that allows users to compose the services available in the LHDL project in an easy and intuitive way. Compared to existing WS-BPEL designers such as Active BPEL Designer and Oracle Business Process Manager, our composition tool has the following benefits for the project:

End-user oriented: The tool hides the complexity of the WS-BPEL process from the end-users, adopts subsets of the WS-BPEL

Figure 3. An example of BPEL Workflow for service composition

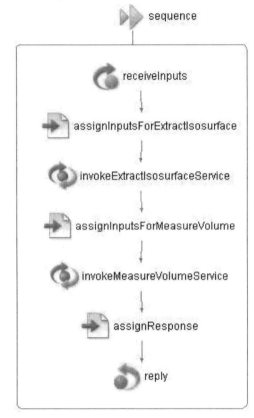

language and gives users a straightforward sequence composition designer;

Dynamic service composition: It automatically generates BPEL processes based on the end-users' configuration inputs and deploys the BPEL process in the ActiveBPEL Engine Community Edition (www.activevos.com/community-open-source.php) on the fly; no extra manual deployment is required to make the process executable on the execution engine.

This framework simulates the data flow combinations and generates a .bpel file that represents the composition process. Figure 3 illustrates an example composition process (*extractisosurface-*

Figure 4. The framework of the LHDL Web service composition

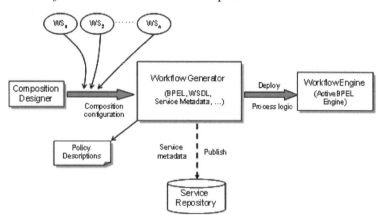

measurevolume) by invoking and combining two existing Web Services.

The process is organized into a sequence with the *receive* activity waiting for an inbound message from outside and the *reply* activity transmitting an outbound message back to the requester. A series of *assign* and *invoke* activities take inputs from *receive*, invoke each service, then pass the response to *reply*.

The current composition framework consists of four main components (see Figure 4):

Composition Designer: A web-based rich application client for composition sequence configuration;

Workflow Generator: This accepts and validates the user's configuration and generates a composite service;

Workflow Engine: This acts as a platform for deploying the newly generated composite service;

Policy Descriptions: These are XML files used by the generator to validate composition configurations.

Figure 5. A screen shot of the LHDL Web service composition tool

As seen in Figure 5, the Composition Designer interface is much simpler and more intuitive than a standard BPEL designer. In the screen shot, the left-hand tree structure displays the available atomic services, which are categorized as *Import*, *Modification*, *Measurement*, *Preview* and *Export* in the LHDL project. The main data grid on the right regulates the composition in the sequence structure. To create a composite service, users first drag and drop services from the service list into the composition sequence, then submit the configuration together with a predefined service name to the generator.

The generator handles the complexities of validating the data flow, creating the composition process and deploying the newly generated service. It accepts the user's configuration inputs and dynamically generates a BPEL process file, a WSDL (Web Service Description Language) file and a process deployment description file.

When all the workflow files have been generated, the workflow generator automatically deploys the process on a workflow engine—an ActiveBPEL Engine in our case. A service metadata file is also generated through the workflow generator, which enables end-users to directly publish the newly created service in the service repository.

Within the LHDL project, this workflow generator is generic and scalable from the developer's perspective. An external XML configuration file is provided which allows newly created services to be easily added into the composition system without much modification within the source code.

CONCLUSION

Web Services, as a part of distributed information systems, play an important role in current business integration. However, many technical issues related to Web Services are still subject to active research. This article has discussed three main aspects: service availability, service performance and service composition.

By considering current Web Service availability techniques and agent technology, we proposed an agent-service pair solution that can offer better service availability—by the use of agents, Web Services can become more context-aware and autonomous. How to find useful information from the context and how to use this information would further challenges.

We defined a method for calculating Web Service request-response time and reviewed current Web Service standards, including XML, HTTP and SOAP. JSON has been proposed in this article as an alternative to XML to achieve better service performance.

We discussed issues relating to Web Service composition including the key concepts, common choreography and orchestration approaches, and possible combinations between them. A graph transformation idea was proposed to transform between choreography and orchestration. Moreover, the article gave a Web Service composition example that has been implemented in the LHDL project.

Furthermore, the article discussed some other technologies distributed information systems including Grid, Agents and Semantic Web. All these technologies can be applied together with Web Services to serve different distributed business goals. The article gave an example of using agents with services to solve the Web Service availability problem.

REFERENCES

Adam, C. (2005). *From Web Services to SOA and everything in between: The journey begins.* Retrieved March 20, 2009, from http://www.webservices.org

Aziz, A., & Mitchell, S. (2007). *An introduction to JavaScript Object Notation (JSON) in JavaScript and. NET.* Retrieved March 20, 2009, from http://msdn.microsoft.com/en-us/library/bb299886.aspx

Camacho, D., Aler, R., Castro, C., & Molina, J. M. (2002). Performance evaluation of ZEUS, JADE, and Skeleton Agent framework. *2002 IEEE Systems, Man, and Cybernetics Conference, 4*(6). IEEE.

Chappell, D. (2004). *Enterprise Service Bus.* USA: O'Reilly Press.

Clabby Analytics. (2004). *The grid report.* Retrieved July 3, 2008, from http://www-03.ibm.com/grid/pdf/Clabby_Grid_Report_2004_Edition.pdf

Crockford, D. (2006). *RFC 4627, The application/ json media type for JavaScript Object Notation (JSON).* Retrieved March 20, 2009, from http:// www.faqs.org/ftp/rfc/pdf/rfc4627.txt.pdf

Erradi, A., Padmanabhuni, S., & Varadharajan, N. (2006). Differential QoS support in Web Services management. *IEEE Intentional Conference on Web Services* (pp. 781-788). Chicago: IEEE Computer Society.

Foster, I., Jennings, N., & Kesselman, C. (2004). Brian meets brawn: Why grid and agents need each other. *3rd International Joint Conference on Autonomous Agent and Multi-agent Systems (AAMAS'04)* (pp. 8-15). New York: ACM Press.

Foster, I., & Kesselman, C. (Eds.). (2000). *The grid: Blueprint for a new computing infrastructure.* San Francisco: Morgan Kaufmann Publishers.

Foster, I., Kesselman, C., & Tuecke, S. (2001). The anatomy of the grid: Enabling scalable virtual organizations. *The International Journal of Supercomputer Applications, 15*(3), 200–222. doi:10.1177/109434200101500302

Jennings, N. R. (2001). An agent-based approach for building complex software systems. *Communications of the ACM, 44*(4), 35–41. doi:10.1145/367211.367250

Konigs, A. (2005). Model transformation with triple graph grammars. *Model Transformations in Practice Workshop, Part of ACM/IEEE 8th International Conference on Model Driven Engineering Languages and Systems (MoDELS 2005),* Jamaica.

Lee, K., Jeon, J., Lee, W., Jeong, S., & Park, S. (2003). *QoS for Web Services: Requirements and possible approaches.* Retrieved March 20, 2009, from W3C: http://www.w3c.or.kr/kr-office/ TR/2003/ws-qos/

McLaughlin, B. (2002). *Building Java enterprise applications.* O'Reilly Press.

Menasce, D. A. (2002). QoS issues in Web Services. *IEEE Internet Computing, 6*(6), 72–75. doi:10.1109/MIC.2002.1067740

Mendling, J., & Hafner, M. (2007). From WS-CDL choreography to BPEL process orchestration. [JEIM]. *Journal of Enterprise Information Management, 21*(5), 525–542. doi:10.1108/17410390810904274

Papazoglou, M. P. (2003). Service-oriented computing: Concepts, characteristics and directions. *4th International Conference on Web Information Systems Engineering (WISE 2003)* (pp. 3-12). Rome: IEEE Computer Society.

Payne, T. R. (2008). Web Services from an Agent perspective. *IEEE Intelligent Systems, 23*(2), 12–14. doi:10.1109/MIS.2008.37

Peltz, C. (2003). Web Services orchestration and choreography. *Web Services Journal, 03*(07), 30–35.

Weber, I., Haller, J., & Mulle, J. A. (2008). Automated derivation of executable business processes from choreographies in virtual organisations. *International Journal of Business Process Integration and Management, 3*(2), 85–95. doi:10.1504/ IJBPIM.2008.020972

Zhao, X., Liu, E., & Clapworthy, G. J. (2008). Service-oriented digital libraries: A Web Services approach. *3rd International Conference on Internet and Web Applications and Services (ICIW2008)* (pp. 608-613). Athens: IEEE Computer Society.

Zhao, X., Liu, E., Clapworthy, G. J., Quadrani, P., Testi, D., & Viceconti, M. *(2008). Using Web Services for distributed medical visualisation.* 5th Intenational Conference on Medical Visualisation (MediVis08) *(pp. 57-62). London: IEEE Computer Society.*

This work was previously published in the International Journal of Distributed Systems and Technologies, Vol. 1, Issue 1, edited by N. Bessis, pp. 1-16, copyright 2010 by IGI Publishing (an imprint of IGI Global).

Chapter 4.5
Successful Web–Based IT Support Services:
Service Provider Perceptions of Stakeholder–Oriented Challenges

Vanessa Cooper
RMIT University, Australia

Sharman Lichtenstein
Deakin University, Australia

Ross Smith
RMIT University, Australia

ABSTRACT

Web-based self-service systems (WSSs) are increasingly leveraged for the delivery of after-sales information technology (IT) support services. Such services are offered by IT service providers to customer firms and increasingly involve business partners. However little is known of the challenges faced by IT service providers as a result of the involvement of the other firms and their employees (end-users). This paper reports related findings from an interpretive study of IT service provider perceptions in six multinational IT service provider firms (Cooper, 2007). The findings highlight that, for IT service providers, (1) it is important to consider and resolve the needs and concerns of other key stakeholders, and (2) significant challenges exist in doing so. The main contribution of the paper is the identification of the key challenges involved. Important implications for theory and practice are discussed.

INTRODUCTION

The continued maturation of the Internet has been accompanied by a corporate shift from the provision of goods to the provision of services, with parallel development of relevant new business models and marketing paradigms (Rust, 2001). Many businesses have developed *E-services,* defined as the provision of services by electronic networks such as the internet (Rust, 2001). Despite the increasing importance of E-services to business success, electronic commerce researchers have been slow to investigate associated issues. As the E-services value chain requires different types of processes and offers greater flexibility in comparison with offline services, there are new research challenges to be explored (Hofacker et al., 2007).

An important new source of value presented by E-services is *supplementary E-services* such as electronic provision of pre- and post-sales customer support for purchased services and products (Hofacker et al., 2007). Experts further suggest that the successful provision of supplementary E-services may be more important strategically to service providers and vendors than the quality of originally-purchased services and products (Otim & Grover, 2006; Piccoli et al., 2004). Marketing of supplementary services (offline and online) can provide differentiation, improve customer service, increase customer retention and lower service costs (Levenburg & Klein, 2006; Reichheld & Schefter, 2000).

This article focuses on the provision by service providers of supplementary E-services to customer firms ("enterprise customers") using the World Wide Web ("Web"). To leverage this market successfully, vendors and service providers aim to improve the implementation and delivery of E-services by employing a systematic approach. One such approach is a Net-Based Customer Service System (NCSS) which has been described as "a network-based computerised information system that delivers service to a customer either directly (e.g. via a browser, PDA, or cell phone) or indirectly (via a service representative or agent accessing the system)" (Piccoli et al., 2004 p.424).

This article focuses on the use of a key type of NCSS based on a Web interface – a *Web-based Self-Service System (WSS)*. Self-service is gaining importance in contemporary organisations primarily for cost reduction reasons (Doyle, 2007). This article explores the context of *managed information technology (IT) support services*. In this setting IT service providers employ WSSs

to provide after-sales IT support to enterprise customers.

Key stakeholders comprise the service provider firm and its employees, business partners and their employees, and enterprise customers and their employees. As this article will show, the involvement of the key stakeholders results in significant challenges for IT service providers aiming to provide successful after-sales support by means of a WSS. These challenges will be explored in the article by examining the IT service provider perspective.

A knowledge transfer lens is used to explore this topic as the transfer of after-sales IT support knowledge (such as IT solutions) from an IT service provider firm to a customer firm is central to the concept of successful after-sales Web-based support services (CSI 2002; Koh et al., 2004).

This article draws on a large study investigating the successful provision of managed after-sales IT support when facilitated by WSSs (Cooper, 2007). The perspectives of six large multinational IT service providers were obtained and analysed. The views of IT service providers are important to understand for improved service provision (Pitt, 1998). Our study focuses on the use of operational IT support services, relating to (1) assembling and operating the core IT environment, and (2) providing key value-adding services such as the Service (Help) Desk (Peppard, 2001).

Five further sections complete this article. Section 2 provides a theoretical background by reviewing representative literature. Section 3 outlines the research design. Section 4 describes the key challenges relating to stakeholders, identified when an IT service provider transfers after-sales IT support-oriented knowledge to enterprise customers when WSSs are used to facilitate service provision. Section 5 discusses the key challenges. Section 6 summarises the main points, draws conclusions, reflects on the limitations of the findings and offers suggestions for future research.

THEORETICAL BACKGROUND

We first situate WSSs within a Customer Relationship Management (CRM) context as the strategic goals of supplementary services - such as after-sales support provision using WSSs - include improving customer service and increasing customer retention (Levenburg & Klein, 2006). We then review the use of WSSs for after-sales IT support provision to enterprise customers. Next a stakeholder-oriented framework of successful Web-based enterprise customer service drawn from earlier findings highlights the importance of stakeholder relationships and related knowledge flows. Finally, the section reviews the knowledge transfer process and the transfer of after-sales support knowledge from an IT support organisation to an enterprise customer.

Customer Relationship Management

In recent years CRM has emerged as a potentially powerful organisational strategy to enable a vendor or service provider to better identify and satisfy customer needs and retain customer loyalty. Enhanced customer relationships may also lead to improved customer-related operational effectiveness and a higher return on investment for the organisation (Barua et al., 2004).

To improve the customer service experience and meet other CRM objectives, the aggregation of data, information and knowledge about the customer is important. Specialised software applications that perform electronic CRM (eCRM) have been developed for this purpose. A common example of an eCRM application is a Web interface, supported by database and data mining tools which record past customer transactions and analyse data to identify customer segments, match products to customer profiles, and better understand target demographics and psychographic characteristics (Brohman et al., 2003). Customer service agents can utilise this

"customer intelligence" to potentially up-sell or cross-sell products and services (Brohman et al. 2003). A WSS is an important type of operational eCRM application (Geib et al., 2005; Khalifa & Shen, 2005) and is discussed below in the context of managed IT support services.

WSS and After-Sales IT Support for Enterprise Customers

A WSS is a Web-based information system that enables organisations to move from labour-intensive manual processes towards low-cost automated Web-based self-service (Pujari 2004). WSSs can facilitate the offering of customer support services for pre-sales, sales, and after-sales activities. They are underpinned by complex information systems, complemented by a customer contact centre, and integrated with a multi-channel service strategy (Negash *et al.* 2003).

WSSs offer important advantages to service providers and customers (Geib et al., 2006; Pujari 2004). Such advantages include electronically leveraging the Web interface, customer/service-provider (and customer/customer) interactions, knowledge management (KM) principles and self-service principles in order to capture and provide information and knowledge useful for pre-sales, sales and after-sales support.

In managed IT service environments, WSSs offer informational, transactional, and proactive support services. Informational support includes "break-fix" support which provides customers experiencing technical problems with resolutions to their problems. This type of support includes (1) unassisted support such as answers to Frequently Asked Questions (FAQs) and the download of software patches and (2) assisted support such as peer-to-peer online fora, e-mail and online chat. Other informational support includes the provision of information and knowledge to assist with enquiries and enable customers to access best-practice – for example, by the publication of White Papers. Transactional support includes case tracking, whereby the customer initially documents their IT problem scenario, requests assistance from the support organisation, and is subsequently able to monitor the support organisation's progress in resolving this problem. Proactive support includes the embedding of problem detection support software on customer end-user computers, and personalised messages directing the customer to potential product or service purchases. In the study reported in this article we consider primarily informational and transactional supplementary support services.

WSSs can reduce customer support expenses by empowering employees (Support Agents). These employees provide support in the form of knowledge such as solutions to customers' IT problems. WSSs boost Support Agent productivity by providing access to a comprehensive knowledge base that includes many solutions, delivering convenient and higher quality support, and increasing customer loyalty and retention.

Non-IT businesses outsource IT support services to service providers because IT is not their core competency, service levels are likely to improve, and Total Cost of Ownership should be reduced (CRMInd, 2006; SSPA, 2004). Furthermore, client firms are often receptive to Web-based support delivery (SSPA, 2004). Thus the Web is considered by customer firms as an important channel for IT support delivery.

Despite the potential benefits of a WSS to service providers and enterprise customers, there has been a long-reported dissatisfaction with Web-based self-service (Barnes et al., 2000; Meuter et al., 2003; Ragsdale, 2007). Clearly success from the use of a WSS cannot be assumed and the critical success factors (CSFs) and challenges involved should be identified and addressed.

The study that is reported in this article identified a set of CSFs (Cooper et al, 2005, 2006a, 2006b; Cooper, 2007) and also identified important challenges, as perceived by IT service providers, many of which relate to other key stakeholders. In the next section we develop a stakeholder-oriented framework which situates WSSs in a broader enterprise customer service context and highlights the interactions with stakeholders.

STAKEHOLDER-ORIENTED RELATIONAL WEB-BASED ENTERPRISE CUSTOMER SERVICE

A broad definition of stakeholders is "all those parties who either affect or who are affected by an organisation's actions, behaviours and policies" (Mitroff, 1983). Management concerns about stakeholders arise because stakeholders have varying perspectives of the underlying problems and their ideal solutions may differ. It is important to business success that a firm resolve conflicting stakeholder needs (Hatch, 1997).

Experts report that the needs, roles, responsibilities, relationships and other interactions of stakeholders are especially important to the success of business-to-business (B2B) commerce (Chua et al., 2005; Kandampully, 2003; Pan, 2005; Ritter & Gemunden, 2003; Schultze & Orlikowski, 2004; Singh & Byrne, 2005). In B2B, businesses are increasingly interdependent and the stakeholder issues must be carefully managed (Kumar & van Dissel, 1996). However stakeholder roles and responsibilities along the value chain are complex (Chi & Holsapple, 2005; Ritter & Gemunden, 2003). Chi and Holsapple propose a model of stakeholder collaboration in B2B highlighting three behavioural processes: knowledge sharing, participative decision-making and conflict governance. Other reasons for understanding stakeholder issues in B2B commerce include the need to manage stakeholder expectations (Singh & Byrne, 2005).

Stakeholder relationships in services are different to mere service encounters and are associated with emotions and expectations (Gutek et al., 1999). Such relationships and associated knowledge flows are important in managed IT services environments (Dahlberg & Nyrhinen, 2006; Xu, 2007) as the quality of knowledge exchange influences the quality of outsourcing relationships (Gong et al., 2007). Of interest to this article, the adoption of WSSs can potentially strengthen stakeholder relationships (Bhappu & Schultze, 2006).

From the evidence above and a review of the literature (Cooper, 2007) we have developed a framework (Cooper et al., 2006a) that conceptualises key stakeholders and relationships in a B2B service context. Such a framework can be helpful in understanding complex knowledge transfer from service providers to customer firms. As mentioned earlier, such knowledge transfer is central to the provision of IT support. The framework in Figure 1 depicts key relationships between the main stakeholder types and a WSS. It shows three key types of stakeholder organisations which may be involved in support provision – a support organisation (previously termed "service provider"), business partner, and customer organisation – and their interaction with one another directly and indirectly via a WSS. At each organisation there are corporate entity representatives (for example, managers) interacting with end-users. The framework clearly highlights the interdependencies found in the multi-stakeholder managed IT support environment.

Knowledge Transfer for IT Support of Enterprise Customers Using WSS

The key knowledge process explored in this article is inter-organisational knowledge transfer. We focus on reviewing staged processual and network models of knowledge transfer for reasons of relevance.

Researchers advocating a staged processual approach to knowledge transfer argue that this can unlock the inner workings of the process and enable a more nuanced identification of barriers and enablers (Szulanski 1996). Staged inter-organisational knowledge transfer models include

Figure 1. A stakeholder-oriented relational framework for web-based enterprise customer service (Cooper et al, 2006a)

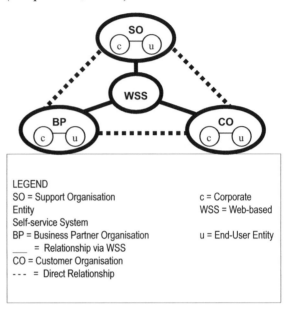

LEGEND
SO = Support Organisation Entity   c = Corporate
    WSS = Web-based Self-service System
BP = Business Partner Organisation   u = End-User Entity
___ = Relationship via WSS
CO = Customer Organisation
- - - = Direct Relationship

those developed by Cranefield and Yoong (2005) and Nieminen (2005). Cranefield and Yoong's (2005) model comprises six stages: engaging; defining; seeking; articulating; integrating; and disseminating. Among the benefits of this model is its identification of key organisational influences on knowledge transfer during each stage. However the factors identified as most relevant to knowledge transfer in an inter-organisational context are the need for fit between the transferred knowledge and the receiving organisation's current organisational objectives and traditional discipline area, and the need to avoid use of "non-transferable examples" which cannot be readily transferred to other organisational contexts. Nieminen's (2005) model of inter-organisational knowledge transfer focuses on the role of a receiving organisation in enabling knowledge transfer. He writes of the need for a receiving organisation to have a range of competencies among its employees in order to reduce any significant absorptive gap (Lane & Lubatkin, 1998) between the two firms involved in the transfer. Researchers proposing a networking approach to knowledge transfer also adopt a relational approach based on understanding how patterns of connections between individuals and groups facilitate knowledge sharing and knowledge transfer (Kakabadse et al., 2003).

We next describe the knowledge transfer process in the managed IT support context (Figure 2) drawing on literature and empirical data from a case study (Cooper, 2007). IT service providers respond to enterprise customers' after-sales enquiries, incidents and problems regarding core IT products and services by providing and transferring support-oriented knowledge. The knowledge is complex and based on solutions to the enquiries, incidents and problems reported.

Both tacit and explicit knowledge may be transferred. Tacit knowledge is knowledge that resides in the mind and is difficult to articulate. Explicit knowledge is a representation of knowledge. An example of explicit knowledge in the managed after-sales IT support context is an IT solution stored in a knowledge base.

As shown in Figure 2, when a customer firm experiences IT incidents or problems, IT professionals at the firm may use the telephone channel or Web interface to obtain a solution. When the telephone is chosen, first tier Support Agents identify potential solutions by accessing tacit knowledge or by using the WSS to search the solutions knowledge base. More complex problems are escalated to more experienced Support Agents. Tiers of Support Engineers resolve the most difficult problems by drawing on valuable tacit knowledge. New and evolving solutions are captured in the knowledge base as explicit knowledge and organised for reuse. Successive efforts are made by Support Agents to address related customer questions. Such efforts aim to assist the customer firm in institutionalising support-oriented knowledge. Business partners may assist in the knowledge transfer process by providing partial solutions or other support and may have access to the service provider's WSS knowledge base.

Figure 2. Knowledge transfer in managed after-sales Web-based IT support (Cooper et al, 2006a)

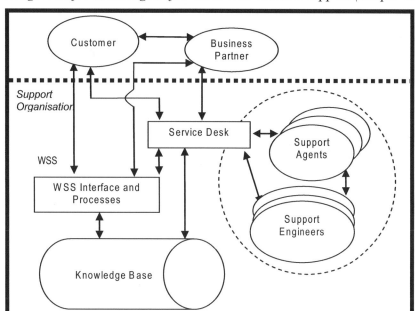

RESEARCH DESIGN

Initially a comprehensive literature review was undertaken. Next, in 2005 an in-depth case study was conducted at the Australian headquarters of a large best-in-class multinational IT services organisation, "ServIT" (a pseudonym). ServIT had previously secured prestigious global awards for its WSS. It defined a successful WSS as one that delivers increased customer satisfaction while reducing service provision costs and this definition of success was used throughout the project. Case data was collected from semi-structured interviews with twelve senior customer service managers, IT support managers and support staff, observations of WSS use, document collection, and a focusing workshop (Rockart, 1979) with participation by five senior customer service managers and IT support managers. Case study data were analysed using qualitative content analysis techniques (Mayring 2000) by two researchers working independently to identify the key challenges relating to stakeholders. A set of CSFs for the transfer of after-sales IT solution-oriented knowledge to enterprise customers when a WSS is used, and a set of key challenges, have been identified.

In 2006 a focus group of Australian senior customer service and IT support managers from an additional five large multinational IT service provider organisations, all with successful WSSs, was conducted, seeking to confirm and extend the findings from the ServIT case study. In the focus group discussion it became clear that, while the WSS of each company was successful, various challenges remained. Two researchers working independently confirmed and extended the set of CSFs and key challenges working inductively from the transcript. *Many of the challenges were found to be related to other stakeholders and it is these challenges which are the focus of this article.*

The quality of the findings was assured by appropriate techniques. Achieving validity in qualitative research requires a fair, honest and balanced account from the viewpoint of someone who lives in the social situation (Neuman, 2006). Construct validity was assured in the study by use of multiple sources of evidence. Participants were also given copies of interview summaries and the outcomes from each phase of the research were provided to participants for confirmation. Reliability was increased via a case study protocol (Yin 2003) to document all procedures and problems. Triangulation was achieved by collecting and analysing data from a variety of sources at ServIT and establishing consistency of results. The results of the cross-organisational focus group added another level of triangulation.

FINDINGS

The six participating IT service providers utilised WSS strategies to increase customer satisfaction while reducing the cost of IT support provision. Each firm offered a suite of informational, transactional and proactive support services using WSSs. Twenty-seven CSFs were identified. While the CSFs are not the focus of this article they are summarised for reference in the Appendix. The CSFs were also classified non-orthogonally into six categories:

- Organisational Commitment and Readiness: The organisation must manage the policies, processes and cultural issues which will affect its ability and willingness to embrace Web-based Self-service.
- Manage for Strategic and Operational Benefits: The WSS strategy must assist the organisation in attaining its strategic and operational objectives.
- KM Capabilities and Processes: The organisation must practice the principles of knowledge management and implement associated knowledge management processes, to maximise the benefits received from the WSS strategy.

- IT Infrastructure Capability: The organisation must have an adequate IT infrastructure in place, to enable it to participate in Web-based Self-service.
- Experience Management: The WSS should manage the stakeholder's experience, both at the corporate and end-user level. The stakeholder experience will directly affect satisfaction levels and therefore ongoing use of the WSS.
- Content: The WSS must contain useful, accurate and up-to-date content in order to resolve the end-user's support issue or knowledge requirement.

These six categories were believed by the IT service provider participants in the study to apply to *all* three stakeholder organisations (that is, those shown in Figure 1). This finding is discussed further in the next section, as it presented one of the main challenges for IT service providers. Further details of the CSFs may be found in earlier publications (Cooper et al, 2005, 2006a, 2006b).

SERVICE PROVIDER PERCEPTIONS OF STAKEHOLDER-ORIENTED CHALLENGES

This section summarises the eight major challenges faced by IT service provider firms, pertaining to key stakeholders. Representative quotes from the ServIT case study and cross-organisational focus group illuminate the challenges. Company names are pseudonyms for reasons of anonymity. The reader is reminded that the findings have been derived from the perspective of the IT support firm only. A further comment on this limitation is made at the end of the article.

First, participants strongly believed that all stakeholder viewpoints should be considered by an IT support organisation when planning, implementing and managing a WSS for after-sales IT support provision. Similar findings were made

for electronic business settings more generally by Kandampully (2003) and Singh and Byrne (2005). However our study highlighted the potential for different stakeholder types to hold unique perceptions. For example, while a support organisation may find the transfer of IT solutions to a customer firm highly desirable, it was questioned by IT service provider participants whether end-users at a customer enterprise would feel the same way:

I think the provider [support organisation] is interested in transferring knowledge so [that] they don't have a problem any more and they can manage their costs and help the customers. [However, the customer firm's end-user is thinking] I am interested, not in receiving knowledge ... [but] I am interested in my problem being fixed. Don't give me all this stuff [the details of the problem and solution]. Tell me what the problem is so I can fix it. I don't want the transferring of any knowledge. (Senior IT Architect, I-Systems)

This is an important finding deserving of further research. If an end-user at a customer firm does not wish to learn from a provided IT solution, how can a support organisation ensure such learning? Proposed cost and efficiency benefits to a support organisation stemming from knowledge transfer may have negative implications for customer satisfaction. It should be noted however that end-users at a customer firm have specialised job roles with role-based knowledge needs. Thus, for example, while some end-users may only desire a resumption of IT operations using a supplied solution, other personnel such as Database Administrators are likely to be highly interested in learning about a solution and gaining more general support knowledge which could be useful at a future time. On the other hand if a professional at an enterprise customer has full knowledge of a solution the customer organisation may become increasingly independent of the support organisation. Ultimately the success of the support organisation can be affected. Thus there may be a level of knowledge which a support organisation may wish to retain and not transfer to customer firms.

Second, participants questioned whether the different stakeholder types might interpret the requirements for CSFs (Appendix) differently. For example, for *CSF-9 Ease of use* participants mentioned that regular end-users of the WSS interface would prefer an efficient interface, whereas novice users would prefer easy-to-use interfaces. As a second example, for *CSF-1 Cost-effectiveness* some participants mentioned that cost-effectiveness to a support organisation, when a WSS is used, is not the same as cost-effectiveness from the perspective of an end-user at the customer firm. End-users are concerned with efficiency gains and usefulness of the knowledge gained from the WSS to perform their jobs (Cenfetelli et al., 2005), rather than the financial costs involved.

Cost effectiveness, from both the end-user of the service and for ServIT, are equally important, but I think you will find some subtleties in [how they are] both explained as cost-effectiveness. For an end-user it's 'Can I actually get the results quickly from my perspective?' From ServIT's perspective, it is 'Can we actually reduce the cost of this service for our customers so that we are actually making a profit? (Consulting Services Division Manager, ServIT)

Third, as described earlier, the six CSF categories were found to apply to *all three* stakeholder organisations. This finding supports prior research by Schultze and Bhappu (2005) who note that customers are often partly responsible for a service provider's success. Clearly, a support organisation will have very little control over whether a customer organisation and business partner organisation do, in fact, address the six CSF categories. As a result, performance measurement and management of WSS strategies in a B2B context will be challenging.

Kurnia and Johnston (2002) note the importance of industry capability in internet trading for corporate adoption of an inter-organisational system. Thus if corporate customers and business partners in a managed IT support situation do not manage the CSFs, the support organisation's WSS may not be successful. As electronic commerce environments are increasingly interdependent (Kumar & van Dissel, 1996; Kurnia & Johnston 2002), a support organisation may benefit from providing further assistance to business partners and customer organisations to better manage the key factors.

One promising strategy may be for a support organisation to conduct education and training programs with partner and customer organisations to increase their awareness and understanding of CSFs. Such education and training could be provided by online support, training, newsletters and so on. Indeed participants also identified the importance of education and training in terms of developing relationships with the customer and ultimately meeting key objectives for CRM. Thus education and training programs will not only provide partner and customer firms with the required knowledge to increase their awareness of WSSs but will provide an opportunity for the support organisation to better understand the needs of the customer and business partners in a WSS context. This finding supports current literature highlighting the importance of developing relationships with enterprise customers when providing support services (Peppers & Rogers, 2001; Pujari, 2004).

A second strategy that is more challenging would be to ensure, when developing external service contracts, that customer and business partner organisations are obliged to meet minimum standards relating to CSFs. Any failure to address CSFs at customer firms and business partners would affect the ability of a support organisation to service them effectively. However such a strategy may be incompatible with the development of improved relationships with business partners and customer firms. It is also important to recall that this study only investigated the IT support organisation perspective. While IT support organisations identified the CSFs as important also for partner and customer firms to address, studies of partner and customer perspectives of CSFs may provide quite different results. This question should be explored in future research.

Fourth, the interesting issue was raised of whether relationships are possible—or even enabled—by a WSS. A two-way relationship was posited by several participants, whereby if an end-user trusts the Web-site and the organisation behind it, this trust forms part of the relationship, with the WSS simply providing the connection:

Although it is a piece of software, it is the front end of a company. For instance, if I feel I have a positive relationship with my Netbank Web-site because I trust it, then that is part of the relationship. (IT Customer Consultant, DistSystems)

Others, however, saw Web-based relationships as perhaps one-way only, whereby it was questioned whether there is a relationship between the end-user and the providing organisation, when the end-user uses the WSS anonymously.

Fifth, it was also suggested that stakeholder relationships can be more complex than Figure 1 allows. Participants observed that relationships with stakeholder types may vary.

We can have the relationship with either both the customer and the business partner or we can have it directly with the customer or we could just have it with the business partner…I mean there are just so many different combinations that that relationship can actually take. (IT Customer Consultant, DistSystems)

Consequently in some instances Figure 1 should be modified. For example, for supporting some customer firms a business partner is involved, while for supporting other customers there are no business partners involved.

The complexity of relationships would also increase as stakeholder organisations increase in size. Multiple relationships would be developed at the individual, departmental and corporate levels. This finding is significant as while it has been acknowledged in a growing body of literature that developing relationships with partners is important (e.g. Vlachopoulou & Manthou, 2003), there is very little literature concerning partner-unit-based relationships.

Sixth, intellectual property (IP), security and privacy issues were found problematic for stakeholder-oriented reasons. Inter-organisational firms in collaborative relationships must protect certain knowledge which may be strategic (Solitander 2006). In the present study, service provider firms were concerned about the loss of IP in the leverage of user fora for customer support. In such fora, end-users may provide solutions to reported problems however it can be unclear who owns the IP that is the solution. Scholars have noted that in customer co-production of service, as illustrated by this situation, new models of digital governance and customer-based innovation are needed (Rai & Sambamurthy, 2006).

IT support organisations, business partners and customers frequently operate across international borders. Support organisations must consider issues of security, privacy and IP within the context of off-shore environments (Rai & Sambamurthy, 2006; Tafti, 2005). The IT service providers in this study expressed uncertainty about the ability of national legal systems to deal with such complex issues. For example, customer end-users may be unaware of the location where their personal information is stored and retrieved. Further, while customer organisations may be aware that, in some instances, third parties such as a support organisation's business partners have access to their stored personal information, they may not be aware of the eventual *use* of this information or its accessibility. A perceived potential privacy violation may lead to unforeseen competitor problems – for example, where business partners compete with a customer enterprise. Sensitive information, knowledge and IP may indeed be compromised (Rai & Sambamurthy, 2006).

A really interesting one that is going through the legal battles now and it comes back to privacy. As a main [support] organisation, you have information that could be of a private nature. If you then make the information available to another organisation that does not have the same privacy policy as you, and then [if they] were to use that information in such a way that it violates somebody's privacy, who is ultimately responsible? That is a huge legal question that is being tested now. Does it come back to the original person or the person who let the information go? (Emerging Technology Consultant, OpSys)

Seventh, understanding the complexities of the business partner alliance was an issue. Not all service providers participating in the study agreed with the distinction between a business partner relationship and a customer/supplier relationship. For example, a participant from one organisation claimed that his organisation did not have business partners, while others claimed that their organisations were, in fact, partners of his organisation. It was advocated that the distinction between a business partner and customer/supplier relationship, surrounds whether the relationship is a one-off transaction, or whether it is an on-going relationship. In an enterprise IT services context, however, there is an apparent blurring of relationships. In some projects, organisations may be considered business partners, while in others they would be considered competitors:

DistSystems, DataCorp, OpSys and I-Systems can say, we have been working together as business partners and as competitors and sometimes even on the same bid…on the one hand you compete, in the next 30 seconds, I might be talking to OpSys

about something we are competitors about, and in another thing we are working together on, you switch hats, you switch alliances, it is just the way things are these days…. (Senior Systems Consultant, I-Systems)

Some of the complexities of business partner alliances surround intellectual property and security and privacy, discussed earlier. Lei (1997) argues that, with respect to strategic alliances, regardless of the various types of legal structures which may be put in place, over time companies will absorb and internalise skills, regardless of the amount of formal, legal ownership that is demarcated by the alliance structure. Further, Ferdinand and Simm (2007) suggest a need for increased research on illegal inter-organisational knowledge transfer. Participants in our research study also expressed a need for greater understanding of this complex area. They believed it likely that associated concerns would continue in the foreseeable future.

Eighth, managing customer contributions to service was considered an important challenge. The growing literature on co-production highlights the productivity benefits as well as the managerial challenges that arise when customers become "partial employees" (Benapudi & Leone, 2003). The advantages of co-production include decreased cost of service provision and greater control and autonomy for the customer, while disadvantages include the difficulty of controlling service quality when customers are actively involved in the production process (Schultze & Bhappu, 2005).

In the study IT service providers raised concerns relating to the contribution of knowledge by customers to their own service fulfillment, optimisation and improvement. At ServIT when customers interacted and shared resolution-knowledge in online for a the knowledge was not captured permanently. Further, the online fora were open to a variety of end-users causing new issues of accuracy and liability:

ServIT has ventured into the hosting of forums. Solutions can be provided by non-ServIT people and that's a potential conflict between the reliability of our knowledge and the fact that we are opening up [knowledge] to end-users, which could have a good result, but there is a danger that we are facilitating the [incorrect] solution. (IT Manager, ServIT)

ServIT invests significant resources in its legal team and explicitly states in the terms and conditions of using the WSS and in support contracts that ServIT will not be responsible for any degradation of a customer's systems, if an enterprise customer decides to act upon information derived from the WSS. Another challenge is that while ServIT monitors fora content, it relies more on a "merit" based system whereby forum users are allocated merit points by original posters (of questions) when they provide valuable responses. A system of points aggregation motivates users to share valuable knowledge and thus contribute to E-service provision. However, the researchers found from forum observations that this scheme occasionally led to highly successful users moving on to create their own sites independently of the service provider, such was their fame and following.

Other potentially negative impacts of customer co-contribution include potential defamation in the fora. While the terms and conditions of posting to online fora state that users should not post defamatory statements, such defamation sometimes eventuates.

DISCUSSION

The findings above suggest a need for industry sector improvement. For the IT support industry to learn to do things better, learning at the industry level is needed. Prior studies suggest the importance of business learning in a network context (c.f. Knight, 2002). This would entail

new collaborative electronic business projects focused on IT support provision involving IT service providers, business partners and customer organisations. According to Cameron's (2005) review of prior relevant studies, there are four important influences to consider for successful electronic business collaboration: motivation, capability, communication and coordination. First, organisations must be motivated to participate in collaborative projects. Second, the desire to increase organisational capability (skills and knowledge) can be a powerful motivator. Third, it is important to communicate about the value of such collaborative projects within organisations. Fourth, industry groups can assist in coordinating such projects for successful conclusions.

As many of the key challenges identified in the previous section centre on the potential for stakeholder conflict, the development of individual IT service contracts (including service requirements) with customer firms and business partners requires attention. This process should entail greater clarification and negotiation of stakeholder needs. The objectives of each organisation should be articulated during joint planning, which is an important aspect of business collaboration in supply chains (Holsapple & Jin, 2007). Holsapple and Jin note several other important collaborative decisions typically made in a supply chain. The findings from our study suggest a need for focused studies seeking to identify key problem points in decision-making where stakeholder conflicts are influential so that the overall process can be improved to avoid or manage such conflicts. Chi and Holsapple (2005) propose a model of stakeholder collaboration in B2B highlighting three behavioural processes: knowledge sharing, participative decision-making and conflict governance. Our study provides support for the importance of such processes.

The findings and discussion above also suggest a need for supporting infrastructure. Electronic marketplaces offer a recognised structure which may be useful to support both collaborative

IT support projects and specific supply chains (Markus & Christiaanse, 2003). However there are also challenges in using electronic marketplaces successfully. In a recent case study of an electronic marketplace, the key influences affecting its success were the loss of social capital, nature of communication channels used, time taken to reach critical mass, and power imbalances among participants (Driedonks et al., 2005).

The risk of reduced service quality was identified in the practice of customer co-contribution to service. This concern was noted more generally for online service provision by Schultze and Bhappu (2005). There may be ways for IT service firms to better monitor customer contributions via user fora and capture the high quality solutions (which currently are not captured). Related questions of knowledge ownership must be resolved. However regulatory issues at different geographic locations cloud the resolution of such questions.

Indeed there were several areas identified where IT service providers suffer from inadequate regulatory support. The security, privacy and IP issues experienced in the often-offshore managed IT support environment highlight the need for clarification and awareness of relevant regulations and laws at industry, national and international levels. IT support companies also seek to understand how to share knowledge with business competitors within strategic alliances while maintaining a competitive advantage. New theories are sought to underpin such knowledge sharing in an increasingly collaborative global business environment.

The six IT service provider companies in our study uniformly noted that the key objective for use of a WSS for after-sales IT support was to increase customer satisfaction while reducing support costs. This objective was expected to be achieved by relational as well as transactional methods. However as the study showed, the successful accomplishment of both goals can be problematic (also found by Bunduchi, 2005). Research is beginning to appear on the enabling

of relationships in service provision when the internet is used to facilitate service provision. In a business to consumer (B2C) context, Sigala (2007) explored online travel service provision and found that the communication aspect of the online service played a key role in relationship development. Where provider-consumer communication was enhanced by use of relevant communication tools, relationships and client satisfaction were improved. Thus IT support organisations may find that the path to satisfying the relational aspect of WSS success is by better leveraging the internet's communication tools and customising communication-oriented content.

Some of the challenges identified in our study relate to the process of knowledge transfer. For example, it was noted that a customer firm end-user may not be interested in institutionalizing transferred IT solutions. Cranefield and Yoong (2005), in identifying key challenges in inter-organisational knowledge transfer, highlighted the need for a fit between the knowledge received and the receiving organisation's objectives. If a customer firm does not prioritise the institutionalization of IT solutions throughout the firm, its employees will not make the effort to learn the solutions transferred from the service provider and will simply apply them to resolve the initial problem. This suggests a need for IT service providers to educate their customers about the importance of institutionalizing IT solutions to their organisation. Nieminen (2005) noted that for knowledge transfer to take place, a receiving organisation must be capable of absorbing shared knowledge. Such capability may be missing from the customer firms which are receiving IT solutions.

CONCLUSION

This article has identified and discussed eight major stakeholder-oriented challenges in the provision of managed after-sales IT support services via WSSs to enterprise customers, from the perspective of multinational IT service providers. Specifically:

- All stakeholder viewpoints should be considered by an IT support organisation when planning, implementing and managing a WSS for after-sales IT support provision;
- Different stakeholder types might interpret the requirements for CSFs differently;
- The six CSF categories identified apply to *all* three stakeholder organisations, however a support organisation will have very little control over whether a customer organisation and business partner organisation do, in fact, address these categories. Thus performance measurement and management of WSS strategies in a B2B context will be difficult;
- It is problematic whether relationships are possible, or even enabled by a WSS;
- Stakeholder relationships can be more complex than Figure 1 allows;
- Intellectual property, security and privacy issues can be problematic for stakeholder-oriented reasons;
- Understanding the complexities of the business partner alliance can be an issue;   and
- Managing customer contributions to service is an important challenge.

The findings demonstrate that best-in-class IT service providers face diverse challenges to better understand and resolve potential conflicting stakeholder needs in this context.

Theoretically this article provides numerous insights into the key challenges faced by IT service providers, relating to the different stakeholders, in the provision of B2B after-sales IT support services via WSSs. The article also highlights a need for new theories which integrate WSS strategies across the multiple stakeholders involved. Our findings further suggest that relationship development by WSSs is poorly understood by the companies involved and that further research is needed to develop new understandings.

This article also assists IT service providers by recommending that all stakeholder viewpoints and issues should be considered when planning, implementing and managing WSSs in the managed after-sales IT support context. Addressing diverse stakeholder needs may be particularly challenging in some areas such as security, privacy and IP. Such emerging challenges highlight the complexities of working with business partners which are also considered competitors. Greater collaboration is needed with better supporting infrastructure and regulation.

While the findings from this article are limited by the context (managed after-sales IT support) and scope (the IT support organisation perspective only was studied), they are indicative of possible concerns that other types of service providers may have in offering supplementary E-services using WSSs. Thus the findings provide a foundation for exploration in other settings. Investigating the customer and business partner perspectives would also provide valuable balance to the views expressed and analysed in this article.

ACKNOWLEDGMENT

This article is a significantly extended and updated version of a article published in the *Proceedings of the 20th Bled eConference (Bled07)*, Bled, Slovenia, 4-6 June 2007. The authors are grateful to the anonymous reviewers whose valuable advice helped improve the quality of this article.

REFERENCES

Barnes, J.G., Dunne, P.A. and Glynn, W.J. (2000). Self-service and Technology: Unanticipated and Unintended Effects on Customer Relationships. Handbook of Services Marketing and Management, Swartz, T.A. and Iabocobucci, D. (eds.), Sage Publications, Thousand Oaks, California, 89-102.

Barua, A., Konana, P., Whinston, A.B. and Yin, F. (2004). An Empirical Investigation of Net-enabled Business Value. *MIS Quarterly.* 28(4), December, 585-620.

Benapudi, N. and Leone, R.P. (2003). "Psychological Implications of Customer Participation in Co-production", *Journal of Marketing.* 67(1), January, 14-28.

Bhappu, A.D. and Schultze, U. (2006). The Role of Relational and Operational Performance in Business-to-Business Customers' Adoption of Self-Service Technology. *Journal of Service Research.* 8(4), 372 – 385.

Brohman, M.K., Watson, R.T., Piccoli, G. and Parasuraman, A. (2003). Data Completeness: A Key to Effective Net-based Customer Service Systems, *Communications from the Association for Computing Machinery.* 46(6), 47-51.

Bunduchi, R. (2005). Business Relationships in Internet-based Electronic Markets: The Role of Goodwill Trust and Transaction Costs. *Information Systems Journal.* 15 (4), 321–341.

Cameron, J. (2005). Ten Concepts for an eBusiness Collaborative Project Management Framework. In *Proceedings of eIntegration in Action: 18th Bled eConference,* June 6-8 2005, Bled, Slovenia.

Cenfetelli, R., Benbasat, I. and Al-Natour, S. (2005). Information technology mediated customer service: A functional perspective. In *Proceedings of ICIS 2005,* Las Vegas, USA.

Chi, L. and Holsapple, C. (2005). Understanding Computer-mediated Interorganisational Collaboration: A Model and Framework. *Journal of Knowledge Management.* 9(1), 53-75.

Chua, C.E.H., Khoo, H.M., Straub, D.W., Kadiyala, S. and Kuechler, D. (2005). The Evolution of E-commerce Research: A Stakeholder Perspective. *Journal of Electronic Commerce Research.* 6(4), 262-280.

Cooper, V.A. (2007). Knowledge Transfer in Enterprise IT Support Provision using Web-based Self-Service, unpublished PhD Thesis, Deakin University, Melbourne, Australia.

Cooper, V.A., Lichtenstein, S. and Smith, R. (2006a). Enabling the Transfer of Information Technology Support Knowledge to Enterprise Customers Using Web-based Self-service systems: Critical Success Factors from the Support Organisation Perspective, in *Proceedings of Seventeenth Australasian Conference on Information Systems (ACIS 2006),* Adelaide, Australia.

Cooper, V., Lichtenstein, S. & Smith, R. (2006b) Knowledge transfer in enterprise information technology support using web-based self-service systems, *International Journal of Technology Marketing,* 1(2), 145-170.

Cooper, V.A., Lichtenstein, S. & Smith, R. (2005) Emerging Issues in After-sales Enterprise Information Technology Support Using Web-based Self-service Systems, in *Proceedings of Sixteenth Australasian Conference on Information Systems (ACIS 2005),* University of Technology Sydney, 30 November – 2 December, 2005, Sydney.

Cranefield, J. and Yoong, P. (2005). Organisational Factors Affecting Inter-organisational Knowledge Transfer in the New Zealand State Sector: A Case Study. *The Electronic Journal for Virtual Organisations and Networks.* 7, December.

[CRMInd] CRMIndustry.com (2006). 2006 State of IT Outsourcing. Summary report, <http://www.crmindustry.com/industry_research/outsourcing.htm> (Accessed 03 June 2008).

[CSI] Consortium Service Innovation (2002). Getting Started with KCS. Official Consortium Service Innovation Site, <http://www.thinkhdi.com/files/pdfs/GettingStartedKCS.pdf> (Accessed 03 June 2008).

Dahlberg, T. and Nyrhinen, M. (2006). A New Instrument to Measure the Success of IT Outsourcing. In *Proceedings of the 39th Hawaii International Conference on System Sciences (HICSS'2006),* IEEE Society Press.

Doyle, S. (2007). Self-service Delivery and the Growing Roles of Channels. *The Journal of Database Marketing & Customer Strategy Management.* 14(2), January , 150-159.

Driedonks, C., Gregor, S. and Wassenaar, A. (2005). Economic and Social analysis of the Adoption of B2B Electronic Marketplaces: A Case Study in the Australian Beef Industry. *International Journal of Electronic Commerce.* 9(3), Spring, 49-72.

Ferdinand, J. and Simm, D. (2007). Re-theorizing External Learning: Insights from Economic and Industrial Espionage. *Management Learning.* 38(3), 297-317.

Geib, M., Kolb, L. and Brenner, W. (2006). Collaborative Customer Management. Financial Services Alliances. In (Fjermestad, J. and Romano, N.C. (eds)), *Electronic Customer Relationship Management*, Armonk, New York.

Gong, H., Tate, M. and Alborz, S. (2007). Managing the Outsourcing Marriage to Achieve Success. In *Proceedings of Hawaii International Conference on the System Sciences (HICSS'07),* IEEE Society Press.

Gutek, B., Bhappu, A.D., Liao-Troth, M.A. and Cherry, B. (1999). Distinguishing between Service Relationships and Encounters. *Journal of Applied Psychology.* 84(2), 218-233.

Hatch, M.J. (1997). *Organisation Theory: Modern, Symbolic and Postmodern Perspectives.* Oxford:UK, Oxford University Press.

Hofacker, C. F., Goldsmith, R.G., Bridges, E. and Swilley, E. (2007). E-Services: A Synthesis and Research Agenda. *Journal of Value Chain Management.* 1(1/2), 13-44.

Holsapple, C.W. and Jin, H. (2007). Connecting Some Dots: E-commerce, Supply Chains and Collaborative Decision Making. *Decision Line.* 38(5), October, 14-21.

Kakabadse, N.K., Kakabadse, A. and Kouzmin, A. (2003). Reviewing the Knowledge Management Literature: Towards a Taxonomy. *Journal of Knowledge Management Practice.* 7(4), 75-91.

Kandampully, J. (2003). B2B Relationships and Networks in the Internet Age. *Management Decision.* 41(5), 443-451.

Khalifa, M. and Shen, N. (2005). Effects of Electronic Customer Relationship Management on Customer Satisfaction: A Temporal Model. In *Proceedings of the 38th Annual Hawaii International Conference on System Sciences (HICSS'05),* IEEE Society Press.

Knight, L. (2002). Network Learning: Exploring Learning by Interorganizational Networks. *Human Relations.* 55(4), 427-454.

Koh, C., Ang, S. and Straub, D.W. (2004). IT Outsourcing Success: A Psychological Contract Perspective. *Information Systems Research.* 15(4), 356-373.

Kumar, K. and van Dissel, H.G. (1996). Sustainable Collaboration: Managing Conflict and Cooperation in Interorganisational Systems. *MIS Quarterly*, 20(3), 279-300.

Kurnia, S. and Johnston, R. (2002). A Review of Approaches to EC-enabled IOS Adoption Studies. In *Proceedings of the 35th Annual Hawaii Conference on System Sciences (HICSS'02),* IEEE Society Press.

Lane, P.J. and Lubatkin, M. (1998). Relative Absorptive Capacity and Inter-organisational Learning, *Strategic Management Journal.* 19(5), 461-477.

Lei, D.T. (1997). Competence-building, Technology Fusion and Competitive Advantage: The Key Roles of Organisational Learning and Strategic Alliances. *International Journal of Technology Management.* 14(2/3/4), 208-37.

Levenburg, N.M. and Klein, H.A. (2006). Delivering customer services online: identifying best practices of medium-sized enterprises. *Information Systems Journal.* 16(2), 135-155.

Markus, M.L. and Christiaanse, E. (2003). Adoption and Impact of Electronic Marketplaces. *Information Systems and E-Business Management.* 1(2), January, 139-155.

Mayring, P. (2000). Qualitative Content Analysis, Forum Quality Social Research, (1)2. <http://www.qualitative-research.net/fqs-texte/2-00/2-00mayring-e.htm> (Accessed 3 June 2008).

Mitroff, I.I. (1983). *Stakeholders of the Organisational Mind.* Jossey-Bass. San Francisco, CA.

Meuter, M.L., Ostrom, A., Bitner, M.J. and Roundtree, R. (2003). The Influence of Technology Anxiety on Consumer Use and Experiences with Self-service Technologies. *Journal of Business Research.* 56(11), 899-906.

Negash, S., Ryan, T. and Igbaria, M. (2003). Quality and Effectiveness in Web-based Customer Support Systems. *Information and Management.* 40(8), September, 757-768.

Neuman, W.L. (2006). *Social Research Methods: Qualitative and Quantitative Approaches*, Sixth Edition. Allwyn & Bacon, Boston, Massachusetts.

Nieminen, H. (2005). Organisational Receptivity – Understanding the Inter-organisational Learning Ability, *Electronic Journal of Knowledge Management.* 3(2), 107-118.

Otim, S. and Grover, V. (2006). An Empirical Study on Web-based Services and Customer Loyalty. *European Journal of Information Systems.* 15(6), 527-541.

Pan, G.S.C. (2005). Information Systems Project Abandonment: A Stakeholder Analysis. *International Journal of Information Management.* 25(2), 173-184.

Peppard, J. (2001). Bridging the Gap Between the IS Organisation and the Rest of the Business: Plotting a Route. *Information Systems Journal.* 11(3), 249-260.

Peppers, D. and Rogers, M. (2001). *One to One B2B: Customer Development Strategies for the Business-to-Business World*, Currency Doubleday, New York.

Piccoli, G., Brohman, M.K., Watson, R.T. and Parasuraman, A. (2004). Net-based Customer Service Systems: Evolution and Revolution in Web-site Functionalities. *Decision Sciences.* 35(3), 423-455.

Pitt, L.F., Berthon, P. and Lane, N. (1998). Gaps Within the IS Department: Barriers to Service Quality. *Journal of Information Technology.* 13(3), 191-200.

Pujari, D. (2004). Self-service with a Smile? Self-service Technology (SST) Encounters Among Canadian Business-to-Business. *International Journal of Service Industry Management.* 15(2), 200-219.

Ragsdale, J. (2007). Self-Service Success Continues to Decline; How Web 2.0 Can Help, Service and Support Professional Association, US.

Rai, A. and Sambamurthy, V. (2006). Editorial Notes – The Growth of Interest in Services Management: Opportunities for Information Systems Scholars. *Information Systems Research.* 17(4), 327 – 331,

Reichheld, F.F. and Schefter, P. (2000). E-Loyalty: Your Secret Weapon on the Web. *Harvard Business Review.* 78(4), July-August, 105-112.

Ritter, T. and Gemunden, H.D. (2003). Inter-organisational Relationships and Networks: an Overview. *Journal of Business Research.* 56, 691-697.

Rockart, J.F. (1979). Chief Executives Define their own Data Needs. *Harvard Business Review.* 57(2), March-April, 81-93.

Rust, R.T. (2001). The Rise of E-Service, *Journal of Service Research*, 3(4), May, 283-284.

Schultze, U. and Bhappu, A.D.P. (2005). Incorporating Self-Serve Technology into Co-production Designs. *International Journal of E-Collaboration.* 1(4), 1-23.

Schultze, U. and Orlikowski, W.J. (2004). Practice Perspective on Technology-mediated Network Relations: The Use of Internet-based Self-serve Technologies. *Information Systems Research.* 15(1), 87-106.

Sigala, M. (2007). Investigating the Internet's Impact on Interfirm Relations: Evidence from the Business Travel Management Distribution Chain. *Journal of Enterprise Information Management.* 20(3), 335-355.

Singh, M. and Byrne, J. (2005). Performance Evaluation of e-Business in Australia. *Electronic Journal of Information Systems Evaluation.* 8(2).

Solitander, M. (2006). Balancing the Flows: Managing the Intellectual Capital Flows in Inter-organisational Projects. *Electronic Journal of Knowledge Management.* 4(2), 197-206.

SSPA (2004). *2005 Support Demand Research Series.* Tech Strategy Partners and Service & Support Professionals Association.

Szulanski, G. (1996). Exploring Internal Stickiness: Impediments to the Transfer of Best Practice Within the Firm. *Strategic Management Journal.* 17, Special Issue, 27-43.

Tafti, M.H.A. (2005). Risk Factors Associated with Offshore IT Outsourcing. *Industrial Management & Data Systems.* 105(5), 549-560.

Vlachopoulou, M. and Manthou, V. (2003). Partnership Alliances in Virtual Markets. *International Journal of Physical Distribution and Logistics Management.* 33(3), 254-267.

Xu, L. (2007). Outsourcing and Multi-party Business Collaborations Modelling. *Journal of Electronic Commerce in Organisations.* 5(2), 77-96.

Yin, R.K. (2003). *Case Study Research, Design and Methods*, Fourth Edition. Sage Publications, Newbury Park.

APPENDIX A

CSFs for Knowledge Transfer from a Support Organisation to a Customer Organisation using WSSs (A)

Critical Success Factor	Description
CSF-1 Cost Effectiveness	The cost equation for providing/using web-based self-service must be better, or at least not worse, than providing/using non-web-based self-service.
CSF-2: Provision of Additional Services and Cross-Selling Opportunities	Current WSS transactions are used proactively as an opportunity to offer the customer organisation additional advice and services
CSF-3: Critical Mass: Knowledge Content and Knowledge Contributors	A sufficient number of end-users must proactively contribute sufficient knowledge content to the WSS knowledge base, to encourage all parties to initially use, and to continue to use, the WSS as a means of resolving their support issues or information requirements
CSF-4: Usefulness: Provision of Knowledge Which Meets User Requirements	The WSS must provide the functionality and knowledge required to meet the objectives of all stakeholders. For example, for the end-user customer, it should resolve a specific technical or business problem, or provide other required knowledge resources.
CSF-5: Ability to Provide Efficiency	Use of the WSS to resolve a support issue or provide other knowledge resources must be perceived as efficient by all parties. This is inclusive of not only the performance of the WSS tool but the surrounding processes for using the WSS.
CSF-6: Access, Connectivity, Availability and Performance	The providing organisation, relevant business partners and the customer organisation must have sufficient technology infrastructure in place, to enable all parties to participate in web-based self-service.
CSF-7: Effective Information Architecture and Search Engine	The WSS must have an effective Information Architecture and Search Engine such that the information system that organises and retrieves knowledge in the knowledge base is perceived as effective by end-users.
CSF-8: Security, Privacy and Assurance	All stakeholders using WSS must feel secure, private and confident in all aspects of WSS transactions including the stored data components of transactions. Issues surrounding information security and information privacy, and the need to keep confidential related company secrets (intellectual property) must be addressed.
CSF-9: Ease of Use/Usability	An end-user must perceive that use of the WSS does not demand excessive cognitive or ergonomic effort.
CSF-10: Early Positive Experience	The first few end-user experiences with the WSS must result in a positive outcome, where end-user needs are met and they feel valued, in order for the end-user to adopt WSS long term.
CSF-11: Positive Experience	Using the WSS on an ongoing basis must result in a positive outcome, where corporate customer needs and all types of end-users' needs are met and they also feel valued. A positive experience is closely related to customer organisation/end-user satisfaction
CSF-12 Confidence in Solution	The customer organisation/end-user must feel confident that the solution provided by the WSS will resolve their issue and will not result in further issues. They must also have self-confidence in their own ability to apply the offered solution.
CSF-13: Customer Focus: Understand Customer and their Requirements	The support organisation (and relevant business partners) must understand the individual business and technical needs of individual customer organisations and their end-users. With this understanding, WSS must be tailored to meet those individual needs.

APPENDIX B

CSFs for Knowledge Transfer from a Support Organisation to a Customer Organisation using WSSs (B)

Critical Success Factor	Description
CSF-14: Positive Relationship	The relationship between the support organisation, business partners and the customer organisation must be one which supports open communication and trust. This positive relationship should exist at both the corporate and end-user levels.
CSF-15: Provision of Additional Support: Education & Training	Additional assistance, or education and training in respect to how to use the WSS must be provided by the support organisation as requested by end-users.
CSF-16: Employee Focus	Management within the support organisation, business partner and customer organisations must have an understanding of the work processes and conditions which will affect the ability and willingness of employees to adopt the WSS and associated strategies. With this understanding, management must focus on meeting the needs of their employees where possible, in order to maximise employee productivity and the benefits received from the WSS strategy.
CSF-17: Culture	The support organisation should foster an environment that recognises that WSS is part of the way it wants to conduct business. In addition, an open, sharing culture is needed. The culture should extend to customer organisations and business partners.
CSF-18: Marketing and Awareness of Web-based Service	Marketing programs which raise awareness of and support for, the adoption of WSS, must be in place.
CSF-19: Knowledge Creation, Capture and Re-Use	Knowledge capture processes to ensure that valuable knowledge is created and captured into the WSS knowledge base by end-users must be in place. Knowledge reuse processes to ensure that this knowledge is subsequently accessed and re-used by end-users, must also be in place.
CSF-20: Knowledge Validation	Processes must be in place to ensure the accuracy of the knowledge which is captured into the WSS knowledge base and to ensure that once it is captured, it is frequently reviewed and updated for currency.
CSF-21: Knowledge Storage/Retrieval	Processes must be in place to ensure that the structure and format of captured knowledge facilitate findability.
CSF-22 : Presentation of Knowledge	The knowledge must be presented in a form which maximizes the understanding acquired by end-users.
CSF-23: Measurement & Feedback of WSS	Sufficient measurement and feedback methods for assessing the effectiveness of the WSS strategy must be in place.
CSF-24: Alignment and Integration	There must be alignment and integration between the WSS and other channels' support processes, as well as with related business processes, in the context of the business/industry environment.
CSF-25: WSS Override and Recovery	The capability for the end-user or WSS to over-ride transactions initially made via the WSS, must be in place, whereby if an end-user is not finding a satisfactory resolution via the WSS, the transaction is directed to an alternative mode of service delivery (e.g. a chat session or telephone call).
CSF-26: Ease of Re-initiation	A process must be in place whereby an end-user can easily re-initiate a support transaction to re-locate a previously retrieved resolution or other knowledge resource.
CSF-27 Top Management Support	Top management must provide ongoing support and commitment to the WSS and associated strategies.

This work was previously published in the International Journal of E-Services and Mobile Applications, Volume 1, Issue 1, edited by A. Scupola, pp. 1-20, copyright 2009 by IGI Publishing (an imprint of IGI Global).

Chapter 4.6
Using Semantic Web Services in E–Banking Solutions

Laurent Cicurel
iSOCO, Spain

José Luis Bas Uribe
Bankinter, Spain

Sergio Bellido Gonzalez
Bankinter, Spain

Jesús Contreras
iSOCO, Spain

José-Manuel López-Cobo
iSOCO, Spain

Silvestre Losada
iSOCO, Spain

ABSTRACT

Offering public access to efficient transactional stock market functionalities is of interest to all banks and bank users. Traditional service oriented architecture (SOA) technology succeeds at providing reasonable, good Web-based brokerage solutions, but may lack extensibility possibilities. By introducing Semantic Web Services (SWS) as a way to integrate third party services from distributed service providers, we propose in this chapter an innovative way to offer online real-time solutions that are easy-to-use for customers. The combined use of ontologies and SWS allows different users to define their own portfolio management strategies regardless of the information provider. In deed the semantic layer is a powerful way to integrate the information of many providers in an easy way. With due regard for more development of security technological issues, research on SWS has shown that the deployment of the technology in commercial solutions is within sight.

DOI: 10.4018/978-1-60566-066-0.ch016

INTRODUCTION

When operating on the stock market, investors make their decisions on the basis of huge amount of information about the stock evolution, economic and politic news, third parties recommendation and other kind of sources. Thanks to the proliferation of the Internet banks the profile of an average investor is changing from a financial expert to common people making small investments on the online stock market. In addition to the business generated around the stock market operations, banks use their online stock market application to attract new and to reinforce the customer commitment.

Banks, as any other commercial organization, needs to optimize the deployment of new products and services to the market. The deployment time of new services or applications is an important issue in a highly competitive market, since it defines the future market share and revenues. Online banks are looking for technologies and architectural paradigms that would allow them to design, implement and deploy new services on a low cost basis and in a short time period. New services often imply integration of many already existing applications, some of them internal and others external to the organization.

This is the case of online stock brokerage solutions adopted by online banks. An online stock brokerage application proposes to the user to buy and sell its stock options via a computerized network. Banks are willing to offer an easy to use application including as much information and as many options as possible without incurring large development costs. We will show that the use of the Semantic Web technology, combined with a service-oriented architecture (SOA), greatly reduces the cost and effort of developing and maintaining an online stock brokerage solution.

A broker based on a semantic service oriented architecture has all the advantages of a service oriented architecture (e.g. modularity, reusability) combined with the advantages of Semantic Web

technologies. Semantic Web technology main advantage is to give a clear semantic inside (and eventually outside) the enterprise which reduces the communication confusions (technical or human). This also leads to higher maintainability of the products and to a better automatisation of the system mechanisms. These advantages applied to SOA will be extended in the proposed solution of this chapter. Next section will first exposes the current situation of brokerage applications based on classical SOA.

CURRENT SITUATION: BROKERAGE APPLICATION BASED ON WEB SERVICES

Banking companies have invested heavily in the last few years to develop brokerage solutions based on a new dominant paradigm in the IT World: service oriented architecture (SOA). The concept of this paradigm is not new: propose a loosely coupled distributed system architecture where independent services provide functionality, so that the difficulty is divided which leads to reduce the development cost and improve the reusability. But the technologies to implement this paradigm are relative new. Web Services are one of the solutions that appeared a couple of years ago and that made the success of this paradigm. For this reason Web Services are often confused with the SOA paradigm.

In this section we first present in more detail the business case for the brokerage application that we propose. We will then explain why a service oriented architecture implemented using Web Services technologies is a suitable solution. The solution properties will be detailed and it will be shown that this kind of architecture is suitable for brokerage application. We then present what the benefits of such an architecture are from both, a technical and a business point of view.

Web-Based Brokerage Applications

Introduction

As a major interface between the financial world and the non-financial world, banks always try to improve their services related to the stock market. As the Internet represents one of the most interesting communication channels of recent years, banks are interested in using this channel to improve the quality of their service and thus increase their image and revenue. Such banks or bank departments have been called eBanks or online banks. We have identified three different strategies for online Banking:

- **Technological leader profile:** Banks that focus their strategy on technology and consider the Internet an opportunity to improve their markets. Also, the Internet specialized banks, usually recently founded banks (not subsidiaries) that have earn a significant market share, even though they do not offer their clients a wide range of products.
- **Follower banks profile:** Banks that first considered the Internet as a threat. When the market has matured, they changed their strategy from a defensive position to a competitive attitude towards those who were the first leaders in Internet banking. In some cases, subsidiary entities were created so as not to cannibalize their own market share.
- **Non "internetized" banks:** Banks that did not invest in the Internet because of their small size, their strategy or other reasons. However, they are a minority in terms of market share.

In these days, banks that already have Web-based brokerage application in place choose the technological leader strategy, while those banks that are only now considering developing their own applications follow the second strategy. Other mediums are also possible:

- **Branches:** Too expensive for Banks. Only for high end clients.
- **Phone banking service:** Expensive for banks. Only for selected clients
- **Mobile services (SMS, mobile phone applications):** Cheap for banks, usually free or at a small fee per service usage.

However, the Internet medium, as a cheap and universal way to perform banking operations is the highlighted solution of this business case.

In current brokerage solutions banks usually only offer the service of making the operations (buy, sell) but rarely integrate the search of relevant information to make the transaction decision. The delivery of this 'hard to integrate' functionality search, is, however, a useful to provide to the end user, who wants to buy and sell stock knowing the most relevant and current information. The user usually searches this information on external pages independently of the bank services. Some of these are free services which propose information of the stock market in real-time or with a minimum delay. Web pages such as Yahoo Finance (http://finance.yahoo.com/), Google Finance (http://finance.google.com), Reuters UK (http://uk.reuters.com/home), Xignite (http://preview.xignite.com/), Invertia (http://www.invertia.com) are good examples of financial information from different providers with different degrees of quality.

However, the need to search the information on several Web pages and then navigate to the brokerage application to execute the transaction is a waste of time and adds unwanted complexity to the end user. The idea is to build an online broker that merges and provides a unified or single point of access to information and operational services. In that way, the user will have an unified environment which integrates most of the tools required to fulfil his/her wishes of buying and selling stocks. A comparison of a traditional brokerage application interaction and the new interaction we proposed is showed in Figure 1. In the traditional interaction, the user must retrieve the information from each Data Provider (Yahoo Finance, etc.) independently and only then do the brokerage action (i.e. buy or sell). In the unified environment we propose, all the interactions are performed through the brokerage application and the brokerage application take care of showing the best data information regarding the user context (user profile, portfolio of the user, etc.).

In the next section we define the functional and non-functional requirements of our business case. The following sections present one relatively new but already commonly used way of using a service oriented architecture (SOA) to implement these requirements. This solution, however, has some problems exposed later on that we resolve exposing a new and innovative way using SOA combined with Semantic Web Technologies.

Functional Requirements

The functional requirements the brokerage application must support in order to fulfil the business case are summarised below:

- **Stock market consultation functionalities:** The application should be able to retrieve information about the stock market such as the price of a share, volume of a share, historical information, etc. Several

sources can be used to obtain the information necessary to the supply the user with the information they require to make the trade.

- **Customer information consultation functionalities:** The application should be able to obtain easily the customer information such as his portfolio, buy and sell history and recent searches by the user.

- **Operational functionalities:** Invocation of operations on the stock market using the bank services: buy, sell.

- **Complex conditional queries:** Possibility to write a complex order in terms of conditions such as "if the stock value of Cisco is higher than X and its volume is lower than Y, ..." that may use different source of information. Logical combinations of the conditions should be possible.

- **Simple entry point of all services:** Complete integration of the conditional queries and operational functionalities within one simple entry point.

Non Functional Requirements

The non-functional requirements that the brokerage application must fulfil are:

- **Highly maintainable:** As the stock market is an entity subject to rapid change, it must be possible to maintain the application in an optimal way.

Figure 1. Brokerage application interaction comparison

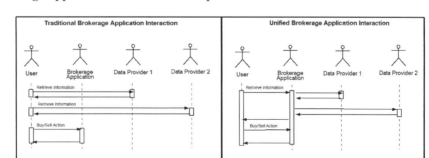

- **Usability:** The application is aimed at non-expert end users. The application should as usable as possible in order to present to the end user a friendly and easy-to-use interface.
- **Extensibility of the information source:** Possibility to easily add and change the providers of the banking information services. And to extend and choose the categories of information that the user wants to see. For example, if the user is executing a buy or sell transaction the user may want to see different sets of information.

Solution Based on SOA/Web Services

Introduction

During the last four decades, software design has been prone to many changes. After abstracting software code from the hardware infrastructure, computer scientists thought to write code in so called black-boxes and invented function oriented software design. The next big revolution was object oriented software design, in which data was intended to be packaged in objects where objects are metaphors of real world entities. Objects were then abstracted in components in order to manage the problem of the increasing number of objects. A component can be defined as a set of objects that has a coherent meaning as a standalone entity. What is the next level of abstraction? A composition of components will always be a component if we only focus on the data that these components contain. The composition must then be thought of a set of components that fulfil a given task. By doing so the packaging is no longer data-oriented but service-oriented, the set of components does no more contain information and methods to access to this information but is a black-box that offers one specific service. The services can then be composed in more abstract services and be part of the entire system, a service-oriented system.

Choosing service-oriented applications allows the clear separation of the users (commonly called 'consumers') from the service implementation (commonly called 'producers'). By having this distinction, the application can then be distributed on several platforms and possibly across networks. Each platform can have its own technology and can be located in any physical place. The software design has fundamentally changed in system design.

The Organization for the Advancement of Structured Information Standards (OASIS) defines the service oriented architecture as follows (MacKenzie et al, 2006):

A paradigm for organizing and utilizing distributed capabilities that may be under the control of different ownership domains. It provides a uniform means to offer, discover, interact with and use capabilities to produce desired effects consistent with measurable preconditions and expectations.

In this definition a service is designed as an entity with on one hand measurable preconditions and on the other hand measurable expectations. It can be reformulated as the input and output of a function in a typical programming paradigm, but in a service the input (precondition) and the output (expectation) are no data but state of the world or effect on the world.

We must clearly separate the architecture from the underlying technology that can be implemented. The Web Services made the fame of the SOA, but there exists other technologies which are totally suitable to be used in a Service-oriented Architecture such as: RPC, DCOM, CORBA, or WCF (Donani, 2006).

In the following subsection we present a standard SOA for a brokerage application using Web Services as the underlying technology.

Figure 2. SOA Architecture of a brokerage application

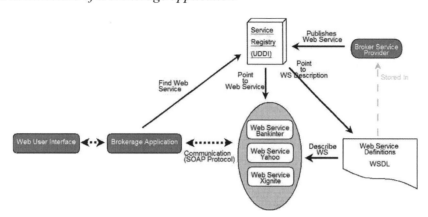

Architecture

An overview of the architecture of a brokerage application based on a SOA/Web Service architecture (Booth et al., 2004) is described in Figure 2.

The Web Services are physically located in either the service provider such as Bankinter or Xignite that provides their own Web Services, or in a specific Web Service container in the case that the Web Service provider does not provide a Web Service Interface and some wrapping mechanisms are needed. This is the case with the above yahoo based Web Service in which analysis (wrapping) of the Web page is needed to extract the right information.

The Web Service Descriptions are stored inside a Broker Service Provider which publishes all the descriptions and is in charge in managing the publication inside a Service Registry.

Through this registry, Web Services can be found and communication between the application and the Web Service is done using the SOAP.

This quite simple and elegant architecture has a lot of advantages that are explained in the following subsections on a technical and business perspective.

Benefits of SOA on a Technical Perspective

SOA is finding increased adoption across more and more business domains. This evolution can be explained by a set of technical benefits. The two most important ones are the following:

- **Reuse:** By decentralizing the systems in self contained atomic Web Services, a SOA allows the redundancy inside the system to be reduced since the Web-services can be used more than once for different purposes. This allows also delivering new functionalities in shorter time.

- **Loosely-coupled:** In a loosely-coupled system, each entity (Web Services) makes its requirements explicit and makes few assumptions about other entities. This permits not being aware where we locate the Web Services and thus increases the IT efficiency (critical Web Services can have an adapted hardware framework), improve the Quality of Service and reduce the costs. Another advantage of a loosely-coupled system is to have standard interfaces. This way there is no need for technical people to know about the whole details of the system and allows a strategically organisational separation of skills inside the project team.

Benefits of SOA on a Business Perspective

As many times the decision of choosing an architecture is done on a business level, it is important for an architecture type to have good benefits on a business perspective. The main SOA advantages are:

- **Business effectiveness:** If one word could be chosen to describe a SOA, it would be the word "agility". By using loosely-coupled services, the responsiveness to market is highly increased. Each process of the system is better controlled and allowed a deployment of resources based on the business needs.
- **Cost efficiency:** Service-oriented architectures Enables reduction of the development costs by separating the skills and efforts in specific development areas. The separation in services allows putting the resources in the technical areas that correspond best to their skills and thus reduce the costs of training or hiring new resources. The maintenance costs of such systems are also highly reduced because of well separated services and technology and location independence. Last cost reduction is the price/performance optimization based on the freedom to select the adequate platform.
- **Risk reduction:** Dividing problems in smaller parts always has the advantage to reduce the risk of a project, thus SOA is based on this division, we can say that the risk of projects based on SOA are inherently reduced. Another point is the risk reduction of the system deployment which can be done incrementally.

Problem Statement

We have presented the benefits of using a SOA based on Web Services to develop brokerage applications. However, there are a number of points in which the standard SOA is unable to respond:

- **Web services heterogeneity:** In the Web Service technologies, the information is described at a syntactical level. For example, in WSDL XML Schema technology is used to describe what the interchanged objects are. However, this kind of technology only allows describing the type of the objects: string, date, integer etc. The semantic of what the objects are is missing. This adds inside the project development a lot of potential problems:
  ○ Misunderstanding of what is interchanged (if the documentation is badly done, errors can be quickly done) Integration problems due to different type definition (for example, one service could describe an address with different fields while the service consumer use an unique string)
- **Poor visibility:** As defined by the standardization group OASIS inside the OASIS SOA Reference Model, the visibility *refers to the capacity for those with needs and those with capabilities to be able to see each other* (MacKenzie, 2006. In standard SOA, the visibility is mainly provided by means of a registry which lists the available services. By having only a syntactic description of the Web Service, the visibility is highly reduced and more efforts in terms of search and analysis are needed by any entity that wants to consume a Web Service.
- **Manual work:** In standard SOA system, an important effort of Web Services integration is needed in order to develop the entire system. The orchestration (composition) of

the necessary Web Services corresponds to one the highest effort time spent inside the project due to the mostly manual work that these efforts imply. Middleware is often used in order to solve the orchestration. Mediation (data conversion) is on this topic the major problem. The previously cited visibility problem also implies a lot of effort time because of the manual effort spent during the localization of each Web Service.

All these points constitute the problems of actual brokerage application based on pure SOA. However, as discussed earlier SOA has a lot of advantages. This encourages us to re-use this solution and improve it. The proposed solution of the next section aims at solving these problems of the actual solution by adding semantic technologies to this SOA paradigm.

SOLUTION: BROKER BASED ON SEMANTIC WEB SERVICES

As seen in the previous section, SOA technology provides a number of powerful concepts that when applied to brokerage applications allow us to construct flexible and easily extensible systems. However, problems have been identified with this kind of technical approach; those problems are responsible for an important part of the cost of such applications. The identified problems were *vocabulary heterogeneity*, *poor visibility* of the services and *manual work* needed in the development and maintenance phases. If we succeed developing a homogeneous vocabulary for Web Services, then we would increase the visibility and reduce the manual work. Three solutions were proposed in (Verma et al., 2007):

- **Pre-agree on all terms (operation name, parameters):** This implies a high oral communication between the development team and a lot of documentation writing. Pre-agreeing on the terms with no formally technical structure implies a high risk for any company due to the risk of losing common knowledge or getting integration problems.
- **Comment all aspects of a service:** In this solution, the comments are added inside the IT components. Each service contains the description of what the service proposes to do. Operation names and the semantic of the parameters are described in natural language.
- **Semantic descriptions:** This solution envisages a formal description of the services, called annotation. The services are not described using natural language but with the proper mechanism of the chosen technology.

This last solution, called Semantic Web Service (SWS), is the one that we propose in this section because it represents the most advanced and thus suitable of these three solutions. The annotation is done by using so called semantic technologies, in which the components of the system (here Web services) are formally described by using semantic resources (usually ontologies). This technology is the base of the vision of Tim Berners-Lee who put the base of a Web where the computer will be able to optimally understand and compute the information (Berners-Lee, 2001). We will explain how the use of ontologies, which is the base of most semantic system, adds visibility to the components by homogenizing the vocabulary used. We will also point out how this enhancement leads to a reduction of manual work and thus a reduction of cost.

Powerful Functionalities

The aim of annotating Web Services is not only to add clarity in the Web Service definitions but also to allow the Web Service to be read by machines.

This machine-readability makes the power of the SWS by adding to the system the following functionalities:

- **Power to reason:** The machine is able to "understand" what the Web Service is doing. It is able to interpret the messages that are interchanged. The messages are no more only pure data structure but are structured in such a way that the data can be analyzed and transformed (mediated). For example, if a SWS receives information of a "client" but expected a "person", he is able to infer that a client is a person and is able to extract the right information. The whole information space is structured and coherent. Axioms are responsible of maintaining this space coherent and reasoners are the medium to do this. As described in the functional requirements, the brokerage system needs a system that is able to handle a unique point entry. The reasoning capabilities given by SWS fit perfectly to these requirements, the queries can be interpreted by the system and the system can identify what the user's wishes are. Additionally, as the machine is able to interpret what the input of the user is, it is able to help the user at the moment of maintaining the system. For example, a company has a brokerage application that allows the user to buy stocks. However, for marketing purposes the number of times that the customer can buy depends on the profile of the customer. In this case, the maintainer of the brokerage system could want to add a new type of client. With a SWS-based system, this is highly simple, as the only action to do is to add the concept of this new type in the ontology and add the information on how many operations he can do. No additional development efforts are needed and no risk of adding errors in the application is run. If the maintainer makes an error in adding

the information inside the ontology, the reasoner will warn him before he put it in production.

- **Automatic discovery:** Formally describing what each Web Service does adds the functionality of automatically discovering them. This means that a query written in a formal language can be interpreted so that the correct Web Services with the appropriate functionalities and Quality of Service parameters are found. This allows a better decoupling between: what the user wants and what the system proposes. By separating these two parts, the system gets more flexible.This SWS functionality responds to the functional requirements about the processing of complex queries. The user expresses a complex query in Natural Language or through a Web Interface, this query is translated into the corresponding formal language and this formal query can then be used to retrieve the best Web Services. More than one Web Service can be accessible for the same functionality; the system takes care at choosing the more adapted one.In terms of maintainability, the separation of the SWS is also important in the sense that adding new duplicated SWS of other providers does not require modifying the application. If new types of SWS are added, some extents must be added to the query generation functionality of the brokerage application. But this task remains relatively easy because of the use of ontologies which takes care of the coherence of the system. The automatic discovery responds to the non functional property of the "extensibility of the information source".

- **Automatic orchestration:** SWS support the automatic orchestration or composition of Web services (Medjahed, 2003). By orchestration, we mean the composition of the Web Services in order to provide a more complex service. As Semantic Web Services are semantically annotated, the system has enough information to handle a user query and respond to it by assembling the Web Services. Automatic orchestration provides an easy way to combine a usable interface to the user, with one entry point that provides the three main requirements: stock market consultation, costumer information consultation and operational invocation.

SWS Technologies

The Semantic Web Service technologies have been in the last few years under intensive research world-wide. In the actual states, two approaches have been developed. Each one of these approach were part of research projects and their validity was proven by the deployment of concrete use-cases. The two approaches are:

- **Pure Semantic Web Services:** These technologies represent a way to write pure Semantic Web Services. By pure, we mean that they are written directly in a formal language and are independent from any non-Semantic Web Services. Of course, all SWS technologies need to be able to be connected with non-Semantic Web Services (called grounding) in order to support any already developed Web service system. But the idea is to be able to build new Semantic Web Services that will not carry on the "old" non semantic technologies. There are two main technologies based on this approach: OWL-S (Martin et al, 2003) based on the OWL ontology language and WSMO (Fensel et al., 2007) (de Brujin, Bussler et al., 2005)based on the WSML (de Brujin, Fensel et al., 2005) ontology language. The first is mainly a North American development effort, while the second one has been developed within

EU-funded projects (Sekt, DIP, Knowledge Web, ASG and SUPER projects). They both are submitted to the W3C and have the necessary specification, development tools and execution engines.

- **Semantic Annotation of Web Services:** The second approach consists in directly annotating the WSDL with semantic information. Two main specification efforts are actually done: WSDL-S (Akkiraju et al., 2005) that is at the Member Submission stage in W3C and SAWSDL(Farell et al., 2007) that is a W3C proposed recommendation. Main advantage of these approaches is that the annotation is done directly in the WSDL / XML Schema. Thus, the evolution of existing systems is facilitated. Other advantage is that these specifications are ontology language independent, thus execution engine can be developed for any chosen ontology language. Both languages have the necessary development tools.

Tools already exist and are operational to model and run Semantic Web Services. Most of them were part of a research project and are freely available on the Internet. For modelling SWS, the following tools are available:

- **WSMO Studio[1]:** A SWS and semantic Business Process Modelling Environment. Also support SAWSDL. As described by the name, this tool supports the WSMO Framework. It is Eclipse-based and the last version is 0.7.2 released on 29/11/2007 (in the moment that this chapter is written: end of 2007)
- **Web Service Modelling Toolkit (WSMT)[2]:** A lightweighted framework for the rapid creation and deployment of the tools for SWS. It supports WSMO Framework. It is Eclipse-based and the last version is 1.4.1 released on 13/09/2007 (in the moment that this chapter is written: end of 2007)

- **Radiant (Gomadam, 2005)[3]:** A WSDL-S / SAWSDL Annotation Tool developed by the University of Georgia. The annotation is made using OWL ontologies. It is Eclipse-based and the last version is 0.9.4beta released on 29/05/2007 (in the moment that this chapter is written: end of 2007).
- **ODE SWS (Corcho, 2003)[4]:** A toolset for design and composition of SWS. It is based on UMPL and some work has been done to integrate OWL-S.
- **OWL-S IDE (Srinivasan, 2006)[5]:** A development environment supporting a SWS developer through the whole process from the Java generation, to the compilation of OWL-S descriptions, to the deployment and registration with UDDI. The last version is 1.1 released on 26/07/2005 (in the moment that this chapter is written: end of 2007).
- **OWL-S Editor (Elenius, 2005)[6]:** A Protégé Ontology Editor plugin for a easy creation of SWS. The last version was released on 04/11/2004 (in the moment that this chapter is written: end of 2007).

The following SWS Engines are available:

- **WSMX[7]:** The reference implementation of WSMO
- **Internet Reasoning Service III (IRS-III)[8]** (Domingue et al, 2004): A SWS framework, which allows applications to semantically describe and execute Web services.
- **OWL-S tools:** A series of tools WSDL2OWL-S, Java2OWL-S, OWL-S2UDDI, etc. are available at: http://www.daml.ri.cmu.edu/tools/details.html

Through these tools represent good proofs of the viability of the technology. That said, further development would be required to adapt them to the needs of real world system. Professional benchmarks would be needed to identify efficiency and security lacks and allow the development of professional SWS frameworks.

We gave a short overview of the existing SWS technologies and we explain now how these technologies can be applied to brokerage applications.

Approach and Architecture

The approach taken for creating a brokerage application with SWS is to use the SWS engine as a central component of the architecture. By taking advantage of the reasoning capacities of the SWS engine, it is possible to build a simple and extendible Brokerage Application. New Semantic Web Services are added directly in the engine and we minimize the development costs of managing new services. The SWS engine "understands" the semantic of the new added SWS and only few modifications are needed inside the Brokerage Application itself. This approach has been proven during the DIP project on a use-case (see the two screenshots Figure 3 And 4) that simulated a brokerage application with Bankinter and external Web Services. The user can enter a complex query composed of several conditions and one action to be taken. The conditions are connected with logical operators (AND/OR). The conditions can be of the types:

- *If the price of a specific stock is higher than a given price.*
- *If the value of an index is lower than a given value.*
- *If the expert recommendation is equal to a specified one.*
- *If the variation of the value of a given stock is higher.*

For each information that needs to be retrieved, the SWS Engine is responsible for discovering the best suitable Semantic Web Service, eventually by composing multiple Semantic Web Services

Figure 3. First screenshot of the SWS based brokerage prototype

Figure 4. Second screenshot of the SWS based brokerage prototype

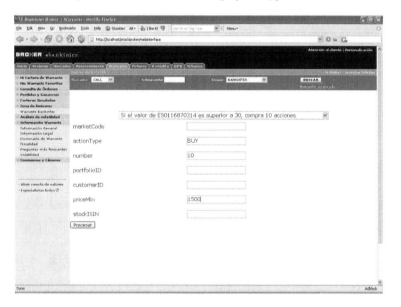

(orchestration) and invoke the one (/ones) that correspond to the given Quality of Services parameters (time to respond, localization, etc.). If a Semantic Web Services is grounded on some other service systems (like normal Web Services), it is in charge of getting the information and converting it into the semantic language. The Brokerage application then returns the result of the execution to the Web Interface.

Figure 5 shows the architecture that implements this approach.The three main components are:

- The Web User Interface that should respond to the Usability non-functional requirement.

- The Brokerage Application that should support all the functional requirements and that is in charge of the communication with the SWS Engine.
- The SWS Engine that is in charge of managing the semantic resources: discovering, invoke and orchestrate the SWS.

The brokerage application prototype developed in DIP has been developed using J2EE technologies. The application makes use of Natural Language Processing technologies to offer a simplified interface to the user. Receiving one sentence as input, the brokerage application is able to identify what is the user intention and automatically retrieve the information that it needs to invoke the SWS. These parameters are used to generate a WSMO goal (de Brujin, 2005) formally describing the user intention. This goal is the entry point to the SWS Engine.

As SWS Engine, WSMX (Bussler et al., 2005)[9] was chosen over IRIS-III (Domingue et al., 2004) (Cabral et al., 2006)[10] in order to prove the correct implementation of this SWS Engine inside the research project. From the input goal provided by the brokerage application and some optional Quality of Service parameters, the SWS engine discovers the necessary SWS and invokes the retrieved SWS in the right order (orchestration). The brokerage application can then have access to all the information it needs to check the condition provided by the user and if the conditions are validated execute the buy/sell order through another call to the SWS engine.

The Financial ontology, exhaustively described in (López-Cobo, 2008) plays a major role in all the tasks of the SWS engine and is the pillar of the whole brokerage application. It describes the vocabulary of the application and is used to annotate the SWS on both levels: the functionality description (capability) and the interface (message exchange).

By using an architecture based on the Financial ontology and the SWS engine, we provide a flexible and maintainable application and provide to the brokerage system the whole benefits of using SWS technologies.

In the next section, we describe in a higher level the cost and benefits of adopting such architecture.

COST AND BENEFITS

From a business point of view, the profits of the proposed solution must not be focused on new incomes neither on costs, although they both exist. The resulting application is intended to create a new product, by giving new options to manage their portfolio. These options could have been developed using a more traditional approach but, due to the

Figure 5. Brokerage application architecture

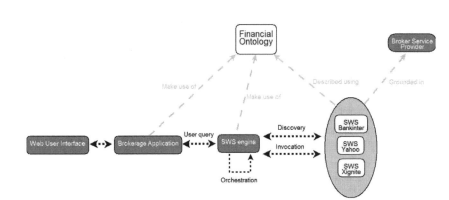

complex and usually mature architectures used by the financial institutions, the costs would have been significantly higher, both the development and the future sub-applications costs.

Also, a more traditional approach (i.e. without semantic technologies) would have implied agreements with the information providers (data formats, relevant data, how to provide the information, how to access to the data, etc), which will usually implied a one-by-one Trading Partner Agreement (TPA). The semantic layer gives us the ability to smartly read the provided data and therefore to manage it easily. It is also easy to add new providers with this approach. Finally, data is accessed when required and if required, making use of the Web Service advantages.

The costs and benefits, from the technical point of view, must be also considered. The Cost/Benefits ratio in terms of adapting actual systems, although not trivial, is not as dramatic change as the one that was performed in the transition to the Internet era.

Banks were usually based on main frame architectures. The scenario in these last 10-20 years has changed from a exclusive main-frame scenario, where only the bank employees had access to the IT transactional systems, to a Web Based scenario where virtually any customer, anywhere at anytime could be using the bank transactional. This transition meant high investments on scaling the main frame architecture to a 24*7 architecture adding several layers: Web servers, application servers, database servers, security layers...

Fortunately a Web Service scenario is more natural in the actual client-servers environment, therefore, in terms of cost/benefits the investment is lower. The same reasoning can be applied to a SWS scenario, where besides the new Web Service layer to be added, semantic pieces appear to complete the puzzle.

Therefore, taking the chance of adding semantic layers to an existing bank architecture implies low economical risk since no major implications are needed to expand the current architecture.

As a result, and taking into account the business opportunity, the small amount of effort required to create and maintain the service, and the technical prerequisites, the SWS approach emerges as a smart solution to create the new service at a reasonable level of cost, both for the developer and, which is more important, for the final user.

RISK ASSESSMENT

From a business point of view, alternatives are almost always more expensive but it could depend on how each Financial Institution manage its own Stock Market Services. What is more, in several cases the solution could be so complex that it could be considered as 'nearly impossible' to develop without studying in depth what is going to be modified, (Stock Market applications are critical tasks for Financial Institutions due to the volatility of the market and the quality assurance that is required in this specific market).

At the same time, the new proposed service is intended to give better utilities to the clients. These kinds of services are actually free, although the final user must manage with them. So the price of the service for the final clients could not be high and thus, it has to be developed at a reasonable cost. There are some risks when the use of SWS is considered:

- **Security issues:** No doubt this is the major functional risk to be considered when deploying SWS technologies. On banking environments security is the mayor column on which all the architecture must be built. All the security issues must be clarified and solved before any transactional application using real customer banking data is deployed to the real world. If this milestone is not achieved all the SWS-based applications will be forced to handle only with public data and the real value of semantic applications will remain as a proof-of-concept not as a real-world-application.

- **Evolution issues:** SWS techniques are in their first steps of use in business environments. As these techniques become more familiar they will evolve and this evolution could mean scalability issues that should be treated as any other scalability issues inside any corporation environment. Although the semantic techniques are mature their wide use could imply changes that would mean changes on the semantic platform. However these two evolution issues are natural to any IT development or to the deploy of any new technology. The IT business, no matter if it is the banking business or any other, has got enough experience to handle these potential risks.

FUTURE TRENDS

The evolution of the Stock Market and its associated services must be forecasted as part of the global social tendencies: people (and investors) are requiring more and more sophisticated products and services allowing them to make their own decisions. If we consider that information aggregators are the Internet 'killer applications' (i.e.: Google, Yahoo, You Tube, etc) investors are expected to make use of Stock Market data aggregators (in fact, the actually use them: Yahoo! Finances, Invertia, etc), making their own buying/ selling decisions and finally performing them in their favourite Stock Market site.

None of these services are designed to perform automatic operations that completely fulfil the investor requirements, nor of them are prepared to perform a personalised strategy when data aggregation is required. There are several solutions for professional investors but they are available at a high cost, thus they are only interesting when high volumes are regularly performed (high volume both in terms of number of transactions and in terms of money invested). But there they are not an option for individuals.

Our tests[11] reveal that people usually make use of at least two Stock Market services just to fulfil their information requirements. The SWS is intended to aggregate them and, in the near future, to automatically perform the actions according to the investor strategy, combining sources and retrieving specific data form them.

CONCLUSION

Responding to the need of maintainable and efficient brokerage applications, we have presented in this chapter a novel approach that combines the SOA architecture and the semantic technologies. By using the proposed solution, we resolve the three identified problems of a non-semantic SOA solution: heterogeneity of the vocabulary used in the services which reduces the maintainability and possibilities of evolution of the application, the poor visibility which reduces the possibility for automatic discovery and the lot of manual work that is generated by this poor visibility and the lack of automatic composition possibilities.

We exposed the advantages of a solution based on Semantic Web services: reasoning functionalities, automatic discovery and automatic orchestration. Such functionalities allow us to build an architecture centralized on the SWS engine and have a really flexible system.

The feasibility to build such brokerage application has been demonstrated during the European project called DIP. The output of these projects is a framework called WSMO associated with an ontology language (WSML) and execution engines (WSMX and IRS-III). The European Commission continues to invest money in the research in Semantic Web Services for example in the SUPER project which aims to take advantage of the Semantic Web Services in order to improve Business Process Management Systems. A lot of research is also done in other technologies such as OWL-S. The high activity of these research projects reflects the important interest that should have industrial investor in such technology. The Semantic Web services are ready and continue to be improved.

Companies should consider the benefits of SWS on two levels: the strategic level and the tactical one. On the strategic level, the SWS give the possibility to build highly maintainable applications and profits from a loosely coupled architecture. On a tactical level, a company should see the benefits on other projects where the ontologies that have been created for the SWS are reused and form a common base for the applications. Using such Semantic technologies is interesting for companies because it promotes the homogeneity of the systems inside the company. The intra-company and inter-company applications are then much easier integrable.

REFERENCES

Akkiraju, R., Farrell, J., Miller, J., Nagarajan, M., Schmidt, M., Sheth, A., & Verma, K. (2005) *Web Service Semantics - WSDL-S,*

Berners-Lee, T., Hendler, J., & Lassila, O. (2001). The Semantic Web. *Scientific American, 284,* 34–43.

Booth, D., Haas, H., McCabe, F., Newcomer, E., Champion, M., Ferris, C., & Orchard, D. (2004) *Web Services architecture.*

Bussler, C., Cimpian, E., Fensel, D., Gomez, J. M., Haller, A., Haselwanter, T., et al. Zaremba Maciej, Zaremba Michal (2005). *Web Service Execution Environment (WSMX).*

Cabral, L., Domingue, J., Galizia, S., Gugliotta, A., Norton, B., Tanasescu, V., & Pedrinaci, C. (2006) *IRS-III: A Broker for Semantic Web Services based Applications,* The 5th International Semantic Web Conference (ISWC 2006), Athens, GA, USA.

Corcho, O., Fernández-López, M., Gómez-Pérez, A., and Lama, M. (2003). *ODE SWS: A Semantic Web Service Development Environment.* VLDB-Workshop on Semantic Web and Databases, 203-216. Berlin, Germany.

de Brujin, J., Bussler, C., Domingue, J., Fensel, D., Hepp, M., Keller, U., et al. (2005). *Web Service Modeling Ontology (WSMO).*

de Brujin, J., Fensel, D., Keller, U., Kifer, M., Lausen, H., Krummenacher, R., et al. (2005). *Web Service Modeling Language (WSML).*

Domingue, J., Cabral, L., Hakimpour, F., Sell, D., & Motta, E. (2004). IRS-III: A platform, and infrastructure for creating WSMO-based Semantic Web services. In *Proc. Of the Workshop on WSMO Implementations.* CEUR Workshop Proceedings

Donani M.H. (2006). SOA 2006: State Of The Art. *Journal of Object Technology,* 5.

Elenius, D., Denker, G., Martin, D., Gilham, F., Khouri, J., Sadaati, S., & Senanayake, R. The OWL-S editor - A Development Tool for Semantic Web Services. In The Semantic Web: Research and Applications. Series: Lecture Notes in Computer Science, Vol. 3532, 78-92. Springer Berlin / Heidelberg 2005. ISBN: 978-3-540-26124-7

Farell, J., & Lausen, H. (2007) *Semantic Annotations for WSDL and XML Schema.*

Fensel, D., Lausen, H., Polleres, A., Brujin, J. d., & Stollberg, M. Romand D., Domingue J. (2007). Enabling Semantic Web Services – The Web Service Modelin Ontology. Springer.

Gomadam K., Verma K., Brewer D., Sheth A. P., Miller J. A. (2005) Radiant: A tool for semantic annotation of Web Services, *ISWC 2005.*

López-Cobo, J. M., Cicurel, L., & Losada, S. Ontology Management in eBanking applications. In Ontology Management. Semantic Web, Semantic Web Services, and Business Applications. Series: Semantic Web and Beyond, Vol. 7. Hepp, M.; De Leenheer, P.; de Moor, A.; Sure, Y. (Eds.) 2008, Approx. ISBN: 978-0-387-69899-1

MacKenzie, M., Laskey, K., McCabe, F., Brown, P. F., & Metz, R. (2006) *Reference Model for Service Oriented Architecture 1.0.*

Martin, D., Burstein, M., Hobbs, J., Lassila, O., McDermott, D., McIraith, S., et al. (2003). *OWL-S: Semantic Markup for Web Services.*

Medjahed, B., Bouguettaya, A., & Elmagarmid, A. K. (2003). Composing Web services on the Semantic Web. *The VLDB Journal*, *12*(4), 333–351. doi:10.1007/s00778-003-0101-5

Srinivasan, N., Paolucci, M., & Sycara, K. (2006). Semantic Web Service Discovery in the OWL-S IDE. In *Proceedings of the 39th Annual Hawaii international Conference on System Sciences - Volume 06* (January 04 - 07, 2006). HICSS. IEEE Computer Society, Washington, DC, 109.2.

Verma K., Sheth A. (2007). Semantically Annotating a Web Service. *IEEE Computer Society,* March/April 2007, 11, 83-85.

ENDNOTES

1.   http://www.wsmostudio.org/download.html
2.   https://sourceforge.net/projects/wsmt/
3.   http://lsdis.cs.uga.edu/projects/meteor-s/downloads/index.php?page=1
4.   http://kw.dia.fi.upm.es/odesws/
5.   http://projects.semwebcentral.org/projects/owl-s-ide/
6.   http://owlseditor.semwebcentral.org/
7.   http://www.wsmx.org/
8.   http://kmi.open.ac.uk/projects/irs/
9.   http://www.wsmx.org
10. http://kmi.open.ac.uk/projects/irs/
11. Done inside the DIP (http://dip.semanticweb.org/) project, Deliverable 10.10.

This work was previously published in Semantic Web for Business: Cases and Applications, edited by R. Garcia, pp. 336-352, copyright 2009 by IGI Publishing (an imprint of IGI Global).

Chapter 4.7
Evolution of Online Financial Trading Systems:
E–Service Innovations in the Brokerage Sector

Alexander Yap
Elon University, USA

Wonhi Synn
Elon University, USA

ABSTRACT

This chapter focuses on the theme of e-service innovation in financial electronic markets. The discussion will cover the theories of "technology bundling" and how bundling creates value-added in servicing electronic markets. More specifically, this chapter looks at innovations created through e-service bundling for online brokers connected to various financial electronic markets. The proliferation of different e-trading systems raises the question of which systems provide better service to online stock traders. Many online brokers (e-brokers) now provide low-cost transactions and financial research capabilities, so where is the next level of innovation? The objective of this chapter is to show that several innovations in broker e-services are critical in the following areas: (a) how order processes are efficiently managed in financial e-markets; (b) how responsive e-trading systems are in handling trading rules and regulations; (c) how different systems address unique niches in financial e-markets; and (d) improving systems stability and reliability.

BACKGROUND

Introduction

In this chapter, we start analyzing an entire sector (the brokerage service sector) rather than one particular business organization in order to understand the case studies. The reason for using the entire sector as the *unit* of analysis is that the e-service problems and challenges are similar for the entire sector and is not unique to one organization alone (see next section, which discusses the problem of

DOI: 10.4018/978-1-60566-064-6.ch012

this sector). More so, the best way to illustrate the e-service innovations of online brokers, we need to relate their unique e-service solutions to the problem facing the entire sector.

E-service in this chapter is defined as the service provided by electronic brokerage systems used to facilitate the buying and selling of publicly traded corporate stocks and financial securities online. If you want to own/buy shares of stocks in companies like Microsoft or IBM, you can trade their shares electronically through e-brokerage systems like Scottrade, E-Trade, and Ameritrade. By trading shares online, you are using an electronic service similar to an online auction system, where sellers and buyers bid for the prices of different stocks and financial securities. Buyers want to get the cheapest prices and sellers want to sell at the highest prices, and the electronic trading systems help them with that objective. This is a critical e-service for the trillion-dollar global financial market, where stocks, futures, options, bonds, foreign exchange, and commodities are traded daily. These electronic brokers do not necessarily own stocks or financial securities. They process the orders electronically by channeling the orders through different networked financial market systems via the New York Stock Exchange, the London Stock Exchange, the Shanghai Stock Exchange, and many other stock exchanges around the world.

Another critical e-service that needs to be defined is the service that assists online investors and traders to make informed decisions whether to buy or sell stocks and when to execute such trade. E-brokers provide bundled e-services like real-time news reports, real-time charting of stock price movements, the demand and supply of stocks, stock analyst ratings, and research on the company's financial health. This is how different e-services are "bundled" to help facilitate critical decisions in electronic financial markets. Different information systems, software applications, real-time databases, and networking technologies are used in the bundling of e-services.

In previous studies (Yap & Lin, 2001), the transaction capabilities of online trading systems as well as their knowledge-based components have been explored. These studies showed that earlier Web-based trading systems took one to three minutes to execute market orders; whereas more current systems can execute orders in one to three seconds. Transaction speed is not the real issue anymore. The real concern is whether traders are getting the "best price" for their trade executions. The demand for financial research and knowledge-base services online also needs to be more innovative to distinguish the uniqueness of e-services provided by different e-brokers. So the issue is what more can e-brokers provide their clients? In what areas can e-service innovation take place in the online brokerage sector? To get an idea of where innovation needs to happen, the problems of the online brokerage sector needs to be defined. Only then can we see how innovations in technologies and its bundling can provide solutions to such problems.

Defining the Problem in the Online Brokerage Sector

The problems with the electronic services provided by most online brokerage outfits are threefold: (1) *Not all systems comply with the U.S. Securities and Exchange Commission (SEC) Trading Requirements (rules and regulations).* Most information systems used for financial trading have loopholes in terms of preventing traders and investors from breaking SEC rules and U.S. government laws. This is important because many amateur traders are not familiar with laws governing the trading of financial instruments in U.S. financial markets. Breaking the law could be very costly and may prevent a trader from trading stocks again. This is a very serious problem not adequately addressed by e-service systems in the brokerage sector. (2) *There is a need to connect fragmented financial electronic markets to reflect more realistic stock quotes.* There are financial e-trading systems that are not as broadly networked to different financial electronic markets as other systems. This means that if your online brokerage service is only connected or bundled to two electronic financial markets while another online brokerage service is bundled to eight electronic financial markets, then your online broker's system may not be able to get you the best "buy" and "sell" price for your stocks like the more connected/networked e-brokers can. Many traders have complained that their orders were not executed at the price they wanted, even if they saw that their stocks momentarily hit those price ranges. This happens when an online trading system is only connected to a few electronic markets. (3) *Problem with systems stability and reliability.* Some online brokerage systems are not very stable and reliable, and therefore disrupting e-service more often during the electronic trading process. This is also a very serious problem. Imagine if your stock went down from $21.50 to $17.63 and you could not sell it because your online broker's system was down for three hours. One of the purposes of this study is to test some of the more popular trading systems for more than a year and see how they hold up over time.

Methodology

This research employs the "case research" methodology. The researchers were involved in the actual use of the financial trading system and so data was acquired on a firsthand basis. The research uses the interpretive approach, which is essentially based on the unique experience of the user. The researchers gather the findings from direct experience and day-to-day interaction with the trading systems, its inherent technological features, and the customer support provided by the e-broker when the system is not working properly.

To be able to do an in-depth analysis, the researchers opened four separate accounts so that four different popular e-trading systems can be tested and compared. However, due to limited space in writing this chapter, we can only cover two

cases discussing two different e-trading systems. The two cases chosen for this chapter offered the more innovative e-services in the industry at the time of data gathering. Each e-trading system was used for more than a year. More than 50 trades were conducted on each system, with a frequency of at least once each week. Several systems features were explored to see what value it provided the user. Trading online naturally meant that the researchers acquired their information/data firsthand. To validate and confirm some findings, the researchers also engage in dialogues with trading communities through message boards with user reviews.

SETTING THE STAGE

The Strategic Role of IT in the Creation of Electronic Markets: A Theoretical Framework

Ciborra (1993) argued that information technology can be used to lower transaction cost, and in turn, enable the creation of cost-efficient electronic markets. Bakos (1991) emphasized that IT-driven electronic marketplaces can lower the "buyer's search costs" as well as the seller's cost.

Bakos (1998) said that electronic markets lead to a more efficient "friction-free" market, because electronic markets match sellers' offer to the buyers' preferences more efficiently than physical markets. The more buyers and sellers there are in an electronic market system, the smoother (less friction) the market mechanism will be in determining a realistic price for goods and services. If we examine global consumer e-markets with millions of users like eBay, prices of goods or services are realistically determined by the supply and demand forces created by multitudes of buyers and sellers. On the other hand, electronic financial markets have been fragmented into smaller electronic market systems called *Electronic Communication Networks* (ECNs).

These financial e-markets have not been as unified, integrated, and as far-reaching as eBay. So, it is not as "friction-less" because price gaps occur in fragmented markets. That is why "arbitrage trading" occurs in financial e-markets. In finance, arbitrage trading is the practice of taking advantage of price gaps/differentials in stocks, options, bonds between two or more financial markets.

Friedfertig and West (1998) enumerated different financial electronic market systems used for trading stocks, to include Instinet, Island, and NASDAQ's Small Order Entry System (SOES). The *National Association of Securities Dealers Automated Quotation System* (NASDAQ) was the first, and as of this writing, the largest electronic stock market. While electronic financial markets have been fragmented, there have been initiatives to start integrating different e-market trading systems. In 2005, NASDAQ acquired Instinet (Ryan, 2005). After that, the Associated Press (2006) reported that the New York Stock Exchange (NYSE) has merged with Archipelago Holdings, a Chicago-based company that owns an electronic market exchange system called ARCA-Ex. The NYSE, a 213-year-old traditional stock exchange, finally adopted its own electronic market system in 2006.

Bakos and Brynjolfsson (2000) argued that the bundling of information goods, systems, and technology is advantageous for service providers as bundling information goods increases the value of a set of goods to the clients/users of the information systems. The bundling of information goods and systems is reflected in the changes seen in financial markets like the merger of Instincts with NASDAQ and ARCA-Ex with NYSE. The purpose of bundling of information goods enabled by information technology relates to Ciborra (1993) and Malone, Yates, and Benjamin's (1987) arguments that information technology brings down the cost of transaction and coordination in electronic markets. In this study, we believe that e-brokerage firms have bundled different information goods, systems, and technology to make their e-services highly innovative and competitive.

This research looks at two e-brokers and investigates if their online trading systems have been "bundled" in such a way that their system can simultaneously transact and access live data from several financial e-markets. The other aspect of "bundling" that will be studied is how various software applications have been combined to provide a comprehensive electronic service to traders/investors. This research believes that the e-trading system with the best bundled information goods, functions, and systems capabilities will provide the best value to traders/investors.

The Changing Service Environment in the Online Brokerage Sector

Considering that instantaneous transaction speed and financial research are already standard capabilities in most e-brokerage services, systems developers for e-brokers need to recognize other unique innovative e-service capabilities that are really needed in this service sector. The following are critical issues to consider:

Order Process Flow - First, there is the issue of how buy and sell orders are channeled to various electronic trading systems and whether traders are getting the "best price" for their orders. The question is to what extent are online trading systems linked to different electronic markets to process orders and get traders the best price for their orders?

Targeting Niche Markets - Second, what differentiates one e-service from another? In what ways do different systems cater to various types of traders? E-brokers need to take advantage of market segmentation and cater to different types of clients/traders.

SEC Regulation - Third, there have been several changes in government rules and regulations that could penalize online brokerage firms if trader violates those SEC rules. The chapter will determine whether there are some loopholes in the systems that are disadvantageous to traders.

Systems Reliability and Security - Finally, there is an increasing risk of system failure and security breaks. Are trading systems as reliable? How are online brokers providing clients safe guards and fail safe systems?

Current Issues in the Stock Market Prompting Changes in Online Trading Services

The growth of electronic markets has caused market fragmentation as alternate market centers are "balkanizing" the order flow process and encouraging internalization. *Internalization* is the situation where brokers buy the stock from their own internal sources or inventory instead of buying from the larger open market. It is not good for orders to be executed in isolated small markets rather than in bigger, more unified, and networked e-markets. Roberts, Pittman, and Reeds (2000) stated this appropriately in their article.

Recent advances in technology and changes in securities regulation have sparked the development of a growing number of alternative market centers. These market centers include regional exchanges and alternative trading systems.

Advancements in technology and regulatory changes have made it possible for these market centers to attract order flow by offering narrower spreads and improved trading efficiencies, including speedier and more reliable executions….The SEC is concerned that fragmentation of the markets has caused or will cause too many customer orders to be executed in isolation, rather than interacting with other market orders.

The objective of having an electronic market is providing accessibility to as many market segments as possible; however, the growing fragmentation or balkanization of electronic markets appears to limit the order flow process

from reaching a wider market given time execution constraints. Moreover, the larger the volume of the trade, the more difficult it is for the online system to match, buy, and sell volumes.

For example, an online brokerage firm may not find 1,000 shares of stocks being sold lower than $20.20/share in their own e-market system, even though another seller in an alternate e-market center may be selling it at $20.00/share. Due to execution time constraint, the system may be able to get the best bid at the fastest execution within its own internal order flow (that is $20.20) but not across other market centers. So, theoretically, the buyer is forced to pay $20.20 instead of only $20.00 and therefore paying $0.20/share more (or $200 for 1000 shares) due to the inability of an electronic market system to search several other electronic market systems for a better price given the constraint of execution time.

Electronic markets seem to be getting more fragmented due to the proliferation of different electronic trading systems in the form of Electronic Communication Networks (ECNs), such as Instinet and Archipelago. Routing orders across different electronic markets can be inefficient in terms of getting the best price of a stock; hence the temptation of brokers to internalize orders. Traditional markets like NYSE and AMEX behave more like a singular unfragmented market where trading occurs on the floor among a network of human specialist.

Figure 1 compares and illustrates fragmented markets (such as ECN1 or ECN2) vs. a single market. In fragmented markets, buyers (B) and sellers (S) may not be properly matched. Some markets have more buyers than sellers or vice versa. If an e-trading system just executes orders within one or two ECNs, their clients may not always get the best traded price.

If an online system can access all ECNs, then it gives its clients the opportunity to access a bigger e-market. In effect, it is unifying all smaller e-markets to a single e-market.

Figure 1. Balkanized or fragmented e-markets (left) and unified single market (right)

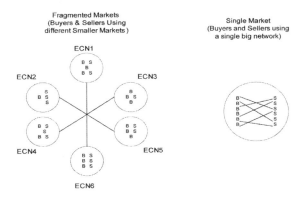

Diversifying E-Services by Targeting Niche Markets

There are different types of traders or investors in the stock market. Different financial brokerage firms target different types of traders or investors. The following are different groups of traders/investors:

- Long-term investors – investors who "buy and hold" and keep their stock portfolio for months or years.
- Swing traders – traders who do not keep stocks for more than a week. They take advantage of the upswing and downswing of stock prices over the course of a few days.
- Pattern Day traders – traders who buy and sell stocks during the same day. They sell stocks at the end of the day, whether they make money or not.
- Micro-day traders – a growing number of traders who only buy and sell within a few minutes or seconds. They do not even hold stocks for an hour. Their objective is to take advantage of small fluctuations in the market and make a small profit spread with these fluctuations.
- Penny stock and small cap traders – traders who trade only micro-caps or small

caps stocks. Micro-cap stocks are often referred to as penny stocks because they can be traded for less than a dollar. Small caps stocks are also cheap and usually below $5.

- Large cap and middle cap traders – a group of traders who believe that they should only buy stocks above $10 or $20. They believe that micro-cap and small cap stocks are cheap for a reason; they are risky and trading for what they are worth.
- Institutional traders – these are large institutions that invest their capital in stocks, like banks, insurance, and mutual fund companies.

Securities and Exchange Commission (SEC) Rules and Regulations

SEC has a number of trading rules that brokers must follow or force its clients to follow. For example, SEC has already limited day trading activities. Pattern daytraders need to have at least $25,000 in their account to meet SEC requirements. This took effect in 2001. Cadway (2001) summarize these new rulings:

As some of you might be aware, the NASD has come out with some new margin rules for day-trading accounts effective September 28th, 2001. Among these rules is the requirement for all pattern daytrading accounts to have a minimum equity of $25,000.

Stock traders have two general paths in trading stocks. One path is to buy low and sell high, while another path is to sell high and buy low (short selling). Selling high and buying low is the processing of shorting a stock. Technically, the trader just borrowing stocks from his broker when he/she short sells a stock that he/she does not own. Sooner or later, the trader must buy stocks to repay or return or cover what he/she borrowed from his/her broker (This is known as "buy to cover"). For a trader to borrow stocks from a broker, the broker must have an inventory of that stock. If the broker does not have an inventory of a particular stock and still lets the individual trader borrow it on paper, then the broker is violating SEC rules by practicing "naked shorting." While naked shorting is illegal, e-brokers are known to violate it all the time. Data show that brokers still allow traders to do naked shorting.

How responsive are online trading systems to SEC rules and regulations? Could users of these systems be allowed to break SEC rules and regulations or does the system stop them from breaking the rules or doing anything illegal? The question is: how are online trading systems keeping up with these SEC rules? Does the trading system inform you if you are violating SEC rules or not?

Systems Reliability

The speed cycle of the trading process is assumingly faster today than it was in the late 1990s with the significant jump of retail traders joining the online trading scenario. The sheer volume of trading may be taxing the trading system of different brokers and also the systems used by different ECNs. The research initiative intends to find out how reliable the systems are.

Dogsofthedow.com posts certain feedback from users of online systems. Some of the feedbacks citing technical problems with online brokers are as follows:

After 2 months of technical issues I have closed my account today. I have lost several thousands of dollars in one day because the price of a particular stock that I shorted...was not at current prices but the day before.... I have filed a fraud complaint on April 20, 2004 with the SEC."

I've had an account with [xxx] since Oct 2002 and have seen a steady decrease in online reliability. Emailed complaints are answered with

form letter responses and after hours trading seem to be farther and farther over the horizon. The problems seem to stem from poor technology implementation and overwhelming the systems with new subscribers before adequately architecting for the heavier load.

From firsthand experience, the research intends to discover how frequent the systems go down and how fast the brokers can bring their systems back running again.

CASE DESCRIPTION

Case One: E-Broker One

E-Broker One (*real name of company withheld*) was launched in 1996 as a discount online brokerage firm, and it quickly gained popularity with its guaranteed one minute execution in 1999. E-Broker One has survived the tight competition among deep discount online brokers. E-Broker One has incorporated new changes into their systems from 2002–2006 which allowed it to offer a system unique to other systems. Over the years, the E-Broker One's system has evolved from a simple transaction processing system to a system that includes several new capabilities.

Order Process Flow

The E-Broker One's system offers three choice of routing orders: (1) INET system, (2) Supermontage, one of NASDAQ's stock market trading systems, and (3) Market Maker, the order gets redirected to a Market Maker handling the particular stock being traded (see Figure 2).

For traders, INET and NASDAQ's Supermontage provide more transparent order routing flows. INET and NASDAQ have their own Web-based system for reflecting orders in real time. So, traders can immediately validate that their orders are posted. Figure 3 shows streaming quotes from

Figure 2. Three order routing for E-Broker One

Figure 3. Java Applet showing real-time buy/ sell orders

INET. The Market Maker route is less transparent because, as most traders know, market makers have notoriety for manipulating trades.

In the E-Broker One trading system, once you choose to place your order in INET e-trading system (an ECN), the INET system has a program, both Java and HTML-based, that will immediately reflect your buy or sell order (see Figure 3).

For traders, it is an instantaneously gratifying experience on their part to see that the order they placed via an online broker's system is reflected immediately in ECNs like INET. The order flow then becomes very transparent and credible.

The transparency of the order flow insures that there is no arbitrage by e-brokers, and that orders are executed directly by the ECNs trading system.

Niche Market

The E-Broker One system has a couple of tools that are not found in any other e-brokerage firms. One of them is a tool called Quotescope. Even if a trader is looking at NASDAQ Level II data, it still takes some time to figure out dynamic moving order volume on the buyer and seller sides. Quotescope provides a more graphic representation of both price and volume. Figure 4 shows

how Quotescope depicts the buying forces on the left side of the pie and the selling forces on the right side of the pie. And traders can also see the prices where most buyers and sellers are putting their trades.

Quotescope is a tool that extracts real-time trading data and converts that data into a real-time graphic representation of the trading volume and price every few seconds. Quotescope is represented by a dynamic pie chart that has two sides. The left side represents the total buyer's volume, while the right side represents the total seller's volume. The volume at each price level is also represented in different colors. It allows traders to make a quick decision to either buy or sell stocks. In Figure 4, the buying and selling pressures are seen as almost equal forces with the left and right sides of the pie almost even. However in Figure 5, the buying force (the left side of the pie) is seen as more powerful than the sell side (the right side of the pie).

Monitoring the buying and selling volume at different price levels in Quotescope is much more simplified with the fast changing graphic format than watching NASDAQ's level II. However, NASDAQ Level II, which E-Broker One also

Figure 4. E-Broker One's Quotescope: a visual representation of volume

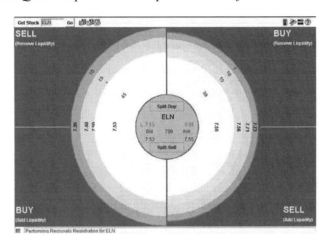

provides, gives traders a sort of microscopic tool to determine the market makers' buying and selling activities. E-Broker One's NASDAQ Level II interface is shown on Figure 6.

For traders, NASDAQ Level II information is important because it lists different market makers who may be scalping for stocks at cheaper prices and selling them a few cents higher. NASDAQ Level II also gives some hint if certain market makers are manipulating prices by dumping a huge amount of share at higher prices, only to buy them back at lower prices. After all, playing the stock market is like a poker game and the more information that is transparent, the better for traders.

Trade Trigger is a feature that E-Broker One introduced in 2004 (Figure 7). This is one of the more advanced automatic programs made available for retail traders. Programmed trading is not new for the professional trader; however E-Broker One has brought it to the mainstream.

E-Broker One's trade trigger can be programmed to buy and sell stocks based on stock or major index movements. For example, if the Dow Jones index loses 50 points, a trader can automatically sell stocks. Or if the NASDAQ falls below the 2000 level, then a sell trigger can be activated. Figure 8 shows the Trade Triggers

Figure 5. Quotescope depicting a bigger left side of the pie due to buying pressure

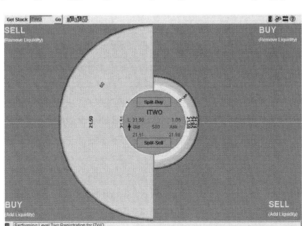

Figure 6. E-Broker One's NASDAQ Level II interface

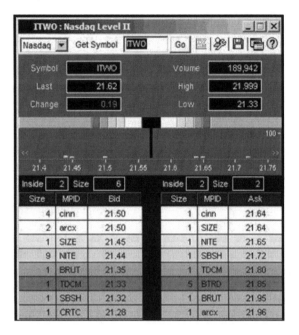

Figure 7. Trade triggers

Figure 8. Trading on the go

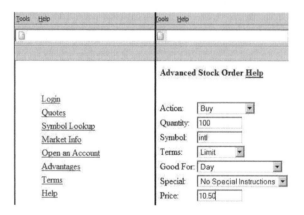

interface of E-Broker One. Not only can a trader set trades based on index movements, but a trader can set trailing stops. Trailing stops are important when a trader wants to trigger a buy or sell order that trails price movements dynamically.

For example, if a trader bought a stock at $7.00 and it is now $7.85. The trader may decide that his target is to sell it at $8.00. However, he is thinking that it may still go up to $8.50. With other online trading systems that only give an option to buy/sell at market or limit price, the trader has no recourse but to set his sell order at $8.00. With trailing stops, the trader can set a trigger to sell at $8.00 or even higher. For example, the stock hits $8.00 but continues to go up to $8.10, $8.20, $8.30, or $8.60. The trader can set a $0.10 trailing stop, so when the stock keeps on going up, the stop sell order also follows it going up. If the stock suddenly goes up from $8.00 to $8.60, the trailing stop follows it $0.10 behind. If the price is at $8.60, the trailing stop should be at $8.50, while at $8.40 the trailing stop is $8.30. Now when the stock does not go up anymore and starts to

fall down from its high of $8.60 to $8.50, the sell order is executed at $8.50. The trailing stop halts when the price movement does not go higher.

Trailing stops also work for buying stocks. If a trader wants to buy a stock at $7.50, the trader can set a trailing stop so that if the stock falls down to $7.00, he could buy it at a lower price. Trailing stops are useful if a trader cannot monitor the trading screen all day.

Although E-Broker One charges $10.99 per trade, free access to Quotescope, NASDAQ Level

II, and Trade Triggers tools actually puts them cheaper than other e-brokers.

Lastly, E-Broker One also caters to traders on the go. They have a WAP-enabled Web site for wireless devices such as Palm Pilots, Blackberries, and mobile phones that have Internet access. The simplified interface for mobile devices is seen in Figure 8.

To summarize the usefulness of these tools:

Quotescope and NASDAQ Level II are excellent tools for daytrading and swing trading because traders can make better decisions with how information is presented to them in real time, thereby enabling them to make quick decisions to sell, hold, or buy.

Trade triggers are good tools for all non-daytraders because it allows investors and traders to automate the trading for them in ways that other online systems do not offer.

E-Broker One seems to have a well-balanced system as it provides diverse tools that cater to the needs of different types of investors and traders.

SEC Ruling

E-Broker One has one of the more comprehensive help information for SEC rules (Figure 9). While its system does not automatically stop traders from violating SEC rules, their information is extensive and well organized regarding the rules.

For new traders who feel that it is too cumbersome to read through voluminous amounts of information in the Help Center, this is still not the best solution for SEC violation avoidance. There are several new traders who fail to study these help files.

A problem with the daytrading rule is that you cannot do more than three roundtrip buy/sell trading in five consecutive moving days. This is the difficult part—tracking five consecutive moving days. So, if you daytraded twice on Thursday and daytraded once on Friday, you cannot daytrade the following Monday, Tuesday, and Wednesday. But suppose that following Monday and Tuesday are holidays, then you cannot daytrade on Wednesday, Thursday, and Friday instead. But how can traders be expected to keep tabs of all the holidays? If the system is not able to track those five consecutive days for you, you can easily forget the holidays in your counting and unintentionally violate SEC rules.

Systems Security and Stability

The streamer of E-Broker One which is Java-based can have difficulties popping up as a separate window in several instances. E-Broker One offers two interfaces for trading. One is in simple HTML format and the other is Java-based. The HTML-based interface is much easier to access and use than the Java applet. Sometimes the Java-based interface takes 15 minutes to open even with a cable modem. However, over the course of three months, E-Broker One has improved the speed of starting the Java applet. Over time, the E-Broker One system was pretty stable.

Figure 9. E-Broker One's comprehensive help center

The Yahoo message boards talked about problems with E-Trade and Scottrade's system but we have not heard about E-Broker One. This confirms our experience that their system was pretty stable at the time we gathered the data.

Technology Bundling

E-Broker One had sophisticated bundling when it came to different software functions and tools. The intelligent trade triggers allowed traders to program their trading based on the movement of the general market like the Dow or NASDAQ. Quotescope provided real time charting of market supply and demand. NASDAQ Level II quote system was also available. These were software functions that other e-brokers did not have. These tools provided good information about the market in real-time. The information goods for investment/trading research were just as about as good as other e-brokers. E-Broker One did not have a fully diversified electronic market network if compared to an interactive broker. It connected to three electronic financial market systems: ARCA-Ex, INET, and Supermontage. E-Broker One could have bundled more market networks, so that traders could get the best execution of buy and sell orders.

Case Two: Interactive Brokers

Interactive Brokers is ranked the 16th largest security firm or among the institutional investor in terms of capital position (2005, Institutional Investor Inc., www.institutionalinvestor.com). Interactive Brokers' consolidated capital of $1.9 billion puts them above other big securities firms such as Jefferies Group, ABN Amro, E-Broker One Holdings, E-Trade Holdings, and Barclays Capital.

Interactive broker claims to have 28 years of experience in creating "direct access trading technology" for professional traders. Interactive Brokers has one of the cheapest commissions at $1 per 100 shares traded or $0.50 per 100 shares if buying more than 500 shares. Interactive Brokers engages not only in stocks and options but also in forex and bonds trading in more than 50 global markets. In 2005, Barron ranked it as "the No. 1 software-based broker."

Order Process Flow

Interactive Brokers can route orders to five different ECNs: ARCA, BRUT, BTRADE, ISLAND, and SUPERSOES. In 2007, they route orders to more ECNs compared to the time data was gathered for this research in 2004–2006. Both BRUT and SUPERSOES are basically NASDAQ systems. The routing also allows you to set the default routing to "SMART." When a trader sets the routing destination to SMART, it means that Interactive Brokers' system will try to find the best price for the buy or sell orders. For example, if the seller wants to sell his/her share at a market price, and ARCA has a buyer at 9.98, ISLAND has another buyer at $9.95, and BRUT has a buyer at $10.00, then the system will route the order to BRUT. That way the seller gets the best price for his/her order. If you are a buyer, then SMART works the opposite way; it will try to find the cheapest seller across the different ECNs and route the order there. (Figure 10)

Niche Market

At first glance, their software application does not appear to be for beginners. While they have an HTML version for trading, their HTML-based interface is not made for advanced trading. To gain the full benefit of their trading system, a trader has to install a Java-based software application called Trader Workstation. The Java-based software is stable and well-protected from security problems related to the Internet, because it uses a different connecting port to pull and push data to the Internet.

Interactive Brokers provides traders a choice of using a single spreadsheet interface that allows

Figure 10. Routing orders to five different ECNs

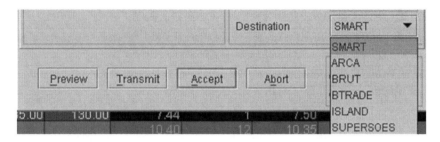

traders to place/cancel orders while watching real-time streaming quotes and some accounting highlights (unrealized gains/loss) all at one glance (Figure 11). The other brokers do not have a one-shop type interface. This is advantageous to traders who need speed, because orders can be executed very fast while monitoring their gains and losses.

For day traders or microsecond traders, Interactive Brokers has an even faster way to executing trades. And that is through a tool called Book Traders (Figure 18). The Book Traders is a tool that could be set to "arm" and the trader is given an array of prices. In Figure 12, the stock AIG is being displayed with different prices from $60.74 to $60.95. The one-click feature allows traders to click either the buy side or the sell side boxes (see marked arrows in Figure 12) and the order goes through with just a single mouse click. Traders need to be really careful with this feature because it is easy to send orders accidentally in one click.

There are advantages of having to be able to access five ECNs all at the same time. In rare occasions, traders can see that the buy (bid) is actually higher than the sell (ask). In one occasion, the researchers saw this discrepancy. To experiment on this, the researchers bought 300 shares of ITWO at $13.20 from the BRUT ECN and then two seconds later sold the 300 for $13.25 at the ISLAND ECN (see Figure 13). The gain was only $15, but it was to prove that some form of pure arbitrage and scalping could be realized if a system can access more ECNs. Many traders only have access to one or two ECNs while Interactive Brokers' can trade across five ECNs.

This shows that electronic market fragmentation has some inefficiency that can be exploited by a system that can network more systems together. It used to be done only by professional traders, but now it could be done by any retail traders.

Like E-Broker One, traders can also access the Interactive Brokers' trading system using their mobile phone or palm pilots (Figure 14).

SEC Ruling

Interactive Brokers has an excellent system that prevents traders from violating SEC regulations. By far, this is one of the best online systems that can warn traders beforehand of possible SEC violations. In Figure 15, the researchers tried to short some STEM stocks. However, because this particular stock was being shorted naked at that time and therefore on the Reg SHO list, it could not be sold short then.

In Figure 16, Interactive Brokers has an accounting window that shows how many trading days you have left on the lower right side. As mentioned earlier, if you have more than $25,000 in your account, daytrading activities are unlimited. However, if you have less than $25,000 in your account, you are only allowed to perform three daytrades within five consecutive days. What is convenient about the Interactive Brokers' system is that if a trader/investor has used up all of his/her daytrading privileges, the system will not allow any more trading to occur. In short, the system actually stops you from breaking SEC rules. No other trading system has this capability. (Figure 17)

Figure 11. Single spreadsheet interface

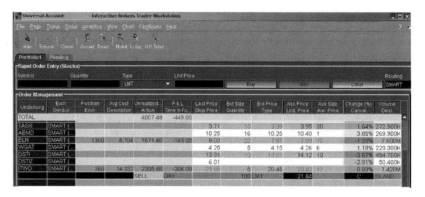

Figure 12. One-click trading

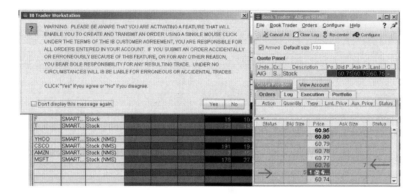

Figure 13. Arbitrage and scalping between two ECNs

Action	Quantity	Underlying	Comb.	Description	Price	Currency	Exch.
BOT	100	ITWO	☐	Stock	13.03	USD	ISLAND
BOT	100	ITWO	☐	Stock	12.76	USD	SUPERSOES
SLD	100	DSTIZ	☐	Stock	6.29	USD	ISLAND
SLD	100	DSTIZ	☐	Stock	6.24	USD	SUPERSOES
SLD	100	DSTIZ	☐	Stock	6.11	USD	SUPERSOES
BOT	300	ITWO	☐	Stock ITWO (NMS)	13.20	USD	BRUT
SLD	300	ITWO	☐	Stock ITWO (NMS)	13.25	USD	ISLAND

Systems Security and Stability

After using Interactive Brokers for a year, there were about five days that the system lost real-time data feed, but not the ability to trade. However, in these instances, they usually rectify the lost data feed within 10 minutes.

There have been instances where data feeds were lost but they informed the traders immediately that it is not their system but data feed coming from the ECNs (or the financial electronic markets). So, Interactive Brokers will actually classify two types of downtime: their own system's downtime and third-party downtime. Their feedback was actually quite informative.

While traders can access the online trading system of E-Broker One on Saturdays and Sunday morning, Interactive Brokers intentionally turns off their system on Saturdays and Sunday morning. They do this because they want a full

Figure 14. Mobile/wireless interface of interactive brokers

maintenance check on all their systems during the weekend. This is a good practice because no one trades on Saturdays and Sunday mornings. Having it available on Sunday afternoon makes

sense because some traders prefer to plan and place their trades before the Monday opening.

Technology Bundling

While Interactive Brokers did not have Quotescope and NASDAQ Level II features bundled like E-Broker One, what was bundled with Interactive Broker was more important. The critical SEC rules and regulations for trading were bundled into their system to make sure that traders/investors do not do something illegal or even become tempted to break SEC rules. For serious matured traders, the way SEC information has been tightly integrated into the system was more important than fancy charts and stock information that can be sourced elsewhere. Interactive Brokers system also had the most extensive electronic market network connections. The comprehensive bundling of

Figure 15. Interactive brokers' system stops naked shorting

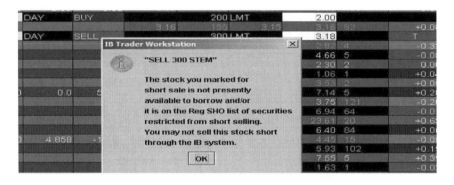

Figure 16. Interactive brokers' system tracks day-trading activity

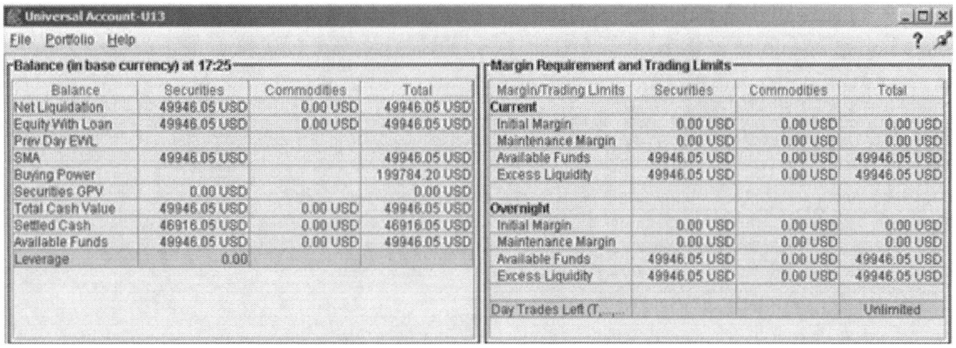

Figure 17. Analytical comparison of online brokers' systems capability

	E-BROKER ONE	INTER. BROKER
ROUTING ORDERS		
Routing Choices	- INET - ARCA - SuperMontage	- INET - ARCA - SuperSoes - BRUT - BTRADE
Automatic Routing For best price	Yes	Yes
Transparency of Order Flow	No	Yes
Routing for Scalping/Daytrading	Good	Best
ADDRESSING NICHE MARKETS		
The Buy and Hold Investors	GOOD	GOOD
Swing Traders	BEST	GOOD
Daytraders	GOOD	BEST
Large & Middle Cap Investors	BEST	GOOD
Small Cap & Penny Traders	GOOD	AVERAGE
Micro-Day Traders	GOOD	BEST
Institutional Traders	AVERAGE	BEST
FOLLOWING SEC REGULATIONS		
Good Warnings on SEC Violation	Average	Very Good
System Force Stops Traders from Violating Daytrader Rule	No	Yes
System Tracks Daytrading Activity Before SEC Violation Occurs	No	Yes
System Stops Traders from Naked Shorting	No	Yes (when stock appears on SHO list)
SYSTEMS STABILITY		
System Down (Cannot Trade)	No	No
Systems Down (Tools and Data Down)	Yes, Java-based tools	Yes, data feed
Internet Intrusion	SSL-Enabled (SAFE)	Non-browser Based (SAFER)

e-market network services provided traders the best execution of trade transactions across the broadest range of financial markets.

COMPARATIVE CASE ANALYSES

After comparing the two online brokerage systems, the observation shows that the different systems cater to very different user and trading needs. In terms of order routing, Interactive Brokers has a better system simply because it covers more ECNs than E-Broker One. This means that traders have a better chance of selling and buying at a better price with more ECNs connected to the Interactive Brokers system. Interactive Brokers also has a smart system that can redirect orders to get the best price for the trader. Once the order is redirected, the order is immediately displayed in the particular ECN the order was sent to, and the Interactive Brokers' system also displays what ECN the order was sent to. E-Broker One also allows traders three choices for routing orders. E-Broker One has an "auto" route that is similar to the "smart" routing; however, once it is set to "auto" routing, traders are left in the dark as to where the order is redirected. Interactive has a more transparent system. Other e-brokers have no routing choice and no transparency at all. The spreadsheet interface of Interactive's system coupled with the various ECN choices also makes it ideal for scalping and daytrading stocks.

In terms of catering to different types of traders, E-Broker One had the best tools for swing traders. The trade triggers are ideal for swing trader because they can help guard traders from short-term losses while maximizing short term gains. The trade triggers can be used to ride the ups and downs of major indices (Dow, NASDAQ, S&P 500, and Russell 2000) and therefore good for swing trading securities that follow the indi-

Figure 18. List of stocks shorted naked, including DSTI

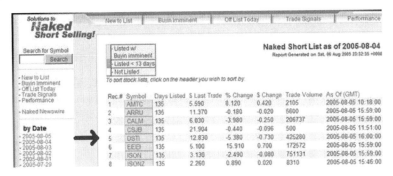

ces movements. Since most of the big cap stocks follow the Dow Jones or NASDAQ indices, the E-Broker One has an excellent programmed trading system for large and mid-cap stocks.

Interactive Brokers' spreadsheet interface that combines real time quotes and one click trading platform is ideal for the speed needed by day traders and micro-day traders that are scalping to make some quick gains. However, at the time of data gathering, Interactive was not fully attuned to penny stocks and small cap stocks that are sold over-the-counter (OTC) or with a pink slip (PK) status. Interactive Brokers did not have full real-time trades for some OTC and PK stocks. Neither is the system useful for trading bankrupt companies that are being restructured (their stock symbol ends with the letter Q).

Interactive Brokers has taken lengths to set up its system for institutional and professional trading. It is only with Interactive Brokers that advisor accounts are available. Advisor accounts are tailor-made for professional traders who manage separate clients' accounts. The clients can electronically transfer money to their accounts but may not do any trading. It is the professional financial advisor that does the trading for clients.

It appears that Interactive Brokers has a system that has broken grounds in areas that other brokers have not. An example of their excellent system is the feature that helps prevent traders from violating SEC regulation. Interactive Brokers' system automatically does not allow traders to daytrade three times in five consecutive days. The system just would not allow a user to buy long or sell short or take any new position once the daytrading requirement hits its limits. Of the two brokerage firms compared here, Interactive Brokers is the one that adheres strictly to the naked shorting rule. As long as a stock is listed on the SHO List (a list that confirms a stock is being naked shorted), Interactive Brokers will not allow that stock to be shorted. Other trading systems did not appear to stop the shorting of a stock on the SHO list. In this particular instance, DSTI (a publicly traded stock) has been heavily shorted naked for almost half a year (see Figure 18). E-Broker One's system tested in this study allowed an order to sell DSTI short without prohibition during that instance (see Figure 19). Very possibly, E-Broker One had their own inventory of DSTI stocks and allowed their inventory to be legally borrowed for short selling. Interactive Brokers' system did not allow short orders to be transmitted if it is listed as a naked short on the SHO list. The reason why naked shorting exists is that brokers and e-trading systems may allow such transaction depending on their rules and situation. As of this writing, there is still a big debate about how SEC needs to tighten controls for naked shorting, because it is common knowledge that brokerage companies allow it based on their own rules and based on their willingness to pay SEC fines.

E-Broker One and Interactive Brokers had some occasional problem with their real-time feed,

Figure 19. Naked shorting allowed by an online trading system

but on the positive side their system still had basic trading functions that allowed buying and selling of stocks. Other e-trading systems (not covered in this chapter) had worst systems downtime and had lost trading functionalities. During the times when E-Broker One and Interactive Brokers had no real-time data feeds, the alternative was to go directly to INET or ARCA's websites to get real-time buy/sell order data.

The Web-based applications of E-Broker One use the socket layer (SSL), which is what most online banks use. So it is generally safe. Interactive Brokers' software is not dependent on a Web browser so it is least susceptible to browser attacks. The researchers noticed that Trade Workstation, Interactive's software, also uses a different port to connect to the Internet, or a different channel from what is used by Internet browsers. It is, therefore, less likely to be attacked or hacked.

After looking at the two online brokers, Interactive Brokers and E-Broker One provided excellent bundling of software and information goods (see Figure 20). Interactive Broker came out on top in terms of being able to bundle their transaction system for multiple access to a broad range of electronic financial markets.

The E-Broker One trading interface was very richly bundled with NASDAQ Level II access, Trade Triggers, Quotescope, and streaming news. However, E-Broker One's rich interface also slowed down the system. Interactive Brokers' interface was noticeably much faster than all of the systems under study. Interactive Brokers' interface was bundled with different features for options trading, real-time accounting, keeping track of SEC regulations, charting, and one-click trading.

CHALLENGES FACING THE ONLINE BROKERAGE SECTOR

One of the challenges that plague the entire online brokerage sector is the service of delivering real-time financial data electronically. Even though

e-trading systems are working properly for buy/sell transactions, the glitch is that various financial electronic market systems occasionally have difficulties transmitting real-time financial data (such as real-time stock price quotes) to various e-trading systems run by different online brokers. During those occasions, clients of online brokers will not get real-time data service, and they will perceive their broker's system as "unstable" and "unreliable" without access to real-time data. Investors and traders find it difficult making decisions on whether they should buy or sell stocks without real-time data. This bundled e-service is normally not within the control of e-brokers, because e-brokers also subscribe to real-time data from the data service providers managing the financial e-markets. If real-time data is not transmitted or available, a good customer service that e-brokers can do for their clients is to honestly inform them in a timely manner that they are not getting real-time data feeds from financial

Figure 20. Rating the value of e-services by the information and capabilities being bundled into different online trading systems

Bundling of E-Services	E-Broker One	Interactive Broker
Software Functions Bundled	*Excellent* (Very Advance Trade Triggers, Quotescope, Streaming Quotes Interface, NASDAQ level II Interface, Charting)	*Excellent* (Some Intelligent Trade Triggers, Charting, Very Fast Streaming Quote Spreadsheet Interface, One-Click Trading Interface; Options Analysis Tools)
Information Goods Bundled	*Excellent* (NASDAQ Level II data, Financial data, Real-time Streaming News, Company Research)	*Excellent* (Multiple-Source Financial Data, SEC Policies Embedded in System, Real-Time Accounting)
E-Market Network Services Bundled	**Good** INET ARCA SuperMontage	*Excellent* INET ARCA SuperSoes BRUT BTRADE

e-market(s). At times, there may be compatibility problems between the e-broker's system and the data providers' system used by financial e-markets. In such cases, e-brokers must resolve any incompatibility problems that prohibit their systems from accepting data feeds from electronic markets. Technological compatibility problems need to be resolved quickly. E-brokers who are able to act fast in resolving these issues will be more successful in satisfying the needs of their clients.

While it seems that each of the online brokerage firm covered in this comparative case study have addressed the diverse needs of online traders through their innovations, the rules and regulations of the financial market can change very quickly. Challenges in the financial market sector continue to push online brokerage firms to upgrade and refine their systems. The Securities and Exchange Commission can drastically change the rules and regulations as the governing regulatory body of the U.S. financial markets, and the U.S. financial market heavily affects the global financial markets. Different markets around the world also have their own rules and regulations, which are not covered in this chapter. Any changes in the rules and regulations of different countries will have an immediate impact on global financial markets. The financial markets in China, for example, are starting to have extensive impact on global financial markets. So if China decides to make regulatory changes to their financial markets, it can have a substantial impact on other financial markets.

The way different financial electronic markets network themselves can continually alter the way stocks, options, and bonds are being bought and sold (the order process flow). As users of different online trading system advance their trading knowledge and skills, they also demand more information, better user-interface, and more intelligence in the trading system. The only way for online brokerage firms to address these challenges is for them to have a rapid application development plan and change processes that will allow them to constantly add new features or subtract outdated ones in their trading systems and bundled e-services. They must continue to look for ways to make their trading system more intelligent in handing trading rules and regulations, forwarding, and receiving orders from different financial electronic markets, and also in giving traders the analytical tools and interface to help them make better trades. The online brokers that can best address these constant changes will be the ones that will survive in this highly competitive e-service sector.

REFERENCES

Associated Press. (2006). SEC approves NYSE, Archipelago Merger. *USA Today.* Retrieved June 5, 2008, from www.usatoday.com/money/markets/us/2006-02-28-nyse-archipelago-ap_x.htm

Bakos, Y. (1991). A strategic analysis of electronic marketplaces. *MIS Quarterly*, *15*(3), 295–310. doi:10.2307/249641

Bakos, Y. (1998). The emerging role of electronic marketplaces on the Internet. *Communications of the ACM*, *41*(8), 35–42. doi:10.1145/280324.280330

Bakos, Y., & Brynjolfsson, E. (2000). Aggregation and disaggregation of information goods: Implications for bundling, site licensing, and micropayment systems. In D. Hurley, B. Kahin, & H. Varian (Ed.), Proceedings of Internet Publishing and Beyond: The Economics of Digital Information and Intellectual Property. Cambridge, MA: MIT Press.

Barber, B. M., & Odean, T. (2001). The Internet and the investor. *The Journal of Economic Perspectives*, *15*(1), 41–54.

Barber, B. M., & Odean, T. (2002). Online investors: Do the slow die first? [Special Issue: Conference on Market Frictions and Behavioral Finance]. *Review of Financial Studies*, *15*(2), 455–487. doi:10.1093/rfs/15.2.455

Battalio, R., Greene, J., Hatch, B., & Jennings, R. (2002). Does the limit order routing decision matter? *Review of Financial Studies*, *15*(1), 159–194. doi:10.1093/rfs/15.1.159

Battalio, R., Greene, J., & Jennings, R. (1997). Do competing specialists and preferencing dealers affect market quality? *Review of Financial Studies*, *10*(4), 969–993. doi:10.1093/rfs/10.4.969

Borrus, A., McNamee, G., Carter, B., & Adrienne, M. (2005, November 24). Invasion of the stock hackers. *Business Week*, •••, 38.

Cadway, R. P. (2001). *New daytrading rules.* Retrieved June 5, 2008, from http://www.princetondaytrading.com/newsletter-princeton/NL-9-31-2001.html

Carey, T. W. (2006, July 3). Tears at Waterhouse. *Barron's National Business and Financial Weekly*, •••, 32.

Ceron, G. F. (2006, August 28). Moving the market: Big board sets expansion in electronic trading: "Hybrid market" to remove volume limits, posing risk for specialists and brokers. *Wall Street Journal*, p. C3.

Ciborra, C. (1993). Teams, markets and systems. Cambridge, England: Cambridge University Press.

Craig, S., & Kelly, K. (2001, November 30). Deals & deal makers: Investors can obtain report card on the execution of stock trades. *Wall Street Journal*, p. C12.

Finance and economics: Moving markets; technology and exchanges. (2006, February 4). *The Economist*, p. 73.

Globerman, S., Roehl, T. W., & Standifird, S. (2001). Globalization and electronic commerce: Inferences from retail brokerage. *Journal of International Business Studies*, *32*(4), 749–768. doi:10.1057/palgrave.jibs.8490993

Hansen, J. V., & Hill, N. C. (1989). Control and audit of electronic data interchange. *MIS Quarterly*, *13*(4), 403–413. doi:10.2307/248724

Island ECN surpasses American Stock Exchange to become largest marketplace in QQQs. (2001, October 22). *Business Wire.*

Kandel, E., & Marx, L. M. (1999). Payments for order flow on Nasdaq. *The Journal of Finance*, *54*(1), 35–66. doi:10.1111/0022-1082.00098

Kim, J. J. (2006, July 11). Online stock trades get even cheaper; Heightened competition among brokerage, banks drives fees as low as $1 per transaction. *Wall Street Journal*, p. D1.

Kim, J. J. (2006, July 19). Trading tools to get a boost. *Wall Street Journal*, p. D2.

Macey, J., & O'Hara, M. (1997). The law and economics of best execution. *Journal of Financial Intermediation*, *6*, 188–223. doi:10.1006/jfin.1997.0219

Malone, T. W., Yates, J., & Benjamin, R. I. (1987). Electronic markets and electronic hierarchies. *Communications of the ACM*, *30*, 484–497. doi:10.1145/214762.214766

Moregenson, G. (1999, November 23). Regulators see need for rules of the road for online trading firms. *New York Times*, p. C1.

Roberts, Pittman, & Reeds (2000). Retrieved June 5, 2008, from www.realcorporatelawyers.com

Ryan, J. (2005). *NASDAQ to Acquire Instinet.* Retrieved June 5, 2008, from www.nasdaq.com/newsroom/news/pr2005/ne_section05_044.stm

Stoll, H. R. (2006). Electronic trading in stock markets. *The Journal of Economic Perspectives, 20*(1), 153–174. doi:10.1257/089533006776526067

Tabb, L. (2004). Perspective: Time for brokers, investors, and regulators to align. Wall Street and Technology. InformationWeek Media Network.

Venkataraman, K. (2001). Automated verses floor trading: An analysis of execution costs on the Paris and New York Exchanges. *Journal of Finance, 56*(4), 1445–1485. New Orleans, LA: Papers and Proceedings of the 61st Annual Meeting of the American Finance Association.

Yap, A., & Lin, X. (2001). Entering the arena of Wall Street wizards, euro-brokers, and cyber-trading samurais: A strategic imperative for online stock trading. *Electronics Market Journal, 11*(3). Related WebSites http://www.buyins.net/ http://www.dogsofthedow.com http://www.tdameri-trade.com http://www.interactivebrokers.com

Chapter 4.8
E–Banking Diffusion in the Jordanian Banking Services Sector:
An Empirical Analysis of Key Factors

Ali Alawneh
Arab Academy for Banking and Financial Sciences, Jordany

Ezz Hattab
Arab Academy for Banking and Financial Sciences, Jordan

ABSTRACT

Grounded in the technology–organization–environment (TOE) framework, we have developed an extended model to examine factors, particularly technological, organizational and environmental factors, which influence e-banking adoption in Jordanian banks. This article added some constructs to (TOE) framework, other factors were excluded. The independent variables are the (technology readiness or competence, bank size, financial resources commitment, IT/Business strategy alignment, adequacy of IT professionals, availability of online revenues, competition intensity or pressure, and regulatory support environment) while e-banking usage constitutes the dependent variable. Our empirical analysis demonstrates several key findings related to the technological, organizational, and environmental aspects of the banks. This article can help further understanding of their role in the adoption of e-banking and examines the impacts of e-banking usage on banks' performance in terms of sales-services-marketing, internal operations and co-ordination & communication. This could enable greater e-banking usage that could improve the overall economy.

INTRODUCTION

The banking and other financial services sector is one of the most advanced in the usage and diffusion of technologies. Being essentially information business, they do not produce physical products and have been trading electronically for decades.

For these reasons hardly any other sector is better suited for e-business which, in fact, is progressing very quickly. ICT impacts on all aspects of the activity and is undoubtedly one of the main driving forces in the sector.

The financial services industry differs in important ways from industries such as manufacturing or retailing, and its use of IT and e-business technologies reflect those differences (Olazabal, 2002). Financial institutions are linked to customers and each other in an extensive network of interrelationships that is more complex, reciprocal, and less linear than traditional manufacturing and retailing industries (Mulligan and Gordon, 2002). There is a primary market in which customers interact with financial institutions such as retail banks, insurance agencies, real estate agencies and stock brokers. There is also a larger secondary market in which those institutions interact with each other and with others such as mortgage brokers, commercial banks, insurance companies, and investment bankers (Hess and Kemerer, 1994). Financial services, which are both immaterial and relatively standardized, and have hence already been widely affected by information technology innovations (Buzzacchi, and Mariotti, 1995), would therefore be one of the first arenas where that "new information economy" would arise (Dewan, Freimer and Seidmann, 2000).

The nature of IT in this industry is complex and heterogeneous. On the front end, IT is used to execute and record customer transactions, whether they are handled in person, by phone, by electronic funds transfer, or on the Internet. On the back end, funds are transferred among institutions via electronic transfer systems, such as Fedwire, CHIPS, and Swift, which handle hundreds of trillions of dollars in transactions yearly. Financial EDI systems are used to support information flows among institutions. Internal IT systems include a mix of packaged and custom applications that maintain account records and support internal financial and managerial functions.

E-business technologies have the potential to add significant value in all of these areas. Most striking is the potential for Web-based applications to improve customer service. Loan applications and insurance forms can be filled out, stock trades initiated, bills paid, and funds transferred online with no human interaction required. Research tools such as mortgage calculators or retirement planning applications can be made available, and account information can be accessed online. On the back end, applications based on common Internet standards can enable data sharing across firms in an industry marked by limited standardization of IT systems. Internally, e-business applications can likewise improve integration of various proprietary systems to move toward "straight-through processing," improving the links between decision (swap, credit extension, trade) and execution (funds transfer, account updates, settlement finality).

There is substantial evidence to suggest that e-banking is being embraced by financial institutions in developed and emerging markets to the extent that explosive growth is almost at hand. There are two different strategies for Internet banking. First, an existing bank with physical offices can establish a web site and offer Internet banking to its customer as an additional delivery channel. A second alternative is to establish an Internet-only bank or virtual bank, almost without physical offices. Recent years have seen the industry rapidly moving towards a "click and bricks" strategy that emphasizes an online supplement to the conventional banking services. Banking institutions are using their web sites not only to provide classical operations such as fund transfer or accounts information, but also to provide stock trading, bill payments, credit card request and investment advice.

Electronic banking (e-banking) covers various operations that can be conducted from home, business or on the road instead of at a physical bank location (Turban et al., 2003). These operations include: retrieving account balances and history of accounts, fund transfers, check-book request, opposition to check and credit card payments. Some banks also offer other services such as security trading, bill payments, etc.

Internet E-banking technology represents a variety of different services, ranging from common automatic teller machine (ATM) services and direct deposit to automatic bill payment (ABP), electronic transfer of funds (EFT), and computer banking (PC banking) (Kolodinsky et al., 2004).

The common motivation for banks to implement e-business is to provide a faster, easier, and more reliable service to clients, to improve the bank's competitive position and image, and to meet clients' demands. E-business may also provide other benefits. For instance, creating new markets, and reducing operational costs, administrative costs, and workforce are increasingly important aspects for the banks' competitiveness, and e-business may improve these aspects as well.

Banks were highly focused on e-business over the last seven years and that is expected to continue in order to achieve varieties of outcomes such as: creating consumer-centric culture and organization, securing customer relationships, maximizing customer profitability, and aligning effort and resource behind most valuable customer groups.

The value of e-banking has become widely recognized, accepted and offered many benefits to banks as well as to customers. Organizations invest in information systems for many reasons, for example cutting costs, producing more without increasing costs, improving the quality of services or products (Lederer et al., 1998).

Jordanian banks have invested heavily to leverage the Internet and transform their traditional businesses into e-businesses in the last ten years (e.g., Arab Bank is the first bank to launch Internet banking service, this service started in Jordan in May 2000). Jordanian banks like their international counterparts have increasingly resorted to e-business to capitalize on the opportunities of business efficiencies. These banks adopted the B2C e-business model to increase market share, to offer better customer service and to reach out to customers at greater geographic distances.

An enhanced extended model based on assumptions of the TOE framework has been developed, and the role and function of each factor in the framework explored. It is expected that the extended model will provide a deeper insight into banks e-banking usage. Then, we will test that model using survey data from banks in the banking services industry in Jordan that had already adopted e-business, i.e., clicks-and-mortars banks which have supplemented their existing business using the Internet in their operations. We chose the above mentioned industry because it was one of the first movers to adopt Internet technologies and to innovate with e-business applications. Data analysis will be performed to determine the role and influence of factors on e-banking deployment and on bank performance.

Our empirical survey was carried out in an interesting and homogenous market, the Jordanian Banking services industry sector. Jordan is one of the regionally leading countries regarding the national IT infrastructure available for online services. Also, the population's motivation and ability to conduct online transactions are one of the highest regionally.

RELATED WORKS

A summary of some of the literature related to technological innovation adoption is given below. Zhu and Kraemer (2005) developed theoretically and evaluated empirically an integrative research model incorporating technological, organizational, and environmental factors for assessing e-business use and value at the firm level based on which a series of hypotheses are developed. The theoretical model is tested by using structural equation modeling (SEM) on a dataset of 624 firms across 10 countries in the retail industry. For e-business use, their study has examined six factors, within the TOE framework, as drivers of e-business use. The study found that technology competence, firm size, financial commitment, competitive pressure, and regulatory support are important antecedents of e-business use.

Zhu et al., (2003) Based on TOE framework they examined the factors: Technology competence , Organizational factors (firm scope, size) and Environmental context (consumer readiness, trading partner readiness, competitive pressure) for studying E-business adoption by European firms using a survey on a sample size of 3100 firms.

Kuan and Chau (2001) confirmed the usefulness of the TOE framework for studying adoption of complex IS innovations. Based on TOE framework they examined the factors: Technological context (perceived direct benefits), Organizational context (perceived financial cost, technical competence) and Environmental context (perceived industry pressure/government pressure) for studying EDI innovation using a survey on a sample size of 575 firms.

Ramamurthy et al. (1999) posited the impact of EDI on firm performance as the consequence of technological, organizational, and environmental factors. Based on TOE framework they examined the factors: Organizational factor (management support, expected benefits, resource intensity, compatibility, costs) and Interorganizational factor (competitive pressure, customer support) for studying EDI innovation using a survey on a sample size of 181 firms. Their empirical results indicated that the impact of EDI on operational and market-oriented performance was significantly affected by these factors.

Thong (1999), based on the TOE framework examined the factors: CEO characteristics (CEO's innovativeness and IS knowledge), IS characteristics (relative advantage/compatibility, complexity), Organizational characteristics (business size, employees IS knowledge) and Environmental characteristics, for studying and developing an integrated model of information systems adoption in small business using a survey on a sample size of 168 firms.

Chau and Tam (1997), based on the TOE framework examined the factors: Characteristics of the innovation (perceived barriers, importance of compliance) Organizational technology (satisfaction with existing systems) and External environment, for studying adoption of open systems using a survey on a sample size of 89 firms.

Damanpour (1996), based on the TOE framework e examined the factors: Organizational complexity (organization size, horizontal complexity) and Contingency factors (environment uncertainty), for studying Organizational complexity and innovation using meta-analysis methodology on various innovations.

Iacovou et al. (1995) developed a model formulating three aspects of Electronic Data Interchange (EDI) adoption—technological factors (perceived benefits), organizational factors (organizational readiness), and environmental factors (Interorganizational context and external pressure)—as the main drivers for EDI adoption, and examined the model using seven case studies. Iacovou et al., using the technology-organization-environment (TOE) framework, found that the impact of EDI on performance was directly affected by its level of integration with other IS and processes. Their model was further tested by other researchers using larger samples.

Grover (1993), based on the TOE framework examined the factors: Organizational factors (IS-related factors, firm size) Environmental factors (market assessment, competitive need) Interorganizational (IOS) factors (compatibility, complexity) and Support factors (top management support) for studying EDI innovation using a survey on a sample size of 226 firms.

Our review indicates that the existing literature is mainly focused on technology adoption. Only a few studies have been done to directly examine how TOE factors affect the impact of technology innovation adoption and usage on performance. Given the relative paucity of research linking TOE factors to performance, we have developed a research model to examine the factors that may affect e-banking adoption, usage and impacts at the bank level.

AIMS AND MOTIVATION FOR THE RESEARCH

In essence, technological innovation diffusion and adoption rests on the three main contexts that surrounded any firm: the technological context, organizational context and environmental context. These are recognized as the source of adoption of any technological innovation. Consideration of each of these various contexts and the relationships between them is necessary for a comprehensive understanding of e-banking deployment in banks.

Why some banks adopted and conducted e-banking in doing their financial transactions whereas others didn't is the problem that motivated this study, and because the lack of empirical examination of e-banking adoption in the Jordanian banking sector is another motivation of this study. In that context, the aim of this study is to contribute to a better understanding of e-banking usage and its application to the sector of financial services to commercial banks in Jordan.

From both research and applied perspectives there are few studies published on this topic. There is a need to combine and concentrate the efforts of academic researchers in a holistic approach to e-banking technology deployment. There is a limited understanding of what are the key factors that affect e-banking adoption in banks and there is currently no tested framework that unifies all relevant factors in an easy to understand and practical way. As such, one of the principal goals of this study is to develop an enhanced framework, which can explain e-banking technology adoption in banks. Such a framework would benefit research in e-business-e-banking and also help to eliminate confusion as to where a bank should focus its efforts, strategies and investments for optimum organizational performance.

There is a lack of substantial empirical studies in e-banking adoption and deployment, as the majority of studies reported in the literature still rely heavily on case studies and anecdotes, with few empirical data to measure Internet-based initiatives or gauge the scale of their impact on bank performance, partly because of the difficulty of developing measures and collecting data. A more fundamental issue is the lack of theory to guide the empirical work. So far, the literature has been weak in making the linkage between theory and measures. Hence, there is a need for theoretical development.

DATA COLLECTION

In order to get insights into e-banking diffusion across banks, a survey was conducted in Jordan in 2008. A questionnaire was designed to collect empirical data of current technological, organizational and environmental elements of the bank. These three aspects of the bank will drive and enact the banks to transform into the online business world, i.e., to be e-banks. Eligible respondents were the individuals in each bank best qualified to speak about the bank's overall e-business or e-banking activities. The respondent profile considered ideal for this study includes executives (CIOs, CTOs, CEOs) as well as top and middle managers (IS/IT managers, directors, planners, e-business managers, e-bankers, ...etc. These respondents are supporting and make use of e-business and e-banking in supporting their bank's online activities.

We gathered detailed data on our sample banks mainly from publicly available sources: annual reports, interviews, and banks' web sites. A structured questionnaire was used to collect information about: (a) the employees (e.g., gender, age, experience, position, and scientific degree); (b) the bank (e.g., size, revenues, and years of experience on the web); (c) potential factors of e-banking adoption (e.g., technological, organizational, and environmental); (d) impacts of e-banking adoption on performance (e.g., impacts on sales-services-marketing, internal operations, and coordination and communication). Most of the approximately 66 questions enumerated in the questionnaire were close-ended, which was consistent with our primary objective of developing a conceptual framework that was informed by empirical evidence.

The questionnaire was sent to 200 employees in seven Jordanian banks. 35 were undelivered because employees were no longer at their positions, and an additional 25 cased had many missing response items. 140 questionnaires were returned in a form eligible for analysis with an overall response rate of 70%. This is regarded as relatively high.

E-BANKING IN THE JORDANIAN BANKING SERVICES SECTOR

Traditional branch-based retail banking remains the most widespread method for conducting banking transactions in Jordan as well as any other country. However, Internet technology is rapidly changing the way personal financial services are being designed and delivered. For several years, commercial banks in Jordan have tried to introduce electronic banking (e-banking) systems to improve their operations and to reduce costs. Despite all their efforts aimed at developing better and easier e-banking systems, these systems remained largely unnoticed by the customers, and certainly were seriously underused in spite of their availability.

In this Internet age when the customer has access to a variety of products and services, it is becoming very difficult for banks to survive. In this situation, when customer inquiries are not met easily or transactions are complicated, the customer will asks for new levels services, and only chose those institutions who are making

a real effort to provide a high level of quality, fast and efficient service through all the bank's touch points, call centers, ATMs, voice response systems, Internet and branches.

The financial sector in Jordan has witnessed media blitzes announcing electronic banking. Banks that have implemented e-banking are showing up as being modernized; some of those that have not are drastically trying to catch up.

The financial sector in Jordan is composed of the Central Bank of Jordan (CBJ), 27 commercial and/or investment banks, 27 insurance companies, 8 special credit institutions, the Social Security Corporation, a number of provident funds, and foreign exchange bureaus. It is considered as one of the better financial sectors in the region and generates in total close to 5% of the GDP (Gross Domestic Product). One of the weakest points in the financial sector is, with the exception of mortgage lending, the lack of long-term lending and the absence of secured loans.

It is worth mentioning that the percentage of Jordanian households who own a personal computer is 15.9%, Internet access 6%, 1,000,000 regular telephone lines, around a 1.6 million mobile telephony subscribers, 21 licensed Internet service providers, more than 500,000 Internet users and close to 250 Internet cafes in the year 2004. However Jordan is in the Guinness Book of World Records as the highest per capita in Internet cafes, and the number of Internet cafes located in the city of Irbid is ranked number one in the world, with regard to so many Internet cafes located in a small region. It is worth mentioning that the number of Internet users in the world will reach three billion in year 2010.

The banking sector is very dynamic and liberal in Jordan. Moreover, some of the commercial banks in Jordan are offering electronic services. Samples of these services are:

1. Internet banking: Arab Bank is the first bank to launch Internet banking service. This service started in Jordan in May 2000.

2. Internet Shopping Card (ISC) provides convenient and easy access to on-line shopping transactions with small limits and can be used at any website that displays the Visa logo.

3. WAP banking: customers can use WAP mobile phone and access their accounts.

4. SMS banking: customers can use a mobile and access their accounts.

5. On-line stock trading: Jordan Kuwait Bank (JKB) offers this service in collaboration with its affiliate United Financial Investment Co. (UFICO). The service allows JKB customers to trade in Amman Bourse through UFICO's website and settle the value of shares traded through JKB's Internet banking service (Net banker) directly from their accounts with the bank.

6. Mobile Banking: this service allows the customers to perform banking transactions by using a mobile.

7. Cyber branch: Jordan Kuwait Bank (JKB) opened its first Cyber branch in May 2001 in the Sweifiyyah area. It is a comprehensive electronic bank providing banking services directly to the clients on a 24 hours basis.

8. Pre-paid mobile cards: customers can buy the mobile prepaid cards electronically.

THE TECHNOLOGY - ORGANIZATION - ENVIRONMENT (TOE) FRAMEWORK

To gain a comprehensive view on what factors may affect the deployment of e-banking, we adopt the TOE framework developed by Tornatzky and Fleischer (1990). A theoretical model for e-business use needs to take into account factors that affect the propensity to use e-business, which is rooted in the specific technological, organizational, and environmental circumstances of an organization. Reviewing the literature suggests that the TOE framework (Tornatzky and Fleischer 1990) may

provide a useful starting point for looking at e-business use. The TOE framework identifies three aspects of a firm's context that influence the process by which it adopts and implements a technological innovation: technological context, organizational context, and environmental context. Technological context describes both the internal and external technologies relevant to the firm. These include existing technologies inside the firm, as well as the pool of available technologies in the market. Organizational context is defined in terms of several descriptive measures: firm size and scope; the centralization, formalization, and complexity of its managerial structure; the quality of its human resources; and the amount of slack resources available internally. Environmental context is the arena in which a firm conducts its business—its industry, competitors, access to resources supplied by others, and dealings with government Tornatzky and Fleischer, 1990). These three groups of contextual factors influence a firm's intent to adopt an innovation, and affect the assimilation process and eventually the impacts of the innovation on organizational performance.

This framework is consistent with the innovation diffusion theory of Rogers (1983, pp. 376–383), in which he emphasized technological characteristics, and both the internal and external characteristics of the organization, as drivers for technology diffusion.

Based on our literature review of Zhu et al. (2003, 2004) we found that the TOE framework has consistent empirical support in various IS domains, such as electronic data interchange (EDI), open systems, and material requirement planning (e.g., Iacovou et al. 1995, Chau and Tam 1997, Thong 1999). As a generic theory of technology diffusion, the TOE framework can be used for studying different types of innovations. According to the typology proposed by Swanson (1994), there are three types of innovations: Type I innovations are technical innovations restricted to the IS functional tasks (such as relational databases, CASE); Type II innovations apply IS to support administrative tasks of the business (such as financial, accounting, and payroll systems); and Type III innovations integrate IS with the core business where the whole business is potentially affected and the innovation may have strategic relevance to the firm. We consider e-business a Type III innovation, in the sense that e-business is often embedded in a firm's core business processes (e.g., making use of the open standard of the Internet protocol to streamline information sharing among various functional departments); e-business can extend basic business products and services (e.g., leveraging Internet-enabled two way connectivity to offer real-time customer service); and e-business can streamline the integration with suppliers and customers (e.g., using XML-based communication to increase the capability of exchanging data on product demand and inventory availability throughout the supply chain).

Prior IS research has sought to study Type I and Type II innovations, but relatively limited attention had been devoted to Type III innovations (Swanson 1994) until the recent studies of EDI and enterprise resource planning (ERP) systems (Iacouvou et al. 1995, Hart and Saunders 1998). E-business is a new Type III innovation and warrants investigation along with these innovations (Straub et al. 2002, Zhu 2004b). In particular, the migration toward the Internet and the transformation of traditional processes require firms and their subunits to orchestrate the co-evolutionary changes to their technologies in use, business processes, and value chain structures to successfully assimilate Internet technologies into their e-business initiatives (Chatterjee et al. 2002).

The TOE framework has been examined by a number of empirical studies in various information systems domains. In particular, electronic data interchange (EDI), an antecedent of Internet-based e-business, has been studied extensively in the past decade. Iacovou et al. (1995) developed a model formulating three aspects of EDI adoption— technological factors, organizational

factors, and environmental factors—as the main drivers for EDI adoption, and examined the model using seven case studies. Their model was further tested by other researchers using larger samples. For example, Kuan and Chau (2001) confirmed the usefulness of the TOE framework for studying adoption of complex IS innovations.

Drawing on the empirical evidence combined with literature review and theoretical perspectives discussed above, we believe that the TOE framework is appropriate for studying e-business usage. Based on the TOE framework, the use of e-business in organizations will be influenced by three types of antecedents: technological factors, organizational factors, and environmental factors (Zhu et al., 2004). One might ask why we need to develop a theoretical model for e-business, given that there are already several studies on EDI adoption. To answer this question, we need to articulate how e-business differs from EDI (or other previous Type III innovations) and explain the theoretical necessity of extending TOE to e-business.

While EDI has some features in common with e-business, it also exhibits significant differences, as EDI is typically a more expensive, proprietary technology operating over a private network controlled by one large manufacturer or supplier. In comparison, e-business is based on the open standard protocol of the Internet. It is more tightly integrated to the value chain at both the front end (sales, customer services) and the back end (coordination, procurement), while EDI is more focused on the back end (invoice exchange, order documents, and inventory management), which is why it is popular in the manufacturing industry (Chau and Tam 1997).

More broadly, the economic characteristics of the Internet are quite different from those of pre-Internet Type III innovations (Zhu 2004). The Internet is characterized by open standard (versus proprietary standard), public network (versus private network), and broad connectivity (back end and front end) (Bakos 1998, Shapiro and Varian 1999). These characteristics may have very different impacts on customer reach and richness of information (Zhu 2004). The global reach of the Internet enables cost-efficient means of reaching out to new markets, attracting new customers, and delivering products and services, as well as improving coordination with suppliers and business partners (Zhu and Kraemer 2002). On the other hand, the open connectivity of the Internet also brings unique issues such as security, privacy, and legal protection of online transactions (Zhu et al. 2004). These issues are particularly important to the banking industry, as they deal with consumers who are especially sensitive to them.

These unique characteristics of e-business imply different antecedents and consequences of its organizational use. For example, while both EDI and e-business may be affected by the technological competence of the user organization, e-business is also influenced by particular organizational factors (such as international scope), environmental factors (such as legal protection of online transactions over the Internet), and website functionalities to serve consumers (while EDI typically does not offer public access). In terms of decision-making processes, EDI use is influenced by a large and powerful company that often requires its suppliers or partners to use EDI (Hart and Saunders 1998). Yet e-business use is more decentralized and is often driven by balanced considerations regarding the organization's technological competence, structural factors (such as size, scope, and resources), and environmental factors related to competition and regulation (Zhu et al. 2003). Combining these factors, we can see that there are significant additional considerations beyond those addressed in the EDI literature. Plus, the EDI literature focuses more on adoption (or intent to adopt) and less on actual use (Iacovou et al. 1995). Thus, we still need a theoretical model for e-business use and value.

Although specific factors identified within the three contexts may vary across different studies, the TOE framework has consistent empirical support. Drawing upon the empirical evidence combined with the literature review, we believe that the TOE framework is an appropriate theoretical foundation for studying e-banking adoption.

THE RESEARCH MODEL AND HYPOTHESES

The proposed outline for the extended framework that will be developed and tested in this research is seen in Figure 1. It depicts the main statement of the problem. An important aspect of the problem is whether e-banking technology is deployed if the bank uses adequately the factors of e-banking technology adoption.

By extending the TOE framework, we developed a conceptual model to assess the adoption and use of e-banking by banks. We present the model first in Figure 1, followed by explanations of the key elements of the model and postulated relationships.

E-banking use is defined as the extent to which e-business and e-banking are being used to conduct value chain activities in the banks. This is measured by the breadth of use for different value chain activities and the depth of use (percentage) for each activity that has been migrated to the Internet platform.

The right-hand side of the conceptual model shows how the use of e-banking impacts bank performance. We posit that e-banking leverages the unique characteristics of the Internet to improve business performance of banks, through betterment of sales-services-marketing, internal operations, and coordination and communication.

The left-hand side of the conceptual model shows the antecedents of e-banking usage. As discussed earlier the extent of e-business use by an organization would be influenced by its technological, organizational, and environmental contexts within the TOE framework (Zhu et al. 2004). Among the wide range of factors that we found from an extensive literature review on previous studies of IT and technological innovation

Figure 1. An extended framework for e-banking diffusion (by researchers)

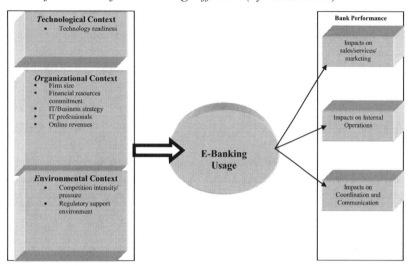

adoption and use, this study focused on technology readiness, firm size, financial resources commitment, competition pressure, and regulatory environment, which were the most commonly studied antecedents in previous literature. Further, we added three factors: IT/Business strategy alignment, adequacy of IT professionals and availability of online revenues, that we consider to be particularly relevant to Internet-based e-banking.

Based on the TOE framework, we developed the following eight hypotheses, corresponding to the eight factors in Figure 1 within the technological, organizational, and environmental contexts of the TOE framework.

Technology Context. The literature suggests that technological capabilities consist of infrastructure, human resources, and knowledge (Bharadwaj, 2000). Consistent with prior studies, technology readiness in this study consists of technology infrastructure and IT human resources, where technology infrastructure refers to technologies that enable Internet-related businesses (e.g., EDI, EFT, intranet and extranet), and IT human resources refer to IT professionals possessing the knowledge and skills to implement Internet-related applications.

Organization Context. Firm size is commonly cited in innovation diffusion literature (Damanpour, 1996). In our study, firm size is defined by the number of employees in the bank. Financial resources constitute another important factor recognized in the innovation literature (e.g., Lacovou et al. 1995). In this study, we tailor this factor to financial resources specially committed to e-banking. Implementing e-banking requires investment in hardware, software, system integration, and employee training. Availability of Online revenues and IT/Business strategy alignment are new factors included in the extended TOE framework (Alawneh and Hattab 2008). Sufficient online revenues attained from carrying out e-banking help banks to develop their e-business functionalities. IT/Business strategy alignment refers to the agreement among business people and IT people corresponding the determinants of e-banking adoption, usage and effect on banks' performance (Alawneh and Hattab, 2007).

Environment Context. Competitive pressure refers to the degree of pressure that the bank feels from competitors within the industry. Porter and Millar (1985) analyzed the strategic rationale underlying competitive pressure as an innovation-diffusion driver. They suggested that, by using a new innovation, firms might be able to alter the rules of competition, affect the industry structure, and leveraging new ways to outperform rivals, thus changing the competitive landscape. Thus, competitive pressure plays a significant role in pushing banks toward adopting e-banking. Regulatory support is another critical environmental factor that tends to affect innovation diffusion. Banks operating in an environment where government policies are restrictive have low technological innovation adoption. The lack of legal protection of online transactions as well as security and privacy tend to be common concerns both for banks and for customers. Accordingly, governments could encourage e-banking usage by establishing supportive business laws to protect e-banking transactions, regulating the Internet to make it a trustworthy business platform (e.g., dealing with fraud and credit card misuse), and providing incentives for using e-banking in government procurements, transactions and contracts.

To examine the points previously discussed and address the issues raised, we have formulated the following eight hypotheses based on the Figure 1.

H1: *The technology readiness or competence positively affects e-banking adoption in the bank.*

H2: *The bank size negatively affects e-banking adoption in the bank.*

H3: *The financial resources commitment positively affects e-banking adoption in the bank.*

H4: *The alignment of IT/Business strategy positively affects e-banking adoption in the bank.*

H5: *The adequacy of IT professionals positively affects e-banking adoption in the bank.*

H6: *The availability of online revenues positively affects e-banking adoption in the bank.*

H7: *The competition intensity or pressure negatively affects e-banking adoption in the bank.*

H8: *The regulatory support environment positively affects e-banking adoption in the bank.*

RESEARCH FINDINGS: TESTING THE THEORETICAL HYPOTHESES

Hypothesis H1 Technological Context vs. e-banking Usage

Tables 1 and 2 summarize the results of simple linear regression for hypothesis 1.

The table shows the standardized regression coefficient of each predicator, R, R^2 and F, for all the predictors in linear regression analysis.

Table 1. Results of simple regression analysis for e-banking usage vs. technological context

Model~	Standardised Coefficient	t
Technology readiness (H1)	.372	4.703**
Equation		
R	.372	
R^2	.138	
F	22.116**	

**p<.01 *p<.05 ~ dependent variable: e-banking usage*

Table 2. Results of multiple regression analysis for impacts of e-banking usage vs. technological context

Independent	e-banking Usage Impacts(Dependent)		
	Sales/services/ marketing R^2=.074 F=11.038**	Internal operations R^2=.064 F=9.514**	Coordination and communication R^2=.187 F=31.718**
Technological Context			
Technology readiness (H1)	β=.272 t=3.322**	β=.254 t=3.084**	β=.432 t=5.632**

The entire model has a significant effect on e-banking usage (p<0.01). R^2 In the entire model of the technological context explains 13.8% of the variance related to e-banking usage. As shown in Table 1, the standardized coefficient (beta) value for the technological context is positive and significant (p<.01), and thus supports hypothesis H1.

Table 2 shows the dependent variable as three impacts of e-banking usage are: sales-services-marketing, internal operations and coordination and communication. The technological context explains 7.4% of the variance of sales-services-marketing as an impact of e-banking usage, 6.4% of the variance of internal operations as an impact of e-banking usage, and 18.7% of the variance of coordination and communication as a impact of e-banking usage. Furthermore, the technology readiness contributes more significantly to e-banking usage on coordination and communication (0.432) more than to e-banking usage on internal operations and sales-services-marketing (0.254, 0.272) respectively.

Hypotheses H2-H6 Organizational Context vs. E-Banking Usage

The entire model has a significant effect on e-banking usage (p<0.01). R^2 In the entire model of the organisational context explains 54.6% of the variance related to e-banking usage. As shown in Table 3, the standardized coefficient (beta) value for the bank size is positive and significant (p<.01), and thus does not support hypothesis H2. the standardised coefficient (beta) value for the financial resources commitment is positive but is not significant and thus, the result does not support hypothesis H3. The standardised coefficient (beta) value for the IT/Business strategy alignment is positive and significant (p<.01), and thus supports hypothesis H4. The standardised coefficient (beta) value for the IT professionals is positive but is not significant and thus, the result does not support hypothesis H5. The standardised coefficient (beta) value for the online revenues is

Table 3. Results of multiple regression analysis for e-banking usage vs. organizational context

Model~	Standardised Coefficient	t
Bank Size (H2)	0.215	3.643**
Financial Resources Commitment (H3)	0.090	1.236
IT/Business Strategy (H4)	0.573	7.110**
IT Professionals (H5)	0.013	0.178
Online Revenues (H6)	0.132	1.923*
Equation		
R	0.739	
R^2	0.546	
F	32.262**	

**p<.01 *p<.05 ~ dependent variable: e-banking usage

positive and significant (p<.05), and thus supports hypothesis H6. Further, IT/Business strategy alignment contributes more to e-banking usage than the other factors.

Table 4 shows the dependent variable as three impacts of e-banking usage are: sales-services-marketing, internal operations and coordination and communication. All of the organisational context variables explain 44.4% of the variance of sales-services-marketing as an impact of e-banking usage, 33.6% of the variance of internal operations as an impact of e-banking usage, and 50.9% of the variance of coordination and communication as an impact of e-banking usage.

On the other hand, the bank size contributes significantly to e-banking usage on sales-services-marketing and coordination and communication (0.271, 0.199) respectively, but the financial resources commitment don't contribute significantly to e-banking usage in any impact, while IT/Business strategy alignment contributes significantly to e-banking usage on sales-services-marketing, internal operations and coordination and communication (0.543, 0.476, 0.475) respectively, but the online revenues contributes significantly

Table 4. Results of multiple regression analysis for impacts of e-banking usage vs. organizational context

Independent	e-banking Usage Impacts(Dependent)		
Organizational Context	Sales/services/ marketing $R^2=.444$ F=21.417**	Internal operations $R^2=.336$ F=13.566**	Coordination and communication $R^2=.509$ F=27.778**
Bank size (H2)	β=.271 t=4.159**	β=.084 t=1.185	β=.199 t=3.240**
Financial Resources Commitment (H3)	β=.027 t=.338	β=.124 t=1.401	β=.086 t=1.127
IT/Business Strategy (H4)	β=.543 t=6.087**	β=.476 t=4.880**	β=.475 t=5.665**
IT Professionals (H5)	β=-.014 t=-.175	β=-.144 t=-1.663	β=.105 t=1.469
Online Revenues (H6)	β=.104 t=1.371	β=.136 t=1.644	β=.174 t=2.335*

to e-banking usage on coordination and communication (0.174) respectively. Finally, the IT professionals don't contribute significantly to e-banking usage in any impact.

Hypotheses H7-H8 Environmental Context vs. E-Banking Usage

The entire model has a significant effect on e-banking usage (p<0.01). R^2 In the entire model of the environmental context explains 29.7% of the variance related to e-banking usage. As shown in Table 5, the standardized coefficient (beta) value for the competition intensity is positive and significant (p<.01), and thus does not supports hypothesis H7. The standardised coefficient (beta) value for the regulatory support environment is positive and significant (p<.01), and thus supports hypothesis H8.

Table 6 shows the dependent variable as three impacts of e-banking usage are: sales-services-marketing, internal operations and coordination and communication. All of the environmental context variables explain 32.9% of the variance of sales-services-marketing as an impact of e-banking usage, 12.4% of the variance of internal

operations as an impact of e-banking usage, and 23.8% of the variance of coordination and communication as an impact of e-banking usage.

On the other hand, the competition intensity contributes significantly to e-banking usage on sales-services-marketing, internal operations and coordination and communication (0.392, 0.219, 0.330) respectively, but the regulatory support environment contributes significantly to e-banking usage on sales-services-marketing, internal operations and coordination and communication (0.311, 0.214, 0.269) respectively.

Table 5. Results of multiple regression analysis for e-banking usage vs. environmental context

Model~	Standardised Coefficient	t
Competition Intensity (H7)	0.363	4.801**
Regulatory Support Environment (H8)	0.306	4.041**
Equation		
R	0.545	
R^2	0.297	
F	28.902**	

**p<.01 *p<.05 ~ dependent variable : e-banking usage*

Discussion of the Findings

Hypothesis H1 was supported by the results of the study, and thus indicated that providing the convenient infrastructure of information and communication technologies, and supplying suited web-based solutions, either separately or together will affect strongly on e-banking adoption and usage in Jordanian banks. Together, the bank size, IT/Business strategy alignment and availability of online revenues as organizational factors strengthen e-banking adoption and usage, as hypotheses H4 and H6 are supported, but hypothesis H2 isn't supported. On the other hand, the adequacy of IT professionals and financial resources commitment as organizational factors do not strengthen e-banking adoption and usage, as hypotheses H3 and H5 are not supported. Finally, the competition intensity and regulatory support environment factors strengthen e-banking adoption, usage and impacts as hypothesis H8 is supported, but hypothesis H7 isn't supported.

CONCLUSION

The main purpose of this research is to provide a context for better understanding of e-banking adoption and how the factors of the technological, organizational, and environmental contexts that surrounding the banks are necessary for diffusion and deployment of e-banking usage and its impacts on bank performance.

This article provides empirical evidence on factors that influence e-banking deployment among commercial banks in Jordan. It contributes to the few pieces of literature on e-banking experiences among banks operating in the Middle East, particularly Jordan. The study contributes several insights into banks e-banking usage. First of all, this study sheds light on the e-banking adoption in Jordanian banks and examines the impacts of e-banking usage on the banks' performance in terms of sales-services-marketing, internal operations and coordination and communication.

Many managers and investors are facing strong pressure to answer the question of what are the most important factors that influence on adoption of any technological innovation they might deploy in their firms, and how their investments on that technological innovation will betterment the performance of firms in terms of sales-services-marketing, internal operations and coordination and communication, because it is not clear to them what are the most important and significant factors that determine adoption or non adoption of that innovation. This study will help managers of banks to make critical decisions toward deployment of e-banking technology in their banks. This study endeavours to find a conceptual model that joins and classifies these factors, unifying them with e-banking usage and bank performance.

The current research is limited to one industry type, the banking services as belong to the financial services industry. Nonetheless, other domains in the financial services industry (e.g.,

Table 6. Results of multiple regression analysis for impacts of e-banking usage vs. environmental context

Independent	e-banking Usage impacts(Dependent)		
Environmental Context	Sales/services/marketing $R^2=.329$ F=33.540**	Internal operations $R^2=.124$ F=9.717**	Coordination and communication $R^2=.238$ F=21.430**
Competition Intensity (H7)	β=.392 t=5.305**	β=.219 t=2.596*	β=.330 t=4.192**
Regulatory Support Environment (H8)	β=.311 t=4.205**	β=.214 t=2.540*	β=.269 t=3.415**

securities, brokerage, credit institutions, trading, loan, mortgage, credit cards and real estate) can be studied.

The current study was conducted only in Jordan, and so future cross-cultural research would be valuable. It is assumed that there will be, to some degree, a difference in the factors affecting the adoption of e-banking technology across different cultures.

REFERENCES

Alawneh, A., and Hattab, E. (2007). E-Business Value Creation: An Exploratory Study. Proceedings of the Seventh International Conference on Electronic Business, Taipei, December 2-6, pp. 181-188.

Alawneh, A., and Hattab, E. (2008). A Framework for E-Business Value Creation: Towards Enhancing the Firms' Performance. Proceedings of International Business Information Management Conference (9th IBIMA) on Information Management in Modern Organizations, January 4-6, Marrakech, Morocco, pp. 1350-1359.

Bakos, Y. (1998). "The emerging role of electronic marketplaces on the Internet", Communications of the ACM 41(8), pp.35-42.

Bharadwaj, A. (2000). A resource-based perspective on IT capability and firm performance: An empirical investigation. MIS Quart. 24(1) 169-196.

Buzzacchi, L. M.G. Colombo and Mariotti, S. (1995). "Technological regimes and innovation in services: the case of the Italian banking industry, Research Policy, vol. 24, pp. 151-168.

Chatterjee, D.; Grewal, R.; and Sambamurthy, V. (2002). "Shaping up for e-commerce: Institutional enablers of the organizational assimilation of Web technologies". MIS Quarterly, 26, 2, 65–89.

Chau, P.Y.K., and Tam, K. Y. (1997). "Factors affecting the adoption of open systems: An exploratory study", MIS Quarterly, 21, 1, pp.1-21.

Cooper, R. B., R. W. Zmud. (1990). "Information technology implementation research: A technological diffusion approach", Management Sci. 36(2), pp.123-139.

Damanpour, F. (1996). "Organizational complexity and innovation: Developing and testing multiple contingency models", Management Science, 42, 5, pp.693-716.

Dewan, R., Freimer, M. and Seidmann, A. (2000). "Organizing Distribution Channels for Information Goods on the Internet". *Management Science*, vol. 46, no.4, pp. 483-496.

Fichman, R. G. (2000). "The diffusion and assimilation of information technology innovations. R. Zmud, ed. framing the Domains of IT Management: projecting the future through the past. Pinnaflex publishing, cincinnati, OH.

Grover, V. (1993). "An empirically derived model for the adoption of customer-based inter organizational systems", Decision Sciences, 24, 3, pp.603-640.

Hart, P. J., and C. S. Saunders. (1998). "Emerging electronic partnerships: Antecedents and dimensions of EDI use from the supplier's perspective". J. Management Inform. Systems, 14(4) 87–111.

Hess, C.M., and Kemerer, C.F. (1994). "Computerized loan origination systems: An industry case study of electronic markets hypothesis". *MIS Quarterly*, 18, 3, 251–275

Kolodinsky, J. M. and Hilgert, M. A. (2004). "the adoption of electronic banking technologies by US consumers, International Journal of Bank Marketing, volume 22, 4, pp. 238-259.

Kuan, K.K.Y., and Chau, P.Y.K. (2001), "A perception-based model for EDI adoption in small business using a technology-organization-environment framework", Information and Management, 38, 8, pp.507-512.

Lacovou, C. L.; Benbasat, I.; and Dexter, A.S. (1995). "Electronic data interchange and small organizations: Adoption and impact of technology", MIS Quarterly, 19, 4, pp.465-485.

Lederer, A. L., Maupin, D. J., Sena, M. P., Zhuang, Y., (1998). "The role of ease of use, usefulness and attitude in the prediction of world wide web usage", Proceedings of the 1998 Association for computing machinery special interest group on computer personnel research conference, 195-204.

Mulligan, P., and Gordon, S.R. (2002). "The impact of information technology on customer and supplier relationships in the financial services". *International Journal of Service Industry Management*, 13, 1, 29–46.

Olazabal, N.G. (2002). "Banking: The IT paradox". *McKinsey Quarterly*, 1, 47– 51.

Ramamurthy, K.; Premkumar, G.; and Crum, M.R. (1999). "Organizational and inter organizational determinants of EDI diffusion and organizational performance: A causal model", Journal of Organizational Computing and Electronic Commerce, 9, 4, pp.253-285.

Rogers, E. M. (1983). Diffusion of Innovations, 3rd ed. Free Press, New York. In Zhu and Kraemer, 2005.

Shapiro, C., H. Varian. (1990). "Information Rules: A Strategic Guide to the Network Economy", Harvard Business School Press, Boston, MA.

Swanson, E.B. (1994). "Information systems innovation among organizations". Management Science, 40,9, 1069-1092.

Thong, J.Y.L. (1999). "An integrated model of information systems adoption in small business", Journal of Management Information Systems, 15, 4, pp.187-214.

Tornatzky, L.G., and Fleischer, M. (1990). The Processes of Technological Innovation, Lexington, MA: Lexington Books, 1990.

Turban, E., King D., Warkentin M., Chung, H. M, (2003). Electronic Commerce 2003: A managerial perspective, Prentice Hall. In Achour and Bensedrine, 2005.

Zhu, K. (2004). "The complementarity of IT infrastructure and e-commerce capability: A resource-based assessment of their business value". Journal of Management Information Systems, 21(1), pp.167-202.

Zhu, K., Kraemer, K. L. (2002). "E-commerce metrics for Net-enhanced organizations: Assessing the value of e-commerce to firm performance in the manufacturing sector". Information Systems Research. 13(3), pp .275-295.

Zhu, K., Kraemer, K., Xu, S., and Dedrick, J. (2004). "Information Technology Payoff in E-Business Environments: An International perspective on Value Creation of E-Business in the Financial Services Industry". Journal of Management Information Systems, Vol. 21, Issue 1, pp.17-54.

Zhu, K., Kraemer, K. L. (2002). "E-commerce metrics for Net-enhanced organizations: Assessing the value of e-commerce to firm performance in the manufacturing sector". Information Systems Research. 13(3), pp.275-295.

Zhu, K., and Kraemer, K. L. (2005). "Post-Adoption variations in usage and value of E-Business by organizations: cross-country evidence from the retail industry". Information Systems Research, Vol. 16, Issue 1, pp.61-84.

Zhu, K., Kraemer, K.L., and Xu, S. (2003). "E-business adoption by European firms: A cross-country assessment of the facilitators and inhibitors". European Journal of Information Systems, 12(4), pp.251-268.

Chapter 4.9
Business to Consumer E-Services:
Australian Accounting Practices and their Web Sites

Stephen Burgess
Victoria University, Australia

John Breen
Victoria University, Australia

Regina Quiazon
Victoria University, Australia

ABSTRACT

This article reports on a study involving analysis of the Web sites of 100 accounting practices located in Melbourne, Australia, and subsequent interviews with twenty practices. This article focuses on identifying the level of e-services that they employ. In this regard, Angehrn's virtual dimensions of Web site spaces were used to classify the various service delivery strategies adopted by the different practices. The results suggest that information technology plays a critical role in the accounting industry and that the use of computer accounting packages is almost mandatory among clients. There is little evidence of the use of Web sites for the delivery of automated e-services. At the moment, the Internet is primarily used to support the delivery of services rather than completely automate it. Overall, the study suggests that Australian accounting firms currently take a fairly conservative approach to Web site use.

INTRODUCTION

Advances in information technology (IT) and the use of the Internet have brought forth new business models for professional services, thus enabling firms to operate more competitively on a wider and more efficient scale (Kotler et al. 2002). Firm-client relationships supported by the Internet will, by many predictions, define the successful accounting firm of the future (Bhansali 2005; Schlageter 2005). Adopters of these new accounting practice models report significant benefits as they move into more productive and satisfying relationships with their clients. These benefits include a reduction in paperwork, the delivery of more responsive services, reduction in errors, and the incorporation of additional services (McCausland 2004). Firms have achieved these benefits by installing online accounting systems through which services are delivered using private and secure Web sites accessible to their clients.

This research investigates the use of the Internet among accounting practices located in metropolitan Melbourne, Australia (and its surrounding suburbs). In particular, this article reports on two phases of the study: firstly, the examination of the Web site content of 100 Australian accounting practices and, secondly, the subsequent interviews with partners in 20 accounting practices to identify the level of current e-service delivery in Australian accounting practices.

DELIVERING SERVICES ON THE INTERNET

The power of information and communication technology in improving business performance is underpinned by the versatility of the Internet as an information medium. Through their Web sites, firms have effectively reached out to their customers in a variety of ways, achieving greater efficiencies and in some cases offering added value. In the late 1990's, Angehrn (1997) identified four Internet 'dimensions' that a business could employ when developing a strategy to engage customers via the Internet. These dimensions are information (dissemination), communication (with customers), distribution (of digital goods or services) and (online) transactions (ICDT). More recently, Jelassi and Enders (2005) have suggested that these dimensions could be used by a business to help them select which Internet features to employ when engaging with customers. They describe Angehrn's dimensions as:

- **Virtual Information Space:** this includes online advertising and posting business information.
- **Virtual communication space:** is where the business engages in a two-way online communication with its customers, typically through email, chat facilities or bulletin boards.
- **Virtual distribution space:** allows for the delivery of digital goods (such as online books, software) and services (such as financial advice). This is an area where innovation in services delivery could provide benefits both to businesses that offer professional services and their clients.
- **Virtual transaction space:** allows for the acceptance of online orders and payments.

The four dimensions provide a useful framework from which to map out existing and potential value-adding activities and are particularly relevant to the subject of this study, accounting practices. In particular, the four dimensions will be used to classify the different e-service strategies of Australian accounting practices. Before this can be carried out, it is necessary to spend some time discussing e-services.

Stafford (2003) suggests that experts have not yet come upon a clear definition of what e-services actually are. One reason for this, as Stafford argues, could be attributed to the range of specialities involved in the delivery of e-services. From a marketing viewpoint, Bolton (2003) suggests that e-services are those services that can take place without buyer involvement. For instance, automatic collection of road tolls as a car passes through a tolling booth is an example of this. E-services can also be related to particular industries. For instance, Laffie (2005) discusses the US Internal Revenue Service (IRS) and describes their e-services as being a suite of online products that allow tax professionals and payers to conduct business electronically with the IRS.

However, other authors suggest a more narrow definition of e-services. For instance, Hsu and Chiu (2004) describe e-services as "highly specialized electronic services" (p.359) for users and suggest that they include "support services such as consulting, outsourcing, Web site design, electronic data interchange, payment transfer and data storage backups" (p.359). Such complex e-services are sometimes known as web services.

E-services can occur between government, business and consumer and, as Chui et al (2005) suggest, from business to business. Despite the potential for complexity in e-service developments, Chui et al claim that the majority of existing e-services are available through interactive web pages in HTML (the well-known Internet formatting language). It has reached the stage where the *quality* of e-service delivery in some areas is becoming an issue when buyers are considering using the services of a business.

As with other services, e-service customers need to be able to assess the quality of e-services in order to make informed buying decisions. (Field, Heim and Sinha, 2004, p.291)

For the purposes of this article we will only be examining the relationship between business and consumer (now known as B2C). In relation to professional services businesses, such as accounting practices, we will take a broad definition of e-services. We define e-services as *those professional services, traditionally performed face-to-face, which are now predominantly delivered online. These might include those services where at least one of the parties (business or consumer) is not required to actively participate for the service to be delivered or, at the less-sophisticated end, where the technology facilitates the delivery of the service.*

ACCOUNTING FIRMS AND THE INTERNET

In recent years, information technology has played a critical role in the services provided by the accounting industry (Banker, Chang and Kao, 2002). The transition to e-commerce provides new opportunities to interconnect various organisational units as well as across different agencies (Gebauer and Shaw, 2002). At the same time, it demands from organisations and individuals new sets of behaviours. Chaston and Mangles (2001) used data from 174 small UK accounting firms to determine that entrepreneurial accounting practices believe that e-commerce offers major new trading opportunities, can deliver competitive advantage and improves internal efficiencies. They concluded that entrepreneurial accounting firms could be expected to be more involved in the adoption of new electronic communications technology before their non-entrepreneurial counterparts.

Further to this, Chen, Tseng and Chang (2005) collected data from 595 accounting firms in Taiwan and found that despite the fact that the impact of the Internet on accounting firms differed in degrees, they were all positive. Douglas (2004, p. 25) also remarks that "an accounting firm with no Web site or a lousy one is at a distinct disadvantage".

The need for access to different levels of accounting information is likely to vary markedly across different individuals and groups. For instance, the financial reporting needs of many are currently met by reports in 'Adobe Acrobat' form, but these present limitations relating to file size and download time (Lymer and Debreceny 2003). The power of the Internet is multi-fold and its capacity to integrate with other information and communication technologies, such as databases and with the support of hypermedia presentations, enhances its capacity for financial reporting (Lymer et al 1999).

For most firms, early Internet reporting merely duplicated traditional 'hard copy' reporting (Bury 1999) and was treated as an additional way to disseminate the same information. There was limited evidence to suggest that the information available through the Internet was, in fact, useful for the users (Taylor 1998). A number of studies have reported problems relating to Internet reporting, such as difficulties associated with locating specific Web site and information items (Debreceny and Gray 2001); information omissions (Ettredge, Richardson and Scolz 2002) and the difficulty of distinguishing between audited and non-audited information (Bury 1999).

Despite these problems, the Internet does have a number of important advantages over the traditional media used for financial reporting. It has the capacity to provide a whole range of additional, non-financial information in annual reports (Green and Spaul 1997). Lymer et al (1997), for instance, identified the advantages of the Internet for financial reporting as being cheap, quick, dynamic and flexible. Xiao, Jones and Lymer (2005) identify the advantages as including the use of digital technology, enhancements through technology integration, the capacity for real time communication, hypermedia presentations and limitless boundaries.

Lymer and Debreceny (2003) argue that the rate of development in technology is such that simply replicating paper reports into Acrobat format is nothing more than a simplistic response to information technology pressure for greater and wider dissemination of financial information. Therefore, they maintain that the professional responses to Internet financial reporting are grossly inadequate in relation to advances in technology developments and that accounting bodies have "a public responsibility to promulgate the most effective and efficient distribution of accounting data via the web." (p 118). Xiao, Jones and Lymer (2005), recognise that when it comes to financial reporting the Internet could, on the one hand, enable or facilitate new and innovative ways of reporting financial information, and, on the other hand, has the potential to unlock databases and provide real time reporting. This suggests that there is a potential for a whole range of services to be delivered by accounting practices over the Internet. The next section introduces a study of Australian accounting practices to examine specifically the level of services that they are currently providing.

THE STUDY

The Institute of Chartered Accountants in Australia (ICAA) have funded a study that examines the Web site practices of Australian accounting practices in the following manner:

1. An analysis of the content of the Web sites of Australian accounting practices to describe the state of play regarding the use of Web sites among local accounting firms.
2. In-depth interviews with the relevant accounting practice staff to uncover drivers and inhibitors for the adoption of Internet technology in accounting firms as well as an investigation of techniques employed to determine the success of existing online initiatives.

This article reports on the results of both phases of the study, the analysis of Web site content of Australian accounting practices and subsequent interviews with 20 Australian accounting practices. The article focuses on the level of services delivered online in those practices and specifically how many of those services could be classified as *e-services* according to our definition.

The analysis of each Web site was carried out in November-December 2006 by one of the authors. For this article, the Web site content was analysed according to Angehrn's (1997) four dimensions of space that businesses could employ to develop a strategy for dealing with customers

Table 1. Examples of services and potential for e-services classified by virtual space

Virtual Space	Example	Potential for e-services
Information	Online advertising and posting business information	There is little potential for delivering *personalised* services as information is basically delivered one-way (business to consumer). The provision of generic advice could, however, be offered
Communication	Email, chat facilities or bulletin boards	Here there is potential for the delivery of enhanced personalised services as individual contact can be made with customers.
Distribution	Delivery of digital goods (such as online books, software) and services (such as financial advice)	There is some potential here, but it is difficult to determine whether or not it is possible to offer a highly personalised service, such as financial advice, in an automated fashion.
Transactions	Acceptance of online orders and payments	If customers are willing and able to pay for business services online and/or set up appointments on an automated basis, then there is potential here.

on the Internet. Table 1 lists each of the virtual spaces and includes some examples provided earlier, along with some of their applications and where the authors see the potential for e-services.

The analysis technique used to identify Web site features was developed by Burgess (2002) and has been subsequently used in studies by Burgess and Zoppos (2002), Shackleton et al (2003) and, more recently, in Burgess, Sellitto and Wenn (2005) and Burgess, Bingley and Sellitto (2005). For this type of content analysis, Henderson and Cowart (2002) quote McMillan (2000) in suggesting specific steps that should be followed in selecting a sample number of Web sites. In our case, the selection process involved the random selection of 100 firms listed on ICAA's Web site that were either located in metropolitan Melbourne or its surrounding suburbs. Some of the studies mentioned here are used for comparative

purposes; for instance, the Burgess, Bingley and Sellitto (2005) study, which examined the Web sites of business services practices, has particular relevance to this study. In order to determine some of the strategies used by accounting practices when developing their Web sites, 20 practices were selected for in-depth interviews in order that their use of the Internet could be explored further. The stratified sampling technique employed in this study was able to generate a useful spread of accounting practices. The technique identified *strata* for practices within different categories in relation to the number of features on their Web sites. In other words, the sample included three types of businesses, those with: few features on their Web sites; an average number of features; and many features. In each case, the interviews were conducted at the premises of the practices with a partner of the practice; although, in a few

Table 2. Main demographics of interview practices

Business type (number of employees)	Number of Interviews	Ave years of Operation	Typical no of clients		% with IT staff
			Individual	Business	
Micro (1-10)	6	19	100	100	17
Small (11-20)	5	40	500-1000	500-1000	20
Medium (21-50)	7	27	1000	500-1000	43
Large (51+)	2	26	1000+	1000+	100

Figure 1. Identification and image features

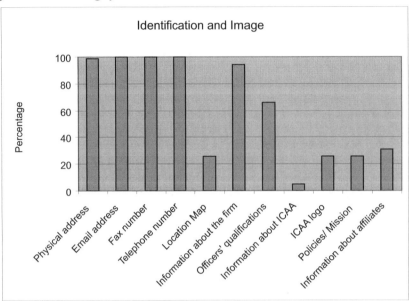

Figure 2. Promotion and contract features

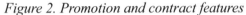

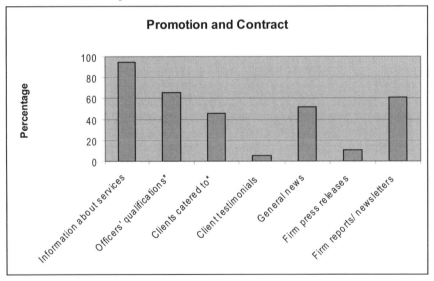

instances, dedicated information technology employees were interviewed. Table 2 shows the main demographics of the interview sample.

Most of the practices interviewed were micro, small or medium sized practices. They had all been in operation for a number of years, ranging from 10 years (a medium sized practice) to 100 years (a small practice). Virtually all of the practices had a combination of individual and business clients. Not unexpectedly, the smaller practices were less likely to employ a dedicated information technology employee. Where dedicated IT employees were not to be found, the role was often carried out by a partner in addition to their assigned accounting duties or was shared between partners. In many of these instances, support also came from external consultants. There were also instances where external support was used when the business had dedicated IT employees. This was especially the case in relation to the design and hosting of Web sites.

RESULTS

Virtual Information Space

Features related to the virtual information space provided the first dimension from which to assess firms' Web site strategy. These features generally provide the Web surfer with information about how to contact or find the organisations, some basic information about the organisations, information about their products and services and news about the organisation or the industry. Alonso Mendo and Fitzgerald (2005) further classify the information provided on Web sites into features related to *identification and image* and those related to *promotion and contract*. We know from previous studies of small business Web sites (Burgess, Bingley and Sellitto 2005; Burgess, Sellitto and Wenn 2005) that most small businesses include a number of contact features. In this part of the study, we examined Web sites to see if they had the following features:

- Identification and Image
  - Physical address; Email address; Fax number; Telephone number; Location map; Information about the firm; Information about the ICAA; ICAA logo*; Policies and/or Mission statement; Information about affiliates*
- Promotion and Contract
  - Information about services offered; Information about how to engage the services of the business; News/ press releases; Customer or member reviews

(*These features were added in during the study when it was noticed that they were prominent).

The percentage of practices that had identification and image features on their Web sites is shown in Figure 1. All accounting practice Web sites had telephone number, email address, and fax number. All but one had their physical location on their Web site. These results differ from other studies, including the analysis of business services Web sites (Burgess, Bingley and Sellitto 2005), where most - but not all - small businesses had these features. Moreover, one in four accounting businesses had a location map on their Web site, whereas none of the business services practices in our earlier study had a location map. If we consider the rationale behind the use of a physical address and a location map on a Web site it might help to explain the differences. The physical address can be used to locate the business, but also for other purposes (such as to send mail). A location map is primarily put on the Web site to help somebody geographically or, rather, *visually locate* the business. It might be typically employed in a situation where businesses may feel their customers need some extra assistance to find the business. It is interesting to note that, although only 5% of the practices had information about their professional association, one in four practices actually had their association logo on their Web site. The authors expected that a higher proportion of Web sites would have one or both of these features. A similar percentage of accounting businesses had their mission or policy statements on their Web site.

Figure 2 shows the percentage of accounting practices that had promotion and contract features.

Some 95% of the accounting practice Web sites we examined had information about the services offered by the practices. This is consistent with the earlier business services study (Burgess, Bingley and Sellitto 2005), where 93% of these businesses had information about the services offered.

An important feature of accounting practice Web sites was the inclusion of the officers' qualifications in two-thirds of the Web sites. Also, 46% of the accounting practice Web sites listed the clients that were catered to.

In the previous business services study only a small number (around 10%) had news or press releases about the business. In comparison, the accounting practice Web sites were more likely to have some type of news or newsletter available on their Web sites. Testimonials from clients were not a prominent feature of accounting practice Web sites.

In relation to the data collected during the interviews, many of the practices interviewed were of the opinion that the Web site has two main objectives: to convey information about the business to the general public and to deliver information from the business to clients (which is consistent with the Web site analysis).

In this regard, especially for those firms that cited the Web site as primarily a client resource, the Web site is used to distribute information such as taxation news updates, changes to superannuation and regular newsletters to clients. For one firm that was interviewed, the most important feature of the Web site is considered to be "content—nothing else" whilst for another firm, importance is placed on the Web site's capacity "to convey information about the staff, their qualifications and specialisation".

Overall, the interviews confirmed that the Web sites are primarily used for the dissemination of information. For example, in one firm that aimed to be technologically efficient, it was pointed out that all documents are either scanned or converted into 'acrobat' format and uploaded onto their Web site. It is important to note that, within the context of eservices delivery, email (refer next section) is sometimes used for the 'one-way' delivery of information, such as news bulletins.

Another important source of information for many clients is via the secure log-in feature, which one in four of the Web sites we analysed provided. Further information about the types of information accessed via this feature is in the 'Distribution Space' section.

Virtual Communication Space

This space covers the use of Internet technologies to provide or support communication between a business and its partners. From the Web site analysis, the only form of two way communication between business and client was via an email address, which was evident on virtually all of the Web sites analysed. The interviews confirmed that by far the most dominant form of Internet-based communication was via email, between employees themselves and between employees and clients. Almost all the businesses interviewed mentioned the importance of email, especially when dealing with clients that were some distance away. Many described it as 'vital' or 'critical'; with others suggesting that it is a useful supplement to their normal operations. The difference between face-to-face and email communications was an interesting discussion point that arose on a number of occasions. In this regard, a few practices conveyed their concerns about the increased use of email insofar as that there is less opportunity for face-to-face dealings and the chance to build relationships with clients.

The convenience and immediacy of reply is considered to be particularly beneficial in the management of interstate and overseas clients in different time zones. Likewise, the immediacy of reply is an important efficiency gain for practices.

Other beneficial reasons cited for use of email included:

- The capacity to send out group emails and information, such as newsletters, to specific (targeted) groups,
- Use as a quality assurance mechanism as there is documentary evidence of the communication,

- There is minimal work interruption to answer simple questions,
- Staff can respond quickly even if they are not in the office (as many firms offer flexible working conditions for their employees, clients are encouraged to email employees rather than call for a faster response).

It is also important to note that, although the firms interviewed regard email as an indispensable business tool, there are different opinions underpinning the firm's use of email communication. In one large firm, for example, "email is regarded as a facilitator only - not a relationship management tool. Major issues are conducted face-to-face". Another firm interviewed also described email as "a supplement, rather than a replacement, to the ways we deliver our services". For example, clients have the option of emailing their data files before booking a face-to-face appointment.

The interviews also revealed concerns associated with the growing use of email. Concerns included:

- The business etiquette or appropriateness pertaining to the (non) use of email, especially with larger or more important clients
- Unsolicited and junk email (SPAM) is becoming an issue
- The difficulty of maintaining relationships which are conducted virtually
- The problems associated with the construction of email correspondence insofar as less formal and more ad hoc decisions are likely to be made compared to the care usually taken with traditional letters.

As will be discussed in the next section, many businesses use email to 'swap' data files as attachments.

Virtual Distribution Space

In Table 1, we indicated that the virtual distribution space might show the most promise for the delivery of e-services (as we have defined it) by accounting practices. The virtual distribution space allows for the delivery of digital goods and services using Internet technologies. The Web site analysis provided little evidence as to any automated e-service delivery occurring via the Web sites, unless it was occurring via the secure log-in areas (which could not be accessed). In the previous section we indicated that many of our interviewees transferred files over the Internet using email attachments. About half of the firms interviewed (9) carried out this practice, but none of these were large businesses. This suggests that, at least for larger firms, the emailing of attachments is not considered to be a suitable work practice. Three other businesses employed the use of file transfer protocol (FTP) to switch files between themselves and clients. Two practices used both FTP and email attachments to transfer files. Our initial Web site analysis showed that approximately one quarter of the Web sites analysed had a 'log-in' feature, which allowed access to restricted areas of the Web site via password. Seven of the practices that were interviewed had a log-in feature. These provided access to special (but not personally tailored) accounting or financial information (3 firms), regular newsletter or reports (2 firms) and access to portfolio accounts (2 firms).

Could any of these be considered to be e-services? Do we have any instances where traditional face-to-face professional services are being delivered online? In relation to the transfer of data files and reports, the Web sites are primarily being used as conduits to *transfer* the results of the professional services (already carried out by a partner or other employee) from business to clients. Certainly, email and FTP features facilitate this process. In relation to the log-in service, most were used for information provision and are therefore not tailored to the client. These could not be classed as e-services. Perhaps the one feature that could be classed as e-services, at least partially, is where there are two practices that allow clients to log-in and access their investment portfolios. In cases where clients are able to manipulate funds it could be argued that this is a professional service offered online. It is interesting to note that a number of practices that do not currently have this feature indicated that they might look to adopt it in the future as a way of enhancing the delivery of their professional services.

Virtual Transaction Space

The virtual transactions space allows for the on-line acceptance or orders and/or payments. From previous studies it is known that certain types of businesses are more likely to encourage ordering/booking (and sometimes payments) online (for example: Burgess, Bingley and Sellitto 2005; Burgess, Sellitto and Wenn 2005). For instance, art galleries are not likely to have any of these features. Bed and breakfast establishments will typically have a facility for customers to book via a web form that sends an email to the business or have the option to print out a booking form that can then be faxed to the business. Small manufacturing businesses are more likely to have interactive order/payment facilities on their Web site.

The earlier study of business services Web sites, however, showed **no** transactional interactivity features on the Web site. This study of accounting practice Web sites is consistent with this finding—with **none** of the Web sites having any of these features. Once again, this reflects the nature of the business and the type of service that is being offered. In other words, the business of accounting can be characterised by its reliance on the provision and delivery of accurate and timely information. The feedback from interviewees

was that there is not yet enough sophistication in the client market to drive the adoption of transactional facilities. More specifically, the concerns in relation to security and low client demand for such services take precedence over their implementation.

OTHER INTERVIEW RESULTS

The interviews revealed a range of attitudes towards IT in general. A number of practices, for example, were quite conservative in their use of IT, either viewing it as a cost and/or a necessity that helps efficiencies and assists them to carry out their day-to-day tasks. Other practices have a more entrepreneurial approach, viewing Internet technologies as a means of differentiation from competitors. The attitudes to Web sites were in some ways very similar. Some firms had Web sites predominantly because of market expectations insofar as they could be seen to be keeping up with their competitors or to convey the image of being 'up to date'. Others saw the Web site as a chance to provide extra value for clients through various features (these features are discussed later in the article). Some of the larger businesses viewed the Web site as a means of attracting new employees to their businesses.

Almost all of the businesses had some control over the management of Web site content, with just over half of those interviewed relying on consultants to provide some content. Some of these consultants provided specialised services in relation to the provision of content for accounting practice Web sites. In regard to design, only seven of the 20 businesses interviewed had some control over this aspect of their Web site, with the majority of businesses relying on a consultant. In some instances, standard 'accounting' Web site templates were used by the consultants.

Only two of the businesses hosted their own Web site. The rest had their Web sites hosted by an external consultant or Internet service provider.

DISCUSSION

Chaston and Mangles (2001) postulated that entrepreneurial accounting firms will be more likely to be involved in the adoption of new technologies. While there was no clear evidence of a measure of entrepreneurial attitude among the firms in this study, the more proactive practices tended to be less conservative in their attitudes to technology adoption and more focused on building their practice.

All interviewees reported that they needed to be 'in the game' with respect to having a Web site. Such a finding is consistent with the views of Douglas (2004) who argued that accounting firms with no Web site are at a competitive disadvantage.

The finding that all accounting practices surveyed have several contact features among the information content on their Web site is consistent with the business services sector studies conducted by Burgess, Bingley and Sellito (2005).

The Burgess, Bingley and Sellito (2005) study found that none of the financial service businesses Web sites that were examined conducted transactions over the Internet and this finding was supported in this study of accounting practices. To date, it is mainly information and communication activity that is being offered over the Internet by accounting practices.

Chen, Tseng and Chang (2005) found that the impact of the Internet on accounting firms differed across firms but all impacts were positive. The findings of this study generally support those findings. There were, however, some negative aspects reported and these included setup and maintenance costs, time spent updating Web sites, dealing with SPAM and client concerns over security.

Xiao, Jones and Lymer (2005) argued that financial reporting using the Internet has the potential to unlock databases and provide real time reporting. While this study did not find substantial evidence to support their view, there were some examples of uses of the Internet that indicate that

the practices are taking notice. These examples include clients' ability to access their investment portfolios in real time; and some practices having direct access to client details through the Australian Taxation Office portal

In relation to service delivery, Banker, Chang and Kao (2002) reported that IT plays a critical role in the services provided in the accounting industry and this study supports that argument. The findings indicated the use of computer accounting packages is almost mandatory among clients, IT supports an improved delivery of information, and email is now seen as enhancing the traditional face-to-face services provided. However there is little evidence of the use of Web sites for the delivery of automated e-services. At the moment, the Internet is primarily used to *support* the delivery of services rather than completely *automate* it. There is no evidence of activity on Web sites at the transaction end of the spectrum.

The interviews conducted in this study provide some real-life context of the current attitudes and Internet practices of accounting practices in and around Metropolitan Melbourne. When combined with the analysis of 100 accounting practice Web sites, the study provides strong evidence that these businesses are very client-focussed and are willing to use the Internet and their Web sites to improve the delivery of services to their clients. However, only a few of these services could be classified as *e-services*. Nevertheless, this does not mean that these practices are shunning the idea of e-services—it is more that they feel that they, and more importantly, their clients, are not yet ready for them.

The authors encourage similar studies to be conducted in other parts of the world. Melbourne would be typical of other Australian capital cities in relation to its accounting practices activities and the level of Internet penetration. Also, Australian practices, whilst connected to the rest of the world electronically, are isolated from much of it in relation to geographic distance and time zone differences. It would be worthwhile to examine how accounting practices attitudes and use of the Internet in other countries would differ, especially where different government regulations, much less distance between neighbouring countries and different levels of Internet penetration were evident.

CONCLUSION

The analysis of Australian accounting practice Web sites reveals a heavy emphasis towards the identification of the business and its services, which is consistent with other Web site studies that have been carried out. More than other businesses, accounting practices rely on the provision of various types of information to clients. The provision of news in various formats on their Web sites is also an important tool for many practices. Interestingly, none of the accounting practices offered transactional interactivity features on their Web sites. The interviews revealed a number of strategies in relation to the use of IT and the Internet, ranging from conservative to entrepreneurial strategies. Following this, it was found that the Web sites were developed for a number of reasons. Although a number of the Web sites discussed during the interviews had log-in features, only two contained features that could perhaps be classed as 'e-services'. We believe this to reflect the nature of the professional services being offered by the practices. At the moment, these services are too personalised, and the practices and clients use of ICTs and the Internet not mature enough, to make effective delivery of e-services maintstream in the practices. Overall, it is reasonable to conclude from our analysis of Web sites and subsequent interviews that the Web sites of accounting practices in Australia, and their Web site strategies, are fairly conservative.

ACKNOWLEDGMENT

This research has been assisted by the Institute of Chartered Accountants in Australia through its Academic Research Grants Scheme

REFERENCES

Alonso Mendo, F. and Fitzgerald, G. 2005, 'Theoretical Approaches to Study SMES E-Business Progression', *Journal of Computing and Information Technology*, 13(2): 123-136.

Angehrn, A. 1997, 'Designing mature internet business strategies: The ICDT model', 15(4): 361-369.

Banker, R., Chang, H. and Kao, Y. 2002. 'Impact of information technology on public accounting firm productivity'. *Journal of Information Systems*, 16(2): 209-222.

Bhansali, C. 2005, 'Successful Firms will be Online on Time', *Accounting Technology*, June.

Bolton, RN. 2003, 'Marketing Challenges of E-Services', *Communications of the ACM*, 46(6): 43-44.

Burgess, S. 2002. *Business-to-Consumer Interactions on the Internet: A Model for Small Businesses*. PhD Thesis. Monash University, Melbourne Australia.

Burgess, S., Bingley, S. and Sellitto, C. 2005, 'A Model for Website Development of Micro Tourism Enterprises', *Illuminating Entrepreneurship: Proceedings of the Institute for Small Business and Entrepreneurship 28th National Conference*, Perlex Associates, UK.

Burgess, S., Sellitto, C. and Wenn A. 2005. 'Maturity in the Websites of Australian Wineries: A Study of Varying Website Content', *International Journal of Electronic Business*, 3(5): 473-490.

Burgess, S and Zoppos, B. 2002. 'The Features of Selected Australian Websites', *E-Conomy: from here to where? (CD Rom Proceedings)*, School of Management Information Systems, Edith Cowan University, Perth, December.

Bury, L. (1999). On Line and on Time. *Accountancy*, August 28-29

Chen, M., Tseng, C. and Chang, J. 2005. 'A survey investigation into the use of the Internet among Accounting firms'. *International Journal of Management*. 22(4): 649-660.

Chaston, L. and Mangles, T. 2001. 'E-commerce and Small UK Accounting Firms: Influence of Marketing Styles and Orientation'. *The Service Industries Journal*, 21(4): 83-99.

Chiu, D. Kok, D., Lee, A. and Cheung, S. 2005, 'Integrating Legacy Sites into Web Services with Webxcript', *International Journal of Cooperative Information Systems*, 14(1): 25-44.

Debreceny, R. and Gray, G. 2001. 'Financial Reporting on the Internet and the Internet and the External Audit', *European Accounting Review*, 8(2): 335-350.

Douglas, A.K. 2004. 'Marketing Your Firm on the Internet', *Tax Practice Management*, January-February.

Ettredge, M., Richardson, V. and Scolz, S. 2002. 'Dissemination of Information for Investors at Corporate Websites', *Journal of Accounting and Public Policy*, 21: 357-369.

Field, J., Heim, G. and Sinha, K. 2004. 'Managing Quality in the E-Service System: Development and Application of a Process Model', *Production and Operations Management*, 13(4): 291-306.

Gebauer, J. and Shaw, M. 2002. 'Introduction to the Special Section: Business-to-Business Electronic Commerce', *International Journal of Electronic Commerce*, 6(4): 7–17.

Henderson, K. and Cowart, L. 2002. 'Bucking E-Commerce Trends: A Content Analysis Comparing Commercial Real Estate Brokerage and Residential Real Estate Brokerage Websites', *Journal of Corporate Real Estate*, 4(4): 375-385.

Hsu, M. and Chiu, C. 2004. 'Predicting electronic service continuance with a decomposed theory of planned behaviour', *Behaviour and Information Technology*, 23(5): 359-373.

Jelassi, T. and Enders, A. 2005. *Strategies for e-Business: Creating Value though Electronic and Mobile Commerce*, Pearson Education, UK.

Kotler, P., Hayes, T. and Bloom, P. 2002. *Marketing Professional Services—Forward Thinking Strategies for Boosting Your Business, Your Image and Your Profits*, 2nd edn, Prentice Hall Press, Paramius, NJ.

Laffie, L. 2005. 'From The Tax Adviser: Expanded E-Services Access', *Journal of Accountancy*, 199(6): 98-98.

Lymer, A. 1997. 'The use of the Internet in company reporting: A survey and commentary on the use of the WWW in corporate reporting in the UK'. *Journal of Financial Information Systems*.

Lymer, A and Debreceny, R. 2003. 'The Auditor and Corporate Reporting on the Internet: Challenges and Institutional Responses'. *International Journal of Auditing*, 7(2): 103-120.

Lymer, A. Debreceny, R; Gray, G. Rahman, A. 1999. *Business Reporting on the Internet*. IASC. London

McCausland, R. 2004. 'Home, Sweet Home Page', *Accounting Technology*, 7 September.

McMillan, S.J. 2000. 'The Microscope and the Moving Target: The Challenge of Applying Content Analysis to the World Wide Web', *Journalism and Mass Communication Quarterly*, 77(1):80-98.

Schlageter, M. 2005. 'Leveraging Technology', *Journal of Accountancy*, 199(6): 14.

Shackleton, P., Fisher, J. and Dawson, L. 2003. 'Town Hall E-Government: A Study of Local Government Electronic Service Delivery', *Proceedings of the 14th Australasian Conference on Information Systems*, Perth, Australia November.

Stafford, T. 2003. 'E-Services', *Communications of the ACM*, 46(6): 26-28.

Taylor, S. 1998). *Web Sites—A missed opportunity?*, Business Briefing. Institute of Chartered Accountants in England and Wales, London.

Xiao, Z.; Jones, M.; Lymer, A. 2002. Immediate Trends in Internet Reporting. *The European Accounting Review*, 11 (2): 245-275.

This work was previously published in International Journal of E-Services and Mobile Applications, Vol. 1, Issue 1, edited by A. Scupola, pp. 38-51, copyright 2009 by IGI Publishing (an imprint of IGI Global).

Chapter 4.10
ICT Usage by Greek Accountants

Efstratios C. Emmanouilidis
University of Macedonia, Greece

Anastasios A. Economides
University of Macedonia, Greece

ABSTRACT

This study investigates Greek accounting offices use of Information and Communication Technologies (ICT). Initially, a comprehensive questionnaire was developed. It contains 35 questions with multiple answers and 2 open questions tailored to the accountants. One hundred accountants' offices in a Greek county answered the questionnaire. The findings present their current ICT infrastructure and their use of ICT and accounting e-services. Greek accounting offices have made improvements in adopting new technology in their everyday work. All use email, antivirus software, and the Web. Most submit VAT (Value Aided Tax), Taxation Statements, and APS (Analytical Periodic Statement) via Internet. However, most are not cautious about backing up their data daily; they do not create electronic files for all their documents; they do not update their software via Internet; and they do not use advanced software applications. Finally, they expect the government and the Accountants' Chamber to finance their ICT infrastructure.

INTRODUCTION

The profession of accountancy has experienced unprecedented change during the past 20 years. It has moved from paper-based to PC-based, and the Internet has become prevailing tendency. Similar to other professions in the service sector (Levy, Murphy, & Zanakis, 2009; Lexhagen, 2009), the recent technological developments have given accountants the opportunity to incorporate information systems in their profession. They use the PC, to a large extent, for customers' book keeping and liquidation of income tax statements. They spend a large amount of time processing and producing many documents (Bhansali, 2006a). Also, they use the Internet extensively for submitting tax statements to the government (Anderson, Fox,

& Schwartz, 2005; Garen, 2006). The recent advances in e-government (Chatzopoulos & Economides, 2009; Economides & Terzis, 2008; Terpsiadou & Economides, 2009) have pushed accountants to follow. Furthermore, more than 2,000 accounting firms have Web sites registered with "The List of CPA Firms Directory" (Roxas, Peek, Peek, & Hagemann, 2000).

Many software packages are available to help accountants with book keeping. However, many of these software packages become quite complicated and present problems of interoperability and usability, among others. Human-computer interface issues are extremely important for online service applications (Pinhanez, 2009). In parallel, many accountants lack the time or the patience to learn the skills needed to take full advantage of these advances. Even worse, the technology continues to move forward, getting more complicated and thus widening the gap between potential and actual use (Zarowin, 2004).

While technology's impact on the accountants' profession has been considerable, there are many more developments to come. Thus, accountants must be technologically proactive (Johnston, 2005). During the next few years, the profession of accountancy will face unexpected new challenges (Bhansali, 2006b).

This study investigates the level of ICT use by accounting offices in a Greek county. In the next section, previous studies on these issues are presented. Then the methodology is described. The presentation of the results follows. Finally, conclusions are drawn and future research is suggested.

PREVIOUS RESEARCH

Not many previous studies exist on the use of ICT by accounting offices. Some detailed studies were conducted by the American Institute of Certified Public Accountants (AICPA).

Gallun, Heagy, and Lindsey (1993) distinguished between small and large public CPAs (Certified Public Accountants) and accountants in large enterprises (industry accountants) in the United States. They found that large accounting offices used more LANs (Local Area Networks) than small ones. Also, most accountants did not appear to worry very much about viruses and other security issues. Most used laser printers along with the essential dot matrix, and the most popular brand was Hewlett-Packard. Finally, a small percentage used portable printers.

Khani and Zarowin (1994) showed that 23% of enterprises in the United States supplemented all forms electronically (e.g., liquidation of income tax statements), and 15% planned to do it in the future. Regarding security, 31% faced virus problems. Also, 37% used an antivirus program, 68% of which used Norton. Regarding backup, 83% backed up their data, 80% of which did this daily and 16% weekly. E-mail was used by 39% of the offices.

Prawitt, Romney, and Zarowin (1997) classified U.S. accountants in the following categories: 1) in big accounting offices (Big 6—national), 2) in intermediate (regional) offices, 3) in small offices (local and individual offices), 4) in organisations (business and nonprofit), 5) in schools (academic), and 6) in governmental organisations. The most popular operating system was Microsoft Windows. All accountants in the first two categories used networks. The most popular application office suite was Microsoft Office (Word, Excel, Access, and PowerPoint). All accountants used applications for managing their contacts and timetables, and the most popular application was ACT! by Sage. (The small use of Microsoft Outlook was interesting.)

Bush (2000) found that 96% of U.S. accountants had access to the Internet. More than half reported that they "surf" every day. Also, 65% of men and 47% of women reported that the Internet created more opportunities for them. Finally, 47% expected an increase in using the Internet for accounting research.

Anders and Fischer (2004) found that the New York accountants were absolutely satisfied with the programs of accountancy that they used for third consecutive year. Also, an increase was observed in the creation of Web pages by accountants aiming at the satisfaction of their customers.

Zarowin (2006) found that many accounting offices of all sizes transformed their offices to electronic ones. In 2003, only 38% prepared invoices electronically. In 2005, the percentage increased to 46%. In 2003, 64% used internal local networks (Intranets) for the storage and processing of customers' data. In 2005, the percentage increased to 72%. Finally, the number of accounting offices that stored their customers' documents only in the computer without printing them (electronic paperless office) showed an enormous increase of 103% from 2003 to 2005.

The use and development of Web pages for advertising by companies in the European Union during 2000–2003 increased, by 19% (Voiculescu, 2003). Advertising was the main reason for using and developing web pages (59%). It is remarkable that income acquisition was in third place (11%), behind customer service (26%).

Gullkvist and Ylinen (2005) found that the most important reasons for the development of e-accounting systems by Finnish accounting agencies were the following: more efficient use of time resources, higher internal performance, availability of accounting information, and perceived requirements from authorities. Lack of time can clearly been seen as one of the key obstacles delaying the adoption of the e-accounting systems among small and medium-sized enterprises.

The accountancy profession is feeling the strain of increased responsibility, away from the traditional roles for which accountants were trained (Mintel International Group Ltd., 2005). Although the triggering factors for stress and increasing staff turnover are high, little is currently being done to improve the situation. A resounding 84% of U.S. companies said their accounting department was leading the compli-ance initiatives in the company. The same 84% stated that increasing compliance requirements have put them under greater pressure due to the increase in scope and volume of their work, and yet 88% were still manually re-keying data into spreadsheets for reporting and analysis (Mintel International Group Ltd., 2005).

Although many Inland Revenue Service offices support electronic tax filling (Economides & Terzis, 2008), many accountants continue not to use these new electronic services. Each of the previous studies investigated only a specific area of accountants' ICT use. For example, one study examined the types of networking technologies adopted; another examined the types of software used; and another examined the accountants' Web sites. Therefore, a comprehensive survey needed to be developed to capture the complete view of accountants' ICT use. Furthermore, most studies investigated accountants in the United States. Thus, a need also existed to investigate accountants' ICT use in other countries.

METHODOLOGY

Based on the OECD (Organization for Economic Co-operation and Development) (2002) model, our experience in surveying other services' areas, opinions of accountants after extensive discussions with them, and the previous studies presented above, we developed a comprehensive questionnaire to find out the utilization of ICT by accountants. Specially, fruitful discussions with members and officials of a local Accountants' Club helped us finalize the questionnaire.

We wanted to discover the ICT infrastructure that accounting offices in a Greek province owned and used. Also, we investigated what kind of accountant-specific software and e-government services the accountants used. We also wanted to identify the problems they faced in their daily accounting work regarding ICT. Suggestions to the Greek government and the Greek Accountants' Chamber could then be made.

The questionnaire contains 30 closed-type questions with multiple choice answers and 2 open-type questions. We classified the questions into four categories:

1. General information about the accounting enterprises (5 questions),
2. ICT infrastructure of the enterprise (18 questions),
3. Internet use and Web presence (4 questions), and
4. Accounting software applications and services (8 closed + 2 open questions).

One hundred twenty accounting offices are in the survey's region. The research was carried out at 100 accounting offices (private as well as belonging to enterprises) in this Greek county, using interviews at each office. The remaining 20 offices did not participate due to their lack of available time. We faced several obstacles in trying to interview the accountants due to their limited time.

We selected the specific survey's region because we have personal relationships with many accountants in this region, and expected that they would take the time to answer our questionnaire. During 2006–2007, we visited 75 offices and personally interviewed the staff. Twenty-five offices were interviewed by phone.

RESULTS

General Information about the Accounting Enterprises

Most accounting offices (53) employed four to nine people, followed by offices (37) with less than three people. There were also 10 offices employing more than nine people.

Almost all offices (98) were autonomous private offices, while 2 were large enterprises. This was expected since most Greek accountants work mainly as free professionals, having their own private offices.

Most offices (63) were active in the profession for more than 15 years. Most (31) were active for 23 years. Only 13 offices were relatively new in the profession (less than 6 years).

ICT Infrastructure

As expected, all offices used Internet and e-mail, since they need to use the e-government services of Inland Revenue Service. Wide Area Networks (WAN) were only used by two offices, the large enterprises (Figure 1).

It is important to note that 63 offices set up LAN networks for better internal office operation. Considering the offices that have LANs, 21% employed 1–3 people, 62% employed 4–9 people, and 17% employed 10 or more people. This shows that

Figure 1. ICT usage

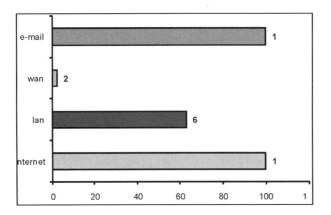

the use of networks in small and medium-sized enterprises is becoming a necessity.

The number of PCs was proportional to the number of personnel. In particular, 58 offices owned 4–10 PCs, and 42 offices owned 1–3 PCs. However, no office owned more than 10 PCs although 11 offices employed more than 10 people. Not all personnel were concurrently working on PCs; some were occupied at exterior works (e.g., visiting the Inland Revenue Service, the Social Security Organization, and banks).

Out of the 63 offices that set up LAN networks, 21 used Client-Server technology and 42 used Peer-to-Peer (P2P) technology (Figure 2). This was expected for such small LANs since the P2P networks cost less and do not require specialised personnel for maintenance. It is also noteworthy that among the 37 offices that did not set up any network infrastructure, 29 planned to set up one in the near future, while 8 did not.

Furthermore, 26 offices used a separate file server for central storage of all their files (in both Client-Server and P2P networks), 4 used Print Server (only in Client-Server networks), 12 used Backup Server (only in Client-Server networks), and none used Mail Server. Since most offices employed few employees, they usually met each other in person at the office. The 26 offices that used a file server realised that they were able to protect important files by placing them centrally

and would not waste time updating the same data on separate PCs.

It is also interesting to note that among the offices that used Client-Server, 10% owned 1–3 PCs (Figure 3). Also, among the offices that used P2P, 62% owned 4–10 PCs. Accountants may not have been fully aware of the different benefits offered by each one of these networking technologies. Usually, an office imitates others and decides to invest in something others suggest. Cost is also a very important factor in this choice. Instead of buying a new server, many small offices transformed an old PC into a File Server.

The offices that did not plan to set up a LAN were small offices, usually with one PC and sometimes two or three. Roughly half of the offices that planned to set up a LAN owned 1–10 PCs (Figure 4).

Only 34 offices owned laptops apart from PCs. Some accountants worked from homes using laptops at these offices.

As expected, 92 offices owned Dot Matrix printers since printing is essential for their daily work, for example printing customers' books (Figure 5). It is interesting to note that 30 offices had black and white Laser printers and 16 offices owned colour Laser printers. These offices were mainly large offices with many customers, as well as the two big enterprises. More than half of the offices owned new multi-machines (fax, Inkjet

Figure 2. LAN types and plans to use LANs

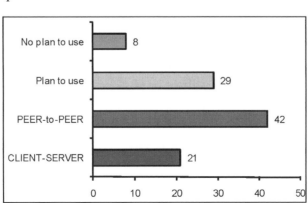

Figure 3. Relationship between "LAN type" and "Number of PCs"

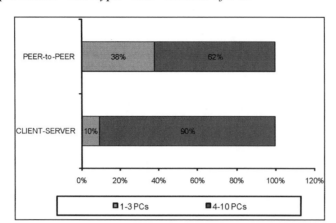

Figure 4. Relationship between the "Plans for LANs" and "Number of PCs"

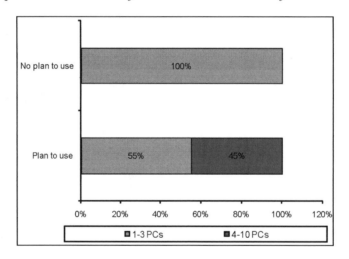

Figure 5. Printers usage

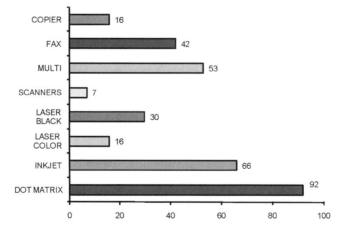

printer, scanner together), which is economically sound for small offices. Forty-two offices owned old fax machines. The new offices preferred to buy multi-machines. Sixty-six owned inkjet printers, which are the most economical for printing a few pages. Seven offices owned separate scanners. Only 16 offices owned photocopy machines (mainly big offices with many customers).

All offices used antivirus programs, while hardly any of the 76 offices used separate firewall programs apart from that included in Windows XP Operating System (Figure 6). Also, 12 offices used full data backup systems. These were mainly big offices and the two large enterprises, which had explicit backup policies. Due to the high cost of such technologies, the remaining offices did not use such technology. Instead, they used more economical ways of backing up their data. The offices that did not use a firewall program were mainly small offices with few PCs; they did not wish to purchase separate programs, since the firewall included in Windows XP worked well.

Regarding security problems faced by the offices during the previous year, 18 faced virus or spy-ware problems, 11 faced unauthorized access into their PCs, and 1 faced a program exploitation problem (Figure 7). The main reason for these problems was that despite being equipped with antivirus programs, they did not update these

programs daily or, in some cases, even have the programs activated. The unauthorized access could be associated with the fact that most offices did not use password and user name to log into Windows.

Seventy-nine offices backed up their critical data daily, 11 did this weekly, and 10 did this monthly (Figure 8). They claimed that the main reason for not backing up daily was the lack of time and their belief that it is not important to back up daily.

Regarding the media used for back up (Figure 9), most offices (86) backed up on the local disk (another partition or another file), 16 used a backup server, 8 used the old zip-drive, and 29 offices used CD-DVD. Twenty-one offices used more modern methods such as USB flash disk and external USB hard disk. Only two offices knew about and had a complete image backup of their hard disk. These two offices were small with less than people people, but these workers were young and familiar with new technology.

As expected, they used Microsoft's software for general use. They used Windows XP as the operating system, and the Microsoft Office 2000–2003 as their office suite. Most companies did not know about open source software.

Sixty-eight offices used password and user name to log in to the Windows system. The re-

Figure 6. Security protection mechanisms

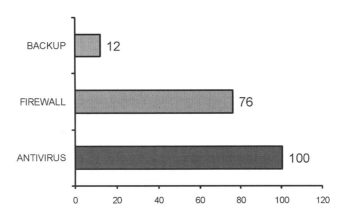

Figure 7. Security problems

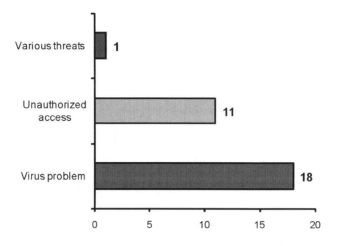

Figure 8. Backup frequency

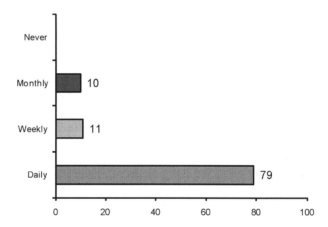

Figure 9. Data media backup

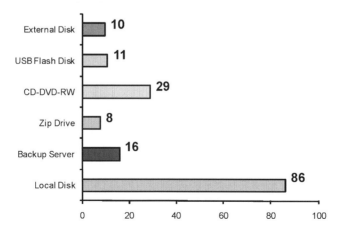

mainder 32 offices were mainly small offices with few PCs, and they did not consider it essential.

Regarding problems due to introducing ICT into their enterprises, 18 offices considered, as a problem, the lack of information and knowledge about ICT; 16 offices had problems with the terminology; and 13 offices were burned up by the time-consuming procedures (Figure 10). However, it is interesting to note that most offices (58) did not face any particular problem, and 5 offices were not interested in any of these problems. (Most offices were staffed by young accountants who eagerly follow any new technological innovations.)

Regarding the use of VoIP (Voice over Internet Protocol) technology, only four offices had used Skype (Figures 11 & 12). Most offices declared that this technology is still unreliable, and they will wait until it becomes perfect to use it again. Sixty-seven offices said they had not used it but intended to do so in the future, while 23 offices declared that they did not intend to use it at all. Their reasons for not using VoIP were that this technology is still new, unreliable, and there is no sufficient information about it. At that time, only two Greek telecommunications companies provided VoIP in parallel with other services, and they did not advertise it enough. Sixteen offices

Figure 10. ICT problems

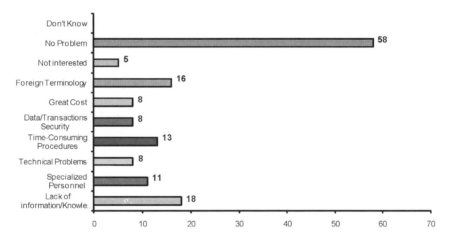

Figure 11. VoIP usage

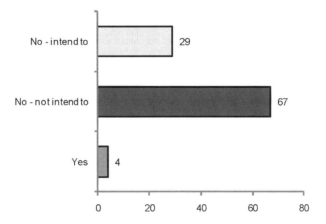

Figure 12. Reasons for not using VoIP

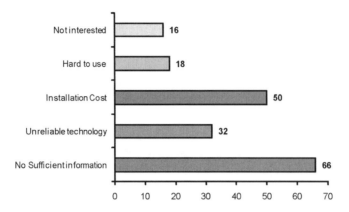

declared that they were not interested in this new technology.

Regarding their degree of familiarization with ICT and their continuing training policy, most offices (58) maintained a continuous training policy and were very familiar with ICT (Figure 13). In these offices, most accountants recognized the benefits of ICT. Internet explosion helped immensely. On the other hand, a few offices (eight) hesitated to use ICT. These were mainly old offices with elderly accountants, who could not keep pace with the new technologies and simply used only the essential items for their daily work. Sixty-four offices were very familiar with ICT, but they

did not have any training policy, which happens mainly in small offices with one or two people.

Regarding their expectations of their Chamber (oe-e.gr, pol.org.gr) or the government, 71 offices wished to be financed to purchase or use new ICT products (Figure 14). Accountants were wiling to use the new technologies, but they needed money to proceed.

Internet Use and Web Presence

In this section, we present the results of our research on accountants' Internet use. It is important to note that a Greek accounting office should have an Internet connection to connect to the Inland

Figure 13. ICT familiarity and training policy

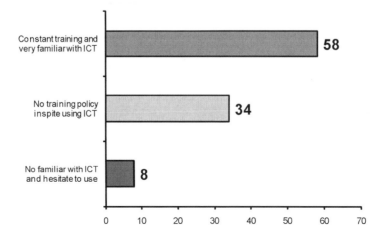

Figure 14. What accountants want from government and chamber

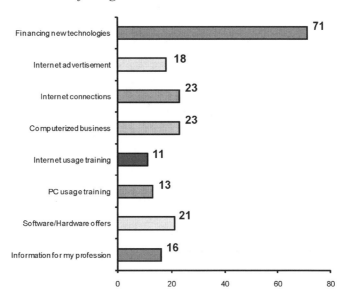

Revenue Service (TAXIS NET: www.taxisnet.gr). Forty-three offices used ISDN (Integrated Services Digital Network), while 53 offices adopted the new ADSL (Asymmetric Digital Subscriber Line) technology (Figure 15). However, four still used simple PSTN (Public Switched Telephone Network) connections via modems; these offices are small and staffed by elderly accountants who did not wish to upgrade their infrastructure. No office used wireless or satellite connections.

More than half of the offices used an ADSL connection due to the aggressive policy of the main Greek telecommunication company (OTE). Recently, OTE lowered the price of ADSL, making it affordable for any office. Correlating these results with their upgrading plans, we see that most of the 53 offices that planned to upgrade their Internet connection used ISDN. Accountants also embraced ADSL technology because it was economically and technically accessible.

Figure 15. Internet connection type

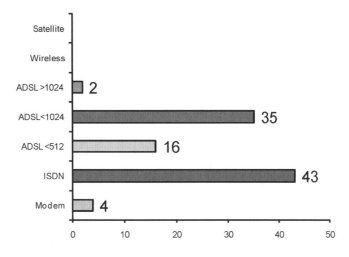

Only three offices had Web sites, which were developed by external personnel and hosted by an ISP server. Most accounting offices did not exclusively employ ICT specialists or an ICT service company, because they believed they needed a Web site only for advertising purposes. However, they did not consider this function essential. This conclusion is also supported by the fact that only five offices planned to create Web pages in the near future.

As we have mentioned, an accounting office must have an Internet connection for transactions with public services, such as the Inland Revenue Service. Consequently, all offices said the main reason they used the Internet was to communicate with public services and ministries (Figure 16). Thirty-four offices also cited e-banking as a reason for their Internet use. Fifty-eight offices used the Web to find information.

They rated the problems that affect their Internet use equally (Figure 17). These problems were related to security, complicated technology, Web site cost, loosing time in surfing, communication costs, and slow and unstable data communica-

Figure 16. Internet usage reasons

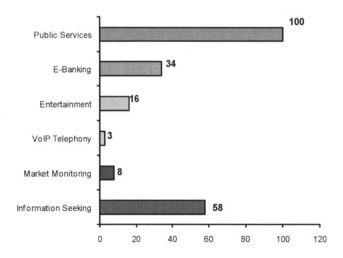

Figure 17. Internet problems evaluation

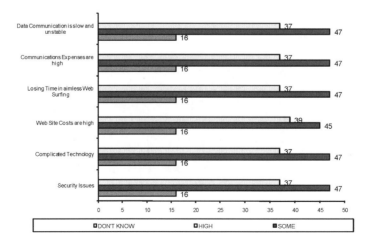

tions. Most offices (47) considered these problems serious, 37 considered them fair, and 13 did not care. Therefore, most accountants were hesitant about the Internet.

Accounting Software Applications and Services

In this section, we report on the accountants' use of accounting software and related services.

The usual work of a Greek accountant is the book keeping of A and B categories. In the Greek market, there are software packages operating in a network environment that are useful for this purpose. These software packages can be used simultaneously by several people, depending on the licence. In 63 offices, such software packages were used by two or more people in a network environment. In the remaining 37 offices, a single person used them. This occurred mainly in small offices.

In Greece, all enterprises are obliged to send a VAT (Value Added Tax) statement periodically (every quarter for A & B categories) to the Inland Revenue Service. According to existing legislation, accountants do not have to send these statements electronically via TAXIS NET even

if such possibility is provided. Most offices (82) periodically sent the VAT statement electronically, exploiting the electronic services offered by the state. Few offices (18) submitted their statement in person to the Inland Revenue Service.

While almost all of these software packages support data exchange with MS Office, no office used this feature. The accountants may not have known about this possibility or did not need it.

Although these software packages could be upgraded via the Internet, in real time (live update), most offices (61) did not download the new versions. They may have not been familiar with this process, or they did not know it existed. On the other hand, 26 offices checked for new versions once per month, and 13 offices did so daily.

When we examined the types of printers used to print out reports from these software packages, we found that 92 offices used all varieties. Eighty-nine did this daily and three did weekly. The remaining eight offices, which are small offices, owned and used only one printer (Figure 18).

Next, we investigated the book keeping of C category. Large enterprises, with high turnover, must keep C category books. Thus, the book keeping of C category is mainly done by large

Figure 18. A' & B' books category services usage

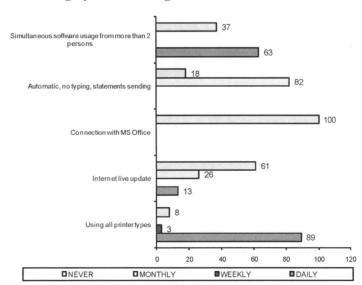

offices with much experience. Regarding the simultaneous use of software packages by two or more people, we have the same results as the book keeping of A and B categories, that is, accountants used networking technology. Sixty-three offices used this technology daily and 37 never. In these 37 offices, offices were included that did not serve customers of the C category.

None of the offices used the software's ability to connect to MS Office. For C category book keeping, accountants must frequently update their software packages. In terms of upgrading via the Internet in real time, 53 offices never updated in this manner, 13 monthly, 5 weekly, and 29 daily. Regarding printing work related to C category book keeping, 66 offices, with many of these customers, printed daily. However, 28 offices did not have such customers and therefore did not need to print this work, 3 offices printed a few times per month because they had one or two such customers, and 3 offices printed a few times per week (Figure 19).

Only eight offices used CRM (Customer Relationship Management) systems daily, and the remaining 92 offices did not know about CRM. These eight offices were mainly large offices with many customers. Similarly, only the two

large enterprises used ERP (Enterprise Resource Planning) systems daily (Figure 20). Only large companies with a specialized accountants' section used ERP.

On the matter of payroll services in Greece, all enterprises that pay personnel are obliged to send the APS (Analytic Periodical Statement) to the Organisation of Social Security (IKA) every month. IKA offers accountants multiple ways to submit this statement. Currently, the two most popular methods are: 1) creating a compatible file using the payroll program and sending it to IKA, and 2) typing the elements into suitable forms on the Web site of IKA (www.ika.gr) and completing the sending of APS (Analytic Periodical Statement). The first method is used by 92 offices monthly (Figure 21). The second method is used by 71 offices monthly. Eight offices did not use any payroll software.

Three offices upgraded their payroll software online daily, 87 monthly, and 10 never.

Concerning electronic communication with banks or other institutions of social insurance (as well as the exchange of electronic data), 79 (respectively 82) offices never had such interactions, 10 (respectively 8) monthly, and 11 (respectively 10) daily (Figure 21).

Figure 19. C' books category services usage

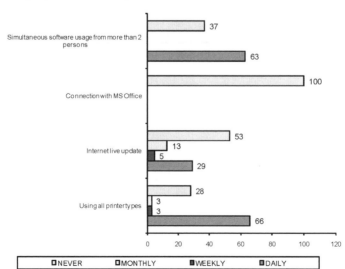

Figure 20. ERP, taxation software and CRM Services usage

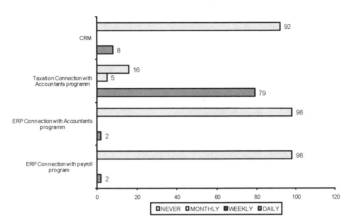

Figure 21. Payroll services usage

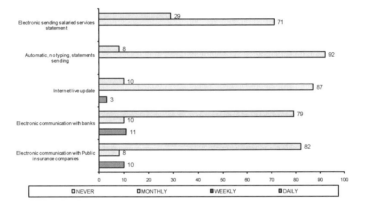

Ninety offices used Windows-based accounting software whereas only three used the old DOS-based software. Greek accounting software companies helped by adapting their products to new technological innovations.

Figure 22 shows the specific accounting software programs offices used. UNION is used by 37 offices, while SINGULAR is used by 24. EPSILON-net is a powerful program, but it is more expensive; therefore, it is used by only 12 big companies.

However, accounting offices did not utilize the new ways of upgrading their software. Seventy-nine upgraded via post (CD) (Figure 23). Although new technology is available, many offices insisted on using old methods. Eight offices upgraded their software directly via the Internet (live update) over a broadband Internet connection, and 34 offices upgraded after downloading and installing the update file.

The accountants kept themselves informed about new developments in their profession via multiple means. Ninety-two offices read periodicals, 53 offices read TaxHeaven (www.gus.gr), 37 offices read e-Forologia (www.e-forologia.gr), 26 offices read the online e-magazine EPSILON7 (http://www.epsilonnetwork.gr/epsilon7), and 29 offices were informed by discussions in various forums (Figure 24). Thus, many accountants were informed not only through traditional written press but also via the Internet.

Figure 22. Program's brands that accountants use

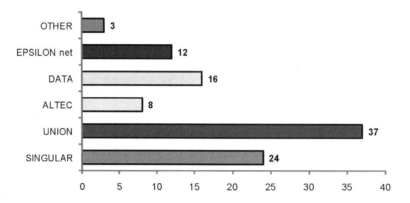

Figure 23. Program's update

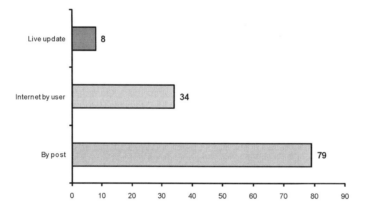

Figure 24. Frequent profession's informing

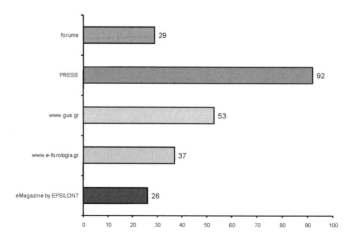

As we have reported, many accountants used the new e-services provided by TAXIS NET. Although sending VAT statements regarding the A and B book keeping categories electronically is not mandatory, 92 offices did in this manner. Also, 95 offices sent their customers' final Taxation Statements to TAXIS NET. The accounting offices realized the benefits of using the new online services that the government provided (Figure 25).

Finally, Greek accountants were not familiar with the "paperless office" that prevails in the United States. Only two offices created an electronic file for each customer by scanning the forms and storing them in e-files. Also, no office could send invoices to their customers in electronic form. Instead, they preferred to key the invoices' data into the corresponding software. They did not use these technologies because 76 offices did not consider them to be important, and 50 did not have much time for such work (Figure 26).

Finally, almost all offices considered the following factors very important for their software packages: convenience of learning, ease of use, reputation of the software's company, live update ability, specifications and functions, customer support, user friendliness, and online service (Figure 27).

Figure 25. Greek government services (TAXIS NET) usage

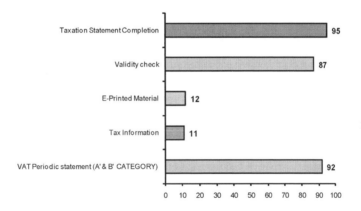

Figure 26. Reasons of not using "paperless Office"

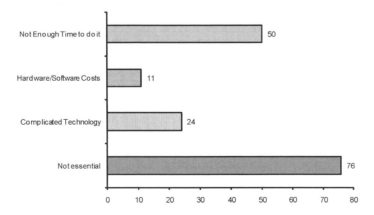

Figure 27. Software evaluation criteria

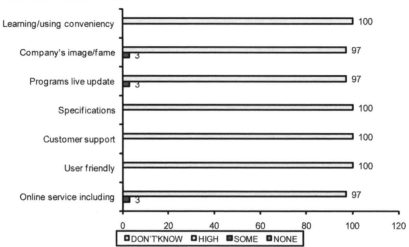

CONCLUSION

The purpose of this study was to provide insights into the level of ICT use by the accounting offices in a Greek county.

The Greek state provided various e-government services to accountants, which urged the accounting offices to use and develop an ICT infrastructure. Various Greek public organizations provide e-services. For example, the Ministry of Finance has the Web site for TAXIS NET (www.taxisnet.gr) and the Ministry of Employment provides the Web site for IKA (www.ika.gr). These e-government services help accounting offices to save time and better serve their customers.

The findings from this survey show that the accounting offices in a Greek county kept pace with ICT technological innovations. For example, Internet was widely used by them. However, elderly accountants seemed to be more resistant to adopt the new technologies.

Briefly, the positive points were the following:

- Many (63) offices set up a LAN, and 29 of the remaining offices planned to do so in the future. The accountants recognized the benefits of having a LAN in their enterprise. Software companies helped with this implementation by allowing their programs to be used in a network environment without extra cost.
- All the offices had antivirus programs for their PCs.
- Few (18) offices faced viruses' problems during the past year.
- Many (58) offices did not face any problems using ICT.
- Many (82) offices used the electronic submission of VAT (in A and B category book keeping) via TAXIS NET, which is not mandatory.

The negative points were the following:

- Few (26) offices used separate file servers to store their data.
- Few (12) offices used complete backup systems for their data.
- Only 79 offices backed up their data daily.
- Very few (2) offices had a complete image backup of their hard disk.
- Very few (4) offices used VoIP for small time duration. They said this service was unreliable, and they did not have much information regarding how to use it.

- Many (43) offices still used the old ISDN Internet connection, although the prices of ADSL had fallen enough to be economically comparable with ISDN.
- Very few (3) offices developed their own Web site.
- Very few (8) offices used CRM programs for daily operations.
- Still, 3 offices used DOS-based professional applications.
- Many (79) offices upgraded their software packages via post (receiving the upgrades in a CD), although almost all software packages had live update ability.
- Very few (2) offices created electronic files of their customers' documents (paperless office).

Although there were two open questions, many accountants did not make any suggestions but the following suggestions were made:

- Enable direct and complete interconnection between their software programs and the public e-services of the Inland Revenue Service (TAXIS NET) and the Organisation of Social Security (IKA) without having to type the same data into forms on the these Web sites. Currently, this ability is provided for some services.

- Provide the possibility of sending a customer's first VAT statement electronically. Currently, a new customer should record his first statement in person with the Inland Revenue Service. Afterward, he can send the statements electronically.
- Provide the possibility of sending the liquidation VAT statement electronically via the Internet. Currently, a pilot project offers this ability.
- Training on accounting software should be offered by the software companies not only in Athens (the capital of Greece) but also in the province.

Limitations of this study include the specific province and country sample of the accounting offices. A future study could cover all Greek regions, as well as other countries. Also, a cross-sector comparison with enterprises in other service professions could be made. Nevertheless, we hope that the results of this study provide an insight into the use ICT and electronic services by Greek accountants. These results could be a starting point for further research in this area.

REFERENCES

Anders, S. B., & Fischer, C. M. (2004). A hard look at tax software: 2004 survey of New York State practitioners. *The CPA Journal*. Retrieved October 14, 2006, from http://www.nysscpa.org/cpajournal/2004/704/infocus/p18.htm

Anderson, T., Fox, M., & Schwartz, B. N. (2005). History and trends in e-filing: A survey of CPA practitioners. *The CPA Journal*. Retrieved October 14, 2006, from http://www.nysscpa.org/cpajournal/2005/1005/essentials/p66.htm

Bhansali, C. (2006a). The question every practicing accountant must ask. *Accounting Technology*, June. Retrieved March 22, 2007, from http://www.webcpa.com/

Bhansali, C. (2006b). A partial solution to a Daunting problem. *Accounting Technology*, September. Retrieved March 22, 2007, from http://www.webcpa.com/

Bush, C. T. (2000). Accountants are thriving on the Web, says survey. [from http://www.aicpa.org/PUBS/JOFA/joaiss.htm]. *Journal of Accountancy*, *190*(5), 20. Retrieved November 23, 2006.

Chatzopoulos, K. C., & Economides, A. A. (2009). A holistic evaluation of Greek municipalities' websites. *Electronic Government, an International Journal (EG), 6*(2), 193-212.

Czech Statistical Office. (2002). *Technology used by enterprises.* Retrieved October 11, 2006, from http://www.czso.cz/eng/edicniplan.nsf/o/9602-04-2003-1__technology_used_by_enterprises

Economides, A. A., & Terzis, V. (2008). Evaluating tax sites: An evaluation framework and its application. *Electronic Government, an International Journal (EG), 5*(3), 321-344.

Gallun, R. A., Heagy, C. D., & Lindsey, H. C. (1993). How CPAs use computers. *Journal of Accountancy, 175*(1), 38–41.

Garen, K. (2006). Driving the firm of the future. *Accounting Technology,* June. Retrieved February 9, 2007, from http://www.webcpa.com/

Gullkvist, B., & Ylinen, M. (2005). E-accounting systems use in Finnish accounting agencies. In M. Seppä, M. Hannula, A-M. Järvelin, J. Kujala, M. Ruohonen, & T. Tiainen (Eds.) *Frontiers of e-Business Research. Proceedings of the e-Business Research Forum 2005* (pp. 109-117). Tampere, Finland: e-Business Resilience Centre.

Johnston, R. P. (2005). A tour of tomorrow's technology. [from http://www.aicpa.org/PUBS/JOFA/joaiss.htm]. *Journal of Accountancy, 200*(4), 95–97. Retrieved November 23, 2006.

Khani, P. E., & Zarowin, S. (1994). The technology used by high-tech CPAs. *Journal of Accountancy, 177*(2), 54–58.

Levy, Y., Murphy, K. E., & Zanakis, S. H. (2009). A value-satisfaction taxonomy of IS effectiveness (VSTISE): A case study of user satisfaction with IS and user-perceived value of IS. *International Journal of Information Systems in the Service Sector, 1*(1), 93–118.

Lexhagen, M. (2009). Customer perceived value of travel and tourism web sites. *International Journal of Information Systems in the Service Sector, 1*(1), 35–53.

Mintel International Group Ltd. (2005). Retrieved October 14, 2006, from http://www.mintel.com

Organization for Economic Co-operation and Development. (2002). *The OECD model survey of ICT usage in the business sector.* Retrieved September 8, 2006, from http://www.oecd.org

Pinhanez, C. (2009). A service science perspective on human-computer interface issues of online service applications. *International Journal of Information Systems in the Service Sector, 1*(2), 17–35.

Prawitt, D., Romney, M., & Zarowin, S. (1997). A journal survey: The software CPAs use. [from http://www.aicpa.org/PUBS/JOFA/joaiss.htm]. *Journal of Accountancy, 183*(2), 52–66. Retrieved November 23, 2006.

Roxas, M. L., Peek, L., Peek, G., & Hagemann, T. (2000). A preliminary evaluation of professional accounting services: Direct marketing on the Internet. *Journal of Services Marketing, 14*(7), 595–605. doi:10.1108/08876040010352763

Terpsiadou, M. H., & Economides, A. A. (2009). (in press). The use of information systems in the Greek public financial services: The case of TAXIS. *Government Information Quarterly.*

Voiculescu, A. (2000). *Strategic implications of electronic commerce for UK businesses.* Retrieved October 14, 2006, from http://www.aurelvoiculescu.com/

Zarowin, S. (2003). Hot stuff: What you need and what you don't your technology setup may be sufficient for your needs. [from http://www.aicpa.org/PUBS/JOFA/joaiss.htm]. *Journal of Accountancy, 195*(4), 28. Retrieved November 23, 2006.

Zarowin, S. (2004). Top tools for CPAs: Technology products that make your work go faster and smoother. [from http://www.aicpa.org/PUBS/JOFA/joaiss.htm]. *Journal of Accountancy, 194*(5), 26. Retrieved November 23, 2006.

Zarowin, S. (2006). Rate yourself in the paperless race: Have you overcome your resistance to the new technology? [from http://www.aicpa.org/PUBS/JOFA/joaiss.htm]. *Journal of Accountancy, 201*(5), 50–54. Retrieved February 17, 2007.

Chapter 4.11
E–Services in Danish Research Libraries:
Issues and Challenges at Roskilde University Library

Ada Scupola
Roskilde University, Denmark

ABSTRACT

This chapter reports the findings of a case study of e-services adoption at research libraries. The case under consideration is Roskilde University Library (RUB), a research library supporting learning activities at Roskilde University. The research focuses on the main issues that RUB had to deal with in the process of adopting e-services and the future challenges that e-services provide for RUB. The chapter also presents the consequences of e-services adoption for Roskilde University library's organization, its business model and the relationships with customers, publishers (providers of knowledge), and other research libraries in Denmark. The main results can be summarized as follows: (1) adoption of e-services has forced RUB to innovate rapidly. Innovation is driven, among other factors, by ICT developments (technology push), but innovation is also user-driven and pervasive throughout the organization; (2) e-services have changed RUB's organizational structure and division of labour by moving more and more towards IT-based jobs and competences; (3) e-services have changed the relationships between users and publishers; (4) e-services have changed and continue to change the business model of the library; and (5) RUB is becoming a combination of a virtual and a physical library, moving more and more towards a virtual library with electronic resources and online communities, but still keeping the traditional function of a "knowledge space."

E-SERVICES AND THEIR CHARACTERISTICS

The networked ICT technologies (such as the Internet) are having a dramatic effect on how services and especially knowledge services are innovated, designed, produced, and distributed. In addition, ICT networks such as the Internet have created

DOI: 10.4018/978-1-60566-064-6.ch014

the basis for the development of new types of services. These networks may also change the way customers or users experience service functions.

E-services are defined here as services that are produced, provided, and/or consumed through the use of ICT networks such as Internet-based systems and mobile solutions. E-services can be used by both consumers and businesses, and can be accessed via a wide range of information appliances (Hoffman, 2003, p. 53). E-services also include the selling of physical goods on the Internet as for instance an airline ticket that is purchased online, but delivered by surface mail to the buyers or government services offered on the Internet or e-government. There are three main characteristics of e-services:

- The service is accessible across the Internet or other electronic networks
- The service is consumed by a person across the Internet or other electronic networks
- There might be a fee that the consumer pays the provider for using the e-service, but that might not always be the case as for example in some e-services offered by the government

Normally the production, provision, or consumption of a service requires the interaction between the service provider and the user of the service. Traditionally, this has been based on personal interactions, most often face-to-face interactions. In e-services, the production, consumption, and/or provision of services takes place through the intermediation of an ICT network such as Internet-based systems or mobile solutions. Examples of e-services are e-banking, e-library services, e-publishing, airline tickets, e-government, information, and location services. However, e-services also include, for example, the online selling of real estate property or the purchasing of physical goods that are then delivered

by other means. The advent of e-commerce and e-services has raised a number of challenges for knowledge intensive service organizations such as consulting companies, libraries, and publishers as well as for companies selling physical goods. For example, companies have to innovate, have to develop strategies and new business models for the production and provision of e-services, and acquire or develop new competences.

The purpose of this study is to investigate the challenges that e-services are posing and will pose for research or academic libraries. The research library is chosen here because it is a particular type of knowledge intensive service organization: it has the role of acquiring and providing research and learning related knowledge as well as storing and preserving such knowledge. More specifically, the study shows how the advent of e-services has revolutionized the whole concept of the library and forced the libraries to innovate at an extremely fast rate. In fact libraries have been using information and communication technologies (ICTs) for more than 20 years, but while the first wave of ICTs and technological change had resulted in automation with consequent rationalization and decreased costs, the advent of e-services is moving the library from automation to digitalization, causing a shift of paradigm in libraries. The study has focused on the issues that RUB has had to deal with as a result of e-services adoption as well as the future challenges that e-services provide for RUB. In addition, the investigation has also focused on the consequences of e-services for Roskilde University Library's organization, its business model, and relationships with customers, publishers (providers of information), and other research libraries in Denmark.

The case is based on a number of interviews with RUB management, other secondary material provided by Roskilde University Library and information provided on the Web page.

THE ROLE AND CONCEPT OF ACADEMIC LIBRARIES

In order to understand how digitalization and e-services are changing the library and its activities, it is important to understand what a library is, and what its major roles in learning are. Libraries have historically had a central role in learning, since the first library was created 2,000 years ago in Alexandria. Libraries can be defined as "an organized set of resources, which includes human services as well as the entire spectrum of media (e.g., text, video, hypermedia). Libraries have physical components, such as space, equipment, and storage media; intellectual components such as collection policies that determine what materials will be included and organizational schemes that determine how the collection is accessed; and people, who manage the physical and intellectual components and interact with users to solve information problems" (Marchionini & Maurer, 1995, p. 68). Marchionini and Maurer (1995) distinguish three major roles that academic and research libraries serve in learning. The first role is sharing expensive resources. These resources are physical resources such as books, periodicals, media, and human resources such as the librarians that provide a number of responsive and proactive services. Responsive services include maintaining reserve materials, answering reference questions, providing bibliographic instructions, developing media packages, teaching users how to use the material. Proactive services include selectively disseminating information to the faculty and students, collaborating with instructors to plan teaching. The second role that libraries serve is a cultural role in preserving and organizing artifacts and ideas. Libraries have historically had the role of preserving material to make it accessible to future learners in addition to ensuring access to materials through indexes, catalogues, and other aids that allow users to find what they need. The third role of the library is that of serving as a physical knowledge space, where people meet to study and read and often to exchange ideas.

DANISH LIBRARY LANDSCAPE

The Danish Library Concept

The Danish library system is based on the concept of the citizen's fundamental right to knowledge and information. Basically the library service is free of charge, but libraries can demand payment for special services (Danish National Library Authority, www.bs.dk/publikationer/english/statistics/). The Danish library system is characterized by extensive and well-functioning cooperation, both within the individual library sector and between the different library types. In Denmark there is an agency that is responsible for all matters that are related to libraries: The Danish National Library Authority. The Danish National Library Authority is an agency under the Ministry of Culture. The Authority is responsible for advising the government on the organization, coordination, and strategy for the Danish Library Service and gives professional advice to ministers and public authorities, as well as local authorities, libraries, and information services. In addition, the Authority has an active role in international collaboration within the field of libraries, documentation, and information. The major duties of the Authority consist of the administration of the Act regarding library services and a number of statutory government grants for library purposes. The Authority is also responsible for collecting and providing statistical information about Danish libraries. The Authority furthermore acts as the administrative base (secretariat) for Denmark's Electronic Research Library. This is a major initiative for the development of e-services in Denmark and the libraries digitalization process.

There are two types of libraries in Denmark: public libraries and research libraries. The purpose of public libraries is to promote information, education, and cultural activity by placing books and other media at the disposal of the public. Libraries therefore offer books, serials, talking books, recorded music, and electronic information resources (including the Internet) to the citizens.

All the public libraries are connected to the Internet. In 2004 there were 224 main public libraries, 428 branch libraries, and 44 mobile libraries.

Danish research libraries are government institutions and serve mainly higher education and research, but most of them are also open to the public at large. In Denmark there are 20 major research libraries connected to universities and other institutions of higher-level education. There are also a large number of smaller research libraries that are connected to educational institutions. The Royal Library located in Copenhagen and the State and University Library in the city of Århus have specific national library functions. The Royal Library functions both as Denmark's national library—including being a legal deposit library—and as the library of the University of Copenhagen. The State and University Library in Århus is similarly a legal deposit library. It houses the national media collection and has the overall responsibility for the Danish Central Library for Immigrant Literature and the Danish Repository Library for Public Libraries. The library acts as the national superstructure for the public libraries. Appendix 1 provides detailed data about Danish research library statistics such as number of staff, stock, expenditures, salaries, interlibrary loans, and so forth (http://www.bs.dk/publikationer/english/statistics/2004/index.htm).

The Important Role of DEFF in the Digitalization of the Danish Research Library System

In the 1990s, the Danish government had made a policy plan focusing on the "IT society" or "IT for all." This vision of IT for all included the digitalization of the libraries to provide all the citizens with access to electronic resources. As a result the Ministry of Culture, the Ministry of Education and the Ministry of Science established an IT working group in May 1996 with the objective of investigating how to transform a number of research libraries into electronic research libraries.

This idea laid the foundation for the establishment of the "Denmark's Electronic Research Library," via a network of cooperating electronic research libraries (http://www.bs.dk). In 1997, the "DEF report" was published with a view to creating a basis for a joint effort for the research libraries' IT development. The report described a model of reference for Denmark's Electronic Research Library (DEF), including the essential electronic functions and services to be delivered by such libraries. Consequently, a budget was allocated by the three ministers involved, a board of directors (steering committee) was appointed, and a vision and a strategy for the project were developed. In 2003, DEF became a permanent activity with the objective of improving the use of IT in supporting research and education. This is done through six programme areas:

- E-learning
- E-publishing
- Licenses
- Portals
- System architecture
- User facilities

Today, Denmark's Electronic Research Library (DEFF) is an organizational and technological partnership between research libraries cofinanced by the Ministry of Science, Technology and Innovation, the Ministry of Culture and the Ministry of Education and based at The Danish National Library Authority. Its purpose is to advance the development of a network of electronic research libraries that make available their electronic and other information resources in a coherent and simple way. This is obtained partly through government funding and partly by joint purchase of licenses (www.deff.dk). According to DEFF's Web page, the strategy of DEFF is "to improve the end user's access to information through cooperation between the Danish special and research libraries. The cooperation includes joint development in cases where cooperation will result in a greater advantage than the sum of local initiatives, including a better and total utilization of the libraries' resources; further development of the joint network of information resources; collective dissemination of the research libraries' information resources to the public" (www.deff.dk).

ORGANIZATION BACKGROUND: ROSKILDE UNIVERSITY LIBRARY

Roskilde University Library (RUB) is a research library serving the students and staff at Roskilde University. Roskilde University is a smaller university located in Roskilde, a city about 35 km from Copenhagen, the capital City of Denmark. The university counts circa 10,000 students. According to Roskilde University Statute (www.ruc. dk/library), Roskilde University Library has the following purposes:

• To give teachers and students at Roskilde University access to information and materials containing information necessary for research and teaching, as well as to ensure information on and access to the university teachers' and students' research.

• As a public research library to make available its collection to external users, among which are regional research and teaching institutions, business, and citizens.

• To participate in the national and international library collaboration.

• To conduct research and development within the library subjects and functions, but also the surrounding community and businesses as well as anybody who would like to use the library being this a public library.

Today the library counts approximately 45 employees, and the number of employees has decreased due to the digitalization process and e-services adoption. The following table (Table

Table 1. Roskilde University Library employees divided by position

Function/Position	Number of Employees
Research Librarian	9.6
Librarian	12.9
Office Functions	14.5
IT	6.5
Other	1.5

1)summarizes some basic information about the library.

The library counts today a number of paper books, paper journals, the entire spectrum of media as for example videos, and a number of e-journals and e-books. The library still acquires 8,000–9,000 books in paper format per year. The cataloguing of these books and paper journals is still done by people employed at the library. However they expect this number to go down, while the number of e-books goes up, especially as the quality of e-books improves. In addition, RUB counts today circa 18,000 e-journals, while the number of paper journals has gone down from circa 5,000 to 2,000. The purchase of the e-journals is based on the gateway model (Scupola, 2002). This model implies that the library buys the license to the e-journals that are stored in a central repository located at the publishing house. Information and communication technologies (ICTs) have made their way into library systems over more than 20 years, and today, in Denmark, libraries are the heaviest users of ICTs among the public sector institutions. At the beginning of the library digitalization process, ICTs contributed to a transformation from a card catalogue to an electronic catalogue. The advent of the World Wide Web roughly 10 years ago has completely revolutionized the way RUB operates and has made possible a number of e-services and self-services. The adoption and implementation of e-services and self-services has resulted in a number of organizational changes, changes in the organizational structure, the competencies of the librarians and relationships between the library and the publishers and the library and the users. In addition, the business model is also changing as RUB is trying to sell the services to private businesses. RUB is moving towards a combination of a physical and virtual library, as many services are getting transformed into e-services and self-services. The advent of e-commerce has raised the question of disintermediation of some actors of the value chain (e.g., Scupola, 2002; Sarkar, Butler, & Steinfield, 1995). Accordingly some speculations have been made about the disintermediation of the research library. However RUB's management believes that the library will still exist due to the value that it adds to the electronic resources provided by the publishers, the need to collect and store the knowledge produced on campus by teachers and students, and the need for a knowledge space where students meet with friends and go to study. Therefore Internet and e-services might change many aspects of the library and its relationships with users and publishers. However, RUB might preserve its historical role of knowledge space, even though after the implementation of library's online communities, such knowledge space can also become a virtual knowledge space.

E-Services Adoption at RUB

Over the last few years RUB has adopted a number of e-services and self-services that are changing many aspects of the way the library operates. Many of the services provided by RUB have been transformed into e-services after the advent of the World Wide Web. The main e-services offered at RUB are as follows:

- Access to electronic journals
- Access to electronic books
- Digital repository of all the students projects
- Chat with a librarian

Examples of self-services include:

- Rucforsk: a self-service system for the online registration of research and other activities of the teachers
- Online reference search, online reservation of material not available in the library, and so on

The library is also working on developing a digital repository of the compendia used in the courses. These e-services and self-services are developed on the base of open source software, although the IT department at RUB modifies it to make the software fit to their needs. However they try to use the original open source software as much as possible since it is very expensive to modify it.

ISSUES AND CHALLENGES IN THE ADOPTION OF E-SERVICES

This section presents the main issues that RUB has encountered in e-services' adoption, the organizational transformations RUB had to go through as a consequence, and the challenges that RUB is presently facing and expecting to face in the future.

Back Office

Back office processes have been completely automated as a result of e-service adoption, and they have changed from being manual to being electronic. All library work is today done with the use of ICTs. Even when they get the paper journal, they insert it into an integrated library system. Everyone working in the library is using ICTs to do their job.

Innovation

Innovation is very important at RUB. The whole e-services and self-services business model is based on it, especially IT-driven innovation. E-services related innovations at RUB are both user-driven and employee-driven. The sources of innovation are very different. A lot of projects are based on ideas coming from people employed at RUB such as librarians, management, the director, and the IT department. Also the librarians provide courses to newly enrolled students and faculty about how to use the e-services, and a lot of ideas come from these teaching sessions. In addition they have a customer-complaint box and library users may send e-mails to the library. These e-mails get screened and RUB may use such suggestions for incremental innovations. DEFF (see above) is also an important source of innovation, especially regarding the technology aspect of e-services implementation. Through DEFF, RUB can get ideas from and share experiences with other libraries. For example, each library might be in charge of testing an IT solution, then they share experiences and finally they decide to choose and adopt a system. DEFF is also important in financing new ideas or innovation projects, as RUB might lack the financial resources to start all the projects they believe are worth pursuing.

The main driving forces of e-services adoption have been the government vision and policy for an "IT society for all," the technological development of the Internet, World Wide Web and related IT solutions mainly in a technology push fashion, the pressure from cutting costs in the public sector coming either from the government or local university authorities, an IT innovation culture that has always existed in the Danish libraries (as the director of reader services says "you want to be a little bit better then your neighbour library"), competition among the different libraries' top management and, even though to a less extent, the customer wishes.

Organizational Change

The digitalization process has changed the structure of RUB's organization in several ways. First of all a new organizational level, a management level, has been introduced that can make the organization look more hierarchical than before, but it cannot really be compared with a classical hierarchical structure. In addition this management level mainly deals with library development and with political issues. Most importantly the division of labour has changed. In particular, the number of IT-related jobs has grown a lot. For example, 13 years ago, RUB had one employee dealing with IT, while today they employee six to seven people in the IT department. The IT department is expected to grow in the future in special fields. In addition almost everybody in the library has to be an IT literate and librarians have to grow together with IT as the trends change rapidly. Each employee is participating in several projects, mostly dealing with e-services and e-services development. When Roskilde University started, RUB employed circa 70 people and was servicing about one third of the number of students and faculties it has today. Nowadays, RUB employees 45 people and serves a number of students and faculties which is three times as large as the one that was servicing when the university was founded. There is a shift from the librarians to the users in the production-consumption of e-services. The use of e-services and self-services is increasing. Circa 80–85% of the users of the library are using e-services and self-services. As a result, while earlier they needed two to three librarians at the reference desk, one is now enough. As in all the organizational changes, this is causing resistance among the employees and users of e-services. As a matter of fact, even though most of RUB users (about 80–85%) are very satisfied with the digitalization trend and the introduction of e-services, there is still a small group that is missing the old library and is unsatisfied with e-services.

RUB Business Model

RUB's business model is changing as a result of e-services and self-service adoption and is going in different directions. Within Roskilde University, RUB is getting more involved with Campus IT, which is presently developed by the IT Department at Roskilde University. However, collaboration is sometimes difficult due to different priorities. RUB believes that they will play a central role in future e-learning projects at Roskilde University. In addition they are trying to collaborate with the teachers and instructors on how to best use the library for teaching and research, including a number of courses on how to use the e-services and self-services that the library offers. Outside Roskilde University, RUB is looking at the possibility of offering consulting in the field of e-services for other libraries, including business libraries. They are also trying to open their market not only to the campus' students and faculties, but also to companies, especially small and medium enterprises. Participation in the DEFF project can influence the future of RUB's business model as well. For example, they presently provide an e-service called "Chat with a Librarian", which they are running not only for RUB, but for all the other research libraries in Denmark as well.

Relationships with Customers/Users

Since the introduction of e-services and self-services, the relationships with the users of the libraries have changed a lot. The number of users coming to the physical reference desk is decreasing quickly, while the number of inquiries at the virtual desk is increasing. The total number of inquiries is decreasing. In addition user behaviour is also changing. For example while paper books are still important for the readers, the total number of library loans is decreasing and the number of downloads of e-books is increasing. This trend is also observed for the journals. While RUB still has a substantial number of paper journals,

more and more downloads of e-journal articles are taking place. They expect that the loans of physical books and journals will not be important in five years and that most of the material will be provided in electronic form. The users that have a log-in to the library can access the e-services 24 hours per day, seven days per week no matter where they are. So they will have everything they need on the computer. Some things are printed; others are not. The relationships with the users are expected to change even more in the future as a result of implementation of library blogs. In fact, RUB is looking at blogs and how to use them or integrate them with e-services such as electronic journals or e-books. Blogs would have the objective of creating online communities around specific topics, specific books, or journal articles. In addition, RUB is negotiating with Google to have all its collection retrievable through Google search engines. Therefore, e-services are leading to a digitalization of knowledge that was already codified in printed form. E-services are making it easier and quicker for users to find, store, and analyze such knowledge. In addition, e-services are making it easier for more users to get access to the same piece of knowledge or information. In fact if only one user at a time could get access to a specific journal in print form, in electronic form many users can get access to the same journal, article, or book chapter simultaneously. Furthermore, e-services are pushing customer relationships towards a virtual form. This is the case both regarding the relationship between the user and librarian and the relationship among the library's users which, after the implementation of blogs, is expected both to become more virtualized and to increase in number due to the formation of online communities.

Relationships with Publishers (or Providers)

This relationship has also changed as a result of e-services. Many of the traditional transactions such as ordering, cataloguing, and so forth, of journals have almost disappeared. The total number of transactions with the publishers has decreased. The e-journals are kept at the publishers' repository and RUB only buys the access or license to them. Initially the publishers offered a huge number of e-journals at extra cost. As a result, RUB cut the number of paper journals from approximately 5,000 to around 2,000 and instead has acquired access to circa 18,000 e-journals. However the publishers are now increasing prices on e-journals, therefore the total costs might increase as a result in the future. This kind of license agreement has contributed to the formation of a Danish library consortium whose purpose is to get better prices for electronic journals and e-books from the publishers.

Relationships with Other Research Libraries

The trend towards the adoption of e-services by the Danish libraries has changed the relationship between RUB and other research libraries in Denmark by increasing collaboration and partnerships among them. While earlier they were competing on services, number, and type of journals and books offered, after the adoption of e-services there is much more collaboration among Danish research libraries. Two key examples of this collaboration and partnerships which RUB is part of are Denmark Licensing Consortium and the DEFF initiative. Denmark Licensing Consortium is a consortium of libraries getting common licenses to publishers' e-journals and e-books. The major purpose is to put pressure on the publishers and decrease costs for the individual library. Therefore, the adoption of e-services is causing a convergence and standardization of the (e-)services offered by the different Danish libraries. Libraries were differentiating from each other much more before the adoption of e-services. Now all the research libraries members of the license consortium offer the same types of e-journals and e-books, and

more or less the same type of e-services. Those few that are ahead get caught up within a six-month period.

DEFF is, as described above, a major initiative undertaken by the Danish government with the purpose of developing a network of electronic research libraries that make available their electronic and other information resources in a coherent and simple way. This is obtained partly through government funding and partly by joint license purchase (www.deff.dk). By participating in DEFF, the libraries can achieve economies of scope and scale in the development of e-services.

FUTURE CHALLENGES

There are many challenges laying ahead for RUB. RUB will continue to exist and keep the role of library as an information centre, but the way the information and knowledge is provided will change. RUB will still face several organizational and technological challenges in the future.

From a technology point of view, the ICTs platforms used in delivering e-services become obsolete quite periodically and new e-services solutions have to be found. For example with the development of Web 2.0, they will have to make new types of systems. Integration of RUB e-services into one simple system is also an important technical future challenge. Presently the e-services located on the Web page are connected to six or seven different systems, and a future challenge is to integrate all these different systems. Standardization is another technological challenge. Customers want a rapid response and RUB is working on this by looking at standardization issues and they have to keep doing so in the future. Standards are very important for library's e-services. Finally, ensuring getting the best and same results for the same search is also a future technical challenge.

Copyrights and licenses are another important obstacle and challenge for the development of

RUB's e-services. For example, they are running a project to convert the library's videos into files to be kept on the local servers. The problem is though that whenever a student wants to see a video, instead of seeing the file on the computer screen, they have to save the file on the tape, since the material that they loan out has to be in analogue form due to copyrights restrictions. So copyrights of what can be digitized are a big barrier to further e-services development and especially use by the customers. Licenses on the other hand limit the use of the e-services for remote users not connected to the university and therefore do not have a log in to the library system. This implies that these users still have to walk into the library to be able to use the e-services, thus limiting to some extent their functionality.

Another future challenge comes from the library users. The users are becoming much more advanced and sophisticated in their online searches; young people have a lot of ideas about how to do things better. Here the challenge is to understand their needs and implement user-driven innovations in e-services. Budget problems are another challenge for RUB. In the last few years the budgets allocated to research libraries have been decreasing. This trend has been worsened by decentralizing the budgets concerning the research libraries from the government to the university the libraries are connected to. This creates the possibility for management at Roskilde University to cut the library's budget in favour of other activities.

Organizational challenges are also lying ahead. As the number of physical loans will decrease and the number of electronic downloads keeps increasing, there is going to be less need for the reference desk and the number of positions in the library might decrease. The way of working in the library is changing, therefore the type of competences needed might change moving more towards IT specialists and going away from the classical librarians skills. Disagreement on e-

services' future development between the different groups in the library is also a major organizational and human resource challenge, even though most RUB's employees like e-services. This requires RUB to explore new functions and new directions to change their business model.

CONCLUSION

This chapter has contributed to understand e-services development by investigating a particular type of e-services: research library e-services. Specifically the study has investigated the implication of the advent of Internet and e-services for Roskilde University library as well as the future challenges that e-services provide for RUB. The study has also investigated the consequences of e-services for Roskilde University library organization, its business model, and relationships with customers, publishers (providers of information), and other research libraries. The picture that emerges is one of rapid innovation, big transformations, and change at organizational and business model level, as well as in the relationships with customers, publishers, and other research libraries. In addition there are a number of challenges that RUB has to face in the future in response to e-services. Some are IT-related; others have to deal with copyrights, licenses, standardization, and user-driven innovation. The general trend is that RUB is becoming a combination of a virtual and physical library, moving more and more towards a virtual library by providing resources and knowledge mainly in digital form and by offering blogs and possibilities of online communities to discuss books and articles. On the other hand RUB is still keeping the traditional library function of a physical knowledge space. What will RUB look like in 10 years? The only certain answer according to RUB management is that it will still exist.

REFERENCES

Hoffman, K. D. (2003). Marketing+MIS=E-Service. *Communications of the ACM, 46*(6), 53–55. doi:10.1145/777313.777340

Marchionini, G., & Maurer, H. (1995). The roles of digital libraries in teaching and learning. *Communications of the ACM, 38*(4), 67–75. doi:10.1145/205323.205345

Sarkar, M. B., Butler, B., & Steinfield, C. (1995). Intermediaries and cybermediaries: A continuing role for mediating players in the electronic marketplace. *Journal of Computer-Mediated Communication, 1*(3).

Scupola, A. (2002). The impact of electronic commerce on industry structure: The case of scientific, technical and medical publishing. *Journal of Information Science, 28*(3).

ENDNOTES

[1]   These statistics are adapted from the Danish Library Authority Statistics (http://www.bs.dk/publikationer/english/statistics/2004/index.htm). The figures apply to the 180 Danish research libraries which are funded by the government, open to the public and employ professional librarian(s) on a permanent basis. There are a further 583 smaller research libraries which do not meet these requirements, including 122 institute (departmental) libraries at universities and institutions of higher education.

[2]   Including the metropolitan municipalities of Copenhagen and Frederiksberg.

APPENDIX : THE DANISH RESEARCH LIBRARY STATISTICS 2004[1]

Table 2. General figures about Denmark

Area	43,094 km²
Local authorities	271
Counties[2]	16

Table 3. Denmarks' population per 1.1. 2005

Adults	4,459,978
Children (0-13)	951,329
Total	5,411,307

Table 4. Number of research libraries in 2004

National library	2
Libraries of institutions of higher education	100
Special libraries	78
Total	180

Table 5. Staff in 2004

National library	563
Libraries of institutions of higher education	788
Special libraries	219
Total	1,570

Figure 1.

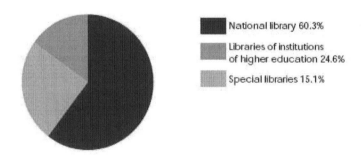

National library 60.3%

Libraries of institutions of higher education 24.6%

Special libraries 15.1%

Table 6. Research libraries stock in 2004

National library	26,573,386
Libraries of institutions of higher education	10,834,470
Special libraries	6,633,201
Total	44,041,057

Table 7. Serials subscriptions

National library	61,270
Libraries of institutions of higher education	32,388
Special libraries	14,021
Total	107,679

Table 8. Research libraries additions in 2004

National library	1,221,707
Libraries of institutions of higher education	251,679
Special libraries	76,085
Total	1,549,471

Figure 2.

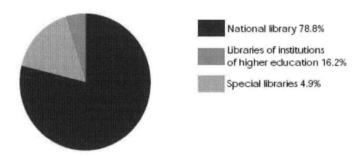

Table 9. Research libraries loans including renewals in 2004

National library	2,759,796
Libraries of institutions of higher education	6,088,009
Special libraries	844,535
Total	9,692,340

Figure 3.

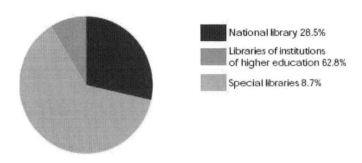

Table 10. Interlibrary loans supplied

by National library	513,604
by libraries of institutions of higher education	507,662
by special libraries	41,423
Total Interlibrary loans supplied	1,062,689

Table 11. Interlibrary loans received

by National library	61,256
by libraries of institutions of higher education	151,862
by special libraries	25,444
Total Interlibrary loans received	238,562

Figure 4.

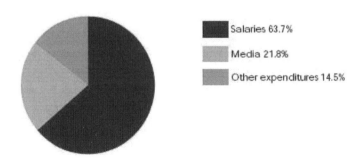

Table 12. Research libraries operating expenditure in 2004

	1,000 DKK
Salaries	537,372
Media	183,687
Other expenditure	122,501
Total	843,559

Table 13. Research libraries operating expenditure in 2004

	1,000 DKK	%
National library	295,588	35.0%
Libraries of institutions of higher education	436,042	51.7%
Special libraries	111,929	13.3%
Total	843,559	100.0%

This work was previously published in Cases on Managing E-Services, edited by A. Scupola, pp. 204-217, copyright 2009 by IGI Publishing (an imprint of IGI Global).

Chapter 4.12

Profightstore.com:
Developing an Online Store for the Niche Market

Mirjana Pejic-Bach
Faculty of Economics & Business—Zagreb, Croatia

Miran Pejic-Bach
Dux Sport d.o.o., Croatia

ABSTRACT

This chapter explores the possibilities for small and medium-sized enterprises (SMEs) to find their way to success in e-business. The basic assumption of this chapter is that the Internet allows SMEs to access the niche markets which have not previously been accessible to them. We are presenting a case study of one Croatian online store developed as a portal which targets the niche market and our focus is on the following issues: subcultures as niche markets, criteria for selecting suppliers, developing a new brand, designing an online store as a portal in order to attract visitors, and opportunities for growth. The authors hope that presenting this particular case will help small companies to take into account niche markets when designing their online stores, but also it will help researchers to further explore niche markets as a possible business strategy for SMEs while entering the e-commerce arena.

INTRODUCTION

The development of the Internet and e-commerce as interrelated phenomena has given small and medium enterprises (SMEs) a new opportunity to present themselves to the global market, both to business-to-consumer (B2C) and business-to-business (B2B) markets. However, it is not realistic to expect SMEs to be able to compete on the mainstream markets with major players like Fortune 500 companies. Therefore, most SMEs found their way to success in e-business by entering niche markets (Barnes, Hinton, & Mieczkowska, 2004).

Firms that pursue niche market strategy are able to make extra profit (Porter, 1998). Those firms focus on the smaller part of the market which is growing fast and which is not yet captured by other firms. The Internet allows SMEs to access the niche markets which have not previously been accessible to them.

DOI: 10.4018/978-1-60566-064-6.ch006

The objective of this chapter is to present the process of developing an online store, developed as portal, for targeting the niche market. The case study approach will be used (Yin, 2003) to answer "how" an online store that targets the niche market was developed and marketed, and "why" niche market strategy was used. The focus of the case study is on the contemporary phenomenon according to which small firms use the Internet as a medium to enter a particular market and to even outmatch the existing competitors who have already established a strong competitive position on the "brick and mortar" market. In addition, the purpose of the case study is to clarify some uncertainties surrounding both the development of online stores by SMEs and to use the established online store for entering niche markets:

- Could a particular subculture be used as a market niche?
- What are the criteria for selecting suppliers?
- Should the firm sell the existing brands or try to develop its own brand?
- What are the most efficient ways of attracting visitors to the online store?
- What is the influence of design on the shopping habits of visitors to the online store?
- Should the firm try to open another online store in order to "scare away" competition?
- What is the possible income from selling advertisements?
- What are other opportunities for growth?

BACKGROUND

The development of modern national economies relies not only on big corporations, but also on SMEs which are often an important generator of growth. In Croatia, for instance, in 2006 there was a total of 72,000 companies, 93% of which were SMEs. The Government of the Republic of Croatia stressed in its strategy of economic development entitled "Croatia in the 21st century"

that SMEs were the main generators of economic development. However, in the era of globalisation SMEs stand the smallest chance of survival, so that one may rightfully question how realistic it is for Croatian SMEs to fulfil such high expectations set by the creators of economic policy. It has been shown in the last couple of years that Croatian SMEs stagnate due to increased competition and higher client demands. On the other hand, the Internet economy fosters the remarkably speedy growth of the national economy because it allows SMEs to direct their marketing strategy toward dislocated markets at smaller business costs. The use of advanced information technologies makes it possible to establish personalised contacts with buyers within the Internet economy, which improves the quality of customer relations. In addition, the growth of e-commerce allows SMEs to achieve competitive advantage if they manage to adjust in a timely manner to the changes of the Internet market. It should also be mentioned that in the Croatian economy, significant growth is recorded in tourism, but also in retail trade. Finally, the Internet users perceive online sales and advertising as increasingly important factors in making their buying decisions (Malic-Bandu, 2006).

The Croatian Internet market (Gfk, 2006) is characterised by a significant number of firms with Web pages which are mainly used as marketing channels. It should be mentioned that only a small number of firms use Web pages as their delivery and selling channel. The number of Internet users in Croatia is one million (45% of the population older than 15), and the total value of e-commerce transactions was over 60 million euros in 2006. According to several researchers (Gfk, 2005), the typical Internet users in Croatia include people from urban areas who have access to the Internet. In contrast, this is true only for a smaller percentage of people from rural areas. Most Internet users come from the Croatian capital city—Zagreb and towns on the Adriatic coast. Approximately one third of men have access to the

Internet, and the same is true only for one quarter of women. Finally, the majority of the users are people younger than 35.

Profightstore.com is an online store established in 2003. It sells equipment for combat sports, which are competitive contact sports where two combatants fight against each other using certain rules of engagement, typically with the aim of simulating parts of real hand to hand combat. Examples of combat sports are: boxing, sports wrestling, and mixed martial arts. The firm was established by the owner who is himself familiar with combat sports and who understands combat sports culture very well. At the time when the firm was established, the owner worked solely by himself. Today (in 2007) the firm employs two part-time journalists and two office clerks. The management structure is very simple, which is to be expected considering the number of people employed. The owner of the firm is the front man of the firm, and he coordinates journalists and office clerks. The firm is situated in Zagreb, the capital city of Croatia (a country in Southeast Europe).

The organisational culture in the firm is informal, meaning that the people who work in the firm are closely connected with each other. As Profightstore.com has become a well known online portal for combat sports in Croatia, journalists are proud to be a part of the Profightstore.com journalist team. However, one has to be aware that journalists working for Profightstore.com are not professionally trained journalists. Instead, they come from the Croatian combat sports community which gathers around online discussion groups like nokaut.com. Therefore, working for a well-known portal like Profightstore.com gives them a chance to become widely recognized as combat sports experts. In addition, the owner of the firm has personal experience in training combat sports, which helps in establishing the network of useful contacts.

Setting the Stage

Combat sports are probably the oldest form of men's competition with each other. Different disciplines/arts like boxing, karate, wrestling, judo, and tae kwon do originate from all over the world (Asia, Europe, and America). The common goal of all combat sports disciplines are twofold: to be able to defend oneself from an attacker, and to be able to hurt the attacker in order to make the attacker incapable of further combat. Therefore, combat sports could be defined as systems of codified practices and traditions of training for combat. The most important characteristic of combat sports fans is that they usually practice combat sports by themselves.

Profightstore.com offers equipment for combat sports which have become increasingly popular in the last 10 years with the appearance of vale tudo events in Brazil, PRIDE Fighting Championships in Japan, and Ultimate Fighting Championship (UFC) in the USA. In 2007, the owners of the UFC bought PRIDE which resulted in the merging of those two greatest combat sports shows into one big championship.

The Internet has allowed combat sports fans to become closely connected through Internet online discussion groups (forums), and through regular visits to Web sites with the latest news. Before the emergence of the Internet, combat sports fans could follow news only through specialised magazines and rare bits of news in the mainstream media (TV and sports journals). They could comment on the latest events only with their friends and acquaintances. However, the emergence of Internet forums allowed combat sports fans to participate in asynchronous communication (Powazek, 2002), when users are able to participate at different times in the debate that can last for a longer period of time (Gurstein, 2000). At the same time, there are a number of Web sites which cover combat sports events with prompt commentaries and which offer their content free of charge. Those Web sites have allowed a greater number of people to become combat sports fans, which certainly would not have occurred if only specialised magazines had been available on the market. Therefore, the Internet has enabled more people to become combat sports fans as a result of the emergence of specialised forums and portals.

Virtual communities could be defined as a network of people who communicate with each other electronically and share common interests (Hagel & Armstrong, 1998). Combat sports fans consider forums to be the most popular form of virtual communities. One of the most popular forums is Sherdog Mixed Martial Arts Forum (www. sherdog.com/forum), whereby joining those free communities, members can post topics, privately communicate with other members, start and vote in polls, update contents, and be able to upload video clips, photos, and other special content.

Combat sports fans could be treated as part of subculture, if we define subculture as "a set of people with a set of behaviours and beliefs, which could be distinct or hidden, that differentiate them from the larger culture of the area from which they are a part of" (Loflin & Winogrond, 1976). According to the owner of Profightstore.com, the following elements constitute combat sports subculture in Croatia:

1. *Styling* – Combat sports fans usually train combat sports by themselves. They usually look similar with shaved heads, strong muscles, tight clothes, and quite eager to look like tough guys. The purpose of such styling is to make the fighter look dominant inside and outside the ring. The intention is also to scare the opponent with all possible means so that even the fighter's gaze is very important.

2. *Strength, courage, skill* – combat sports are the best way to express emotional stability and physical readiness. People who practice combat sports aim to enhance their physical ability to their maximum. The best way to test physical readiness is to fight with someone of similar size and strength. Combat sports give athletes an opportunity to test to what extent they are better than other fighters. The greatest challenge is to test if one is emotionally ready. Some fighters will rely more on their strength, and some on their skills. Some do not have strength or skill, but will rely on their courage instead. Those three components are crucial for practicing combat sports. Expressing aggression is not the main goal of practicing combat sports. It is all about two people who compete against each other.

3. *Combat sports and other sports* – The difference between combat sports and other individual sports is not as great as it seems at first sight. Group sports do not have such strong "one-against-another feeling," but rather stress the importance of team spirit. Tennis is also characterised by strenuous practice, physical effort, and pain. However, physical confrontation with the opponent is not as important as in combat sports. To the outside observer, combat seems like violence, but it is competition as in any other sport. Most men possess an impulse to fight with each other, and combat sports give them the opportunity to fulfil this desire.

4. *Who practices combat sports* – It is hard to give a description of a typical person who practices combat sports. Combat sports are practised by different kinds of people: young, old, and with different educational backgrounds. However, most of them are young males. Another important characteristic of people who practice combat sports is that they work out as hard as any other athlete. It is a common prejudice that people who practice combat sports do not do anything else in their lives and want to earn money "easily" through fighting. Quite the opposite,

most people who practice combat sports in their private lives work in different areas. Some of them are even experts in their fields, while most of them seem eager to obtain college education or some other form of education.

5. *Media* – Most men like to watch combat sports fights. Some people will even wake up at 3 a.m. to watch a fight in real time, while other people will read the report on the fight in tomorrow's newspaper. All fans are extremely happy when their hero wins and all the people who watch combat sports fights seek reality in fights. That is why some time ago the reality show called Ultimate Fighter (tv.com, 2007) gained strong media attention. It seems that people want to watch real fighting and really appreciate the efforts of the show participants so that the same dedication is expected in the ring. In the past, movies were important for the popularity of a particular combat sport discipline. However, today there are fighters like Randy Couture or Mirko Filipovic Cro Cop (Ultimate Fighting Championship, 2007) who have a bigger charisma and are more appealing to the media than some actors who played in action movies 20 years ago. Today, media competition is getting stronger and stronger so that fights are not covered only on TV and in the newspaper, but increasingly on the Internet.

Combat sports subculture could be best described if we resort to the description of a typical combat sports fan. He is a young male who trains in combat sports at the neighbourhood club or somebody who regularly practices at home by himself. His look is specific (shaved head, tight clothes, masculine look). He informs himself on combat sports events using the mainstream media and even more so using online portals. He regularly participates in discussions in one or more Internet forums dedicated to combat sports. In private life,

he is not violent, but has ability to defend himself in dangerous situations, and the possibility to test his strength with equally strong and capable opponents are very important to him.

According to the facts on the demographic features of Internet users in Croatia, a typical Croatian Internet user is a young male. The owner decided to use that fact at the time when he realised that there was growing demand for online shopping. Four years ago (in 2003) the supply side was rather weak and it was the right time to launch combat sports equipment through the online market. At that time, only two online shops offering combat sports equipment existed, but they did not succeed in attracting a sufficient number of visitors. Those online shops only offered combat sports equipment but did not offer any other additional information.

In addition, combat sports are very popular in Croatia where a strong tradition exists in training world-class combat sports fighters. However, the owner soon realised that it was not enough to just open an online store and expect customers to come shopping automatically. The owner's concept was based on four steps: content, traffic, trust, and selling. The owner believed from the start that people on the Internet were not looking for a particular store, but for information. Therefore, the store was built as an information portal (Chiou & Shen, 2006; Kennedy & Coughlan, 2006) for people interested in combat sports. Good content should attract visitors who will develop trust in the Web site and eventually buy combat sports equipment.

CASE DESCRIPTION

At the time of the development of Profightstore. com (in year 2003), it was widely accepted that digital and information-based products that customers did not have to physically inspect by themselves were the most appropriate for e-commerce (Hsein & Lin, 1998; Poon & Matthew, 2000). Therefore, the owner decided to sell combat sports equipment (gloves, punch bags, etc.) through an online store. He realised that the customers who bought combat sports equipment had a distinct set of needs, and were willing to pay a premium price for high-quality equipment. In addition, none of the existing competitors who also sold combat sports equipment had an online store in combination with a news portal. At the same time, the number of combat sports fans was growing because the Internet had increased the popularity of combat sports and created combat sports subculture. Therefore, the market for combat sports equipment could be defined as a niche market according to the characteristics defined by Kotler (2003). The owner's idea was that the name of the store should indicate its purpose, and that is how the name Profightstore.com was chosen. However, the firm registered another name esport. hr (hr is the Croatian domain) if ever a need for selling other sports equipment appeared.

Finding the Supplier

Different world-known combat sports equipment brands were considered for sales in Profightstore. com. However, the prices were rather high, and profit margins were too narrow. Electronic marketplaces (Ems) were considered as a second source for possible suppliers.

Electronic marketplaces (Chircu & Kauffman, 2001) have great potential of stimulating disintermediation (Shunk, Carter, Hovis, & Talwar, 2007). They connect buyers and suppliers from all over the world who would otherwise have a very small chance of communicating with each other. Apart from encouraging disintermediation, Ems manage other functions like checking customers' and suppliers' credibility, and checking product quality. First, customers and suppliers give basic information on their credibility in the registration process. Then, the credibility of customers and

suppliers is examined through personal contacts of Ems representatives at their headquarters and trade fairs. Finally, providers of credit information and credit reports give information. Dun and Bradstreet provide information mainly on U.S. firms, and FriedlNet provides information on Chinese firms (Duffie & Singleton, 2003). The quality of products offered by suppliers is checked in a similar way. In addition, Ems give additional advice to both suppliers and customers which helps them in conducting secure trade transactions. However, Ems usually do not accept any legal responsibility for lost products, product damage, and non-ethical customers who do not pay for the received products. Finally, contracts that customers and suppliers conclude do not mention Ems.

The owner registered in one of the electronic marketplaces (Ems), that is, Web sites which connect buyers with suppliers, and he announced that he wanted to buy combat sports equipment. Around 20 offers arrived by e-mail, and it took about three months to choose the supplier. The final choice of the supplier was based on several criteria: good communication, good assortment, convenient prices, and no request for a minimum quantity. The owner also checked if the supplier was well-known through some online discussion groups which discuss dishonest suppliers of combat sports equipments. In addition, the chosen supplier sent a trial order. As it seemed that everything was going well, the first bulk of combat sports equipment was ordered in the form of airplane delivery. It was agreed that the goods would be paid 50% in advance, and the remaining amount would be paid as Cash Against Documents, which is "a method of payment for goods in which documents transferring title are given to the buyer upon payment of cash to an intermediary acting for the seller, usually a bank" (Reyndols, 2003).

Developing a New Combat Sports Equipment Brand

The owner decided to sell combat sports equipment under the new brand name PFS (ProFightStore). He also designed a logo for the new brand and sent it to the supplier. In other words, the owner followed embryonic brand orientation which presumes developing its own brand from the start, although this approach is highly risky especially for SMEs (Groucutt, 2006). In developing the brand, the owner relied solely on himself and his own familiarity with combat sports subculture. He examined the design of different combat sports equipment brands but also colours and shapes that combat sports online communities use on popular Web sites. Clear shapes and dark colours have proven to be popular and widely accepted, because they indicate strength and masculinity typical for combat sports subculture. Such an approach, coupled with the owner's passion for the brand, his active role as the entrepreneur as well as his creativity, are a recipe for successful brand management proposed by Frank and Krake (2005). In addition, the decision was made that PFS brand would be priced within the medium-quality price range, which is the usual pricing setting in SMEs (Carson, Gilmore, Cummins, O'Donnell, & Grant, 1998).

Developing an Online Store

The stages of e-commerce development and their characteristics include (Rao Subba, Metts, & Mora Monge, 2003) presence, portals, transactions integration, and enterprise integration. Transactions integration presumes that the Web site offers goods and/or services to potential customers, and that it is possible to order goods through an online store. In addition, two general Web site design strategies are proposed by Wen, Chen, and Hwang (2001): (1) informational/communicational strategy, which presumes using the Web site as a supplement to traditional marketing, and (2) online transactional

strategy which is suitable for companies that use the Web to construct "virtual business" existing only on the Internet and independent from the main business activity. Wen et al. (2001) identify several models of e-commerce Web site design. One of those models is the community model based on user loyalty which emerges from the fact that users invest both time and emotions in the site.

Profightstore.com is designed as a transactions integration online store based on the community model because it is the only Web portal which delivers the latest daily news on combat sports events and intriguing interviews with combat sports fighters. Most visitors access Profightstore.com daily where they read the latest news written in an unbiased and objective tone. Journalists who write for Profightstore.com are instructed not to incorporate their personal opinions if they report on personal conflicts which are frequent in the combat sports world. At the same time, online combat sports forums are more than just a place where visitors exchange information, they are also the "arena" for pursuing personal conflicts. By being objective, Profightstore.com differentiates itself from such trivial issues. However, when reports on fights are given, personal opinions of journalists are welcome. In that way, visitors can be sure that Profightstore.com will give them the most objective view of current personal conflicts in the combat sports community and the juiciest report on the latest fights.

The development of the online store was conducted by a professional provider who offered a convenient price. The owner did not choose the developer who offered the lowest price, but instead he made a decision based on the recommendations of customers who have already established a strong and reliable relationship with the developer. Also, Web stores that the developer had already set up were thoroughly examined in order to detect if the quality and depth of the design were acceptable to the owner's high standards. The store design was made by a professional designer employed by the developer of the online store, following widely accepted standards such as: accessibility, naviga-tion, readability, and download speed (Thelwall, 2000). In addition, Profightstore.com was created with such colours, shapes, and photos that turned it into a place where visitors could encounter virtual experience (Gilmore, 2002). The store is designed as content management system (CMS), which means that the content to the online store is added by journalists and the owner himself.

The store is organised as a portal, and at least several relevant pieces of news are published on the Web site, together with interviews, TV programs with combat sports shows, and other contents (the best fighter, the best fighting club).

The process of ordering goods is very simple. First, customers browse through the offer of combat sports equipment products, and add the products to the basket. When all the goods are added to the basket, customers give their personal information (name, address, contact phone num-ber, and e-mail address). An automatic e-mail is sent both to customers and the selling staff. It is not possible to pay by credit card in this online store. Therefore, customers pay for the goods at the time of either door-to-door or post-office delivery.

Attracting Visitors

The first day of launching Profightstore.com was the day when the first order was made, which indicated that the future was bright for this par-ticular online store. However, things did not go as smoothly as expected. In the beginning, the number of visits was rather small, and the owner realised that although the Web site content was attractive, potential visitors should be additionally informed about Profightstore.com. Therefore, the owner of Profightstore.com pursued three ways of attracting visitors: (1) guerrilla marketing ap-proach through online combat sports community, (2) paid search, and (3) sponsorship of combat sports events and fighters.

Guerrilla Marketing Approach

The owner of Profightstore.com thought it would be unreasonable to use broadcast advertising techniques that appeal to the general public, when he is targeting the niche market of combat sports equipment. Expensive prime time television ad-vertisements would surely be a waste of money, especially because they are unfocused. The only time when TV advertisements would yield results would be TV broadcasts of combat sports fights, but their price is beyond Profightstore.com's marketing budget.

Guerrilla marketing, a term coined by Jay Conrad Levinson, uses "unconventional marketing intended to get maximum results from minimal resources." Some of the guerrilla marketing prin-ciples are (Cohen, 2003):

- Setting clear goals and objectives
- Learning the media usage and business habits of your target
- Posting advertisements in the media that reach your target audience
- Using e-mail and virtual marketing
- Alerting the media with the public rela-tions campaign

Therefore, the guerrilla marketing approach was employed to target online discussion groups. This approach was also chosen because of a tight marketing budget. Hagel and Armstrong (1998) point out in their book on virtual communities that great marketing potential lies in the fact that a group of people communicates virtually to each other because of their common interests and, even more importantly, because they trust each other. Most online discussion groups have some kind of administrators or moderators who take care that certain rules are respected, e.g. people should not be offensive to each other; no commercials should be posted on the online discussion group Web site etc.

Profightstore.com has therefore decided to benefit from such great potential of virtual communities and the owner's vision was to use online discussion groups dedicated to combat sports. He made this decision based on his gut feeling, although procedures for estimating the success of an online community could have been applied (Cothrel, 2000). At this point the owner hired several members of such groups. They started to write news for Profightstore.com, and at the same time they mentioned Profightstore.com in their posts in online discussion groups.

Paid Search

Search engines are the most frequently visited Web sites in virtual Internet space. They enable visitors to easily find the content they are interested in. The most popular search engines today have gained their popularity due to their simple design and lack of banner ads. Google, for instance, has based its strategy on innovations, among which paid search stands out as the greatest source of its revenue. It might be mentioned at this point that synonyms used for the term *paid search* are pay-per click, pay for payment, pay-for-performance, paid listing, and sponsored search (Laffey, 2007). However, there are some problems with paid search such as the infringement of trade mark (Tyacke & Higgins, 2004).

Paid search is based on the following four steps (Google, 2007): (1) advertisers choose keywords related to their business; (2) advertisers create the text of the ad by themselves; (3) the ads appear on the search engine next to search results, and (4) visitors can click on the ad in order to make a purchase or because they are curious about the advertiser. Although Profightstore.com is highly rated in search engines, and visitors generally prefer nonsponsored links to paid ads (Jansen, Brown, & Resnick, 2007), the owner started Google Adwords campaign two years ago with great success. This was the result of a very careful keyword selection, and constant monitoring of campaign performance.

Sponsorship of Combat Sport Events and Fighters

Sponsorship in today's world has changed its role from a special form of advertising to an important relationship in which the sponsoring firm and the sponsored subject (person, nonprofit organization, event, etc.) form a strategic alliance (Urriolagoitia & Planellas, 2006). In addition, sponsorship is an important opportunity for operationalising brand strategy (Cliffe & Motion, 2005). As it gained popularity, Profightstore.com became sponsored by numerous combat sports events and fighters. However, fighters and event organisers tend to stress that money is not the main reason for collaborating with Profightstore.com. Instead, they focus on the Web site objective and ability to cover combat sports events in the fastest possible manner.

Change of the Web Site Design

The development of the Web site is a continuous process which should never end. Many technological innovations, user capabilities and needs, competitor actions, and the growth of supporting business reinforce the change of Web design (Waite & Harrison, 2007). Profightstore.com was designed by a professional designer in light colours. After one year the design changed into much darker colours following the model of some world famous combat sports Web sites, like sherdog.com. Surprisingly enough, the number of visits remained the same. However, after such drastic changes in design, the number of orders diminished (fewer orders were made for almost one month after the change). The owner again changed the design to the new one that resembled more the original one. Sales again started to increase. A possible explanation of the decrease in the number of orders was the use of dark colours in combination with white letters, which diminished the visibility of the Web site. However, an important lesson was learned: design should not be changed drastically and suddenly.

Developing One More Combat Sports Online Store

Additionally, the owner of PFS launched another online store with more expensive combat sports equipment brands. However, the store only offered combat sports equipment, and did not have any other additional content that could attract visitors. Google Adwords were not enough to attract more visitors, and sales were infrequent. This online store still exists, but the owner does not plan to improve it any further.

Selling Advertisements

Banner ads were the first form of Internet advertising that appeared on Web sites in the late 1990s. They were priced similarly to TV ads on a flat fee, cost per thousand, or on the basis of audiences (Hoffman & Novak, 2000). After initial enthusiasm with banner ads, the revenue from such advertisements dropped because Web site visitors simply ignored them. However, Profightstore. com succeeds in selling banner ads of combat sports events because of their great design, which gives visitors a genuine feeling of what they will experience in real combat sports events—pure fighting. For now, those banners are designed with as few Flash effects as possible because of the slow Internet connection. The goal is to develop more vivid banner ads as soon as fast Internet connections become more widespread among the Croatian population. Advertisers are given access to Profightstore.com Web-site metrics: number of unique visitors, visitors' countries and search engines, the most popular pages of the Web site, statistics per hours, days, months, and years.

Current Challenges Facing the Organization

The main business objective of the owner of Profightstore.com is to position his store as regional leader with the English version of the Web site as soon as Croatia becomes member of the European Union. (Once Croatia joins the EU, export procedures will be less complicated.) Currently, the majority of visitors of Profightstore.com come from Croatia and neighbouring countries but there is quite a number of visitors from English speaking countries as well despite the language barrier. Therefore, the English version of Profightstore. com is planned in the near future.

Internationalisation is usually connected with larger firms. However, SMEs also use internationalisation as growth strategy, but it is usually successful only if the owner of a small firm is strongly dedicated to it, and has knowledge and resources to conduct it properly. Some common problems that SMEs encounter when trying to internationalise their operations include (Lloyd-Reason & Mughan, 2002): lack of language skills, poor understanding of foreign cultures, poor development of international marketing skills, and skills of other supporting activities (finance, operations, IT, human resources, strategy development). Only if the owner/manager pursues a very strong international orientation of his firm and only if he has well developed skills and resource base of the firm will Profightstore.com succeed in achieving the goal of becoming a regional leader. In addition, the issue of the impact of local culture on the Web site content, design, and structure (Fletcher, 2006) should be taken into account when new Web sites are developed.

Sandy and Burgess (2003) list the following levels of facilitation of Web sites: electronic brochure, electronic brochure and order, electronic brochure and order and payment, and finally, interactive publishing. Currently, Profightstore. com is at the stage of electronic brochure and order and should move to the higher levels of facilitation of Web sites. However, the owner's opinion is that the current facilities of Profightstore.com (news, product catalogue, order) are sufficient for attracting customers, so that he is more oriented on enhancing the number of products offered.

REFERENCES

Barnes, D., Hinton, M., & Mieczkowska, S. (2004). Avoiding the fate of the dotbombs: Lessons from three surviving dotcom start-ups. *Journal of Small Business and Enterprise Development, 11*(3), 329–337. doi:10.1108/14626000410551582

Carson, D., Gilmore, A., Cummins, D., O'Donnell, A., & Grant, K. (1998). Price setting in SMEs: Some empirical findings. *Journal of Product and Brand Management, 7*(1), 74–86. doi:10.1108/10610429810209755

Chiou, J., & Shen, C. (2006). The effects of satisfaction, opportunism, and asset specificity on consumers' loyalty intention toward internet portal sites. *International Journal of Service Industry Management, 11*(1), 7–11. doi:10.1108/09564230610651552

Chircu, A. M., & Kauffman, R. J. (2000). Reintermediation strategies in business-to-business electronic commerce. *International Journal of Electronic Commerce, 4*(4), 7–42.

Cliffe, S. J., & Motion, J. (2005). Building contemporary brands: A sponsorship-based strategy. *Journal of Business Research, 58*(8), 1068–1077. doi:10.1016/j.jbusres.2004.03.004

Cohen, N. (2003). Early-stage marketing for start-ups. Retrieved June 3, 2008, from http://www.clickz.com/showPage.html?page=825181

Cothrel, J. P. (2000). Measuring the success of an online community. *Strategy and Leadership, 28*(2), 17–21. doi:10.1108/10878570010341609

Duffie, D., & Singleton, K. J. (2003). Credit risk: Pricing, measurement and management. Princeton University Press.

Fletcher, R. (2006). The impact of culture on Web site content, design, and structure. *Journal of Communication Management, 10*(3), 259–273. doi:10.1108/13632540610681158

Frank, B. G., & Krake, J. M. (2005). Successful brand management in SMEs: A new theory and practical hints. *Journal of Product and Brand Management, 14*(4), 228–238. doi:10.1108/10610420510609230

Gfk (2005). Number of Internet users in Croatia. Retrieved June 3, 2008, from http://www.gfk.hr/press/internet6.htm

Gfk (2006). Citizens and the Internet. Retrieved June 3, 2008, from http://www.gfk.hr/press1/internet.htm

Gilmore, J. H., & Pine, J. II. (2002). Customer experience places: The new offering frontier. *Strategy and Leadership, 30*(4), 4–11. doi:10.1108/10878570210435306

Google.com. (2007). Learn about AdWords. Retrieved June 3, 2008, from http://adwords.google.com/select/Login

Griffin, T. (1994). International marketing communications. Oxford: Butterworth Heinemann.

Groucutt, J. (2006). The life, death and resuscitation of brands. Handbook of Business Strategy, 7(1), 101–106.

Gurstein, M. (2000). Community informatics: Enabling communities with information and communications technologies. Hershey, PA: Idea Group Publishing.

Hagel, J., III, & Armstrong, A. G. (1998). Net gain: Expanding markets through virtual communities. Boston: Harvard Business School Press.

Hoffman, D. L., & Novak, T. P. (2000). How to acquire customers on the Web. *Harvard Business Review, 78*(3), 179–183.

Hsein, C., & Lin, B. (1998). Internet commerce for small business. *Industrial Management & Data Systems, 3*(1), 113–119.

Jansen, B. J., Brown, A., & Resnick, M. (in press). Factors relating to the decision to click on a sponsored link. *Decision Support Systems*.

Kennedy, A., & Coughlan, J. (2006). Online shopping portals: An option for traditional retailers? *International Journal of Retail & Distribution Management, 34*(7), 516–528. doi:10.1108/09590550610673590

Kotler, P. (2003). Marketing management (11th ed.). New York: Prentice Hall.

Laffey, D. (2007). Paid search: The innovation that changed the Web. *Business Horizons, 50*(3), 211–218. doi:10.1016/j.bushor.2006.09.003

Lloyd-Reason, L., & Mughan, T. (2002). Strategies for internationalization within SMEs: The key role of the owner manager. *Journal of Small Business and Enterprise Development, 9*(2), 120–129. doi:10.1108/14626000210427375

Loflin, M. D., & Winogrond, I. R. (1976). A culture as a set of beliefs. *Current Anthropology, 17*(4), 723–725. doi:10.1086/201810

Malic-Bandu, K. (2006). Electronic media as a key of competitiveness of transition countries. *Informatologija, 39*(4), 280–285.

Poon, S., & Matthew, J. (2000). Product characteristics and Internet commerce benefit among small businesses. *Journal of Product and Brand Management, 9*(1), 21–34. doi:10.1108/10610420010316311

Porter, M. E. (1998). Competitive advantage of nations. New York: The Free Press.

Powazek, D. M. (2002). Design for community: The art of connecting real people in virtual places. Indianapolis: New Riders.

Rao Subba, S., Metts, G., & Mora Monge, C. A. (2003). Electronic commerce development in small and medium sized enterprises: A stage model and its implications. *Business Process Management Journal, 9*(1), 11–32. doi:10.1108/14637150310461378

Reyndols, F. (2003). Managing exports: Navigating the complex rules, controls, barriers, and laws. New York: Wiley.

Sandy, G., & Burgess, S. (2003). A decision chart for small business Web site content. *Logistic Information Management, 16*(1), 36–47. doi:10.1108/09576050310453723

Shunk, D. L., Carter, J. R., Hovis, J., & Talwar, A. (2007). Electronics industry drivers of intermediation and disintermediation. *International Journal of Physical Distribution & Logistics Management, 37*(3), 248–261. doi:10.1108/09600030710742443

Thelwall, M. (2000). Effective Websites for small and medium-sized enterprises. *Journal of Small Business and Enterprise Development, 7*(2), 149–159. doi:10.1108/EUM0000000006836

Tv.com. (2007). The Ultimate Fighter. Retrieved June 3, 2008, from http://www.tv.com/the-ultimate-fighter/show/31862/summary.html

Tyacke, N., & Higgins, R. (2004). Searching for trouble: Keyword advertising and trade mark infringement. *Computer Law & Security Report, 20*(6), 453–465. doi:10.1016/S0267-3649(04)00090-1

Ultimate Fighting Championship. (2007). Fighters. Retrieved June 3, 2008, from http://www.ufc.com

Urriolagoitia, L., & Planellas, M. (2007). Sponsorship relationships as strategic alliances: A life cycle model approach. *Business Horizons, 50*(2), 157–166. doi:10.1016/j.bushor.2006.10.001

Waite, K., & Harrison, T. (2007). Internet acheaeology: Uncovering pension sector Web site evolution. *Internet Research, 17*(2), 180–195. doi:10.1108/10662240710737031

Wen, H. J., Chen, H., & Hwang, H. (2001). E-commerce Web site design: Strategies and models. *Information Management & Computer Security, 9*(1), 5–12. doi:10.1108/09685220110366713

Yin, R. K. (2003). Case study research design and methods. London: Sage Publications.

FURTHER READING

Aragon-Correa, J. A., & Cordon-Pozo, E. (2005, Jun.). The influence of strategic dimensions and the environment on the introduction of Internet as innovation into small and medium-sized enterprises. [Article]. *Technology Analysis and Strategic Management, 17*(2), 205–218. doi:10.1080/09537320500088856

Brache, A., & Webb, J. (2000). The eight deadly assumptions of e-business. *The Journal of Business Strategy, 21*(3), 13–17. doi:10.1108/eb040084

Gilmore, A., Gallagher, D., & Henry, S. (2007). E-marketing and SMEs: operational lessons for the future. *European Business Review, 19*(3), 234–247. doi:10.1108/09555340710746482

Grandon, E. E., & Pearson, J. M. (2004). Electronic commerce adoption: an empirical study of small and medium US businesses. *Information & Management, 42*(1), 197–216.

Hedbor, L. D. H. (2005). Small Business Projects / Internet. Indiana: AuthorHouse.

Ihlström, C., Magnusson, M., Scupola, A., & Tuunainen, V. K. (2003). SME barriers to electronic commerce adoption: nothing changes-everything is new. In G. Gingrich (Ed.), Managing IT in Government Business & Communities. (pp. 147-163). Hershey, PA: IDEA Group/IRM Press.

Krug, S. (2005). Don't Make me Think: A Common Sense Approach to Web Usability. Indianapolis: New Riders Press.

Chapter 4.13

The Role of E–Services in the Transition from the Product Focus to the Service Focus in the Printing Business:
Case Lexmark

Esko Penttinen
Helsinki School of Economics, Finland

Timo Saarinen
Helsinki School of Economics, Finland

Pekka Sinervo
Lexmark, Finland

ABSTRACT

Today, many manufacturing companies are focusing on their service operations, which are often seen as a better source of revenue than the traditional product business. E-services can accelerate this process by offering companies new ways to control products and monitor equipment from a distance. This chapter describes the changes which are taking place in the printing business. It tells the story of Lexmark, a printer manufacturer that has recently created differentiated offerings to its business customers. In the case of Lexmark, this repositioning of offerings has been enabled by e-services. Here, the e-services consist of the Lexmark Fleet Manager system which monitors the use and availability of the equipment and makes suggestions on how to improve the printing processes on the customer site. The case ends with a description of the actual challenges that Lexmark is currently facing.

BACKGROUND: THEORY SUGGESTS MOVING TOWARDS SERVICES

Management theory suggests that product manufacturers should move downstream closer to the customer and provide different kinds of services

DOI: 10.4018/978-1-60566-064-6.ch011

along with their tangible products (Oliva & Kallenberg, 2003; Penttinen & Palmer, 2007; Quinn, 1992; Vargo & Lusch, 2004; Wise & Baumgartner, 1999). Manufacturers' traditional value-chain role—producing and selling goods—has become less and less attractive as the demand for products has stagnated throughout the economy (Wise & Baumgartner, 1999). The demand for different kinds of services, on the other hand, has grown considerably. Increasingly, the customers of manufacturing companies are concentrating on their core competencies and, often, do not regard the maintenance of machines as being part of their core business.

Services within the manufacturing business include, for example, maintenance services, condition monitoring services, training services, consultation services, installation services, and documentation services (Oliva & Kallenberg, 2003). Increasingly, these services are in electronic format. As an example of an electronic service, manufacturing companies have innovated information systems that enable condition monitoring from a distance. These systems allow companies to keep an eye on their equipment on the customer site more effectively.

Service industries have grown in importance compared to the agricultural and manufacturing industries. Steady productivity increases in agriculture and manufacturing have meant that it takes ever fewer hours of work to produce or buy an automobile, a piece of furniture, or a home appliance. While productivity has improved, the demand for goods is somewhat capped; people can only consume limited quantities of automobiles, sofas, and washing machines (Quinn, 1992). At the same time, the installed base of products has been expanding steadily in many industries, thanks to the accumulation of past purchases and to longer product life spans (Wise & Baumgartner, 1999). The combination of this stagnant product demand and an expanding installed base has pushed economic value downstream, away from manufacturing and toward providing services

required to operate and maintain products (Wise & Baumgartner, 1999).

Many manufacturing companies have learned their lesson and have turned to services in search for growth and increased profitability (Penttinen & Palmer, 2007). Examples of successful companies include the elevator company KONE and the bearing producer SKF (Penttinen, 2007; Penttinen & Palmer, 2007; Penttinen & Saarinen, 2005). These companies have been actively inventing electronic services. For example, SKF has innovated intelligent bearings which report the status of the bearings to SKF. This is done by inserting a sensor to the bearing core which measures the vibration and motion status of the rotating components. These e-services allow SKF to provide maintenance contracts more economically than before. Similarly, KONE has added intelligence to their elevators, allowing a more efficient monitoring of their products from a distance.

Others have not been as successful in making the transition from product manufacturer to service provider. According to Oliva and Kallenberg (2003), there are three successive hurdles to overcome the problems related to the transition from products to services. First, firms might not believe in the economic potential of the service component for their product (e.g., engineers are more excited about building a multimillion-dollar piece of equipment than about a service contract for cleaning it). Second, firms might not have the capabilities and competencies to provide services for their products. Third, firms might fail in deploying a successful service strategy (e.g., Ford Motor Co.'s attempt to enter after-sales services was blocked by its network of independent dealerships) (Oliva & Kallenberg, 2003).

What Are Electronic Services?

In the marketing literature, services have been defined according to the IHIP framework (Zeithaml, Parasuraman, & Berry, 1985). The IHIP framework lists intangibility, heterogeneity, inseparability of production and consumption, and perishability as the distinguishing traits of services. Compared to tangible goods, services are intangible. Services are heterogeneous, meaning that services are customized to individual customers. The production and consumption processes of services cannot be separated. Services are perishable, meaning that it is impossible, for example, to store services for later use. More recently, services have been defined as processes, activities, performances, or changes in the condition of an economic unit. In short, services are the "application of specialized competencies through deeds, processes, and performances for the benefit of another entity or the entity itself" (Vargo & Lusch, 2004, p. 2).

In the case of manufacturing companies' e-services, we define and conceptualize e-services as service systems that enable the dissemination and transmission of information from the manufacturers' products to the manufacturer. At the current case company, the printer manufacturer Lexmark, the core of the company's e-services is the Lexmark Fleet Manager system, which is described later in the chapter.

SETTING THE STAGE: SELLING PRINTERS AND PRINTER CAPACITY TO COMPANIES

In this chapter, we look at the manufacturers of printing machines. We tell the story of Lexmark which has recently turned to services in their B2B activities and launched the e-services concept, Lexmark Fleet Manager system. Increasingly, the turnover of Lexmark comes from services: for example from maintenance services and from consultation services. The objective of this case study is to familiarize the reader to case Lexmark and to describe the e-services that the company has innovated. The core of the e-services is the Lexmark Fleet Manager system. We will also discuss the transition from products to services taking place in this company. We begin by giving some basic facts of the printing business, then, we introduce case Lexmark and describe how their business model has changed recently. We conclude by listing some key challenges that the company faces.

According to the Gartner Research Group, document handling and printing expenses can amount to 1–3% of a company's turnover. Whereas the other parts of the IT-related activities have often been outsourced outside, printing and document handling activities are the last islands of the IT services that have not been thoroughly considered from the perspective of outsourcing. Generally speaking, relatively little effort has been put to optimizing the printing processes in offices. Procurement processes related to printers and printing material are scattered and seem to fall between the IT side with printers and the office equipment side with copy machines. Even though there is potential for considerable savings, very few companies are interested in optimizing their document handling and printing processes.

When aiming to optimize the printing processes in an office, an important ratio to understand is the ratio describing the number of employees to the amount of equipment within the company. According to Lexmark Finland, currently, this ratio is usually two to one; meaning that there are, on average, two employees per one piece of output equipment (printer, copy machine, fax, etc.). Lexmark has encountered companies, where the ratio has been one to one, meaning that each employee has one printer or copy machine or fax at his/her disposal. In most cases, this represents a considerable waste of resources in offices. Naturally, individual employees have individual printing needs. For example, in some companies, printing may be seen as a critical operation (due to, e.g., confidentiality issues); and therefore, each employee must have his/her own printer. However, in general, we can try to find the optimal ratio of employees per printer; and, according to the Gartner research group, the optimal ratio, in office work on average, is eight to one.

CASE DESCRIPTION: LEXMARK

Lexmark is a manufacturer and supplier of printing solutions including laser and inkjet printers, multifunction products, associated supplies and services. The company employs 13,000 people worldwide and has a turnover of around 4.3 billion euros. Lexmark International Inc. was founded in 1991 when IBM decided to hive off its printing business to retail investors. All business functions from new product development to sales departments were shifted to the new company. Lexmark entered the New York Stock Exchange as an independent company in 1995. Lexmark initially focused on business-to-business (B2B) companies but extended its product range to providing business-to-consumers (B2C) printers in the mid-1990s when ink jet technology came to the market. This case description and the following challenges focus on the B2B activities of the company.

In the B2B activities, during the recent years, we can observe an important change in focus: "In B2B, we printer manufacturers compete over printed papers, not machine sales. It is more important for us to provide MRO (maintenance, repair and operations) products and services for our customers than selling the actual printing machines" (CEO Lexmark Finland). The margins on product sales (namely printers in this case) have decreased sharply lately. This is due to increased competition in the market. The printer market went through a period of rapid change and this was due to the digitalization of office printing. Copy machines moved from the analogical to the digital world. Suddenly, copy machines were able to be used as printers through office networks. Printer manufacturers responded by innovating multifunction products that could function as printers and copy machines simultaneously. Today, in offices, 55–60% of sheets of paper are printed using traditional printers and 45–50% are printed or copied using copy machines. The trend is toward the increasing use of printers. More and

more of information can be stored in electronic format, either by originally entering the data in electronic form or by scanning the existing information in electronic format. This favors the use of printers.

The change in the product market described above has affected the focus of the printer manufacturers, including our case company Lexmark. Today, the focus is not in product sales, but, rather, in providing companies service contracts. "By providing service contracts, we can ensure the MRO business for our company" (CEO Lexmark Finland). Under the service contract, the equipment is delivered as part of the monthly contract and the charges are based on the number of printed sheets of paper, or cost per page, and not based on the aggregation of the equipment cost over a period of time.

E-Services: The Fleet Manager System

How to provide these service contracts? For doing this, Lexmark has created new e-service offerings. The core of Lexmark's electronic services is the fleet manager system depicted in Figure 1. It is an information system which essentially monitors the equipment located on the customer site, transmitting automatically updated information on, for example, the number of printed sheets, type of sheets, location of printers and users, and change patterns of use. This information can be used to control the costs on the customer site: by analyzing printing information and by making suggestions on how the printing operations could be optimized on the customer site. The system is located within the customer company provided there are less than 500 devices on the customer site. For global customer companies and for those clients whose number of devices exceeds 500 devices, Lexmark proposes the ARMS system. Here, Lexmark manages the system on a server which is located outside the customer company. Lexmark then provides the customer company a

Figure 1. The Lexmark fleet manager system

customized view to the system, including all the information the customer wants to see.

The core system, fleet manager, consists of five parts: the Asset Manager, the Billing Manager, the Consumables Manager, the Availability Manager, and the Optimization Manager. The Asset Manager is used to manage the equipment. It identifies and registers the equipment in the customer environment and enables the collection of data from printers and other related equipment. It tracks the life cycle of the equipment and makes suggestions when certain equipment needs to be updated or renewed. The collection of the data is automated, and the data are directly transmitted to the system. The Billing Manager uses the data from the Asset Manager system to produce billing information and reporting analyses based on the number of pages printed at the customer site. The customer can choose from a variety of billing options: a recurring monthly charge, a monthly per page charge, or a combination of the two.

The Consumables Manager observes the machinery and alerts Lexmark when, for example, the toner level is getting low. The system automatically sends out an e-mail indicating that the machine needs maintenance. The customer can also choose the option that the new spare part is delivered automatically to the customer site. The Availability Manager monitors the device and reports changes in the condition of the machine. It automatically reports the down time of the equipment; and, based on this information, the availability of the printing equipment can be obtained as a service level percentage. For example, the customer can be guaranteed to have a 95% service level, which guarantees that the printer will be available for 95% of the time. The Availability Manager then notifies whether this objective has been achieved or not. The Optimization Manager observes the printing processes on the customer site and evaluates whether the processes could be improved by changing the setup of the equipment. It alerts if some devices are overloaded most of the time and makes suggestions on how such problems could be resolved.

Differentiated Offerings

Generally speaking, today, the customer usually pays for printed sheets of paper. In 2002, Lexmark launched the concept of "print-move-manage." These three levels can be described as steps toward a more service-oriented market offering. Within the "print-move-manage" framework, each step basically means transferring some responsibility of the functioning of the printers to Lexmark. Moving towards the "manage" part means that Lexmark does more for the company and the company can free its human resources to more productive activities.

Print" relates to the hardware and technical printing solutions that are used for market entry. Here, the main idea is the consolidation of the equipment base. There are many advantages that the customer company can gain by consolidating the printers and the related equipment. First, it is easier to arrange maintenance contracts for the machines when the equipment is more uniform. Second, the MRO (maintenance, repair, and operations) logistics is more efficient whereby the company can compare and choose their MRO suppliers in a more efficient manner. Third, IT support becomes more straightforward when the number of servers and the variety of brands are decreased. Finally, it is easier to take backups when the systems and machinery are consolidated.

"Move" is about combining activities, making the most use of multifunction machines and about scanning documents into electronic format and saving them as well as distributing them electronically. Here, the main idea is about changing the culture of the customer company. For example, by using two-sided printing, the company can save in printing costs but it also has considerable environmental effects. Most of the pollution from paper printing is concretized when the paper is produced. By using two-sided printing, approximately 40% of the negative environmental effects can be avoided. Scanning documents into electronic format and archiving them electronically can further reduce these effects.

"Manage" is about controlling the output environment: becoming conscious of the costs and trying to find ways to control and lower these costs. For doing so, Lexmark has created differentiated offerings for different customer segments. Figure 2 depicts these offerings. On the left side of Figure 2, Lexmark provides the equipment through dealers. On the right side, Lexmark interacts directly with the customer, delivering equipment directly to the

customer, and providing maintenance services and consultation services.

Beginning from the lower left corner of Figure 2, the ValuePrint Partner concept is offered to small companies and organizations through the dealer network. The offering is made primarily to copier dealers, giving them tools and techniques to improve printing processes on their customers' sites. The main idea for Lexmark here is to use the dealer network efficiently by providing the dealers guarantees on hardware, software, and spare part warranties.

ValuePrint Business concept is offered directly to customer companies without the use of the dealer network. Lexmark proposes simple, unbundled offerings without reporting or value-adding services. The main challenge here is to accommodate the offering to customer needs. The billing is based on the number of printed pages; this information is provided by the customer through the Web portal.

The ValuePrint Partner and the ValuePrint Business concepts are acquisition/copier based, which means that the customer purchases equipment and services separately. In other words, the offering that Lexmark makes to the companies

Figure 2. Differentiated offerings at Lexmark

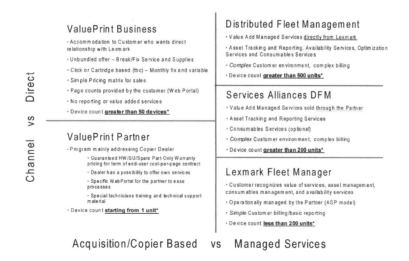

and dealers is not bundled. The main difference between the ValuePrint Partner and the ValuePrint Business offerings is that the ValuePrint Business offering is made directly to customers whereas the ValuePrint Partner is made to the copier dealers. The ValuePrint Business is also directed to somewhat larger customer companies than the ValuePrint Partner.

The Lexmark managed services are depicted on the right side of Figure 2. For a simple customer setting with basic reporting, Lexmark proposes the use of Lexmark Fleet Manager. The Lexmark Fleet Manager is essentially an information system and was described in the previous section. Here, the customer recognizes the value of services provided by the Fleet Manager system and is willing to pay for these services. Services Alliances Distributed Fleet Management (DFM) is basically the Fleet Management offering that is made to a more complex customer environment which requires more complex billing processes. The Lexmark Fleet Manager and Services Alliances concepts are made to the market through Lexmark's partners, the application service providers (ASPs).

Interacting directly with customers, Lexmark proposes the Distributed Fleet Management concept which is basically an outsourcing contract in which the customer company can choose from a variety of service levels. The highest service level means that the customer outsources everything from the physical printers to the maintenance and technical support to Lexmark. Here, everything ranging from technical equipment (printers, copying machines, networks, etc.) to technical support is outsourced to Lexmark. These outsourcing contracts are maintained either by controlling the client's machines from a distance or by placing Lexmark employees on the customer site. These concepts are offered primarily to large companies and organizations: for example in Finland, the Distributed Fleet Management contracts are targeted to the top 150 companies and organizations.

CHALLENGES AND NEW REQUIREMENTS

An important challenge in selling the service contracts to large companies is finding the right negotiation partner from the client company. The decision to outsource output management is a strategic one. Therefore, the decision should be taken by top management. In Finland, companies have been criticized for having too few marketing and IT people in their top management. Often, the company names an IT director who is responsible for the IT budget. Usually, the IT director has previously worked as an IT manager and has very seldom had the opportunity to take part in the strategic development of the company. This means focusing on costs and not looking at the big picture of making processes more efficient. Therefore, the customer's decision to outsource or not to outsource is made based on hard numbers and cold facts. It is Lexmark's job to convince the customer that Lexmark will be able to provide the service contracts more efficiently than the customer's own current practices.

Lexmark has recognized that it cannot provide these service contracts on their own: they need to partner with application side partners, outsourcing partners, and other product manufacturers. When providing service contracts for large customer companies, it is essential to try to partner even with competitors such as Hewlett Packard. It would be somewhat arrogant to think that Lexmark alone can provide service contracts for large companies that have tens of thousands of employees. Providing document-handling service contracts for large companies requires more than printers, scanners, and the necessary network to combine the existing equipment. It is about making different kinds of equipment from various product and service providers work well together. This is why Lexmark needs partners, even from the competitor side.

Besides networking with other companies and even competitors, Lexmark has had to re-educate its current staff. The role of sales managers has changed quite dramatically. Today, the sales managers really need to have knowledge of their customers' internal processes, and they need to interact with their customers more than they used to do. Lexmark has put considerable effort in re-educating its sales managers and giving them tools and techniques to deal with the new sales situation.

Transferring Responsibility and Risks

As already mentioned above, when Lexmark proposes these service contracts, it takes more responsibility of the customer's document-handling and printing processes. This brings up the question of risk management. What happens when something goes wrong? Fortunately, printing is very rarely a critical function within a company (although, for example, there are examples of instances where a failure to print out an offer has resulted in losing an important business opportunity). Nevertheless, risks related to product failure and its consequences, for example, are stipulated within the service contract.

The risks for Lexmark include the client's unwillingness to trust Lexmark in improving the document handling and printing processes. This might lead to wasted resources on Lexmark's side without any compensation. What risks might there be for the client? In some companies and organizations in Finland, some service providers have been too ambitious in decreasing the number of printers in the workplace. In other words, the ratio of employees/equipment has been too high. Now, if the client company has taken a 5-year leasing and service contract, it might be very difficult to get it cancelled and to improve the situation.

CURRENT CHALLENGES FACING THE ORGANIZATION

At Lexmark, we can see four main challenges when moving from product focus to service focus. They are related (1) to acquiring of new resources, (2a,b) to convincing the customers and Lexmark employees, (3) to finding the right negotiation partner, (4) to determining the level of service for each customer, and (5) to innovating new e-services.

1.   **New Resources in the Form of IT Solutions and Human Resources:** As described in the text, the role of the sales manager has changed dramatically. What kinds of innovations could be used to help the sales managers transfer from mere salespeople to consultants who have to understand the client's internal processes and needs and wants? What kinds of IT innovations, besides the asset management system described in the text, could be used?

2a. **Convincing the Customers to Purchase Printers As Services:** It is very challenging for Lexmark to find arguments to convince the customer company that it should outsource its printing activities to Lexmark. Very often, taking this decision would mean that the customer company's own staff is made redundant and should be moved to more productive activities. Currently, these arguments are made using hard facts describing how much the company would save in monetary terms if document-handling and printing activities were optimized and made more efficient. What kinds of novel arguments could there be?

2b. **Convincing the Personnel of Lexmark and Tackling the Internal Processes:** Besides convincing the customers of the new business deal, there are several internal challenges in the transition. In the past, the Lexmark sales managers were compensated according to their hardware revenue, in other words, the amount of printers they sold to their customers. Today, the situation is reversed. The managers are remunerated according to the revenues from the number of the printed pages that their customers print. The transition has an effect on how the different divisions within the company are evaluated. The CEO must understand that when the company moves to the service focus, some divisions may actually show negative results, even though the overall performance of the company has improved. What kinds of solutions could there be for getting the message through to the personnel? What kinds of new internal performance measurement instruments could the company use?

3. **Finding the Right Negotiation Partner in the Client Organization:** Every outsourcing decision is a strategic one, and it should be made by the top management. However, printing process and document-handling optimization is not seen as important activities within the customer companies of Lexmark. Therefore, it is very challenging to get face-to-face meetings with appropriate negotiation partners within the customer company. What kinds of strategies could Lexmark use in order to get the top management interested?

4. **How to Determine Whom to Target with the Service Contracts:** Lexmark proposes their Distributed Fleet Management and outsourcing services mainly to large firms, with more than 500 pieces of output equipment (printers, copy machines, faxes, etc.). Smaller firms are not equally attractive to Lexmark because they do not have the critical mass of document-handling and printing needs. Current challenges facing Lexmark include: How to determine what level of service contract is suitable for each customer? What should be the level of service contract offered to large firms/smaller firms? What other determinants than the customer company size should there be?

5. **How to Innovate New Services with the Fleet Manager Electronic Information System:** The Lexmark Fleet Manager system currently includes the Asset Manager, the Billing Manager, the Consumables Manager, the Availability Manager, and the Optimization Manager systems. These systems were described in the chapter. What kinds of new innovative systems could Lexmark incorporate to this Fleet Manager system?

REFERENCES

Oliva, R., & Kallenberg, R. (2003). Managing the transition from products to services. *International Journal of Service Industry Management, 14*(2), 160–172. doi:10.1108/09564230310474138

Penttinen, E. (2007). Transition from products to services within the manufacturing business. Doctoral dissertation, Helsinki School of Economics, Finland. Retrieved June 5, 2008, from http://hse-publ.lib.hse.fi/FI/diss/?cmd=show&dissid=343

Penttinen, E., & Palmer, J. (2007). Improving firm positioning through enhanced offerings and buyer-seller relationships. *Industrial Marketing Management, 36*(5), 552–564. doi:10.1016/j.indmarman.2006.02.005

Penttinen, E., & Saarinen, T. (2005). Opportunities and challenges for B2B industrial manufacturing firms: Case SKF. In T. Saarinen, M. Tinnila, & A. Tseng (Eds.), Managing business in a multi-channel world: Success factors for e-business (pp. 117–127). Idea Group Publishing.

Quinn, J. (1992). Intelligent enterprise: A knowledge and service based paradigm for industry. New York: Free Press.

Vargo, S., & Lusch, R. (2004). Evolving to a new dominant logic for marketing. *Journal of Marketing*, *68*(1), 1–17. doi:10.1509/jmkg.68.1.1.24036

Wise, R., & Baumgartner, P. (1999). Go downstream: The new profit imperative in manufacturing. *Harvard Business Review*, *77*(5), 133–141.

Zeithaml, V., Parasuraman, A., & Berry, L. (1985). Problems and strategies in services marketing. *Journal of Marketing*, *49*(2), 33–46. doi:10.2307/1251563

Chapter 4.14
Quality Assessment of Digital Services in E-Government with a Case Study in an Italian Region

Flavio Corradini
University of Camerino, Italy

Alberto Polzonetti
University of Camerino, Italy

Barbara Re
University of Camerino, Italy

ABSTRACT

The quality assessment of e-government services is more and more emerging as a key issue within public administrations. Ensuring a proper quality of digital services is mandatory to satisfy citizens and firms' needs and to accept the use of ICT in our lives. We propose a methodology for quality assessment that takes e-government quality features into account. We also define a reference model to provide a single quality value starting from a set of service parameters. To validate our approach we assess the goodness of the 'TecUt' shared services management system.

INTRODUCTION

Information and communication technologies (ICTs) are widely used within public administrations. In this context, e-government refers to the "use of ICT in public administrations combined with organizational changes and new skills in order to improve public services and democratic processes and strengthen support to public policies" (Commission of the European Communities, 2003, p. 7). These technologies allow governments to improve both the delivery of government services to citizens and the interactions with the business and the industry world. Digital government services represent one of the most critical areas of the whole service domain and several definitions are available in the

DOI: 10.4018/978-1-60566-064-6.ch003

literature (see, for instance, Elmagarmid & McIver, 2001; Tiwana & Ramesh, 2001) and references therein). In a broad sense, they can be thought as the provision of service, including pure services or tangible physical products, over electronic networks such as the Internet (Rust & Lemon, 2001). In particular, digital government services encapsulate public administration functionalities and informative resources making them available through the use of digital interfaces.

The growing diffusion of e-government requires services with high standard level of quality. Nowadays, quality of services is a hot topic of research. There is a very extensive research activity towards quality assessment in different application domains such as software development, multimedia applications, networking, mobile computing, real time and embedded applications, and so forth. According to the International Organization for Standardization, the term "quality" is intended as all the features of an entity (resource, service, and tool) that influence its capability to satisfy declared or implied needs (ISO, 1994).

Unfortunately, quality of services receives little attention by the e-government research community (see Papadomichelaki, Magoutas, Halaris, Apostolou, & Mentzas, 2006) and references therein for a review on quality dimensions in e-government services). Within the application domain of our interest—e-government—we could rephrase the above definition of quality as "all the features of digital services in public administrations that influence their capability to satisfy declared or implied citizens and firms' needs."

Certainly, quality in e-government plays a significant role. A proper quality of digital services is mandatory to satisfy citizens and enterprises' needs, to accept the use of information and communication technology in our lives as well as improve "government management."

In this chapter, we propose a framework to analyze the quality of digital services in e-government. Our methodology takes e-government quality features into account and is composed by three different phases: (i) quality definition, (ii) quality measurement, and (iii) quality interaction. We define (within the first phase) a comprehensive quality model. It is based on a taxonomy of four parameters subcategories related to services and their implementation (e-government, presentation, behavioral, and infrastructural). Our main efforts were to identify those parameters and their relationships that are necessary to assess the quality of e-government services. For each parameter, we pursue a proper analysis to determine the more appropriate metrics and measurement procedures. At the same time, we define a mathematical model that aggregates the detected parameters values into a single one. The model plays a fundamental role allowing a high abstraction level of the problems description and a formal background of the applicative solutions so to avoid possible structural mistakes and inaccurate descriptions.

To validate our approach, we rely on an existing shared services management system—the so-called TecUt portal (www.tecut.it), a portal developed in collaboration with one of the italian regions, the Marche Region (Corradini, Sabucedo, Polzonetti, Rifón, & Re, 2007). In more details, we have considered the TecUt digital services and we have compared the quality of services (with the same functionalities) provided by several Italian Municipalities to discover those that are more suitable to users requests.

The rest of the chapter is organized as follows. The second section provides a comprehensive understanding of the case study. Th third section introduces related works that have somehow contributed to the development of our work. The fourth section presents our methodology for quality assessment taking into account e-government quality features, while the fifth section introduces service quality model based on taxonomy of parameters related to service and its implementation. The sixth and seventh sections propose the measurement model and the mathematical model, respectively. Finally, the eighth section introduces experimental results, and the final section completes the chapter with conclusions and future work.

BACKGROUND

Several Italian Regions have been involved to implement e-government solutions to increase interactions between public administrations and citizens/enterprises by means of ICT infrastructures. To reach such a goal, key aspects of services distribution have been taken into account (authentication, accounting, discovery, etc.). According to the investigation on one-stop government (Corradini, Forastieri, Polzonetti, Riganelli, & Sergiacomi, 2005), the UeG group (Unicam e-Government research group) and the Marche Region public administration have developed the TecUt portal (Corradini et al., 2007), a fully integrated government portal for shared and standardized municipalities services. TecUt supports activities of small and medium municipalities providing a "gateway" between citizens/enterprises and public administrations. It allows a rapidly access to services by means of a single access point.

A global vision of the Marche Region stakeholders includes financial arrangements and aggregations, enterprises, banks, and citizens. This clearly boosts the national and international chances to increase relations with public administrations (PAs) and drives advanced ways to improve standards of living. As a matter of fact, the Marche Region is among the first places in Italy as far as welfare, cohesion, and competitiveness are concerned. At the same time Marche Region is characterized by a lot of small municipalities that are not able to support the fully digital services distribution. TecUt represents an opportunity to e-government diffusion in such an environment.

RELATED WORK

In application domains such as marketing, e-commerce, bioinformatics, and multimedia, the literature on quality of services contains interesting approaches. All of these contributions somehow influenced the development of our work, though we differ from them significantly. As far as we know, our chapter is the first attempt to introduce a comprehensive methodology for quality assessment of e-government digital services focusing on the role of users and ICT technologies. In our opinion, an in-depth analysis of quality literature gives us the necessary input for both the definition of the methodology for quality assessment and related models. In this section we essentially concentrate our attention on those papers that have more directly contributed to the development of our work. We put together domain and implementation related aspects focusing on the role of ICT in the services provision.

Starting from government quality literature, we identify two main areas of interest:

i. organizational performance: CAF (CAF Resource Center, 2006), Balanced Scorecard (Kaplan & Norton, 1992), Six Sigma (De Feo & Barnard, 2005), and Baldrige Criteria (Baldrige National Quality Program, 2006);

ii. site quality: SiteQual (Webb & Webb, 2004), Portal Usage Quality (Lin & Wu, 2002), IP-Portal (Yang, Cai, Zhou, & Zhou, 2005), Norwegian Approach (Jansen & Olnes, 2004), and G-Quality (Garcia, Maciel, & Pinto, 2005).

Regarding organizational performance, the authors mainly discuss the role of organizations while services play a marginal role. The authors define quality models but do not introduce ICT and implementation related aspects. Our approach takes into account organization elements for the identification of implicit relationships in the e-government domain but also focuses on the distribution of digital service and related issues. On the other hand, item (ii) above, the site quality area, introduces facilities to measure the quality of Web site focusing on the e-government front-end aspects. We refer to this stream of research for the definition of parameters and metrics related to the front-end layer of the services. Indeed, the evaluating and monitoring of digital government services must take into account aspects like adaptability, accessibility, and so on. The introduction of a proper client site represents a fundamental part of e-government services distribution. Regarding the e-government domain, we also mention e-government in a Thai approach (Sukasame, 2004). This latter presents a conceptual framework and some factors (content, linkage, reliability, ease of use, and self-service) affecting the e-service provided on the Web portal of Thailand's government. Unfortunately, it does not introduce a complete discussion on the objective assessment of digital services quality.

Interesting works done within services marketing literature have been taken into account, such as SERVQUAL (Parasuraman, Zeithaml, & Berry, 1998). The marketing literature always states that services quality perceptions are important elements of customers' satisfaction. The e-government setting heavily relies on technological and domain dependent constraints. Interesting suggestions also came from the business management domain with a special focus on quality policies (see Seth, Deshmukh, & Vrat, 2005 and references therein). In particular, Yang and Jun (2002) introduce a business service quality model that underlines the role of users (purchaser and nonpurchaser). Also in this setting their satisfaction plays a role. In the e-government domain, of course, we do not rely on business executives but the customers' perception of services quality is crucial. Santos (2003) introduces a model of e-quality, to achieve high customer retention, customer satisfaction, and profitability for the organizations in e-business. He proposes a model of e-service quality that takes into account static and dynamic parameters.

Unfortunately, none of the presented models proposes a complete set of parameters and a specific process for run time measurement. It has to be said that the literature on marketing and business

contributed to our approach on the subjective part of the assessing methodology. They are useful to investigate the users feeling on the services.

Related to the technological aspects, we underline the role of Web services as the most common implementation of digital services. In Ran (2003), Farkas and Charaf (2003), and Maximilien and Singh (2004), there is a first approach to define nonfunctional aspects in Web services discovery. From these works we have selected interesting parameters. In particular, Ran (2003) suggests an UDDI quality extension as solution for Web services discovery. In such a way, during the discovery phase, functional and nonfunctional service aspects are introduced. In Farkas and Charaf (2003), a software architecture is proposed to provide Web services with high quality. They implement a quality of service (QoS) broker for services discovery to reflect quality parameters stored in UDDI. Maximilien and Singh (2004) discuss the standard lack of description of nonfunctional attributes needed for Web services discovery. They propose an ontology-based framework to describe quality in order to improve the stakeholders' interaction. Moreover, in Cardoso, Sheth, and Miller (2002); Menascé (2004a, 2004b); and Zeng, Benatallah, Dumas, Kalagnanam, and Sheng (2003), a quality composition approach is investigated. Unfortunately, they consider a short list of quality parameters that are meaningless for e-government application domain and do not introduce a formal measurement and assessment process.

In Nahrstedt, Xu, Wichadakul, and Li (2001) and Tsetsekas, Manitias, Funfstuck, Thoma, and Karadimas (2001), QoS is introduced in a middleware domain. In Nahrstedt et al. (2001), the authors discuss QoS middleware information able to support quality-based applications like streaming and e-commerce. This work presents key aspects about service quality introducing application and process quality information at low abstraction level. In Tsetsekas et al. (2001), a middleware that drives service presentation to the users is proposed. It allows description and selection of QoS parameters and related resources preemptive reservation. In general, distributed applications and their quality provide several hints to quality of services in e-government.

Finally, Menascé (2003) and Corradini et al. (2004) introduce digital service quality in e-commerce and bioinformatics, respectively. They propose an approach for domain related quality investigation and parameters modularization. In Menascé (2003), a QoS controller is introduced. It uses aggregated metrics to take into account performance parameters. In particular, a QoS controller continuously supervises e-commerce sites and fixes the best configuration to achieve the quality objectives. Corradini et al. (2004) proposes a quality model for biomedical service discovery using a MAS approach and in particular matchmaker functionalities. This is an agent contacted by other agents which want to obtain the best service for specific task. In order to ensure the best quality service to the client, the matchmaker communicates with the QoS certification authority that provides a quality level to each registered service.

QUALITY ASSESSING METHODOLOGY

We propose a methodology suitable for quality assessment of digital services. Our methodology (Figure 1) takes into account e-government quality features and relies on the following activities: (i) development of a quality vocabulary, (ii) formalization of the measurements, and (iii) definition of a quality aggregation function. We can also cycle through the methodology activities to propose the more accurate solution for quality assessment.

The first phase—quality definition—refers to the identification of parameters and related metrics starting from a review of the e-government domain. This phase defines a comprehensive e-government quality model. We have investigated the domain at different abstraction levels and we have developed a quality vocabulary. We consider parameters as usability, attraction, availability, and execution time (just to cite a few). In particular, we split the parameters into two sets of the same importance: subjective parameters and objective parameters (see, for instance, Shewhart, 1980) that describe quality in term of subjective and objective parameters in the manufacturing domain. The

Figure 1. E-government quality assessing methodology

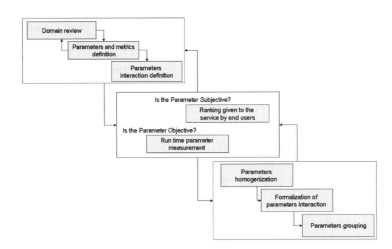

former is conditioned by individuals experience or knowledge and by personal mental characteristics or states, whereas the latter is individual independent. Related to metrics, we define a unit of measure that is in line with a specific procedure for quality measurement. In this phase, we also find parameters dependences to measure dynamic relationships among them and overall quality.

The second phase—quality measurement—refers to the formalization of the measurements. We have introduced a model that allows a suitable abstraction level of the problem description and a formal background of the applicative solutions so to avoid possible structural mistakes and inaccuracies. The model is scalable with respect to the considered set of parameters. Starting from the parameters taxonomy previously detected and the classification in subjective and objective parameters, we investigated on a proper measurement model. In particular, subjective parameters are measured using ranking given by the end users to a specific service. A rank is based on the user profiles and the user preferences and is collected starting from a sample of population (Devore, 1995). The target of population and the number of people to interview are critical aspects. If you do not interview the right kinds of people, you might not meet your goals. We define a sample group composed of 30 people aged 25–45. At the same time, objective parameters are measured performing an automatic run-time monitoring.

Finally, the third phase—quality interaction—introduces a mathematical model to define a quality function and assess a quality value starting from the sets of parameters. The model relies on parameters homogenization, interaction, and grouping. In particular, homogenization of the input is useful to reason over different metrics (for instance, time-based measurements need to be aggregated with security-based boolean measurements or some other metrics). The homogenization takes also into account whether a given parameter grows in a proportional or in an inverse proportional way with respect to the

overall quality measurement. Interaction between different parameters is also considered by the mathematical model. In such a way we can take into account how parameters influence each other's (for instance, how trust parameter influences usability, Bedi & Banati, 2006). Finally, the proposed model groups parameters and manages them with different importance.

QOS CRITERIA OF QUALITY MODEL

In this section we present the parameters of our quality model able to assess the quality of services. They can be classified in a taxonomy of four subcategories (Table 1): (i) *e-government parameters* that take into account how digital services of public administrations are perceived by the final users, (ii) *presentation parameters* that analyze front-office services with respect to the final users needs, (iii) *behavioral parameters* that describe the implementation of back-end services, and (iv) *infrastructural parameters* related to the basic infrastructures enabling digital services. At this stage of presentation we do not introduce the further classification related to subjective and objective parameters because we give them the same importance.

Service Related Aspects

As previously mentioned service parameters are split in two parts: (i) e-government and (ii) presentation.

In the e-government group we introduce the

Table 1. QoS categorization for digital e-government service parameters

Service	e-Government
	Presentation (front-end)
Implementation	Behavioral (back-end)
	Infrastructural

following items. *Popularity* considers the amount of population interested to the service as well as the utilization frequency with respect to time and the number of interactions between government and users. *Usability* considers easiness of learning the service and easiness to benefit of the service information. Moreover, we introduce *attraction* and *multicanality* to detect e-government maturity. Attraction measures the users' incentive to use online services rather than traditional ones (offered by public administrations through off-line channels), while multicanality points out service distribution solutions (Web, mobile computing, etc.). We also consider *internationalization* that refers to the languages used for service description and distribution and *reputation* that represents the service trustworthiness. We introduce *originality* and *contents* that are related to service contents quality. Originality focuses on the service innovation level, while contents indicate public administrations capabilities to provide useful and proper information. *Legality* represents laws and norms that regulate the provision and the service user fruition. A further significant parameter is *domain security* that measures the process and information control level. *Trust* represents the level of confidence among stakeholders in the services execution. This parameter involves citizens, enterprises, public administration employee, software agents, and organization focusing the attention on proper skills and tasks. At the same time a digital service underlines privacy and communication security levels. A proper service distribution allows a certain level of trust and promotes the service utilization. Moreover, *promoting e-democracy* represents a useful parameter to evaluate the impact of a service on the society. This supplies a quantitative value to show how a service can promote digital citizenship. Namely, the set of practices of ICT used by citizens to take part to political choices at any level. The presence of forums, FAQs, mailing lists, nd so forth, related to the service has a good impact on the value of this parameter. Finally, we consider the *completeness*

of a service, representing the e-Europe levels. It is evaluated starting from different way to interact with the services. An high level corresponds to a complete online service presence to perform proper transactions.

About front-end related aspects, we take into account *cost, accessibility,* and *adaptability*. The cost parameter measures the mean amount of money involved in a complete service transaction, capturing the economic condition of the service use. It summarizes every cost related to the service provision such as execution price and pricing model. Accessibility measures the users' easiness to detect and to use the needed service capabilities. It is particularly relevant related to disadvantaged people. Finally, adaptability evaluates the service capacity to change (or be changed) and make itself suitable for a new context.

Implementation Related Aspects

As well as service parameters, the implementation parameters are split in two parts: (iii) behavioral and (iv) infrastructural.

In the first group, we introduce *interoperability* levels achieved by the services. It represents the amount of cooperative work between consumer applications, software agents, and services in different development environments that implement and deploy procedures. From this perspective, the use of standards affects service interoperability. It is measured by *supported standard/regulatory*. Moreover, *applicative security* represents the security level of Web services introducing authentication and authorization policies and procedures. *Integrity,* about data and transactions, is another important element. It measures service ability to prevent unauthorized access to—or modification of—computer programs or data. It remarks on the ACID properties: atomicity, consistency, isolation, and durability (Gray, 1981). At the same time, *robustness/flexibility* measures the service capabilities to work correctly even when invalid, incomplete or conflicting inputs occur. It is affected by service stability in terms of its interface and/ or implementation.

About infrastructure parameters, we analyze the following items. *Availability* represents how the service is available when a client attempts to use it. *Performance* represents how fast a service request can be completed. It measures the speed in completing tasks using service response time, latency, and execution time. *Scalability* refers to the capability of increasing the service capacity in terms of operations or transactions processed in a fix time. Moreover, *scheduling* refers to the quality level of the service assigning resources. *Throughput* represents transfer rate for information in a given time interval. It is measured using Successful Execution Request and Successful Execution Rate. Finally, *reliability* represents the ability of a service to perform its required functions under stated conditions for a specified period of time.

QUALITY MEASUREMENT

In this section we present measurement algorithms and we focus on a representative subset of parameters. The parameters are chosen according to the classification in the previous section.

Terminology and Algorithms

The measurement model refers to the following elements.

- Σ is the set of digital e-government services that we would like to monitor, where S, R, V range over Σ.
- Π is the set of parameters in our quality model, where par_1, par_2, par_3 range over Π.

Over parameters and services we need a couple of predicates. Assume $par \in \Pi$ and

$S \in \Sigma$. Predicate $qt(par, S)$ indicates whether parameter *par* can be measured for service S (or, in other words, *par* is relevant for service S). As an example consider security parameters are introduced when sensible data are involved in a service behavior. Predicate $PAR(par)$ indicates whether parameter *par* can be measured for all services in Σ *PAR(par)=true* if *qt(par,S)=true* $\forall S \in \Sigma$. For instance, usability parameter is related to all the services in e-government domain.

- T is the set of time instances, where t_1, t_2, t_3 range over T. Of course, we assume an ordering among time instances in a discrete time domain. Ω denotes the set of time intervals. They take the form (t_1, t_2), where $t_1, t_2 \in T$ (and $t_1 \leq t_2$). Time is needed in a quality assessment framework due to the dynamic environment.
- Λ is the set of service locations, where loc_1, loc_2, loc_3 range over Λ. A spatial environment for quality measurements allows an overview of the services context (Lee & Helal, 2003).

Assume $S \in \Sigma$, $t \in T$, and $loc \in \Lambda$. We can measure the parameters in a fixed time instance and in a spatial location according to the following algorithm. Parameters measurement represents the input of the mathematical model described in detail in the "QoS Assessment Model" section (Figure 2).

Array Q stores the measurements of the parameters related to a service. The list of array QoS stores the measurement of the parameters related to the service S and all the digital government services measured in different time by the algorithm. Starting from the measures, we define upper bound using the following algorithm. (Figure 3)

Finally, the parameters trend is represented by *Tr(par)*. It assumes value true or false depending on the behavior related to the overall quality value: proportional parameter in the former case,

Figure 2.

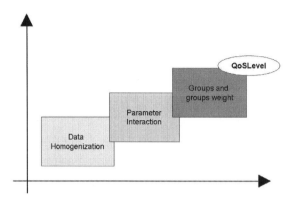

inverse proportional parameter in the latter one. In other words:

- the parameter trend is positive (true) if whenever the overall quality at t_1 is bigger than the overall quality at t_2 then the value of *par* in t_1 is bigger than the value of *par* in t_2, and
- the parameter trend is negative (false) if whenever the overall quality at t_1 is smaller than the overall quality at t_2 then the value of *par* in t_1 is bigger than the value of *par* in t_2.

Of course, the above considerations on measurements and trends at time instants apply also at time interval.

Measured Parameters

This section proposes the measurement on a subset of parameters related to the "measure" procedure in the "measure" algorithm. The service response time (*rt*) (6.2.1) measures the delay (at client site) between sending a request and receiving response.

$$rt = t_{clientReceive} - t_{clientSend} \qquad (6.2.1)$$

The service execution time (*et*) (6.2.2) measures the time needed to process service instructions. In particular, it measures the delay between request reception and response forwarding by the service. The measure is executed at service site.

$$et = t_{serviceSend} - t_{serviceReceive} \qquad (6.2.2)$$

Figure 3.

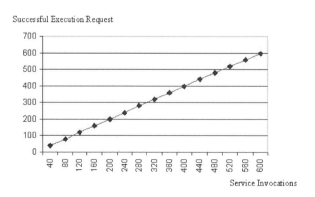

The service latency (*lat*) (6.2.3) measures the delay between sending a request and receiving a result at client site, without taking into consideration the execution time of the service.

$$lat = rt - et \qquad (6.2.3)$$

The service reliability (*rel*) (6.2.4) measures ability to perform required functionalities under stated conditions for a fixed period of time. In (6.2.4), $F(S)$ indicates the number of executions that the service has not been successfully completed within the interval t_1, t_2 interval.

$$rel = \frac{F(S)}{t_2 - t_1} \qquad (6.2.4)$$

The service successful execution request (*sereq*) (6.2.5) is the number of service requests completed successfully in a given time interval. In (6.2.5), $N_C(S)$ indicates the number of times that the service has been successfully completed within the interval t_1, t_2.

$$sereq = \frac{N_C(S)}{t_2 - t_1} \qquad (6.2.5)$$

The service successful execution rate (*serat*) (6.2.6) is the rate of service requests successfully completed in a given time interval related to the executed requests. It is related to the successful execution request. In (6.2.6), $N_C(S)$ indicates the number of service executions that has been successfully completed in the interval t_1, t_2 while $N_{Cmax}(S)$ indicates the maximum number of executions that the service is able to complete with success within the same time interval. $N_{Cmax}(S)$ can be computed starting from $N_C(S)$ and $F(S)$.

$$serat = \frac{N_C(S)}{N_{Cmax}(S)} \qquad (6.2.6)$$

The service availability (*ava*) (6.2.7) represents capability to reply immediately to the users requests. In (6.2.7), $T_A(S)$ is the total amount of time where the service is available during the interval t_1, t_2 and it is computed through service site measures. If $T_A(S) = t_2 - t_1$, then we have the maximal availability.

$$ava = \frac{T_A(S)*100}{t_2 - t_1} \qquad (6.2.7)$$

The service attraction (*att*) (6.2.8) represents the users incentive to use online services rather than traditional ones. Different end users may have different opinions on the same services. The value of the attraction is computed using the (6.2.8) formula and it is defined as the average ranking given to the service by end users. In (6.2.8), $R_i(S)$ is the *i*-th end-user ranking on the service attraction and *n* is the number of time that the service has been graded in t_1, t_2 time interval.

$$att = \frac{\sum_{i=1}^{n} R_i(S)}{n} \qquad (6.2.8)$$

Finally, the service reputation (*rep*) (6.2.9) represents trustworthiness of the service. It is measured using an approach similar to that one used in attraction assessment. In (6.2.9), $G_i(S)$ is the *i*-th end-user ranking on service reputation and *n* is the number of time that the service has been graded in t_1, t_2 time interval.

$$rep = \frac{\sum_{i=1}^{n} G_i(S)}{n} \qquad (6.2.9)$$

Given the above consideration, quality parameters can be aggregate using the mathematical model explained in "QoS Assessment Model" section. In this way we can associate to a specific service a single quality value starting from quality measurements on a set of heterogeneous parameters.

QOS ASSESSMENT MODEL

In this section we introduce our mathematical model for QoS quantification of e-government digital services. The model provides an assessment, after three normalization phases, of the quality level for a digital service. Starting from a set of quality parameters, the model estimates a value in the $[0...100]$ range. This model is inspired by Liu, Ngu, and Zeng (2004), but we introduce further elements like data homogenization and parameters interaction. In detail, (i) homogenization of the input is useful to reason over different e-government parameters metrics and behavior. The homogenization takes into account whether a given parameter grows in a proportional or inverse proportional way with respect to the overall quality measurement. For example, infrastructure related criteria measured against time needs to be aggregated with security parameters measured with boolean values, or some other metrics, and if the quality of infrastructure grows up, then the quality of security also grows up. At the same time we introduce (ii), interaction among parameters to measure dynamic relationships. In such a way we can take into account how parameters influence each other (for instance, usability parameter influence on service trust).

Input of the Model

Let S be a service. The mathematical model uses the following input parameters.

- $Q = (q_1, q_2, ..., q_n)$ is an array of n natural numbers representing the measured value of parameters (*par*) related to the service S. Each q_i, for $1 \leq i \leq n$, is collected during measurement process and represents a specific view of the service.
- $Z = (z_1, z_2, ..., z_n)$ is an array of n boolean values used in the normalization phase. It is defined starting from *Tr(par)*. Each z_i for $1 \leq i \leq n$, assumes a value as in (7.1.1).

$$z_i = \begin{cases} 1 & \text{if the } q_i \text{ parameter in } Q \text{ grows in proportional way with respect to the overall quality value;} \\ 0 & \text{if the } q_i \text{ parameter in } Q \text{ grows in inverse proportional way with respect to the overall quality value. (7.1.1)} \end{cases}$$

- $C = (c_1, c_2, ..., c_n)$ is an array of n not zero natural numbers used during the normalization process. It is defined starting from *Ub(par)*. Each c_i $1 \leq i \leq n$ represents the upper bound of the q_i parameter in Q vector. The C elements are bound to parameter analysis and they depend on the specific metrics used to express them and on the methodology for the measurements.

- MI is a matrix of $[0...1]$ values composed of n rows and n columns. It shows the interaction level between parameters in Q. Each $m_{i,j}$, for $1 \leq i,j \leq n$, assumes a value as it follows:

$$m_{i,j} = \begin{cases} [0...1] & \text{if } q_i \text{ and } q_j \text{ interact} \\ 0 & \text{if } q_i \text{ and } q_j \text{ not interact} \end{cases} \quad (7.1.2)$$

In particular, in the MI diagonal all the values are 0 to represent a not relevant interaction of a parameter with itself. For instance, cost parameter cannot interact with itself in the same spatial-temporal location.

- D is a matrix of boolean composed of n rows (representing the parameters) and l columns (that refers to the number of quality groups). D is used to group the parameters with similar features. Each parameter can take part to one and only one group. The matrix complies with the followed constraint.

$$\forall i \quad 1 \leq i \leq n \quad \sum_{j=0}^{l} d_{i,j} = 1 \quad (7.1.3)$$

In particular, we indicate groups cardinality using h_i.

- $W = (w_1, w_2, ..., w_l)$ is an array of l natural numbers with each w_i $1 \le i \le l$ that indicate the weight of the specific group i. Moreover, the array complies with the following constraint $\sum_{i=1}^{l} w_i = 100$. The weights can be also associated to parameter if and only if the groups are composed of only one of them.

Figure 4 shows the phases to evaluate the overall service quality.

Phases of the Model

Phase 1: Data Homogenization. As a first step, let Q, Z and C be the input. We introduce a normalization function f_1. It takes triples of the form (q_i, z_i, c_i), where q_i, z_i, c_i are the i-th elements of the arrays Q, Z, and C respectively, and returns a value in the range $[0...100]$. We obtain a new array Q' of elements $q_i' = f_1(q_i, z_i, c_i)$. The formal definition of function f_1 is proposed in (7.2.1).

$$f_1(q_i, z_i, c_i) = z_i \left(\frac{q_i * 100}{c_i} \right) + (1 - z_i) * \left(100 - \frac{q_i * 100}{c_i} \right) \quad (7.2.1)$$

Phase 2: Parameters Interaction. In the second phase we consider the interaction factors of the quality parameters. We obtain, using (7.2.2), the interaction factor φ_k $\forall k$ such that $1 \le k \le n$.

$$\phi_k = \frac{\sum_{j=1}^{n} m_{j,k}}{n-1} \quad (7.2.2)$$

The proposed interaction factor does not take into consideration recursive impact on parameters; as matter of fact MI is a matrix with null diagonal elements. Moreover, each element q' must be normalized to obtain a new arrays Q'' (its elements will be denoted by $q_1'', q_2'', q_3'', ...$) using function f_2 in (7.2.3). It takes pairs of the form (φ_i, q_i') where φ_i and q_i' are the i-th interaction factor and element of the array Q' respectively.

$$f_2(\varphi_i, q_i') = \varphi_i q_i' \quad (7.2.3)$$

Phase 3: Grouping and Group Weight. At this point we introduce the possibility to group the parameters and manage them as groups with different importance (exploiting to this purpose the matrix D and array W). In the first step of this phase we use matrix D and we obtain a new array G (its element will be denoted by $g_1, g_2, g_3,$ ... range over G) of QoS values for each group with $G = Q'' D$.

Finally, it is possible to evaluate an overall quality value for a service considering the QoS-

Figure 4. QoS assessment model phases

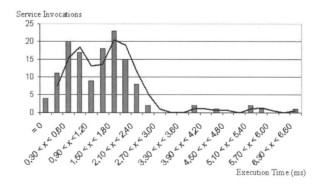

Level function showed in (7.2.4). It takes triples of the form (g_i, h_i, w_i) where g_i and w_i are the *i*-th elements of the arrays G and W respectively and h_i is the cardinality of *i*-th group. It gives a value in the range $[0...100]$.

$$QoSLevel(g_i, h_i, w_i) = \frac{\sum_{i=1}^{l} \frac{g_i}{h_i} * w_i}{\sum_{i=1}^{l} w_i} \qquad (7.2.4)$$

EXPERIMENTATION

In order to examine the effectiveness of our quality approach we carried out a set of simulations to study step-by-step the impact factor of the digital e-government services parameters on quality.

TecUt is an ASP.NET Web application running on IIS6 (Windows Server 2003 Environment). The server is a Pentium IV 3.0GHz with 1Gb of RAM located inside the Marche Region Demilitarized Zone.

In this section we present the most important experimental results related to the

1. behavior of some service parameters under growing amount of stress;
2. dependence among parameters;
3. behavior of the overall quality of service value starting from a subset of parameters, in this case we have verified also parameters and interaction variation;
4. global trend of the quality function.

The specific service under experimentation in the TecUt portal is the "Residence Certificate" request. It is used to certify personal information with respect legal residence/domicile.

Parameters Behavior

We perform parameters measurement to under stress service. The outputs of measurement are represented in the following graphs. We immediately observe that the successful execution request behavior is proportional to the number of service invocations that are done simultaneously. Parameter behavior depends on the lack of time constraints (meant as upper bound on the service execution) on the execution time of the service. In this case all the service requests are satisfied (Figure 5). We also observe service execution time, in the range 0.3–3 milliseconds (Figure 6) and latency in the range 10–16 milliseconds. Their distribution follows a normal trend (Figure 7). Also response time follows a normal trend and shows a stable behavior, its values are in the range 6–24 milliseconds (Figure 8). Finally, reliability and availability assume constant values (we do not observe fault and types mismatch) and during the measurements service was always achievable. In general, a good quality level and stable behavior characterize the service, thanks to a proper service context and a good connectivity level.

Parameters Dependence

In this subsection we observe different kinds of dependences among objective parameters presented in the measurement model. We mention some of them; others are not very relevant or will be investigated deeply in the future. We observe that response time and successful execution request are inversely proportional, and the increasing of the first yields a reduction of the second. Also latency and execution time impact the successful execution request; we observe some waving due to the growing of service requests. The growing of service requests and the complexity of service behavior play a fundamental role. Moreover, response time is related to latency and execution time

Figure 5. Service successful execution request

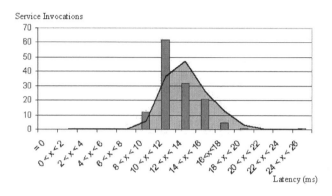

Figure 6. Service execution time distribution

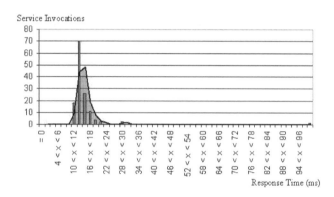

Figure 7. Service latency distribution

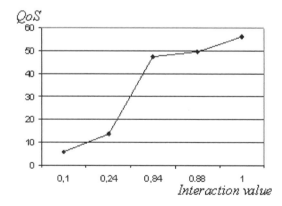

in a proportional way. Their decreasing reduces the response time of the services, and vice-versa.

Finally, we also individualize dependences between successful execution request and reliability-availability. Service faults (or mismatch) bring out a successful execution request reduction. Moreover, reliability and availability grow in inverse proportional and proportional way related to successful execution request respectively.

Figure 8. Service response time distribution

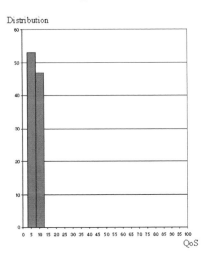

Experimental Result Related to a Specific Service

In this section we introduce our quality approach to TecUt "Residence Certificate" and we analyze two quality parameters: availability and response time.

- $Q = (350,120)$ represents parameters values in particular availability (measured in minutes) and response time (measured in second).
- $Z = (1,0)$ introduces trend relations between overall quality and individual parameter. We underline that quality grows in a proportional way respect to availability value and in an inversely proportional way respect to response time value.
- $C = (1440,600)$ proposes the upper bound of the two parameters; in particular a service can be available at most for 1440 minutes and the delay allow to receive a valid response from the service is 600 seconds.
- MI shows a positive and symmetric interaction between the considered parameters.

$$MI = \begin{pmatrix} 0 & 0,84 \\ 0,84 & 0 \end{pmatrix}$$

- D represents the groups; in our case it is meaningless; and each parameter represents a group.
- $W = (40, 60)$ shows the weight given by the users to availability and response time.

Starting from this set of input, the output value of *QoSLevel* is 47,60. We observed parameters and interaction variations.

First case—availability. We observe a variation of availability values from 350 to 1460 minutes. Availability grows in a proportional way respect to the value of *QoSLevel* and we expect an increase of the quality value. Indeed, the quality rises from a value of 47,60 to 70,13.

Second case— response time. We observe a variation of response time values from 120 to 300 seconds. Response time grows in an inversely proportional way respective to the value of *QoSLevel* and we suppose a decrease of the quality value. Indeed, the overall quality changes from 47,60 to 32,39.

Third case—interactions. The experimental results are shown in Table 2 and in Figure 9 for some values of interaction. We can observe that quality is proportional to interaction function value.

Moreover, the model limits interaction function to nonzero values. It represents the lower bound of the quality. Overall quality is next to zero when the interaction function is next to zero. This means that quality parameters choice on non-interactive parameters is not very good to analyze the overall quality of the service. More generally, in e-government domain we underline the importance of interaction to reach the full users' satisfaction.

General Considerations

We would also like to observe the quality behavior by introducing random values as inputs. The

Table 2. Quality variation

Interaction value	QoS
1	56,33
0,88	49,57
0,84	47,60
0,24	13,52
0,1	5,63
0,00001	0

following cases are proposed:

a. We analyze the behavior of quality function observing the variation of quality parameters by fixing all the other model entities.

b. We analyze the behavior of frequency distribution of the quality values starting from random values both for parameters and for other inputs of the model.

c. We analyze the quality frequency distributions underlying the role of parameters interactions (we observe bound behaviors).

After several experiments we were able to assess the QoS trend. Experiments in item (a) above show a linear trend of QoS value. It increases or decreases steadily with respect of the parameters trend. We take into account the properties of the parameters; some of them are proportional whereas others are inversely proportional with respect to the quality value (i.e., the quality increases if the execution time decreases and/or the usability increases). The behavior of frequency distribution of the quality values follows a normal trend. We observe this kind of behavior starting from random values both for parameters and for other inputs of the model in item (b). Taking into account the central limit theorem, the sum of large and independent quality observations has an approximate normal distribution (Gaussian Distribution) under certain general conditions. Finally, in item (c) it is clear that parameters interactions affect quality upper bound. If the interaction decreases

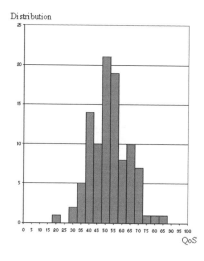

Figure 9. Quality variation

the quality level assume low values, while with height interaction also the QoS values increase. Finally, we observe with low interactions a close quality frequency distribution, while it is stretched to a normal trend with high interactions. The increase of parameters interaction support the goodness of our approach; as matter of fact, the e-government process is influenced by different dependent factors.

CONCLUSION

We have presented a methodology to assess the maturity of digital government services in public administrations. In our opinion, quality assessment of services, together with a shared service management system as TecUt, represents the main element to monitoring services capabilities and implement optimal resources allocation saving time and costs.

Nonfunctional services aspects awareness and specific measurement and assessment models allow complete and fine services governance. Our final aim is to improve people trust and access to e-government services through a dynamic ICT infrastructure that responds quickly to changing needs.

Quality approaches, which are discussed in detail in the "Background" section, present a global view of the problem. Most of them do not introduce both domain and technology related features. These aspects are usually discussed separately. Some works focus also on the role of users and introduce subjectivity users experiences in service utilization but do not merge them with objective ones. Vice versa works in that the objective quality aspects do not take into account users roles. Moreover, they usually define metrics but only a few of them introduce careful measurement on the detected parameters. The closest approach to this work is Sukasame (2004) about e-government in Thai. Unfortunately, it does not introduce neither a complete list of quality parameters nor specific and careful measurement activities. It focuses only on subjective parameters and does not introduce a complete discussion on the assessment of quality of digital services. As previously mentioned, this work presents the first attempt to introduce a complete assessment methodology for quality of e-government digital services focusing both on the role of users and ICTs. In such a way, we combine different aspects in a formal and homogeneous way.

Our methodology, together with the formal treatment, provides several benefits. First of all it allows a certain level of confidence on the service capabilities and enhances reliability and efficiency of inspection procedures. We can analyze (i) the behavior of parameters under growing amounts of stress, (ii) the dependence among parameters related to government domain, and (iii) the behavior of the overall quality of service. We can also control parameters value, interactions, upper bound, and the trend of overall quality.

Starting from the set of experimentation carried out on the TecUt portal, we observe a good quality level of the services. In practice, we have effectively noticed a stable behavior. The main reasons are related to services location and connectivity level. The quality value indicates the maturity of the services and it is also useful to analyze offered solutions (on the hand of service providers). Public administrations can plan the development of new services and the adaptation of existing ones by using the results of the application of this kind of quality assessment. However, the most important result, after the application of quality assessment, is the utilization improvement of the TecUt services (62%). In this way TecUt trustworthiness is improved.

We plan to extend this work taking into consideration dynamic aspects related to quality of services. We are going to introduce more e-government parameters to extend the goodness of the models. In particular, we are going to refer also to those parameters that cannot be measured in an objective way but that rely on data collected from the evaluations given by end users. At the same time, we must study complexity reduction algorithms for the proposed mathematical model. This kind of algorithm will be able to maintain the models' expressivity.

REFERENCES

Baldrige National Quality Program. (2006). *Criteria for performance excellence*. Retrieved June 8, 2008, from http://www.quality.nist.gov/

Bedi, P., & Banati, H. (2006). Assessing user trust to improve Web usability. *Journal of Computer Science, 2*(3), 283–287.

CAF Resource Center. (2006). *Common assessment framework*. Retrieved June 8, 2008, from http://www.eipa.nl/CAF/CAFmenu.htm

Cardoso, J., Sheth, A., & Miller, J. (2002, April). Workflow quality of service. In *Proceedings of the IFIP Tc5/Wg5.12 International Conference on Enterprise Integration and Modeling Technique: Enterprise Inter- and Intra-Organizational Integration: Building International Consensus*, Valencia, Spain (pp. 303–311).

Commission of the European Communities. (2003). The role of e-government for Europe's future (Communication from the commission to the council, the European parliament, the European economic and social committee, and the committee of the regions). Brussels.

Corradini, F., Ercoli, C., Merelli, E., & Re, B. (2004, November). An agent-based matchmaker. In Proceedings of WOA04 Sistemi Complessi e Agenti Razionali, Torino, Italy (pp. 150–156).

Corradini, F., Forastieri, L., Polzonetti, A., Riganelli, O., & Sergiacomi, A. (2005, February). Shared Services Center for E-Government Policy. In *Proceedings of the 1st International Conference on Interoperability of eGovernment Services (eGov-Interop '05)*, Geneva, France (pp. 140–151).

Corradini, F., Sabucedo, L. A., Polzonetti, A., Rifón, L. A., & Re, B. (2007, September). A case study of semantic solutions for citizen-centered Web portals in eGovernment: The TecUt Portal. In *Proceedings of the 6th International EGOV Conference 2007, DEXA*, Regensburg, Germany (pp. 204–215, LNCS).

De Feo, J. A., & Barnard, W. W. (2005). JURAN Institute's Six Sigma breakthrough and beyond: Quality performance breakthrough methods. Tata McGraw-Hill Publishing Company Limited.

Devore, J. L. (1995). Probability and statistics for engineering and the sciences. Duxbury Press.

Elmagarmid, A. K., & McIver, W. J. (2001). Guest editors' introduction: The ongoing march toward digital government. *IEEE Computer, 34*(2), 32–38.

Farkas, P., & Charaf, H. (2003). Web services planning concepts. *Journal of WSCG, 11*(1).

Garcia, A. C., Maciel, C., & Pinto, F. B. (2005, August). A quality inspection method to evaluate e-government sites. In *Proceedings of the 4th International EGOV Conference 2005, DEXA*, Copenhagen, Denmark (pp. 198–209, LNCS).

Gray, J. (1981). The transaction concept: Virtues and limitations. In *Proceedings of the 7th International Conference on Very Large Data Bases*, Cannes, France (pp. 144–154).

ISO. (1994). ISO 8402: Quality management and quality assurance (Vocabulary, 2nd ed.). Geneva: Author.

Jansen, A., & Olnes, S. (2004, June). Quality assessment and benchmarking of Norwegian public Web sites. In *Proceedings of the 4th European Conference on E-government*, Dublin.

Kaplan, R. S., & Norton, D. P. (1992). The balanced scorecard: Measures that drive performance. Harvard Business Review.

Lee, C., & Helal, S. (2003). Context attributes: An approach to enable context-awareness for service discovery. In *Proceedings of the 2003 Symposium on Applications and the Internet, SAINT* (p. 23). IEEE Computer Society.

Lin, S., & Wu, C. S. (2002, January). Exploring the impact of online service quality on portal site usage. In *Proceedings of the 35th Annual Hawaii International Conference on System Sciences (HICSS'02)*, Maui, Hawaii (pp. 2654–2661).

Liu, Y., Ngu, A. H., & Zeng, L. Z. (2004, May). QoS computation and policing in dynamic Web service selection. In *Proceedings of the 13th International World Wide Web Conference on Alternate Track Papers and Posters*, New York (pp. 66–73).

Maximilien, E. M., & Singh, M. P. (2004). A framework and ontology for dynamic Web services selection. *IEEE Computer Society, 8*(5), 84–92.

Menascé, D. A. (2003). Automatic QoS control. *IEEE Computer Society, 7*(1), 92–95.

Menascé, D. A. (2004a). Composing Web services: A QoS view. *IEEE Computer Society, 4*(6), 88–90.

Menascé, D. A. (2004b). Response-time analysis of composite Web services. *IEEE Internet Computing*, *8*(1), 90–92. doi:10.1109/MIC.2004.1260710

Nahrstedt, K., Xu, D., Wichadakul, D., & Li, B. (2001). QoS-aware middleware for ubiquitous and heterogeneous environments. *Communications Magazine, IEEE*, *39*(11), 140–148. doi:10.1109/35.965372

Papadomichelaki, X., Magoutas, B., Halaris, C., Apostolou, D., & Mentzas, G. (2006). A review of quality dimensions in e-government services. In *Proceedings of the 5th International EGOV Conference 2006, DEXA*, Krakow, Poland (pp. 128–138).

Parasuraman, A., Zeithaml, V. A., & Berry, L. (1998). SERVQUAL: A multiple-item scale for measuring consumer perceptions of service quality. *Journal of Retailing*, *64*(1), 12–40.

Ran, S. (2003). A model for Web services discovery with QoS. *SIGecom Exchange*, *4*(1), 1–10. doi:10.1145/844357.844360

Rust, R. T., & Lemon, K. L. (2001). E-service and the consumer. *International Journal of Electronic Commerce*, *5*(3), 85–101.

Santos, J. (2003). E-service quality: A model of virtual service quality dimensions. *Managing Service Quality*, *13*(3), 233–246. doi:10.1108/09604520310476490

Seth, N., Deshmukh, S. G., & Vrat, P. (2005). Service quality models: A review. *International Journal of Quality & Reliability Management*, *22*(9), 913–949. doi:10.1108/02656710510625211

Shewhart, W. (1980). Economic control of quality of manufactured product. American Society for Quality.

Sukasame, N. (2004). The development of e-service in Thai government. *BU Academic Review*, *3*(1), 17–24.

Tiwana, A., & Ramesh, B. (2001, January 3–6). e-services: Problems, opportunities, and digital platforms. In *Proceedings of the 34th Annual Hawaii International Conference on System Sciences (HICSS-34)*, Maui, Hawaii (pp. 3018). IEEE Computer Society.

Tsetsekas, C., Manitias, S., Funfstuck, F., Thoma, A., & Karadimas, Y. (2001). A QoS middleware between users, applications and the network. In *Proceedings of the 8th International Conference on Advances in Communications and Control*, Crete, Greece.

Webb, H. W., & Webb, L. A. (2004). SiteQual: An integrated measure of Web site quality. *Journal of Enterprise Information Management*, *17*(6), 430–440. doi:10.1108/17410390410566724

Yang, Z., Cai, S., Zhou, Z., & Zhou, N. (2005). Development and validation of an instrument to measure user perceived service quality of information presenting Web portals. *Information & Management*, *42*(4), 575–589. doi:10.1016/S0378-7206(04)00073-4

Yang, Z., & Jun, M. (2002). Consumer perception of e-service quality: From Internet purchaser and non-purchaser perspectives. *The Journal of Business Strategy*, *19*(1), 19–41.

Zeng, L., Benatallah, B., Dumas, M., Kalagnanam, J., & Sheng, Q. Z. (2003, May). Quality driven Web services composition. In *Proceedings of the 12th International Conference on World Wide Web*, Budapest, Hungary (pp. 411–421). ACM Press.

Chapter 4.15
Business Process Change in E–Government Projects:
The Case of the Irish Land Registry

Aileen Kennedy
Dublin Institute of Technology, Ireland

Joseph P. Coughlan
Dublin Institute of Technology, Ireland

Carol Kelleher
University College Cork, Ireland

ABSTRACT

This research investigates one of the first e-Government services launched as part of Ireland's Information Society programme, the Irish Land Registry's implementation of their award winning Electronic Access (EAS) project. In-depth enquiries into how public sector organisations manage IT-enabled transformations have remained relatively limited and this case contributes to this emerging body of literature. The analysis highlights that the implementation of e-Government initiatives beyond basic service levels necessitates business process change in order to reap rewards. This study fulfils an identified need for research in Business Process Change (BPC) in the implementation of e-Government initiatives. In this way the research attempts to add to, and complement, the existing pool of studies exploring e-Government induced change. The conclusions from the research stress the importance of planning for process change and the support of top management in the achievement of the efficiency gains and improved customer experience that are outcomes of e-Government.

INTRODUCTION

In response to a growing range of demands, the governance process of the public sector is undergoing modernisation (Pärna & von Tunzelmann, 2007). Although organisations in this sector may not operate within competitive environments in the traditional sense, changes in management philosophies are causing these organisations to think and act more like private sector ones

(Gulledge & Sommer, 2002, Hughes *et al.,* 2006). One of the consequences of adopting a private sector mentality has been an increased level of Information Technology (IT) projects, with a concurrent need for organisational transformation (Tan & Pan, 2003). These new technologies have the potential to provide higher levels of efficiency and the ability to reduce costs for government while simultaneously increasing productivity and delivering better quality services for stakeholders in public management (Weerakkody & Dhillon, 2008). Given the pressure on government to deliver services in a more efficient and effective manner, the drive to reap the benefits of these changes is intensifying.

Although various perspectives are available for the analysis of e-Government initiatives (Tan & Pan, 2003), a process perspective of e-Government initiatives, examining the areas of government where IT can be effectively utilized to enhance the efficiency of service delivery as well as the redesign of governmental processes and its impact on customers, is adopted in this article. O'Donnell *et al.* (2003) deduce that technology radically affects public organisations not only by reengineering current processes and structures but by also inducing fundamental changes to the strategic role of government. Bellamy & Taylor (1994) agree that IT in public administrations presents opportunities for increased efficiencies but also opportunities to adapt bureaucracy and in this way they suggest that IT is in fact identified as key to the reinvention and the reinvigoration of public administrations.

This research investigates one of the first e-Government services launched as part of Ireland's Information Society programme. The Irish Land Registry office implemented the award winning e-Government Electronic Access (EAS) project, which provides a unified national system of title registration for land administration, between 1999 and April 2005, as part of a strategic initiative to improve the quality of service delivered to customers. The study generates insights into the implementation and management of strategic process change by describing, analysing and explaining how the agency changed their fundamental structures and processes through this project, and the consequent effects on their employees and their customers.

It also highlights the opportunities now available to the organisation having successfully redesigned its fundamental processes. The data used in the case is derived from a variety of sources, both primary and secondary, that combine to generate a comprehensive retrospective picture of e-Government induced change in the public sector in Ireland.

Comprehensive studies of how public sector organisations manage IT-enabled transformation are relatively scarce (Tan *et al.*, 2005). This research contributes to the understanding of Business Process Change (BPC) within the public sector and highlights the key factors observed in process change which may explain its success. The study also highlights the motives for process redesign and the strategic approach taken within the organisation. The case analysis is also useful for business process management researchers as it gives insights into the application of IT and its influence on government processes. This case fulfils an identified need for research in BPC in the implementation of e-Government initiatives (Hughes *et al.*, 2006). In this way the research attempts to add to, and complement, the existing pool of studies exploring e-Government induced change from a BPC perspective. The article proceeds with a review of the relevant literature. The qualitative research methodology is outlined and the case material presented. The case findings are highlighted and discussed. Conclusions are drawn for future e-Government projects of this nature.

E-Government and Public Sector Change

e-Government refers to the use of information and communication technologies to change the structure and processes of government organisations

(Beynon-Davies, 2005). In the implementation of e-Government applications governments seek efficiency, effectiveness and data quality improvement gains (Groznik *et al.*, 2008). Weerakkody & Dhillon (2008) suggest that governments will need to radically transform most public agencies to achieve these benefits. Considering the complexity of business today, and especially in the public sector, all organisations will have to prune outdated procedures and routines in exchange for structures that are malleable to changing environmental conditions (Tan & Pan, 2003).

Public administration service delivery benefits from e-Government initiatives at a number of levels. At its most basic, e-Government can harness modern technology to enable departments to achieve efficiency improvements in the processing of large volumes of data and other administrative operations (Scholl, 2005). However, Al-Kibsi *et al.* (2001) suggest that the real value of e-Government derives less from simply using IT, or placing public services on line, than from the ability to force an agency to rethink, reorganise, and streamline their delivery before doing so. In this way, through the use of technology, organisations are challenged to redesign their processes in order to achieve the potential benefits of increased efficiencies, cost reductions and improvements in customer service (Hughes *et al.*, 2006).

When introducing transformative government initiatives and their constituent projects, the key problems to be resolved are normally not technological in nature (Gulledge & Sommer, 2004); rather they are in the organisational and process domains (Sundberg & Sandberg, 2006). In this way, e-Government implementation represents not just a technological change but also an organisational one (Beynon-Davies, 2005). It is therefore suggested that business process change methods should be used in the framework of e-services introduction (Stemberger & Jaklic, 2007). Mutula & van Brakel (2006) agree suggesting also that the root of the problems to be solved in introducing e-services has moved from the technological domain into the information and process management domains.

Business Process Change (BPC)

Business process change, also known as Business Process Redesign (BPR), has been accepted as an appropriate conceptual lens with which to assess e-Government induced change within the public sector (McAdam & Donaghy, 1999, Thong *et al.*, 2000, Gulledge & Sommer, 2002, 2004, Groznik *et al.*, 2008, Weerakkody & Dhillon, 2008). It has been instrumental in the redesign of governmental structures (Moon & Bretschnedier, 2002, Burn & Robins, 2003) to meet the needs of stakeholders (Ho, 2002). This research focuses on change as a result of IT-enabled transformation so the term Business Process Change (BPC) is used throughout to emphasise that change is required to reap the benefits of the process.

A significant success factor in process change and improvement is management support (Thong *et al.*, 2000) and sincere commitment of top management is considered as a critical success factor in project implementation (Al-Mashari & Zairi, 1999, Stemberger & Jaklic, 2007). Harnessing the full power of e-Government requires reorganising departmental processes around the needs of the business and clear leadership is essential to make this effort work (Al-Kibsi *et al.*, 2001).

Venkatraman (1994) identified five levels of IT enabled business transformation. The first two evolutionary levels include localised exploitation and internal integration corresponding to a relatively low level of business transformation. These two initial levels suggest that only minor advantages occur when superimposing IT on existing organisation conditions and require only minimal changes to business processes. The next three levels of the framework, business process redesign; business network redesign and business scope redefinition are deemed to be revolutionary in nature and require major changes in existing business processes. To achieve significant results the organisation needs to move to the first revolutionary level and engage in BPC (Hughes *et al.*, 2006).

This principle is reinforced within an OECD (2003) report which suggests that a problem in past implementation of initiatives has been that governments have tended to use technology as a patch to provide a seamless service interface with users to a complex administrative structure with IT overlaid on existing organisational structures without adequate attention to how these structures could be improved. The report suggests that this amounts to information being rearranged without the necessary fundamental shift in processes and/ or procedures. Overall, it is generally agreed that e-Government technologies are only capable of potential success if introduced in tandem with business process change (Gulledge & Sommer, 2002, Murphy, 2002, Groznik *et al.* 2008).

Through empirical research (Thong *et al.*, 2000, Golden *et al.*, 2003), the absence of a clear strategy for process redesign when undertaking an e-Government project, has been shown to be detrimental to the success of the project and indeed higher levels of e-Government adoption in the future. These change initiatives are usually highly complex and challenging not just for the government department but also for the constituent stakeholders of the department. As a result, the need for a coherent strategy not only for the individual projects but also for the organisation as a whole is essential.

Another key issue with BPC is the need to avoid an over emphasis on the technology side of operations which can lead to a redesigned process that becomes obsolete in the extended business process (Stemberger & Jaklic, 2007). In order to avoid such errors BPC should be a deliberately planned effort where the customer is the focus of all efforts (Tan & Pan, 2003). A key factor to achieve this target is to expend sufficient time at the beginning of BPC projects to set clear strategic targets and plan accordingly (Tennant & Wu, 2005). An important enabler of success is

the ability to build upon the experience of others. O'Donnell *et al.* (2003) suggest the use of external consultants. Guha *et al.*, (1997) also comment on the importance of external experience in the success of projects of this nature.

In terms of process change outcomes, profitability and market share improvement may not be relevant within public sector operations, however as many firms now acknowledge their dependence on employees in achieving their objectives, employee quality of work life issues are now becoming an important feature of assessments of process change outcomes (Guha *et al.*, 1997). Often with well managed process change employees should experience improved working conditions in redesigned process tasks which should increase job satisfaction ultimately leading to productivity gains and improved customer satisfaction (Guha *et al.*, 1997). Effectively then improved quality of work life can now be considered as a measurable outcome of organisational process change.

RESEARCH METHODOLOGY

The objective of this research is to explore and investigate the role of business process redesign in creating efficient and seamless service delivery in a citizen centric model of process change and revitalisation within the Irish public sector, specifically the Land Registry. The research presents the business case for e-Government induced process change initiatives which may allow the organisation to achieve economies of scale, reduce duplication and provide seamless service. The research is exploratory in nature and a case study is presented detailing how the Land Registry's strategic approach to process improvement was devised and implemented.

The case study methodology was chosen to provide an understanding of the dynamics present within a single, real-life setting (Yin, 1994). The case study method is recognised as an appropriate method of empirical enquiry when the complex phenomena to be studied cannot easily be separated from their organisational contexts (Langley, 1999). The Land Registry was selected as a case study as it is an exemplar organisation (Yin, 2003) as evidenced by the fact that it won an award at the National Showcase in Public Service Excellence event in 2004 and was the overall winner of the Irish e-Government Awards in 2005 in recognition of its success in utilizing electronic services (Taylor, 2005).

The case study was conducted at the Land Registry over a period of 12 months. The research proceeded in three phases. Kaplan & Duchon (1988) argue that collecting different kinds of data by different methods from different sources provides a wider range of coverage resulting in a fuller picture. Firstly, a documentary analysis of the Land Registry using offline and online sources was undertaken. Secondly, an analysis of internal operational and project documentation was carried out. Finally in-depth interviews, considered by some as being "the best" method of data collection (Yeung, 1995) were conducted with senior management directly responsible for the implementation process within the Land Registry.

The focal contact was a senior level manager in the organisation who was directly responsible for, and integrally involved with, the project from the beginning. In this instance this manager was a process champion, capable of discussing strategy and process implementation, organisational culture, learning and effectiveness. With over thirty years experience within the public sector he also provided valuable insights into the management teams' perspective on e-Government, their project vision and the organisational challenges encountered pre and post implementation. He was also able to situate the EAS project within the overall strategy of the agency, and the other government organisations it interacts with.

The second interviewee was a senior team member who was intimately involved with the development and implementation of all stages of the initiative and who had an objective knowledge-able view of the entire project (Burn & Robins,

2003). He also had detailed technical expertise relating to system implementation challenges and the business process changes mandated by the system. This interviewee was also actively involved in working with other government agencies who were implementing initiatives which would in turn be linked to the EAS project. Both interviewees provided copies of internal documentation on the project from inception to final roll out to complement the externally available material available to the researchers.

A team approach to interviewing was taken (Eisenhardt & Bourgeois, 1988) which improved the reliability of the study and built confidence in the findings (Eisenhardt, 1989). The two participants were interviewed twice and generated over six hours of dialogue. The theme sheet for conducting the interviews focused on the background of the initiative and the organisational processes and structures prior to commencement; the drivers and the rollout and implementation of the project; the planning process including change management procedures; and the benefits delivered to the organisation and to the customer in terms of efficiency and productivity. The issues of organisational change and the managerial and financial implications of the initiative were investigated as well as challenges encountered and future development plans. Each interview was recorded and subsequently transcribed and coded in NVivo. An a-priori coding framework developed by the authors was used to analyse each transcript.

The research methodology acknowledges the limitations inherent within qualitative research, such as arguments against validity and generalisation of findings. Validity concerns the integrity or credibility of results derived from qualitative research (Saunders *et al.*, 2000). However carefully conducted interviews can yield high levels of validity. Data triangulation was also used to compare and contrast the outcomes of the interviews with the external and internal documentary analysis to further validate and verify the findings (Saunders *et al.*, 2000). This aimed to ensure that bias from either the participants or the researchers was not an issue in the conclusions of the research (Yin, 2003) The inherent limitations of a single case study not withstanding, this study has offered an analytical account of experiences of process redesign of the Land Registry.

THE LAND REGISTRY PROJECT

Throughout the developed world, there are a variety of systems for the recording of the ownership (title) to land. In Ireland, the Land Registry is the State agency responsible for the registration of property transactions and operates under the aegis of the Minister for Justice, Equality and Law Reform. Its role is to provide a system of registration of title (ownership) to land, which is comprehensive and readily accessible. The principal aims of the Registry are to maintain and develop a uniform and efficient land registration system; to guarantee legal title on behalf of the State to interests in land; to provide ready access to accurate land information and to achieve continuously improving levels of service delivery to customers. The core business of the organisation involves examining legal documents and related maps and recording their legal impact on the registers and maps. It includes the registration of title for the first time, the registration of subsequent transactions, the recording of deeds and the supply of evidence of title and a comprehensive range of associated services. The principal customers of the agency are the legal profession and associated commercial communities within the State.

The Paper Chase

Since its inception in 1707, the Land Registry has maintained a significant repository of paper documents to carry out its functions. Approximately eight million pages of title records and over two million pages of map records were held on file prior to the implementation of the e-Government initiative. Duplicates of all title records (but not the maps) were held in the local office for each county (of which there are 26). Over 200,000 records were categorised as active at any time, with over 5,000 records accessed each day. A library type system for recording the movement and whereabouts of documents was also maintained. Over two million named index records were held in 4,000 loose leaf books. 4,000 duplicate books were also held in the local offices. Over 100 large ledgers were created each year to record applications for title and their whereabouts. Circa 10 million active historical files - the collection of documents presented for registration since the foundation of the organisation were permanently stored. Over 36,000 large-scale map sheets – A0 size were also maintained.

The Business Imperative

The Electronic Access (EAS) Project sought to provide a comprehensive record that was clear, readily accessible, minimised risk of fraud and was responsive to customer needs. The demand for the services of the Land Registry grew steadily over the past decade, consistent with the growth in the economy and with the expanding property and mortgage markets. Through various government initiatives in the e-Government domain, the organisation has been actively seeking innovative ways of making that information available in the most efficient, convenient and effective manner while fulfilling its key strategic business objective to improve the quality of service delivered to customers. Analysis undertaken concluded that the organisation could not continue to provide the levels of service demanded by customers in a paper environment. This approach caused the organisation to focus on projects that would decrease the reliance on paper records, reduce turnaround times on services and increase the quantity and quality of information that could be provided on-line. Three separate but integrated projects, namely the Integrated Title Registration

Information Systems (ITRIS), the Electronic Access (EAS) project and the Document Imaging Project (DIS) were implemented to achieve these strategic objectives.

Integrated Title Registration Information System (ITRIS)

In July 1999, the Land Registry launched a new computerised system known as the Integrated Title Registration Information System (ITRIS), which was developed by EDS Ireland Limited. This was the culmination of a project, which had commenced in 1990 as a result of a major study linking the organisations IT strategy with the organisation's business requirement to move from a paper register to a system of electronic registration. ITRIS provides direct support for internal staff members across the registry.

Electronic Access Services (EAS)

Paragraph A.42 of *Implementing the Information Society: A Framework for Action* (December 1998) mandated the Land Registry to undertake a 'flagship project' to provide 'an electronic service for folio access'. This was achieved through the successful implementation in August 1999 of the *Land Registry Electronic Access Service* (EAS), the first e-Government project to 'go live' in the Irish Civil Service, which provided on-line access to the organisation's then existing computerised database of folios and related indices. The EAS has particular benefits for the legal profession, professional law searching firms, commercial property companies, government departments and the law departments of public and private corporations. The on-line EAS service is the public access element of ITRIS. It supports several key Land Registry functions including: electronic storage and retrieval of folios; the tracking and processing of cases and applications submitted to the Land Registry by its customers and generation and electronic transmission of case-related correspondence and provision of key statistics.

Authorised users of the EAS can conduct on-line searches by referencing to the name of registered owner; view and print folios and filed plans in their office. All folios are now available for inspection online in addition to the 'Dealings Pending' on a particular folio.

Document Imaging Project

With the early success of the EAS, a critical task facing the Land Registry was the conversion of over 110 years of historical paper records into electronic format. Having undertaken a detailed situational analysis with the assistance of expert external advice, a number of options were considered. The solution chosen, in addition to providing a mechanism to have all folio records available at a much earlier date, allowed for the provision of the filed plan map as well as the folio thereby providing a complete set of information for customers. The Land Registry undertook a major project to implement document-imaging technology accompanied by a programme to have all its paper folios and filed plans systematically converted into electronic records and to make these available on-line to customers through the EAS. This project has also won a national award in 2007, and is due to be completed for all land parcels in the state by end 2010.

DISCUSSION

The EAS system has introduced significant modifications to the underlying business processes of the Land Registry. Process change has occurred with respect to complete digitization of information; customer services; acceptance of electronic submissions; online transactions and data quality, security and storage. By using IT as a catalyst for, and enabler of, organisational process redesign, the Land Registry has effectively reinvented itself from an inflexible, slow, labour intensive service to an efficient, speedy and customer centric one.

In this way the reality reflects the suggestion put forward by Bellamy & Taylor (1994) that IT can in fact be identified as the key to reinvention and reinvigoration of public administrations. However this project illustrates that these IT projects are not implemented within a vacuum and must be fused with business process change to increase the chances of successful implementation (Venkatraman, 1994, Hughes *et al.,* 2006, Sundberg & Sandberg, 2006).

The key themes underlying the success of this project implementation are strategic leadership and commitment; customer satisfaction and service achievements via operational efficiencies and astute human resources strategies. The key organisational benefits achieved include increased efficiencies, productivity gains and reputational benefits for the entire organisation. The findings are presented and discussed in the context of the actions of top management, their impact on employees and their combined impacts on the end customer.

Strategic Approach, Leadership & Commitment

Process change usually begins with strategic initiatives enabled by the senior management team. The reasons can be reactive or in the case of the Land Registry they can be due to a proactive push to leverage potential opportunities (Guha *et al.,* 1997). The Land Registry initiative was enabled by change agents such as the Strategic Management Initiative and the Delivering Better Government programmes, both of which were wider Irish government initiatives across the public sector. These resulted in the organisation actively seeking innovative ways of improving the information and the services available to all stakeholders. It also ensured the funding to support the project.

In the case of the Land Registry this e-Government initiative was driven by local management who made a strong business case for the initial project. Senior management concede that the Land Registry "*probably would not be able to*

function today if it had not gone this route and this was recognized at an early stage". As suggested by Bellamy & Taylor (1994) the economic and business logic of the information age gradually drives all service organisations, including those from the public sector, towards public sector transformations in the design of their processes and structures.

Any significant business process change requires a strategic initiative where top managers act as leaders in defining and communicating a vision of change (Guha *et al.,* 1997). Within the Registry the CEO and her senior management team were fully committed to the project implementation and led from the top in terms of providing leadership and vision. Given that change initiatives are usually highly complex and challenging, strategic leadership, management support and the obvious commitment of top management is considered as a critical success factor in project implementation (Al-Mashari & Zairi 1999, Thong *et al.,* 2000, Stemberger & Jaklic, 2007). Such levels of support and commitment have also proven to be essential enablers of additional projects and higher levels of e-Government adoption in the future. Internal documentation showed that this project enjoyed an exceptionally high level of management support, and interviewees also commented on this factor as a key issue in the success of the project.

These strategic initiatives involve delineation of a specific plan of action and then motivation of the entire organisation towards achievement of this goal. As suggested by Tennant & Wu (2005) the key is to expend sufficient time at the beginning of BPC projects to set clear strategic targets and plan accordingly. This is clearly reflected in the Land Registry operations. A cross-functional steering committee was created and the team teased out at a very early stage the essential enablers to the successful introduction of new technologies including issues related to people and process, "no stone was left unturned" and no last minute surprises appeared.

Such planning and attention to detail are vital ingredients in ensuring the smooth introduction of new systems and associated work practices. This is reinforced by the view of senior management where the suggestion is that the Land Registry

had a very enthusiastic and strongly focused approach at both a top and middle management level. There was a strong contribution from people at all levels, so this went right through the organisation.

In this case, clear strategic leadership, commitment from the team and ongoing planning and consultation have been key elements in sustaining this project. This has also benefited the organisation for the future development of their services and has been instrumental in the Registry being a flagship for e-Government initiatives across the public sector.

Human Resource Strategies

From a human resources (HR) perspective, the Land Registry faced challenges at the time of implementation as:

this (project implementation) was a dramatic change and the fact that we (Land Registry) were the first to do it in the public service did in itself cause some difficulties; also the fact that we are such an old organisation, over 300 years old, there is a lot of historical baggage.

The Land Registry used astute HR policies in two regards; firstly in the utilisation of external consultants and secondly in gaining increased productivity from staff through creating the possibility of redeploying staff to core functions and roles within the organisation.

O'Donnell *et al.,* (2003) suggest that one of the key factors facilitating transformational aspects of e-Government implementation is the development and use of private sector companies when insufficient in-house expertise or resources are

identified as project constraints. In the case of the Digital Imaging project the contract was awarded to a consortium headed by EDS Ireland Limited in September 2001. EDS established a 36-month program of work to cover the development of a document imaging system, the implementation of the hardware and software infrastructure and the provision of a bureau service to capture images of the documents and converting them to electronic format. The EDS team integrated EAS and ITRIS to enhance the capabilities that the Land Registry could provide to its customers and staff online.

It has been argued that the success of consultants in BPC is determined by their level of experience in implementing similar projects (Al-Mashari & Zairi, 1999). Their understanding of the organisations operations is also vital and EDS had previous experience of working with the Registry. Guha *et al.,* (1997) suggest that the more successful process change projects tend to be enabled in organisations that leverage external information and experts while also learning from best practice and customer needs. All of these elements are in evidence within the Land Registry where best practice internationally informed their decision to use an external company for the Digital Imaging project to create a customer centric organisation.

Productivity gains have been a key outcome for Land Registry operations. For example, the preparation and issuing of certified copy folios and filed plan maps was formerly a very labour intensive activity. Also in terms of the work load involved, it is estimated that by the time the computerised system went live for the entire country over 500,000 changes were made to the register each year. An estimated 40 to 50 staff was required for this purpose. These functions have now been effectively automated. Now, once an entry is made on the central register, it is automatically available at all 24 offices and significant productivity gains have accrued. This in turn has allowed the Land Registry to *redeploy staff away from manual work into registration. There is still a need for staff to certify documents but this is now undertaken by five or six people compared to approximately 40 previously, who have now been redeployed.*

The Land Registry has invested somewhere in the region of €20 million in the initiative to date and feels that the cost has been well justified as the operation *"makes more than sufficient money to run this organisation, largely because of greater efficiencies within the office now".*

Process change within organisations directly affects the employee's quality of work life (Guha *et al.,* 1997) and within the Land Registry this change has had a positive impact. Since the EAS solution is self-service-based, the re-organisation has now enhanced job satisfaction for staff by reducing or eliminating many of the routine processing duties which previously demanded time and also releasing staff for more rewarding and satisfying work. This also reflects the fact that public services are being reconfigured to steer away from traditional book keeping functions (Tan & Pan 2003). The EAS solution has also provided for greater flexibility in staff assignments, for example, allowing employees in the Southern region to process cases for the Eastern region online. This has helped in the removal of cross-functional boundaries, a problem noted by Gulledge & Sommer (2002). In this way well managed process change has led to job satisfaction and productivity gains (Guha *et al.,* 1997). These internal efficiencies have in turn impacted customer satisfaction in a positive manner, thus meeting the core aim of the organisation more effectively.

Customer Satisfaction

This project implementation has moved the organisation in the direction of a customer based organisational model where business processes are seamlessly integrated for the benefit of the customer (Tan & Pan, 2003) thus generating in-

Table 1. Annual customer transactions

Year	2000	2002	2004	2006	2007
No of subscribers	1,700	4,400	7,500	10,900	12,741
No. of business transactions through EAS per annum	0.2 million	1.2 million	1.7 million	2 million	3 million

creased levels of customer satisfaction. The real test of the success of an e-Government initiative is the level of customer usage. As can be seen from Table 1, which presents a snapshot of some of the key performance indicators, uptake and usage continues to grow and this trend is likely to continue.

Since the project launch, over three million fee-paying transactions had been conducted, with over 90% of services conducted on a self-service basis making it one of the busiest e-Government services available in Ireland. The Land Registry initiative has been all about giving customers access to the information they need in a timely and convenient manner. As the size of the electronic database increases, the Registry expects to see the current upward usage levels for its on-line services to continue.

It has been suggested that the outcomes of process change should be monitored through the measurement of performance variables such as quality, cycle time, costs and ultimately customer satisfaction (Guha *et al.,* 1997). In terms of quality, as well as enhanced levels of customer service, the Land Registry can now also offer a better quality product. All certified copy folios and maps are now issued in colour whereas previously they were issued in black and white only. Data quality gains are a highly desired outcome of e-Government applications (Groznik *et al.,* 2008), and feedback from customers available through internal documentation has shown a greater level of satisfaction with the improved service.

The Registry has been able to reduce turnaround times for services dramatically which also impact on overall customer satisfaction levels. Delays in, for example, inspections of folios and filed plans and provision of name index searches, have been eliminated. Customers and employees can now access title information online using a variety of search criteria, with access document times reduced from days to minutes. Customers can apply for certified copies of records and track the progress of their applications throughout their life cycle in the Registry.

Other waiting times have also been significantly reduced. Previously for a postal application the average turnaround time was 5 to 6 weeks. Now with the availability of the EAS and the completion of imaging, where an application is made electronically, over 80% of such applications (over 1,000 each day) are completed inside 24 hours (when the filed plan is available). In this way the benefit of e-Government in integrating underlying processes (Layne & Lee, 2001) is clearly demonstrated in this case, and is an example of how information technology can transform government for the better (Weerakkody & Dhillon, 2008).

Al-Kibsi *et al.,* (2001) suggest that a benefit of e-Government is a reduction in error rates. In the case of the Land Registry, some of the main sources of error were the incorrect folio numbers, the non-lodgement of the Land Certificate, omission of documents and the calculation of fees. Such potential errors have been eliminated by the design of the electronic system, which automatically matches the folio number to registered owner details, shows the status of the Land Certificate and automatically calculates fees payable.

Improvements in customer access to the service have also been dramatic. Historically in order to avail of services, customers had to attend at the public offices, in Dublin and Waterford, and spend considerable periods working within the paper environment. By August 2004, all folios, names indices and filed plan maps became accessible via the EAS thereby removing the need for personal attendance in offices. An additional advantage has been that, now that data is maintained on

servers, much less office space is needed and all paper records are kept in permanent deep storage. Three public offices in Waterford have been merged into one, and two Dublin offices have been reduced to one. Bearing in mind the BPC stages proposed by Venkatraman (1994), it is clear that this project has achieved Business Network Redesign with the closure of surplus offices and the redeployment of staff. The final stage of Business Scope Redefinition was not within the remit of the project.

The case clearly demonstrates that customer focus is now emphasised more within the public sector, and customer friendliness and simplification of procedures is the imperative of the administration, in keeping with the stated aim of the organisation. Often this is the main motive for business process change within the public sector (Stemberger & Jaklic, 2007). This motivation is particularly interesting given that the goal in most cases is not to attract new customers as customers are often obligated to use the service, as is the case with Land Registry services (Stemberger & Jaklic, 2007). This reinforces the idea that the motive for process change is a genuine interest in improving service provision for customers.

CONCLUSION

This research has closely scrutinized the implementation of an e-Government initiative within a public agency through the conceptual lens of BPC. Specifically the study traces the evolution of the initiative from 1999 to 2005. The case study has explored issues in the implementation of the initiative with the aim of contributing to the theoretical and managerial knowledge in the area of e-Government induced business process change. This research supplements current knowledge on the strategic factors that public sector organisations are pre-occupied with in the transformation from paper-based government to e-Government. It highlights that fundamental process change is required in order to get the full benefit from technological interventions. It also illustrates how IT projects have a resonance throughout the organisation and are catalysts for process change (Al-Kibsi *et al.*, 2001).

Due to the extent of changes needed and complexities of implementation of e-Government applications practitioners are challenged to strategically manage such initiatives, often with little experience of the issues involved. The case analysis attempts to leverage the organisational experiences observed to generate actionable guidelines for future projects of this kind. It does so by analysing the managerial perspective of the implementation process to the exclusion of other employees involved. Though beyond the scope of this particular study an interesting avenue for further research would be the employee's perceptions of, and perspectives on, the business process changes implemented in a vein similar to the work of McAdam and Donaghy (1999). Also further public sector cross-case analysis would also be useful in validating the themes which have emerged from this research.

The Registries focus on improving customer service through technological exploitation has been a lead project within the public service and the outputs have benefited individual customers, the legal profession, financial institutions, and both public and private corporations. The change in the organisation itself has been phenomenal and is evidence of the modernisation suggested by Pärna and von Tunzelmann (2007). The Land Registry has been to the forefront of e-Government in Ireland and is now strategically well placed to move forward with further e-Government initiatives in the areas of e-registration and e-conveyancing. The optimisation of the business process through the e-Government project (Fagan, 2006) has yielded not only efficiency gains but a real transformation of government activities (Weerakkody & Dhillon, 2008).

ACKNOWLEDGMENT

The authors would like to acknowledge the support of the Land Registry in this research.

REFERENCES

Al-Kibsi, G., de Boer, K., Mourshed, M., & Rea, N. P. (2001). Putting citizens on-line, not in line. *McKinsey and Co.* Retrieved February 6, 2008, from http://www.mckinsey.com

Al-Mashari, M., & Zairi, M. (1999). BPR Implementation process: An analysis of key success and failure factors. *Business Process Management Journal*, 5(1), 87–112. doi:10.1108/14637159910249108

Bellamy, C., & Taylor, J. A. (1994). Exploiting IT in public administration – toward the information polity? *Public Administration*, 72(1), 1–12. doi:10.1111/j.1467-9299.1994.tb00996.x

Beynon-Davies, P. (2005). Constructing electronic government: The case of the UK Inland Revenue. *International Journal of Information Management*, 25(1), 3–20. doi:10.1016/j.ijinfomgt.2004.08.002

Burn, J., & Robins, G. (2003). Moving towards e-government: A case study of organisational change processes. *Logistics Information Management*, 16(1), 25–35. doi:10.1108/09576050310453714

Eisenhardt, K. (1989). Building theories from case study research. *Academy of Management Review*, 14(4), 532–550. doi:10.2307/258557

Eisenhardt, K., & Bourgeois, L. J. (1988). Politics of strategic decision making in high velocity environments. Toward a mid range theory. *Academy of Management Journal*, 31(4), 737–770. doi:10.2307/256337

Fagan, M. (2006). Exploring city, county and state e-government initiatives: An East Texas perspective. *Business Process Management Journal*, *12*(1), 101–112. doi:10.1108/14637150610643797

Golden, W., Hughes, M., & Scott, M. (2003). Implementing e-government in Ireland: A roadmap for success. *Journal of Electronic Commerce in Organizations*, *1*(4), 17–33.

Groznik, A., Kovacic, A., & Trkman, P. (2008). The role of business renovation and information in e-government. *Journal of Computer Information Systems*, *48*, 81–89.

Guha, S., Grover, V., Kettinger, W., & Teng, J. T. C. (1997). Business process change and organisational performance: Exploring an antecedent model. *Journal of Management Information Systems*, *14*(1), 119–154.

Gulledge, T. R. Jr, & Sommer, R. A. (2002). Business process management: Public sector implications. *Business Process Management Journal*, *8*(4), 364–376. doi:10.1108/14637150210435017

Gulledge, T. R. Jr, & Sommer, R. A. (2004). Splitting the SAP instance: Lessons on scope and business processes. *Journal of Computer Information Systems*, *44*(3), 109–115.

Ho, A. T. K. (2002). Reinventing local governments and the e-government initiative. *Public Administration Review*, *62*(4), 434–444. doi:10.1111/0033-3352.00197

Hughes, M., Scott, M., & Golden, W. (2006). The role of business process redesign in creating e-government in Ireland. *Business Process Management Journal*, *12*(1), 76–87. doi:10.1108/14637150610643779

Kaplan, B., & Duchon, D. (1988). Combining qualitative and quantitative research methods in information systems research: A case study. *MIS Quarterly*, *12*(4), 571–586. doi:10.2307/249133

Langley, A. (1999). Strategies for theorising from process data. *Academy of Management Review*, *24*(4), 691–710. doi:10.2307/259349

Layne, K., & Lee, J. (2001). Developing fully functional e-government: A four stage model. *Government Information Quarterly*, *18*(2), 122–136. doi:10.1016/S0740-624X(01)00066-1

McAdam, R., & Donaghy, J. (1999). Business process re-engineering in the public sector. A study of staff perceptions and critical success factors. *Business Process Management Journal*, *5*(1), 33–49. doi:10.1108/14637159910249135

Moon, M. J., & Bretschneider, S. (2002). Does the perception of red tape constrain IT innovation in organizations? Unexpected results from Simultaneous Equation Model and implications. *Journal of Public Administration: Research and Theory*, *12*(2), 273–291.

Murphy, M. (2002). Organisational change and firm performance. *OECD Directorate for Science, Technology and Industry Working Paper Series*. Retrieved March 10, 2008, from http://www.oecd.org/sti/

Mutula, S. M., & van Brackel, P. (2006). An evaluation of e-readiness assessment tools with respect to information access: Towards an integrated information rich tool. *International Journal of Information Management*, *26*, 212–223. doi:10.1016/j.ijinfomgt.2006.02.004

O'Donnell, O., Boyle, R., & Timonen, V. (2003). Transformational aspects of e-government in Ireland: Issues to be addressed. *Institute of Public Administration (IPA) Ireland*. Retrieved March 12, 2009, from http://www.ipa.ie

OECD. (2003). OECD e-government flagship report "The e-government imperative". *Public Management Committee*. Retrieved October 12, 2008, from Http://www.oecd.com

Pärna, O., & von Tunzelmann, N. (2007). Innovation in the public sector: Key features influencing the development and implementation of technologically innovative public services in the UK, Denmark, Finland and Estonia. *Information Polity, 12,* 109–125.

Saunders, M., Lewis, P., & Thornhill, A. (2000). *Research methods for business students* (2nd ed.). Essex, UK: Pearson.

Scholl, H. J. (2005). E-government induced business process change (BPC): An empirical study of current practices. *International Journal of Electronic Government Research, 1*(2), 27–49.

Stemberger, M. I., & Jaklic, J. (2007). Towards e-government by business process change – A methodology for public sector. *International Journal of Information Management, 27,* 221–232. doi:10.1016/j.ijinfomgt.2007.02.006

Sundberg, H. P., & Sandberg, K. W. (2006). Towards e-government: A survey of problems in organisational processes. *Business Process Management Journal, 12*(2), 146–161. doi:10.1108/14637150610657503

Tan, C., Pan, S., & Lim, E. (2005). Managing stakeholders' interests in e-government implementation: Lessons learned from a Singapore e-government project. *Journal of Global Information Management, 13*(1), 31–53.

Tan, C. W., & Pan, S. L. (2003). Managing e-transformation in the public sector; an e-government study of Inland Revenue authority of Singapore. *European Journal of Information Systems, 12*(4), 269–281. doi:10.1057/palgrave.ejis.3000479

Taylor, C. (2005). *Land registry picks up top award.* Retrieved October 9, 2008, from http://ElectricNews.net

Tennant, C., & Wu, Y.-C. (2005). The application of business process reengineering in the UK. *The TQM Magazine, 17*(6), 537–545. doi:10.1108/09544780510627633

Thong, J. Y. L., Yap, C. S., & Seah, K. L. (2000). Business process reengineering in the public sector: the case of the Housing Development Board in Singapore. *Journal of Management Information Systems, 17*(1), 245–270.

Venkatraman, V. (1994). IT enabled business transformation: from automation to business scope redefinition. *Sloan Management Review, 35*(2), 73–87.

Weerakkody, V., & Dhillon, G. (2008). Moving from e-government to t-government: A study of process reengineering challenges in a UK local authority context. *International Journal of Electronic Government Research, 4*(4), 1–16.

Yeung, H. W. C. (1995). Qualitative personal interviews in business research: Some lessons from a study of Hong Kong transnational corporations. *International Business Review, 4*(3), 313–339. doi:10.1016/0969-5931(95)00012-O

Yin, R. (1994). *Case study research: Design and methods* (2nd Ed.). Beverly Hills, CA: Sage Publications.

Yin, R. (2003). *Applications of case study research* (2nd Ed.). Beverly Hills, CA: Sage Publications.

This work was previously published in the International Journal of Electronic Government Research, Volume 6, Issue 1, edited by V. Weerakkody, pp. 9-22, copyright 2010 by IGI Publishing (an imprint of IGI Global).

Chapter 4.16
Morethailand.com:
Online Travel Intermediary

Pongsak Hoontrakul
Sasin of Chulalongkorn University, Thailand

Sunil Sahadev
University of Sheffield, UK

ABSTRACT

The case study showcases 'morethailand.com' an e-intermediary in the tourism industry. Based out of Thailand, the firm is in the process of finding a niche for itself through innovative online and offline marketing strategies with the constraint of limited resources. The case study attempts to focus on the e-business challenges in the travel and tourism sector especially in a developing country like Thailand. It specifically highlights the clash between the traditional and modern form of intermediaries in the travel and tourism sector and how it is bound to evolve in the future. A comparison between different approaches to search engine marketing offers an interesting perspective to the literature pertaining to on line e-commerce. An economic view on the case is also presented.

MORETHAILAND.COM – ONLINE TRAVEL INTERMEDIARY

It was a challenging task - to grow by more than ten times a year. That was the objective set by Mrs. Nontana Thanabatchai, the founder and Managing Director of Morethailand.com for the coming two years. Morethailand.com was at a turning point in terms of its future performance. While the present increase in the visitor rate and enquiry conversion rate were quite creditable, to emerge as a dominant player in its field, a growth of over ten times a year was absolutely important. Yet it was achievable if the latest efforts in improving, dynamic pricing and searching engine optimization bears fruit.. The opportunities were immense, the need was to implement a coherent set of strategies that would attract more customers and generate a high transaction rate.

DOI: 10.4018/978-1-59904-831-4.ch018

Morethailand.com is an online travel intermediary based in Bangkok, Thailand. The company acts as an intermediary that helps customers round the world to book rooms in Thailand hotels through the internet. Motherthailand.com was founded in the year 2002 after the need was felt for setting up a Thailand based on-line travel intermediary. The company has a clutch of interconnected websites that together provide potential travelers a means for searching for and booking hotel rooms in Thailand. These web-sites also enable potential tourists to book tour packages as well as airline tickets. The website displays a list of hotels which are part of the network. A potential tourist can enquire about the availability of rooms as well as to book accommodation in the hotels listed in the websites. Provision for tour packages, airline booking and travel related products are also available. The sites normally get around 5000 hits a day. Attachment-I gives a screenshot of the website.

Having established itself as a B2C site, morethailand.com is looking forward to strengthen its position in its primary line of activity ie. online travel intermediation. The primary area of focus was in increasing site traffic by attracting more and more potential tourists to its web-sites. The company was also keen to strengthen its supply side by forging partnerships with more and more IOO hotels in Thailand. This would in turn enable morethailand.com to offer rooms to its customers at more competitive rates than the off-line travel agents who presently occupy the dominant position in the market. The biggest challenge in this endeavor was to compete with large travel wholesalers in gaining acceptance and support from the hotels. This was an extremely difficult task as most of the hotels in Thailand presently depend heavily on large travel wholesalers or consolidators to sell their rooms in bulk. The offline intermediaries who are well entrenched in the market ensure a steady cash flow for the hotels through bulk buying. The travel wholesalers, in turn gain greater power and influence over the hotels who would not like to risk themselves by aligning with a relatively new player like morethailand.com. However, hotels that depend on travel wholesalers have to sell their rooms at a heavy discount to the wholesalers. It is estimated that many hotels sell their rooms to travel wholesalers at almost 30% of their walk-in price. The hotels are compelled to offer such heavy discounts since the travel wholesalers are in a position to ensure high occupancy rates for the hotels. Morethailand.com, on the other hand, demand considerably less discounts from the hotels though it is presently not in a position to match the travel wholesalers in terms of the number of rooms sold. The critical success factor for morethailand.com is therefore about consistently ensuring higher occupancy rates to its partner hotels so as to gain their commitment and confidence. This in turn has to be achieved by attracting greater traffic to its websites and then converting these visitors to enquirers. The case study illustrates the operation of a small start up in the on-line travel industry and its efforts at capturing market share from much stronger and well entrenched off-line competitors through various e-commerce strategies. It is indeed a great challenge in the face of the turmoil that the Thai tourism industry is presently going through.

Technology Adoption for Travel and Tourism Marketing-a Theoretical Perspective

The importance of information and communications technology in the travel and tourism sector has been well acknowledged. In fact, technology has become the main source of sustainable competitive advantage and a strategic weapon, especially in the tourism and hospitality industries owing to the pivotal role information plays in the description, promotion, distribution, amalgamation, organization and delivery of tourism products (Poon, 1993; Sheldon, 1997). Within the larger ICT adoption, the adoption of internet and e-commerce in the travel and tourism industry has lead to wide ranging transformations both in the Industry structure and basic processes. UNCTAD (2000) in its E-commerce and development report states: "The tourism industry is learning fast that the Internet can satisfy the acute need for information at all stages of the tourism product life cycle far better than any other existing technology". The extent of adoption of the Internet as a medium for transaction in the travel and tourism sector is testified by the fact that in the year 2001 almost half of America booked either airfare, hotel reservations or car rentals on-line (UNCTAD, 2000) since 2001, it has only increased even further. It is a well-known fact that small or remote destinations and products with well-developed and innovative websites can now have equal Internet access. However, the usage of Internet as a viable medium for promotion and transaction of travel and tourism related services have not been so widespread in the developing countries. The rate of adoption has been hampered by several factors both economic and historical. There has been very little research trying to look at the adoption of e-commerce in the travel and tourism sector in the developing countries. The case study of morethailand.com attempts to contribute to this stream of research. It brings out the main challenges and the unique contextual factors that hamper this adoption in the hotel industry in Thailand - a country that finds a prominent place in the tourism map of any traveler.

Tourism Industry in Thailand

Tourism is one of the most important sectors in Thailand with about 6% of its GDP being contributed by the tourism sector alone (TAT 2003). In 2003 the tourism authority of Thailand (TAT), the nodal agency for tourism promotion in the country, estimated that about 9.31 million people had visited Thailand. The tourist arrivals in Thailand are expected to increase to 12 million in 2004 and are ultimately posed to reach 20 million by 2007 (TAT 2003). Figure1 below shows the trend in tourism arrival over the past several years.

Figure 1. Tourist arrivals in Thailand over the past five years (TAT 2003)

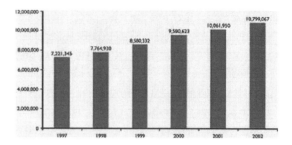

As the Figure 2 indicates, Most of the tourists who come to Thailand, stay for an average of 8 days. This implies that a greater proportion of tourists who arrive in Thailand are holiday makers, with the proportion of business travelers being comparatively less.

The Travel Intermediary Sector in Thailand

The intermediaries in the travel and tourism sector exist mainly because of the lack of expertise and inclination of the eventual service providers to indulge in direct sales. Being primarily service providers, hotels generally consider it difficult to attract customers on their own. They are therefore quite happy to stick to their area of expertise and thus don't have the inclination or resources to shoulder the responsibility of selling rooms

Figure 2. Average length of stay in Thailand

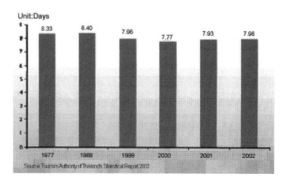

directly. On the other hand, without expending adequate selling effort it is quite difficult to achieve high occupancy rates in large hotels with more than 200 rooms because word-of-mouth as a means of promotion is very limited in scope. Further, in the travel and tourism sector the customers and service providers are normally separated by large geographical distances. This makes the position of the intermediary at close contact with the customer absolutely indispensable. It is for this reason that most hotels rely heavily on travel agencies or tour operators to market their properties. The travel agencies perform the task of managing the inventory of the hotels, especially for new hotels and new destinations. The hotels in turn offer rooms to these intermediaries at a heavy discount which serves as the operating margin for the travel agent. Figure.3 shows the different types of distribution channels in the travel and tourism industry that sell hotel rooms on behalf of the hotels to the travelers.

The basic inability and disinclination of hotels to market their products directly to its customers can be attributed to certain fundamental economic reasons. If hotels attempt to promote their properties on their own, they will be: (i) unable to achieve economies of scale and (ii) unable to achieve economies of scope. The inability to achieve economies of scale is due to the highly dispersed customer base spread across all the continents that in turn necessitates that any marketing effort has to be truly global in nature. Further, the atomized nature of demand necessitates the presence of an extremely large sales network for a hotel is to be in a position to achieve sales targets consistently. Consequently, the promotional expenditure associated with selling tourism products on a global scale will be very high. Since a large sales and marketing network is economically feasible only when large numbers of rooms (may be tens of thousands of room-nights) are sold through it, a single hotel or even a relatively large hotel will not be in a position to achieve any economies of scale if it attempts to market directly without the help of intermediaries.

The potential customer on the other hand will be more interested if a whole host of choices are provided like a beach resort, a golf holiday, a river cruise etc. at the point of sale so that he/she can choose a particular hotel or destination according to his/her preferences. When a single hotel offers its products in an individual basis, the choice set presented to the potential customer will naturally be very limited and thereby reduces the potential customer's motivation to search and select. Therefore it becomes absolutely essential to rely on intermediaries who can achieve both economies of scale and scope in distribution by bundling an attractive choice set for the customers.

The preeminence of intermediaries can also be justified on the basis of the unique features of the tourism product. At the point of sale, tourism is little more than an information product since the customer decides about consuming a product mostly based on the information that he/she gets about the product from various sources. Further, during the period leading up to the time when the product is actually consumed, consumers must be confident that the experience purchased will materialize and satisfy their expectations. Tourism is also thus considered as credence good as discussed by Hoontrakul (2004). This is because experience attributes predominate in a tourism product (Cooper et al, 1998). While a potential customer can see photos and get a very general feel of the destination he/she is going to visit, it is extremely important that the customer is made to imagine the experience of visiting a destination. This is probably possible on a large scale only with the help of intermediaries who could explain and give a credible idea about what the visitor can expect. Intermediaries therefore are required to reduce the high level of information asymmetry that exists between the potential customer and the service provider. During the transaction phase, it is hence important that the customer is fed with the right information which he/she can feel confident about. This fact puts the established intermediary located at the customer's end in a position of great advantage.

As can be seen from figure 3, there are four possible ways through which a customer can book his/her accommodation in a hotel. Of the four, the first channel which involves the wholesaler and the travel agent is the most established and popular one. The wholesalers are large intermediaries with links to several hotels and several travel agents. The wholesalers demand huge discounts from the hotels as they deal with big volumes. The discounts normally are in the range of 50 to 60% (sometimes even 70%) of the room rent eventually charged by the hotel from the guest. A part of this discount is passed on to the travel agent who is in direct contact with the customer. The other part becomes the operating revenue for the wholesaler. Due to the huge volume handled, the wholesalers are very powerful in the market. It is estimated that about 70% of the hotels are highly reliant on the wholesalers for their marketing effort. The wholesalers are typically based in Europe from where most of the tourists originate. It is widely acknowledged that the large tourism wholesalers have been instrumental in developing the Thai tourism market. When most of the destinations were relatively unknown, the wholesalers had marketed it quite enthusiastically especially in the developed countries. This rapidly led to the development of these destinations. The travel wholesalers like LTU, TUI and Thomas Cook with monopsony like market power thus enjoyed the first mover advantage in dealing with most of the hotels especially in gaining access to a large inventory of rooms at a relatively bargain price.

The second channel comprising of the travel wholesaler, tour operator and the travel agent is the second most popular channel. Tour operators package the tour for the customer and sell these packages through the travel agent. The customer in fact may not even know in which hotel he/she will be staying while he/she books for the tour. The third channel viz. the direct channel or walk-ins are not very practicable to depend upon especially for large hotels with more than 200 rooms. This is because intense competition among the hoteliers has made it impossible to sell their rooms entirely on the support of word-of-mouth. Further, since there is a huge geographical barrier between the tourist and the hotel, creating awareness about the hotel itself is a stupendous task. However some rooms (less than 10%) gets sold directly.

The online channel is the latest and emerging channel, which was expected at one time to revolutionize the sector. However, the utility of the channel for a hotel still remains quite limited,

Figure 3.

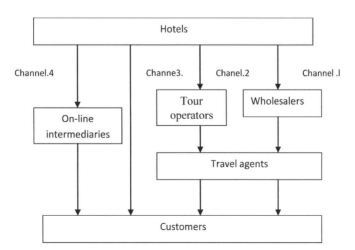

as the business generated by this channel for an average hotel is still not significant. The on-line channel it self comprises of different routes. For instance, a hotel can be a member of a large web-site like expedia.com or rely on an emerging on-line intermediary like moterthailand.com.

The On-line Travel and Tourism Channel

With increasing Internet penetration, the on-line travel industry has seen phenomenal growth over the years (Marcussen, 2004). The on-line travel industry consists of large Global Distribution systems, on-line travel agents who operate on a global basis as well as on-line travel agents with a regional presence. The GDS like SABRE, Amadeus, World Span, Galileo etc. have been in existence since the late 70s. These systems span the entire world and enable travel agencies to book airline tickets or hotel rooms any where in the world. Of these systems only World Span is available through the internet.

Large global intermediaries like expedia.com, orbitz.com, Travelocity.com etc. have a worldwide presence. They enable customers anywhere in the world to search for and book rooms in any part of the world. These websites often cater to large hotels or hotel chains that have a well-known brand. Another type of on-line travel intermediaries are the global marketing representatives like utell.com, best western, Concorde etc. These companies cater to independent owned hotels which are not large enough to invest in being a part of the GDS. These companies provide an interface between the hotels and the travel agencies (O'Conner, 1999).

The latest entrants in this field are e-intermediaries that operate exclusively through the internet. While they are similar to large e-intermediaries like expedia.com or orbitz.com, the new intermediaries normally concentrate on particular regions and cater to small or independent hotels. Some of the main players in this field in Thailand apart from morethailand.com are asiatravel.com,

sawadee.com, phuket.com and hotels-hailand.com. However, except morethailand.com most of the other e-intermediaries are nothing more than electronic directories since they operate mostly on a commission basis. These intermediaries basically provide a much cheaper and easier way for hotels to sell their rooms through cyberspace. The business model for these intermediaries is quite simple. They enter into a contract with hotels in a destination and include their names in their website. Customers who visit the websites of these companies can search and book a room matching their requirements through the website. The e-intermediary receives a commission/profit for each room booked through their website. The main cost for the e-intermediaries is to maintain staff for the back office activities and promotion of their websites. The back office activities include receiving and answering to the enquiries from the customers, contacting the hotels for availability of rooms and finalizing the transactions. The marketing activities include search engine optimization, e-mail marketing and other means of off-line promotion. Hotels which find it costlier to have electronic interfaces can easily make themselves available to a global audience through the internet by contracting with these e-intermediaries. Customers are also benefited since it makes it easier for them to search and book rooms at affordable rates.

The emergence of e-intermediaries as a strong contender against off-line travel wholesalers and consolidators can be attributed to several technological and market-related factors (Buhalis and Licata, 2002). With the rapid expansion of the internet in the developed countries- the prime market for Thailand, the advantage enjoyed by the travel wholesalers due to their close proximity to the customers has been blunted to a substantial extent. With the 'death of distance', the information delivery through the internet satisfies most of the customers quite well. Further, e-intermediaries were in a position to operate with considerably less operating costs than the large travel wholesalers located in some of the most expensive cities with a large employee contingent. This enabled the e-intermediaries to match the travel wholesalers in terms of the discounts charged from hotels. In fact e-intermediaries often are able to offer more attractive benefits to the hotels than large travel wholesalers.

The Hotel industry in Thailand

Hotels in Thailand are typically classified into two: tier-I and tier-II. Table 1 gives the number of hotels in each category at the most favorite destinations in Thailand. The tier-I hotels are typically large hotels and generally form part of a hotel chain. These hotels are mostly associated with a Global hotel chain like group Accor or Holiday Inn. They are often professionally managed and use a global distribution system like SABRE, AMADEUS etc. and/or are attached to a global website like expedia.com. or Travelocity.com. The potential customers book rooms in these hotels when they use any of these intermediary networks. Out of the estimated 10,000 hotel properties in Thailand not more than 10% are considered as belonging to tier-I. Almost all international hotel chains like Group Accor, Marriott, Holiday Inn, Hilton etc. are present in Thailand apart from Thailand based chains like Dusit Thani, Central etc.

The tier-II hotels are normally known as IOO (Independent Owned and Operated). Many of these hotels are small with less than 200 rooms, though a few large IOO hotels also exist. However, most of the IOO hotels are stand alone hotels. These lodges were normally owned by a local landlord and the management structure in these hotels present a typical principal-agent problem in the Jensen and Meckling (1976) sense. These properties would typically have an owner, a general manager and a sales director. The owner would often be a local landowner, not quite competent to run the affairs of the hotel and is only interested in the profits generated. Normally these landlords had constructed the hotel in their land by managing to secure funds from different sources. Once the property is build, they expect a steady stream of profits. The general manager and the sales directors are professionals but often have conflicting interests with the owners. The owner is more interested in the amount of profit and cash flow generated from operations and thus not too keen to give huge discounts to the travel wholesalers. The sales director in turn is more interested in incentive payout from the total sale, while the general manager would like to improve occupancy rates and hotel food and beverage sale. Thus, they would not be wary of teaming up with travel wholesalers who would often demand high levels of discounts in return

Table 1. The number of hotels (accommodation establishments) in the important destinations in Thailand.

		Bangkok	Krabi	Pattaya	Phuket	Samui
Source:	www2.tat.or.th/stat					
Year	2003					
Supply						
Number of Accom. Estab.		259	290	250	549	357
Grade 1		78	53	12	178	33
Grade 2		46	192	14	304	30
Grade 3		35	45	25	3	23
Grade 4		69	-	84	10	70
Grade 5		31	-	116	54	200

for ensuring a steady occupancy rate. This agency problem leads to high turnover of executives in many of these IOOs. It is estimated that a sales director's average tenure in an IOO is not more than two years. These conflicting interests and the differences in perceptions make it difficult for the e-intermediaries to enter into contracts with these hotels. While the management teams will often be pro-travel wholesaler, the owner may be more appreciative of the efforts of the e-intermediary. Since the level of discounts provided by the hotel to the e-intermediary as well as the commitment of rooms during high season are two major issues that determine viability of e-intermediaries, such internal problems within hotel organizations often prove to be very difficult to tackle. It is hence conjectured that online intermediaries would have a much easier time with the IOO hotels, when are managed by the owner.

The IOOs don't have any major presence in the world wide web though they may have their own websites. Very few transactions take place directly between the customers and the hotels through their websites. This is because it is very unlikely for a potential customer to come and visit the website without any promotion of the website on the part of the hotel.

The IOOs find e-intermediaries like morethailand.com an attractive proposition to collaborate with since they don't have the manpower or expertise to manage the inventory transactions if they become part of a GDS or other centralized reservation systems. Only chain hotels can afford to become part of a GDS since they require a well developed and constantly updated electronic data base to be a part of the GDS. Further, it is estimated that even in those hotels which are linked to the GDS, hardly 10% of the rooms are being booked through that route. This is mainly because of the fact that a GDS is only a network that enables online reservation on a global scale doesn't indulge in any kind of promotion activities with regard to the hotels. On the other hand, the e-intermediaries through their promotional campaigns market it self as well as the hotels that are part of it.

Moterthailand.com offers the hotels that are part of their network; (i) flexibility in managing their inventory and (ii) support by means of internet marketing and other type of promotional activities. Hotels can also promote themselves through the motherthailand.com website by renting out a preferred area in the site which could catch the attention of the web-surfers when they open the web page. For the hotels, morethailand.com is of course only one of the avenues for selling rooms. Usually hotels will form linkages with several intermediaries like travel agents, tour operators, e-intermediaries etc.

Contractual Agreements with Hotels

Morethailand.com has contractual arrangements with around 500 hotels located all over Thailand. The number of hotels having linkages with morethailnd.com from the different regions of Thailand is given in Attachment II. For morethailnd.com to make available rooms of a particular hotel to be booked through its website, the company has to enter into contractual agreements with the concerned hotels. These agreements cover aspects like commission sharing, clauses on cancellation of rooms, procedures for payment etc. Hotels usually sell rooms to intermediaries in three ways: (i) the commission rate (ii) the contractual rate and (iii) the merchant system. In the commission rate system, the hotels decide the eventual selling price and give a commission to the intermediary as per the contract while in the contractual rate system, the hotels sell rooms to the intermediary at a particular rate and the intermediary in turn has the freedom to sell the rooms at whatever rate it deems fit. In both the systems however, there is no commitment from the intermediary's side to sell a certain number of rooms. In the merchant model followed by a few large on-line intermediaries like expedia.com, the intermediary actually buys rooms at a very low rate from the hotel and then resells it to the travelers. In this system the intermediary looses money if it is not capable of selling the rooms to the customers. In the case of morethailand.com, about 20% of its contracts are at commission rates while 70% are in contract rates.

Each of the contracts will be valid for a year. It takes at least a week to more than a month to get a contract signed from a hotel. On an average the commission (either in the form of commission or discounts) given to morethailand.com will be in the range of around 30%. The contract with the hotel also mentions the policy with regard to cancellations. Almost 70% of the hotels in the list charge an average room rent of Thai baht. 3000 to 5000 per night. It is estimated that about 50% of the hotels in the list don't get any enquiries at all while most of the bookings are for about 20% of the hotels. Morethaniland.com is very selective in inducting hotels into its network for cost-effectiveness. Only hotels of a particular standard are included in the network. The main reason is that the firm wants to ensure a certain standard in the service provided by the hotels to its customers who book rooms through morethailnd. com. Subsequently, the partner hotels would be visited for inspection at least once in a year by the staff from morethailand.com. Accommodations which give poor service constantly as reported by the customers are deleted or suspended from the list by morethailand.com.

Morethailand.com has just started with the merchant system with a few hotels. In the merchant model, moretailand.com purchases room inventories prepaid at a cheaper rate for a specific period of time and promotes through its website. The potential customers are offered these rooms at a competitive rate as morethailand.com is able to pass on the benefits of the heavy discounts to the customers. In addition, Morethailand.com is experimenting with the dynamic pricing model by varying prices offered to the customers on the basis of their time of booking. Customers who book in advance are offered rooms at a cheaper rate than those who book later.

Morethailand.com Visitor Statistics

Presently there are 12 websites for the company and each website contributes directly and indirectly to the traffic. Maintaining 12 websites is part of a well thought out strategy. Other than morethailand.com, all the other websites are mainly meant to provide information. For instance a website like www.moresamui.com is primarily meant to provide information about hotels in a destination called Samui. Morethailand.com on the other hand is primarily meant to be a transaction site. Though you could do transactions through an allied site like www.moresamui.com, transaction is not the primary purpose behind maintenance of the website. Most of these allied websites serve the purpose of increasing the company's visibility when potential customers search using destinations as key words in search engines. This is because travelers familiar with Thailand often search using destination specific key words like Smaui, Phuket or Krabi and having a website with the key word as a part of its url increases the possibility of achieving a higher rank in the website listings of search engines.

Together, all the 12 websites generate around 22,000 hits and 5,000 unique visitors per day. Table 2 gives the number of hits and no. of unique visitors to morethailand.com and its associated sites during the month of October 04. Analysis of the traffic shows that most of the competitors are generating more hits than this figure. Sawadee.com, which is the closest competitor for morethailand. com is estimated to generate four times more hits than morethailand.com. As table 2 indicates, the number of hits received by the websites allied to morethailand.com also varies considerably. Table 3 gives details for the total hits and the break up of the sources through which these hits originated. It is estimated that about 300 hits are generated per day from google.com while Yahoo.com generates 100 hits and msn.com generates another 100 hits.

Table 2. hits and unique visitors for the major web-sites in the morethaildand.com stable

Website	Hit/week	Avg./Day	Unique Visitors	Avg./Day
morethailand	4,429,170	142,876	64,250	2,073
morebangkok	484,810	15,639	20,866	673
morekrabi	238,436	7,691	6,316	204
morephuket	241,337	7,785	6,432	207
moresamui	344,760	11,121	9,395	303
morepattaya	92,957	2,999	2,288	74
morethilandmap	398,344	12,850	4,927	159
thaiparks123	1,309,091	42,229	15,311	494
total	7,538,905	243,190	129,785	4,187

The Customer Profile

It is worth noting that most of the visitors to the morethailand.com websites are repeat travelers having traveled in Thailand before. Nearly all website visitors are well educated and have good knowledge of the destinations they are about to choose. About 70% of the customers are from Europe and the rest are from the other parts of the world including the US. In terms of volume of transactions around 80% are for leisure travel while the rest are for business travel. This skewed ratio for leisure travel is explained by the fact that most of the hotels listed in the websites are located in destinations that are better known for leisure travel. Business travelers usually visit just Bangkok and since morethailand.com has less than 100 hotels listed down in Bangkok, it is quite natural that the website caters mostly to the leisure traveler.

The customers generally progress through three stages before they indulge in a transaction. In the initial stage the customers just visit the site. Once they are serious about traveling to Thailand, the visitors post an enquiry about the rooms and the price at which these rooms are available. This is considered as the enquiry phase. It is estimated that just 4 to 5% of the visitors end up enquiring about the product displayed in the website. Out of the enquirers about 35 to 40% eventually end up transacting with the company during the normal season. The transaction rate for the five main destinations focused by morethailand.com is shown in figure 4.

High season in Thailand would mean the months of November to March of every year. It is estimated that about 70% of the tourists visit Thailand during these five months (TAT 2004). As the attachment shows, the enquiry conversion rates vary from one location to another and also from one season to another. Except in Bangkok where there is little impact of seasonal demand, in all other destinations, the number of enquiries is considerably less in low season than in high season. The conversion rate doesn't seem to be determined by the seasonal fluctuation since it

Table 3. Details about traffic to morethailand.com

Overview	% Change	19-25 Jun.04		12-18 Jun.04	
		Visitor	Avg.	Visitor	Avg.
Unique Visitor (Webtrend)	-4.56%	17228	2461	18051	2579

Figure 4. Details about the enquiries and conversion rates across major destinations

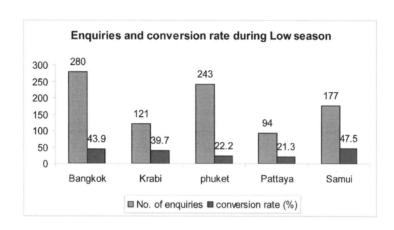

is seen to be varying unevenly across different seasons across different destinations.

It has also been observed that 80% of the bookings are for rooms with rents ranging between 1500 Thai bahts to 3000 Thai bahts. Enquiries are classified on the basis of the price of the rooms as well as the actual sales are classified on the price of the rooms is shown in figure 5.

Before the enquiry culminates into a transaction the potential customer may require more information about the destination, the hotel to stay, even about the possibility of reducing the price. The entire process normally takes about a week. Hence the sales cycle is about 5 to 7 days. Once the visitor transforms to an enquirer, it is assumed that the enquirer is in touch with other websites offering similar products to compare the price. The communication normally progress through e-mail during this phase. Once the enquirer is convinced about the right hotel and the right price, he/she transacts with the morethailand.com. Once the transaction is complete with the amount paid, either through credit card or through bank transfer, the amount net its commission is passed on to the respective hotel at least three days before the customer checks in.

While this is the normal process of transaction with the customer through morethailand.com, two types of transactions are actually possible. The normal transactions explained above are not instant and has a sales cycle of about 5 to 7 days. In the second type called instant transactions, the traveler gets instant confirmation for a room booked through the website. However, such instant

Figure 5. Type of enquiries and sales classified in terms of the price per room

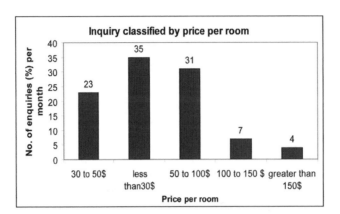

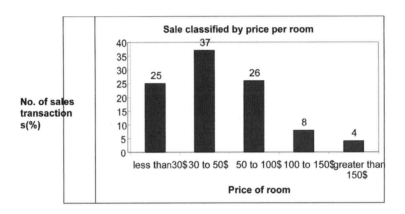

transactions are normally less than 10% of the total transactions. Moreover the instant booking facility will not be available with all the hotels listed in the website. For making available the instant booking facility, morethailand.com has to enter into a special contract with the hotel so that some rooms are kept apart for morethailand.com for a particular period of time.

Since the site also offers lucrative tour packages almost one new package is introduced every week. At a time there can be about 60 such packages. Among the variety of packages offered, the long stay packages in turn are very popular since the price at which they are offered are very low compared to the normal rates. It is in fact estimated that about 50% of the customers who book through

morethailand.com opt for long stay packages.

It is difficult to list down factors that lead to greater conversion from the enquiry. The room rent quoted by the hotels in the list is considered to be a main reason. Other factors include the service provided by the website in terms of the variety of packages, confidence of the traveler with the service providers listed in the site etc. Since it is difficult to understand the real factors that lead to greater conversion, it is also difficult to either differentiate or position the services. The average duration of stay of a traveler who books through morethailand.com is estimated to be about 3 to 7 days. It is of course clear that most of the travelers who transact through morethailand.com are price-sensitive customers as they have a definite threshold as far as the price of a room is concerned. Since the website also offers, but not focused, airline booking facility, a small percentage (about 10%) of the travelers also use morethailand.com for composite booking of their stay and travel. For packages the main attraction seems to be the price reduction offered through the long stay packages as well as the pick up and transfer arrangements. Another trend that has been noticed is the increase in customer traffic caused due to the popularity of certain hotels. Certain properties, end up becoming very attractive with the travelers either due to the superior service that they provide, or because of the scenic beauty of their location, and thus attract customers to the website. The positive word of mouth about the hotel also contributes to the increase in traffic.

On-line Marketing Effort of the Morethailand.com

The main marketing activities of the company comprises of search engine optimization (SEO) and search engine marketing (SEM) carried out on some of the most popular search engines like google.com, yahoo.com and msn.com. SEO relates to altering the content of the website in order to make it easier for the search engines to find and understanding the content's essence. A search engine's mission is to deliver the most relevant results to searchers and therefore, the search engine rank that a website will enjoy is dependent on the content and your linking strategy. This is a constant process and involves the full time attention of about four staff members. It has been found that increasing the traffic to the site is a major way of increasing the transaction levels. SEO aims to keep the company's websites in the first ten positions in the list that emerges when the customer types the most popular key words in the three search engines. This is ensured through positioning specific keywords in strategic positions in the web pages, trying for achieving links from other sites to morethailand.com etc. Reputation management, online PR, and content freshness based on seasonal search behavior, as well as trend adjustments, are ongoing processes that will enhance a search engine friendly site

Apart from SEO, the company also conducts SEM whereby it advertises in google.com to obtain sponsored links for certain key words. These sponsored links appear in the right side of the screen when certain key words are used for searching through google.com. In order that a website URL appears as a sponsored link in the first screen for a keyword, google.com charges a certain amount per click through. This click through rate varies from one key word to another based on its popularity. This is because, for each key word, there will be more than one claimant for the first few spaces in the sponsored link. In order to be in the first three positions in the sponsored link space, each of the sites have to bid for the keyword. The bidding is for the click through rate. If you bid the highest for a key word like "Phuket", then, when the customer searches using the key word 'Phuket' in google.com, the link to a relevant site will appear as the first among three or four sites in the sponsored link portion of the screen. It is always important to be in the first three as otherwise a website may not appear in the first page of the keyword results and as a consequence, the sponsored link will be of little use. The most crucial part in SEM is therefore to identify the most popular keywords and successfully bid for it. This is because there are thousands of keywords that are used by the customers to search in google.com and it is virtually impossible to get sponsored links for each of these keywords. The paid campaigns through google.com, are classified into two: (i) nationality specific campaigns in which Google sites of specific countries are considered and (ii) destination specific campaigns where the sponsored links for destinations are sought and paid for.

Comparison between Destination and Nationality Based Campaigns through Google.com

The destination specific campaigns and nationality specific campaigns use two different approaches. In destination based campaigns, keywords associated with specific destinations like Bangkok, Samui, Krabi etc. are booked in google.com so that when web searchers type any of these destinations based keywords, a link to morethailand.com or any other associated website appears in the search screen on the right side. Morethailand.com has to pay a specific click through amount for obtaining a specific position in the screen. Table 4 shows a report of the outcome of a destination campaign through google.com. Overall during the week when this report was taken, morethailand.com paid about $475.00 for 2277 clicks and 31 enquiries. The summary table (table 6) shows the total transactions that directly resulted from the 31 enquiries and the volume of the transactions from these enquires. A total of 15 enquiries were converted to orders with a value of $4730.57. With an order processing cost of roughly about 7$ per order and a margin of roughly 15%, this works out to an ROI of about 10%.

For nationality specific campaigns, morethai-

Table 4. Outcome of the destination specific campaign carried out between 24 to 30 November 2005.

Campaign	Impression	Clicks	Clicks last week	Cost	Conversions	Cost / Conv.	CTR	Avg CPC	average position	average position last week
Samui	13,287	124	140	$42.47	1	$42.47	0.90%	$0.34	4.6	3.8
Bangkok	4,169	83	61	$26.43	5	$5.29	2.00%	$0.32	6.6	7.4
Phuket	14,554	305	271	$102.79	7	$14.68	2.10%	$0.34	5.5	5.7
Krabi	20,115	289	285	$51.00	4	$12.75	1.40%	$0.18	3.6	3.4
Pattaya	7,133	103	111	$43.14	4	$10.78	1.40%	$0.42	5.4	5.4
Koh Chang	10,463	249	285	$35.84	4	$8.96	2.40%	$0.14	2.9	3
Chiang Mai	8,597	126	125	$34.13	3	$11.38	1.50%	$0.27	4.2	2.6
Chiang Rai	24,742	172	11	$27.15	0	$0.00	0.70%	$0.16	na	na
Phitsanulok	1,144	23	16	$2.07	0	$0.00	2.00%	$0.09	1.7	1.7
Sukhothai	0	0	43	$0.00	0	$0.00	0.00%	$0.00	3.5	3
Koh Tao	6,976	160	12	$27.14	0	$0.00	2.30%	$0.17	4.4	4.7
Trang	778	12	12	$1.15	0	$0.00	1.50%	$0.10	na	na
Hua Hin	8,642	83	95	$23.88	3	$7.96	1.00%	$0.29	na	na
Kanchana-buri	2,088	32	39	$2.38	0	$0.00	1.50%	$0.07	na	na
Ayuthaya	2,636	21	26	$3.02	0	$0.00	0.80%	$0.14	na	na
Khon Kaen	2,506	39	44	$2.75	0	$0.00	1.60%	$0.07	2.1	1.8
Ubon Rat-chathani	1,000	25	32	$1.25	0	$0.00	2.50%	$0.05	2.3	1.9
Udon Thani	2,467	70	45	$4.77	0	$0.00	2.80%	$0.07	5.8	3.8
Nakhon Ratchasima	1,157	26	16	$1.89	0	$0.00	2.20%	$0.07	2.4	1.9
Overall	177,971	2,277	2,076	$475.80	31	$15.35	1.30%	$0.21		

land.com pays for sponsored links in nationality specific google.com sites for instance to cater to the Italian audience, morethailand.com pays for sponsored links in the Italian version of google.com via google.co.it. The details of the outcome of the nationality specific campaign for a particular week in November 2005 are given in table 5. The nationality campaign is much less profitable, but more targeted oriented to achieve other marketing objectives [e.g. strategic coverage, visibility, branding, etc.]. The total amount spent was about $ 306 which generated 927 clicks and 6 direct conversions. The campaign during the week considered generated to confirmed orders with a total volume of about $1787.00. This turns out to a ROI of about -20% after considering the order processing cost.

However, it is not always vital to look at specific conversions; the click through that has been achieved is an immense advantage in terms of promotion of the website. Especially in terms of achieving greater visibility and patronage in the long run. Further the conversions registered in the

calculations are just the direct registrations. In reality there will be several customers who might click and browse the web on a particular occasion and transact much later. The ROI calculation mentioned above does not capture such transactions which are the indirect effects of the google based promotion campaigns. Overall, it can be said that campaigns which are essentially based on click through rates are much less profitable in the short run. Their major contribution is in the long run. For a firm like morethailand.com, it is more profitable to have organic enquiries which are attracted through word of mouth or through repeat customers the search engine based marketing campaigns only serve the purpose of attracting first time customers and developing a brand image in the market for the firm.

Offline Marketing

About the offline marketing effort and public relations (PR) of the company, Mr. Tri Pramoj, non-executive director to morethailand.com on offline marketing has this to say:

Table 5. Results of a nationality based campaign carried out during 24 to 30 November 2005

Campaign	Clicks	Clicks last week	Cost	Conversions	Conversion %	Cost / Conv	Impressions	CTR	Avg CPC	Avg Position	Avg Position last week
Australia	20	17	$7.98	0	0.00%	0	1751	1.10%	$0.40	6.6	6.6
Canada	1	0	$0.20	0	0.00%	$0.00	171	0.60%	$0.20	5.6	6.2
China	8	7	$1.20	0	0.00%	$0.00	925	0.90%	$0.15	3.7	4.1
Denmark	63	68	$25.17	0	0.00%	0	4783	1.30%	$0.40	4	5
England	57	63	$17.60	0	0.00%	0	5709	1.00%	$0.31	5.9	6
Finland	24	17	$8.47	1	4.20%	$8.47	4179	0.60%	$0.35	4.8	5
Hong Kong & Taiwan	10	7	$1.81	0	0.00%	$0.00	403	2.50%	$0.18	5.6	5.2
India	14	11	$2.25	0	0.00%	$0.00	576	2.40%	$0.16	4.6	4.3
Japan	15	15	$8.41	0	0.00%	0	1068	1.40%	$0.56	4.3	4.6
Netherland	16	34	$4.86	0	0.00%	$0.00	2907	0.60%	$0.30	6	5.6
Norway	29	42	$10.38	0	0.00%	0	7835	0.40%	$0.36	3.9	3.9

Table 6. Total enquiries and sales due to the search engine marketing activities during the time period 24 to 30 November 2005 for Morethailand.com and associated sites

	Enquiry		Sale		
	total number	Volumn(US$)	total number	Volumn(US$)	
Total Inquiry	93	29,762.63	44	12,739.69	43%
Adword Track Inquiry	37	15,550.18	17	6,517.95	42%
- Destination	31	11,826.43	15	4,730.57	40%
- Nationality	6	3,723.75	2	1,787.38	48%

"The offline marketing efforts and public relation campaign of the company mainly focuses on building relationships for branding and brand awareness with the supply side of the tourism service delivery chain. It is increasingly being realized that only through developing stronger relationships with hotels can the company expect more favorable prices and thus be able to offer rooms at competitive process to its customers."

During high season, good relationships with hotels assume a strategic importance since often it is only through such good relationships that rooms are made available in the most attractive hotels. The main activities in relationship building include conducting seminars for hoteliers, participating in Tourism fares and public relation campaign to make hoteliers understand the significance of e-intermediaries. The idea is to position morethailand.com as a knowledge-based intermediary that doesn't limit itself to mere room booking activities. The company conducts around one seminar every three months where hoteliers are invited to attend a series of talks for half a day by the founder and top executives of the company. This also serves as an occasion for the executives of the company to interact with the hoteliers and develop relationships with them. Since the e-intermediary concept is relatively new and the hoteliers are yet to get substantial bookings through this channel, it is felt that these efforts are required to get greater cooperation from the hoteliers. Another activity promoted by the company is a PR campaign through professional PR agency. The PR campaign aims to improve the visibility of the company among the trade. The campaign involves publishing articles about the website, general articles about the tourism industry and the role of the intermediaries as well as publishing interviews with the founder and the CEO of the company in various media like the national television network and major newspapers. These activities attempt to improve the stature of the company among the travel and tourism industry so that it becomes possible for the company to get the support of the hoteliers in its endeavor.

Organizational Structure

Morethailand.com has a small organization comprising of mostly young professionals. Presently there are 30 employees in the company. This is in line with the company's philosophy of being technology driven and purposeful in all its endeavors. However, the employees of the company are presented with a good learning opportunity. The operations of the company are divided into five departments:

1. *Reservation department*: Headed by a manager with sufficient experience in the travel industry, the department looks after the communication with the customers. The department is the actual direct interface with the customer for the company. Apart from

the manager, the department has 3 staff members. The department is also responsible for developing the products like designing special packages, negotiating with hotels etc

2. *Online marketing and SEM staff*: The online marketing staff is responsible mainly for search engine optimization. The department has apart from a manager, four staff members. They undertake all the search engine promotional activities of the organization including SEM and content writing. This activity is of prime importance in attracting customers

3. *Webmaster and SEO Department*: This department is responsible for updating the website, ensuring the overall attractiveness of the website and SEO. Apart from a manager there are four other staff members working in this department. They prepare a site traffic report every Wednesday for analysis by the company.

4. *IT- Department*: This department looks after the hardware and software aspects of the website. In this department there are three programmers and, one systems engineer apart from the manger who heads it.

5. Key-in department: The main task of this department is to look after the main paper work including the responsibility of up-keeping the contracts with the hotels and other service providers. There are two staff members in this department. The key in department reports to the reservation department

6. *Finance and Accounting department*: The finance and accounts department consists of three staff members.

Each of the departments also has an external advisor who provides a strategic vision for the functioning of the departments. The employees are given performance-based incentives.

It is estimated that about 70% of the company's costs are incurred as salaries and about 20% on advertisements in google.com. The company also incurs expenditure on off-line promotion like participating in travel and tour fairs conducting seminars for hoteliers etc. It is estimated that to process each order, the company has to spend about 40bhat (almost equivalent to $1.00)

CONCLUSION AND DISCUSSION

As is evident from the case study, a start up morethailand.com is trying to establish itself in an industry that is itself in its infancy. The future of this industry is as yet quite uncertain. The main challenge the industry has to face is the market power dominance of the conventional off-line travel wholesalers who are moving onto online in the market. The hotels are often not in a position to come out of the clutches of the travel wholesalers and help the on-line intermediaries wholeheartedly. On the other hand, only if the hotels give adequate support by allotting sufficient rooms to the e-intermediaries can the intermediaries give a stiff competition to the travel wholesalers. In addition, the customers will adopt e-intermediaries in a big way only when the e-intermediaries are able to sell hotel rooms at rates comparable to that offered by travel agents. The industry therefore is in a transition phase with the e-intermediaries trying their level best to break the stranglehold of the travel wholesalers. Though at presently the market power of offline travel wholesaler is declining, it is still a long way to go before online travel intermediary may emerge significantly. From an e-commerce perspective this provides an interesting scenario as it illustrates how e-commerce and IT can change the relative power structure in an industry. It is an instance where the traditional loyalties and economies of scale enjoyed by conventional intermediaries are challenged by the cost efficiencies of the new age Internet based companies. In the developed countries the transition to a predominantly Internet based intermediation has already happened in the hotel industry. It is in the developing economies like Thailand with significantly big tourism industry that the new wave of e-commerce based intermediation is taking root. Morethailand.com as a representative of this new wave of companies is traversing through a path which is abounding in opportunities and challenges. Morethailand.com considers itself as a bridge between the Independently Owned and Operated Hotels and the worldwide tourism market. The IOOs hitherto had very little direct access to the international tourist market. Morethailand.com believes that through linking IOOs in Thailand to the worldwide tourism market, it is actually opening up more choice and more possibilities to the global tourist. An activity that it feels is quite sustainable.

On supply side, the IOOs continue to face an agency problem between the owners and management. This may be a major obstacle to ICT adaptation and E-Commerce usage since the management is very keen to keep in existing off-line channels and their networks for their own benefit. On the other hand, in the long run, due to increasing competition and the consequent reduction in margins, if the owner can not resolve this agency problem, IOOs would end up being part of a large hotel chain or sold out rightly.

The biggest challenge for morethailand.com however is to promote its offer in the world wide web with its limited resources. Morethailand.com has selected search engine optimization (SEO) and search engine marketing (SEM) as the two main means of increasing its presence in the B2C space. The business model selected by morethialand.com, though very promising is not totally unique. Moreover, in Thailand itself there are numerous e-intermediaries that follow the similar business models. The main differentiating factor between morethiailand.com and many of its competitors is its high reliance on IOOs and its adoption of the merchant model. By featuring a large number of hotels in the website, morethailand.com hopes to improve the choice for its visitors. For those

who want to explore new areas and visit hitherto unknown destinations will find morethailand.com would be a better option to search. Further, through the merchant model morethailand.com intends to offer rooms at a cheaper rate to the customers than most of its competitors including the travel wholesalers. Morethailand.com has to grapple with the challenges posed by two domains. At the supply side, the company has to contact and negotiate with hotels to get them listed in their websites and once an enquiry is received from a potential customer, to get the rooms allotted during the dates required for the customer. On demand side, the company has to market it website to its customers. The demand side activity requires such responsibilities like developing the content in the website, search engine optimization so that potential customers could access the site when they search for any information on hotels in Thailand or other associated subjects. The company has to deal with both on-line competitors as well as off-line competitors both in the supply as well as the demand side.

REFERENCES

Buhalis, D., & Licata, C. M. (2002). The Future of eTourism Intermediaries. *Tourism Management*, *23*, 207–220. doi:10.1016/S0261-5177(01)00085-1

Cooper, C., Fletcher, J., Gilbert, D., & Wanhill, S. (1998). Tourism Principles and Practice, Pearson, Essex.

Freely downloadable at www.Pongsak.Hoontrakul.com

Hoontrakul, P. (2004*). "Value Revelation in Differentiated Goods for Travel Industry", Discussion Paper, Sasin of Chulalongkorn University, Bangkok

Jensen, M. C., & Meckling, W. H. (1976). Theory of the firm: Managerial behavior, agency costs and ownership structure. *Journal of Financial Economics*, *3*, 303–360. doi:10.1016/0304-405X(76)90025-8

Marcussen, C. H. (2004) Trends in European Internet distribution of Travel and Tourism Services, available at www.rcb.dk/uk/staff/chm/trends.htm accessed on 3/December/2004

O'Conner, P. (1999). Electronic Information Distribution Tourism and Hospitality, CABI Publishing, Cambridge.

Poon, A. (1993) "Tourism, Technology and Competitive Strategies, CAB International, Oxford.

Ryan, Peter and Pongsak Hoontrakul (2003*) "An Economic Analysis of the Tourism Industry – Implications for Online intermediary", *Chulalongkorn Journal of Economics*.

Sheldon, P. (1997) "Tourism Information Technology", CAB, Oxford.

TAT. (2003) "Tourism Authority of Thailand Statistical Report 2003", Tourism Authority of Thailand. Bangkok.

UNCTAD. (2000) Electronic Commerce and Tourism New Perspectives and Challenges for Developing Countries, United Nations Conference on Trade and Development.

APPENDIX
Table 7.

Northern Region	
Location	no. of hotels
Chiang Mai	32
Ghiang Rai	8
Pitsanulok	7
Rest	16
Total	**63**

This work was previously published in E-Business Models, Services, and Communications, edited by I. Lee, pp. 372-393, copyright 2008 by IGI Publishing (an imprint of IGI Global).

Chapter 4.17
Online Services Delivered by NTO Portals:
A Cross–Country Examination

Marco Papa
University of Bari, Italy

Marina Avgeri
Monte dei Paschi di Siena Bank, Italy

ABSTRACT

This study compares the online services currently delivered by the official National Tourism Organizations (NTO) portals of the 25 European Union states, to assess their capability in evolving into powerful marketing communication tools. A conceptual framework that identifies 129 online service quality attributes is developed based on the 2QCV3Q model (Mich et al., 2003) and on four different perspectives: marketing, customer, technical and information for the destination (So and Morrison, 2004). The 25 portals are compared by means of content analysis. Our rankings provide a first time assessment of the NTO online offerings and indicate high variability in their performance. Surprisingly, Greece and Italy, two of the most popular tourism destinations, underperformed with respect to all four perspectives examined. We provide out-of-sample evidence that affluence levels explain the variation in the observed scores, while e-readiness, popularity of tourism destination and cultural richness are not statistically significant.

INTRODUCTION: THE ROLE OF NATIONAL TOURISM ORGANIZATIONS' PORTALS

Among the Destination Management Organizations (DMOs), prominent is the role of the National Tourism Organizations (NTOs[1]) in marketing a destination at a national level. Prior to the Internet era the DMOs have been rather passive and limited to the distribution of printed tourist promotional material on demand (So and Morrison, 2004; King, 2002). However, the adoption and the diffusion of e-commerce applications have provoked unprecedented changes (Wöber,

2003). All European Union (EU) members have invested in the development of websites with different levels of interactivity (Morgan et al., 2002). Essentially, these portals undertake the management of "content information" relating to a tourist destination, arriving from a wide variety of different sources (Turban et al., 2004: 322). By assuming the role of on line brokers of information providers, they become responsible for matching cross cultural demand of individual tourists with the destinations' tourism service supply (Scharl et al., 2004).

Different studies indicate that NTO portals should not be perceived exclusively as information seeking facilitators (Morgan et al., 2002). Instead, they should aim to evolve into powerful interactive marketing communication tools (Sainaghi, 2006; Griff and Palmer, 1999²; Cano and Prentice, 1998) that have the potential to enhance the overall attractiveness of a travel destination and to evoke an optimal experience for their on line users, offering superior value to different customer groups (Nysveen et al., 2003). However, while the trend of internet being the first point of embarkation for prospect tourists is gaining *momentum* (Buhalis and Licata, 2002) and the presence of NTOs through internet is becoming better established (Feng et al., 2002), there is still a *paucity* of empirical research regarding the online offerings and the internet marketing strategies undertaken from them.

Under the recognition that it is important to examine NTOs in an *exploratory way*, where the dimensions of online quality from a customer perspective will serve as a framework, this study compares the official European NTO portals online offerings. The aim is to examine *what* information and services of value added each of the 25 EU portals is offering and *why* their offerings differ. To this end, as first objective, there were identified the online services that may facilitate the tourist search, evaluation of information and purchase of services via the NTO sites, based on a deep inspection of the e-Service Quality (e-SQ)

and the DMO empirical literature. Secondly, these portals were compared by means of content analysis in order to study the service quality attributes provided and to investigate the extent to which four country context variables explain differences in the NTOs' performance.

E-SERVICE QUALITY AND DMO OFFERINGS

The way e-SQ is conceptualized is still at an exploratory stage. Researchers not only have tried to combine known dimensions that influence product quality and Service Quality (SQ), but also to discover some unique factors, relevant to the virtual operations only. The e-SQ attributes seem to depend on the level of web-based technology readiness of the different users (Zhu et al., 2002) and do not to demonstrate a linear relationship, since "more" of an attribute is not necessarily perceived as better (O'Neill et al., 2001).

In order to define e-SQ, some authors take into account both the *pre* and *post* web sites services aspects (Santos, 2003; Liu and Arnett, 2000), while others consider only the interaction with the site itself (Zeithaml et al., 2002). Additionally, in contrast to the traditional service offerings, online users tend to regard e-SQ more as a universal concept, deriving from their overall online experience, rather than from sub-processes (Van Riel et al., 2001).³ The *focus* of each individual research (e.g., consumer buying procedure), as well as the *types of web sites* used (e.g., portals, retailing sites, etc.) determine how the definition of e-SQ may be conceptualised (Kim et al., 2006). Given that the NTO portals' core activity is to help customers at different stages in the information search process, the definition of website quality used in this study is based on the concept of value added services as provided by Nysveen (2003) and Lexhagen (2004): "Services giving access to various forms of information about the tourism products offered on a website", disregarding approaches tailored for e-commerce shopping (Zeithaml et al., 2002), or based on an ex-ante definition of e-services (Santos, 2003: 235).

Not only defining, but also measuring the multidimensional construct of e-SQ continues to generate increased academic debate. Many different scales have been proposed during the last eight years based on different classifications of quality dimensions and attributes (O'Neill et al., 2001; Madu and Madu, 2002; Zhu et al., 2002; Yoo and Donthu 2001; Santos, 2003; Zeithmal et al., 2002; Parasuraman et al., 2005, etc.), either emphasizing the *human and soft* elements of service quality or the *technical dimensions* of on line efficiency, or both (Sigala, 2004).

An extended framework, which incorporates many of the e-SQ dimensions proposed by previous approaches, has been developed by Madu and Madu (2002). Their model included some of the product quality dimensions according to Garvin (1984), as well as the 5 quality dimensions of the SERVQUAL scale (Parasuraman et al., 1988), while it identified some unique, new dimensions, appropriate only for virtual contexts. Even if the proposed dimensions have never been tested empirically, it is interesting the evolutionary approach it adopts, encompassing both product and services features.

Barnes and Vidgen (2000)[4] based on 54 students' evaluations of British online bookstores, have extended the SERVQUAL scale of Parasuraman et al. (1988) to an online context, encompassing softer service related attributes by introducing 24 different measurement items under their index named WebQual. They focused on the following aspects: *reliability, competence, responsiveness, access, credibility, communication and understanding*. Later on, Loiacono et al. (2002)[5] proposed the WebQual™ scale which emphasised again the technical aspects of the website in the evaluation of its online quality, developing 12 web design features. This approach has been criticised by Zeithaml et al. (2002) and Parasuram et al. (2005), for having limited capabilities in

capturing important quality dimensions (e.g., "fulfilment", customer service), since these scales have been produced by using convenience samples of students rather than actual online purchasers. A further drawback derives from the fact that the participating students have rated researcher specified categories that had not emerged through a qualitative study.

Parasuraman et al. (2005) recently have developed the well known E-S-QUAL model. Under the latter, e-service quality dimensions have been divided into 7 categories: *efficiency, availability, fulfilment, privacy, service recovery dimension, compensation and contact*. A recent application of the E-S-QUAL model has been undertaken by Kim et al. (2006) which evaluated the performance of 111 US apparel retail websites in providing on line service attributes that facilitate efficient and effective shopping, purchasing and delivery of garments. Such on line service attributes were examined by means of content analysis, by considering the E-S-QUAL categories, accommodated to include other dimensions: *personalisation, information and graphic style*, regarded as relevant for the specific retail context. Overall, it was found that the e-SQ level of the sample companies was unsatisfactory.

Previous studies have investigated tourism websites from three different perspectives: a) from a business, b) from a customer perspective and c) a combination of the previous two. The former implies that the on line quality is evaluated as superior according to where the business is in the transformation process: *if a site is only informative or whether it offers more advanced features such as on line booking services, etc.* (Larson and Ankomah, 2005; Hart et al., 2000[6]; O'Connor, 1999[7]; Doolin et al., 2002). Representatives of this strand: Doolin et al. (2002), extended and applied an internet commerce adoption metric (eMICA) developed by Burgess and Cooper (2000)[8] for benchmarking the relative maturity of 26 New Zealand's Regional Tourism Organizations (RTO) websites and concluded that the majority of them displayed moderate to high levels of interactivity. The customer perspective encompasses two different approaches: the first assesses the websites according to their level of customer support during the information searching process, thus following a "consumer behavior theory"; whereas the second according to their level of design features superiority. Finally, under the last approach the business and customer perspectives are combined together, within different contingent evaluation frameworks, ranging from technical approaches, such as the Balanced Scorecard (Morrison et al., 1999; Ismail et al., 2002; Feng et al., 2002; So and Morrison, 2004), to more theoretical ones, such as the Marketspace model (Blum and Fallon, 2002), which emphasized the marketing mix and the customer relationships.

Moreover, so far, research in assessing websites effectiveness in the tourism sector, has been mainly focused on either a) opinions of experts of tourist services providers (Chung and Law, 2003; Hudson and Lang, 2002; Jung and Butler, 2000) or b) end users (tourists) evaluations (e.g. Jeong et al., 2003, Tierney 2000)[9] or c) by applying quantitative measures (e.g., Scharl et al., 2004, Wöber, 2003). Regardless of whether the end users or the tourist experts have been focused upon, both directions' research findings seem to converge in one common admittance: *the importance of the online content* in terms of richness of information, features and services (Huizingh, 2000; Scharl et al., 2004; Cai et al., 2004b) and *content quality* (Aladwani and Pavia, 2002) as critical success factor of tourism websites. In particular, as far as destination portals are concerned, their content has been broadly recognised (Doolin et al., 2002, Cano and Prentice, 1998) as being responsible for creating the perceived image of the destination. Finally, there is also a recent research stream (Skadberg et al., 2005; Chen and Wells, 1999, Hoffman and Novak, 1996)[10] which supports that since tourism is mainly experiential, the overall web site effectiveness depends on the

flow experience of the online visitors in tourism destination websites.

Recently, Feng et al. (2002), Ismail et al. (2002) and So and Morrison (2004), in three papers, by means of content analysis, compared the performance of DMO websites of different countries, based on the Balanced Scorecard (BSC) approach, developed by Kaplan and Norton (1996)[11]. These studies acknowledge tourism website performance in a holistic way, encompassing four different perspectives. The first study compared 36 Chinese DMO websites to 30 US DMO websites and concluded that the latter were superior in terms of marketing strategies and destination information provided. The second study examined website's information content and photos from a cultural point of view, while the third one compared 15 East Asian NTO sites, concluding that none of them had been particular effective as an online marketing tool.

Finally, Mich et al. (2003, 2002) have developed a meta-model 2QCV3Q, to compare the regional tourist boards (RTB) websites in the area of Alps. In their approach, quality of web site has been identified as the ability to satisfy the needs and objectives of all the online users involved. Their model, by asking a set of questions, identifies seven dimensions of quality, according to which the tourism websites' overall quality was assessed, revealing a poor performance in terms of dissemination of information and use of modern technology.

From the above e-SQ and DMO literature, it can be concluded that regardless of the numerous different approaches developed through the last years, there still does not exist a detailed framework that provides a comprehensive understanding of e-SQ which could be used for the evaluation of websites and portals *independently* of sector of belonging. A common practice instead has been to tailor the different e-SQ models to the specific study under investigation.

DETERMINANTS OF NTO PORTALS SERVICE QUALITY ACROSS THE EU

The main objective of this study is to examine the characteristics of the NTO online offerings and to analyse which factors can explain the level of service quality observed. Our sample consists of the 25 EU official NTO portals, evaluated between June and July 2006. The latter organizations have been chosen, due to their unquestionable importance as primary suppliers of online information and services to market a destination and as coordinators of the other local/regional tourism authorities initiatives (Ismail et al., 2002; Cai et al., 2004a). By observing the global tourism statistics (United Nations Conference on Trade and Development, UNCTAD, 2005; World Tourism Organization, WTO, 2005), in terms of international arrivals and volume of tourist receipts, it was decided to focus on the whole population of EU states NTO portals since it was confirmed that the majority of the most significant tourism markets (e.g., France, Italy, UK, Spain, Germany, Austria, etc.) are found among those.

To the extent of our knowledge, no empirical study has defined and tested, through empirical analysis, any variables which could be particularly relevant to explain NTO portal service quality. Under the recognition that important regional differences do exist, four main country variables have been examined: affluence, tourism popularity, e-readiness and cultural richness.

It is widely believed that the extent of e-business adoption is associated with a country's economic development. For example, Di Gregorio et al. (2005) provide empirical evidence of e-business activity differences between high income nations and emerging markets. This disparity could support the initial claims that developing countries would benefit from the wide diffusion of the Internet and e-business. Different definition may be used to classify developed and emerging countries (e.g., the International Monetary Fund classification, the World Bank, the World Economic Outlook Report, etc.), this paper uses the 2005 Gross Domestic Product (GDP) per capita of the EU states, at purchase power parity, expressed in international $ (Euro monitor, 2006) to detect the "level of affluence" of each country. In this way it is possible to avoid that the results are dependent up on a specific definition. Based on the average GPD the EU states were dived into two different groups: affluent (less affluent) countries (see Table 1).

Along with the economic factor, a country's tourism industry and its popularity will likely influence NTO portals offerings. Buhalis and Deimezi (2004), explain that the inadequacy of the national planning process and the lack of infrastructures have affected the development of a comprehensive portal to promote Greek tourism. The popularity of a destination has been used as a proxy to enable a *first* appreciation of tourism industry. The popular (less popular) destinations (see Table 1) were identified by using the average number of tourist arrivals in the EU states for the year 2004 (WTO, 2005).

Certain academics (e.g., Di Gregorio et al., 2005), and consulting companies (e.g., Economic Intelligence Unit, Forester Research, etc.) have examined the extent to which "e-readiness" could be associated with the development of e-business adoption. Similarly, it could be the case that the "state of play" of a country's Information and Communication Technology (ICT) and the ability to use the latter, will explain difference in the on line offering of NTO portals. To examine this relation, the EU member states were divided into two groups: e-advanced (e-early stages) destinations (see Table 1) according to their e-readiness rankings, as emerged from the 2005 Economist Intelligence Unit study (Economist, 2005).

Apart from the country's e-readiness, "cultural richness" is a further variable that is supposed to have an impact on the present NTO offerings. In our case, the number of world heritages listed by the United Nations Education, Scientific and

Table 1. Proxy measures used to cluster the 25 EU states

EU member state	International tourist arrivals (1000) for 2004[a]	Destination tourism popularity above the EU average	GDP per capita at ppp in $ (2005)[b]	Levels of affluence above the EU average	Economist E-readiness classification 2005	2005 E-readiness classification above average	No of UNESCO heritages	Cultural richness
Austria	19.400	1	33.822	3	8	5	8	8
Belgium	6.710	2	31.196	3	8	5	9	8
Cyprus	2.349	2	21.602	4	n.a	7	3	8
Czech Republic	6.061	2	18.404	4	6	7	12	8
Denmark	3.358	2	34.673	3	9	5	4	8
Estonia	1.750	2	16.452	4	6	5	2	8
Finland	2.840	2	31.237	3	8	5	7	8
France	75.100	1	30.356	3	8	5	30	7
Germany	20.100	1	30.489	3	0	5	32	7
Greece	14.000	1	23.314	4	6	5	16	7
Hungary	12.200	2	16.852	4	6	7	8	8
Ireland	6.982	2	41.767	3	8	5	2	8
Italy	37.100	1	28.597	3	7	5	41	7
Latvia	1.080	2	12.666	4	5	7	2	8
Lithuania	1.491	2	14.236	4	5	7	4	8
Luxembourg	874	2	68.869	3	8	5	1	8
Malta	1.156	2	19.708	4	n.a	7	3	8
Netherlands	9.600	2	30.784	3	8	5	7	8
Poland	14.300	1	12.864	4	6	7	13	7
Portugal	11.600	2	19.387	4	7	7	13	7
Slovakia	1.401	2	16.168	4	6	7	5	8
Slovenia	1.499	2	21.846	4	6	5	1	8
Spain	53.600	1	26.642	3	0	5	39	7
Sweden	3.003	2	30.049	3	9	5	14	7
UK	27.800	1	30.648	3	9	5	27	7
mean	13.414		26.505		6		12	

Notes: 1 (2) means popular tourism (less popular tourism) countries; 3 (4) means affluent (less affluent) countries; 5 (6) means e-advanced (e-early stages) countries; 7 (8) means rich cultural (less cultural rich) countries; a) source: WTO , 2005; b) source: Euromonitor database, 2006.

Cultural Organization (UNESCO) has been used as a proxy (http://whc.unesco.org/en/list/) of "cultural richness". According to the average number of listed sites, the 25 EU states were divided into two groups: cultural rich (less cultural rich) destinations (see Table 1).

As no one of the empirical literature on DMO has examined the effects of the above factors on the e-quality of NTO portals and because there may be different competing explanations, the hypotheses have been stated in the null from:

- **Affluence levels:** The online offerings performance of NTO portals' is equal, in affluent destinations and in less affluent destinations, within the EU;

- **Tourism popularity:** The online offerings performance of NTO portals' is equal in popular tourist destinations and in less popular tourist destinations, within the EU;

- **E-readiness:** The online offerings performance of NTO portals' is equal in e-advanced destinations and less e-advanced destinations, within the EU;

- **Cultural richness:** The online offerings performance of NTO portals' is equal in cultural rich destinations and in less cultural rich destinations within the EU.

While the two control variables associated with H_1 and H_4 contribute to the assessment of a positive relationship between institutional factors (economic development and country's cultural richness) and online NTO performances, the variables associated with H_2 and H_3 might explain the extent to which tourism infrastructures and e-readiness, including Internet and ICTs infrastructure, are factors that contribute to the development of NTO tourism portals, providing clear implications for policy makers.

RESEARCH METHOD AND PERFORMANCE MEASUREMENT

In order to carry out the comparative analysis of the online offerings of the NTO portals in EU, content analysis was used to capture and quantify both the richness of the NTOs' information content and the number of useful services provided to the customers, which in turn shape important e-SQ dimensions, from a customer perspective. According to Weber (1985: 21–25), content analysis is process of creating and testing a coding instrument to identify the characteristics of a written message.

A prior-research driven approach (Boyatzis, 1998: 99) was followed in order to define the coding categories. The developed conceptual framework has emerged after taking into account the e-SQ literature discussed above (e.g., Kim et al., 2006), previous empirical studies on website evaluation (Mich and Franch, 2007), and best practices recommended by the World Tourist Organization (WTO, 2005). Together, it was generated a list of 129 attributes which were accommodated into 4 qualitative categories: *destination information, marketing, customer and technical perspective*, following the framework of the modified Balance Scorecard (BSC), as applied by So and Morrison (2004). The latter, was chosen due to its strong emphasis on customer service and marketing, both important features in evoking high levels of perceived e-SQ in tourism portals. Figure 1 and

Figure 1. Balance scorecard (BSC) framework (adapted from Ismail et al., 2002)

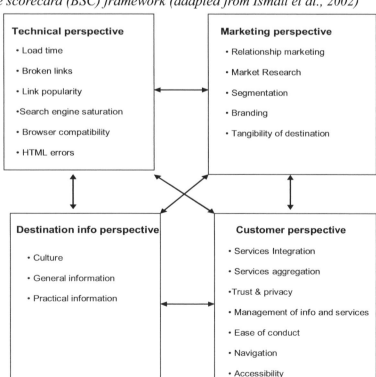

Table 2. List of performance items

	Frequency in percentage
Marketing perspective (43)	51
Segmentation	51
No hotel lodging alternatives	88
Spa	92
Fitness	60
Dining per categories	48
Nightlife	44
Kids corner	36
Youth section	32
Business tourism	84
City break	52
Gay/lesbian	32
Religious tours	32
Wedding organisations	20
Educational courses	36
Thematic forms of tourism	52
Tangibility of destination	58
Photos different landscapes, all regions	88
Maps	100
Photo gallery	76
Virtual tours	40
Video clips	52
Web cams	12
E-cards	40
Branding	59
Environment statements	20
Quality certification	28
Logo in homepage	100
Logo in other webpages	84
Information behind public entity	96
URL among the first 5 findings	76
Site popularity	60
Data on use	4
Relationship marketing	34
Customised research	32
Feedback forms	44
Sharing of information to counterpaters	52
News letters	72
Send comments	8
View reviews	12
Travel plans favourites	36
Memory settings	12
Marketing research, customer database	55
Links to lower level tourist organisations	84
Tracking country of origin	52
Portal versions according to country of choi	44
Registration within the site	76
Online surveys	24
On line competitions	48
Customer perspective (45)	47
Privacy and trust	24
Identification of information source	24
Un registration option	24
Statements of personal data privacy	36
Terms of use	44
Security certification	8
Last update date	8
Service integration	12
Accomodation booking on line	32
Holiday package on line	8
Air plane ticket on line	4
Other facilities on line	12
Track state of orders	8
Virtual community	8
Service aggregation	47
Native language expression	28
Press office	60
List of articles, books, guides	24
Weather forecast	60
Exchange convertor	64

	Frequency in percentage
Management of information	61
Option to search for lodging by type (e.g. stars)	72
Directions of how to reach destinations	36
List of "highlights" (e.g. main attractions)	56
Option to request material on line	56
Option to download on line	84
Printing options (e.g. full page, some areas etc.)	80
Audio	28
Route planner	40
Interactive maps	92
Information updated	52
FAQ section	40
Advanced search engine	100
Ease of contact	61
NTO address	80
NTO operating hours	28
Web-master e-mail	84
NTO telephone number	88
NTO fax number	76
Call centre	12
Navigability	73
Graphic design changes for each different section	76
Site map	68
Advanced search engine	40
Link avoiding homepage	84
Link to homepage from all pages	80
Principal elements visible before entire loading	84
Web site visible without images loaded	80
Accessibility	28
Information for disabled accessability in hotels	68
Portal version in "bigger fonts"	8
Seperate specialised accessibility section	8
Destination information (35)	67
Culture	76
Artistic heritage	100
Local culinary traditions	100
Local handicraft/trades	64
Local famous people	68
UNESCO listed sites	84
Local events	84
Food recipes	40
General information	66
Popular sports	56
Dining facilities	56
Natural assets	92
Political information	64
Religion	68
Economic information	40
information	76
Geographical information	96
Highlights for the next year	8
Practical information	65
Public transportation	100
Car rental	72
National public holidays	88
Opening/business hours	76
Pricing and payment methods	80
Currency information	76
Discounts	40
Custom/taxes information	68
Immigration/work permit	24
Entry requirements	84
Real estate information	4
Traffic & parking rules	68
Regulations for pets	52
Taxis	64
Voltage	72
Embassies and consulates	36
International phone access code	76
Climate	84
Emergency numbers	68

Table 2 illustrate the four categories and the full list of items, respectively.

Contrary to web evaluation based on a Likert type scale (Davidson and Yu, 2004; Morrison et al., 1999), a binary code was followed where a score of 1 was given if the item was available, and 0 if not[12]. According to the coding instrument's rules, multiple references of the same item were ignored. Following coding, the overall score (*Score*) for each of the three categories (j) was quantified as follows:

$$Score_j = \sum_k S_k / TOTS \qquad (1)$$

where: j = the perspective category, j = 1, 2, 3; k = the item subscript, k = 1, ….129; s_k = the number of items found in each NTO portal (answered as "yes"); TOTS = the total maximum number of possible items for each perspective (i.e. 45 for customer perspective). Based on this score, each portal, within each of the 3 perspectives (marketing, destination information and customer), was ranked in a descending order from 1 to 25, with means assigned to ties. In the case of the technical perspective, each portal has been ranked within each of the 6 technical criteria used, as illustrated in Table 3.

Kendall's Coefficient of Concordance (W) was calculated to test the degree of association among the 4 different rankings as follows (Siegel and Castellan, 1988: 271):

$$W = \frac{\sum_{i=1}^{N} (R_i - \overline{R})^2}{N(N^2 - 1)/12} \qquad (2)$$

where: N = the number of portals to be ranked; $\overline{R}_i$ = the average of the ranks assigned to the *ith* portal, $\overline{R}_i$ = the average (or grand mean) of the ranks assigned to a portal across all the categories. Since

the sample consisted of 25 EU NTO portals, this coefficient can be approximated by a chi-square distribution (X^2) with 24 degrees of freedom. Inter-coder reliability test (Krippendorff's *alpha* coefficient) has been performed in order to assess the consistency of the coding process.

FINDINGS AND ANALYSIS: DESTINATION INFORMATION CATEGORY

The results of the BSC approach to evaluate the EU NTO portals are summarised in Table 4. It emerges that Denmark achieved the best overall ranking (4.8), implying that currently the Dan-

Table 3. Technical rankings

NTO EU member state	HTML errors[a]		Compa tibility Problems[b]		Link Popularity[c]		Search Engine Saturation[d]		Down loaded time at 56K[e]		Broken Links[f]		Sum of Rankings
Netherlands	0	1	0	1	12.105	18	230.900	4	0,2	3	8	3	30,0
Poland	1	2	3	2	10.834	19	153.895	9	3,09	4	1	2	38,0
Czech Republic	3	4	8	7	76.155	7	96.028	12	0,02	1	21	8	39,0
Austria	1	2	14	12	101.019	3	145.404	10	19,37	13	17	6	46,0
Cyprus	2	3	3	3	17.937	15	58.818	14	18	11	0	1	46,0
Italy	6	7	12	10	56.231	8	2.492.975	2	17,76	10	26	11	48,0
Malta	1	2	7	6	31.427	11	177.388	8	26,98	14	25	10	51,0
France	2	3	4	3	86.426	6	58.169	15	14,73	6	72	19	52,0
Finland	2	3	0	1	33.628	10	98.689	11	39,69	17	26	11	53,0
UK	16	12	3	2	163.552	1	3.318.441	1	48,65	21	38	16	53,0
Lithuania	0	1	0	1	6.262	22	30.201	18	0,06	2	27	12	56,0
Denmark	11	10	6	5	154.463	2	186.448	6	74,12	23	26	11	57,0
Slovenia	0	1	10	8	6.283	21	36.699	16	7,2	5	17	6	57,0
Estonia	5	6	4	3	43.130	9	22.289	20	16,87	9	33	15	62,0
Germany	0	1	16	14	90.997	5	77.148	13	35,39	16	31	14	63,0
Slovakia	0	1	0	1	10.522	20	23.030	19	47,57	20	12	4	65,0
Greece	2	3	3	2	3.453	23	819	24	14,76	7	22	9	68,0
Portugal	4	5	5	4	12.205	17	230.330	5	45,84	19	67	18	68,0
Spain	48	16	29	16	93.293	4	177.489	7	42,55	18	18	7	68,0
Sweden	19	13	11	9	22.384	13	2.287	22	16,74	8	14	5	70,0
Latvia	2	3	8	7	523	25	59	25	18,61	12	8	3	75,0
Luxembourg	27	15	7	6	13.510	16	255.001	3	194,12	24	64	17	81,0
Belgium	9	9	13	11	23.522	12	1.180	23	34,56	15	29	13	83,0
Ireland	8	8	23	15	1.718	24	32.096	17	54,13	22	0	1	87,0
Hungary	24	14	15	13	21.189	14	5.650	21	241,22	25	38	16	103,0

Notes: a) refers to the number of errors, as estimated by www.netmechanic.com; b) refers to any unsupported Hypertext Markup Language (HTML) tags and attributes that block viewing on specific NTOs' browsers, as estimated by www.netmechanic.com; c) refers to the number of pages in each search engines index that contains a link to a portal's domain, as estimated by www. marketleap.com; d) refers to the number of pages a given search engine has in its index for the NTO website domain, as estimated by www.netmechanic.com; e) refers to the download times (seconds), as estimated by www.watson.addy.com; f) refers to the total links, as estimated www.netmechanic.com.

Table 4. Overall rankings through the BSC framework

EU Member state	URL	Marketing Ranking	Customer Ranking	Destination Info Ranking	Technical Ranking	Total
Denmark	http://www.visitdenmark.com	3	1	2,5	12,5	4,8
UK	http://www.visitbritain.com	1	2,5	7	9,5	5,0
Netherlands	http://www.holland.com	7,5	12,5	1	1	5,5
Austria	http://www.austria.info	9,5	5	7	4,5	6,5
Spain	http://www.spain.info	2	2,5	7	18	7,4
France	http://franceguide.com	4,5	8,5	18	8	9,8
Malta	http://www.visitmalta.com	4,5	15	13,5	7	10,0
Sweden	http://www.visit-sweden.com	9,5	8,5	7	20	11,3
Slovenia	http://www.slovenia.info	6	4	24	12,5	11,6
Czech Republic	http://www.cheztourism.com/	14	10	23	3	12,5
Ireland	www.discoverireland.com	11	11	4	24	12,5
Finland	http://www.visitfinland.com	16,5	18	7	9,5	12,8
Cyprus	www.visitcyprus.org.cy	16,5	22	10	4,5	13,3
Germany	http://www.germany-tourism.de	7,5	15	16	15	13,4
Hungary	http://www.hungary.com/	12	6	16	25	14,8
Belgium	http://www.visitbelgium.com	14	21	2,5	23	15,1
Estonia	http://www.visitestonia.com	20	12,5	16	14	15,6
Luxembourg	http://www.ont.lu	20	7	13,5	22	15,6
Slovakia	www.slovakiatourism.sk	20	17	11,5	16	16,1
Portugal	http://www.visitportugal.com	14	15	19,5	18	16,6
Poland	http://www.poland-tourism.pl	20	24	21,5	2	16,9
Italy	http://www.enit.it	20	19,5	25	6	17,6
Lithuania	http://www.travel.lt	24	19,5	19,5	11	18,5
Latvia	http://www.latviatourism.com	23	24	11,5	21	19,9
Greece	http://www.visitgreece.gr	25	24	21,5	18	22,1

ish portal is the most customer led, whereas the Latvian (19.9) and the Greek portal (22.1) occupy the last positions, with the latter being the worst of all in terms of the marketing perspective.

Kendall's coefficient of concordance was found W=0.410, considering the four rankings of the BSC approach, adjusted for ties, and equal to 0.647 excluding the technical ranking. It is evident that this value is not satisfactory, however X^2 (39.35) is statistically significant at 5 per cent level and it can support the conclusion that the Danish portal has the best performance in terms of the four perspectives combined.

Table 5 presents the descriptive statistics of our sample. The average scores in the three categories indicate that the NTOs' performance was higher in terms of Destination information in comparison to the Marketing and Customer categories of the BSC approach. Of the overall sub-categories of

the scoring list, "culture" and "navigability" are the ones with the highest performances averaging 76 and 73 per cent respectively (see Table 2 for the sub-totals and frequencies of the single items).

Figure 2 shows the distribution of Destination information scores across the 25 portals. It reveals that the NTO portals are performing quite similarly, implying high degrees of standardisation in the levels of information provided online. This pattern may be further investigated by considering Table 2. For example, as expected, the vast majority of NTO sites provide practical advices covering basic useful travelling information (e.g. transportation, public holidays, entry requirements, etc.). However, less than half of them (40%) show increased sensitivity for the tourists' needs by including useful tips, such as information regarding tourist discounts, or information

Table 5. Descriptive statistics

Perspectives	Minimum	Maximum	Mean	Std. Deviation
Marketing	0.28	0.77	0.507	0.146
Customer	0.29	0.73	0.478	0.130
Information	0.17	0.86	0.674	0.143
Technical	30.00	103.00	60.760	16.741

Figure 2. Distribution of BSC scores across portals

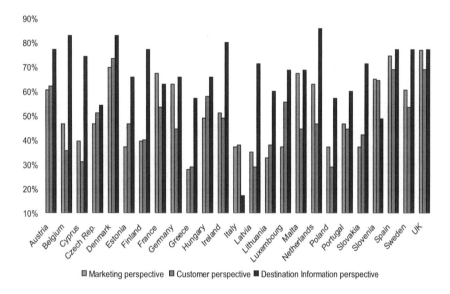

☐ Marketing perspective ☐ Customer perspective ■ Destination Information perspective

regarding foreign embassies and consulates in their country (36%).

The Dutch portal manages better to promote Holland through the provision of an impressively rich and well organised content. The practical advices provided go beyond the "typical" basic practical information before visiting the destination, covering aspects such as immigration and work permit regulations. The last place in this category is occupied by the Italian NTO portal since the latter fails completely to transmit a comprehensive picture about the diversity of the different Italian regions and it pays very limited attention to the Italian cultural assets such as local events. In addition, its content is poor and sometimes even outdated. By consulting the sub-category *Culture* (Table 2), it appears that EU members have understood the power of internet for marketing their own culture. All the websites maintain separate sections where the artistic heritage of the destination such as castles, churches, museums, as well as the local culinary traditions are thoroughly described. Moreover, the majority of them (21 portals) is in the position to provide an updated database, which covers the main incoming local events, with a particular emphasis on the small characteristic local festivals. Although it is evident that some destinations put more effort in marketing online their culture more extensively (e.g., Belgium, Netherlands, etc.), again it can be argued that the cultural cues used to promote a destination are characterised by relatively high degrees of standardisation. Only when it comes to examining the promotion of local handicrafts, trades and local food recipes, some higher degrees of individualism arise, with only 64% of them promoting the former and 40% of them providing the latter. Finally, interestingly enough, the relatively low destination information percentages of countries possessing rich cultural heritage such as Italy, France, Greece and Spain imply that the latter do not appear to leverage particularly successfully their NTO portals to promote it. Thus, it is confirmed the realisation of the Ismail et al., (2002: 175), that there is no evidence of particular effectiveness of NTO websites from destinations with high number of cultural attractions and resources. The latter statement has been tested statistically in section 6.

CUSTOMER PERSPECTIVE FINDINGS

Among the 25 portals, Denmark and UK scored higher within this category with the former having 33 out of the 45 identified items (73.3%) and the later having 31 (68.9%) respectively. Both these NTO have realised the importance of "one site shop" as a driver of superior customer service for the contemporary demanding and time sensitive visitors. Both of them are offering direct online booking for accommodation, holiday packages and even more specialised vacation items, such as theatre and other attraction tickets. In addition, the British portal supports the acquisition of airplane tickets and it is offering a well organised online shop, where buyers can track the state of their orders.

By consulting the sub-category *Privacy and trust* (Table 2), it emerges that a) a "terms of use" section, b) a "privacy statement" for the collection of personal data and c) a "security certification" are often missing. In particular, the lack of the above, combined with: "neglecting to mention the source of information provided" in 19 out of 25 portals (76%), and to "guarantee any last updating date for the site's content, antecedent

of the last 2 months" in a stunning: 23 out of 25 portals, definitely influence the building of trust between the entity behind the website and its online visitors. Since trust and control of online users have been regarded as key components of e-SQ (Parasuraman et al., 2005; Nysveen et al., 2003) there is an emerging margin for improvement.

The three web sites with the most disappointing performance in the customer perspective are the Latvian, the Polish and the Greek one (Figure 2). These portals can be regarded as "product driven" ones, where emphasis is given on the presentation of as much as possible information about the country, failing to organise this information and to "empower" their visitors, through the provision of advanced search engines which allow them to discover on their own *only* that kind of information they are mostly interested about.

Disappointing is the picture regarding the measures undertaken by the portals for assuring *accessibility*, accommodating different users' needs and capabilities. More specifically, while the majority of the websites under examination (17) include sufficient information regarding accessibility for travellers with special needs, only 2 of them (the Spanish and the British NTO) declare that their portals are adhering with the legal imperatives for accessibility according to the web content accessibility guidelines (http//w3.org). This is consistent with the findings of Williams et al. (2004) who found discouraging low levels of accessibility for tourism related websites in Germany and UK. A further category where the sample portals are performing particularly weakly is *service integration*, averaging 12 % across the total sample. Virtual communities are recognised as value added services (Nysveen et al., 2003; Hjalager, 2001) however, only 2 NTO websites (the Slovenian and the Irish one) are making use of them. As far as it concerns the category *management of information* the majority of portals (23 portals, or 92%) make extensive use of modern internet applications such as interactive maps, whereas less than half of them (9 portals or 36%)

offer a complete value added service including the provision of directions of *how* to reach different destinations and/or a route planner (10 portals, or 40%) and even fewer are providing directions for alternative ways of transporting. Finally, it is worthy mentioning that, regardless of the portals' large size, the majority of them (73%) include functions which enhance navigability.

MARKETING AND TECHNICAL PERSPECTIVE FINDINGS

As Figure 2 reveals, the UK NTO website has scored higher in the marketing category, with 33 out of the 43 examined items (76,7%) being present. It appears as highly interactive with strong brand identity and satisfactory information customisation and personalisation features. Moreover, its design effectively supports market research and targeted marketing activities, and finally it assists the tangibility of destination through the provision of a wide variety of helping cues. On the other hand, the Greek and the Lithuanian portal have the poorest on line presence in terms of marketing functions (27.9% and 32.6% respectively) and need urgently to improve their efforts in marketing segmentation, tangibility of destination and market research. Finally, many websites such as the NTO portals of Estonia, Italia, Poland, Luxembourg and Slovakia have scored equally low (37,2%) implying the existence of significant margins for improvement.

A closer examination of the single items highlights some specific features within the *relationship marketing* category. First of all, it can be argued that the websites employ relatively low levels of interactivity, with only 11 or 44% of them supporting online feedback forms, and only two of them (Slovenia and Portugal) including users' ratings on: a) price offers and/or b) usefulness of the information received. Once more, very few of them (only 3) seem to have realised the importance of "word of mouth" and provide the possibility to browse other users' experiences and comments on certain issues. Similarly, there have been detected varying levels of customisation and personalisation of information. In terms of personalisation items, the sample websites did not perform well since only 36% of them (9 portals) are allowing online visitors to select, organise, and store personal interest information into a "favourites section" and even less (12% or 3 portals) maintain in memory previous settings such as "choice of language".

As far as it concerns the *segmentation category*, the vast majority of them (23), in conformity with one of the strongest trends of the recent years, are providing extensive information for spas and fitness centres, in an attempt not only to satisfy better the needs of their online users, but also to target more effectively the most valuable market segments. To a further extent, slightly more than half of these portals (52%) are including a city break section, another important trend gaining popularity among the time sensitive tourists of nowadays. On the other hand, segmentation according to lifestyle is not extensively used. Indeed the provision of a separate nightlife section, with information regarding entertainment options shows a less strong trend (only: 44% or 11 portals). The other emerged targeted segment is business tourism, with 21 portals (84%), providing separate, specialised web-sites within their main portal.

In terms of the number and kind of cues used to enhance the *tangibility of the destination*, despite that almost every portal makes use of tools such as maps (100%) and photographs of landscapes of different regions (88%), other more sophisticated and advanced tools such as virtual tours (10 portals or 40%) or video clips (13 portals or 52%), and webcams (3 portals or 12%) are not yet fully employed.

Eight items have been used to examine whether the NTO are *branding* their site sufficiently. Among these: a logo is included in the homepage of all the portals (100%), as well as in the rest of pages (84%). However, the sites often miss a quality certification (only 7 out of 25 portals do have one), failing to assure their visitors for the content of the information provided. Finally, they hardly include data on their use, such as number of registered users, number of hits, etc. (1 out of 25 portals only). By consulting the *marketing research and customer database* category, it emerges that the majority of the NTO portals (76%) are maintaining a customer database since they allow their visitors to register online. A less popular way to gather personal data regarding their visitors is through online competitions (12 portals or 48%). In terms of market research and targeting: 52% of the websites (in total 13 portals) track the country of origin of the different visitors and 11 portals provide multiple versions of their website, with content adjusted to reflect the local tourist market conditions of each country.

As Table 3 reveals, the Dutch NTO portal was the one which scored higher in the technical perspective. Indeed, the latter portal gained the highest ranking position in terms of Hypertext Markup Language (HTML) errors and browser compatibility problems, an equally high classification in terms of broken links and overall downloaded time at a 56K speed connection (3rd position), and the 4th position in terms of search engine saturation (Table 3). On the other hand, the Hungarian website was rated as the least techni-cally sound NTO portal with serious delays in downloading time. Finally, the high positions of some of the accession states, such as the 2nd position of Poland, the 3rd position of Czech Republic in contrast to the lower classifications of more e-advanced nations such as Sweden and Ireland (Economist, 2005) support the claim that Internet empowers new players and boosts competitiveness regardless the smaller internet penetration rates of the latter.

HYPOTHESIS TESTING

The Wilcoxon-Mann Whitney has been calculated to test whether the online performance were equal in the 8 groups of countries defined in section 3. It emerged that the variable affluence (see Table 6), has a significant influence on the online performance in terms of marketing, destination information and customer perspective. On the contrary, the "affluence" variable does not have any significant influence on the online performance of the NTO portals in terms of technical perspective. The remaining three independent variables were not found to have a statistically significant influence on the NTO portals' online performance.

Table 6. Wilcoxon-Mann Whitney test

Perspectives	Groups	N	Mean Rank	Sum of Ranks	Z
Marketing	Affluent	13	16.31	212.0	-2.352**
	Less affluent	12	9.42	113.0	
Customer	Affluent	13	15.85	206.0	-2.017**
	Less affluent	12	9.92	119.0	
Information	Affluent	13	16.96	220.5	-2.817***
	Less affluent	12	8.71	104.5	
Technical	Affluent	13	13.31	173.0	-0.218
	Less affluent	12	12.67	152.0	

*Notes: ** and *** indicate statistical significance levels of 5 percent and 1 per cent , respectively, in two-tailed tests.*

Finally, a univariate correlation analysis was performed to assess the relationship between the four perspectives. All correlation coefficients were positive, except between customer and technical and between technical and destination information perspectives. Marketing was the most significant contributor to the total score at 0.907 (p<0.01) followed by the customer category at 0.765 (p<0.01). Moreover, a positive and high correlation (0.749) was found between the Marketing and the Customer perspective (p<0.01), a realistic result since e-marketing excellence by definition is closely related to customer orientation. The correlation among the other perspectives was low and insignificant.

CONCLUSION AND FURTHER RESEARCH

This study analyses the online offerings of 25 EU NTOs using a framework that captures four e-quality categories. It is found that NTOs have realised that by just including basic information on their websites and waiting for online visitors to arrive is not a viable solution anymore. However, even if the vast majority of them demonstrates "acceptable" levels of online performances significant margins for improvements do exist. In particular, relatively high degrees of standardisation were observed in the areas of: content of information and cultural cues used to promote the destination. This implies that the NTOs are failing, up to a certain extent, to create a "unique sales proposition" to promote their destination. In most of the cases, some basic features necessary to promote "trust" for the online users were missing, and basic features enhancing accessibility for *all* online users were almost absent. It can be argued that the use of a simple binary code offers a partial valuation of the on line service quality and uniqueness[13]. In particular, neither differences in the content itself nor accessibility of selected features are always captured by the presence of different attributes.

Nevertheless, this research is a necessary *first step* in order to make inferences about the current level of online offerings and e-quality provided by the NTO web sites and to investigate possible determinants of on line performances in terms of marketing, destination information and customer perspective. Moreover, *customer perceptions* of e-quality need to be explored in order to form a complete picture of online quality. Thus, future research could concentrate on increasing our understanding of: a) *which of the information and services present here contribute the most* in achieving a high level of overall service quality, as perceived by the end users and b) if the latter perceptions are *culturally sensitive*. A survey could be addressed to online users with the scope to capture which of the identified online services are rated as most important by prospect tourists when seeking tourism information on line and in what order of importance. The latter would be of particular value to the NTO, since it would reveal eventual gaps between their current offerings and customers preferences of on line value added services. A further interesting direction would be: to examine if these findings can be generalized in *other categories of tourism websites* more profit oriented.

REFERENCES

Aladwani, A. M., & Pavia, P. C. (2002). Developing and validating an instrument for measuring user perceived web quality. *Information and Management, 39*(6), 457-476.

Blum, V., & Fallon, J. (2002). Welsh visitor attraction websites: multipurpose tools or technological tokenism? *Journal of Information Technology and Tourism, 4*(34), 191-201.

Boyatzis, R. E. (1998). *Transforming qualitative information: thematic analysis and code development*, Thousand Oaks, CA: Sage Publications.

Buhalis, D., & Licata, M. (2002). The future of eTourism intermediaries. *Tourism Management, 23*(3), 207-220.

Buhalis, D., & Deimezi, O. (2002). E-tourism developments in Greece: information communication technologies adoption for the strategic management of Greek tourism industry. *Tourism and Hospitality Research, 5*(2), 103-128.

Cai, L. A., Card, J. A., & Cole, S. T. (2004a). Content delivery performance of world wide web sites of US tour operators focusing on destinations in China. *Tourism Management, 25*(2), 219-227.

Cai, L. A., Feng, R., & Breiter, D. (2004b). Tourism purchase decision involvement and information preferences. *Journal of Vacation Marketing, 10*(2), 138-148.

Cano, V., & Prentice, R. (1998). Opportunities for endearment to place through electronic "visiting" WWW homepages and the tourism promotion of Scotland. *Tourism Management, 19*(1), 67-73.

Chen, Q., & Wells, W. D. (1999). Attitude towards the site. *Journal of Advertising Research, 39*(5), 27-38.

Chung, T., & Law, R. (2003). Developing a performance indicator for hotel websites. *International Journal of Hospitality Management, 22*(1), 119-125.

Davidson, A. P., & Yu, Y. (2004). The internet and the occidental tourist an analysis of Taiwan's tourism websites from the perspective of western tourists. *Journal of Information Technology and Tourism, 7*(2), 91-102.

Di Gregorio, D., Kassicieh, S. K., & De Gouveva R. (2005). Drivers of e-business activity in developed and emerging markets. *IEE Transactions on Engineering Management, 52*(2), 155-166.

Doolin, B., Burgess, L., & Cooper, J. (2002). Evaluating the use of web for tourism marketing: a case study from New Zeland. *Tourism Management, 23*(4), 557-561.

Economist Intelligence Unit, IBM Institute for Business value (2005). *The 2005 e-readiness rankings*. White Paper. Retrieved June 23, 2006, from http://www.eiu.com/site_info.asp?info_name=eiu_2005_e_readiness_rankings.

Feng, R., Morrison, A. M., & Ismail, J. A. (2002). East versus West: a comparison of online destination marketing in China and the US. *Journal of Vacation Marketing, 10*(1), 43-56.

Garvin, D. A. (1984). What does "product quality" really mean? *Sloan Management Review,* Fall, *26*(1), 25-43.

Hjalager, A. (2001). Research and concepts: quality in tourism through the empowerment of tourists. *Managing Service Quality, 11*(4), 287-295.

Hudson, S., & Lang, N. (2002). A destination case study of marketing tourism on line: Banff, Canada. *Journal of Vacation Marketing, 8*(2), 155-166.

Huizingh, E. K. R. E. (2000). The content and design of web sites: an empirical study. *Information and Management, 37*(3), 123-134.

Ismail, J. A., Labropoulos, T., Mills, J. E., & Morrison, A. M. (2002). A snapshot in time: the marketing of culture in European Union NTO websites. *Tourism Culture and Communication, 3*(3), 165–179.

Jeong, M., Ohand, H., & Gregoire, M. (2003). Conceptualizing Web quality and its consequences in the lodging industry. *International Journal of Hospitality Management, 22*(2), 161-175.

Jung, T. H., & Butler, R. (2000). Perceptions of marketing managers of the effectiveness of the Internet in tourism and hospitality. *Journal of Information Technology and Tourism, 3*(3-4), 167-176.

Kim, M., Kim, J., & Lennon, S. (2006). Online service attributes available on apparel retail web sites: an E-S-QUAL approach. *Managing Service Quality, 16*(1), 51-77.

King, J. (2002). Destination marketing organizations-connecting the experience rather than promoting the place. *Journal of Vacation Marketing, 8*(2), 105-108.

Krippendorff, K. (1980). *Content analysis: an introduction to its methodology*, Beverly Hills, CA: Sage Publications.

Larson, C., & Ankomah, P. (2005). Evaluating tourism web site complexity. The case of international tourism in the U.S. *Service Marketing Quarterly, 26*(2), 23-37.

Lexhagen, M. (2004). The importance of value-added services to support the customer search and purchase process on travel websites. *Journal of Information Technology and Tourism, 7*(2), 119-135.

Liu, C., & Arnett, K. P. (2000). Exploring the factors associated with website success in the context of electronic commerce. *Information and Management, 38*(1), 23-33.

Madu, C. N., & Madu, A. A. (2002). Dimensions of e-quality. *International Journal of Quality & Reliability, 19*(3), 246-258.

Mich, L., Franch, M., & Gaio, L. (2002). *Evaluating and designing the quality of web sites*, Working paper, 70, DISA, University of Trento.

Mich, L., Franch, M., & Cilione, G. (2003). The 2QCV3Q quality model for the analysis of web site requirements. *Journal of Web Engineering, 2*(1-2), 115-127.

Mich, L., & Franch, M. (2007). *Un approccio multi-step per la valutazione dell'usabilità del sito web di una destinazione turistica.* Paper presented at the 4th Annual Conference of the Italian Marketing Academy: Il Marketing dei Talenti, Roma, 5-6 October.

Morgan, N., Pritchard, A., & Pride, R. (2002). *Destination branding. Creating the unique destination preposition*, Oxford: Butterworth-Heinemann.

Morrison, A. M., Taylor, S., Morrison, A. J., & Morrison, A. D. (1999). Marketing small hotels on the world wide web. *Journal of Information Technology and Tourism, 2*(2), 97-113.

Nysveen, H., Methlie, L. B, & Pedersen, P. E. (2003). Tourism web sites and value added services: the gap between customer preferences and web sites' offerings, *Journal of Information Technology and Tourism, 5*(3), 165-174.

O'Neill, M., Wright, C., & Fitz, F. (2001). Quality evaluation in online service environments. *Managing Service Quality, 11*(6), 402-417.

Parasuraman, A., Zeithaml, V. A., & Berry, L. L. (1988). SERVQUAL: a multi-item scale for measuring consumer perceptions of the service quality. *Journal of Retailing, 64*(1), 12-40.

Parasuraman, A., Zeithaml, V. A., & Malhotra, A. (2005). E-S-QUAL: A multiple-item scale for assessing electronic service quality. *Journal of Service Research, 7*(3), 213-233.

Sainaghi, R. (2006). From contents to processes: versus a dynamic destination management model. *Tourism Management, 27*(5), 1053-1063.

Santos, J. (2003). E-service quality: a model of virtual service quality dimensions. *Managing Service Quality, 13*(3), 233-246.

Scharl, A., Wober, W. K., & Bauer, C. (2004). An integrated approach to measure web site effectiveness in the European hotel industry. *Journal of Information Technology and Tourism*, *6*(4), 257-271.

Siegel, S., & Castellan, N. J. Jr. (1988). *Non parametric statistics for behavioral sciences*, Second edition, McGraw-Hill international editions.

Sigala, M. (2004). Measuring ASP service quality in Greece. *Managing Service Quality*, *14*(1), 103-104.

So, S., & Morrison, A. M. (2004). Internet marketing in tourism in Asia: an evaluation of the performance of East Asian National Tourism Organization web sites. *Journal of Hospitality & Leisure Marketing*, *11*(4), 93-118.

Skadberg, Y. X., Skadberg, A. N., & Kimmel, J. R. (2005). Flow experience and its impact on the effectiveness of a tourism website. *Journal of Information Technology and Tourism*, *7*(34), 147-156.

Turban, E., King, D., & Viehland, D. (2004). *Electronic commerce 2004: a managerial perspective*, Upper Saddle River, New Jersey: Pearson education, Inc.

UNCTAD (2005), *Taking off: E-tourism opportunities for developing countries*, Chapter 4, United Nations Conference on Trade and Development, e-commerce and development information economy report 2005. Retrieved April 01, 2006, from http://www.unctad.org/en/docs/sdteecb20051ch4_en.pdf.

Weber, R. P. (1985). *Basic Content Analysis*, 49 Beverly Hills, CA: Sage Publications.

Williams, R., Rattray, R., & Stork, A. (2004). Website accessibility of German and UK tourism information sites. *European Business Review*, *16*(6), 577-589.

Wöber, K. W. (2003). *Evaluation of DMO web sites through interregional tourism portals: a European cities tourism case example*. Paper submitted for the 2003 ENTER Conference, January 29-31, Helsinki. Retrieved April, 10, 2006, from http://tourism.wuwien.ac.at/lehrv/lven/03ws/vk5/EuropeanCitiesTourismPortal.pdf.

World Tourism Organization (2005). *Evaluating and improving websites*. The Tourism Destination Web Watch' Report. Retrieved March, 22, 2006, from http://www.world-tourism.org.

Yoo, B., & Donthu, N. (2001). Developing a scale to measure perceived quality of an internet shopping site (SITEQUAL). *Quarterly Journal of Electronic Commerce*, *2*(1), 31-46.

Zeithaml, V. A., Parasuraman, A., & Malhotra, A. (2002). Service quality delivery through websites: a critical review of extant knowledge. *Journal of the Academy of Marketing Science*, *30*(4), 362-375.

Zhu, F. X., Wymer, W., & Chen, I. (2002). IT-based services and service quality in consumer banking. *International Journal of Service Industry Management*, *13*(1), 69-90.

ENDNOTES

[1] NTO is defined by WTO, (1996)as: *"An autonomous body of public, semi-public or private status, established or recognised by the state as the body with competence at the national level for the promotion and in some cases, marketing of inbound international tourism"* as cited in Law *et al.*, 2004:100

[2] cited in Santos, 2003:236

[3] cited in Santos, 2003:235

[4] cited in Sigala, 2004: 105

[5] cited in Zeithmal *et al.*, 2002: 366

[6] cited in Blum and Fallon, 2002:193

[7] cited in UNCTAD, 2005:159

[8] cited in Doolin *et al.*, 2002:558

[9]   cited in Scharl *et al.*, 2004: 258

[10]   cited in Skadberg *et al.*, 2005: 148

[11]   cited in So and Morison, 2004:101

[12]   The material analyzed consisted of the English homepage including links, pictures and text information. However, links as hypertexts within a unique resource locator (URL) that would lead to a separate and independent web page, were not further considered. Neither it was analyzed information accessible to registered users.

[13]   We thank one of the reviewers for this observation.

This work was previously published in the International Journal of Information Systems in the Service Sector, Volume 1, Issue 3, edited by J. Wang, pp. 65-82, copyright 2009 by IGI Publishing (an imprint of IGI Global).

Chapter 4.18
Exploring the Adoption of Technology Driven Services in the Healthcare Industry

Umit Topacan
Bogazici University, Turkey

A. Nuri Basoglu
Bogazici University, Turkey

Tugrul U. Daim
Portland State University, USA

ABSTRACT

Recent developments in information and communication technologies have helped to accelerate the diffusion of electronic services in the medical industry. Health information services house, retrieve, and make use of medical information to improve service quality and reduce cost. Users—including medical staff, administrative staff, and patients—of these systems cannot fully benefit from them unless they can use them comfortably. User behavior is affected by various factors relating to technology characteristics, user characteristics, social environment, and organizational environment. Our research evaluated the determinants of health information service adoption and analyzed the relationship between these determinants and the behavior of the user. Health information service adoption was found to be influenced by service characteristics, user characteristics, intermediary variables, facilitating conditions, and social factors.

INTRODUCTION

The healthcare industry has grown rapidly over the past three decades and projected growth is likely to continue or even expand in the coming decades. As a result it is facing significant challenges on a number of fronts: healthcare reimbursement is decreasing, demand for larger volumes of healthcare services, and increased pressure to publicly report quality data are a few of the factors driving change. While the healthcare industry has been slow to adopt technology, it will be forced to do so in the coming decade to meet not only the known challenges identified above but also other challenges that have not yet been identified in this rapidly changing marketplace.

Health expenditures per capita, as a percent of gross domestic product (GDP), doubled between 1970 and 2001 in the United States for a total expenditure of $14.1 trillion in 2001 (Levit, Smith, Cowan, Lazeby, Sensening, & Catlin, 2003). This growth is driven by a number of factors, the primary drivers being increased demand for healthcare services and increasing cost of services. The number of Americans over the age of 65 is projected to increase by a factor of 2.5 by 2040 (Lee & Tuljapurkar, 1994). As a result of improved economic and technical environments, these "baby boomers" will not only increase the total volume of healthcare services provided (Reinhardt, 2000) but also drive the type of healthcare services required. Baby boomers also have more disposable income than previous generations and as a result elect to have more elective procedures than any generation before them (Knickman, Hunt, Snell, Marie, Aleczih, & Kennell, 2003).

In the healthcare sector, electronic information and communication technologies are intensively used to provide and support healthcare operations (Hsieh, Hjélm, Lee, & Aldis, 2001). However, compared to other industries diffusion of such technologies have been slow in the healthcare sector. This article focuses on this problem and identifies factors that may influence the adoption of such services. Telemedicine, and specifically remote monitoring, was picked as the case to analyze in this article. Telemedicine systems were deployed in many medical fields. Remote monitoring systems were developed to capture disease specific measurements electronically. For example, data from insulin-dependent diabetes (Biermann, Dietrich, Rihl, & Standl, 2002) and asthma patients (Glykas & Chytas, 2004) are being captured remotely. Also, some systems are used

for consultation purposes (Berghout, Eminovic, Keizer, & Birnie, 2007).

Therefore, this research will have the following objectives

1. To search and find major determinants of health information service adoption among users (medical staff, administrative staff and patients)
2. To find individual, social, service and technological components of adoption
3. To assess desirability of a service electronic interface prototype
4. To establish a more general framework that can be tested statistically in future studies

In this study, we developed an electronic health service prototype for patients suffering from diabetes and obesity where its foundation had been set in preliminary work (Topacan, Basoglu, & Daim, 2008). Patient data is collected through various devices, such as a mobile phone, stethoscope, and glucose meter. Collected data is then stored on a medical server. Healthcare providers can monitor the patients through this system and make suggestions as necessary. As a result, we found that health information service adoption decisions of users were influenced by service characteristics, user characteristics, intermediary variables, facilitating conditions, and social factors.

LITERATURE REVIEW

Adoption Theories

Service adoption is influenced by various factors including user characteristics and requirements, service characteristics, and social factors. During the past decades, many theoretical models were developed by researchers to explain the human behaviors in the adoption process. Theory of Reasoned Action (TRA) (Fishbein & Ajzen, 1975) is one of the well known models. Fishbein and Ajzen (1975) used two main constructs, namely attitude toward behavior and subjective norm, to predict the behaviors. Following the TRA model, many researchers attempted to expand it by adding new constructs or by applying it in different contexts. Theory of Planned Behavior (TPB) (Ajzen, 1991) was developed by adding perceived behavioral control to the TRA (Figure 1). Technology Acceptance Model (TAM) (Davis, 1989) was applied in the IS context to predict technology acceptance. TPB and TAM (Figure 2) are just two of such models expanding TRA. According to Davis (1989), two fundamental determinants of system use are perceived ease of use and perceived usefulness. The relative strength of usefulness-utilization relation is stronger than that of the relationship between ease of use and utilization (Davis, 1989). These findings are validated in many different studies (Venkatesh & Davis, 2000; Chau & Hu, 2002).

Healthcare Systems

Healthcare providers use various technologies to decrease cost, increase access to healthcare and improve quality in the medical services (Gagnon et al., 2003). Telemedicine is one of these technologies that enable "remote medical procedures and examinations between patients and medical providers via telecommunication technologies such as the Internet, or telephone" (Al-Qirim, 2007). Chau and Hu (2002) studied healthcare professionals' decisions regarding acceptance of telemedicine. They compared TRA and TAM and found that TAM is a more suitable model than TRA in predicting the technology acceptance in the medical sector (Chau & Hu, 2002). Others found factors that influence acceptance of both medical providers and patients. How the service is perceived and used by the users significantly affects adoption process.

With the rapid development of telecommunication systems, intelligent monitoring and control systems have become the major application areas of telemedicine. Such applications include 'Smart homes' for telecare by means of movement detectors, oxymeters, tansiometers, and various other devices (Rialle, Lamy, Noury, & Bajolle, 2003), such as a ring-sensor that monitors patient's blood oxygen saturation (Yang & Rhee, 2000) and a Web-based electrocardiogram monitoring application facilitating collection, analysis and storage of patient data (Magrabi, Lovell, & Celle, 1999). Many different devices and techniques are used to collect more accurate patient information. A spoken dialogue system was designed by Giorgino et al. (2005) to test the reliability of a speech recognition system. Finally, compared to traditional patient care, telemedicine systems provide many benefits to the physicians and patients. Brink, Moorman, Boer, Pruyn, Verwoerd, and Bemmel (2005) found electronic health information and monitoring systems help physicians in early detection of occurring head and neck cancer problems. Telemedicine systems are reported to reduce number of clinic visits significantly (Chae, Lee, Ho, Kim, Jun, & Won, 2001).

Figure 1. Theory of planned behavior (Ajzen, 1991)

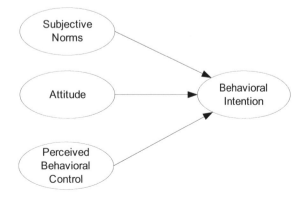

Figure 2. Technology acceptance model (Davis, 1989)

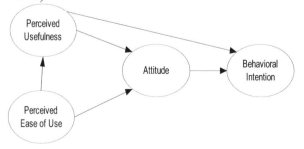

Factors Influencing Adoption

Effort expectancy, defined as "the degree of ease associated with the use of the system," (Venkatesh, Morris, Davis, & Davis, 2003) is one of the factors related to service characteristics. The more users think that the service is complex to use, the slower their adoption. Also, compatibility, which is defined as "the degree to which an innovation is perceived as being consistent with the existing practices, values, needs and experiences of the healthcare professional," influences acceptance of information and communication technologies in the case of occupational therapists (Schaper & Pervan, 2003). Besides, availability, quality, and value of the information provided by the service are other important characteristics (Aubert & Hamel, 2001). In addition, some of the adoption factors are related to individual characteristics. Chen, Yang, Tang, Huang, and Yu (2008) studied user specific characteristics such as age, educational level, and job experience to explore the intention of nurses towards Web-based learning. Also, user satisfaction which is defined as "the overall evaluation of a user's experience in using the system and

the potential impact of the system," significantly influences the adoption process (Yusof, Kuljis, & Papazafeiropoulou, 2008). Moreover, users' intrinsic motivation about adoption and perceptions about ease of use are influenced by the satisfaction of the user with the medical care (Wilson & Lankton, 2004). Apart from service and users, adoption is influenced by the organizational, environmental, or external characteristics as well. Rewarding and financial incentives were found to accelerate adoption of computerized physician order entry with clinical decision support systems (Simon, Rundall, & Shortell, 2007). Gagnon et al. found that social norms are one of the significant predictors of physicians' intention toward using medical technology (Gagnon et al., 2003). Table 1 summarizes the factors cited in the literature.

METHODOLOGY

Research Method

Prior to the study, a health information service prototype was developed for patients and their healthcare providers. The service was designed to

Table 1. Factors influencing adoption

Class	Literature
User Characteristics	Aubert & Hamel, 2001; Bruner & Kumar, 2005; Chang, Hwang, Hung, Lin, & Yen, 2007; Chau & Hu, 2002; Chen et al., 2008; Dishaw & Strong, 1999; Gagnon et al., 2003; Schaper & Pervan, 2003; Thompson et al., 1991; Venkatesh & Davis, 2000; Venkatesh et al., 2003; Wilson & Lankton, 2004; Yusof et al., 2007
Service Characteristics	Aubert & Hamel, 2001; Bruner & Kumar, 2005; Chang et al., 2007; Dishaw & Strong, 1999; Karahanna, Straub, & Chervany, 1999; Liu & Ma, 2005; Schaper & Pervan, 2003; Thompson et al., 1991; Tung et al., 2008; Venkatesh & Davis, 2000; Yusof et al., 2008
Ease of Use	Aubert & Hamel, 2001; Bruner & Kumar, 2005; Chang et al., 2007; Dishaw & Strong, 1999; Chen et al., 2008; Chau & Hu, 2002; Karahanna et al., 1999; Liu & Ma, 2005; Schaper & Pervan, 2003; Taylor & Todd, 1995; Thompson et al., 1991; Tung et al., 2008; Venkatesh & Davis, 2000; Venkatesh et al., 2003; Wilson & Lankton, 2004
Social Factors	Aubert & Hamel, 2001; Chau & Hu, 2002; Karahanna et al., 1999; Schaper & Pervan, 2003; Taylor & Todd, 1995; Thompson, et al., 1991; Venkatesh & Davis, 2000; Venkatesh et al., 2003
Usefulness	Aubert & Hamel, 2001; Bruner & Kumar, 2005; Chau & Hu, 2002; Chen et al., 2008; Dishaw & Strong, 1999; Karahanna et al., 1999; Liu & Ma, 2005; Schaper & Pervan, 2003; Taylor & Todd, 1995; Tung et al., 2008; Venkatesh & Davis, 2000; Venkatesh et al., 2003; Wilson & Lankton, 2004; Yusof et al., 2008
Facilitating Conditions	Aubert & Hamel, 2001; Chang et al., 2007; Gagnon et al., 2003; Karahanna et al., 1999; Schaper & Pervan, 2003; Thompson, et al., 1991; Venkatesh et al., 2003;

- Collect patient data via various devices like stethoscope, treadmill, bascule, mobile phone
- Support collecting patient information and transmitting to the healthcare providers
- Facilitate the early detection of health problems by means of monitoring patient data

Qualitative research method was applied in the study to analyze the topic and to take advantage of interviewees' creative ideas and experiences. Semi-structured open-ended questions were asked to the potential users, physicians, and nurses. The interviewee list was prepared such that distributions of gender, age, and work experience were balanced. At the beginning of the interview, interviewees were informed about the service with a presentation that takes approximately 5 minutes. After presentations, physicians used the prototype developed for physicians and potential users the one developed for them. Finally, the interview was conducted by asking 14 questions (see Appendix A for questions).

In the analysis phase, the following steps have been realized

- Interviews' audio-records were deciphered and written in a file sentence by sentence.
- The sentences were examined so that we can extract casual relationships where an outcome is attributed by one or more factors and consequently dependent and independent variables were set. A sort of modified attribution coding has been realized (Silver, 2004). The variables list also grew out of this conception.
- A second expert also repeated the same relationship coding. In case of any discrepancy, a discussion has occurred to resolve the conflict.
- All produced casual relationships that were weighted based on how critical they were perceived by the interviewees. The weight was accepted as 1 by default. If the participant mentioned the same factor more than once or gave special emphasis, the relationship was assigned a score of 1.5.
- After content analysis and coding, the relationship scores were summed and divided by total weights, and depicted in Table 5 for further analysis.

Proposed Service

A home based telemonitoring service was designed for obesity and diabetic patients. The service (Figure 3) mainly consisted of

- Hypothetical devices that were capable of sending data via Bluetooth technology
  ○ Treadmill for cardio information
  ○ Bascule for weight information
  ○ Stethoscope for blood pressure
  ○ Glucose meter for blood glucose level
- Prototype of the patients' application developed for mobile devices to collect information about patient

Figure 3. Proposed service

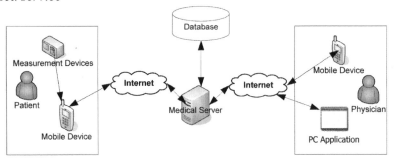

- Prototype of the physicians' application developed for mobile devices to get patient information
- Prototype of the PC application installed in the desktop computer of physicians to monitor patient status
- A medical server to store and manage patient data collected from various sources

Both the patients' and physicians' prototypes work as follows:

The mobile device reads the menu to patient/physician. The patient/physician selects operation by pronouncing the operation name and saying the keyword "OK." The service listens the voice of patient/physician and syntheses it. After the service hears "OK," it goes onto the next step based on the selected operation. Thus, a dialogue occurs between patient/physician and the service. In Appendix B, many typical dialogue examples have been given. Table 2 shows the functions of the electronic service.

The proposed system also has reminder services for both patients and physicians. If the patient takes medicine at regular times, the service warns him or her when this time comes. Also, if the patient does not enter any information at a specific time, the service prompts him or her to enter. Moreover, physicians can define reminders based on specific patient data. As an example, they can

Figure 4. PC application screen

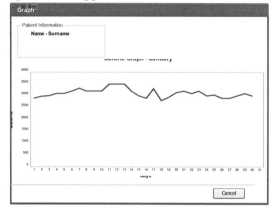

define so that the service can warn them when the patient's blood glucose level decreases to below "3 mmol/l" (dialogue and sample warning texts are in the Appendix B). Developed PC application prototype enables physician to monitor all of the patient's data, such as what the patient eats, how much calorie he or she gets, and what exercises he or she does. Figure 4 shows a sample screen of the prototype. In this screen, physicians can generate calorie, fat, protein, blood sugar, and weight graphs of the patient for a specific period.

RESULTS

Profile of Interviewees

Twenty-five people participated in this study. Educational level, age group, gender, computer literacy, and mobile phone experience variables were taken into consideration in the selection process. Age of the interviewees ranged between

Table 2. Menu of the services

Patients Menu	Physicians Menu
- Enter Meal - Enter Information ---- Enter movement or exercise ---- Enter Trauma ---- Enter pain ---- Enter drug ---- Return main menu - Meal Suggestion - Get Calorie Information - Exit.	- Calorie Information - Blood Glucose Information - Blood Pressure Information - Exit

Table 3. Interviewees' profile

	Number	Average Age (in years)	Computer Experience (in years)	Mobile Phone Experience (in years)
Doctor	6	40	18	10
Nurse	2	32	8	7
Potential User	17	27	10	9
Total	25	31	12	9

22 and 50. Fifteen were female and 10 were male. Educational level of the sample consisted of high school graduates, university graduates, and graduate students. Table 3 contains details about the profile of interviewees.

Findings

Service Characteristics

Service characteristics should match the user needs and requirements for better performance and effortless adoption (Goodhue, 1995).

Content: Potential users attempt to use services that meet their needs and requirements. Thus, required information content differs based on doctors' area of specialization and patients' disease types in the case of health information services. As an example, general surgery doctors need cardio information and diabetic patients show concern for blood glucose level. One of the comments was:

...As a general surgeon, I do not care what patient eats or drinks. I just care about his/her blood pressure, electrocardiogram ... if I were an internal specialist; I probably would use the service because information content fits with an internal specialist's or a dietician's data requirements. (Male, Doctor, 32)

An anesthesia expert said the following about the content;

... I do not care about the weight, the calories, or the blood pressure. Pruritus, headache, and nausea information are more useful in my profession. (Female, Doctor, 32)

Users think that appropriate, comprehensive, and quality content improve the usefulness of the service. The relationship between content quality and usefulness is also supported in the literature (Ozen & Basoglu, 2006).

Cost: One of the major predictors of behavior intention to use an IS system is the perceived cost

(Mathieson, Peacock, & Chin, 2001). Tung, Chang, and Chou (2008) defined cost as the monetary expense for using the electronic information system. It negatively affects the adoption of the service. One of the participants said the following:

... my usage preference of the service depends on the cost of it. If it costs much, I do not prefer to use it. (Male, Potential User, 25)

Another comment is given below:

If the cost of using the service exceeds the cost of visiting a doctor, I prefer face-to-face communication with a doctor. (Female, Potential User, 23)

Based on the participants' comments, the more costly the service, the less people prefer to use it. Thus, the findings about the cost were parallel with the literature (Tung et al., 2008).

Sound quality: The voice used in the mobile device to communicate with the patient/physician was that of a mechanical male. Most of the participants disliked the voice and proposed a more human one.

The voice of the service is mechanical and hoarse. Sometimes, it is very difficult to understand what it says. (Female, Potential User, 30)

Also, another comment from a participant:

It should be a female voice. (Male, Potential User, 30)

Participants are more comfortable with a non-mechanical female voice in the conversation with mobile device.

Security: Security affects the adoption of IT services (Cheng, Lam, & Yeung, 2006). Security is the condition of protecting user specific data against others.

Security is very important for me. I do not prefer to share the data that shows my health status with others. (Male, Potential User, 47)

Mobility: Users can benefit from a mobile service anywhere at any time. According to Klein-rock (1996), two of the well-known dimensions of mobility are time and place independence. What participants said about the mobility also supports these findings. Especially, doctors pay more attention to the mobility characteristics of the service in the adoption process because they could reach patient data even if they were outside of the hospital. One of the doctors commented about mobility:

I may refer this service to my colleagues because doctors can monitor their patients on the weekends and holidays. You are not confined to office hours to access the patient information. (Female, Doctor, 32)

Mobility affects usefulness of the service in a positive way. Another comment about mobility indicated:

... there are similar services on the Internet. You enter what you eat to the application and it calculated how many calories it has. The most significant advantage of the proposed service is that it can be used in a mobile device. You can get advice whenever you need." (Female, Doctor, 37)

Thus, mobile applications were found more useful by the potential users because they could use these applications whenever the need arose.

Time factor: Time factor is a person's belief about the time spent interacting with the service and the response time of the service concerning patient status. If entering data to the service takes too long, users prefer seeing the doctor. Biermann et al. (2002) also found that 30% of the patients prefer entering extra data into a system if it is not time-consuming.

... the time I spend during data entrance affects my usage decision. If I spend a lot of time while entering information about me, I would not prefer using it. I visit the doctor instead of using it. (Female, Potential User, 23)

Participants emphasized that time is a significant factor that affects adoption. Thus, designers should develop services that do not require much time. Users do not prefer to spend much time using the service.

User Characteristics

Health status: With some health conditions, like chronic illness, patients need more healthcare than normal conditions. Although Wilson and Lankton (2004) did not find a strong relationship between patients' healthcare need and intention to use provider-delivered e-health, participants in the study would use an e-health service if they had a disease.

I do not need to use the service because my health status is good. However, I wish to use it on account of ill health. (Male, Potential User, 47)

Age: Behavior of the user toward computer use is also influenced by the user's age (Liu, Pothiban, Lu, & Khamphonsiri, 2000). Chen et al. (2008) studied age as a determinant of intention of nurses toward Web-based learning. Others examined age as a moderator variable in the technology adoption context (Chau & Hu, 2002; Venkatesh et al., 2003). The following is one of the participants' comments about age:

I do not need the help of others while using the service. I think all of the doctors can use it except aged ones. (Male, Doctor, 50)

In the study, it was found that both potential users and doctors considered age as a factor that affects effortless use of the service. It is a general belief that older people would have difficulties adopting or using a technological device.

Users' time constraint: Participants think that people who do not have enough time to visit a doctor may prefer to use the service.

Hard-working people who do not spare time to visit a doctor, but they want to be under control of the doctor may prefer to use. (Male, Potential User, 47)

Subsequently, in addition to service-related time factors like quick data entry and rapid response, users' time limitations also affect the attitude of users toward using health services.

Intermediary Characteristics

Usefulness: Usefulness is the key determinant of attitude in the technology acceptance research field. Davis (1989) defined usefulness as "the degree to which a person believes that using a particular system would enhance his or her job performance," and found that usefulness is the strongest predictor of behavioral intention. Many researchers support Davis' findings about usefulness (Taylor & Todd, 1995; Venkatesh et al., 2003). Venkatesh et al. (2003) called usefulness as performance expectancy and defined it as "the degree to which an individual believes that using the system will help him or her to attain gains in job performance." One of the comments of the participants about usefulness is:

I ask people who use the service for its functionalities and try to understand how I can benefit from it in my job. Then, I make a decision whether or not to use the service. (Female, Nurse, 25)

Another comment:

If I think that information given from the service is useful for me, I start using the service. (Male, Potential User, 25)

Many comments were about the usefulness of the service. Therefore, it can be said that health information service users pay great attention to how the service would improve their job performance. These findings are in parallel with previous research findings (Davis, 1989; Taylor & Todd, 1995; Venkatesh et al., 2003).

Ease of use: Perceived ease of use (EoU) defined as "the degree to which a person believes that using a particular system would be free of effort" is one of the core constructs in TAM (Davis, 1989). Significant effect of EoU on behavior intention was also confirmed by many other researchers (Taylor & Todd, 1995; Venkatesh & Davis, 2000). Moreover, comments of potential users about the EoU supported these findings. Two of these comments are given below:

There are some questions in my mind. One of them is about ease-of-use. Effortless use of the service affects my intention about service usage. (Male, Potential User, 25)

... the more the service is simple and easy to use, the more people will intend to use it. (Male, Doctor, 50)

Social Influence

Social influence contains three main constructs: subjective norms defined as "The person's perception that most people who are important to him think he should or should not perform the behavior in question" (Ajzen, 1991), social factors, which is "The individual's internalization of the reference group's subjective culture, and specific interpersonal agreements that the individual has made with others, in specific social situations" (Thompson, Higgins, & Howell, 1991), and image defined as "The degree to which use of an innovation is perceived to enhance one's image or status in one's social system" (Moore & Benbasat, 1991; Venkatesh et al., 2003). In the study, eight of the interviewees answered the question that stated "Do you attempt to use the service if you notice someone who uses it?" as follows:

I try the service if I see someone who uses it. (Male, Doctor, 50)

In the study, participants referred to the subjective norms and image constructs of social influence. People are influenced by others' opinions and behaviors. People may use a service if he or she believes that becoming one of the service users will improve his or her social status.

Facilitating Conditions

User guidance: In the previous studies, facilitating conditions were found significant when they were examined with intermediary variables like age or experience. For example, it was found that they only matter for older users (Venkatesh et al., 2003). However, in the research, participants did not mention age or other variables when talking about the facilitating conditions. They indicated that all of the users need some help to use the service:

Users may need a user's guide that explains how to use the service. (Female, Potential User, 22)

Table 4. Weights of health service adoption taxonomy

Class	Study
Service Characteristics	55%
User Characteristics	26%
Intermediary	8%
Social Factors	6%
Facilitating Conditions	5%

DISCUSSION

As a result of the data gathered through these interviews, we propose a health service adoption taxonomy, which is shown in Figure 5 and the weights of variables in Table 4. It has been produced with the constructs that were found significant by the participants and researchers cited in this article.

According to the taxonomy, health service adoption has five main aspects: service characteristics, user characteristics, intermediary variables, social factors, and facilitating conditions. Three of these aspects contain some subcategories. While cost, content, sound quality, security, mobility, and time factor constitute subcategories of the service characteristics, health status, age, and time constraint compose users' sub categories.

Figure 5. Proposed health service adoption taxonomy

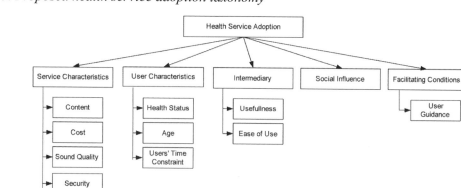

Figure 6. Propositions for future research

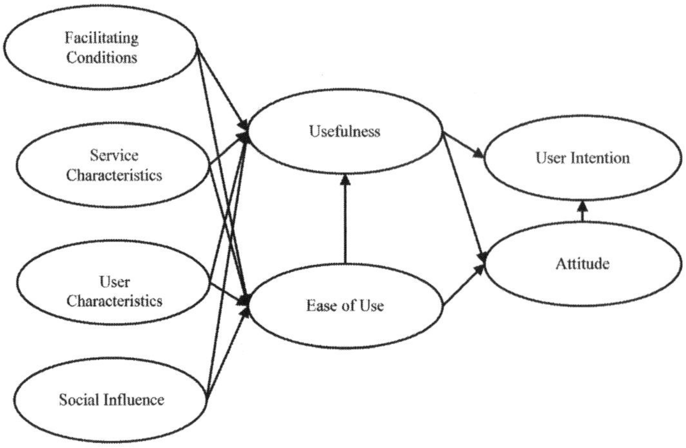

Usefulness and EoU are two of the intermediary variables.

Finally, a theoretical framework is developed (Figure 6). This framework draws upon both prior research, such as TAM and TRA, and the findings of this study. A larger scale data would help us to test the relationship proposed in this framework.

We found that service characteristics have more impact on usefulness when compared with other variables. Rich and accurate content were indicated to be more useful by the interviewees. Also, two of the participants said that the service capabilities, such as reminders for medicine time, make the service more useful. Mobility offers advantages to the service by enhancing job performance of the doctors as well. Variables in

Table 5 are collected from 17 different technology acceptance and adoption papers (see Table 1 for details), and grouped according to relevant classes. Then, occurrence number of these classes has been determined to calculate the percentage values in the *literature* column in Table 5. Values in the *study* column in Table 5 are computed by dividing sum of weights of each class studied in this article to the grand total weight of these classes. According to Table 5, classes are examined equally in the literature. However, most of the comments in this study were about the service characteristics, indicating a major need to research service characteristics.

Table 5. Literature and study comparison

Class	Literature	Study
User Characteristics	24%	26%
Service Characteristics	21%	55%
Ease of Use	16%	3%
Social Factors	15%	6%
Usefulness	15%	5%
Facilitating Conditions	9%	5%

Table 6. Propositions developed for future study

Ease of Use is influenced by the following attributes of the health services: user guidance, sound quality, age, and language.
Usefulness is influenced by the following attributes of the health services: content, service capability, mobility, and job fit.
Attitude of the potential users is influenced by the following attributes of the health services: cost, health status, social influence, usefulness, content, users' time constraint, and security. Content quality is influenced by the following attribute of the health services: communication standards. Service quality is influenced by the following attribute of the health services: sound quality, communication standards, and language.

When we examined the data acquired from the interviews (see Appendix C), we observed further implications of our findings. These implications can be interpreted as future propositions as listed in Table 6.

These propositions will need to be tested with further data collection.

CONCLUSION

This article contends that health information service adoption decisions of users are influenced by service characteristics like cost, content, sound quality, security, mobility, and time factor; user characteristics like health status, age, and users' time constraint; social factors; and facilitating conditions like user guidance. In line with previous technology adoption studies, usefulness and ease of use are found two significant determinants of user behavior.

Based on the findings, electronic health service designers and developers may focus on financial cost of the developed service. The cost of the service should be less than the cost of visiting a doctor. Moreover, content of the service should be related to the doctors' profession and users' requirements. Users attach importance to reach accurate, relevant, and quality information in a minimum response time. Another implication is that security and time factors should be taken into consideration when designing such services. Users do not prefer using services that are insecure and require a lot of time. Also, similar to prior research (Tung et al., 2008; Venkatesh & Davis, 2000), people intend to use systems that are effortless and improve job performance of the user.

For future study, a comprehensive quantitative research with large sample size can be conducted to test validity of the results. Proposed prototype can be expanded by adding new functionalities and capabilities to examine their affect on the health service adoption process.

REFERENCES

Ajzen, I. (1991). The theory of planned behavior. *Organizational Behavior and Human Decision Processes*, *50*(2), 179–211. doi:10.1016/0749-5978(91)90020-T

Al-Qirim, N. (2007). Championing telemedicine adoption and utilization in healthcare organizations in New Zealand. *International Journal of Medical Informatics*, *76*, 42–54. doi:10.1016/j.ijmedinf.2006.02.001

Aubert, B. A., & Hamel, G. (2001). Adoption of smart cards in the medical sector: The Canadian experience. *Social Science & Medicine*, *53*, 879–894. doi:10.1016/S0277-9536(00)00388-9

Berghout, B. M., Eminovic, N., Keizer, N. F., & Birnie, E. (2007). Evaluation of general practitioner's time investment during a store-and-forward teledermatology consultation. *International Journal of Medical Informatics*, *76*, 384–391. doi:10.1016/j.ijmedinf.2007.04.004

Biermann, E., Dietrich, W., Rihl, J., & Standl, E. (2002). Are there time and cost savings by using telemanagement for patients on intensified insulin therapy? A randomised, controlled trial. *Computer Methods and Programs in Biomedicine*, *69*, 137–146. doi:10.1016/S0169-2607(02)00037-8

Brink, J. L., Moorman, P. W., Boer, M. F., Pruyn, J. F. A., Verwoerd, C. D. A., & Bemmel, J. H. (2005). Involving the patient: A prospective study on use, appreciation and effectiveness of an information system in head and neck cancer care. *International Journal of Medical Informatics*, *74*, 839–849. doi:10.1016/j.ijmedinf.2005.03.021

Bruner, G. C., & Kumar, A. (2005). Explaining consumer acceptance of handheld Internet devices. *Journal of Business Research*, *58*, 553–558. doi:10.1016/j.jbusres.2003.08.002

Chae, Y. M., Lee, J. H., Ho, S. H., Kim, H. J., Jun, K. H., & Won, J. U. (2001). Patient satisfaction with telemedicine in home health services for the elderly. *International Journal of Medical Informatics*, *61*, 167–173. doi:10.1016/S1386-5056(01)00139-3

Chang, I. J., Hwang, H. G., Hung, M. C., Lin, M. H., & Yen, D. C. (2007). Factors affecting the adoption of electronic signature: Executives' perspective of hospital information department. *Decision Support Systems*, *44*, 350–359. doi:10.1016/j.dss.2007.04.006

Chau, P. Y. K., & Hu, P. J. H. (2002). Investigating healthcare professionals' decisions to accept telemedicine technology: An empirical test of competing theories. *Information & Management*, *39*, 297–311. doi:10.1016/S0378-7206(01)00098-2

Chen, I. J., Yang, K. F., Tang, F. I., Huang, C. H., & Yu, S. (2008). Applying the technology acceptance model to explore public health nurses' intentions towards web-based learning: A cross-sectional questionnaire survey. *International Journal of Nursing Studies*, *45*(6), 869–878. doi:10.1016/j.ijnurstu.2006.11.011

Cheng, T. C. E., Lam, D. Y. C., & Yeung, A. C. L. (2006). Adoption of internet banking: An empirical study in Hong Kong. *Decision Support Systems*, *42*, 1558–1572. doi:10.1016/j.dss.2006.01.002

Davis, F. D. (1989). Perceived usefulness, perceived ease of use, and user acceptance of information technology. *MIS Quarterly*, *13*(3), 319–339. doi:10.2307/249008

Dishaw, M. T., & Strong, D. M. (1999). Extending the technology acceptance model with task-technology fit constructs. *Information & Management*, *36*, 9–21. doi:10.1016/S0378-7206(98)00101-3

Fishbein, M., & Ajzen, I. (1975). *Belief, attitude, intention and behavior: An introduction to theory and research*. Reading, UK: Addison-Wesley.

Gagnon, M. P., Godin, G., Gagné, C., Fortin, J. P., Lamothe, L., & Reinharz, D. (2003). An adaptation of the theory of interpersonal behavior to the study of telemedicine adoption by physicians. *International Journal of Medical Informatics*, *71*, 103–115. doi:10.1016/S1386-5056(03)00094-7

Giorgino, T., Azzini, I., Rognonia, C., Quaglinia, S., Stefanelli, M., & Gretter, R. (2005). Automated spoken dialogue system for hypertensive patient home management. *International Journal of Medical Informatics*, *74*, 159–167. doi:10.1016/j.ijmedinf.2004.04.026

Glykas, M., & Chytas, P. (2004). Technological innovations in asthma patient monitoring and care. *Expert Systems with Applications*, *27*, 121–131. doi:10.1016/j.eswa.2003.12.007

Goodhue, D. L. (1995). Understanding user evaluations of information systems. *Management Science*, *41*, 1827–1844. doi:10.1287/mnsc.41.12.1827

Hsieh, R. K. C., Hjelm, N. M., Lee, J. C. K., & Aldis, J. W. (2001). Telemedicine in China. *International Journal of Medical Informatics*, *61*, 139–146. doi:10.1016/S1386-5056(01)00136-8

Karahanna, E., Straub, D. W., & Chervany, N. L. (1999). Information technology adoption across time: A cross-sectional comparison of pre-adoption and post-adoption beliefs. *MIS Quarterly*, *23*(2), 183–213. doi:10.2307/249751

Kleinrock, L. (1996). Nomadicity: Anytime, anywhere in a disconnected world. *Mobile Networks and Applications*, *1*(4), 351–357.

Knickman, J. R., Hunt, K. A., Snell, E. K., Marie, L., Alecxih, B., & Kennell, D. L. (2003). Wealth patterns among elderly Americans: Implications for healthcare affordability. *Health Affairs*, *22*, 168–174. doi:10.1377/hlthaff.22.3.168

Lee, R. D., & Tuljapurkar, S. (1994). Stochastic population forecasts for the United States: Beyond high, medium and low. *Journal of the American Statistical Association, 89*, 175–189. doi:10.2307/2290980

Levit, K., Smith, C., Cowan, C., Lazeby, H., Sensenig, A., & Catlin, A. (2003). Trends in U.S. healthcare spending 2001. *Health Affairs, 22*, 154–164. doi:10.1377/hlthaff.22.1.154

Liu, J. E., Pothiban, L., Lu, Z., & Khamphonsiri, T. (2000). Computer knowledge, attitudes, and skills of nurses in People's Hospital of Beijing Medical University. *Computers in Nursing, 18*(4), 197–206.

Liu, L., & Ma, Q. (2005). The impact of service level on the acceptance of application service oriented medical records. *Information & Management, 42*, 1121–1135. doi:10.1016/j.im.2004.12.004

Magrabi, F., Lovell, N. H., & Celle, B. G. (1999). A web-based approach for electrocardiogram monitoring in the home. *International Journal of Medical Informatics, 54*, 145–153. doi:10.1016/S1386-5056(98)00177-4

Mathieson, K., Peacock, E., & Chin, W. W. (2001). Extending the technology acceptance model: The influence of perceived user resources. *The Data Base for Advances in Information Systems, 32*(3), 86–112.

Moore, G. C., & Benbasat, I. (1991). Development of an instrument to measure the perceptions of adopting an information technology innovation. *Information Systems Research, 2*(3), 192–222. doi:10.1287/isre.2.3.192

Ozen, Ç., & Basoglu, N. (2006, July 9-13). Impact of man-machine interaction factors on enterprise resource planning (ERP) software design. In *Technology Management for the Global Future, 2006 (PICMET 2006)* (Vol. 5, pp. 2335-2341). IEEE.

Reinhardt, U. E. (2000). Healthcare for the aging baby boom: Lessons from abroad. *The Journal of Economic Perspectives, 14*, 71–83.

Rialle, V., Lamy, J. B., Noury, N., & Bajolle, L. (2003). Telemonitoring of patients at home: A software agent approach. *Computer Methods and Programs in Biomedicine, 72*, 257–268. doi:10.1016/S0169-2607(02)00161-X

Schaper, L. K., & Pervan, G. P. (2003). ICT and OTs: A model of information and communication technology acceptance and utilization by occupational therapists. *International Journal of Medical Informatics, 71*, 103–115. doi:10.1016/S1386-5056(03)00094-7

Silver, J. (2004). *Attributional coding in essential guide to qualitative methods in organizational research*. Thousand Oaks, CA: SAGE Publications.

Simon, J. S., Rundall, T. G., & Shortell, S. M. (2007). Adoption of order entry with decision support for chronic care by physician organizations. *Journal of the American Medical Informatics Association, 14*, 432–439. doi:10.1197/jamia.M2271

Taylor, S., & Todd, P. (1995). Assessing IT usage: The role of prior experience. *MIS Quarterly, 19*(4), 561–570. doi:10.2307/249633

Thompson, R. L., Higgins, C. A., & Howell, J. M. (1991). Personal computing: Toward a conceptual model of utilization. *MIS Quarterly, 15*(1), 124–143. doi:10.2307/249443

Topacan, U., Basoglu, A. N., & Daim, T. U. (2008, July 27-31). Exploring the success factors of health information service adoption. In *Portland International Conference on Management of Engineering & Technology, 2008 (PICMET 2008)* (pp. 2453-2461). IEEE.

Tung, F. C., Chang, S. C., & Chou, C. M. (2008). An extension of trust and TAM model with IDT in the adoption of the electronic logistics information system in HIS in the medical industry. *International Journal of Medical Informatics, 77*, 324–335. doi:10.1016/j.ijmedinf.2007.06.006

Venkatesh, V., & Davis, F. D. (2000). A theoretical extension of the technology acceptance model: Four longitudinal field studies. *Management Science, 45*(2), 186–204. doi:10.1287/mnsc.46.2.186.11926

Venkatesh, V., Morris, M. G., Davis, G. B., & Davis, F. D. (2003). User acceptance of information technology: Toward a unified view. *MIS Quarterly, 27*(3), 425–478.

Wilson, E. V., & Lankton, N. K. (2004). Modeling patients' acceptance of provider-delivered e-health. *Journal of the American Medical Informatics Association, 11*(4), 241–248. doi:10.1197/jamia.M1475

Yang, B. H., & Rhee, S. (2000). Development of the ring sensor for healthcare automation. *Robotics and Autonomous Systems, 30,* 273–281. doi:10.1016/S0921-8890(99)00092-5

Yusof, M. M., Kuljis, J., Papazafeiropoulou, A., & Stergioulas, L. K. (2008). An evaluation framework for health information systems: Human, organization and technology-fit factors (HOT-fit). *International Journal of Medical Informatics, 77,* 386–398. doi:10.1016/j.ijmedinf.2007.08.011

APPENDIX A. INTERVIEW QUESTIONS

1. Have you ever used a mobile service?
    a. If you have used, which mobile service(s) did you use?
    b. Are you interested in new technologies?
2. Would you want to use the proposed service?
    a. According to you, which functionality/properties of the service are beneficial?
    b. In your opinion, which functionality/properties of the service are inadequate?
3. Do you advise the service to your colleagues and friends?
    a. According to you, which functionality/properties of the service do you advice?
    b. According to you, which functionality/properties of the service do not you advice?
4. If you encounter someone who uses the service, do you attempt to use it?
5. What do you think about the one that uses the service?
6. Did you need help while using the service?
    a. If you need, in which part of the service do you need help?
7. Do you think the service is ease of use? What type of difficulties did you encounter while you were using the service?
8. Is the information given by the service useful? Which information is the most useful for you?
9. Do you suggest any extra information for the service?
10. How much money would you want pay for using the service?
11. Do you mind privacy and security of your data stored in the service?
12. Do you think that people intend to use this service? In your opinion, who are the people that need this service at most?
13. What do you think about the interface's sound used in the service?
14. Do you have any additional comment for the proposed service?

APPENDIX B. DIALOGUE BETWEEN PATIENT/PHYSICIAN AND THE SERVICE

Patient Dialogue

Service: Hello. What is your username?
Patient: Tiger *(okay)*
Service: Enter your password.
Patient: Enter 1224 *(okay)*
Service: Select your operation. Enter Meal, Enter Information, Meal Suggestion, Get Calorie Information, Exit.
Patient: Enter Meal *(okay)*
Service: What did you eat or drink?
Patient: I eat hamburger *(okay)*
Service: How much you eat or drink
Patient: One *(okay)*
Service: Do you eat or drink anything else?
Patient: Yes *(okay)*
Service: What did you eat or drink?
Patient: I drink coke *(okay)*
Service: How much you eat or drink?
Patient: I drink one bottle *(okay)*
Service: Do you eat or drink anything else?
Patient: No *(okay)*

Service: Select your operation. Enter Meal, Enter Information, Meal Suggestion, Get Calorie Information, Exit.

Patient: Meal Suggestion *(okay)*

Service: You can eat 1 Cups of Spaghetti, 3/4 Cup Tossed Salad, 1 Cup Apple Juice. Do I repeat or return main menu.

Patient: Repeat *(okay)*

Service: You can eat 1 Cups of Spaghetti, 3/4 Cup Tossed Salad, 1 Cup Apple Juice. Do I repeat or return main menu.

Patient: Return main menu *(okay)*

Service: Select your operation. Enter Meal, Enter Information, Meal Suggestion, Get Calorie Information, Exit.

Patient: Enter Information *(okay)*

Service: Select your operation. Enter movement or exercise, Enter Trauma, Enter pain, Enter drug, Return main menu

Patient: Enter Pain *(okay)*

Service: What is your pain?

Patient: I have headache and chest pain *(okay)*

Service: Select your operation. Enter movement or exercise, Enter Trauma, Enter pain, Enter drug, Return main menu

Patient: Enter movement or exercise *(okay)*

Service: What type of movement or exercise you did?

Patient: Today, I run 3000 meters and ride a bicycle 6000 meters.

Service: Select your operation. Enter movement or exercise, Enter Trauma, Enter pain, Enter drug, Return main menu

Patient: Enter drug *(okay)*

Service: Enter drug information.

Patient: I get one sulfonylurea.*(okay)*

Service: Select your operation. Enter movement or exercise, Enter Trauma, Enter pain, Enter drug, Return main menu

Patient: Return Main Menu *(okay)*

Service: Select your operation. Enter Meal, Enter Information, Meal Suggestion, Get Calorie Information, Exit.

Patient: Get Calorie Information *(okay)*

Service: Today you got 4200 cal and you can got 1000 more in today. Do I repeat or return main menu.

Patient: Return main menu *(okay)*

Service: Select your operation. Enter Meal, Enter Information, Meal Suggestion, Get Calorie Information, Exit.

Patient: Exit

Service: Bye bye

Warning to Take Medicine

Service: Hello Mrs. James. This is a reminder service of the Medical Record Server. It is time to take sulfonylurea. Bye Bye.

Warning to Enter Information

Service: Hello Mrs. James. This is a reminder service of the Medical Record Server. You do not enter any information to the system last 8 hours. Thank you. Bye Bye.

Physician Dialogue

Service: Hello. What is your username?
Physician: Tiger *(okay)*
Service: Enter your password.
Physician: Enter 1224 *(okay)*
Service: Select your operation. Calorie Information, Blood Glucose Information, Blood Pressure Information, Exit
Physician: Calorie Information *(okay)*
Service: What is your patient name?
Physician: Peter Brown *(okay)*
Service: Peter Brown got 3000 calories in today. He can take 1230 more calories. Do I repeat or return main menu.
Physician: Return main menu *(okay)*
Service: Select your operation. Calorie Information, Blood Glucose Information, Blood Pressure Information, Exit
Physician: Blood Glucose Information *(okay)*
Service: What is your patient name?
Physician: Mary Brown *(okay)*
Service: There are two Mary Brown. What is the birth date of Mary Brown?
Physician: 4th of April *(okay)*
Service: Blood glucose of Mary Brown is 6 mmol/l and recorded at 10:00 am in today. Do I repeat or return main menu.
Physician: Repeat
Service: Blood glucose of Mary Brown is 6 mmol/l and recorded at 10:00 am in today. Do I repeat or return main menu.
Physician: Return main menu *(okay)*
Service: Select your operation. Calorie Information, Blood Glucose Information, Blood Pressure Information, Exit
Physician: Exit
Service: Bye Bye

Warning to Physician

Service: Hello Mr. James. This is an alert service of the Medical Record Server. Blood Glucose level of patient Mary Brown decreases under 3 mmol/l. Bye Bye.

APPENDIX C. DATA EXTRACTED FROM THE INTERVIEWS (TABLE 7)

Table 7.

Class	Independent	Content Quality		Service Quality		Ease of Use		Usefulness		Attitude		Grand Total	
		No.	%	No.	Percent	No.	Percent	No.	Percent	No.	Percent	No.	Percent
Service Characteristics	Communication standards	2	0.71%	2	0.71%							4	1.42%
Service Characteristics	Sound Quality			5	1.77%	8	2.84%					13	4.61%

Class	Independent	Content Quality		Service Quality		Ease of Use		Usefulness		Attitude		Grand Total	
		No.	%	No.	Percent	No.	Percent	No.	Percent	No.	Percent	No.	Percent
Service Characteristics	Language			2	0.71%	5	1.77%					7	2.48%
Service Characteristics	Accurate Input			1	0.35%			2	0.71%	3	1.06%	6	2.13%
Service Characteristics	Output Quality			1	0.35%			2	0.71%	2	0.71%	5	1.77%
User Characteristics	User Involvement			1	0.35%			2	0.71%	2	0.71%	5	1.77%
Service Characteristics	Customizable			1	0.35%			1	0.35%			2	0.71%
Facilitating Conditions	User Guidance					10	3.55%					10	3.55%
User Characteristics	Age					7	2.48%			8	2.84%	15	5.32%
Service Characteristics	Input Type					4	1.42%			3	1.06%	7	2.48%
User Characteristics	Experience					4	1.42%			3	1.06%	7	2.48%
Service Characteristics	Input Quantity					3	1.06%			1	0.35%	4	1.42%
Service Characteristics	Sound					3	1.06%			1	0.35%	4	1.42%
Service Characteristics	Length of Menu Items					3	1.06%				0.35%	3	1.06%
User Characteristics	Tech-savvy					2	0.71%			5	1.77%	7	2.48%
Facilitating Conditions	Help Button					2	0.71%			2	0.71%	4	1.42%

Class	Independent	Content Quality		Service Quality		Ease of Use		Usefulness		Attitude		Grand Total	
		No.	%	No.	Percent	No.	Percent	No.	Percent	No.	Percent	No.	Percent
Service Characteristics	Device Type					2	0.71%					2	0.71%
Service Characteristics	Service Complexity					1	0.35%			1	0.35%	2	0.71%
Service Characteristics	Input Quality					1	0.35%					1	0.35%
Service Characteristics	Content							16	5.67%	12	4.26%	28	9.93%
Service Characteristics	Service Capabilities							5	1.77%	2	0.71%	7	2.48%
Service Characteristics	Mobility							3	1.06%	6	2.13%	9	3.19%
Service Characteristics	Job Fit							3	1.06%	4	1.42%	7	2.48%
Service Characteristics	Rapid Response							1	0.35%	1	0.35%	2	0.71%
Service Characteristics	Service Accuracy							1	0.35%	1	0.35%	2	0.71%
Service Characteristics	Cost									16	5.67%	16	5.67%
User Characteristics	Health Status									16	5.67%	16	5.67%
Social Influence	Social Influence									15	5.32%	15	5.32%
Intermediary	Usefulness									14	4.96%	14	4.96%
User Characteristics	Users' Time Constraint									9	3.19%	9	3,19%

Class	Independent	Content Quality		Service Quality		Ease of Use		Usefulness		Attitude		Grand Total	
		No.	%	No.	Percent	No.	Percent	No.	Percent	No.	Percent	No.	Percent
Service Characteristics	Security			1	0.35%					9	3.19%	10	3,55%
Service Characteristics	Time Factor									8	2.84%	8	2.84%
Service Characteristics	Face-to-face Communication									6	2.13%	6	2.13%
Intermediary	Ease of Use			1	0.35%			1	0.35%	6	2.13%	8	2.84%
User Characteristics	Income									4	1.42%	4	1.42%
User Characteristics	Educational Level									3	1.06%	3	1.06%
User Characteristics	Gender									3	1.06%	3	1.06%
User Characteristics	Requirement									3	1.06%	3	1.06%
Social Influence	Image									2	0.71%	2	0.71%
Service Characteristics	Service Quality									1	0.35%	1	0.35%
User Characteristics	Trust									1	0.35%	1	0.35%
Grand Total		2	0.71%	15	5.32%	55	19.50%	37	13.12%	173	61.35%	282	100.00%

This work was previously published in An the International Journal of Information Systems in the Service Sector, Volume 2. Issue 1, edited by J. Wang, pp. 71-93, copyright 2010 by IGI Publishing (an imprint of IGI Global).

Chapter 4.19
GuiMarket:
An E-Marketplace of Healthcare and Social Care Services for Individuals with Special Needs

M. Manuela Cruz-Cunha
Polytechnic Institute of Cávado and Ave, Portugal and University of Minho, Portugal

Ricardo Simões
Polytechnic Institute of Cávado and Ave, Portugal and University of Minho, Portugal

António Tavares
Polytechnic Institute of Cávado and Ave, Portugal

Isabel Miranda
Câmara Municipal de Guimarães, Portugal

ABSTRACT

The healthcare sector has been continuously growing in importance in the past years throughout the entire world, and particularly in most Western countries and the U.S., where we witness an increase of expenditure in health per capita every year. This is related to many aspects of contemporary society, including an increase in life expectancy, the public demand for a better quality of life and better health services. This must be met with more cost-efficient approaches, and new technology-based solutions for providing health and other services. The chapter contextualizes the utilization of electronic marketplaces (e-marketplaces) for the social and healthcare sectors, how this field has been evolving in recent years, current challenges and trends, and their contribut to society. The authors also discuss a pilot project of an e-marketplace for healthcare and social services currently being developed in the Guimarães Municipality, including its goal, definition and implementation, as well as the commercially available enabling technology and tools.

DOI: 10.4018/978-1-61520-670-4.ch043

INTRODUCTION

The March 2000 Lisbon European Council set the objective of making the EU 'the most competitive and dynamic knowledge-based economy in the world, capable of sustainable economic growth with more and better jobs and greater social cohesion' (European_Commission, 2002b). According to the strategy defined by the European Council in Lisbon, e-Health has a clear role in the European Union strategy – eEurope – and is the key to attain a stronger growth and create qualified employment in a dynamic and knowledge-based economy (European_Commission, 2002a, 2004, 2005). However, this intention requires specific actions, from research and development of new models for application and/or integration of existing technology, new technological advances, the widespread reach of broadband internet access to all population (particularly remote areas) and overcoming the digital divide due to ability to use technology, specific public health actions, and the problematic issues of integrating the population with special care needs, such as elder people, in the e-Health systems.

If continuous health care systems and care to people with special needs are performed in an unarticulated and fragmented manner, provided by entities that do not communicate among themselves, the results will be wholly undesirable. Often, those two specific areas of health care and social services must be provided at the patient's home. On the other hand, the existence of a network of health care, social care and professional services providers, working articulately with an underlying effective management and intermediation service, based on an e-Marketplace for health care and social care services, can be a powerful tool and result in effective and efficient service to people with special needs (elderly and permanently or temporarily disabled people)

A wide range of supporting technologies already exist that can contribute to such purpose. What is needed is an integrating environment to identify user needs transmitted over an e-marketplace platform and the allocation of services providers to answer these needs, integration and management, performance monitoring and evaluation, commitment control, etc.

The authors are developing a pilot project for the Municipality of Guimarães[1] envisaging the definition and implementation of an e-marketplace for healthcare and social services, integrating healthcare professionals and professionals of social services with people with special needs (or their relatives) and institutions willing to accede to these services.

The service is focused on the needs usually fulfilled by day care hospitals and continuous care units, home care, and support to the elderly and people with special needs. The effectiveness and efficiency on providing health care and the population well-being, particularly the previously mentioned segments of the population, are based on correctly orienting resources that can comply with their problems and specific needs, as well as their expectations of quality and comfort.

More precisely, the objectives of the proposed project consist of offering new solutions in the area of health care and social care, provision of home services, making available privileged communication means between:

- The individual and the entities with social concerns, or entities that provide social and healthcare services or independent service providers
- Institutions that provide social /healthcare services and independent service providers
- Two institutions providing social / healthcare services, for complementarily solve a given situation

Secondly, this project will give more flexibility and quality of live to individuals that for any reason (incapacity temporary or permanent, age, etc) should stay at home can find in the eMarketplace of Social and Healthcare Services (GuiMarket) many of the services that they require for their day-to-day life.

A first phase of the project design is already going, with the identification of user needs and system requirements analysis. After this phase it will be implemented a pilot installation with two pilot groups in two different parishes – one with rural characteristics, the other with urban characteristics. After validation, the platform will be worked on regarding its extension to the entire Municipality.

The chapter contextualizes the utilization of Electronic Marketplaces (e-Marketplaces) for the social and healthcare sectors, describes the actors of the project in the third section, and in the fourth part it frameworks this e-Marketplace able to co-ordinate and manage the matching between offer and demand of services, i.e. between the delivery of social and healthcare services and their users. The final section draws some conclusions and presents directions for further developments.

BACKGROUND: CONTEXT AND NEW APPROACHES

In this section we present some data about the dimension of Health expenditure in some parts of the globe to understand the importance that should be devoted to solutions that at the same time increase the well-being of people, allow an optimization in the delivery of services in the sector of health and social care, and contribute to a desirable reform of making these services demand oriented, and simultaneously to cope with the population ageing.

The Magnitude of Health Expenditure and Policies

As we know, the healthcare sector is a huge industry in many Western countries. Health expenditure in USA was US$ 2.2 trillion in 2007, correspond-

ing to 16% of the Gross Domestic Product, with an expected growth rate of 6,2% per year until 2018, reaching US$ 4.4 trillion, corresponding to 20% of the Gross Domestic Product in 2018 (Medicare.gov, 2007). In Europe (EU-25) in 2006 the total Health expenditure corresponded on average to 7.76% of its GDP; the average in the EU-15 was 8.6% and in the new member states 5.8% (OECD 2008).

However, there are many different aspects that contribute to the increased expenditure in health. A main cause is based on the combined effect of the projected increase in the share of older people and the tendency for health expenditures per capita to increase with age (Martins & Maisonneuve, 2006). The increase in life expectancy has a fairly straightforward impact on expenditure; as people live longer, their health costs increase. However, this is not a linear effect. Not only do people require treatments for a longer period, but the number of treatments required increases. At the threshold of life expectancy, the needs in terms of both medication and physical care can increase substantially.

Also, in the past years, science and technology have provided healthcare professionals with a much wider range of tools. Advances in pharmacology, materials science, nanotechnology, information technology, and medical practice, have all contributed to new or improved mechanisms of healthcare. The market driver towards innovation and competitiveness among companies has also pushed for many new medical devices. However, all these new (or improved) solutions involve costs. According to An European Action Plan for the eHealth area (European_Commission, 2004) for some years European countries have been facing rising demand for health and social services as a result of an ageing population and higher income levels, although the funding available remains limited. At the same time, citizens have higher expectations and the mobility of patients and of health professionals has increased. The eHealth Action Plan identified a challenging list of implementation actions to be undertaken by both the European Commission and the Member States; it includes a roadmap that extends until 2010 (which is embedded in the wider context of achieving the Lisbon Strategy) (European_Commission, 2005).

According to a recent European report on eHealth priorities and strategies (European-Commission, 2007), when compared to other sectors of European economies, the deployment of ICT applications by health systems has been severely lagging behind; however, Europe's healthcare policy makers are now aware of this crucial gap, and an improvement is at hand. The information from current policy papers and national experts, collected by the eHealth European Research Area (ERA) project, show that an important step towards wider deployment of eHealth solutions has been made. The creation of a European eHealth area, free patient mobility, and empowerment of the citizen through eHealth services are now core policy objectives of the Union (European-Commission, 2007).

Some main challenges Europe healthcare systems is facing includes the rising demand for health and social services, due to an ageing population, with previsions for 2051 pointing to 40% of the Union's population older than 65 years old (Braun, Constantelou, Karounou, et al, 2003), and the increasing expectations of citizens who want the best care available, and at the same time to experience a reduction in inequalities in access (European-Commission, 2004).

Strategies for eHealth vary from country to country, but the general objective is to provide increased quality of care as efficiently and effectively as possible. The role of the patient is clearly evident in the ICT strategies of certain countries such as Ireland, Portugal and England. Ireland, for instance, plans to build an ICT framework placing ICT in the context of healthcare reform and citizen-centered services, while England is focused on implementing an integrated IT infrastructure which will enable patients to make informed health choices and which will lead to greater efficiency. Likewise, Portugal plans to use ICT to place the citizen at the centre of the health system, while increasing the quality of services provided, increasing the efficiency of the system and reducing costs (European-Commission, 2007).

Characterization of the Social and Health Providers in the Region

Local health care and social care systems are geographically dispersed units, covering both urban and rural areas, according to geographic-population criteria. These units have specific capabilities that intend to answer the needs of the serviced community, defined in terms of risk. Among these units are health centers, hospitals, private and non-profit institutions, non-governmental organizations, and community / communitarian institutions active in the health and social care area. These units develop on logic of resource complementary and coordination, aiming at taking full advantage of the existing or required capabilities, and demanding careful management to local specificities and characteristics.

As part of the Social Development Plan that the Department of Social Intervention has conceived for the period 2007-2009, several pilot actions were previewed in order to put technologies on the service of population, in particular of individuals with special needs and elderly.

In the framework of the current project, the focus is on the needs usually fulfilled by day care hospitals and continuous care units, home care, and support to the elderly, disable and people with special needs (temporarily or permanently). The effectiveness and efficiency on providing social and health care and the population well-being, is based on correctly orienting resources that can comply with their problems and specific needs, as well as their expectations of quality and comfort.

If continuous health care systems and care to people with special needs are performed in an unarticulated and fragmented manner, provided by entities that do not communicate among themselves, the results will be wholly undesirable. Often, those two specific areas of health care must be provided at the patient's home. On the other hand, the existence of a network of health care providers, which work in an articulated manner, but with an underlying effective management, based on a logic of user-demand can be a powerful tool and result in effective and efficient service.

It is required an ICT-based environment /platform able to coordinate and manage the delivery of professional social and healthcare services to elderly people or people with special care needs, promoting the match between the delivery of healthcare services (provided by healthcare professionals) and the users (individual users with special needs or institutions), that in a particular moment need the intervention a professional or a specific social service to support /increase their well-being.

Day care centers, continuous care units, and health centers face sometimes shortage of capability of response / insufficiency to meet the demand or internal needs that should be strength by reinforcing some services available at other institutions or that can be provided by specialized professionals.

New ICT-Based Solutions

Due to the magnitude of Health expenditure, market oriented healthcare reforms are being considered in many countries (Smits & Janssen, 2008).

One of the goals of the reforms in the European Healthcare systems over the last two decades has been to make them more demand oriented. Several studies as well as official documents evidence that Internet and telecommunications technologies and infrastructures may contribute significantly to health care system performance (Babulak, 2006; European-Commission, 2007; Kerzman, Janssen, & Ruster, 2003; Séror, 2002; Smits & Janssen, 2008).

Several examples exist of Internet-based markets between users of care and providers of care, such as the CareAuction.nl, a new intermediary on the market for maternity care in the Netherlands(Smits & Janssen, 2008). The authors analyze the influence of Electronic Auctions on Healthcare Markets, which might serve as a potential solution to national health care policy problems, and additionally might lead to a reduction in transaction costs. In Netherlands, about 30% of all maternity care sector was contracted through CareAuction.nl by the end of 2006.

According to a Report on eMarketplaces for the Health sector (Kuller, 2005), the European Health and Social Services sector it is a complex web of 'businesses' and 'customers', characterized by a combination of public and private providers who control the strategic direction and finances. The services are delivered by micro-businesses, that is, hospitals, clinics, general practitioners and specialists, and delivered through government, public or non-profit bodies, not the private sector (although this is slowly changing in some countries) (Kuller, 2005). The resulting absence of the profit goal means that the motivation for changing business processes and implementing tools is driven by a need to improve 'patient care', and not a desire to make or save money. This partly explains why the Health and Social Services sector lags behind others with regards to IT infrastructure in place and e-Business usage.

Electronic Marketplaces implemented the concept of Market (where offer and demand meet) were developed to bring together large numbers of buyers and sellers expanding the choices available to buyers, and giving sellers new opportunities and access to new customers (buyers), simultaneously reducing transaction costs for all participants (Kaplan and Sawhney, 2000).

e-Marketplaces are a third party, mediating offer and demand, offering important value-added mechanisms (Christiaanse et al., 2001; Bailey and Bakos, 1997): facilitate multiple buyers and sellers to connect to negotiate prices on a dynamic real-time basis; promotes trust and support transaction phases.

We are currently witnessing an attempt to use in the Health sector some solutions already in use by the business sector, to optimize processes of product sourcing and supply chain improvement, such as the several well-succeeded "last generation" eMarketplaces (e.g. www.broadlane.com, www.Med2med.com, www.labx.com, www.saniline.com), and many others referred by directories like eMarketServices, available online at http://www.emarketservices.com (eMarketServices, 2007; Zallh, 2005).

But this concept is far from being adopted to improve networks of services providers in the sector, creating true synergies of resources and capabilities for service delivery.

GUIMARKET: AN E-MARKETPLACE FOR HEALTH CARE AND SOCIAL CARE SERVICES

Offer and demand are usually matched under several different circumstances, from unregulated search to oriented search, from simple intermediation mechanisms to the market mechanism, all of them with the possibility of being either manually performed or automated. GuiMarket is a marketplace of healthcare and social care resource providers to facilitate the matching between users looking for service providers and individuals / institutions offering their resources, in a context of geographical proximity. In this section we explain who are the participants / actors of GuiMarket, the functionalities that the pilot service is expected to provide and the main requirements for its implementation and

Users and Their Requirements

The environment or market herein introduced – a Marketplace for healthcare and social care services – is an environment to coordinate and manage the match between the offer of healthcare and social

care services (provided by healthcare social care professionals and specialized institutions) and the individuals (users or patients) with special needs or institutions, that in a particular moment need the intervention of a professional

The offer and demand side is represented as follows:

- *Offer* or services providers can be (a) entities providers of services in the covered domain of health or social care and services and (b) individuals and enterprises providers of special services, that use the e-Marketplace to make available information about their products and services.

- The *demand* side consists of both individuals or entities that use the service to search for the satisfaction of their needs.

  a. **Individuals-users or patients of health care services:** The service is designed having in mind firstly individuals with special needs, elder or disabled (temporarily or permanently), but it is accessible to all population of the Municipality. Currently a large majority of these targeted users cannot access these technologies, but this task can be performed by their relatives, neighbors or friends. They can require daily home assistance of hygiene, special care, health care, physiotherapy, care giving, baby sitting, nursing.

  b. **Individuals and enterprises-providers of specific services:** Individuals and enterprises certified to provide social care, health care or home specific services, such as gerontology services, transportation, plumbing, catering, cleaning, transportation, home assistance, or massages and therapists.

  c. **Entities – providers of services:** Certified entities of the social network of services and care providers, the health care network.

d. **Entities – users of services:** In a perspective of complementarities to the services they offer, or as demanders of services provided by the other classes of providers represented in the e-Marketplace.

Figure 1 represents these classes of participants and their interaction with the e-Marketplace

Functionalities / Specification

A wide set of services can be identified. At this pilot stage, we have selected the following services to be implemented, represented in Figure 2:

Considering the type of user that this system is directed to, one fundamental aspect is accessibility. The e-Marketplace portal must include the following features:

• Possibility to be accessed from different communication platforms
• Intuitive and optimized navigation
• Large fonts and easily identifiable buttons

The portal should be compatible with the interfaces expected at desktop computers, laptops, and even PDAs. The idea is that users can interchangeably use any of these platforms, depending on which is more easily available to them at the

Figure 1. Interaction between participants in the GuiMarket

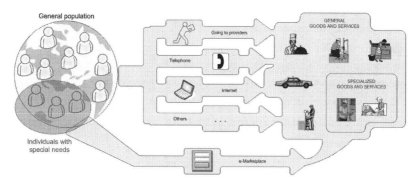

Figure 2. Functionalities implemented

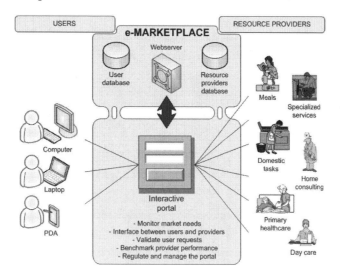

time. User preferences should be saved between sessions, obviously dependent on authentication.

GuiMarket Manager

The e-Marketplace portal has a manager, who is responsible for the major maintenance and coordination tasks. Considering the type of services offered, and the need to ensure a high standard of quality and reliability of the services, the portal manager is a vital component of the system. He is responsible for creating new service categories (either requested by users or by providers), validating that new providers are legally allowed to offer the service, benchmarking the quality of providers based on user feedback (including discriminating useful feedback), and ensuring the system is functional (quickly acting whenever there are problems).

Aside from these logistic tasks, the portal manager has two critical roles in the growth and sustainability of the business: (1) communicate with users along time in order to identify new possible areas of activity and also implement modifications to improve the usability of the portal; and (2) use the necessary traditional communication mechanisms to allow people access to the market without the use of the portal. The later allows all types of interaction with the market, including the personal and direct contact like any traditional business.

Requirements for the GuiMarket

Two relevant requisites are identified within the project: (1) identification of an adequate professional able to take care of the user's needs and flexible and fast access to it; (2) minimization of the time required to respond, from the identification of the need until the identification of the services provider to be allocated.

The first requisite implies the existence of a market of services providers, to assure:

a. The environment, technology and procedure protocols for the efficient access to the most suitable providers to a particular need;
b. An efficient and user-friendly platform to support the market interactions;
c. A domain for selection of service providers covering a broad domain of situations, large enough to assure a "good" solution to the need;
d. Permanent monitoring of the service to assure a continued quality;
e. Utilization of business intelligence tools to monitor the ability of the market to respond to user demands.

The second requisite is mandatory, in order to provide a response as fast as possible, and involves the utilization of mobile technologies by some service providers, like for instance health professional services.

If the providers selection domain, to satisfy the user needs, within his neighbourhood represents the lower limit of the *providers selection domain* space, the global providers selection domain, to satisfy the user needs, involving all the professionals or providers for the required service represent the upper limit of the *providers selection domain* space. The global domain provides virtually, and from a practical point of view, an almost infinite providers selection domain size provides the highest level of competitiveness, however, the search in the global domain is prohibitive, because of the infinite effort required.

The selection problem is by nature a very complex problem (NP class) and if manually performed, it is not possible to assure high performance. The search of providers in the universal/global domain, even using agent technologies is extremely time consuming, and the lack of standardisation and uniformity in the description of the desired services cannot assure an efficient selection in useful time. In the GuiMarket all the entities in interaction in a selection process must be described in a normalised format to allow automatic selection and decision-making. The second way to assure efficient selection is to limit the search domain to a subset of the universal domain, registering the providers and describing them in a normalised basis, to enable the application of the automated brokerage mechanisms (designated as *algorithm for search* in the IDEF diagram of Figure 3).

GUIMARKET: SPECIFICATION AND DIRECTIONS FOR IMPLEMENTATION

In this section, the GuiMarket is introduced, firstly with a description of the main activities offered, and followed by a brief specification of its overall structure using an IDEF0 diagram[2].

The main activities involved resources providers search and selection using GuiMarket are the following:

- **Request:** Request involves the specification of the required service. This can be done navigating through the market of resources providers (or more narrowed sets of providers called focused markets), or for complex situations, using a chat facility with the "broker" of the market, when the specification requires "knowledge" about the required service.

- **Search and selection:** Search, negotiation and selection consist of several steps: the identification of potential providers, separation of eligible resources, negotiation among these to identify the candidate resources (according to availability, price, conditions to provide the service), and finally the selection of the most suitable. Negotiation is a facility that is possible for certain classes of professional services (request for quotations is the most usual). When it is not needed negotiation, selection is made from the services directory or catalogue. For complex situations, the final selection can be controlled by the broker or in interaction with him.

- **Contractualization:** An automated contractualization by which the user and the provider agree on the conditions to be respected in the service to be provided.

The overall functioning of GuiMarket is represented by an IDEF0 diagram in Figure 3. It consists of the creation and management of the Market of Resources (GuiaMarket database) (Process A.1.), as the environment to support search, negotiation, selection and contractualization of resources providers (Process A.2.) that, after the conclusion of the service, are evaluated (Process A.3.).

Figure 3. IDEF0 representation of the global process for the GuiMarket creation and maintenance, the resources providers search and selection and the final evaluation of the service provided

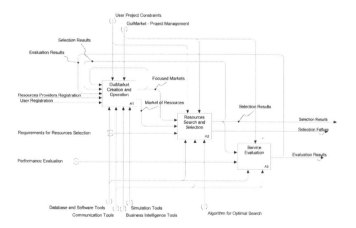

GUIMARKET IMPLEMENTATION

The technical requirements to support the electronic market (GuiMarket) can be grouped under three heads, and are bounded by a project management guide to regulate the implementation and operation of GuiMarket, and to manage the participation of the elements (providers, users and brokers). These are systematized in Table 1.

- **An information infrastructure:** The information infrastructure must provide information exchange, security, access, monitoring, recovery and emergency handling and contingency operations. Technology elements include functional engines (file servers, network servers, distributed database engines, search engines and security mechanisms), distributed information resources built upon these engines (such as catalogues, distributed databases) and services to access these resources (building on the existing techniques as HTML, File Transfer Protocol, messaging, collaboration techniques, etc.).

- **Appropriate support mechanisms and tools for the supra infrastructure:** An information infrastructure *de per si* is not enough; participants require mechanisms and tools to operate within the infrastructure, namely coordination and performance evaluation, electronic negotiation systems, authentication and other supporting tools. Participants (clients and providers) need supporting tools to quantify service levels and to evaluate the performance, assess targets, etc., Brokers need also specific management tools (search algorithms, business intelligence tools to evaluate search and selection, level or capacity of solution that the market offers etc.

- **Project management and regulation:** Management and regulation of the market are critical aspects. In defining this component, we considered the following:
  - Various user profiles in terms of computer skills, level of education, etc. The purpose is to look out for the interests of those with more difficulties in using this type of services, ensuring an overall level of quality and satisfaction.
  - Various service provider profiles, according to their specific characteristics. In all cases, providers must be legally enabled to provide that service before they are added to the portal. They are required to deliver legal supporting documentation for that.

This is related to the role of the portal manager, which has been described in detail above.

In Table 2 we summarise some of the components required for the GuiMarket and the existing technologies able to support them

Table 1. Technologies for the implementation of the market of resources technical requirements

	Technical Requirements		
	Information infrastructure	**Support mechanisms and tools**	**Project Management/ GuiMarket Regulation**
Technologies / Tools	- Servers - Distributed database systems - E-Marketplaces development platforms - Electronic catalogues - Communication technologies - Messaging and collaboration techniques	- Benchmarking and metrics - Electronic negotiation mechanisms - Electronic contracting - Algorithms or protocols - Market regulation - Intelligent decision making systems - Computer aided tools	- Market organisation - Management procedures - Business models - Performance evaluation - Contract management - GuiMarket management (maintenance, control, coordination, enforcement, etc)

Table 2. Technologies to support the main Gui-Market components / processes

Market of Resources components /processes	Support technologies and tools
- Market contents: user profile, catalogues, historic, database of resources	- Database management systems - Distributed database management systems - eBusiness development platforms - Portals
- Negotiation: request for quotes, optimal selection	- Electronic negotiation tools - Algorithms or protocols - Regulation of negotiation - Intelligent decision making systems
- Authentication and contractualisation	- Digital signature - Certification - Other security mechanisms
- Management: monitoring, performance evaluation, analysis of operation results, decision making,	- Simulation tools - Business intelligent tool - Regulation - Social networks analysis tools
- Brokerage: expert advice, monitoring and coordination	- Messaging and conferencing - Database management systems - Algorithms - Management procedures
- Providers final selection (optimal combination)	- Algorithms, heuristics and computer aided tools - Intelligent decision making systems

The technological requirements of the system are vast and complex. Some of its components are only effective when the system has reached a certain critical size which allows for its full analysis and evaluation. Thus, the strategy employed is based on development and gradual integration of the different components, dependent on the natural evolution of the market.

The current state of the pilot implementation, developed under a PHP Web Framework, aims at concept validation, mainly before the promoters and potential service providers, in order to establish the market's initial service list.

CONCLUSION AND FURTHER DEVELOPMENTS

This project is still at an early phase. The user needs analysis allowed the identification of a service with the characteristics of GuiMarket, to meet the needs felt by individuals with special needs. It is certain that at this moment many potential users will be excluded by the well-known digital divide; however this is a global concern of our times and progresses are being made at this level, and new actions and efforts such as active ageing and the e-inclusion will gradually allow going beyond these limitations.

This project here roughly drafted represents a good opportunity to develop a totally innovative service with high potential for individuals with special needs, as we have been able to conclude in all the public presentations, anticipating a good adhesion to the project being developed.

REFERENCES

Babulak, E. (2006). Quality of service provision assessment in the healthcare information and telecommunications infrastructures. *International Journal of Medical Informatics, 75*(3-4), 246–252. doi:10.1016/j.ijmedinf.2005.07.019

Braun, A., Constantelou, A., Karounou, V., Ligtoet, A., & Burgelman, J.-C. (2003). *Prospecting ehealth in the context of a European Ageing Society: Quantifying and qualifying needs. Final report.* Sevilla, Spain: IPTS/ESTO.

Cunha, M. M., & Putnik, G. D. (2008). Market of Resources for Healthcare Teleservices Management. In G. D. Putnik & M. M. Cunha (Eds.), *Encyclopedia of Networked and Virtual Organizations.* Hershey, PA: IGI-Global.

eMarketServices. (2007). *eMarket Directory.* Retrieved March 2007, from http://www.emarket-services.com/start/eMarket_Directory/index.html

European-Commission. (2007). *eHealth - Priorities and Strategies in European Countries.* Luxembourg: Office for Official Publications of the European Communities.

European_Commission. (2002a). *eEurope 2005: an information society for all* (Communication from the Commission to the Council, the European Parliament, the European Economic and Social Committee and the Committee of the Regions. No. COM(2002) 263). Brussels: Commission of the European Communities.

European_Commission. (2002b). *The Lisbon Strategy - Making Change Happen* (Communication from the Commission to the Spring European Council in Barcelona. No. COM(2002) 14). Brussels: Commission of the European Communities.

European_Commission. (2004). *e-Health - Making Healthcare better for European Citizens: An Action Plan for a European e-Health Area* (Communication from the Commission to the Council, the European Parliament, the European Economic and Social Committee and the Committee of the Regions No. COM(2004) 356). Brussels: Commission of the European Communities.

European_Commission. (2005). *i2010 - A European Information Society for growth and employment* (Communication from the Commission to the Council, the European Parliament, the European Economic and Social Committee and the Committee of the Regions No. COM(2005) 229). Brussels: Commission of the European Communities.

Kerzman, E., Janssen, R., & Ruster, M. (2003). e-Business in Health Care: Does it Contribute to Strengthen Consumer Interest? *Health Policy (Amsterdam), 64,* 63–73. doi:10.1016/S0168-8510(02)00139-2

Kuller, E. (2005). *e-Marketplaces in the Health Sector: eMarket Services.* Australian Trade Commision.

Martins, J. O., & Maisonneuve, C. (2006). The Drivers of Public Expenditure on Health and Long-term Care: an integrated approach. *OECD Economic Studies, 2006*(2).

Medicare.gov. (2007). *National Health Expenditure 2008-2018, Forecast summary.* Retrieved April 05, 2009, from http://www.cms.hhs.gov/NationalHealthExpendData/downloads/proj2008.pdf

OECD. (2008). *OECD Health Data 2008.* Retrieved April 10, 2009, from http://ec.europa.eu/health/ph_information/dissemination/echi/echi_25_en.pdf

Séror, A. C. (2002). Internet infrastructures and health care systems: a qualitative comparative analysis on networks and markets in the British National Health Service and Kaiser Permanente. *Journal of Medical Internet Research, 4*(3), e21. doi:10.2196/jmir.4.3.e21

Smits, M., & Janssen, R. (2008). Impact of Electronic Auctions on Health Care Markets. *Electronic Markets, 18*(1), 19–29. doi:10.1080/10196780701797607

Zallh, S. (2005). *Significant e-Marketplaces.* eMarketServices. Retrieved from http://www.emarketservices.com/clubs/ems/artic/SignificanteMarkets.pdf

KEY TERMS AND DEFINITIONS

Electronic Marketplace (e-Marketplace): An Internet-based platform where several buyers and several sellers meet to do business. It is a third party mediating offer and demand, offering value-added services and promoting trust and support to negotiation and transactions

Individuals with Special Needs: Individuals with disabilities, temporary or permanent, that require special attention (healthcare and social care).

GuiMarket Manager: The e-Marketplace portal (GuiMarket) has a manager, who is responsible for the major maintenance and coordination tasks.

GuiMarket: A pilot project of an e-marketplace for healthcare and social care services currently being developed in the Municipality of Guimarães, Portugal. GuiMarket is a marketplace of healthcare and social care resource providers to facilitate the matching between users looking for service providers and individuals / institutions offering their resources.

ICT: Information and communication technologies. This is a term that covers all advanced technologies in manipulating and communicating information.

IDEF0: Integration Definition for Function Modeling. A function modeling methodology which offers a functional modeling language for the analysis, development, reengineering, and integration of information systems; business processes; or software engineering analysis.

ENDNOTES

[1] Guimarães is a city and a municipality in the northeast of Portugal, with a population of around 160,000 inhabitants in 241,3 km2. A survey of living conditions undertaken in 2007 by the "Expresso" newspaper ranked Guimarães as number 2 in the most attractive Portuguese cities.

[2] IDEF stands for ICAM DEFinition methodology (ICAM – Integrated Computer-Aided Manufacturing). IDEF diagrams illustrate the structural relations between two processes and the entities present in the system. The processes (represented as boxes) transform the *inputs* into *outputs* (respectively the left and the right arrows of a process), using the *mechanisms* for the transformation (the bottom arrows of a process) and constrained by *control information or conditions* under which the transformation occurs (the top arrows).

This work was previously published in the Handbook of Research on Developments in E-Health and Telemedicine: Technological and Social Perspectives, edited by Maria Manuela Cruz-Cunha; Antonio J. Tavares; Ricardo Simoes, pp. 904-917, copyright 2010 by IGI Publishing (an imprint of IGI Global).

Chapter 4.20
Lotus Workforce Management:
Streamlining Human Resource Management

Jerh. O'Connor
IBM, Ireland

Ronan Dalton
IBM, Ireland

Don Naro
IBM, Ireland

ABSTRACT

Human Resources departments are often burdened with administrative tasks performed on behalf of employees who lack the tools necessary to complete these tasks themselves. A software approach known as self-service aims to streamline HR processes by providing employees with access and control of their personal information. Different approaches to self-service have been developed, including solutions offered by SAP, Sage Software, and IBM®. This article examines the approach taken by IBM Lotus® Workforce Management, which is a self-service solution for IBM WebSphere® Portal. Most of the self-service solutions available in the marketplace do provide HR capabilities for an organization's workforce, however, these solutions are usually designed as "out-of-the-box" software that require an organization to adopt a particular approach and a specific set of functionality. Lotus Workforce Management, on the other hand, focuses on providing three key features that allow organizations more choice and control over the implementation of a self-service solution. These features are extensibility, customization, and ease of integration. Extensibility is provided through the WebSphere Portal framework that lets users add or remove components and functionality and determine the structure of communication between portal resources. Integration with IBM WebSphere Portlet Factory gives users the ability to customize and design a solution that is tailored to their needs. Finally, ease of integration with HR resources that reside in a back end system is important as most organizations would be reluctant to change or make complex configurations to that system. For this reason, Lotus Workforce Management uses existing components for SAP ERP systems and provides functional code for rapid and simple integration without extensive configuration.

INTRODUCTION

This article describes an approach taken to develop a solution that streamlines Human Resource Management tasks with an emphasis on openness and flexibility to focus on the work performed by employees, managers and HR staff.

Interaction with Human Resource departments is not without problems. These issues affect all participants from average employees to managers to customer service representatives. All these users stand to benefit from a solution that streamlines their tasks and processes and removes or reduces pain points. In this article we share our experiences and insight gained during the design and development of Lotus® Workforce Management, a framework solution built on WebSphere® Portal. This framework provides a foundation to create flexible, extensible, and readily customisable HR self-service applications.

This article begins with a description of the Human Resources Management space, the major players within this space, and the issues and ideas that led to the creation of the Lotus Workforce Management framework. This article then describes the main components of the framework and explains how these components collaborate to fulfil the solution requirements. The article closes with a summary of what we have learned about the technical challenges in the HR self-service domain from our customers as well as some plans for the future.

Human Resource Management

Human Resource Management (HRM) is the professional practice and academic theory that relates to the structure and management of a workforce. In nearly every major organization today, there exists a Human Resources (HR) department. Regardless or whether public or private, profit or non-profit, organizations rely on HR departments to ensure that they not only attract a talented and competent workforce, but that the individuals who make up that workforce gain a sense of personal fulfilment and are encouraged to improve their skills and professional abilities, thereby assuring the organization's retention of the workforce.

As HR evolved, the level of associated administrative duties increased proportionally. Research suggests that as much as 70% of the time spent by the personnel of many HR departments was performing administrative tasks (Barron, 2002). These tasks were largely manual, paper-based, and focused on maintaining employee records. Information was often difficult to locate and changing it was a time-consuming affair. Data inaccuracy was common. Correcting mistakes diverted even more time and effort away from business-related activities.

However, HR departments have increasingly been able to make use of software systems that streamline these administrative processes. In turn, HR departments have been able to gain back valuable time to focus on strategic goals such as the recruitment and training of employees, the development of specific business practices and policies, and all the other functions that focus on the efficiency and effectiveness of an organization's workforce.

Numerous HRM systems have been developed and implemented, all with varying degrees of success. For the most part, though, currently available HRM systems fail to deliver true value to HR departments. The failures of these software systems stem from a single cause; employees are unable to take control of their own information and must ultimately depend on the HR department to complete common tasks. Whether because their information was spread over multiple systems, requiring multiple passwords, or because they were unable to access their information at the time when they needed to, employees often find HRM systems problematic and end up contacting their HR department to either enter the required information or to verify that the information was entered correctly. This failure has two effects: the first is that employees feel frustrated and dissatisfied; the second is that HR departments become weighed down in unnecessary administrative work.

A software approach known as self-service has taken shape to deal with the failures of previous HRM systems and not only give HR departments the ability to focus on their strategic objectives, but also to deliver a solution that is truly of benefit to a workforce.

Self Service

In the context of HRM, self-service is the ability of employees to manage their own HR information easily and at any time. Research has shown that HR departments benefit from self-service solutions, whether ESS (Employee Self-Service) or MSS (Manager Self-Service). Such benefits include gaining back time that would have been spent processing information and reducing data inaccuracy.

In one case study of a public sector organization in Australia, SAP's HR/Payroll module (4.0b), which included the ESS module and SAP's Workflow tool, was used to replace the existing system (Hawking, Stein, & Foster, 2004). In this study, the ESS module was shown to provide a number of benefits to the HR department such as an reduction of time spent processing payroll, an improvement in productivity, and an increase in strategic focus, while overcoming initial resistance from the workforce who were adapted to the previous system. The view taken by Hawking et al. was that the adoption of the ESS solution led to increased satisfaction among the workforce.

However, studies do suggest that the adoption of a self-service solution depends largely upon a positive reception by the workforce. Furthermore that the success of the self-service solution depends upon an intuitive user interface and verification of transactions (Marler & Dulebohn, 2005). Additional research indicates that employee satisfaction with self-service was also influenced by a single authentication mechanism and prompt access to HR information (Rahim, 2006).

Taking into account the conclusions drawn from such research, Web portals can be seen to offer much value to self-service applications as users can access portals through Web browsers, which presents a familiar and comfortable environment for users. Users do not need to learn how to use an entirely new client application and are familiar with entering data through Web forms and views. Additionally, when the Web interface to HR management systems are rendered through a Web portal, value can be added by connecting other Web applications and integrating more closely with the work environment. This integration makes the transition to self-service a much more seamless and cohesive experience for the workforce.

LOTUS WORKFORCE MANAGEMENT

IBM® Lotus® Workforce Management is a self-service accelerator for IBM WebSphere® Portal that improves employee productivity and performance by streamlining employee and manager-related activities. Lotus Workforce Management provides employees with personalised, online views into the specific content, self-service transactions, company intranet applications and third-party applications and services they require to operate more efficiently.

Lotus Workforce Management consists of a number of high-level components that collaborate to expose a wealth of Human Resource information and processes that are not traditionally accessible in a user friendly fashion.

The two Lotus Workforce Management components that users interact with most frequently are two portlets known as the checklist framework and the unified task list, UTL. Working together, these two components provide a means of launching and completing profiled events and activities in a uniform way even though individual activities may, and frequently do, occur on disparate back-end systems.

Lotus Workforce Management also provides specific pages and portlets that give managers a dynamic overview of the timesheets, leave requests, and general calendar-related activities for their employees.

The other components that give the checklists and UTL functionality are:

- An innovative approach to SAP data access
- A dynamic and flexible authentication framework
- IBM WebSphere Portlet Factory
- IBM WebSphere Portal and all its various features

The following diagram shows how all the UX and other components collaborate at run-time (Figure 1). The sections that follow the diagram describe the illustrated components in more detail.

Figure 1. Diagram showing how all the UX and other components collaborate at run-time

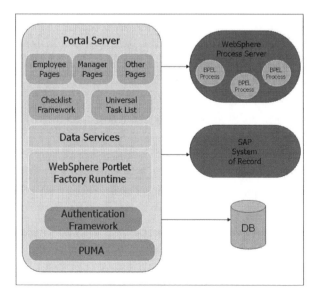

IBM WebSphere Portal

IBM WebSphere Portal provides the runtime environment for the Lotus Workforce Management application. As well as a JSR compliant portlet container there are a number of specific components for both Portal and the underlying IBM WebSphere Application Server, which make the resulting Lotus Workforce Management application more extensible and robust. This section provides a list of the most important of these components along with a brief description of what they do and which parts of Lotus Workforce Management use them.

Application Extension Registry

WebSphere Application Server has enabled the Eclipse™ extension framework that applications can use. Applications are extensible when they contain a defined extension point and provide the extension processing code for the extensible area of the application.

An application can be plugged in to another extensible application by defining an extension that adheres to what the target extension point requires. The extension point can find the newly added extension dynamically and the new function is seamlessly integrated in the existing application. It works on a cross Java™ 2 Platform, Enterprise Edition (J2EE) module basis. The application extension registry uses the Eclipse plug-in descriptor format and application programming interfaces (APIs) as the standard extensibility mechanism for WebSphere applications. Developers can use WebSphere Application Server extensions to implement their functionality to an extensible application, which defines an extension point. This is done through the application extension registry mechanism.

The architecture of extensible J2EE applications follows a modular design to add new functional modules or to replace existing modules, particularly by those outside of the core development team. Each module is a pluggable unit, or plug-in, that is either deployed into the portal or removed from the J2EE application using a deployment tool that is based upon standard J2EE and portal Web module deployment tooling. A plug-in module describes where it is extensible and what capability it provides to other plug-ins in the plugin.xml file.

The Lotus Workforce Management authentication and checklist frameworks both rely on the application extension registry to provide their dynamic extensibility.

PUMA

The Portal User Management Architecture (PUMA) System programming interface (SPI) provides interfaces for accessing the profiles of a portal User or Group. PUMA SPI is used to find, create, modify and delete users and groups. Profile information about the currently logged in user can also be retrieved.

PUMA is used extensively by Lotus Workforce Management, particularly by the authentication framework and in all components which profile content based on the logged in users and the groups to which users are members.

Credential Vault

The Credential Vault is a service that stores credentials and allows portlets to log in to applications on behalf of a user. The Credential Vault manages multiple identities for portlets and users. Using the Credential Vault, a portlet can retrieve a user's authentication identity and pass the information to a backend application.

The Credential Vault is a mature and easily used component which is core to the default authentication implementation that the Lotus Workforce Management authentication framework provides.

Portlet Wires

Portlet Wires are used to direct the information flow between portlets that communicate with one another using portlet events.

A wire connects a publishing event to a processing event of another portlet. When the source portlet fires an event source event has outgoing wires, the information is propagated to the target portlet(s). At the same time the corresponding handler code is invoked. Conversely, if an event is produced that is not wired to any targets, the event is simply discarded.

Creating wires is a part of page administration and requires appropriate access permissions. It is separated from the portlet development or deployment process, so that the portlet developer does not need to know the actual structure of inter-portlet communication. Communicating portlets can be developed independent of each other, as long as they agree on the same data type and semantics for data exchange.

Wiring is used wherever Lotus Workforce Management requires portlets to communicate with one another. Wiring not only provides the means of this communication but also enhances the ability of users to customise the solution by allowing for the wiring to be changed after deployment without any need to redevelop the core application.

IBM WebSphere Portlet Factory

WebSphere Portlet Factory is an Integrated Development Environment (IDE) and run-time environment for developing Java Web applications and portlets. While WebSphere Portlet Factory has many different capabilities and can run on various platforms, we used WebSphere Portlet Factory to create solutions hosted on IBM WebSphere Portal. Most of the components of the Lotus Workforce Management solution are developed on WebSphere Portlet Factory as it provides foundational artefacts that deliver the functionality that Lotus Workforce Management required much faster.

WebSphere Portlet Factory has a design time component and a run-time component. The WebSphere Portlet Factory designer is an Eclipse plug-in that provides the IDE for developing with

WebSphere Portlet Factory. To develop applications in WebSphere Portlet Factory, developers assemble builders into models and then build portlets from the models. Models are XML documents that define the order in which builders are called and what parameters are passed to the builders. Builders themselves are snippets of Java code that can do many things from generating a simple piece of HTML to retrieving data from a remote service. The builders assembled into a model are used to generate the contents of a Web application and a model is usually either consumed by other models or deployed as a portlet. Taken all together the models and builders in a WebSphere Portlet Factory project within the designer result in a web application for deployment on a portal server.

At run-time time the automation engine (a servlet) handles incoming requests and in conjunction with the WebSphere Portlet Factory profiling functionality provides dynamically profiled content.

SAP

SAP is a leading European software provider that is based in Germany. SAP products primarily focus on Enterprise Resource Planning (ERP). The company's main product is called SAP ERP. The current version is SAP ERP 6.0, which forms part of the SAP Business Suite. The previous version was R/3 and is still in widespread use.

SAP ERP is one of five enterprise applications in SAP's Business Suite. The other four applications are:

- Customer Relationship Management (CRM)
  - Helps companies acquire and retain customers as well as gain marketing and customer insight
- Product Lifecycle Management (PLM)
  - Helps manufacturers with product-related information
- Supply Chain Management (SCM)
  - Helps companies with the process of resourcing manufacturing and service processes

- Supplier Relationship Management (SRM)
  - Enables companies to procure from suppliers

SAP in HRM

SAP HRM or HCM (Human Capital Management) is also a part of SAP ERP and it is the part in which we are most interested as SAP is one of the leading providers of HCM solutions. Given SAP's dominance in the marketplace, engaged customers, and pre-existing software artefacts, SAP was chosen as the first system of record that Lotus Workforce Management would support.

The other driving force behind the decision to support SAP initially was the general dissatisfaction amongst customers with the user experience when interacting with SAP. This is especially true with regard to the older versions. To move to a more modern interface was not a simple upgrade when staying within the SAP product suite, which remains to be true today. The Lotus Workforce Management solution offers an attractive, nonproprietary, and complementary route to enhanced data interaction as well as the potential for integration with multiple other systems by leveraging the underlying capabilities of the WebSphere Portal and Application Server products.

SAP Integration

As discussed in the preceding section, SAP provides Enterprise Resource Planning software. Lotus Workforce Management leverages SAP's HR component as a system of record for its Employee and Manager Self Service functionality. Integration with SAP from Lotus Workforce Management is achieved by the use of SAP's Java Connector library. This Java Connector library, the SAP JCo, allows applications developed using the Java programming language access to SAP data via Remote Function Calls (RFCs). These RFCs are essentially remote enabled applications running on a deployed SAP system. SAP provides a suite of RFCs that can be called to perform a variety of operations. These RFCs provided by SAP are known as BAPIs. Lotus Workforce Management interacts with these BAPIs but also provides a set of additional RFCs that are deployed on an SAP system. These Lotus Workforce Management RFCs allow for a greater degree of access to information stored on SAP's HR component.

Data in SAP's HR component is structured as a set of infotypes. Infotypes are logical representations of data as this data exists inside the SAP HR component. The data to which we refer here is essentially employee related information. For example, you'd expect a HR management system to capture data about an employee's address, pay details, emergency contact information and so on. Each of these examples are stored on SAP's HR component as infotypes. Each infotype in turn can have a number of subtypes. As a generic infotype becomes specialised, this specialised infotype is referred to as a subtype. Again, an example may help with the understanding here. Take the address infotype, this address can be of varying types, for example a permanent address, a temporary address, a holiday address and so on. Each of these specialised types of address is considered a subtype of the address infotype.

SAP's BAPIs, the remote enabled applications we introduced above, provide access to these infotypes and subtypes, but do so in a defined and somewhat restrictive manner. Calling a BAPI to read an instance of an infotype, requires that a defined set of parameters be passed when making the remote call and in turn a defined set of return values are made available. The return values made available when calling a BAPI on SAP do not reflect the entire Infotype data structure. Rather, a limited set of fields are returned, which may not meet the requirement of the calling application. Let us use an example to help illustrate. Let us say for example, we wanted to read an employee's permanent address from an SAP system. When reading a permanent address using a BAPI, we have access to only a subset of the infotype information on SAP. So where a permanent address infotype on SAP may include 50 fields, we have access to only 10 for example.

For this reason, the Lotus Workforce Management application delivers an implementation of an approach to retrieving all infotype data via remote function call. The implementation is delivered as ABAP code (the SAP specific programming language) by Lotus Workforce Management and is a fully functional RFC. By deploying this ABAP code on an SAP system, access is provided to all infotypes and subtypes available on the SAP HR component. This ABAP once deployed and configured as an RFC, can be called by a remote Java application using the SAP JCo connector. In this manner any application developed using the Java programming language has access to all SAP infotypes.

Lotus Workforce Management provides a tight approach to integration with this RFC by delivering a specially designed WebSphere Portlet Factory builder. This builder, called the SAP Infotype builder, leverages the existing SAP builders delivered by WebSphere Portlet Factory to connect with SAP via the SAP JCo Connector library. Having established a connection, the SAP Infotype builder interacts directly with the custom RFC delivered with the Lotus Workforce Management solution, providing services to create, retrieve, update and delete infotypes on SAP.

Using this and other builders as it's foundation, Lotus Workforce Management provides a means of interacting with the SAP system of record that is not possible using the traditional BAPI approach.

Custom Components

The following components are those we developed specifically to resolve issues in streamlining the HRM interaction action experience. These components leverage underlying application features as mentioned in previous sections.

Checklist Framework

When we need to do tasks that comprise a number of steps we work from a checklist. We do this in everyday day life when we work from a recipe or use a grocery list. In the content of human resource interaction these lists are for tasks such as hiring a new employee or changing of one's marital status. As we progress through these lists we check off completed items. So put simply a checklist is a list of activities to be carried out to accomplish a particular task. Within Lotus Workforce Management this task, or event, can be anything and comprises a list of activities which can involve interaction with people and applications. An oft used example of a checklist is that of the change address event.

To extend flexibility there are many attributes which activities possess:

- They can be organised into related groups
- They can be mandatory or optional
- They can have a required completion order
- They can integrate with various external systems
- They can exist on various backend repositories

Moreover the containing checklist can:

- Be unique or multiply occurring for the owning user
- Restricted in access particular groups
- Have its status changed based on its age

Both checklist templates and in-flight checklists are represented as xml documents the storage of which is provided and abstracted by a persistence layer. This representation allows for simple manipulation of the checklists as well as enhanced readability of the checklist contents outside of the Lotus Workforce Management application.

Presentation

Checklists are presented to the user by one of three portlets.

The My Resources Portlet

The My Resources portlet (Figure 2) provides a profiled and categorised list of checklists to the logged in user. This profiling provides for targeting of function so that a manager can for example exploit resource management events such as promotion which would not be presented to an employee.

Figure 2. The My Resources portlet

The UTL Task List Portlet

The task list portlet of the UTL displays in-flight checklists that are owned by the current logged in user. This is the users' primary means of accessing active checklist instances.

The Checklist Portlet

The checklist portlet is responsible for rendering checklists and presenting the activities to the user. Most of the heavy lifting here is performed by the checklist builder, a custom built WebSphere Portlet Factory artefact.

Operation

New events are initiated by the user via the My Resources portlet. A user simply selects one of the categorised events and typically a new checklist instance is created and displayed in the checklist portlet. If however the selected event is unique and pre-existing it is the pre-existing instance of the checklist which is presented to the user. An example of one such event is the change marital status event which is unique per user at any given time.

With the checklist available in the checklist portlet the user can proceed with completing the listed activities. Unsequenced activities can be completed in any order and non-mandatory activities can marked complete by the user or simply ignored. At any stage the user may save the state of the checklist and proceed to do other things.

To return to an in-flight checklist the user typically uses the UTL task list portlet. On the selection of the required task from this portlet the checklist portlet restores the previous state of the checklist and work can proceed.

Each individual activity in a checklist delegates its function to an activity handler. Activity handlers can be as simple as URL handlers handling redirection to another portal page or as complex as a handler to interact with a workflow engine.

Lotus Workforce Management ships with a number of pre-built handlers including those for interacting with WebSphere Portlet Factory

models and portal page redirects. Additional handlers can easily and dynamically be added via the implementation of an extension class or statically added with the creation of a new WebSphere Portlet Factory model.

As in real life as time passes the status of incomplete checklist instances changes, the checklist sub-component of the checklist framework runs on a configurable schedule and visits each in-flight checklist in turn. For each instance it compares the current time with the creation time of the checklist and based on a set of customer configurable values it changes the status of the checklist and/or sends email alerts to specified parties.

Unified Task List

The UTL task list portlet aggregates tasks and activities from multiple systems into a single user interface. WebSphere Portal users access the unified task list portlet to complete these tasks and activities in order to advance workflows.

Presentation

The UTL presents a simple and easily understood interface to the business user as well as a comprehensive range of configuration options to an administrative level user. As with all the major components used in Lotus Workforce Management the UTL is also flexible and dynamically extensible. Some of its capabilities are listed in the following table by user role (Table 1).

Table 1. UTL capabilities

Role	Task
All	add task list providers at runtime via the portlet configuration view
All	enable the filtering and sorting of the aggregated task list
Administrator	enable or disable caching
Administrator	configure how task pages should be launched

Figure 3. Unified task list

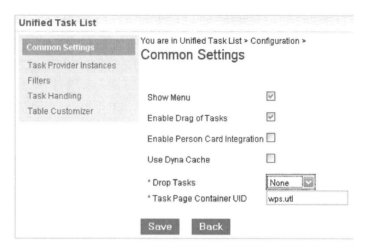

The tasks presented to the user are those the individual task providers decide the user is eligible to see (Figure 3). This may mean simply that the user is the owner of the task as in the case of a checklist task or that the user is one of the potential owners of a WebSphere Process Server hosted process task.

Operation

When the task list portlet is loaded it determines the logged in users attributes via PUMA, the Portal User Management Architecture, SPI. The central task dispatcher then passes this information to each of the listed task providers. It is then the individual task provider's responsibility to return a list of relevant tasks to sort and display. In the current version there are task providers for Checklist tasks, IBM WebSphere Process Server tasks, and SAP workflow tasks.

The user can now select any task from the list. Each task type is handled by a task details portlet the launching of which is user configurable. We have already seen that the checklist portlet provides the task details UI for checklist tasks and whilst a generic UI is provided for the out of the box task types the pattern of usage would be that the details portlets would very much be task specific and need to be developed by the customer of a case by case basis.

Authentication

The Lotus Workforce Management authentication solution was designed to provide a dynamic and extensible framework for single sign-on between the portal resident Lotus Workforce Management application and the HR repository of choice at the backend. It has a generic approach to authentication which allows for the dynamic alteration of authentication mechanism with no observable impact on the end user. The framework comprises largely WebSphere Portal server artefacts with companion WebSphere Portlet Factory client artefacts to allow for its use in portlet factory base applications.

The framework leverages WebSphere Application Server's implementation of the Eclipse extension framework and it is this which allows for the flexibility and extensibility of the solution. Additional authentication mechanisms can be added to the application server and these are automatically detected by the Lotus Workforce Management authentication administration portlet. This portlet then allows the administrator to chose a new authentication mechanism and configure its settings all without any code change to the pre-existing deployment.

An authentication broker, implemented as WebSphere Portal service, is the single point of contact between the Lotus Workforce Management application and the pluggable authentication mechanisms. This allows applications to be developed without being tied to a particular authentication mechanism.

Identities

There are three main artefacts when it comes to authentication and identification between the Lotus Workforce Management application and the HR backend. These are the credentials used to authenticate with the portal system, the credentials used to authenticate with that backend, and the employee's identifier in the HR backend.

The following sections describe each of these artefacts in turn and explain how they interoperate to surface information to the Lotus Workforce Management user.

Portal Authentication

By default WebSphere Portal uses the Custom Form-based Authentication mechanism of IBM WebSphere Application Server to prompt users for identity. Users type their user ID and password in the login portlet or the login screen of the portal. It has support for many other types including SSL, custom forms, and third party authentication with Tivoli® Access Manager for example.

SAP Personnel Number

In SAP employees are identified but their personnel number, a system wide unique string which is used in most interactions with the SAP backend system. The personnel number supplied to the backend ensures that the employee information specific to that personnel number is returned to the requestor. For example a call to get an address will only return address information for the personnel number passed to the get address call. There are temporal and other standard parameters that also affect the information returned but for the purposes of this section we are only interested in the personnel number.

Backend Authentication

Obviously before one can retrieve information from the HR system the request must be authenticated. As our solution is Java based we use the SAP Java Connector to connect to the SAP backend. The connection methods of the java connector require credentials to authenticate requests and subsequently return information. The Java Connector supports SSO with username and password credentials and logon tickets. It also supports x509 certificates. Whilst the Lotus Workforce Management authentication framework is flexible enough to accommodate all there, and more, the out of the box authentication implementation uses the common username and password credential combination. The username has no relation to the personnel number. It is used purely to authenticate with the backend and determine authorisation rights. Depending on the rights of the username, information on more than one personnel number may be retrieved or altered.

Interoperation

WebSphere Portal stores information about it's users in a user registry and access to this registry is provided programmatically via PUMA, the Portal User Management Architecture, SPI. Our solution leverages the WebSphere Portal user registry and its credential vault component to provide a single sign-on mechanism between the Lotus Workforce Management application and the HR backend.

We map the SAP personnel number to an attribute in the Portal user registry. This provides the linkage between the user's identity in Portal and their identity in SAP. Independently if this link we store the SAP logon credentials in Portal's credential vault. The credentials stored are determined by the mapping type chosen by the portal administrator. The default mapping is n-1 where multiple portal users logon to SAP with the same shared credential. The other mapping supported by the username and password authentication mechanism is a 1-1 mapping where each portal user has their own SAP credential in the vault.

These mappings provide two distinct runtime paths on initial logon to the Lotus Workforce Management application:

- n-1 mapping
  - There is no credential challenge as only the administrator can set the password. If the password is set and valid the user notices nothing. If the password is invalid (unset or expired for example) the user is presented with a customisable error message.
- 1-1 mapping
  - If a valid credential exists in the vault for the user they seamlessly go to the Lotus Workforce Management application. If the password is invalid the user is presented with a challenge. On successful completion of the challenge the new valid credential is persisted to the vault and the user continues to the Lotus Workforce Management application.

The challenge is determined by the authentication mechanism in use and in the case of the default username and password implementation the challenge is the familiar dual text entry field for username and password. The framework allows for any type of challenge as long as the accompanying authentication mechanism can handle the returned credential.

Builders

A set of WebSphere Portlet Factory builders we developed and released with the Lotus Workforce Management solution. These builders were designed to provide rapid application development capabilities for the Portlet Factory developer creating HR portlets in particular. The builders themselves are broken into three broad categories:

1. Base builders
2. SAP builders
3. Checklist builders

The Checklist builders form part of the previously discussed checklist framework and provide a solution for lightweight workflow type applications running on WebSphere Portal. SAP builders and Base builders are designed specifically to build HR portlets using data from SAP. The sections that follow discuss each category in more detail.

Base Builders

The Base builders delivered with Lotus Workforce Management provide essentially two core services for the SAP builders. Firstly the Base builders operate as a point of integration with the Authentication Framework. Tightly coupled with services provided by the Authentication Framework, the Lotus Workforce Management Credential builder will determine whether a user has already supplied valid credentials to access SAP. If no valid credentials are present, the user will be asked to enter a user name and password for SAP. Once these credentials are verified, the builder will then store these values in WebSphere Portal's credential vault. Secondly, the Lotus Workforce Management Base builder will provide access to a range a valuable data from SAP to a Portlet Factory model developed using the Lotus Workforce Management SAP builders. This data is core information about the logged in user that may be required numerous times in the life of the application. This Lotus Workforce Management Base builder will retrieve relevant information via a one time call to SAP, store the information in local variables and make this information available via a set of public methods that can be called by other builders in the model.

SAP Builders

The SAP builders delivered with Lotus Workforce Management aim to abstract away from the complexity of calling Remote Function Calls on SAP. Five builders are included in this category of builders with specialised functions to

- Read table data on SAP
- Perform create, retrieve, update and delete (CRUD) operations on HR data on SAP

- Provide a presentation layer for the data access functions listed above

The SAP Infotype builder is one of the foundational builders in this category. Responsible for performing the CRUD operations on HR data mentioned above, this builder is designed for use by the business analyst that has no specific knowledge of working with SAP APIs known as BAPIs. Creating a web application or portlet that interacts with SAP as a HRM system would typically require expert knowledge of SAP's BAPIs. Clever logic inside the SAP Infotype builder removes this onus from the developer, empowering the business analyst to develop SAP HR portlets in just minutes.

This category of SAP builder should not be confused with the SAP builders delivered with the WebSphere Portlet Factory product itself. WebSphere Portlet Factory's SAP builders are raw data access builders that require the user be skilled in working with SAP's BAPIs when developing a web application. These builders certainly have a place in the SAP web application development space but the Lotus Workforce Management SAP builders are of particular value when leveraging SAP as a Human Resources Management System. Technically, the Lotus Workforce Management SAP builders have a dependency on the WebSphere Portlet Factory SAP builder and in fact leverage the SAP Function Call builder delivered with WebSphere Portlet Factory. This dependency is of course by design, leveraging the connection pooling already implemented by Portlet Factory.

CONCLUSION

In this article we described the motivations behind the development of the Lotus Workforce Management solution; the desire for a customisable solution, the need for ease of integration, and the requirement for extensibility. We showed how each of these goals were met and what technologies and assets were used to create Lotus Workforce

Management. During the course of the project we strove to reuse as much as possible of the underlying stack components. Both WebSphere Portal and WebSphere Portlet Factory provided us with a significant amount of functionality out of the box, for example, the user management feature of Portal and the SAP feature set in Portlet Factory. WebSphere Portal and WebSphere Portlet Factory also provided the ability to customise and extend Lotus Workforce Management. The Eclipse extension framework in Portal and the builder/model architecture in Portlet Factory are perhaps the most pertinent examples of the capacity for customising and extending Lotus Workforce Management.

The following sections enumerate some of the experiences of the team during this project and provide a view on the future direction of work on Lotus Workforce Management.

Lessons Learned

The development of the Lotus Workforce Management solution involved a relatively large team of developers, some with experience of Java, some with SAP, and some more with Portal. During the course of the project we encountered the usual issues development teams hit as well as some more specific ones. This section aims to share a synopsis of those issues.

Knowledge Acquisition

Throughout this project we had SAP domain experience in two key areas of SAP; the functional area of human resources within SAP and the development of Advanced Business Application Programming, ABAP, the COBOL like language used to develop on SAP.

These skills enabled us to develop the SAP resident functionality we required and administer the SAP systems we used for test. However, even with such expertise onboard there was still much effort involved in determining the information we required to interact with SAP at the level we wanted to. The experience of our SAP resources allowed us the mine this information more quickly but knowledge acquisition was still something that took longer than originally anticipated.

User Experience

The main purpose of this project was to streamline access to HR data. The presentation of such data to the end user, as well as the paths to access this data, is one of the most important means of achieving this streamlining. With the use of the Universal Task List, the My Resources portlet and its companion the checklist framework, as well as the themed portal pages we feel we successfully achieved this user experience goal.

As always some things slip through however and in our case the most obvious of these is the need for a user to specifically save a checklist to persist state. It would be better if activities could be auto-saved on completion. So doing would prevent users losing state if they were to forget to manually save a checklist before moving on.

The lesson here is that experienced UX resource involvement at all stages of the project and most especially at the beginning and end is invaluable.

Testing

As we have shown the Lotus Workforce Management solution comprises a number of collaborating components used at both design time and run-time. Both of these types of components presented their own challenges from a test point of view.

The design time builders had to be tested for integration with the rest of the WebSphere Portlet Factory artefacts and also for integration with the WebSphere Portlet Factory builders on which some of them are built.

The run-time components, both those produced via WebSphere Portlet Factory and the authentication framework, naturally had to be system and performance tested as a whole. The development of a test harness and the allocation of unearthed defects proved to be the most troublesome aspects here due to the number of moving parts.

When going through a similar project in future planning and implementation effort will be expended to system and performance the larger components in isolation before the whole solution is subjected to these tests.

AUTHOR NOTES

IBM®, the IBM logo, and ibm.com® are trademarks or registered trademarks of International Business Machines Corporation in the United States, other countries, or both. If these and other IBM trademarked terms are marked on their first occurrence in this information with a trademark symbol (® or ™), these symbols indicate U.S. registered or common law trademarks owned by IBM at the time this information was published. Such trademarks may also be registered or common law trademarks in other countries. A current list of IBM trademarks is available on the Web at http://www.ibm.com/legal/copytrade.shtml

Java™, and all Java-based trademarks and logos are trademarks of Sun Microsystems, Inc. in the United States, other countries, or both.

Lotus®, is a trademark or registered trademark of IBM Corporation and/or Lotus Development Corporation in the United States, other countries, or both.

REFERENCES

Barron, M. (2002). *Retail web-based self-serve isn't just for customers, it's for employees.* Chicago: Internet Retailer.

Hawking, P., Stein, A., & Foster, S. (2004). e-HR and Employee Self Service: A Case Study of a Victorian Public Sector Organisation. *Issues in Informing Science and Information Technology, 1.*

Marler, J. H., & Dulebohn, J. H. (2005). A Model of Employee Self-Service Technology Acceptance. *Research in Personnel and Human Resources Management, 24*, 137–180. doi:10.1016/S0742-7301(05)24004-5

Rahim, M. M. (2006). *Understanding Apdotion and Impact of B2E E-Business Systems: Lessons Learned from the experience of an Australian University.* Melbourne, Victoria, Australia: Monash Univesity. 5 Trademarks Trademark information is provided to identify terms that are exclusively reserved for use by the owner.

Tivoli®, and WebSphere®, are trademarks of the IBM Corporation in the United States, other countries, or both.

Chapter 4.21
Virtual Tutoring:
The Case of TutorVista

Beena George
University of St. Thomas, USA

Charlene Dykman
University of St. Thomas, USA

EXECUTIVE SUMMARY

This case presents the story of TutorVista, an e-business organization based in India that provides online tutoring services to students in different parts of the world. TutorVista had been able to meet growth expectations and gain recognition in the lucrative private tutoring market because of its innovative technology platform and business model. As a fledgling organization charting new territory, TutorVista faced the dual challenges of creating and capturing the demand for online tutoring and managing resources to satisfy the shifting demand. Note: this case was constructed based on interviews with individuals at TutorVista.

ORGANIZATION BACKGROUND

TutorVista was established in Bangalore, India, in July 2005, with the goal of providing personalized, convenient, and affordable education to students at any location. The mission statement read:

Our mission is to provide world-class tutoring and high-quality content to students around the world. TutorVista.com is the premier online destination for affordable education—anytime, anywhere, and in any subject. Students can access our service from the convenience of their home or school. They use our comprehensive and exhaustive lessons and question bank to master any subject and have access to a live tutor around the clock. TutorVista helps students to excel in school and at competitive examinations.

The primary target markets were the United States and United Kingdom, since English would be the medium of instruction. Students used TutorVista to gain access to a personal tutor, 24/7, from their home or dorm room, and received personalized tutoring on subjects or assistance in preparing for competitive exams like SAT, ACT, and so on. The price was set at $99.99 a month for unlimited sessions in various subjects, making it a viable option for many who would never have considered it before. As one satisfied parent remarked, "I like to tell people I did private tutoring (*for my child*) every day for the cost of a fast-food meal or a Starbucks' coffee [*sic*]" (Szep, 2006).

The business model at one level was similar to models employed in outsourcing of IT and IT-enabled services, but there were significant differences.

1. TutorVista was the first business-to-consumer (B2C) company focused on the U.S. and European consumer markets, operating directly from India, leveraging Web 2.0 features. Annual revenues from such "person-to-person offshoring" (PPO) of services was estimated to top $2 billion by 2015 by Evaluserve, a business research services firm based in Gurgaon, India.

2. TutorVista functioned as a virtual organization. Tutors were recruited, hired, and trained over the Internet. The tutors worked from home, tutoring their students Figure 1. TutorVista's global B2C model

3. Technology developed in-house at TutorVista provided the means to manage and conduct tutoring sessions online. TutorVista could connect tutors and students from any location (see Figure 1) and serve more students without having to build centers; the virtual nature of the organization made scalability easier than in typical IT and IT-enabled services outsourcing organizations. For example, when a student from U.S. wanted to learn Chinese, TutorVista found a tutor in Hong Kong within a week and offered tutoring to the student.

4. Moving away from the hourly charges model, TutorVista was the first to offer a flat-price tutoring plan. While traditional tutoring in the U.S. could cost $15-$75 per hour depend-

Figure 1. TutorVista's Global B2C model

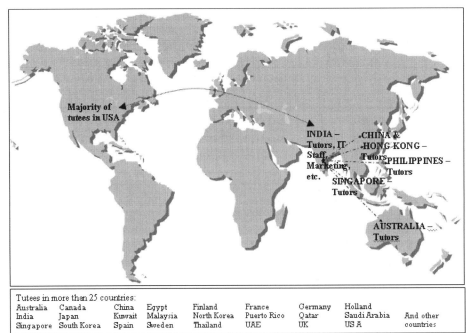

Table 1. Comparison of pricing for different modes of tutoring in the U.S. (based on rates published on various Internet sites)

Private tutoring	Hourly charge	$20 to $75, depending on subject for K-12
Center-based tutoring (e.g., Sylvan)	Hourly charge	$30 to $45, depending on location of center and subject
Online tutoring	Hourly charge	$15 to $30
TutorVista	Monthly, unlimited	$99

ing on mode of tutoring, TutorVista charged $99.99 per month in the U.S. for unlimited online tutoring in all subjects. For similar services, charges in the UK were £50 per month.

While other companies had been offering tutoring services on the Internet for some time, what differentiated TutorVista were their pricing model and their capability for scalability. TutorVista prided itself in belonging to a new generation of companies in the realm of knowledge process outsourcing.

TutorVista – An Idea Takes Shape

TutorVista was founded by Krishnan Ganesh, a serial entrepreneur, after a visit to the United States in the early part of 2005, when he noticed two concerns being emphasized recurrently in the American media—education and healthcare. Ganesh had a successful record in entrepreneurial activities, having recently sold his third venture, Marketics, a market analytics firm based in Bangalore, to WNS, a leading provider of business process outsourcing services. Interested in leveraging Indian resources for global markets, he was intrigued by the possibility of addressing the U.S. education crisis by deploying overseas resources.

Ganesh saw a paradox in the American educational system:

"United States produces the highest number of Nobel laureates in the world and probably has the best higher education systems in the world…but at the school level, there is a glaring deficiency. In a comparison of students from the top thirty nations in the world, American students were ranked twenty-ninth in Math skills and twenty-sixth in Science skills."

Investigating further, he realized that the problem is not a lack of schools, teachers, or funds, but a lack of personalized attention. Ganesh believed that every child, whether struggling or excelling in school, required this attention. In his words:

The amount of attention needed may vary, the goal may vary – it could be passing a course, changing a C to A, or getting into Harvard, but each person requires some amount of handholding that they are not getting now.

A very lucrative tutoring market had been made visible by the No Child Left Behind Act of 2001, signed into law in January of 2002. The NCLB Act provided a focus on the output and accountability of the primary and secondary educational processes. The intent was to assure that all children in the public school system (K-12) received the support needed for academic success. The performance of schools was measured in a variety of ways, including testing. Those schools that did not meet certain standards were required to make supplemental academic services, such as tutoring, available to their students. This tutoring was often made available, free to students, through contracts with profit-making organizations that specialized in subject-specific (such as mathematics, reading, etc.) tutoring as well as learning-enhancement-focused tutoring (such as critical thinking, study skills, etc.) (Vergari, 2007).

The NCLB mandate, and subsequent media attention, increased public awareness of the dismal state of the educational system and brought to guardians' attention the need for tutoring for their student. Several U.S.-based companies were struggling to reach profitability in this market, and Ganesh quickly saw the potential for a new business model that would bring together a highly educated, but low wage, Indian population with a demand for subject-specific experts to tutor students via the Internet. However, the NCLB market was very complex. Though there was a U.S. government-funded guaranteed market for the services, regulations, such as background checking of all tutors, would present significant complications for a company with tutors based in India. Ganesh studied the tutoring market beyond that presented by the NCLB ACT and saw great potential in a general demand for tutors in the one-on-one private tutoring market, if the pricing model could be made attractive.

TutorVista, with a new business model, would provide a B2C service from India directly to the overseas consumer, and TutorVista would own the full experience, brand, and share of the wallet. Previously, for the end consumer in the United States or Europe in a business-to-business (B2B) relationship, the Indian offshore organization provided only a small and largely invisible part of the value chain, with no brand recognition for the Indian company. As the business plan was developed, there were many issues to consider. Would it be possible to create a consumer brand based in India and owned completely by an Indian organization? Would it be possible to create a B2C e-business where the U.S. consumer's experience was completely provided by the Indian organization? Would it be possible to create a service where a hundred percent of the revenue accrued to the Indian organization?

The credibility of the India Inc. brand also played a part in the decision to offer tutoring services from India. A market research study was conducted in the United States; 25 parents were asked if they would purchase online tutoring services from India. The results were uniformly encouraging. The parents who were surveyed based their positive responses on the perception of India as a nation that values education and that produces a number of graduates excelling in the Math and Science disciplines. The success of Indians in the school and college education system in the U.S. also contributed to the level of comfort of the parents with this offshore online tutoring model.

Ganesh's previous experiences in turning greenfield ventures in different domains into successful organizations gave him the confidence to forge ahead. He knew that he could get the domain expertise by hiring experienced educators. What TutorVista needed to be able to do was to hire, train, and deploy staff who understood specific aspects of the target environment well enough to provide the required services. The "hire, train, deploy" process had been a common refrain in his past ventures, and he was comfortable with that.

Ganesh knew that the commitment and quality of the tutors would play a key role in TutorVista's success. Qualified tutors were identified through a stringent recruitment process and trained in different pedagogical styles, technology, and cultural differences. TutorVista offered flexible work scheduling and an attractive remuneration package to its tutors, and tutor achievements were recognized in internal documents and Web sites. Further, plans for growth of the organization were communicated to the employees on a timely basis through meetings in different towns and over the Web.

Technology would play a critical part in TutorVista's success. Ganesh recognized the need to leverage the advances in information and communication technology. Information technology professionals were recruited to develop a system that would connect tutors and tutees in different locations and enable TutorVista to manage the process and quality control from a central location (Bangalore). To the consumer, the tutee, the technology should be invisible and, as TutorVista's slogan stated, provide "world-class tutoring just a click away."

SETTING THE STAGE

Public school K-12 education in the United States had been under great scrutiny during the last few decades (McCluskey, 2004) as local, state, and national governments tried to understand and address the gaps between the realities of U.S. public school education and the need to have an educated and competent workforce to meet the needs of the evolving and rapidly changing economy. The No Child Left Behind Act offered opportunities for tutoring companies, but also brought significant governmental oversight through an array of regulations. Nevertheless, several new companies—including SmarThinking and Tutor.com—jumped into this market with online tutoring offerings. Technology capabilities made this a real possibility, building upon increased acceptance of online education in general within the U.S. population. Even established companies, such as Sylvan Learning Centers, entered this market with eSylvan in 2002—offering group tutoring sessions for three students or less for each session.

However, low-performing schools were often in low-income areas with limited home access to technology. In such communities, technology is often available through the public library system, and Tutor.com addressed this market through acquisition of Real Time Learning, which provided customized tutoring services to libraries (Cigale, 2005). Tutor.com began in 1998 as an online registry for tutors in partnership with Princeton Review, a standardized test preparation firm (BusinessWire, 2000). Profitability was not assured, in spite of the built-in market offered by the NCLB. The labor costs using U.S.-based tutors were high, and the unpredictability of demand made it difficult to manage the supply side of the business.

The U.S. government provided financial support directly to the schools to provide these services for their students (NEA, 2001); however, the NCLB did not provide exact specifications for how these services were to be made available.

Nor did the NCLB Act require that students avail themselves of these support services. Since schools could use the NCLB funding in a variety of ways, there was a reluctance to promote the tutoring services to the parents involved (Education Notebook, 2006). Often schools were directing these funds for other activities that were considered critical for the individual school's performance scores.

In addition to the NCLB-inspired tutoring services, private tutoring to meet academic challenges represented a significant market in the U.S., although estimates of potential varied widely. Reports based on research by Eduventures, an educational market research firm in Boston, placed the private tutoring market in the K-12 space at $4 billion and growing at an annual rate of 15% (Daria, 2007). Roughly $132 million was spent on online tutoring in 2005, and nearly $25 million of this went to tutors based in India (Hua, 2006). The significantly lower wages paid to online tutors in India, coupled with increased sophistication and reliability in technology, represented serious market opportunities. India's highly educated population excelled in many of the subjects for which students in the U.S. required tutoring support, most notably, mathematics and sciences.

Ganesh's plan was to leverage this human capital and technology resources to provide personalized services to tutees in the U.S. and elsewhere. He sought needed funding, securing $2 million in series A round funding, led by Sequoia Capital and prior angel investors in June 2006. TutorVista was an attractive investment because of Krishnan Ganesh's successful entrepreneurial track record and TutorVista's innovative business model. TutorVista used these early funds primarily to expand operations in the U.S. and the UK. A second round of venture funding brought in $10.75 million. With these additional funds, TutorVista planned to enter the new markets for English language teaching in the Far East and expand its offerings into the Indian market. Currently, all of TutorVista's operations are fully funded.

Table 2. Funding in two rounds—2006-2007

Round A	Sequoia Capital	$2.0 million
Round B	Sequoia Capital	$3.0 million
	Light Speed	$7.0 million
	Manipal Education and Medical Group	$2.5 million
	Silicon Valley Bank Financial Group	$0.75 million
Total		$14.75 million

CASE DESCRIPTION

In Spring, 2008, Krishnan Ganesh was about to convene a meeting of his colleagues and managers at TutorVista. It was time to step back from the last two years of explosive growth and determine a strategy for the next stage of his firm. The competitive environment was changing, technology continued to rapidly evolve, and significant changes were occurring in the labor markets in India as the technology revolution progressed offshore.

The United States K-12 tutoring market was maturing, and yet for most firms in the market, there was a startling dependency on the demand created by the No Child Left Behind Act. TutorVista was in a good position because it had focused on direct-to-consumer marketing. The NCLB Act was clearly the result of political and legislative efforts in the U.S. and was vulnerable to elimination, with a new president to take office in January 2009. Would this significantly impact the overall tutoring market?

Ganesh recognized that this was a critical time in the life of his company. He needed to develop a clear strategy if he were to realize his dream of becoming "part of a household's monthly budget if the family contains a student who is studying something." TutorVista was "trying to make tutoring on demand a part of the household monthly budget, like a health club membership." The road ahead presented real challenges. How could Ganesh leverage TutorVista's investments in infrastructure, both human and technological, to create a sustained acceptance of tutoring originating in India? His managers were convened to help brainstorm about the possibilities ahead.

The Key Managers

One of TutorVista's first moves after inception had been to acquire domain expertise, by hiring Jarrod Brown as academic director. Brown joined TutorVista in November 2005 in Bangalore, India, where he prepared tutor training seminars focused on one-on-one pedagogy, the tutoring cycle, and key differences between the Indian and American educational and communication models. He worked in Bangalore for six months creating a large repository of online resources to provide tutor training and serve as an online reference as tutors prepared their tutoring sessions.

After his time in Bangalore, Brown worked from his offices in Lexington, Kentucky, leading the development of resources in different subject areas and for test preparation courses. He was also involved in design and delivery of tutor certification and training. Other responsibilities included research in one-on-one pedagogy, and managing existing alliances between educational institutions in the U.S. and TutorVista. For example, TutorVista works to match the curricula in various independent school districts in the U.S.

In December 2006, Dr. John Stuppy joined TutorVista as president, managing TutorVista's U.S. operations, increasing brand awareness, and identifying partnership opportunities for TutorVista. Stuppy earned undergraduate and graduate degrees in Curriculum Studies & Teacher Education from Stanford University, an MBA from Kent College, and a PhD in Education Policy Analysis from UCLA. He joined TutorVista from The Princeton Review, where he served as chief information officer. Prior to that he was at Sylvan Learning Systems, where he was awarded 12 patents for various instructional delivery and assessment systems. Stuppy then joined Educational Testing Services as the vice president for product development. He also served as chief operating officer for Software Technology, Inc. a provider of information technology solutions for school systems. Stuppy was also a successful entrepreneur who founded Articulate Publications, Inc. in 1981. He brought not only educational expertise to TutorVista, but also the experience of successfully creating and growing an organization.

Another key manager was Martin Baker, recruited in the United Kingdom, TutorVista's second target market. Baker had a MBA and over 17 years of experience working and building businesses in the UK. He managed country-wide operations of FedEx Kinko's for the UK and The Netherlands prior to joining TutorVista. While Baker's qualifications were not in the educational field, he had intimate knowledge of the market that TutorVista wanted to conquer. Ganesh had surrounded himself with significant entrepreneurial, educational, and technological expertise.

Marketing

Though TutorVista started operations in late 2005, it started marketing aggressively only in late 2006 (Hamm, 2007). The experienced marketing team worked to establish a strong consumer brand and took a multi-pronged approach to marketing the tutoring service, including search engine optimization and other search engine marketing strategies. Most of TutorVista's customers came to it by word-of-mouth or through viral marketing, an online advertising approach that functions like word-of-mouth. TutorVista had established alliances to ensure that the TutorVista name appeared on Web sites most likely to be visited by target customers. These B2B partnerships were established with educational providers and other organizations on a revenue sharing basis and with search engine companies on a pay-per-click basis.

- In November 2006, TutorVista inked a pay-per-click agreement, to be the exclusive online tutoring provider, with Microsoft's MSN Encarta online education portal.
- In March 2007, TutorVista announced a limited-time offer to customers of Educere, which provides over 2,000 virtual education courses and programs, to provide two weeks of free online tutoring and test preparation.
- In April 2007, TutorVista provided a limited-time offer to students of Vocabulary.com, a service that offers free vocabulary-enrichment programs.
- In April 2007, TutorVista inked an agreement with the American Book Company, a publisher specializing in standards-based state test preparation, to give their customers a free online diagnostic assessment for state exit, end of grade, or end of course exams and two free hours of online tutoring services.
- In May 2007, Lifelong Solutions, which provides resources in legal, financial, and medical solutions areas, chose TutorVista as its exclusive online provider of tutoring solutions, offered as part of Lifelong Solution's membership package.
- In the first quarter of 2008, TutorVista entered into an agreement with the public library system in Englewood, Colorado, to provide tutoring for patrons from kindergarten through the first year of college.

TutorVista also continues to offer promotional pricing packages on its Web site in pursuit of its growth targets. For example, for a short period in August 2007, TutorVista offered a promotional deal of $24.99 for the first month.

TutorVista hired RLM Public Relations, whose services included media relations development and competitive analysis, to create awareness of the TutorVista brand name. RLM's goals for TutorVista were to generate media coverage and public curiosity about TutorVista, to establish

TutorVista as a credible solution for parents and students, and to introduce TutorVista spokespeople as trustworthy sources on tutoring, online services, and the need for these services in the U.S. Further, RLM also worked with TutorVista to differentiate itself from existing supplemental educational service organizations.

RLM had a time-tested methodology to establish organizations in the public eye, focused on alerting media organizations to the availability of TutorVista spokespeople, and their expertise in areas of tutoring, test prep, and outsourced education. TutorVista garnered media attention to an extent that other tutoring service organizations had not achieved. Articles in local newspapers, and Time® magazine were followed by segments on ABC News, CNN, and NBC's Today. TutorVista was poised, with adequate funding and market recognition, to secure an important niche in this online tutoring marketplace. Ganesh predicted TutorVista would be profitable by the end of 2008 (Economist, 2007).

Technology

A TutorVista one-on-one tutoring session had to be tailored to meet the needs of the individual tutee through the use of its global network of resources—tutors located in six different countries. The information system developed by TutorVista's IT team would be the lynchpin of this organization. This posed a challenging technical task. The technology had to enable the student to schedule, pay, and interact with the tutor online while allowing the tutor to manage the tutoring session, access supplementary resources, and interact with the tutee. TutorVista's managers needed to use the technology for monitoring of the tutoring sessions for session initiation and completion, quality control, customer care, knowledge management, and administrative purposes. If a tutor was unexpectedly absent, the system needed to recognize this and help identify a substitute tutor. Breaks in connections during sessions had to be

minimized. According to one of the IT managers, the goal of the IT team was that "technology should be a black box for the student. The student experience should be focused on the tutoring and not be about overcoming technology problems."

To meet these objectives, TutorVista deployed an online portal, the entryway into TutorVista's service offerings online. This portal was developed completely by the in-house technology team, for tutor and student management. While course management tools existed, a tool that could provide the functionalities required for managing the tutoring environment did not exist. Being in Bangalore, dubbed the Silicon Valley of India, the resources to develop such a tool were also readily available. The portal was built on an open-source platform using Linux, Apache, MySQL, and PHP (George, 2007). Hundreds of tutors, managing schedules and completing tutoring session administrative tasks, and thousands of students, viewing and managing their accounts, were able to log on to this portal simultaneously. TutorVista filed for two patents on this tutoring management tool in 2007 (Bulkley, 2007).

For managing tutor-student interaction, TutorVista initially relied on the WebEx platform. According to TutorVista management, they were the first to use WebEx in a home environment (George, 2007); they were also probably the first to use WebEx in sessions with school-age kids. Given the size of their target market segment, TutorVista management believed that WebEx would not be adequate to meet its future needs. In the first half of 2007, the technology team at TutorVista completed the development of a tutoring tool, TutorVistaNow. With the development of this system, TutorVista was able to integrate multiple functions in one system: the portal, commerce, session timing and management, conferencing, and other programs.

TutorVistaNow, an Internet application, provided collaborative whiteboard and chat functionalities and allowed completely Web-based communication between tutors and tutees while integrating tightly with TutorVista's portal, providing a convenient way to manage and complete the tutoring session. With ownership of the tool, TutorVista had eliminated issues related to download and performance of third-party software, like WebEx. TutorVistaNow allowed tutees to access tutoring sessions on any computer that had Internet access, including public machines, and was designed to support the completion of thousands of simultaneous tutoring sessions (George, 2007).

TutorVistaNow offered an interactive environment which the tutors were trained to leverage. The tutors encouraged student participation and were able to elicit responses from students multiple times during the tutoring session. The online environment allowed the tutors to share resources from the online repository with the students to facilitate and enhance their understanding of a concept. Animations were also available in the system to help tutees grasp a concept.

One of TutorVista's considerations in creating the online repository of resources was reusability. TutorVista identified units that could be reused across curricula across the world. For example, any Physics student would have to learn Newton's laws of motion. The goal of TutorVista's IT staff and learning resource developers was to develop a resource base that could be leveraged for maximum benefit. Pursuing this goal further, in November 2007, TutorVista acquired Edurite, a company that provided content for educational CD-ROMs.

TutorVista decided not to use video to connect the tutors and tutees because of the potential for misuse. Some tutees had enquired about the possibility of using video with their tutoring sessions, making the argument that it would provide a richer experience. However, satisfaction surveys showed that the tutees appeared satisfied with the quality of the tutoring that was provided to them in the existing interactive online environment.

Customer-Facing Roles at TutorVista

TutorVista's hiring strategy avoided the turnover and workforce availability issues that offshore service organizations in hotspots like Bangalore faced. With increased availability and decreasing costs of broadband connectivity in Tier II and Tier III towns in India, TutorVista management realized that they could hire tutors from any part of the country. Individuals with the requisite educational qualifications who do not work outside the home formed TutorVista's hiring pool. In April 2007, TutorVista had 500 tutors, working from their homes in 23 Indian cities (Hamm, 2007). At the end of 2007, of the 845 TutorVista employees, 600 were tutors. They were based in India and five other countries (see Figure 1).

TutorVista required that tutors have a graduate degree in the tutoring subject as well as teaching experience. The recruitment process was composed of testing and interviews completed online. The job offer was made only after the applicants completed the online training and certification. The applicants' references and qualifications were scrutinized very closely. In cases where the applicant had excellent educational qualifications, but lacked experience, the applicant would be conditionally accepted by TutorVista. The inexperienced applicant was not assigned independent tutoring sessions immediately after completing training, but was apprenticed to an experienced tutor.

TutorVista had to ensure that tutors operated at world-class standards; hence, training was seen as a critical component for successful tutors. One poor quality training session could result in loss of many consumers, with customer use of review sites on the Internet. Thus, training in new topics, assessment, continuous monitoring of the tutors, and remedial training based on student feedback must be provided consistently to maintain a well-trained and prepared tutoring force (O'Rourke,

2003). At the end of 2007, TutorVista had 25 employees devoted to training and recruitment alone.

Training included sessions on use of technology, school district-specific curricula, expectations and behavior of the target student group, differences between the Indian culture and the culture of the customer group's country of residence, preparation of material for a tutoring session, and accent neutralization (Times, 2006). In a one-hour session each tutor had to teach a topic and help a student understand the material thoroughly. This session had to be entertaining and educational to provide a satisfactory experience and ensure customer retention. The duration of the tutor training was three to four weeks. Written and oral tests were conducted throughout the training process, with feedback being provided at every stage. In the last phase of the training, the trainees were tested on their capabilities to plan and execute a tutoring session using TutorVista's technology tools. Each tutor was assigned a topic and grade level based on their interest and qualifications, and was then asked to prepare and present a tutoring session.

When the trainees attained certification, they were assigned to tutor managers, each responsible for approximately ten tutors. In the TutorVista database, the tutor manager maintained the tutor profile of information about the subjects and grade levels the tutors were qualified to teach. Besides administrative functions such as handling vacation requests, the tutor manager also monitored the tutors' sessions and collected feedback information from the tutors.

Tutors committed to work three, four, or eight hours each day for six days a week; another option was to work eight hours for five days every week. Scheduling was not done on a freelance or ad hoc basis. These workload options helped TutorVista avoid problems of employee burnout. TutorVista was accommodative of tutor needs, according to a tutor who was interviewed; tutors were allowed to change session timings with prior notice. The tutors were content with the schedule

that required them to work very early in the day or late at night since they were able to work from home. The remuneration was excellent with a salary of $300-400 a month, which was quite high, compared to the Indian national average (Hua, 2006).

Training was an ongoing process; tutors were required to take periodic assessment tests in their subject and were retrained in an area, if necessary. Tutors could also be retrained based on student feedback, collected online at the end of a session. Research has shown that the value of online tutors is in the fact that they guide and assist in the learning process, rather than lecture (MacDonald, 2006). An internal TutorVista wiki, maintained by the IT staff, had syllabi, curricular, and best practices pedagogical resources. Tutor managers passed information from the tutors to the IT team for inclusion on the wiki site; all updates were made by the IT staff. A biweekly magazine chronicling tutor experiences and student comments was also circulated within TutorVista.

TutorVista management wanted to keep tutors invested in the well-being of the company and periodically hosted meetings in different locations for tutors from surrounding areas. TutorVista executives attended these meetings, talked to the tutors about their concerns, and kept them informed of plans for TutorVista's growth. These meetings were purely informational and social gatherings—not coupled with training sessions—and created a feeling of belonging among the TutorVista tutors. In-house surveys indicated that the tutors were satisfied with all aspects of their work.

There were two other customer-facing roles at TutorVista. Customer relationship managers were assigned approximately 15 students, contacting them and/or their guardians via telephone to ensure that the needs of the tutee were being met. The Customer Care team, on the other hand, took a more passive role; their interactions with the customer were instigated by the customer and often centered on problem resolution.

Figure 2. Screenshot of TutorVistaNow (www.tutorvista.com)

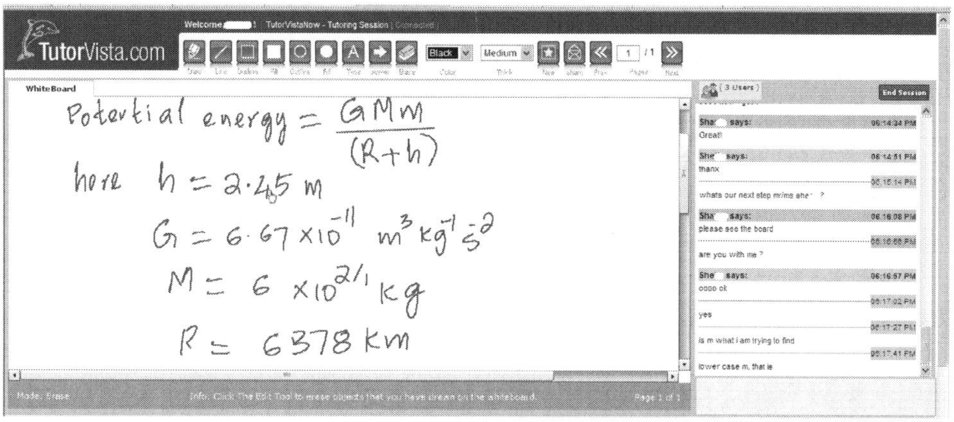

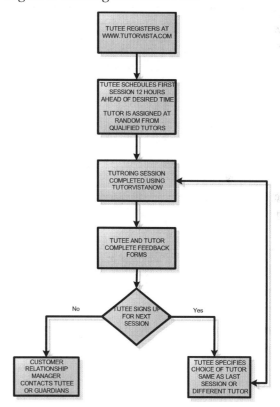

Inside a Tutoring Session

At the TutorVista site at www.tutorvista.com, a student had the option of taking a one-hour free trial session or signing up for one of two tutoring plans—either the $19.99 per hour of one-subject tutoring, or $99.99 per month for unlimited tutoring. Following registration, future sessions could be scheduled on the TutorVista site with 12 hours advance notice, for a time that was convenient for the student. For the first tutoring session, the tutor was assigned at random. When signing up for a second session of the same subject, students saw a calendar showing, through color coding, the availability of the tutor from the first session. A tutee could choose another tutor for the second session. TutorVista wanted tutees to be comfortable with the tutor. Figure 3 depicts this process.

During the session, the tutee and teacher used headsets and a "whiteboard"—an area of the screen on which both can write—using a graphics tablet and a digital pen. Whatever was written by one was visible to the other (see Figure 2). The tutee could choose to conduct a voice chat or a text chat with the tutor. At the start of the first session, the tutor would explain the use of the technology and provide appropriate contact information to the tutee. If the tutee wanted to work on specific material or assignments during a session, there was a toll-free number available to

Figure 3. Tutoring with TutorVista

fax the documents to TutorVista. The tutor would then use the documents to prepare for the session.

At the end of the session, tutor and tutee both completed feedback forms. The tutor provided information on the tutee's progress with a topic and experience using different pedagogical techniques during the session. The feedback from the tutees included several parameters such as the tutee's satisfaction with the session overall, relevance of what was taught to the tutee's curriculum, teaching style of tutor, tutor's communication skills, responsiveness of tutor, and preparation of the tutor for this session. The increasing diversity in schools and communities seemed to contribute to the comfort of the tutees in these sessions where they were interacting with a tutor from the other side of the world.

Tutoring was available in a wide variety of subjects and for all grade levels from second grade to college level. Eighty percent of lessons to date were in mathematics. English as a Second Language (ESL) tutoring was offered in some countries. There were plans to offer Spanish tutoring as well in the near future. Besides tutoring on different subjects and languages, TutorVista also offered competitive test preparation classes. These test preparation classes were available at any time, and TutorVista made arrangements with select tutors so that tutors were available around the clock for this tutoring.

Results

TutorVista's tutoring services were positively reviewed in the popular media based on glowing recommendations from satisfied guardians and tutees. The fees for these services were paid, in the majority of cases reported in the media, by parents who were very satisfied with the unbeatable combination of budget pricing and quality tutoring backed by guarantees.

The growing number of students was also a testament to TutorVista's success since referrals from satisfied customers were one of the primary sources of acquiring new customers. Some of the customers had been with TutorVista since the inception of the company. In the short period from 2005 to 2007, the number of tutees had grown from 100 to around 1,200 (in 2006) to 10,000.

Table 3. Composition of employees at TutorVista, December 2007

Tutors	600
Technology	40
Customer Service	25
Sales and Marketing	100
Academic Resources	25
Tutor Management	15
Training and Recruitment	25
HR, Administration, and Support	15
Total	845

These tutees were from 12 different countries with the majority from the United States.

A significant number of the students reported grade improvements as a result of the tutoring. Using aggregate data gathered from students, TutorVista concluded that students could expect to increase their grade by two levels if they worked continuously with TutorVista tutors for an eight-month period.

By the end of 2007, TutorVista had already moved beyond break-even at the unit level, generating positive cash flow. The costs of adding and servicing a new customer were more than covered by the revenue from the customer. At an organizational level, TutorVista expected to break-even by the end of 2008. Plans to expand into new services and areas would impact that goal.

CURRENT CHALLENGES AND PROBLEMS

TutorVista management realized that their market was unlimited by geographical boundaries. Ganesh and his colleagues planned to move into new markets in Australia and Canada, offering similar services as in the U.S. and the UK. Their other target markets were in Korea and China, where they offered English language tutoring and competitive exam preparation classes (Jin-Seo,

2007). In addition, TutorVista had plans to enter the Indian market, offering a mix of classroom and online tutoring sessions.

While TutorVista had created public interest and faith in offshore online tutoring and was registering an increasing number of students every month, it could not rest on its laurels. The competition was heating up on all fronts. Other tutoring organizations, established and new, were also pursuing the online tutoring market aggressively. Educomp had established a fully owned subsidiary in the U.S. for marketing and customer relationship management. CareerLauncher had signed a deal with two U.S.-based online tutoring companies (Prystay, 2005). Publishing companies were also offering their own tutoring services online: Pearson, a leading publisher of textbooks, was launching its own tutoring service online to accompany its textbooks (Blakely, 2007).

Growth Expectations and Competition

With TutorVista meeting growth expectations, Ganesh and his managers considered the future of the highly successful venture. These new entrants to the market realized that TutorVista had created a successful business model. TutorNext, one of these new companies, is a Washington, DC-based company founded at the end of 2006 by Anu Bhave, an MIT Sloan graduate of Indian origin. TutorNext had already raised its first round of funding in April 2007 to develop proprietary software that would enhance its learning platform and to create more math content, which would be made available freely online (Hammer, 2007).

TutorVista management needed to formulate a growth strategy. While the business model and the technology platform could sustain current enrollment, they had to decide whether to focus on geographic growth or offer additional subjects and services. Though their current online business model did not set any geographic limitations, TutorVista tutors and resources were not equipped to handle requests from tutees from different countries, each with its own curriculum and instructional patterns. Offering additional subjects and services would also be a challenge, since programs and resources would need to be developed in these new areas. Multiple lesson plans built around different curricula could be hard to maintain and could create confusion for the tutors as well. How would they manage to successfully meet the increasing multitude of differing curricular needs as the company grew?

The processes required to initiate and use the online tutoring environment should remain simple and user friendly. TutorVista also needed to be able to offer strong guarantees of availability and reliability to sustain its credibility with customers. Given the prevalence of online consumer reporting, a company like TutorVista that relies on word-of-mouth could not afford a technological failure that would cause problems for its clients. How would they assure 24/7 availability as the company grew, and what would it cost?

TutorVista had to remain flexible to meet the changing demand and continued growth, with its subsequent impact on capacity utilization. TutorVista's overhead costs to add additional tutors were relatively low compared to some competitors. However, there were significant costs associated with managing a large technology platform and ensuring that the tutors were current in their subject area and pedagogical techniques. While TutorVista had experienced success with its tutees, ensuring that a student scheduled sessions regularly and remained engaged during a session could be difficult. Additionally, monitoring and ensuring quality in tutoring sessions and other interactions of students and their guardians with TutorVista would certainly be more difficult as the client base and the number of tutors grew.

Given his entrepreneurial mindset, Ganesh was already considering leveraging his business model to offer other services. Certainly the India Inc. brand would be an advantage in this area. Further, there was a large educated population that he could recruit and train to meet the expected standards. In fact, Ganesh believed that his expertise in "hiring, training, and deploying" was a core competency that could be transferred to other areas. Were there new associated businesses on the horizon for Krishnan Ganesh?

Being the first player of its kind in the offshore outsourcing market meant there was no precedent to help TutorVista gauge the viability of a B2C model from India. Selling a consumer brand from India to overseas consumers who were more brand conscious was not easy. The ROI using traditional marketing channels was not high, and TutorVista had relied primarily on word-of-mouth advertising and Web-based marketing and sign-up to promote the services, since there were too many low-value clients to support a face-to-face sales force. The question facing the marketing group was whether there could be a convergence of the traditional marketing channels in an online medium for TutorVista. How could they ensure continuing visibility in their core markets?

By all reports, the market for online tutoring was huge. However, not everyone viewed online tutoring with rose-colored glasses (Price, Richardson, & Jeffs, 2007). There had been considerable opposition from teachers and teachers' organizations in the United States (Gewertz, 2005). Further, there was a possibility that the NCLB Act and its mandates could be amended to exclude online tutoring. A shift in the public opinion would not bode well for all offshore online tutoring services. Could TutorVista secure it place in the psyches of its target population before others began to question such online offerings?

Ganesh knew that TutorVista was blazing new trails with a virtual company based in India offering services to consumer markets in many parts of the world. Developing and managing resources to meet shifting demand posed an ongoing challenge. Creating and capturing that demand also required careful planning and management of marketing resources. While the possibility of solving educational problems of different societies

and countries was exciting, the orchestration of resources needed to achieve that goal profitably was challenging. The meeting was convened to begin addressing these issues.

REFERENCES

Allen, I.E., & Seaman, J. (2006). *Making the grade—online education in the United States, 2006.* Retrieved December 27, 2007, from http://www.sloan-c.org/publications/survey/pdf/making_the_grade.pdf

Blakely, R. (2007, March 28). *Indian takeaway as learning goes offshore.* Retrieved December 27, 2007, from http://business.timesonline.co.uk/tol/business/industry_sectors/technology/article1577313.ece

Bulkley, K. (2007, April 26). *The U.S. really has an educational crisis there* (Interview: Krishnan Ganesh). Retrieved June 17, 2007, from http://technology.guardian.co.uk/weekly/story/0,,2065086,00.html

BusinessWire. (2000). *Tutor.com breaks new ground in distance learning.* Retrieved January 12, 2008 from http://findarticles.com/p/articles/mi_m0EIN/is_2000_Jan_28/ai_59034903

Cigale, G. (2005). Partners in advocacy. *Library Journal, 30*(13), 46-48.

Daria, I. (2007, September). *Does your child need a tutor?* Retrieved December 27, 2007, from http://www.parents.com/parents/story.jsp?storyid=/templatedata/fc/story/data/1187639893738.xml

Economist. (2007, June 21). *Krishnan Ganesh: The outsourcer.* Retrieved August 13, 2007, from http://globaltechforum.eiu.com/index.asp

Education Notebook. (2006). *Public schools deny low income children tutoring.* Retrieved January 12, 2008, from http://www.heritage.org/Research/Education/EdNotes22.cfm

George, N. (2007, September 27). *TutorVista's in-house technology empowering education.* Retrieved December 18, 2007, from http://www.tech2.com/biz/india/casestudies/education/tutorvista's-inhouse-technology-empowering-education/1912/0

Gewertz, C. (2005, April). Critics question use of offshore firms for online tutoring. *Education Week, 24*(32), 14.

Hamm, S. (2007, April 17). *A new angle on distance learning.* Retrieved June 17, 2007, from http://www.businessweek.com/globalbiz/blog/bangaloretigers/archives/2007/04/a_new_angle_on.html#more

Hammer, B. (2007, April 6). *Online tutoring firm aims for first round of capital.* Retrieved August 6, 2007, from http://washington.bizjournals.com/washington/stories/2007/04/09/story13.html?b=1176091200%5E1443086

Hua, V. (2006, October 22). *One for the books*: *tutoring gets outsourced.* Retrieved June 25, 2007, from http://www.sfgate.com/cgi-bin/article.cgi?f=/c/a/2006/10/22/MNGTILTVRR1.DTL&hw= tutoring+gets+outsourced&sn=001&sc=1000

Jin-Seo, C. (2007, August 2). *Indians to teach English via Internet.* Retrieved August 14, 2007, from http://www.koreatimes.co.kr/www/news/biz/biz_view.asp?newsIdx=7682&categoryCode=123

Kode, B.V. (2007). *RIA product launch: Introducing TutorVistaNow (R.F. Developers, message from discussion at Flex India Community).* Retrieved August 15, 2007, from http://groups.google.com/group/flex_india/msg/141513150c391553

MacDonald, J. (2006). Review by Gower. Review of blended learning and online tutoring. *British Journal of Educational Technology, 37*(6), 998-999.

McCluskey, N. (2004). *Policy analysis—a lesson in waste. Where does all the federal education money go?* Retrieved January 10, 2008, from http://www.cato.org/pubs/pas/pa518.pdf

NEA. (2001). *America's top education priority—lifting up low performing schools.* Retrieved January 12, 2008, from http://www.nea.org/priorityschools/priority.html

O'Rourke, J. (2003). *Tutoring in open and distance learning.* Vancouver, BC: Commonwealth of Learning.

Pandey, A., Aggarwal, A., Devane, R., & Kuznetsov, Y. (2004). India's transformation to knowledge-based economy—evolving role of the Indian diaspora. *Evaluserve,* 36.

Price, L., Richardson, J., & Jeffs, A. (2007). Face-to-face versus online tutoring support in distance education. *Studies in Higher Education, 32*(1), 1-20.

Prystay, C. (2005, July 12). *Help with calculus online—from India.* Retrieved June 25, 2007, from http://www.careerjournal.com

Szep, J. (2006, September 29). *U.S. homework outsourced as "e-tutoring" grows.* Retrieved August 12, 2007, from http://www.boston.com/news/local/massachusetts/articles/2006/09/29/us_homework_outsourced_as_e_tutoring_grows/

Times Educational Supplement. (2006, August). Call India for homework aid. Issue 4700, 3.

Vergari, S. (2007). Federalism and market-based education policy: The supplemental services mandate. *American Journal of Education, 113*(2), 311-339.

This work was previously published in the Journal of Cases on Information Technology, Volume 11, Issue 3, edited by M. Khosrow-Pour, pp. 45-61, copyright 2009 by IGI Publishing (an imprint of IGI Global).

Chapter 4.22
Web Service Enabled Online Laboratory

Yuhong Yan
Concordia University, Montreal, Canada

Yong Liang
National Research Council, Canada

Abhijeet Roy
University of New Brunswick, Canada

Xinge Du
University of New Brunswick, Canada

ABSTRACT

Online experimentation allows students from anywhere to operate remote instruments at any time. The current techniques constrain users to bind to products from one company and install client side software. We use Web services and Service Oriented Architecture to improve the interoperability and usability of the remote instruments. Under a service oriented architecture for online experiment system, a generic methodology to wrap commercial instruments using IVI and VISA standard as Web services is developed. We enhance the instrument Web services into stateful services so that they can manage user booking and persist experiment results. We also benchmark the performance of this system when SOAP is used as the wire format for communication and propose solutions to optimize performance. In order to avoid any installation at the client side, the authors develop Web 2.0 based techniques to display the virtual instrument panel and real time signals with just a standard Web browser. The technique developed in this article can be widely used for different real laboratories, such as microelectronics, chemical engineering, polymer crystallization, structural engineering, and signal processing.

INTRODUCTION

In science and engineering education, experimentation plays a crucial role. The classic university science course entails lecture and lab: students' active participation in experiments enhances their understanding of the principles described in the lectures. However, not every educational institution can afford all the experimental equipment it would like. Moreover, colleges and universities increasingly offer distance-learning programs, allowing students to attend lectures and seminars and complete coursework using the Internet. In situations such as these, access to online laboratories or experiment systems can greatly enhance student learning - increasing the range of experiments available at an institution and giving the distance learners hands-on, real-time experience. Online laboratories, however, are not as mature as online courses. There is no matured software system to support online experimentation. Experimentation is also an important approach for scientific discovery. Sharing expensive equipment is a common practice in the scientific community. Some research facilities, e.g. synchrotrons and accelerators, are very expensive that a country normally invests to build one of the kind. These facilities are shared by the scientific community national wide and/or international wide. Currently, the scientists need to reserve a time slot in these facilitates and travel to the site to conduct the experiments. With the capacity of online experimentation, traveling cost can be saved. More importantly, online experimentation can allow the users to reserve shorter time slots, because the users do not need to finish an experiment during their travel. Therefore, the resource sharing can be more efficient.

Current online experiment systems fall into two categories (Naef, 2006): *virtual laboratories* provide a simulation environment in which students conduct experiments; and *remote laboratories*, with real instruments and equipments at the remote sites. The later is the scope of our

research. The ultimate goal of our research is to provide IT techniques for remote experimentation over Internet. Our focus in this article is to let students use a Graphic User Interface (GUI) to operate actual instruments via remote control.

The difficulty with creating an effective laboratory operated by remote control is making scattered computational resources and instruments operable across platforms. Existing online experiment systems commonly use a classic client-sever architecture and off-the-shelf middleware for communication (Hardison, *et al.* 2005, Auer and Gallent, 2000, Latchman, *et al.* 1999). Normally, to ensure interoperability, these systems rely on instruments from a single company—such as National Instruments or Agilent—and Microsoft Windows as the common operating system. Users must then install additional software to operate the remote instruments. For a student using an old laptop or the computer at a public library, this could be difficult. So, online labs configured this way can't achieve the ultimate goals of sharing heterogeneous resources among online laboratories and easy access via the Web. Our solution to these shortcomings is to base online experiment systems on Web services, which are designed to support interoperable, machine-to-machine interaction over a network and can also integrate heterogeneous resources. We have devised a service-oriented architecture for online experiment systems, enabled by Web service protocols, and a methodology for wrapping the operations of the instruments into Web services. Although these methods probably aren't suitable for time-critical missions or applications that need real-time control, such as robot operation, they do work for controlling standard commercial instruments over low-speed or unreliable communication networks—the types of networks available to many college students. Using this framework, we can create an online experiment system for students—or an online research lab for scientists—that incorporates a great variety of instruments and that users can access without installing special software.

This article is organized as follows: following the present of service oriented architecture for online experiment systems, we present the solution to wrap instruments as Web services and to display dynamic graphics for real time signals. Then we discuss the management of stateful instrumental Web services and benchmark the performance of Web services in this application and present the optimization methods to improve performance. At the last is the discussion and conclusions.

SERVICE ORIENTED ARCHITECTURE FOR ONLINE EXPERIMENT SYSTEMS

A Web service is a software system that typically relies on a set of W3C standards. Identified by a Uniform Resource Identifier (URI), a Web service has public interfaces and bindings defined and described in Extensible Markup Language (XML), specifically, the WSDL format (W3C, 2004a). Other software systems can discover the Web service definition—for example, via a registry server using Universal Description Discovery and Integration (UDDI) protocol (UDDI.org, 2004). These other systems can then interact with a Web service as its definition prescribes, using Simple Object Access Protocol (SOAP) (W3C, 2004b), an XML-based messages format, conveyed by Internet protocols such as Hypertext Transfer Protocol (HTTP).

An Online Experiment System (OES) uses the scattered computational resources and instruments on the networks for experiments. It is a Web-enabled distributed system: the user accesses an OES via the Web interface; and the heterogeneous resources and devices interoperate with each other using Web service protocols. Our major efforts in this study are the service oriented architecture for OES and the techniques to operate remote instruments wrapped as Web services.

Figure 1 diagrams our service oriented architecture for an OES. It combines two client-server architectures. The first client-server architecture mediates between the client's browser and the Web server associated with the online lab management system. The second client-server architecture mediates between the online lab management system and scattered resources wrapped as Web services. The online laboratory uses SOAP messages to communicate with the remote resources. The online lab management system is the key component in this architecture. It has standard learning management functions such as tutorial management, student management, and so on. The system uses service oriented architecture to invoke remote services. It works in a series of steps, indicated by the numbered green circles in Figure 1:

Figure 1. Service oriented architecture for an online experiment system

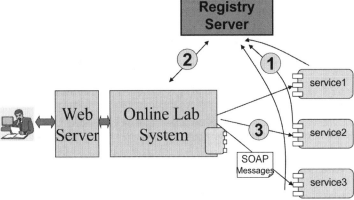

1. A service provider registers its services in a UDDI registry server.
2. A service requester searches the registry server and finds all the potential resources. It selects the proper services based on its own criteria.
3. The service requester sends SOAP messages directly to the service provider to invoke the remote service.

Figure 2 shows our implementation of the online laboratory management system. We use Moodle, an open source learning management system, to realize the learning management functions. These modules are an authoring tool to generate tutorials, quizzes, and homework; a student management system to manage the enrollment, marks and progresses of students; a booking and scheduling module to book timeslots for the experiments; and multiple collaboration tools, such as discussion forums, wikis, and chat rooms for students to communicate and work in group. The tutorial pages contain Instrument GUI for displaying instrument panels and real time signals. The students can press the buttons and enter inputs from the Web interface to operate the remote instruments. The GUI code is designed to be very light weight, and no particular installation is needed at the client side. Our major focus of this

article is on wrapping instruments as Web services and designing the light weight GUI interface for operating the remote instrument Web services.

A Sample Experiment

Our research targets the online education at college level. We are especially interested in electronic circuit experiments, because the instruments in this domain commonly have digitalized interface to computer. A sample experiment is common emitter NPN transistor amplifier. The circuit diagram is as in Figure 3. The common emitter circuit comprises the load resistor R_C and NPN transistor with the output connected as shown. The resistors R_1 and R_2 are chosen to ensure the base-emitter voltage is approximately 0.7 volts, which is the "on" voltage for a transistor. These resistors, along with R_E, also determine the quiescent current flowing through the transistor and therefore its gain. The input signal V_{in} is generated by a waveform generator. The amplified signal is the output V_{out}.

We use a waveform generator, Agilent 33220A, to generate the input signal V_{in}. And we use a data acquisition and switch unit, Agilent 34970A, to read in V_{in} and V_{out}. Please notice that in a real lab, people normally use an oscilloscope to observe the signals, but for online lab, everything has to

Figure 2. An implementation online laboratory management system

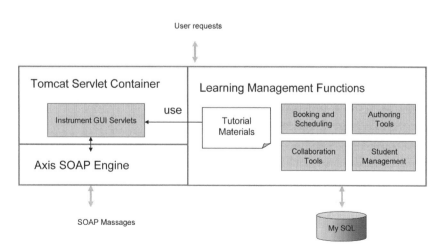

Figure 3. Common emitter amplifier

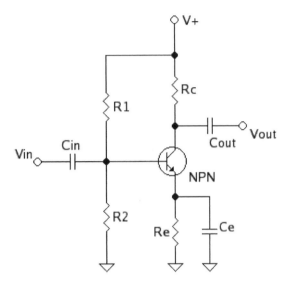

be digitalized. Therefore, we need to use data acquisition devices. That means that we need to change the usual way to do experiment for putting an experiment online. In order to operate the instruments via GUI interface and via Web service protocols, we develop some techniques below to wrap the instruments into Web services and to display the instrument panels and the real time signals on Web pages.

WRAPPING INSTRUMENT OPERATIONS AS WEB SERVICES

A WSDL file contains the operations of the Web service and the arguments to invoke operations. When instrument functions are wrapped as Web services, the interface of the instrument Web service is described in a WSDL file. An instrument service needs to provide three kinds of information: 1) the input/output parameters to operate the instrument; 2) the information about rendering the GUI of the instrument panels; and, 3) the metadata about the instruments. These issues are described individually below.

Generic Approach to Wrap Instrument Operations based on VISA standard

Instrument I/O is a well studied topic for which industrial standards have been established. Two methods to control instruments are by using an instrument driver or by making direct calls to the I/O library. If using an instrument driver, the user will call functions that cause the instrument to take some action. If using the I/O library, the user will control the instrument by sending an ASCII string to it and reading ASCII strings back from it. The commonly used languages to operate instruments are C, C# or Visual Basic. The commonly accepted industrial standards are Virtual Instrument System Architecture (VISA) and Interchangeable Virtual Instruments (IVI) (Aglient, 2005). Most commercial products follow these standards. The purpose of these standards is to enable interoperability of instruments, which means using common APIs of the instruments. Therefore, it is possible to generate generic WSDL interfaces for instruments based on these standards. The relationship between VISA and IVI is shown in Figure 4. The individual instruments – Instr. A, B and C – have their own drivers. These drivers are wrapped by VISA complaint drivers. The IVI compliant drivers are built still on the top of VISA standard.

Both VISA and IVI standards operate the instruments by reading and sending ASCII strings to the instruments. Compared with VISA, IVI can operate the instrument by referencing its properties. The IVI standard classifies the instruments into eight classes. Each class has basic properties that are shared by all the instruments in the same class, and extension properties that are unique to the individual instrument. As an example, Figure 5 shows the code to set the frequency of an Agilent Waveform Generator 33220A to 2500.0HZ, using IVI COM. Figure 6 is the code of VISA COM to implement the same function. Using VISA COM, people do not know the semantics of the

Figure 4. The relations of the instrument I/O standards

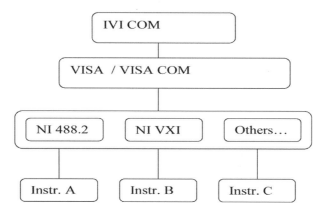

Figure 5. Sample code of IVI COM

```
IAgilent33220Ptr Fgen;
.......
Fgen->Output->Frequency = 2500.0;
.......
```

Figure 6. Sample code of VISA COM

```
Fgen->WriteString("FREQuency 2500")
```

parameters. That is to say, setting the Frequency or Voltage, people will use the same API.

We consider that using the VISA standard, the methodology of wrapping the instrument services can be generic to any of the instruments, which means that many instruments can share the same Web services interface. Indeed, using the VISA standard, we need only to define an operation *writeString* for sending commands or data to the instrument. The argument of this operation is always string, which is the same for any instrument. Figure 7 is the snippet of WSDL for defining the operation of *writeString*. Similarly, we can define an operation *readString* for getting status or data from the instrument, which is eliminated from Figure 7.

In the example in Figure 8, we demonstrate how to operate the waveform generator to generate a sinusoid waveform. The set of control parameters for the sinusoid waveform contains "instrument address", "wave shape", "impedance", "frequency", "amplitude", and "offset".

In order to improve performance by reducing the time taken to send SOAP messages (ref Section 5), those parameters are put into one string. This means that only one SOAP message is transported to pass all the parameters from the client to the server. After the server gets the string from the client, it will parse the string according to the delimiter (here we use ";") and send the command to the instrument.

Although we prefer to use the VISA standard to wrap the instrument functions, it is also possible to use the IVI standard. The difference is that each instrument class will have a common WSDL file in which the operations for the basic properties of this instrument class are defined. For instruments having extension properties, the WSDL has to be generated separately to include the operations for the extension properties. Therefore, if using the IVI standard, the interoperability is satisfied if the instruments are in the same class and if they have the same extension properties.

Figure 7. The snippet of WSDL to operate an instrument

```
<?xml version="1.0" encoding="UTF-8"?>
<wsdl:definitions ......>
      ......
  <!--define the response message -->
<wsdl:message name="writeStringResponse">
  <wsdl:part name="writeStringReturn" type="xsd:int"/>
</wsdl:message>
 <!--define the request message -->
  <wsdl:message name="writeStringRequest">
   <wsdl:part name="in0" type="xsd:string"/>
  </wsdl:message>
  <!--define the operation -->
<wsdl:operation name="writeString" parameterOrder="in0">
  <wsdl:input message="intf:writeStringRequest" name="writeStringRequest"/>
  <wsdl:output message="intf:writeStringResponse" name="writeStringResponse"/>
      </wsdl:operation>
      ......
</wsdl:definitions>
```

Figure 8. Sinusoid waveform parameters in one string

```
"*RST;FUNCtion SINusoid;OUTPut:LOAD 50;FREQuency
2500;VOLTage 1.2;VOLTage:OFFSet 0.4;OUTPut ON";
```

Interfaces of Metadata

The IEEE Learning Object Metadata (LOM) standard defines metadata for a learning object (LTSC, 1999). Any entities which can be used, reused or referenced during technology supported learning are learning objects. Examples of learning objects include multimedia content, instructional content, learning objectives, instructional software and software tools, and persons, organizations, or events referenced during technology supported learning. The LOM standard focuses on the minimal set of attributes needed to allow these learning objects to be managed, located, and evaluated.

An online course is a most common learning object. Relevant attributes of LOM for online courses are author, owner, terms of distribution, language, teaching or interaction style, grade level, and prerequisites etc. A part of an online experiment is similar to an online course as it also has tutorial materials and pedagogical attributes. (Bagnasco, Chirico, and Scapolla, 2002) extended the LOM standard for experimentation context to include instrument attributes and assignments. In their work, instruments are a part of an entire experiment and the information about them are not sufficient for searching and booking. Our work studies how to share instruments and operate instruments in more detail. Therefore, we need to extend their LOM extension for instrument attributes. Figure 9 shows the extended LOM attributes for instruments.

The LOM metadata information is defined in an XML file. In the WSDL, we define the operation, *getLOMMetaData*, to download the information (c.f. Figure 10). The LOM information can be used to search, evaluate, and utilize the proper instrument for an experiment. The information about availability and Quality of Service (QoS) are especially useful for evaluating and booking the instrument service. Therefore, we generate two operations, *getAvailabilityInfo* and *getQoSInfo*, for the two attributes. From *getAvailabilityInfo*, we can get all the available timeslots during a time

Figure 9. LOM attributes for instruments

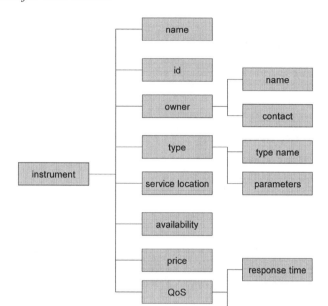

Figure 10. The operations to get metadata information in WSDL

```
<!--define the operation -->
<wsdl:operation name="getLOMMateData">
 <wsdl:output name="getLOMDataResponse">
 </wsdl:output>
<!--define the operation -->
<wsdl:operation name="getAvailabilityInfo">
 <wsdl:input name="getAvailabilityRequest">
 </wsdl:input>
 <wsdl:output name="getAvailabilityResponse">
 </wsdl:output>
<!--define the operation -->
<wsdl:operation name="getQoSInfo">
 <wsdl:output name="getQoSResponse">
 </wsdl:output>
```

interval, or query if the instrument is available for a specific time period.

QoS information is accumulated from history and can become an important selling and differentiating point of Web services with similar functionality. We record the successful connecting rate to the instrument and the response time to the instrument. QoS information is used when selecting available instruments for an experiment. The higher QoS of the instrument service, the more likely the OES selects this instrument or recommends it to the user to use. The operation *getQoSInfo*, is designed for this.

LIGHTWEIGHT WEB GUI FOR INSTRUMENTS

The primary advantage of a Web application over a desktop application is universal access. The client side of a Web application, in the best case, does not require local installations other than a standard Web browser. Therefore, Web applications are highly portable and platform independent. The Web interface to remotely operate an instrument needs to be user friendly and interactive, and gives the user a similar look and feel as the real instruments. For efficient reason, we should also reduce the amount of data transferred from the server to the client. We have solved the following two problems using only JavaScript enabled Web browser at the client side: to display the instrument panel graphical; to display dynamic graphics for real time signals.

The Web GUI for Virtual Instrument Panels

The panel of a remote instrument should be displayed graphically on a Web browser. The user operates the GUI to control the instruments. The methodology to describe instrument panels is presented in (Fattouh and Saliah, 2004). The principle is to design an XML schema which defines the syntax of the panel of a kind of instruments. An XML file compliant to the schema describes the panel of an individual instrument. Then the XML file can be parsed and rendered at the client side. We use the multimeter Agilent 34401A as an example. A snippet of the XML for its panel is in Figure 11.

One can see the container panel objects are the *parentFrame*, *parentPanel* and *childPanel*. A container object can contain other panel objects, such as labels and text boxes. A container object has a layout that describes how to render the objects inside the container. If one is familiar with java, one can see the objects can be mapped one by one to the classes in a java swing GUI package.

Figure 12 shows the principle to display the panel from its XML description. The XML schema for the Digital Multimeter is in DMM_GUI.xml. It validates the file DMM_Agilent_34401A_GUI. xml which defines the GUI for the Aglient 34401A. The JAXB is used to parse DMM_Agilent_34401A_GUI.xml. Then a java servlet is used to display the panel object on an HTML page. The generated GUI page is displayed on the right bottom section of Figure 12.

Display Real Time Signal on Web GUI

A large number of instruments display a coordinate diagram (graphs and charts) in a panel. A vital feature of the instrument Web interface is to display experiment results that closely resemble the output of the instrument itself. Displaying dynamic textual results in a browser is straightforward. However, displaying dynamic pictorial results is challenging due to the limited graphical capabilities of prevalent Web browsers.

AJAX, shorthand for "Asynchronous JavaScript and XML", is a development technique for creating interactive Web applications (Garrett, 2005). The main technologies used in an AJAX enabled web application are asynchronous data retrieval using XMLHttpRequest and dynamic manipulation and display of html elements based on the retrieved data using Document Object Model (DOM). The intent is to make Web pages feel more responsive by exchanging small amounts of data with the server behind the scenes, so that the entire Web page does not have to be reloaded each time the user requests a change. AJAX is a good solution for displaying and updating the real time signals. We can transfer just the discrete data points for the signals and update just part of the screen for displaying the data points. Then

Figure 11. A snippet of the XML to describe the panel of Agilent 34401A

```
<parentFrame parentFrameName="Frame Container">
  <parentFrameLayout> ... </parentFrameLayout>
</parentFrame>
<parentPanel parentPanelName="Parent Panel">
  <parentPanelLayout>GridBagLayout</parentPanelLayout>
<parentPanelDimension>...</parentPanelDimension>
</parentPanel>
<childPanel childPanelName = "ExternalParametersChildPanel">
  <childPanelLayout> ... </childPanelLayout>
  <component className="jLabel">
     <componentName> ... </componentName>
     ...
  </component>
  ...
</childPanel>
```

Figure 12. The principle to display instrument panel from its XML description

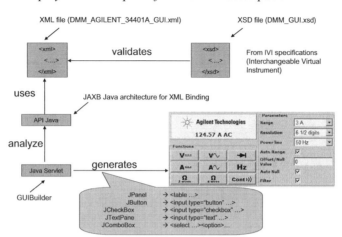

whole screen looks still and the signal is updating. Bandwidth requirement is reduced making Web pages load faster. This approach also allows keeping data independent of the presentation layer.

JavaScript Object Notation (JSON) is used for transferring the data points between the end user and the servlet. JSON is a text based data interchange format (JSON.org, 2007). What makes JSON rather useful is its inherent support within JavaScript. JavaScript, being the most widely supported scripting language for Web browsers, is very efficient in parsing JSON messages. JSON is not going to replace XML anytime soon, but it provides a viable alternative.

Parsing XML messages within a browser results in a Document Object Model (DOM) tree, which makes the code to manipulate it complicated. On the other hand, parsing JSON results in JavaScript objects and the code to manipulate it is straight forward. Table 1 shows a JSON text and Table 2 shows the equivalent JavaScript objects that can be obtained from parsing the above JSON text. In JSON, an object can be represented by a name value pair separated by a colon and surrounded by curly brackets. An array can be represented within square brackets, and values can be separated by a comma. The value of an object can be a string, an integer, another object, or arrays. In addition, the Boolean literals "true" and "false" are supported. The void concept of "null" is also supported. JavaScript "eval" function, which invokes the JavaScript compiler, can be used for parsing JSON text.

JSON can represent semi-structured data very efficiently compared to XML. Table 3 provides a comparison between XML and JSON representation that shows the similarity and differences between these two formats. XML is relatively verbose and would almost always require more characters to represent the same data. JSON has been touted as the "fat free alternative to xml".

Figure 13 depicts the technique used for creating dynamic coordinate diagrams for the Web interface. As stated earlier, a browser is not

Table 1. Code snippet: a JSON document

```
{
    "name": "Jack Sullivan",
    "student": true,
    "subjects": ["Web Programming", "Discrete Math",
"Psychology", "Operating Systems"]
}
```

Table 2. Code snippet: JSON string to Java Script Object

```
var name = "Jack Sullivan";
var status = true;
var subjects = new Array("Web Programming","Discrete
Math",
"Psychology", "Operating Systems");
```

Table 3. Code snippet: comparing XML and JSON

XML ... 146 characters without blanks	JSON ... 103 characters without blanks
<student fulltime="false"> <name>Wallace</name> <subject>Rabbit psyche</ subject> <subject>Carrot care</ subject> <subject>Cage building</ subject> </student>	{ "student": { "fulltime": false, "name": "Wallace", "subjects": ["Rabbit psyche", "Carrot care", "Cage building"] } }

an ideal platform to construct dynamic images. HTML 4.01 specifications recommended by the W3C does not even state the basic unit of graphics – the pixel as one of the HTML elements. Lutz Tautenhahn, a German software developer, has created a JavaScript library that can be used to display coordinate diagrams (Tautenhahn, 2005). The JavaScript Diagram Builder library is available as a freeware. In our solution we utilise this library to draw the coordinate space and to translate coordinates to positions within a Web page.

The div html element of 1px width and 2px height is used to mark a coordinate in the graph panel. The divs are placed within the Web page according to the translated coordinate. The AJAX engine as seen in Figure 13 is JavaScript method that creates XMLHttpRequest object binds it with

Figure 13. Web page dynamic graphics technique

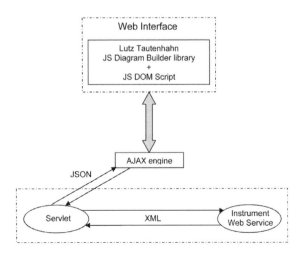

a timer and fetches the data from the Servlet. AJAX technique is used to fetch the coordinates from the application server in JSON format and is dynamically displayed over the output panel. In order to mimic the constant output of a wave generator we continuously call the server periodically for new data. The final interface looks like in Figure 14. The demo can be found at our testing Web site http://flydragontech.com/prototypes/lms/oisee/OISEE.htm.

MANAGING STATEFUL INSTRUMENT WEB SERVICES

Instrument Web services involve remotely operating real devices in real time. Improper design of the Web services can cause damage to the instrument, and can lead to false measurement and control, which in turn will result in failure of the online experiment. In (Yan, *et al.*, 2005), we present the special requirements for the instrument Web services, such as reliability mechanisms and communication strategies. By using proper software technologies, these requirements can be satisfied. In the following sub-sections, we will focus on how to manage the instruments as resources.

Stateful Service for Stateless Resources

It is well known that classic Web services is stateless, i.e. it does not maintain states between different clients or different invocations. HTTP, the commonly used transport protocol for Web services, is a stateless data-forwarding mechanism. There are no guarantees of packets being delivered to the destination and no guarantee of the order of the arriving packets. Classic Web services are suitable for services providing non-dynamic information. In this subsection, we discuss if additional effort is needed to manage the instrument Web services.

An instrument itself is a stateless resource. This is because an instrument itself does not record client information or invocations. Indeed,

Figure 14. Display real time signal on Web GUI with AJAX and JSON

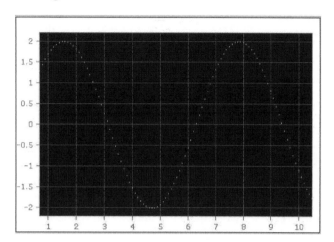

an instrument acts in a reactive way. It receives commands, executes them accordingly, and returns the results. If we say an instrument has "states", these are the parameters of its working mode, which have nothing to do with the states of a Web service.

An instrument can only be occupied by one user at a time. Unlike the resources in Grid Services, instruments can only accept one user at a time because an instrument needs to be set to a specific working mode before it can work for a certain experiment. Normally it is not possible to recover an instrument's status without a proper procedure, so many mechanisms in Grid Services are not useful in our application. The use of an instrument is booked by time slots. On some occasions, the tasks of an instrument can be managed by a queue (Hardison, *et al.*, 2005).

An instrument service needs to be stateful for several reasons. It must be stateful when it needs to record the operations from one user for payment accounting, or to support booking and scheduling, or to control how the user can use this instrument, or when the results need to be transported among several resources asynchronously. In the next subsection, we present a method to build the stateful instrument Web services.

Design the Stateful Service for Instrument Resources

As stated previously, we know that the instrument service has to identify clients and maintain a history of the operation. This kind of stateful service is different from the available stateful framework in Grid Services and WSRF. We design the stateful service for instrument resources as in Figure 15. The states are managed by the resource management layer. The client ID is transferred in SOAP to identify the states of the services. In detail:

1. The client sends the request to the Web service. The request should contain the ID of the client to identify the session.
2. The Web service returns the identifier of the reference.

Figure 15. The stateful service for instrument resources

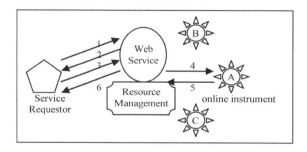

3. The client always contacts the service using the resource identifier.
4–5. The online experiment is executed and the results are returned to the Web service.
6. The Web service records the results in a proper manner and returns the results to the client.

Compared to Grid Services, our method does not use a service factory to create service instances for different users, because an instrument service is a single user service, thus no service instances are created. Compared to WSRF, the resource in our method itself remains stateless. We add a layer to manage the states.

THE PERFORMANCE ISSUES FOR WEB SERVICES FOR ONLINE EXPERIMENT

Although Web services have strong advantages on interoperability, it has intrinsic weaknesses on latency and scalability because it uses more transport layers.

The trade-off of the high interoperability of Web services is its lower performance. Web services have intrinsic performance weaknesses for two main reasons: there are more transport layers than for middleware; and the overhead of using SOAP. Many researchers have analyzed the problem of SOAP efficiency and identified some factors that can affect the latency performance of Web services and SOAP (Chiu, Govindaraju and Bramley, 2002) (Litou, 2002) (van Engelen, 2003). For each factor that could cause the latency, there are some proposed methods to improve the performance. In this article, we benchmark the SOAP efficiency in this context and propose the solutions to improve performance.

Benchmark of Latency

This benchmark test is aimed at determining the time to transport a service request from the requester to the provider. The time involves marshalling the SOAP message and binding it to the HTTP protocol at the request side, and the trans-

portation time and decoding time on the service side. This test takes place when the instrument Web service and the OES are on the same host, thus, the delay by the Internet is not considered. In above, we described that instruments accept ASCII strings as input according to VISA and IVI standards. Therefore we use ASCII strings for encoding a volume of the floating numbers in SOAP message. In our test, we assumed each of the floating numbers had 16 digits to provide adequate precision. Therefore the size of the strings for floating numbers is directly proportional to the number of digits. We measured the time delay starting before the call of the service and ending as the request reaches the service endpoint.

Figure 16 shows the relation of the delay time vs. the number of data points per message. One can see that the delay increases quasi-linearly as the data points increase. There is also a basic overhead for the transportation, which is primarily the time for setting up the TCP/IP connection.

Optimize the SOAP Efficiency

Latency of SOAP message is caused by the time of transportation, which is proportional to the size of SOAP, and the delay caused by the TCP/IP layer.

The most straightforward method of optimization is to reduce the SOAP message size by extracting the string out of the XML, compressing it into binary format (we use ZIP compression format here) and sending it as an attachment. The size of the payload is reduced to approximately 40 to 50 per cent of its original size. The SOAP messaging protocol supports Multipurpose Internet Mail Extensions (MIME) or Direct Internet Message Encapsulation (DIME) attachments. The difference is that MIME is designed to provide flexibility, while DIME is designed to be simpler and to provide more efficient message encapsulation. The results of applying different attachment approaches are shown in Figure 17. One can see that the transportation time can be reduced dramatically by compressing the SOAP content.

Figure 16. The delay vs. number of data point

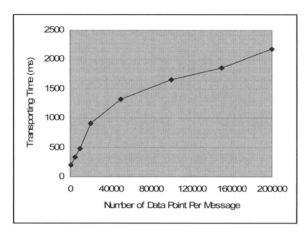

Figure 17. Different methods to send string data through SOAP

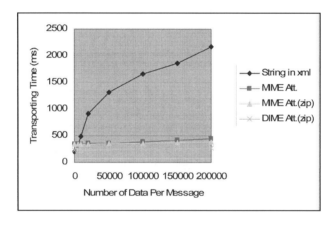

We can also optimize the underlying HTTP and TCP protocols for SOAP messaging. We present the possible methods below without testing results:

Persistent HTTP Connection

Persistent connection could "keep-alive" a connection and save the time needed to establish HTTP connection every time. For HTTP 1.0, the persistent connection works only if there is no proxy between the client and server. For HTTP1.1, the persistent connection can be used with more than one proxy between a client and a server.

Disable Nagle Algorithm and Remove TCP Delay ACK

The Nagle algorithm in combination with the TCP delayed ACK (the acknowledge response in TCP) are used to prevent network congestion (Litou, 2002), but they cause unnecessary delays when sending a SOAP message (Elfwing, R., Paulsson, U., and Lundberg, L., 2002). It is possible to disable Nagle on both the server and client side to get considerable improvement for the response time.

Better Pipelined Connection by Using HTTP 1.1

The use of HTTP inherits some of the TCP features such as the three-way handshake. This can cause delays. HTTP1.1 attempts to solve these problems. The result shows that HTTP1.1 can reduce the RTT (Round Trip Time) to half of HTTP1.0 implementation (Nielsen, *et al.*, 1997).

DISCUSSIONS

Service oriented architecture is the new technique to build distributed system. It has attracted attention for building online experiment systems as well. iLab at MIT adopts SOAP for communications between users and labs (Hardison, *et al.* 2005). Their architecture has three roles: lab server, end user and service broker. The service broker mediates the communication between the user and the lab server and provides storage and administrative services that are generic and can be shared by multiple labs within a signal university. Their focus is on providing such a kind of broker. In our architecture, the broker role is rather weak and not more than the function of registration. Our focus in this article is to study how to control a remote device via Web service protocol and how to design lightweight Web GUI for remote instruments using Web 2.0 techniques. We consider that the communication between the end user and the online lab should be very light that SOAP is too heavy to use. So far as we know, our work is unique in this domain.

During our study, we find that the current devices and the way of experiments are not completely suitable for online experiments. For example, the users have to do everything by sending command, not using their hands. In our sample experiment, the users cannot assemble the circuits, nor tune the resistor to change the amplitude. Therefore, we need to design a special circuit to allow the users to configure the circuit by sending commands. Technically it is possible in our experiment. But in some other cases, to achieve reconfiguration is not so straightforward. Moreover, in real lab, the input and output signals are observed by oscilloscopes. In this article, we digitalize the signals and display them on the Web site. We consider it is a cheaper way than using digital oscilloscopes. So people can see that we have different ways to do online experiments than real experiments. We have also found that not all the instruments can be shared online. For example, waveform generator produces analog signals which are not sharable without digitalization. Therefore, it is hard to say that it is useful to share a waveform generator online. Under current experiment devices and methods, it is commonly feasible to share a whole experiment or share a group of devices that has digital interface. We suppose more devices and experiment methods will be designed for online experiment and online engineering domain.

Collaborative working environment is helpful for online experiment. Currently, we just use the standard online tools. In the future work, we would use camera and video conferencing tools to enhance our environment. Other future tasks are to optimize the SOAP messaging and to analyse the resource description and integration issues.

CONCLUSION AND FUTHER WORK

Our vision is to share expensive equipment and educational materials associated with lab experiments as broadly as possible within higher education and beyond. In this article, we propose to wrap the remote instruments as Web services for online experiment systems. The advantage of Web services is its inter-operability across platforms and programming languages. Its trade-off is low efficiency caused by SOAP messaging. This article covers the essential issues to build instrument Web services, such as WSDL design, stateful service management and performance issues. This article also presents the lightweight Web GUI to display virtual instrument panels and real time signals using Web 2.0 techniques. The technique developed in this article can be widely used for different real laboratories, such as microelectronics, chemical engineering, polymer crystallization, structural engineering, and signal processing.

As the article is published, we have got a Canarie (http://www.canarie.ca/about/index.html) funded project called Science Studio for enabling remote experimentation with the synchrotron within Canada Light Source (CLS) (http://www.lightsource.ca/), a national science research laboratory. Currently the scientists who use the facilitate to do experiments need to travel to Winnipeg where the CLS is located and reserve the beamline time for 3 days as a minimum unit. With the capacity of remote experimentation, the scientists can save traveling time and cost. Furthermore, the occupy time of an experiment can be shrunk to hours instead of days. Therefore, the facilitate can be more efficiently shared in the scientific community. Our work within Science Studio is much beyond the topics touched in this article.

REFERENCES

W3C, (2004a). *WSDL Specification*. http://www.w3.org/TR/wsdl.

W3C, (2004b). *SOAP Specification*. http://www.w3.org/TR/soap12-part1/.

Agilent Inc. (2005). *About Instrument I/O.* http://adn.tm.agilent.com/index.cgi?CONTENT_ID=239, retrieved in 2005.

Auer, M. E., & Gallent, W. (2000). The 'Remote Electronic Lab' as a Part of the Telelearning Concept at the Carinthia Tech Institute. *Proc. Interactive Computer-Aided Learning (ICL),* Kassel University Press.

Bagnasco, A., Chirico, M., & Scapolla, A. M. (2002). XML Technologies to Design Didactical Distributed Measurement Laboratories. *IEEE Instrument and Measurement Technology Conference (IMTC),* Anchorage, Alaska, USA.

Chiu, K., Govindaraju, M., & Bramley, R. (2002). Investigating the Limits of SOAP Performance for Scientific Computing. 11th *IEEE international Symposium on High Performance Distributed Computing* HPDC-11.

Elfwing, R., Paulsson, U., & Lundberg, L. (2002). Performance of SOAP in Web service Environment Compared to CORBA. *Proceedings of the Ninth Asia-Pacific Software Engineering Conference (APSE'02).* IEEE.

Fattouh, B., & Saliah, H. H. (2004). Model for a Distributed Telelaboratory Interface Generator. *Proceedings of Int. Conf. On Engineering* [), Czech Republic.]. *Education and Research,* (June): 27–30.

Garrett, J. J. (2005). *Ajax: A New Approach to Web Applications.* Available at http://adaptivepath.com/publications/essays/archives/000385.php, last retrieved March 29 2007.

Hardison, J., Hardison, D. J., Zych, D., del Alamo, J. A., et al. (2005). The Microelectronics WebLab 6.0—An Implementation Using Web services and the iLab Shared Architecture. *Proc. Int'l Conf. Engineering Education and Research (iCEER2005), Int'l Network for Engineering Education and Research,* 2005. http://wwwmtl.mit.edu/~alamo/pdf/2005/RC-107%20paper.pdf.

Hardison, J. D., Zych, J. A., & del Alamo, V. J. Harward, et al. (2005). *The Microelectronics WebLab 6.0 – An Implementation Using Web services and the iLab Shared Architecture. iCEER2005,* March, Tainan, Taiwan.

JSON.org. (2007). *Introducing JSON.* Available at: http://www.json.org/. Last retrieved in March 29 2007.

Latchman, H. A., Salzmann, Ch., Gillet, D., & Bouzekri, H. (1999, November). Information Technology Enhanced Learning in Distance and Conventional Education. *IEEE Transactions on Education*, 247–254. doi:10.1109/13.804528

Litou, M. (2002). Migrating to Web services – Latency and Scalability. *Proceedings of Fourth Int. Workshop on Web Site Evolution (WSE)*. IEEE.

LTSC (IEEE Learning Technology Standards Committee). (1999). *IEEE 1484 Learning Objects Metadata (IEEE LOM)*.http://www.ischool.washington.edu/sasutton/IEEE1484.html.

Naef, O. (2006). Real laboratory, virtual laboratory or remote laboratory: what is the most efficient way? *International Journal of Online Engineering, v2*(n3). http://www.i-joe.org/ojs/sitemap.php.

Nielsen, H., Gettys, J., Baird-Smith, A., Prud'hommeaux, E., Lie, H., & Lilley, C. (1997). *Network Performance Effects of HTTP/1.1, CSS1, and PNG*.http://www.w3.org/Protocols/HTTP/Performance/Pipeline.html, June 1997.

Salzmann, C., & Gillet, D. (2002). Real-time Interaction over the Internet, *Proceedings of IFAC2002. UDDI.org*. http://uddi.org/pubs/uddi_v3.htm.

Tautenhahn, T. (2005). *JavaScript Diagram Builder 3.3*.http://www.lutanho.net/diagram.

van Engelen, R. (2003). Pushing the SOAP Envelop With Web services for Scientific Computing. *Proceedings of the International Conference on Web services (ICWS)* (pp. 346-354).

Yan, Y., Liang, Y., Du, X., Saliah-Hassane, H., & Ghorbani, A. (2005). Design Instrumental Web services for Online Experiment Systems. *Ed-Media 2005*, Montreal, Canada.

This work was previously published in the International Journal of Web Services Research, Volume 6, Issue 4, edited by L.-J. Zhang, pp. 75-93, copyright 2009 by IGI Publishing (an imprint of IGI Global).

Chapter 4.23
Student Support Services

Scott L. Howell
Brigham Young University, USA

Wendi Wilcken
Brigham Young University, USA

INTRODUCTION

Success secret number one for a successful online learning program, according to Jeffrey Feldberg, chairman and CEO of Embanet Corp. and who has launched several successful online programs, is "live technical support" (Feldberg, 2001, p. 1). Many student support services, like technical support, are critical to the successful learning experience of all students, but especially for students who are engaged in online learning at a distance. One director of student support services for an online learning program said it this way: "If they're having trouble with the technology, it's like showing up at class and the door's locked and they can't get in" (Kelly, 2001, p.5). And, just as trouble with technology may keep the class door locked for one student, so can any other unmet student need for another student.

Like campus students, students at a distance or online expect high-quality, effective student support services to help them achieve their academic goals. Even though the student should be the number one concern, student support services are often not considered when distance-education programs are discussed, designed and developed (Moore, 2000). Tony Bates agrees and identifies the "incorporat[ion of] student services" as one of the 12 important lessons for distance education administrators to learn. He also makes the point that, "If your distance-education program is part of a university-wide plan for learning, then you will likely find that it is equally attractive to both traditional and distance students" (Bates, 2003, p. 1), thereby expanding the reach and role of student support services.

MEETING STUDENT NEEDS

Traditional student-support services for distance-education and online students may not be enough. As one dean of continuing education and distance learning noted: "I think we need to ... admit that a good distance-learning program may have to deliver more services to the student than the traditional program, particularly in the administrative/student services area" (Bothel, 2001, para. 3). Moore (2000,

DOI: 10.4018/978-1-60566-198-8.ch288

p.1) suggests that support services for learners "should include at least the following elements: pre-enrollment activities such as recruiting and orientation, admissions and registration support, academic advising, financial planning and management, access to library and bookstore resources, personal and career counseling, degree and transcript services, and technical support." At one institution, approximately one-fourth of the surveyed students "reported interest in various types of social function services such as … a student newspaper, academic clubs, … and access to an online psychologist" (LaPadula, 2003, p. 127). In short, the most appropriate student services are those the students at a particular institution need most. "Knowing student needs is essential to an effective student services program" (Ambler, 1989, p. 255).

After identifying what student services students would most like, program administrators must then differentiate among essential student services and those that would be "nice." The balancing of institutional resources with student needs and wants will determine how many of the nice-but-not-so-necessary student services are made available. However, accommodating the disabled is one of those student-support services that should always be considered necessary and not just "nice" – for both moral and legal reasons.

THE ORGANIZATIONAL FIT

Not only does the online or distant learner need "more services" – or at least a different configuration of services – the online program administrators also depend on better services to complement their marketing efforts to not only current but also prospective students. It is a well-documented fact that the marketing costs to retain one student are significantly less than those costs to recruit one new student. Knowing and attending to students' needs will inform marketing strategies (Malan, Rigby & Glines, 1991). And once students' needs

are identified and fitting support services are mapped to these needs, both the enrolled as well as the prospective students should be informed of their availability. One study found that many students are not aware of the services available to them. Marketing excellent student services can not only help retain current students in the program but also attract new students to it (Cain, Marrara, Pitre & Armour, 2003).

Excellent student service is sometimes the only distinguishing characteristic of two comparable online or distance education programs. The best course content and faculty coupled with the best marketing efforts cannot compensate for deficient or even mediocre student support services. Students served well serve the program well by telling their friends; students disappointed in the services of a program can easily and quickly hurt a program by discouraging other students from enrolling. The programs with the best student support services will not only retain current students but also attract new ones.

While competent and inspiring online instructors with well-designed content are frequently associated with program success, student support services cannot be ignored. Some theorists have linked student satisfaction with the academic support services to educational outcomes (Cain & Lockee, 2002). A distance education program that recruits outstanding faculty and develops exceptional courses may no longer be enough for students if support services are lacking, especially as more and more educational providers compete for online and distant learners. All three dimensions of the online or distance learning experience – that is, faculty, instruction and support services – are vital to the success of the whole academic experience. Furthermore, well-designed courses and properly trained online instructors will mitigate the demand on support services just as a well-staffed and -trained student support department will influence student perception of course quality and instructor effectiveness.

PROGRAM RETENTION AND COURSE COMPLETION

An important characteristic of a successful distance education program is high rates of course completion and student retention at the program level. Effective student services not only meet students' needs but can also contribute to both student retention and course completion. While "effective student services are student-centered and value added, superb student services not only … meet the student needs, but also go the extra mile to help them become successful. Student-focused services create a positive experience, which may lead to higher retention" (Burnett & Oblinger, 2003, p.28). The literature on the role of student services in the online learning process, though not abundant (Cain & Lockee, 2002), does yield significant findings, particularly in the areas of course completion and program retention rates.

Mary Hricko of Kent State University identifies seven support services to assist students in completing their courses of study:

1. Provide students an orientation to the course.
2. Allow students to engage in a formative assessment throughout the course.
3. Educate students that the technology and content of the course are two different elements of the course.
4. Bring campus life to the class.
5. Be innovative, and establish an online learning community.
6. Be available.
7. Partner students with study buddies (2003).

Another researcher, Kasworm (2002), lists 10 support service strategies for improving student retention:

1. Provide initial entry advisement, orientation and career counseling.

2. Offer financial assistance or financial counseling.
3. Provide academic and basic skill development opportunities.
4. Establish policies and procedures oriented to adult learners.
5. Use information technology (e.g., listservs, online forums) to build community.
6. Establish programs that incorporate family and spouse support.
7. Increase opportunities for personal interaction with and attention from faculty.
8. Provide assistance in finding special-needs services, such as housing, transportation, and so forth.
9. Establish adult support networks.
10. Get to know and treat students as individuals.

STANDARDS AND ACCREDITATION

Not only have researchers and practitioners identified critical support services for the online and distant learner but so have organizations with oversight responsibility – regional, state and technical or professional accrediting bodies. Many of these organizations have adopted standards, benchmarks or best practices for student service and support within the past 3 years. For example, the Council for Higher Education Accreditation (CHER) announced 32 distance education standards in August 2000 – those relating to student services are listed under the third major competency standard entitled, "Responsiveness to Students." An example of one of these standards is, "The institution has clear procedures for addressing student grievances."

This same standard of addressing grievances is listed under the major category "Student Services" in the document "Guidelines for Distance Education" prepared by the Western Interstate Commission for Higher Education (WICHE). Another institutional expectation identified by

WICHE is that "students ... possess the knowledge and equipment necessary to use the technology employed in the programs and provide aid to students who are experiencing difficulty using the required technology" (Oblinger, Barone & Hawkins, 2001, p. 34).

The Institute for Higher Education released in April 2000 its "Benchmarks for success in Internet-based distance education," with seven major categories identified, including one called "Student Support Benchmarks." The institute defined two important student support benchmarks at a degree of specificity not used by CHER and WICHE:

- "Students receive information about programs, including admission requirements, tuition and fees, books and supplies, technical and proctoring requirements, and student support services.
- "Students are provided with hands-on training and information to aid them in securing material through electronic databases, interlibrary loans, government archives, news services, and other sources" (Oblinger, Barone & Hawkins, 2001, p. 40).

Finally, the Association of Colleges and Research Libraries (ACRL) announced in Fall 2000 its distance education guidelines for libraries. An ACRL document states: "Access to adequate library services and resources is essential for the attainment of superior academic skills in post-secondary education, regardless of where students, faculty and programs are located. Members of the distance learning community are entitled to library services and resources equivalent to those provided for students and faculty in traditional campus settings" (para. 1). In many ways, these standards, benchmarks and best practices are defining what student support services are for online and distant learners.

EMERGING MODELS

As distance education and online providers and the number of students enrolled in online and distance learning programs increase, the existing student support infrastructures for many programs will be stretched. For online learning to scale, student support service areas will need to reinvent themselves. Several student service models are beginning to emerge in response to the demand for improved student service support at a time when institutional resources are scarce. Student support services of the future must be available anytime and anywhere to support anytime and anywhere learning (Smith, 2001).

Student support service administrators from Washington State University have identified two support service models that can help meet this demand:

- "Moving to a convenient – any time/any place delivery modality – which implies an asynchronous system, part of which is probably a self-service model, [and]
- "One-stop shopping, which means our student service staffs will have to be trained across functions and able to address at least the first 5 or 8 questions about every element of our programs" (Moore, 2000, p. 8).

Self-Service

Self-service functionality allows students to complete many common transactions anytime from anywhere. In the self-service model, students can access their updated academic plan, check on their financial aid, register and pay for their courses, request tests and order transcripts, and find answers to process or policy questions at will and convenience. This model, analogous to "paying at the pump," allows students to complete transactions at a time convenient for them and frees up student services staff to focus on value-added services. The self-service model can be implemented in complement with or as a component of other models.

Knowledge bases fit well into a self-service paradigm. Once built, students and staff can quickly and easily find answers to questions previously answered and placed online. The University of Houston recently implemented a knowledge base, AskShasta, which has reportedly cut down the number of student service calls by as much as 25% (Roberts, 2004).

One-Stop Services

Portals are personalized and customized Web pages that anticipate in one stop or in one place most of the service needs of the student. These portals are not limited to the students, either, as they also customize to the roles and interests of faculty or student services staff (Burnett & Oblinger, 2003). For example, a student just admitted to an online program will be presented information suited to the new student still in need of orientation, as opposed to the experienced student preparing for graduation.

In addition to many services being readily available with the help of "high-tech" portals and knowledge bases, the "high touch" of staff members communicating with students by phone, e-mail or chat will remain a critical element of a student support service strategy. A well-trained staff can address student needs in one stop or one call. They solve the problems and remove the obstacles that keep the student from having the best possible learning experience. The chief student services officer should be concerned with the staff's effectiveness, morale, training and welfare (Ambler, 1989). All efforts to help and to train the student services staff will benefit students as they receive more caring, knowledgeable help (Dalton, 1989). "Immersion" (intense and simulated) training for staff employees is a good way to sensitize them to the student experience and identify potential problems in the service (Burnett & Oblinger, 2003).

The more student services staff is cross trained and the more individualized and robust are portals and knowledge bases, the more direct and successful the student support.

CONCLUSION

Student support services are a critical component of any successful online and distance education program. Student service standards, benchmarks and best practices are emerging that help institutions plan and redefine their programs and measure their effectiveness in meeting expectations of administrators, faculty and, especially, students. These support services focus on essential student needs and help meet them by providing an appropriate mix of self-serve and staff-serve services. The opportunity for providing better and more efficient student support services has never been better, as technology enables personalized student support services to complement online courses and instructors. Student support services can help students reach their academic goals, remove obstacles to learning, improve student completion and retention rates, and help ensure program success.

ACKNOWLEDGMENT

Authors express special thanks to Jennifer Tolman, their research assistant, for her help in preparing this entry.

REFERENCES

Ambler, D. (1989). Designing and managing programs: The administrator role. In U. Delworth, G. Hanson et al. (Eds.), Student services: A handbook for the profession (pp. 247-264). San Francisco, CA: Jossey-Bass.

Association of Colleges and Research Libraries. (2000, Fall). *Guidelines for distance learning library services.* Retrieved February 5, 2004, from www.ala.org/ala/acrl/acrlstandards/guidelines distance.htm

Bates, T. (2003). Tony Bates' twelve lessons for distance education administrators. *Distance Education Report, 7*(8), 1–3.

Bothel, R. (2001). Bringing it all together. *Online Journal of Distance Learning Administration* 4(1). Retrieved February 4, 2004, from www.westga. edu/~distance/jmain11.html

Burnett, D., & Oblinger, D. (2003). Student academic services: Models, current practices and trends. In G. Kramer (Ed.), Student academic services (pp. 27-52). San Francisco, CA: Jossey-Bass.

Cain, D., Marrara, C., Pitre, P., & Armour, S. (2003). Support services that matter: An exploration of the experiences and needs of graduate students in a distance learning environment. *Journal of Distance Education, 18*(1), 42–56.

Cain, D.L., & Lockee, B. (2002). *Student support services at a distance: Are institutions meeting the needs of distance learners?* (ERIC Document Reproduction Service, No. ED468729)

Dalton, J. (1989). Enhancing staff knowledge and skills. In U. Delworth, G. Hanson, et al. (Eds.), Student services: A handbook for the profession (pp. 533-551). CA: Jossey-Bass.

Feldberg, J. (2001). Seven secrets of successful online learning programs. *Distance Education Report, 5*(16), 1–3.

Hricko, M. (2003). Retention resources. Message posted to The Distance Education Online Symposium electronic mailing list. Retrieved April 10, 2003 from http://lists.psu.edu/cgi-bin/ wa?A2=ind0304&L=*deos-l&F=&S=&P=4114*

Kasworm, C. E., Polson, C. J., & Fishback, S. J. (2002). Responding to adult learners in higher education. Malabar: Krieger Publishing.

Kelly, R. (2001, March 15). An integrated approach to student services. *Distance Education Report, 5*(6), 5.

Kendall, J., Moore, C., Smith, R., & Oaks, M. (2001). Student services for distance learners: A critical component. *NASPA's E-zine for Student Affairs Professionals.* Retrieved February 6, 2004, from http://naspa.org/netresults/PrinterFriendly. cfm*?ID=229*

LaPadula, M. (2003). A comprehensive look at online student support services for distance learners. *American Journal of Distance Education, 17*(2), 119–128. doi:10.1207/S15389286AJDE1702_4

Malan, R., Rigby, D., & Glines, L. (1991). Support services for the independent study student. In B. Watkins, & S. Wright (Eds.), The foundations of American distance education: A century of collegiate correspondence Study (pp. 159-172). Dubuque, IA: Kendall/Hunt.

Moore, C. (2000, May 23). Comprehensive student services for distance education programs. Paper presented at *Second Annual California Community College Online Student Services Conference*, Victorville, CA.

Oblinger, D., Barone, C., & Hawkins, B. (2001). Distributed education and its challenges: An overview. Washington, D.C.: American Council on Education Center for Policy Analysis.

Roberts, B. (2004). Transforming your Web site into a 24/7 service center. *Syllabus, 17*(12), 50–51.

Smith, S. (2001). Beyond face to face: One institution's journey to develop online student services and ways to get started. *Student Affairs Online, 2*(Spring). Retrieved February 6, 2004, from www.studentaffairs.com/ejournal/Spring_2001/services.html

KEY TERMS AND DEFINITIONS

Accreditation: The process of certifying whether a program meets the standards and expectations of any association to which it belongs.

Completion Rate: The most common measure for success in an online or distance learning course, frequently associated with program persistence and retention rates. No standardized algorithm currently exists for calculating completion rates; they are best used in comparing one cohort of the same course with another.

Immersion Training: The University of North Carolina at Greensboro provides a one-day "immersion" as a part of their staff training. The staff trainee works in a student-simulated environment to better experience their program services from the student perspective.

One-Stop: The one-stop model allows students the convenience of talking with one person at one location to find all the services and answers needed. Staff who work at one-stop call, e-mail or chat centers have a very broad knowledge of the services and are able to address a high percentage of student questions and service requests.

Portal: A Web-based environment customized to provide users' information needs. In contrast to the typical Web page, where a large amount of information is available to all, portals provide information specific to the user's need and role. The user is able to customize what information is revealed and what is hidden.

Self-Service: Online students register, request and pay for services, receive basic academic advising, and so forth, without accessing student support personnel. Under this model, students are no longer bound by the office hours of the provider. They can individually access their services anytime from anywhere.

Student Support Services: Student services are all the services provided by the distance education's provider to the students (prospective and matriculated) to facilitate their success at the learning institution.

This work was previously published in the Encyclopedia of Distance Learning, Second Edition, edited by P. Rogers; G. Berg; J. Boettcher; C. Howard; L. Justice; K. Schenk, pp. 1951-1956, copyright 2009 by IGI Publishing (an imprint of IGI Global).

Section V
Organizational and Social Implications

This section includes a wide range of research pertaining to the social and organizational impact of electronic service. Chapters included in this section analyze the enablers and inhibitors of Internet technology adoption, discuss consumer attitudes towards different electronic services, consider the challenges of consumer trust and electronic services, and demonstrate the positive impact of early user involvement and participation on electronic self-services. The inquiries and methods presented in this section offer insight into the implications of electronic services at both a personal and organizational level, while also emphasizing potential areas of study within the discipline.

Chapter 5.1
Factors Relating to the Adoption of Internet Technology by the Omani Banking Industry

Salim Al-Hajri
Higher College of Technology, Oman

Arthur Tatnall
Victoria University, Australia

ABSTRACT

The banking industry in Oman is of major importance to Oman's economy, yet Omani banks continue to conduct most of their transactions using traditional methods. A strong banking industry significantly supports economic development through efficient financial services, and their role in trying to achieve the objectives outlined by the Sultan of Oman will depend heavily on the industry's capabilities. Omni banks will need to introduce change at both procedural and informational levels that includes moving from traditional distribution channel banking to electronic channel banking. This chapter addresses the question: What are the enablers and the inhibitors of Internet technology adoption in the Omani banking industry compared with those in the Australian banking industry? The chapter does not attempt a direct comparison of the banking industries in these two very different countries, but rather presents a discussion of Internet technology adoption in Oman, informed by the more mature Australian experience.

INTRODUCTION

In developed countries such as Australia Internet technologies have been embraced by the banking industry and, for several years, banks have pursued strategies to encourage their clients to engage in Internet banking. In an article relating to on-line banking portals, Ayadi (2007) notes the diversity of competitive, technical and strategic challenges faced by banks on the Internet. In developing countries, financial institutions have been less inclined to adopt Internet technology and thereby capitalize on the benefits of simplicity, convenience and usefulness claimed to be associated with its implementation (Kurihara, Takaya, Harui, & Kamae, 2008). Oman is an example of a developing country committed to economic growth but with a banking industry that is yet to embrace Internet technology.

Traditionally, Oman has been heavily reliant on oil as its main income source. Fluctuations in world oil prices, however, can leave the country exposed to commodity price risk and during the 1990s Oman began to diversify its income sources. His Majesty,

DOI: 10.4018/978-1-60566-964-9.ch015

the Sultan of Oman, summarized his vision for Oman's economy as follows:

"The government has made major efforts in recent years to achieve comprehensive development in all fields. Now that it has succeeded, with the help of God, in moving the country from a traditional economy to a modern developed one, our future plan will be based on the balanced management of income and expenditure and the preservation of that balance so that Oman's present high prestige in the economic sphere, will be preserved. Therefore, the duty of the private sector in playing an active role in the development of economic process and in the achievement of national goals by taking appropriate initiatives, as is the case in all developed countries, is of great importance" (Qaboos bin Said's speech, June 2, 1995, reported in Oman Ministry of Development (1996)).

Since the development of the Omani banking industry in 1948 all banks have relied heavily on traditional distribution channels for banking services. However, in 1997 the Oman telecommunication company, Omantel, introduced Internet services to home and business users. According to the statistics provided by Omantel (2002) in their annual report, the number of Internet technology users had reached 12,348 in 1998 one year after of its introduction. By 2002 Omantel reported that the number of Internet users had reached 48,000, making up around 2% of the general population. Indeed, Internet technology infrastructure has grown steadily over the years but has only had a moderate effect on the Omani economy. The Omani banking industry has been very slow and cautious in moving from traditional distribution channel banking services to electronic distribution channel banking services (Al-Hajri, 2005).

Paradoxically, the growing number of users of Internet technology in the Omani economy has not yet motivated the Omani banking industry to adopt Internet technology the way the Australian banking industry has done. The Market Intelli-

gence Strategy Centre (MISC, 2002) reported that in 2002 there were six million Internet banking users in the Australian banking industry reinforcing the observation that Internet technology is far more developed in the Australia than in Oman. Other analysts (Wright & Ralston, 2002) expect Internet technology to grow substantially in the Australian banking industry which means that the Omani banks will be left lagging further behind global competitive markets.

In every country the banking industry is important, as a strong banking industry can have a significant affect in supporting economic development through efficient financial services. In Oman the role of the banking industry in trying to achieve the objectives outlined by the Sultan depends heavily on the industry's capabilities and banks need to introduce change, both at the procedural level and at the informational level. This change includes moving from traditional distribution channel banking to electronic distribution channel banking. Given the prevalence of Internet technology adoption by the banking industry in developed countries, reasons for the lack of such innovation in developing countries such as Oman are of considerable importance.

There are, of course, huge cultural differences between Oman and Australia and a direct comparison of the two is not the intent of this paper. The backgrounds, economics, societies and indeed the very way of life in the two countries are all very different. Australian banks have already largely adopted Internet technologies while Omani banks are just beginning to do so. The goal of this paper is to discuss adoption of Internet technology in the banking industry in Oman, with reference to the Australian experience in order to identify possible ways forward. This paper will thus address the question of determining inhibitors and enablers to the adoption of Internet technology in the banking industry in Oman, and inform the Oman experience by the more mature Australian experience.

TECHNOLOGY ADOPTION AND DEVELOPING COUNTRIES

Internet technology has played a major role in economic development in developed countries (Ghosh, 1998; Kalakota & Whinston, 1997; Kurihara et al., 2008; Raisinghani, 2000), but less so in developing countries and economies. A good deal has been written about adoption of new technologies and techniques in *agriculture* in developing countries (e.g. (Lee, 2005; Michelsen & Hartwich, 2004; Paarlberg, 2003), but not so much has been recently written on adoption of other technologies apart from a classic article published some fifteen years ago by Besley and Case (1993).

Montealegre (1999) describes a study of Internet adoption in four Latin American countries in which he notes a gradual but progressive course of institutional adoption actions including knowledge building, subsidy, knowledge deployment, innovation directive, and standard setting. Basant, Commander, Harrison and Menezes-Filho (2006) report on the determinants of Information and Communication Technology (ICT) adoption and its impact on performance on manufacturing firms in Brazil and India. They suggest that while Brazilian firms on average use ICT more intensively than their Indian counterparts, in both countries ICT intensity is strongly related to size, ownership structure, share of administrative workers and education. Rajapakse and Seddon (2007) explore the adoption of ERP software in Asia using Hofstede's dimensions of national cultures and conclude that contrasting dimensions of the cultural practices embedded in ERP software are a barrier to adoption. Molla and Licker (2005) report that their studies of eCommerce in developing countries emphasize the influence of contextual impediments including economic, technological, legal, and financial infrastructure as major determinants of adoption. Talukdar, Sudhir and Ainslie (2006) investigate new product diffusion across products and countries, and note

that diffusion is much slower in developing than developed countries.

THEORETICAL FRAMEWORK

It has been suggested that "… explaining human behavior in all its complexity is a difficult task" (Ajzen, 1991:179). Further to this we will argue that the main complexity in understanding Internet technology adoption behavior, or that lack of it, within the context of the banking industry in Oman (a non-adopter) and Australia (an adopter) is that this involves people such as bank managers and customers, and people behave in different ways. In deriving a framework for this study, four existing research frameworks were considered: The Theory of Reasoned Action (TRA), The Theory of Planned Behavior (TPB), The Technology Acceptance Model (TAM) and Diffusion of Innovations.

The Theory of Reasoned Action (TRA)

Fishbein and Ajzen (1975) originally developed the Theory of Reasoned Action (TRA) in 1975, before later comprehensively refining it with empirical evidence to support its validity and reliability (Ajzen & Fishbein, 1980). In developing their theory they integrated various studies on attitude from social psychology with the aim of developing an integrated conceptual framework to predict and explain an individual's behavior in a general situational setting. In sum, their study focused on three major determinants of an individual's behavior: **Behavioral Intention**, **Attitude** and **Subjective Norm**. They illustrated their model using these three major variables in a hierarchical sequence to facilitate understanding. In summary they postulated that:

1. An individual's behavioral intention is the immediate determinant of behavior

2. His/her attitude and subjective norm are mediated through behavioral intention

3. His/her behavioral and normative beliefs are mediated through attitude and subjective norm respectively.

In predicting and explaining behavior, TRA has been applied in various fields including consumer behavior (Engel, Blackwell, & Miniard, 1995; Taylor & Todd, 1997; Thomson, Haziris, & Alekos, 1994), moral behavior (Vallerand, Pelletier, Deshaies, Cuerrier, & Mongeau, 1992), ethical/unethical behavior (Chang, 1998; Gibson & Frakes, 1997; Loch & Conger, 1996), environmental behavior (Goldenhar & Connell, 1993), coupon usage behavior (Bagozzi, Davis, & Warshaw, 1992; Shimp & Kavas, 1984), fast food consumption behavior (Bagozzi, Wong, Abe, & Bergami, 2000), adoption of strategic information systems (IS) behavior (Mykytyn & Harison, 1993), system investment decision behavior (Clark & Soliman, 1999), information technology (IT) adoption behavior (Karahanna, Straub, & Cherveny, 1999) and Internet use behavior (Bobbitt & Dabholkar, 2001).

Although TRA has gained wide acceptance in the behavioral sciences and the IS literature due to its well integrated paradigm, the likelihood that a person will actually perform the specific behavior described has been questioned by many researchers (e.g. Warshaw and Davis (1985) and Davis et al. (1989)). For example, in a situation where there is a gap between behavioral intention and actual behavior, some studies have found a low correlation between behavioral these (Bonfield, 1974; Harrell & Bennett, 1974).

The Theory of Planned Behavior (TPB)

After identifying problems with TRA Ajzen (1991) came up with a modification: the Theory of Planned Behavior (TPB). His main criticisms of TRA were that it was designed to predict and

explain behavior, or actions, based on the assumption that the behavior was under a person's volitional control. He argues, however, that some behavior that is not under a person's volitional control might be problematic due to the differences in individuals' abilities and in external forces. This may have an influence on actual performance of the behavior and, therefore, consideration should be given to the concept of behavioral control to overcome these volitional control problems. To achieve this Ajzen extended the Theory of Reasoned Action by adding another construct called Perceived Behavioral Control, which refers to an individual's perception of the "... presence or absence of requisite resources and opportunities" (Ajzen & Madden, 1986:457) required to perform the specific behavior.

Like the theory of Reasoned Action, the Theory of Planned Behavior assumes that Behavioral Intention is a function of two determinants: the individual's attitude towards the behavior, and the subjective norm within the social environment. Ajzen (1991) argues, however, that the inclusion of Perceived Behavioral Control is important, and provided two rationales for this: it is expected that Perceived Behavioral Control will increase the likelihood of success in performing the behavior, and it is expected that it will provide a measure of actual control. Its validity as a measure to predict the likelihood of achieving the target behavior will depend on the individual's capability (e.g. having the requisite opportunities and resources) to exercise control over the specific behavior. This means that a person who believes that they have the resources and opportunities expects fewer problems in performing the specific behavior and hence perceives that they have complete control over the specific behavior.

Ajzen (1991) reviewed several studies employing TPB and found support for it, more evidence also being found in various situational settings. These studies include: task performance (Locke, Fredrick, Lee, & Bobko, 1984), attending class and weight loss (Shifter & Ajzen, 1985), obtaining grades (Ajzen & Madden, 1986), investment decisions (East, 1993), consumer behavior (Sparks & Shepherd, 1992), dishonest behavior (Beck & Ajzen, 1991), ethical behavior (Kurland, 1995; Randall & Gibson, 1991), leisure activities (Ajzen & Driver, 1992), executives' adoption of IT in small business (Harrison, Mykytyn, & Riemenschneider, 1997), adoption of virtual banking (Liao, Shao, Wang, & Chen, 1999), learning to use the Internet (Klobas & Clyde, 2000) and Internet purchases (George, 2002). However, Liao et al. (1999) did not find support for the Theory of Planned Behavior and research studies by Randall and Gibson (1991), Beck et al. (1991) and Kurland (1995) found only weak support. These studies thus show rather mixed and confusing results.

Technology Acceptance Model (TAM)

The Technology Acceptance Model (TAM) is a theoretical model that evaluates "… the effect of system characteristics on user acceptance of computer-based information systems" (F. D. Davis, 1986:7). In a similar fashion to the Theory of Reasoned Action, TAM assumes that a computer user is generally quite rational and uses information in a systematic manner to decide whether to use, or not to use this technology in the workplace. The main goal of TAM was:

"… to provide an explanation of the determinants of computer acceptance that is general, and capable of explaining user behavior across a broad range of end-user computing technologies and user populations, while at the same time being both parsimonious and theoretically justified" (Fred D. Davis et al., 1989:985).

In attempting to fulfill this aim, Davis' (1986) conceptual framework proposed that a user's motivational factors are related to actual technology usage and hence, act as a bridge between technology design (e.g. system features and capabilities) and actual technology usage. This means that

information obtained from the prediction of actual usage at the early stage will guide designers and implementers to enhance the chance of implementing technology successfully or even avoid the risk of failure. In the conceptual framework Davis (1986) assumes that stimulus variables (e.g. system features and capabilities) trigger organism factors (e.g. user motivation to use the technology) and in turn users respond by actually using the technology. Davis identified three major determinants of technology acceptance (or adoption) suggested by previous research studies that relate to cognition and effectiveness. He began with the Theory of Reasoned Action (Ajzen & Fishbein, 1980; Fishbein & Ajzen, 1975) and adapted this as a basis for causal links between **Perceived Usefulness**, **Perceived Ease of Use**, **Attitude Toward Using Technology** and **Behavioral Intention** to explain technology adoption.

Benefits claimed for the use of TAM are twofold: (1) it provides IS designers with information about how and where to modify design to enhance IS acceptance, and (2) it provides IS implementers with information about how and where to manage IS implementation.

Many studies (e.g. (F. D. Davis, 1989; Segars & Grover, 1993; Taylor & Todd, 1995b) have examined TAM across various technologies and have found TAM to be a reliable and valid model for predicting and explaining technology adoption or acceptance behavior. Various studies utilized TAM to assess users' acceptance or rejection of various computer technologies such as microcomputers (Igbaria, Guimaraes, & Davis, 1995), DOS and Windows (Speier, Morris, & Bridggs, 1995), word processing software (Adams, Nelson, & Todd, 1992; Fred D. Davis et al., 1989; F. D. Davis & Venkatesh, 1996; Hendrickson & Collins, 1996; Venkatesh & Davis, 1996), spreadsheets (Mathieson, 1991), groupware (Taylor & Todd, 1995a), database management systems (Szajna, 1994), e-mail (Adams et al., 1992; F. D. Davis, 1989; Szajna, 1996) and the World Wide Web (Lederer, Maupin, Sena, & Zhuang, 2000). Other studies extended TAM by including other variables such as perceived credibility (Wang, Wang, Lin, & Tang, 2003), gender difference (Gefen & Straub, 1997), and enjoyment (Al-Gahtani & King, 1999). In summary, although several authors (Fred D. Davis et al., 1989; Venkatesh & Davis, 2000) assert that TAM is a useful model for predicting user technology adoption behavior, the above studies showed mixed results. Moreover, most of these studies concentrated on the fundamental prescriptions of TAM with the exception of the study by Wang et al. (2003) which included Perceived Credibility.

Diffusion of Innovations

The theory of Diffusion of Innovations as described by Rogers (1995) is well known. Rogers describes diffusion of innovations as: "… the process by which an innovation is communicated through certain channels over time among the members of social systems. It is a special type of communication, in that the messages are concerned with new ideas" (Rogers, 1995:5).

In the diffusion process, Rogers stresses the importance of communication in an attempt to educate the customer about the innovation concerned. He identifies four main elements: an innovation, communication channels, time and the social system. Rogers suggests that consumers' reactions to the innovation can be measured based on how an innovation is different, how well it is communicated, how long it takes to persuade customers to adopt it, and whether the social system is structured towards achieving a common goal. According to Rogers the four elements of the diffusion of innovation provide an indication of how an innovation is passed to the consumer from first knowledge of this innovation to its final adoption or rejection. The adoption decision for an innovation such as Internet technology in the banking industry is defined as:

"… the process through which an individual (or other decision-making unit) passes from first knowledge of an innovation to forming an attitude toward the innovation, to a decision to adopt or reject, to implementation and use of the new idea, and to confirmation of this decision" (Rogers, 1995:21).

A decision not to adopt an innovation relates to the rejection of the available new idea. However, in order to explain the rate of adoption of innovations Rogers suggests measurement of the following **Perceived Characteristics of Innovations**: (1) relative advantage; (2) compatibility; (3) complexity; (4) trialability; and (5) observability. Rogers (1995) postulated that the adoption of innovations is influenced by these five characteristics, and that they can explain the rate of technology adoption.

Innovation Translation (from Actor-Network Theory)

Innovation Translation (Latour, 1986, 1996; Law & Callon, 1988), informed by Actor-Network Theory (ANT), makes use of a model of technological innovation which uses the concept of heterogeneity in a world that is full of hybrid entities (Latour, 1993) containing both human and non-human elements. It notes that innovations are often not adopted in their entirety but only after 'translation' into a form that is more appropriate for use by the potential adopter, and uses these notions in an explanation of the adoption, or non-adoption of technology (Tatnall & Davey, 2007).

Callon et al. (1983) have proposed that translation involves all the strategies that an actor goes through to identify other actors and to arrange them in relation to each other. Latour (1996) speaks of 'chains of translation' and suggests that with the translation model the initial idea hardly counts and the innovation is not endowed with autonomous power, but moves only if it interests one group of actors or another.

Developing a Framework for this Study

This study involved an exploratory investigation of Internet technology adoption in the Omani banking industry, informed by the situation in the Australia. The various technology adoption models described above suggest that a number of factors might affect adoption. Relative advantage and ease of use, suggested by Moore and Benbasat (1991), were firstly considered in the analysis. Rogers (1995) originally identified these two perceptions of technology adoption as relative advantage and complexity. Moore and Benbasat (1991) and Taylor and Todd (1995b) explained that these two constructs are similar to those of TAM (F. D. Davis, 1986). They highlighted the fact that relative advantage is similar to the perceived usefulness construct and perceived complexity is similar to perceived ease of use, due to the similarity in their definitions and in the operation of their measurements. Two additional perceptions, organizational performance and customer/ organizational relationship, not previously identified in the ICT literature, were also considered. From an analysis of this literature, and from some preliminary discussions with bank managers, a theoretical framework was devised that suggests that bank managers' perceptions of only four adoption factors:

- **Relative Advantage**
- **Organizational Performance**
- **Customer/Organizational Relationship**
- **Ease of Use**

might affect any decision to adopt Internet technology in the banking industry. The results of the study, specifically investigating the major enablers and inhibitors of Internet technology adoption in the banking industry in Oman, suggest that these four adoption factors do indeed provide a useful explanation of this adoption.

RESEARCH METHOD

The Australian banking industry was considered in this investigation because of the advanced development of its Internet technology adoption. By examining Internet technology adoption in the banking industry of a developing country in relation to a developed country, the study hoped to provide a richer understanding of the industry and to enrich the analysis of how to improve Internet technology adoption in the banking industry in Oman. Twenty-seven interviews were conducted with strategic, tactical and operational managers at each of nine major banks, five in Oman (Bank of Dhofar, Oman Arab Bank, Oman International Bank and National Bank of Oman) and four in Australia (National Australia Bank, WestPac, Commonwealth Bank and Australia New Zealand Bank).

Selection of interviewees was made from available and willing bank officers so that roughly equal number from each management group were considered. A significant difficulty was encountered in arranging interviews with Australian bankers, but eventually some bank officers of appropriate standing did agree to participate and

Table 1. Classification of participants according to country and level of management

Country	Number of banks	Interviews – Strategic	Interviews – Tactical	Interviews – Operational	Total Participants
Australia	4	4	4	4	12
Oman	5	5	5	5	15
Total	9	9	9	9	27

gave willing of their time, however several hoped for interviews did not eventuate thus restricting the depth of the information gathered about some Australian banks. Given the exploratory nature of this investigation, data was gathered through semi-structured interviews with these managers, and available internal and public reports were used to facilitate understanding and to explore Internet technology adoption. Interview questions were devised to cover the issues identified from the literature and the research framework. Statements by participants are very important sources of evidence, and interviews were thus tape-recorded for later analysis. The average interview time was around 35 minutes.

A schedule of semi-structured interviews with these managers was set up to gather field evidence of perceptions of the four adoption factors: Relative Advantage, Organizational Performance, Customer/ Organizational Relationship and Ease of Use. Interviews were based on issues identified from the literature to explore in-depth the major enablers and inhibitors of Internet technology adoption in the banking industries of Oman and Australia. The four interview factors are further described below:

Perceived Relative Advantage

Discussion here concentrated on the extent to which a manager perceives that Internet technology would enable their organization to gain relative advantage in the industry. From NVIVO analysis of the interviews, issues related to perceived relative advantage were identified as: convenience of services; innovation of ideas, and management of services.

Perceived Organizational Performance

This explored the extent to which a manager perceives that Internet technology could improve organizational performance in the industry.

Clearly, if an organization expects to improve its performance with Internet technology then the likelihood of their adopting it will be greater. From NVIVO analysis of the interviews, perceived organizational performance related issues were: profitability, market environment and employees' productivity.

Perceived Customer/ Organizational Relationship

Here the discussion emphasized the extent to which a manager perceives that Internet technology would improve their organization's relationship with customers. If an organization perceives that Internet technology can improve its relationship with its customers then the likelihood of their adopting it will be higher. From the literature it was possible to identify focused issues as: customer trust, customer commitment, and customer satisfaction.

Perceived Ease of Use

If a bank officer perceives that Internet technology is easy to use then they will most likely be motivated to adopt this technology. The issues identified here by NVIVO analysis of the interviews include: easy to navigate, easy to learn, and easy to manage.

Analysis of Data

The elaborated responses from the 27 managers were analyzed, and the findings reported according to suggestions for data reduction and display offered by various authors (Miles & Huberman, 1994; Strauss & Corbin, 1990). NVIVO (version 2) qualitative research software was utilized in analyzing the data. Specifically, NVIVO assisted the analysis in both reducing (organizing and sorting) and displaying the evidence (creation of thematic conceptual tables) in a way that made it easier to see. A case-by-case matrix display was prepared using NVIVO to compare participants' perceptions on various issues. A thematic conceptual matrix display was then produced to compare and identify similar or different patterns of concerns within both banking industries to facilitate understanding of Internet technology adoption. Another thematic conceptual matrix display was produced to compare and identify similar or different concerns within different levels of management (strategic, tactical and operational). From the analysis it was possible to:

- Identify major patterns to facilitate in-depth understanding of Internet technology adoption.
- Reduce the data through the process of generating categories and establishing links (e.g. open and axial coding) as suggested by Strauss and Corbin (1990) using a grounded theory approach where a code is attached to a segment of text and then links between the coded data are explored.
- Display thematic conceptual tables to compare issues within a case and across cases.
- Identify patterns that facilitate understanding and lead to useful conclusions.

MAJOR FINDINGS OF THE STUDY

The study found that Omani bank managers' perceptions of four issues, namely:

- Perceived Relative Advantage
- Perceived Ease of Use
- Perceived Organizational Performance
- Perceived Customer/Organizational Relationship

jointly provided a broader understanding of Internet technology adoption in the banking industry than that proposed by previous theories and models including the Theory of Reasoned Action, the Theory of Planned Behavior, the Technology Acceptance Model and the theory of Innovation Diffusion.

The Omani and Australian banking industries were both found to perceive that Internet technology was important and that it could enable the industry to gain relative advantage. In relation to Perceived Relative Advantage, the enablers of Internet technology adoption found in both the Omani and Australian banking industry include:

A number of authors (e.g. (Dedrick, Gurbaxani, & Kraemer, 2003; King & Teo, 1996) have argued from a theoretical perspective that it is possible to increase the rate of Internet technology adoption if a manager perceives that Organizational Performance could be improved. The study showed that in the Omani banking industry, the majority of managers' responses indicated that this was indeed the case. Specifically it was found that perceived improvement in productivity of employees (e.g. improvement in business efficiency) could increase the rate of adoption. On the other hand, perceived problems in profitability, such as technology investment cost and the need for economies of scale for Internet technology use, could inhibit the banking industry from adopting Internet technology. The majority of the respondents in the Australian banking industry also suggested that perceived organizational performance was associated with Internet technology adoption. However, Australian managers expect to face a problem in the market environment in the difficulty of expanding their customer base. One reason for this is that the Australian banking industry is now facing intensive competition (Ramsey & Smith,

Table 2. Enablers relating to the factor of Perceived Relative Advantage

Major enablers in both Oman and Australia
Convenience of services (- convenience of available service and convenience of location)
Innovation of ideas (- rapid development of innovative ideas)
Management of services (- easy to follow up requests/complains)

1999; Sathye, 1999). Moreover, major Australian banks have already adopted Internet technology as a strategic tool to expand their markets and offer the same services online, making it harder for others to differentiate their offerings. So the real challenge here is how banks will be able to expand their market on the Internet. Table 3 below shows the major enablers and inhibitors of Internet technology adoption in relation to Perceived Organizational Performance.

The role of perceived customer/organizational relationship in IT adoption has attracted considerable attention in the literature (Anderson & Srinivasan, 2003; Athanassopoulos, 2000; Sathye, 1999). In this study, participants were asked whether or not they perceived that Internet technology adoption could improve the relationship with their customers in relation to three focused issues identified in the literature: customer trust; customer commitment; and customer satisfaction. Results of the study suggests that the decision to adopt Internet technology is indeed based on what managers perceive about the customer/organizational relationship in the banking industry.

Omani managers expect to satisfy their customers, but this creates several challenges including: customer trust (e.g. Internet security) and customer commitment (e.g. customer loyalty). Most respondents did not think that Internet technology adoption could improve their customers' trust as they thought that their customers feared that their privacy might be invaded on the Internet. They also did not think that Internet technology could improve their customers' commitment as this related to a close personal relationship with bank branches. This finding has implications for the way banks conduct their business as they have the option of conducting banking business either on the basis of pure Internet banking or using branches and the Internet.

In the semi-structured interviews participants were asked whether or not they believed that Internet technology was easy to use in the context of the banking industry. The literature identified three major issues: easy to navigate, easy to learn and easy to manage. The findings of this study suggest that the decision to adopt Internet technology is consistent with the literature and that managers' perceptions about Ease of Use are very important. Australian managers perceived no difficulties in using Internet technology whereas their Omani counterparts saw some difficulty in navigating on the Internet. They highlighted part of this difficulty as lack of awareness and knowledge about Internet technology, and the accessibility of services. These findings suggest that the Omani banking industry faces a major challenge in using the Internet. Al-Wohaibi et al. (2002) claim that human resource deficiency is a major problem in Oman, however, Abdul-Ghadir and Kozar (1995) argued that computer knowledge,

Table 3. Enablers and inhibitors relating to the factor of Perceived Organizational Performance

	Major enablers	*Major inhibitors*
Omani banks	Productivity of employees (- business efficiency)	Profitability (-technology investment cost and the need for economies of scale for Internet technology use)
Australian banks	Profitability (- reduction of communication cost)	Market environment (- customer base expansion)
	Productivity of employees (- business efficiency)	

Table 4. Enablers and inhibitors relating to Perceived Customer/Organizational Relationship

	Major enablers	**Major inhibitors**
Omani banks	Customer satisfaction (- reduce conflict)	Customer trust (- Internet security)
		Customer commitment (- customer loyalty)
Australian banks	Customer commitment (- customer loyalty)	Customer trust (- Internet security)
	Customer satisfaction (- reduce conflict)	

experience and educational level would contribute to the process of increasing the rate of Internet adoption in the Gulf countries. Other authors (F. D. Davis & Venkatesh, 1996; Venkatesh, 1999) have suggested that it would be more beneficial to focus on training rather than on system design.

DISCUSSION: IMPLICATIONS AND RECOMMENDATIONS FOR OMANI BANKS

The banks that stay behind will not be able to embrace Internet technology and the benefits it is claimed to bring and hence will not be able to compete in the industry or in international markets (Porter, 2001). This will also have consequences on the economy. For example, the Omani economy will not improve if banks stay behind, meaning that Internet technology is an important tool in the new economy and should not be ignored. The findings of this study have practical implications for Internet technology adoption in the Omani banking industry and below we offer some guidelines.

Table 5. Enablers and inhibitors relating to the factor of Perceived Ease of Use

	Major enablers	**Major inhibitors**
Omani banks	Easy to learn (- increased automation of process)	Easy to navigate (- awareness/knowledge about Internet technology and accessibility of services)
Australian banks	Easy to navigate (- user friendly and accessibility of service)	
	Easy to learn (- awareness/knowledge about Internet technology)	
	Easy to manage (- customization of banking services and online tracking of banking/financial services)	

Perceived Organizational Performance

The major inhibiting concern here is profitability. This concern relates to high technology investment cost and the need for economies of scale for Internet technology use.

Implications

Internet technology adoption has major implications on banks' performance and hence the economy, and could affect the marketing mix in industry (Al-Hajri, 2005; Kettinger, Grover, Guha, & Segars, 1994). The privatization of the Oman Telecommunication Company (Omantel) is a good forward step allowing Omantel to play a role in the economy. This means that the banking industry can also expect changes such as improvement in telecommunication services, the expansion of telecommunication services, quality of delivery in telecommunication services and lower cost of delivering the service (Oman Telecommunication Company, 2002). Of course the change in telecommunication services will have positive implications on the growth of the Internet population as well as on the geographical distribution of Internet services. In addition it is expected that the number of Internet cafés will grow in addition to home and business Internet use. Moreover, the development of an Internet village is expected to offer awareness of Internet technology in the region and e-government is also expected to play a major role in e-payment as it expands. Improvement in telecommunication infrastructure and services, Internet village and t will have positive implication on the economic scale of Internet use and the cost of offering Internet banking services. This suggests that banks should be motivated to invest more in Internet technology (Molla & Licker, 2005).

Recommendations

To reduce this inhibiting factor, King and Teo (1996) suggested a focus on economies of scale for Internet technology use. However, others (Lavender, 2004; Reichheld & Schefter, 2000) argued that most ICT decision-makers ignore intangible cost/benefits. Thus the Omani banking industry ought to consider intangible cost/benefits in their ICT decisions.

Perceived Customer/ Organizational Relationship

For this factor, the major inhibiting concerns are customers trust (e.g. Internet security) and customer commitment (e.g. customer loyalty).

Implications

Internet technology adoption has the potential to affect the relationship between customers and banks: it could improve or destroy this relationship.

Recommendations

To improve customer/bank relationships the banks ought to consider reducing factors inhibiting improvement in the relationship. For example, Whitman (2004) argued that people lack understanding of threats to information security and others (Gefen, 2002; Khalfan, 2004; Mukherjee & Neth, 2003) reported that Internet security was a major concern in trusting the Internet. Therefore the Omani banking industry needs to continually address Internet security concerns through learning, making backups, and implementing secure systems, databases and networks (Held & Bowers, 2001). On the other hand, some authors (Julian & Ramaseshan, 1994; Reichheld & Schefter, 2000; Vatanasombut, Stylianou, & Igbaria, 2004) mentioned that it is hard to win customer loyalty on the Internet so the Oman banking industry will

need to focus on continually creating values as well as having a long-term plan.

Perceived Ease of Use

The major inhibiting concern here is ease of navigation on the Internet (e.g. lack of awareness/ knowledge about Internet technology and accessibility of service).

Implications

Successful adoption of ICT depends on how easy it is for people to use it (Fred D. Davis et al., 1989; Moore & Benbasat, 1991; Taylor & Todd, 1995b).

Recommendations

To reduce these inhibiting concerns Venkatesh and Davis (1996); Davis and Venkatesh (2004); and Abdul-Gader and Kozar, (1995) suggest that training could improve awareness/knowledge about Internet technology and hence increase favorable perceptions about ease of use. On the other hand Karahanna and Limayem (2000) suggested that users should have both physical and informational access to the ICT. To ensure this, customers of Omani banks need to address the issue of Internet navigation with telecommunication companies.

Al-Wohaibi et al. (2002) suggested that Omani government organizations need to focus on the development of ICT awareness in schools and universities if they want to increase the rate of successful ICT implementation. They also suggested that banking should consider IT training in its strategic plan as well as supporting it financially to make it work. Consistent with Al-Wohaibi et al. (2002) these suggestions have two important benefits. One is that the Omani banks would be able to develop Internet technology/bank services awareness smoothly when they introduce it to their customers in the industry through a series of seminars, training, online manuals and online support without having to invest a lot of money to train and educate their customers. The second benefit would be that Omani banks would also be able to educate their employees through a series of technical seminars and short-term courses to advance their employees' skills so that they could support their Internet technology infrastructure.

CONCLUSION

This study has shown that analysis of four perceptions of managers in the banking industry: Relative Advantage, Ease of Use, Organizational Performance and Customer/Organizational Relationship, can shed light on the reasons for adoption (or non-adoption) of Internet technology. As expected, the findings confirm that Australian managers perceived less inhibitors to the introduction and implementation of Internet technology than Omani managers, meaning that the Australian banking industry has less challenges to confront than that of Oman.

It has revealed that despite cultural differences there are many similarities in the attitude to technology adoption in the banking systems of the two countries. Bankers in both countries see the use of Internet technologies as offering advantages including: convenience of available service and location, being able to rapidly develop innovative ideas, and the ease with which requests and complaints could be followed up. Both saw ease of learning to use this technology, improvements in productivity of bank employees and customer satisfaction as important enabling factors. Omani and Australian banks each saw issues of customer trust relating to privacy and Internet security as inhibitors to use of Internet technologies.

There were also, however, some important differences. While profitability was regarded as an enabler by Australian banks, which had already installed this technology, it was regarded as an inhibitor by the Omani banks due to the high cost of setting this up. Customer commitment

(loyalty) was seen as an enabler to use of the Internet by Australian banks but as an inhibitor in Oman where bank customers still appreciate the personal attention available in local bank branches. Finally, with their greater experience in using computers and the Internet Australian banks found the services easy to use, easy to navigate and quite accessible. In Oman, however, where such experience was lacking, issues of Internet navigation were seen as an inhibiting factor to use of the technology.

This study should provide useful information to the banking industry in Oman to assist it with decisions regarding the adoption of Internet technology. A report provided to Omani bank managers will make them more aware of the problems of technology adoption and of recommendations to take action to improve their competitive position in the global market.

REFERENCES

Abdul-Gader, K., & Kozar, K. A. (1995). The Impact of Computer Alienation on Information Technology Investment Decisions: An Exploratory Cross-National Analysis. *MIS Quarterly*, *19*(4), 535–559. doi:10.2307/249632

Adams, D., Nelson, R., & Todd, P. (1992). Perceived Usefulness, Ease of Use, and Usage of Information Technology: A Replication. *MIS Quarterly*, *16*(2), 227–247. doi:10.2307/249577

Ajzen, I. (1991). The Theory of Planned Behavior. *Organizational Behavior and Human Decision Processes*, *50*(2), 179–211. doi:10.1016/0749-5978(91)90020-T

Ajzen, I., & Driver, B. (1992). Application of the Theory of Planned Behaviour to Leisure Choice. *Journal of Leisure Research*, *24*(3), 207–224.

Ajzen, I., & Fishbein, M. (1980). *Understanding Attitudes and Predicting Social Behavior*. London: Prentice-Hall, Englewood Cliffs.

Ajzen, I., & Madden, T. (1986). Prediction of Goal-Directed Behavior: Attitudes, Intentions, and Perceived Behavioral Control. *Journal of Experimental Social Psychology, 22*, 453–474. doi:10.1016/0022-1031(86)90045-4

Al-Gahtani, S., & King, M. (1999). Attitudes, Satisfaction and Usage: Factors Contributing to Each in the Acceptance of Information Technology. *Behaviour & Information Technology, 18*(4), 277–297. doi:10.1080/014492999119020

Al-Hajri, S. (2005). *Internet Technology Adoption in the Banking Industry.* Victoria University, Melbourne.

Al-Wohaibi, M., Masoud, F., & Edwards, H. (2002). Fundamental Risk Factors in Deploying IT/IS Projects in Omani Government Organisations. *Journal of Global Information Management, 10*(4), 1–22.

Anderson, R., & Srinivasan, S. (2003). E-Satisfaction and E-Loyalty: A Contingency Framework. *Psychology and Marketing, 20*(2), 123–138. doi:10.1002/mar.10063

Athanassopoulos, A. (2000). Customer Satisfaction Cues to Support Market Segmentation and Explain Switching Behavior. *Journal of Business Research (Bangladesh), 47*, 191–207. doi:10.1016/S0148-2963(98)00060-5

Ayadi, A. (2007). Business Challenges of Online Banking Portals. In A. Tatnall (Ed.), *Encyclopaedia of Portal Technology and Applications* (Vol. 1, pp. 102-105). Hershey, PA: Information Science Reference.

Bagozzi, R., Davis, F., & Warshaw, P. (1992). Development and Test of a Theory of Technological Learning and Usage. *Human Relations, 45*(7), 659–670. doi:10.1177/001872679204500702

Bagozzi, R., Wong, N., Abe, S., & Bergami, M. (2000). Cultural and Situational Contingencies and the Theory of Reasoned Action: Application to Fast Food Restaurant Consumption. *Journal of Consumer Psychology, 9*(2), 97–106. doi:10.1207/S15327663JCP0902_4

Basant, R., Commander, S. J., Harrison, R., & Menezes-Filho, N. (2006). ICT Adoption and Productivity in Developing Countries: New Firm Level Evidence from Brazil and India. IZA Discussion Paper No. 2294

Beck, L., & Ajzen, I. (1991). Predicting Dishonest Actions Using the Theory of Planned Behavior. *Journal of Research in Personality, 25*(3), 285–301. doi:10.1016/0092-6566(91)90021-H

Besley, T., & Case, A. (1993). Modeling Technology Adoption in Developing Countries. *The American Economic Review, 83*(2), 396–402.

Bobbitt, L., & Dabholkar, P. (2001). Integrating Attitudinal Theories to Understand and Predict Use of Technology-Based Self-Service: The Internet as an Illustration. *International Journal of Service Industry Management, 12*(5), 423–450. doi:10.1108/EUM0000000006092

Bonfield, E. (1974). Attitude, Social Influence, Personal Norm and Intentions as Related to Brand Purchase Behavior. *JMR, Journal of Marketing Research, 11*(Nov), 379–389. doi:10.2307/3151284

Callon, M., Courtial, J. P., Turner, W. A., & Bauin, S. (1983). From Translations to Problematic Networks: An Introduction to Co-Word Analysis. *Social Sciences Information. Information Sur les Sciences Sociales, 22*(2), 191–235. doi:10.1177/053901883022002003

Chang, M. (1998). Predicting Unethical Behavior: A Comparison of the theory of Reasoned Action and the Theory of Planned Behavior. *Journal of Business Ethics, 17*, 1825–1834. doi:10.1023/A:1005721401993

Clark, J., & Soliman, F. (1999). A Graphical Method for Assessing Knowledge-Based Systems Investments. *Logistics Information Management, 12*(1-2), 63–77. doi:10.1108/09576059910256277

Davis, F. D. (1986). *A Technology Acceptance Model for Empirically Testing New End-User Information Systems: Theory and Results*. MIT, Boston.

Davis, F. D. (1989). Perceived Usefulness, Perceived Ease of Use, and User Acceptance of Information Technology. *MIS Quarterly, 13*(3), 318–340. doi:10.2307/249008

Davis, F. D., Bagozzi, R., & Warshaw, P. (1989). User Acceptance of Computer Technology: A Comparison of Two Theoretical Models. *Management Science, 35*(8), 982–1003. doi:10.1287/mnsc.35.8.982

Davis, F. D., & Venkatesh, V. (1996). A Critical Assessment of Potential Measurement Biases in the Technology Acceptance Model: Three Experiments. *International Journal of Human-Computer Studies, 45*(1), 19–45. doi:10.1006/ijhc.1996.0040

Davis, F. D., & Venkatesh, V. (2004). Toward Preprototype User Acceptance Testing of New Information Systems: Implications for Software Project Management. *IEEE Transactions on Engineering Management, 51*(1), 31–46. doi:10.1109/TEM.2003.822468

Dedrick, J., Gurbaxani, V., & Kraemer, K. (2003). Information Technology and Economic Performance: A Critical Review of the Empirical Evidence. *ACM Computing Surveys, 35*(1), 1–28. doi:10.1145/641865.641866

East, R. (1993). Investment Decisions and Theory of Planned Behaviour. *Journal of Economic Psychology, 14*, 337–375. doi:10.1016/0167-4870(93)90006-7

Engel, J., Blackwell, R., & Miniard, P. (1995). *Consumer behaviour* (8th ed.). Fort Worth, Texas: Dryden Press.

Fishbein, M., & Ajzen, I. (1975). *Belief, Attitude, Intention, and Behavior: An Introduction to Theory and Research*. Reading: Addison-Wesley.

Gefen, D. (2002). Customer Loyalty in e-Commerce. *Journal of the Association for Information Systems, 3*(2), 27–51.

Gefen, D., & Straub, D. (1997). Gender Differences in Perception and Adoption of E-Mail: An Extention to the Technology Acceptance Model. *MIS Quarterly, 21*(4), 389–400. doi:10.2307/249720

George, J. (2002). Influences on the Intent to Make Internet Purchases. *Internet Research: Electronic Networking Applications and Policy, 12*(2), 165–180. doi:10.1108/10662240210422521

Ghosh, S. (1998). Making Business Sense of the Internet. *Harvard Business Review*, (March-April): 126–133.

Gibson, A., & Frakes, A. (1997). Truth or Consequences: A Study of Critical Issues and Decision Making in Accounting. *Journal of Business Ethics, 16*, 161–171. doi:10.1023/A:1017914713375

Goldenhar, L., & Connell, C. (1993). Understanding and Predicting Recycling Behavior: An Application of the Theory of Reasoned Action. *Journal of Environmental Systems, 22*, 91–103.

Harrell, G., & Bennett, P. (1974). An Evaluation of the Expectancy Value Model of Attitude Measurement for Physician Prescribing Behavior. *JMR, Journal of Marketing Research, 11*(3), 269–278. doi:10.2307/3151142

Harrison, D., Mykytyn, P., & Riemenschneider, C. (1997). Executive Decisions About Adoption of Information Technology in Small Business: Theory and Empirical Tests. *Information Systems Research, 8*(2), 171–195. doi:10.1287/isre.8.2.171

Held, J., & Bowers, J. (2001). *Securing E-Business Applications and Communications*. Boca Raton, FL: Auerbach.

Hendrickson, A., & Collins, M. (1996). An Assessment of Structure and Causation of IS Usage. *The Data Base for Advances in Information Systems*, *27*(2), 61–67.

Igbaria, M., Guimaraes, T., & Davis, G. (1995). Determinants of Microcomputer Usage Via a Structural Equation Model. *Journal of Management Information Systems*, *11*(4), 87–114.

Julian, C., & Ramaseshan, B. (1994). The Role of Customer-Contact Personnel in the Marketing of a Retail Bank's Services. *International Journal of Retail and Distribution Management*, *22*(5), 29–34. doi:10.1108/09590559410067316

Kalakota, R., & Whinston, A. (1997). *Electronic Commerce: A manager's Guide*. Reading, Mass: Addison-Wesley.

Karahanna, E., & Limayem, M. (2000). E-mail and V-mail Usage: Generalizing Across Technologies. *Journal of Organizational Computing and Electronic Commerce*, *10*(1), 49–66. doi:10.1207/S15327744JOCE100103

Karahanna, E., Straub, D., & Cherveny, N. (1999). Information Technology Adoption Across Time: A Cross-Sectional Comparison of Pre-Adoption and Post-Adoption Believes. *MIS Quarterly*, *23*(2), 192–213. doi:10.2307/249751

Kettinger, W., Grover, V., Guha, S., & Segars, A. (1994). Strategic Systems Revisited: A Study in Sustainability and Performance. *MIS Quarterly*, *18*(1), 31–58. doi:10.2307/249609

Khalfan, A. (2004). Information Security Considerations in IS/IT Outsourcing Projects: A Descriptive Case Study of Two Sectors. *International Journal of Information Management*, *24*(1), 29–42. doi:10.1016/j.ijinfomgt.2003.12.001

King, W., & Teo, T. (1996). Key Dimensions of Facilitators and Inhibitors for the Strategic Use of Information Technology. *Journal of Management Information Systems*, *12*(4), 35–53.

Klobas, J., & Clyde, L. (2000). Adults Learning to Use the Internet: A Longitudinal Study of Attitudes and Other Factors Associated with Intended Internet Use. *Library & Information Science Research*, *22*(1), 5–34. doi:10.1016/S0740-8188(99)00038-9

Kurihara, Y., Takaya, S., Harui, H., & Kamae, H. (Eds.). (2008). *Information Technology and Economic Development*. Hershey: Idea Group Reference.

Kurland, N. (1995). Ethical Intentions and the Theories of Reasoned Action and Planned Behavior. *Journal of Applied Social Psychology*, *25*(4), 297–313. doi:10.1111/j.1559-1816.1995.tb02393.x

Latour, B. (1986). The Powers of Association. In J. Law (Ed.), *Power, Action and Belief. A New Sociology of Knowledge? Sociological Review monograph 32* (pp. 264-280). London: Routledge & Kegan Paul.

Latour, B. (1993). *We Have Never Been Modern* (C. Porter, Trans.). Hemel Hempstead: Harvester Wheatsheaf.

Latour, B. (1996). *Aramis or the Love of Technology*. Cambridge, Ma: Harvard University Press.

Lavender, M. (2004). Maximizing customer Relationships and Minimizing Business Risk. *International Journal of Bank Marketing*, *22*(4), 291–296. doi:10.1108/02652320410542563

Law, J., & Callon, M. (1988). Engineering and Sociology in a Military Aircraft Project: A Network Analysis of Technological Change. *Social Problems*, *35*(3), 284–297. doi:10.1525/sp.1988.35.3.03a00060

Lederer, A., Maupin, D., Sena, M., & Zhuang, Y. (2000). *The Role of Ease of Use, Usefulness and Attitude in the Prediction of World Wide Web Usage.* Paper presented at the ACM SIGCPR Conference on Computer Personnel Research, Boston, MA.

Lee, D. R. (2005). Agricultural Sustainability and Technology Adoption: Issues and Policies for Developing Countries . *American Journal of Agricultural Economics, 87*(5), 1325–1334. doi:10.1111/j.1467-8276.2005.00826.x

Liao, S., Shao, Y., Wang, H., & Chen, A. (1999). The Adoption of Virtual Banking: An Empirical Study. *International Journal of Information Management, 19*(1), 63–74. doi:10.1016/S0268-4012(98)00047-4

Loch, K., & Conger, S. (1996). Evaluating Ethical Decision Making and Computer Use. *Communications of the ACM, 39*(7), 77–83. doi:10.1145/233977.233999

Locke, E., Fredrick, E., Lee, C., & Bobko, P. (1984). Effect of Self-Efficacy, goals, and Task Strategies on Task Performance. *The Journal of Applied Psychology, 69*(2), 241–251. doi:10.1037/0021-9010.69.2.241

Mathieson, K. (1991). Predicting User Intentions: Comparing the Technology Acceptance Model with the Theory of Planned Behavior. *Information Systems Research, 2*(3), 173–191. doi:10.1287/isre.2.3.173

Michelsen, H., & Hartwich, F. (2004). *University-based Agricultural Research: A Comparative Study in Sub-Saharan Africa* Addis Ababa: International Service for National Agricultural Research

Miles, M., & Huberman, A. (1994). *Qualitative Data Analysis: An Expanded Sourcebook* (2nd ed.). Thousand Oaks, CA: Sage Publications.

MISC. (2002). 6 Million Internet User Registration Milestone Reached, After 1st Quarter, As Banking Usage (Transactions) Grow 15% in Latest Quarter. Retrieved 17 December 2004, from www.marketintelligence.com.au

Molla, A., & Licker, P. S. (2005). Ecommerce Adoption in Developing Countries: a Model and Instrument. *Information & Management, 42*(6), 877–899. doi:10.1016/j.im.2004.09.002

Montealegre, R. (1999). A Temporal Model of Institutional Interventions for Information Technology Adoption in Less-Developed Countries. *Journal of Management Information Systems, 16*(1), 207–232.

Moore, G., & Benbasat, I. (1991). Development of an Instrument to Measure the Perception of Adopting an Information Technology Innovation. *Information Systems Research, 2*(3), 192–222. doi:10.1287/isre.2.3.192

Mukherjee, A., & Neth, P. (2003). A Model of Trust in Online Relationship Banking. *International Journal of Bank Marketing, 21*(1), 5–15. doi:10.1108/02652320310457767

Mykytyn, P., & Harison, D. (1993). The Application of the Theory of Reasoned Action to Senior Management and Strategic Information Systems. *Information Resources Management Journal, 6*(2), 15–25.

Oman Ministry of Development. (1996). *Vision for Oman Economy* (Qaboos bin Said speech, June 2 1995). Muscat: Ministry of Development.

Oman Telecommunication Company. (2002). *Annual Book 2002.* Muscat: Oman Telecommunication Company.

Paarlberg, R. L. (2003). Technology Adoption in Developing Countries: The Case of Genetically Modified Crops. Retrieved April 2007, from http://www.au.af.mil/au/awc/awcgate/cia/nic2020/technology_adoption_nov6.pdf

Porter, M. (2001). Strategy and the Internet. *Harvard Business Review*, (March): 63–78.

Raisinghani, M. (2000). *Electronic Commerce at the Down of the Third Millennium - Electronic Commerce: Opportunities and Challenges*. Thousand Oaks: Sage Publications.

Rajapakse, J., & Seddon, P. B. (2007). ERP Adoption in Developing Countries in Asia: A Cultural Misfit Unpublished Working paper. University of Melbourne.

Ramsey, J., & Smith, M. (1999). Managing Customer Channel Usage in the Australian Banking Sector. *Managerial Auditing Journal*, *14*(7), 329–338. doi:10.1108/02686909910289812

Randall, D., & Gibson, A. (1991). Ethical Decision Making in the Medical Profession: An Application of the Theory of Planned Behavior. *Journal of Business Ethics*, *10*(2), 111–122. doi:10.1007/BF00383614

Reichheld, F., & Schefter, P. (2000). E-Loyalty: Your Secret Weapon on the Web. *Harvard Business Review*, *78*(4), 105–113.

Rogers, E. M. (1995). *Diffusion of Innovations* (4th ed.). New York: The Free Press.

Sathye, M. (1999). Adoption of Internet Banking by Australian Consumers: An Empirical Investigation. *International Journal of Bank Marketing*, *17*(7), 324–334. doi:10.1108/02652329910305689

Segars, A., & Grover, V. (1993). Re-Examining Perceived Ease of Use and Usefulness: A Confirmatory Factor Analysis. *MIS Quarterly*, *17*(4), 517–525. doi:10.2307/249590

Shifter, D., & Ajzen, I. (1985). Intention, Perceived Control and Weight Loss: An Application of the Theory Planned Behaviour. *Journal of Personality and Social Psychology*, *49*, 843–851. doi:10.1037/0022-3514.49.3.843

Shimp, T., & Kavas, A. (1984). The Theory of Reasoned action Applied to Coupon Usage. *The Journal of Consumer Research*, *11*(Dec), 795–809. doi:10.1086/209015

Sparks, P., & Shepherd, R. (1992). Self-Identity and the Theory of Planned Behaviour: Assessing the Role of Identification with Green Consumerism. *Social Psychology Quarterly*, *55*(4), 388–399. doi:10.2307/2786955

Speier, C., Morris, M., & Bridggs, C. (1995). *Attitudes Toward Computers: The Impact of Performance*. Paper presented at the AIS, Pittsburgh, PA.

Strauss, A., & Corbin, J. (1990). *Basics of Qualitative Research: Grounded Theory Procedures and Techniques*. Newbury Park: Sage Publications.

Szajna, B. (1994). Software Evaluation and Choice: Predictive Validation of the Technology Acceptance Instrument. *MIS Quarterly*, *18*(3), 319–324. doi:10.2307/249621

Szajna, B. (1996). Empirical Evaluation of the Revised Technology Acceptance Model. *Management Science*, *42*(1), 85–94. doi:10.1287/mnsc.42.1.85

Talukdar, D., Sudhir, K., & Ainslie, A. S. (2006). Investigating New Product Diffusion across Products and Countries. Unpublished Working paper. Yale SOM Working Paper No. MK-06.

Tatnall, A., & Davey, B. (2007, 19-23 May 2007). *Researching the Portal*. Paper presented at the IRMA: Managing Worldwide Operations and Communications with Information Technology, Vancouver.

Taylor, S., & Todd, P. (1995a). Assessing IT Usage: The Role of Prior Experience. *MIS Quarterly*, *19*(4), 561–570. doi:10.2307/249633

Taylor, S., & Todd, P. (1995b). Understanding Information Technology Usage: A Test of Competing Models. *Information Systems Research, 6*(2), 144–176. doi:10.1287/isre.6.2.144

Taylor, S., & Todd, P. (1997). Understanding the Determinants of Consumer Composting Behavior. *Journal of Applied Social Psychology, 27*(7), 602–628. doi:10.1111/j.1559-1816.1997.tb00651.x

Thomson, K., Haziris, N., & Alekos, P. (1994). Attitudes and Food Consumption. *British Food Journal, 96*(11), 9–14. doi:10.1108/00070709410074632

Vallerand, R., Pelletier, L., Deshaies, P., Cuerrier, J., & Mongeau, C. (1992). Ajzen and Fishbein's Theory of Reasoned Action as Applied to Moral Behavior: A Confirmatory Analysis. *Journal of Personality and Social Psychology, 62*(1), 98–109. doi:10.1037/0022-3514.62.1.98

Vatanasombut, B., Stylianou, A., & Igbaria, M. (2004). How to Retain Online Customers. *Communications of the ACM, 47*(6), 65–69. doi:10.1145/990680.990682

Venkatesh, V. (1999). Creation of Favorable User Perceptions: Exploring the Role of Intrinsic Motivation. *MIS Quarterly, 23*(2), 239–260. doi:10.2307/249753

Venkatesh, V., & Davis, F. (1996). A Model of the Antecedence of Perceived Ease of Use: Development and Test. *Decision Sciences, 27*(3), 451–481. doi:10.1111/j.1540-5915.1996.tb01822.x

Venkatesh, V., & Davis, F. (2000). A Theoretical Extension of the Technology Acceptance Model: Four Longitudinal Field Studies. *Management Science, 46*(2), 186–204. doi:10.1287/mnsc.46.2.186.11926

Wang, Y., Wang, Y., Lin, H., & Tang, T. (2003). Determinants of User Acceptance of Internet Banking: An Empirical Study. *International Journal of Service Industry Management, 14*(5), 501–519. doi:10.1108/09564230310500192

Warshaw, P., & Davis, F. (1985). Disentangling Behavior Intention and Behavioral Expectation. *Journal of Experimental Social Psychology, 21*, 213–218. doi:10.1016/0022-1031(85)90017-4

Whitman, M. (2004). In Defence of the Realm: Understanding the Threats to Information Security. *International Journal of Information Management, 24*, 43–57. doi:10.1016/j.ijinfomgt.2003.12.003

Wright, A., & Ralston, D. (2002). The Lagging Development of Small Business Internet Banking in Australia. *Journal of Small Business Management, 40*(1), 51–57. doi:10.1111/1540-627X.00038

This work was previously published in E-Commerce Trends for Organizational Advancement: New Applications and Methods, edited by Khosrow-Pour, M, pp. 264-282, copyright 2010 by IGI Publishing (an imprint of IGI Global).

Chapter 5.2
Limitations and Perspectives on Use of E–Services in Engineering Consulting

Hanne Westh Nicolajsen
Aalborg University, Denmark

Morten Falch
Aalborg University, Denmark

ABSTRACT

In this chapter we analyse organizational challenges when an engineering consultancy in the building industry integrates information and communication technologies (ICT) in the production and delivery of their services, and discuss how the e-service concept can be applied in this context. The analysis is based on a field study on introduction of 3D-modeling tools within one of the leading engineering companies in Scandinavia (Ramboll). The analysis focuses on the changes in knowledge creation and transfer both within the company and in inter-organizational relations. The analysis points towards a need to change the business model as the project engineering part of the technical engineering service becomes standardized.

INTRODUCTION

This chapter analyses how the use of information and communication technologies (ICT) in an engineering consultancy has led to increasing codification of the knowledge delivered, and how this affects the potential for using the e-service business concept within this particular industry.

Knowledge Intensive Business Services (KIBS), such as engineering consultancy, produce and sell knowledge to other businesses. The knowledge service they sell is often customized to a particular customer and made in interaction with the customer, but builds on in-house expertise from the consultancy. Engineering consultancies must continuously upgrade and develop knowledge if they want to be capable of delivering unique and competitive services. On the other hand it is necessary to reuse

DOI: 10.4018/978-1-60566-064-6.ch010

the same knowledge in several projects in order to reduce costs. Knowledge management is therefore a key parameter for the success of an engineering consultancy.

The organization of production of engineering consultancy services is like production of other KIBS highly affected by use of ICT. However engineering services cannot be termed e-services in a narrow sense because engineering service is only partly subject to electronic delivery. Engineering consultancy is a complex service involving intensive communication between several parties, including suppliers, contractors, architects, and customers. The end product is to a large extent a physical product in the form of a building. However, the different KIBS involved within this "production" process deliver various knowledge services. The service delivery can thus be seen as a large number of separated deliveries to the building owner (as the primary customer) or to the other partners as "internal customers," which is further complicated through the feedback cycles involving the customer or other parties in the building process. Some of these services may be partly produced or delivered through e-mail communications and other Web-based interaction, others at business meetings, and so forth. It is however unlikely that electronic communication will be able to replace all types of communication in full. The e-service concept must therefore be understood more widely as the use of ICT to produce, collaborate, or deliver parts of the service package. ICT is used both as a means of producing services in the sense of new production tools and for creating an electronic communication infrastructure enabling communication with partners and customers, thus facilitating both production and delivery of services.

This chapter analyses how ICT is used to facilitate intra- and inter-organisational collaboration in production and delivery of engineering consultancy services within the area of building construction. Based on information from a field study of the engineering consultancy Ramboll,

the chapter studies how use of ICT affects internal organisational issues in relation to securing future innovations, development of new ways of working, and building and maintenance of staff competences needed. First, the chapter provides background information on the field study and a description of the drivers for introducing ICT systems in provisioning of engineering services. Thereafter a general presentation of Ramboll follows together with a detailed description of its building division. This is followed by an outline on the usage of ICT within engineering consulting. Finally organisational implications and the status of engineering consultancy as an e-service are discussed.

BACKGROUND

For decades the building industry has been characterised by increasing costs, low productivity, and often poor quality. This is in part due to labour intensive production processes in design, projection, and construction, which have proved to be hard to automate. Another problem is lack of coordination between the large numbers of partners involved in building projects. Knowledge that flows between partners from different companies is often limited by lack of common standards, lack of common understanding on how the building process is organised, and the varying division of labour and responsibilities between the partner companies. This results in unnecessary conflicts and errors. In addition the lack of knowledge flow within building projects reduces accumulated learning both across projects and across partners. These problems are reinforced by the temporary character of partnerships within the building industry, where each project in general presents a new partner constellation. Moreover, along with increased competition, the ongoing globalisation taking place in segments of the building industry will further complicate coordination between partners.

The use of ICT in the production of service offers a number of advantages addressing these problems. In general the digitalisation of data used in the design and planning phases enables reuse of data both within the organisation and by collaborating partners. In addition the growth in inter-organisational and intra-organisational networks makes it easier to connect and exchange data and communicate on a more ongoing and direct basis providing for closer collaboration across time and space within and between organisations. Also new ICT based production tools have proved to reduce the need for manpower and have automated some of the processes and at the same time create information, making the content of the jobs more abstract (Zuboff, 1989).

In the building sector both industrial players and governments have become aware of the need to advance implementation of ICT systems in order to address the problems sketched above. Engineering consultancy firms as well as other players in building projects are now more focused on using ICT as a tool to reduce costs and improve quality in order to respond to growing international competition. This is supported by growing maturity of both ICT based design and calculation tools as well as new Web based communication tools. This development is in large part based on learning from other industrial sectors that are more advanced in the use of ICT in their production processes. In order to facilitate this development, since the early 1990s the Danish Government has launched a number of projects including "Project House" and later "Digital Construction." In addition the seven largest companies in the Danish building sector created a sector wide organisation in 2003 called BIPS (Building, Information technology, Productivity and Collaboration). BIPS is a non-profit membership organisation of companies that represents all parties within the building trade. The aim of BIPS is to develop collective tools and methods to aid collaboration between all players involved in the construction of buildings. Through BIPS and similar initiatives, the Danish

government stimulates the development and integration of ICT based solutions. The government has created a growing awareness of the need for change, and companies are becoming more alert and engage more actively in investments related to the integration of new ICT in the production process.

The use of ICT within the building sector offers a wide range of new possibilities including seamless flow of information within and between organisations. This enables more flexibility in organisation of design and project management in relation to the service production. However realisation of these potential benefits demands agreement on common formats, investments in tools, learning of how to use the tools, adjustment of the qualifications needed as well as changes in the established practices and adjustment of business models in order to comply with new products and changes in production processes. In order to analyse these challenges a field study was conducted in the building division of the Danish engineering consultancy company Ramboll. The field study is further described in Box 1. We investigated the use of ICT systems in the building section of the Danish division. The objective was to analyse how the use of ICT tools (in particular a 3D-modeling system) affected the organisation of work and the business models pursued. Especially the study aimed to study how the use of ICT tools affected creation and dissemination of knowledge within the organisation.

The area of technical engineering consulting was chosen as it is a service area of importance in any economy and at the same time it is a service area with special conditions due to its relation to a physical product and the involvement

From January 2005 to June 2007, 14 interviews with 10 employees from the building section in the headquarters of Ramboll Denmark were carried out. This information was supplemented by secondary material in the form of internal documents and annual reports. The findings of the study were tested in an interactive finalising workshop session with participation of representatives from Ramboll.

of customer and partners. Ramboll was chosen from among technical engineering companies because the company is specialised in designing unique solutions for prestigious buildings, rather than developing standard solutions used for mass production. The subsequent analysis focuses on the integration of 3D models, as the use of such models highlights a wide range of possibilities and challenges within the organisation as well as the inter-organisational collaboration.

A key challenge is to maintain a reputation for being among the most advanced with regard to technical expertise in building construction. Innovation and knowledge management is therefore crucial for success. The service provided is increasingly dependent on the use of ICT based tools, in which much of the knowledge and know-how needed are embedded. It is therefore a challenge for a company like Ramboll to maintain its position as ICT based design tools are being developed and offered as software packages available on the market. This may potentially enable competitors with less technical expertise to develop technical solutions similar to those offered by Ramboll without having the same level of technical knowledge.

THE BUILDING SECTION IN RAMBOLL

Ramboll has provided technical engineering services for more than 60 years and is a leading player in the Danish market of technical engineering. In 2003 Ramboll and the Swedish engineering company Scandia Consult merged, and Ramboll developed from being among the top three in the Danish market to become a leading player in the Nordic market with 104 offices in the Nordic region and 21 permanent offices in the rest of the world. (Figure 1 and Box 2)

Ramboll group provides engineering, consultancy services, product development, and operation services within the areas of buildings, infrastructure, industrial processes, energy, water and environment, telecommunication, management, and IT.

The organisation in Ramboll reflects three different dimensions: geography, business areas, and technical competences. The first level of

• Traditional assignments • Overseas consultancy • Turn-key projects • OPP and BOT

Figure 1. Organisation chart of Ramboll

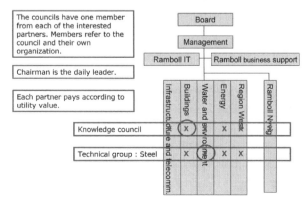

organisation reflects mainly national borders; the Ramboll group includes six different companies covering each of the Nordic countries: Denmark, Sweden, Norway, and Finland. In addition, Ramboll Informatics and Ramboll Management are defined as separate companies. Ramboll Denmark generates 42% of the group's revenue. At present, the national offices generally serve their own home markets, but Ramboll intends to strengthen international coordination in order to enable their companies to use their special competencies in the entire Nordic region.

Ramboll Denmark includes both regional divisions and divisions defined by business area. In some business areas such as telecommunications the activities are concentrated in one division, while activities in other business areas such as building are distributed among a number of regional offices. However more specialised competences in the building area are concentrated in the building division in Copenhagen.

In addition to this Ramboll has an IT department and a support function supporting the entire organisation). Lately, the number of support staff has been drastically reduced. Instead a number of different councils working across the different sections have been established. However, these councils are embedded in the organisation, as all divisions with an interest in the actual council have a member. The idea is to avoid the costs of having expensive staff functions out of touch with what is going on, and instead let new initiatives grow out of the prioritized needs in and across the different divisions.

The building division in Copenhagen is organised according to technical disciplines such as steel constructions, concrete, electrical installations, and so forth. The blend of geography and professional focus in the departments are seen to provide the best conditions for developing expert knowledge and educating experts. Locating people from the same professional area together gives them daily contact with colleagues from the same discipline and facilitates further development of their competences. This happens, however, at the expense of the coordination between different fields and development of interdisciplinarity within the projects. Other consultancy firms have chosen a structure where offices are defined by market segmentation. In such a structure each office possesses a broad range of technical expertise, and will be able to carry out many projects without consulting other parts of the organisation; however, they face the challenge of keeping each employee updated within their field of expertise.

In Ramboll, it is thus necessary to involve several parts of the organisation in a project. Therefore Ramboll uses a kind of matrix organisation. Most assignments are defined as projects and a project structure operates across the line structure. Engineers can be allocated to several different projects at the same time. When big and long lasting projects are running such as the Opera House in Copenhagen, many employees are allocated full time and a new department, where project members are placed together during the implementation of the project, is established.

TRADITIONAL BUILDING PROJECTS: PHASES AND PARTNERS

Ramboll consultancy services in building include four different types of assignments (see Box 1). Eighty percent of the business still comes from so-called traditional consultancy projects and design and project engineering of new and unique buildings. Another service area is overseas consultancy following Danish customers in their need to establish buildings in other countries. This is mainly a management assignment and includes identification and recruitment of local companies to do the job. Third, Ramboll provides turn-key projects, where standard solutions such as power plants are provided. In these projects, Ramboll provides everything from design, purchase, construction, inspection, and decommissioning.

Last, new types of assignments, such as build-operate-transfer (BOT) projects and private public partnering (OPP), following concepts coming from the UK and the USA, are being introduced. Here maintenance and operation are part of the responsibilities and require Ramboll to assume more financial and operating responsibilities. During the field study it was discovered that it has been possible to avoid involvement in financing of projects through cooperation with pension funds. OPP and BOT imply very different ways of operating and managing the entire project cycle and include several new partnerships. This chapter concentrates on the use of ICT in traditional assignments as they still account for the majority of the services delivered. (Figure 2)

Traditional assignments are related to a specific building project. The assignments may vary in size but they are all limited by time. This implies that the organisation continuously must adapt to carry out new tasks. Project groups with participants from line groups are created and closed down, when an assignment is completed.

The first task in a project is to get a contract. Contracts are obtained either through direct negotiation with a potential customer or through public tenders. Ramboll may identify new possibilities themselves and initiate projects by contacting potential investors and partners. Ramboll may also be contacted directly by customers who know the company from previous assignments or from its good reputation. Following the initial contact Ramboll may prepare a more detailed offer on the project. Sometimes Ramboll gets a contract by winning a public tender either alone or as part of a consortium with external partners. Such consortia will usually include at least an architect firm and an engineering consultancy company. (Figure 3)

When the consortium has got a contract the project is designed. In larger projects, this will be done in several phases, where still more detailed solutions are prepared and discussed with other partners and the building owner. Following the preproject phase a tender may be made in order to select one or more contractors to carry out the construction. During the construction phase Ramboll may be responsible for supervision and the management parts of the project. Finally the project is handed over to the building owner. Sometimes a maintenance contract is also included as a separate part of the project.

The role of the engineering consultancy company often varies from project to project. Sometimes the consultancy has responsibilities during the construction phase or during the maintenance/operation phases. These responsibilities may include either carrying out certain tasks themselves, employing somebody else to do it, or supervising the work. However there is a flexible division of work between the architects or the suppliers and

Figure 2. Project phases in a building project

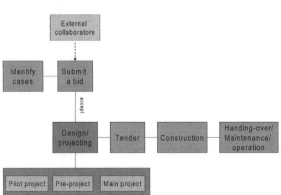

Figure 3. Overview of overlap in competences and need for negotiation of responsibilities

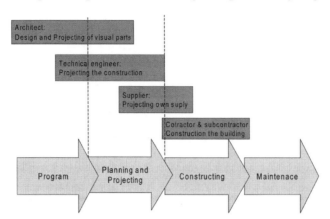

the technical engineering company. It is important that the sharing of specific tasks is agreed in detail from the outset, as lack of clarity may otherwise be a constant source of conflicts.

Management of the various partners, each with their own responsibilities, is in itself a big challenge in all building projects. The building process is often described as a stepwise process with a serial relation with some overlap between the companies involved: the output of the architects in the form of an architectural design or a program (see the lower part in Figure 4) forms the basis for the planning and project engineering work, which includes preparation of a detailed plan with technical solutions considering choices of material, sequences, forces, weights, and so forth, this

service is primarily carried out by the engineering consultancy. However, the visual parts of the building such as facades, walls, and the like are often project engineered by the architects. Some suppliers may also carry out the project engineering for the instalment of their own deliveries. In the construction phase, the chosen building contractor and the subcontractors construct the buildings based on the service delivered from the engineering consultancy in the form of detailed descriptions and plans.

When a building project is understood as a process of sequential interconnected phases (Thompson, 1967), this indicates that each phase is thought to present well defined tasks and clear responsibilities separated from other phases, as

Figure 4. Building project with mutual adjustments

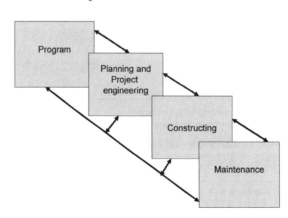

illustrated in the four phase model presented above. However, describing the building process as a well defined and stepwise process is not without complications, as strong dependencies exist between the different phases and partners. Solutions and choices made by one partner affect possible alternatives and choices to be made by other partners involved in the subsequent project phases. Seeing the building process as sequential phases thus might inhibit some useful knowledge from flowing, which could otherwise provide for better solutions (in terms of quality and price). Approaching the building process as integrated across the different partners is seen as a solution to this challenge. An integrated approach requires what Thompson (1967) has termed mutual adjustments between the involved partners, meaning feedback loops between all the different phases.

For instance, both the contractor and the engineering consultancy should contribute to the design phase with their knowledge on solutions, conditions, and effectiveness of materials and constructions in order to optimise the entire project. The integration of knowledge and agreement on optimal technical solutions is complicated by the division of labour between financially independent partners, each with their own contractual obligations and interests.

USE OF ICT IN ENGINEERING CONSULTING

Digitalisation of administrative processes and work in Ramboll has been going on for quite some time. However it has mainly concerned introduction of Microsoft office tools and other standard tools; more recently internal and external networks have been implemented with applications like project webs, digital library systems, e-mail, and calendar systems as well as administrative systems of different kinds. A digital infrastructure has emerged and much of the communication taking place from ongoing information and exchange of process information has been digitalised, and this has removed some of the time and space limits for interaction within the company and for exchange of information with external partners involved in the same project.

IT has also been used in production tools for quite a while, especially CAD systems are well implemented in the processes for project engineering for buildings. The early implementation of CAD systems in Ramboll resulted in an estimated reduction of around 80% in the number of technical assistants. Before the introduction of CAD, engineers drafted drawings, which later were refined by technical assistants. Due to the possibility of manipulating and changing in the initial drawings, much of the technical assistant work has disappeared, just as secretarial work did in other sectors. However the introduction of CAD changed working conditions for engineers, as it required the engineers to learn to use computers as part of their work and to complete their own drawings themselves. Still, some calculations of weight and forces were still made outside the CAD system by using pencils and paper. The integration of these systems mainly affected internal work relations within each department, while work relations to other departments and to external partners basically remained unchanged.

Introduction of CAD systems has been followed by introduction of advanced 3D modeling systems. The use of 3D modeling systems has proved advantageous both internally and at the inter-organisational level. However to take advantage of these possibilities some quite major changes are needed within the companies involved. In Ramboll some steps have been taken already, but many considerations and decisions about the future remain unsettled.

3D modeling was initiated by a project on renovation of a plant for water purification. At that time there was a general interest in experimenting with new 3D production systems. However due to the business concept of Ramboll, this type of new investment needed to be justified by specific projects. In the renovation of the water purification plant, 3D modeling was an explicit request in the tender material due to a complicated piping system and fear of collision of pipes. Winning this project provided the necessary goodwill to purchase and to experiment with 3D modeling tools. In 2005 20% of all projects used 3D modeling and a number of opinions existed on how complicated constructions should be to justify use of this method. However in the middle of 2007 it is being used in most projects of a certain size. It is less costly and cumbersome to use now as people have acquired the needed competences through using the system along with process-related experiences and adaptations. The introduction was a bit difficult, the software was expensive, and only a few licenses were purchased in the beginning, making it a limited resource. Second, it was impossible to operate the system without any specific knowledge of it. A few employees were trained in the system and the system was used in a few projects. However after using it for a while it was taken into broader use in all big projects and more licenses were purchased and more people sent on courses.

3D modeling has proved advantageous in a number of different ways, especially combined with calculation modules and CAD systems which

have made it a very strong production tool. In addition it can also be combined with a 3D Gypsum printer making detailed plaster models. Or it can be combined with virtual reality technology from the gaming world making it possible to make virtual tours visualising the construction from different angles. The combination of these digital models and the different visualisation tools has improved the work and thus the services along with the creation of new subservices in a number of different ways: (Figure 5)

Marketing
Understanding between partners
Modeling of complex geometry
Collision control
Geometry control
Reuse of data in models
Reuse of data across partners

Whereas the above advantages (described in details below) are already reality, other advantages are expected in the near future, such as possibilities of compatibility with other systems resulting in new possibilities for time management, resource management, and maintenance management closely linked to the production line.

3D models are a very convincing marketing

Figure 5. Layered plaster model

tool. Many people have difficulties in visualising a spatial construction from drawings and descriptions. The Gypsum printer, which is expensive to purchase, makes it possible to make plaster models in many layers with a lot of details at a cost of 13 euros.

The model can be cut in pieces or made in parts and opened up to look at the construction inside. In the virtual model people can move around inside a building by using a computer. These kinds of models specifically reveal the spatial consequences of the design and can thus be used to get a feeling of the final result and help in discussing different solutions with the customer. This can thus be seen as an additional service to the customer. Where a virtual tour is an e-service and the plaster model is a service based on ICT used in the production.

The same methods can be used in cooperation with partners in the building process, even though these professionals are trained in using drawings and numbers to visualize the construction in their heads. The solid models help to reveal where construction and design might be problematic because a common model is created which makes it easier to discuss and point at the specific part discussed.

Furthermore Web-based 3D models allow for more people to work on the same model and in addition, this model can be transferred and combined with models from other partners. The 3D model thus unites different angles and interests in the model that can be read in different ways thus serving the various professionals' distinct yet related information needs. Thus the 3D-model acts as a so called boundary object (Star & Griesemer, 1989), connecting distinct worlds through a common model whereby different practices focusing on different issues meet. Formerly, different models were used for different purposes. Now data from different models can be integrated into one, and in this way inconsistency errors can be avoided. The 3D models also provide for data reuse between the partners, helping projects to move on much faster.

Internally in Ramboll the 3D modeling tool allows for more people to work on the same model at the same time. The 3D programs make the drawings intelligent, it is possible to reuse data around the model, and changes in reused data just need to be changed in one place to become updated throughout the model. It is also possible to copy one part of the model, for instance, the design of a floor into another part (for instance, another floor), or making small changes, which rationalises the project engineering phase tremendously. This method has been used in the project engineering of the 12 stock building in Nuuk, Greenland (see Figure 6). Formerly, reuse also occurred; however in those cases either new calculations were needed or a "too good" solution was reused; that is, it was a balance between material costs and time resource aspects. Today's combination with calculation tools has made it possible to design models with greater geometrical complexity, which is an improvement in the technical engineering service that allows for new and geometrically more complex buildings.

Another area of 3D model use is control. Collision control reveals all collisions in the model, for example, if a pipe runs into a wall or another pipe. A whole report of collisions can be made in the system and used to manage the resulting corrections. Another type of control is geometry control, for example, revealing too short beams and other similar inconsistencies. These control types are where the most immediate financial advantages have been found. This is because they reduce almost all these types of faults which are normally not revealed before the construction phase, a factor which is very expensive and time consuming. Again the service delivered from the technical engineering consultancy to the constructor has an improved quality.

However, obtaining these advantages is not without cost as the use of 3D models changes the practice of project engineering. Much more time must be invested before drawings can be made, as a consistent model needs to be drawn first. Second, using the tool requires specific qualifications in

Figure 6. Intelligent model of steel tower

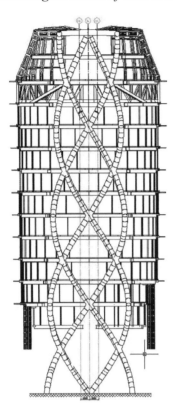

ORGANIZATIONAL CHALLENGES

The advantages of moving towards the e-service business concept by using ICT in the production and delivery of technical engineering services are numerous. However, as already mentioned, this process is quite demanding and requires major changes in the organisation. Here the demands for change will be further discussed. What we see on an overall level is that the digitalisation and the use of ICT based tools for calculations and presentation of results implies (1) codification of knowledge which (2) results in a move towards standardisation of both processes and final products. These two trends have tremendous impact on the work to be done, the needed qualifications,

Figure 7. Collision control of the Elephant house

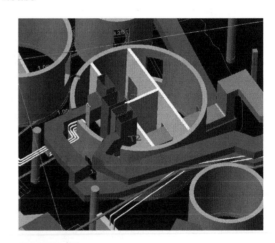

using the modeling system. Third, experience and expertise is still highly needed as 3D modeling has some limitations and weaknesses that need to be understood and spotted. The problem here is that the technology is black-boxing part of the process where less understanding and expertise in calculation is needed. The use of 3D modeling for inter-organizational use requires some standardisation or knowledge of the different measures across the different partners as well as common formats to actually make it possible to exchange, read, and understand the models across the different sorts of partner. This is complicated due to the numerous partners in the value chain and the shifting partners from project to project. However the emergence of BIPS has succeeded in supporting these needs by uniting all different partners in an organisation working towards these needs. (Figure 7) and not least the core of the business. The impacts on the business models will be discussed in the next section.

So far innovation in technical engineering services in Ramboll happens through experimenting in the production of a service. This means that all service-product innovation takes place in relation to projects. The input for innovation is mainly the competences, knowledge, and creativity of the employees combined with wishes and requests from customers or partners. The management of innovation and knowledge follows what Hansen, Nohria, et al. (1999) call personalisation. In a personalisation strategy the knowledge of the employee is the most important asset as opposed to codification, where knowledge is built into practices or products. With the current development we see a move from personalisation towards codification as a lot of the competencies and thus the knowledge are built into the modeling and calculation systems. This move is not unproblematic according to the theory as it demands less qualified employees.

However the conclusion is not as straight forward as saying that project engineering is becoming a standardised and codified process. The experience in Ramboll so far is that the modeling of the constructions seems easy and straight forward and eliminates the number of people needed due to reuse and manipulation of the data in the system. However, an additional experience is that use of these models in complex buildings does have some severe limitations; they thus need to be drawn or corrected taking forces and other factors into account. This means that highly experienced technical consultants are needed to do the modeling or check the model. We thus reach a different conclusion that less but highly technically competent people are needed (the routine work is taken over by the technology). In addition the project engineering itself is not the whole job. Whereas the standard methods (embodied in software tools) do improve productivity to some extent, the design process can be further

facilitated and enhanced if reuse of solutions from different projects is supported, which demands transfer of knowledge. This process is still mainly supported through the employee and his earlier experience; however the modeling tools do open up for implementation of macros for standard solutions. Such use of technology is confronting the values of being a good engineer and point to the differences between definitions of work in a company having a personalisation strategy and those within a company having a codification strategy—different types of employees are needed!

Using a system that black-boxes the process and at the same time calls for high qualifications raises a problem of competence building. Due to increasing use of ICT based modeling tools engineers engage in less assignments and exercises of project engineering. Engineers using the tools need to have an intuitive understanding of the complex relations between the various technical parameters in order to use the tools properly, and to evaluate alternative solutions. Part of this understanding can only be gained through practical experience, but when still more parts of the design process are being embodied in various modeling tools, it becomes harder for engineers employed in a consulting company to obtain such experience. A competence trap may thus be the result and the companies need to take actions to provide new ways of gaining this knowledge.

If Ramboll decides to make project engineering even more standardised by implementing macros in the system, this may provide an additional opportunity to resolve or reduce the problems related to engineers lacking understanding of the contractors' working conditions. Engineering consultants work on a more abstract level than those responsible for the implementation, and they need to develop an understanding of how the invented solutions will work in practice. In some departments, tours to constructing sites are made to help engineering consultants gain this insight. However, making knowledge flow across the different phases and partners is still a major and unsolved problem. In addition to the internal use of modeling tools and the possibilities of developing macros, there are also visions about integrating knowledge from the different partners, especially knowledge from the constructors. In other words macros on "good" and "workable" solutions should be used instead of newly made solutions which often do not consider construction issues. This would greatly improve the cost of the entire building project; however there are fears about the extent to which such an approach leaves room for creative solutions needed in unique building design and project engineering and that it may undermine project engineering as a unique service that demands high technical engineering competencies.

Making a system with macros that build on the knowledge from different projects and partners will probably restrain the creativity in the work of the technical engineers and make a strong move from personalisation towards codification of knowledge. Such an approach would imply that knowledge development is carried out centrally or becomes more closely linked to an overall coherence.

A final organisational issue limiting the codification of knowledge and thus restraining part of the digitalisation of technical engineering service is the need for local presence. In principle all codified knowledge can be delivered electronically to anywhere in the world, and increasingly digitalised production with the services delivered through inter-organizational networks will therefore facilitate international competition, as is seen for other KIBS. But even though both final and intermediary engineering services to a large extent are delivered as electronic information, local presence is still an important parameter for winning contracts. Local contact is needed to enable good contact with customers and the usually local contractors and suppliers during the project. This is related to issues of trust, cultural understanding, and so forth. Also knowledge of national and local conditions, regulations, and traditions such

as weather and working culture is important and it might be difficult to serve a lot of different and dissimilar markets in this respect. These issues are among the reasons for having offices in the different countries and even regional offices within a small country like Denmark.

CHALLENGES TO THE BUSINESS MODEL

Ramboll's building section is specialised in providing consultancy services related to construction of unique buildings, which demands use of innovative design and project engineering. It is therefore crucial for Ramboll to be a leader in using state of the art technologies and in development of new technical solutions. Use of calculation models has had a substantial impact on both productivity and quality, as engineers can develop faster and more complex solutions. The latter is of particular importance for a company like Ramboll, as the possibility of complex solutions can be turned into highly unique constructions. So far only few direct financial gains have been harvested through standardisation. There is a clear understanding of productivity gains that are mainly due to reduced production time. These gains are used to provide better and more complex solutions, and occasionally to reduce prices. This improves competitiveness, but has no immediate impact on the bottom line.

The use of ICT based calculation models greatly increase possibilities for reuse of data in other projects. It therefore becomes even more important to facilitate knowledge transfer between different projects. Reuse of data across partners is another area where productivity gains can be achieved. However standardised formats for intensive exchange of information with partners are needed at many levels, and include more than agreement on common data formats. It is not easy to develop common standards in an industry with many small and medium sized players. The current trend is that the use of ICT leads towards more standardisation across the building process at the very basic level. Since its creation in 2003 BIPS has worked towards the creation of compatible IT infrastructures, common languages, and well defined partner roles and responsibilities. This supports better and closer collaboration among cooperating partners in building projects. One task has been to develop common formats in order to make it possible to exchange files. Another area of action has been development of tools to settle the division of responsibilities among partners in order to make a better foundation for collaboration by reducing potential conflicts. These agreements can be seen as a way to reduce the need for trust and thus a reduced need for social interaction, which again can be seen as a way to make a foundation for moves towards the creation of e-services.

A strategic disadvantage of the digitalisation of the project engineering process is related to the use of standard models, especially standard models included in commercial software packages available on the market. This service can easily be duplicated by other companies as much of the technical expertise needed for design and project engineering is embodied in the software. Ramboll might thus lose part of its competitive edge. However using these models on complex buildings still requires high project engineering competencies to ensure that models are consistent and to take special conditions not foreseen by the models into account. It is therefore important that Ramboll maintains these competences and also build up new competences which are difficult to duplicate and contribute to better and more sophisticated solutions. Ramboll find itself at a crossroads. Project engineering is expected to become less important for competition and there will therefore be more focus on consulting. In order to stay competitive, new areas of expertise are developed. One example is design of lighting. This has developed into an important market where Ramboll offers highly sophisticated solutions.

Another big challenge is to what degree

organisations should allow integration of their production processes with other partners. For the entire building project, there is no doubt that this would lead to overall productivity gains. However it might be difficult for companies involved both to actually realise these gains and to ensure their share of the benefits without losing control of their own part of the production. Especially there is a fear that integration will happen at the expense of the uniqueness and special technical competences provided by an engineering consultancy company like Ramboll. However if Ramboll choose to focus less on project engineering and more on consultancy, this problem becomes less important. One way to solve these problems would be the creation of companies which are able to carry out the entire building project alone or to engage in more stable strategic partnerships or other types of extended enterprises. However due to, for example, insurance, it is often required that certain functions are carried out by separate independent companies. Moreover integrated companies and stable partnerships will not be as flexible as shifting constellations, where the optimum consortium of partners can be created to win a particular contract.

CONCLUSION

The use of ICT in the production of technical engineering services is changing the services tremendously, along with the practices and competences needed. Ramboll is at a crossroads with regard to project engineering. Despite the need for high competences in technical skills the use of ICT reduces the importance of project engineering for competitiveness, and project engineering is becoming a smaller business area as the number of man hours needed is drastically reduced. Ramboll thus needs to move their focus towards other areas in order to create added value and remain competitive. However, the move towards codification and standardisation of project engineering along with the need for closer integration requires Ramboll and its (shifting) partners to consider how closely they want to integrate. The integration can be on a basic level with use of common formats and ongoing communication. However the integration can also move a step further towards more standardised processes with integration of knowledge from the different types of partner.

Although some processes are becoming more codified and standardised, a substantial part of the processes will not. This will be the case especially for a company like Ramboll that focuses on those processes that require most specialised technical expertise and with most value added. If e-service is defined narrowly as a service, delivered via the Internet or a similar electronic communication infrastructure (as defined in an earlier chapter by Henten), engineering consulting can be provided as an e-service in only few cases. However as noted in the beginning of this chapter, engineering consultancy cannot be seen as (1) one service or (2) a service with one delivery to one customer; rather it is a much more complex service product with several service deliveries and highly complex services with ongoing interaction with a number of players including the building owner and several partners. Some of these separated services are delivered as e-services by using ICT, for example, the virtual models as well as drawings and plans that are communicated to the partners electronically. These e-services are often combined with a meeting to provide further explanation. The use of ICT can thus be seen as a way of providing additional services (the virtual model) or extended services (electronically delivered drawings and plans). In addition multiple examples of improvements in the service have been given, emphasising how the new technology is used in the production of the technical engineering service, including communication with the partners. The knowledge service is improved due to a combination of new tools such as the 3D models, the infrastructure, and common formats that enable more streamlined

processes based on interactive communication and sharing and reuse of data between different partners. This can be seen as internal e-services facilitating processes of production in different phases of the building project. Thus if we define e-service as services which are delivered and/ or produced using ICT, the answer to whether technical engineering services can benefit from the e-service concept is definitely yes. Technical engineering will never become a full e-service, but many subparts of the service can indeed be delivered as an e-service.

The limitations to becoming a full e-service lie first in the complexity of the product and second in the distributed process involving many partners. Building a construction is extremely knowledge intensive, part of this knowledge is easy to obtain as it lies within regulations, standardised methods, and so forth; however part of the knowledge is related to the particular situation, that is, the building environment and conditions, which is also knowledge that can be obtained. However part of the knowledge is developed in interaction with the building owner and the other partners; this need for interaction reduces the possibility of a full e-service greatly as it demands ongoing contact to build an understanding of the wishes and possibilities along with trust between project partners. The amount of actors is another issue that limits the possibilities of becoming a full e-service, collaboration requires a division of responsibilities which to a large extent builds on trust, which has so far been developed through interaction. However this need may be reduced when standards on responsibilities are developed further.

REFERENCES

Hansen, M.T., Nohria, N., et al. (1999, March–April). Whats your strategy for managing knowledge? *Harvard Business Review*.

Star, S. L., & Griesemer, J. R. (1989). Institutional ecology, translations and boundary objects: Amateurs and professionals in Berkeleys Museum of Vertebrate Zoology, 1907-39. *Social Studies of Science*, *19*, 387–420. doi:10.1177/030631289019003001

Thompson, J. D. (1967). Organizations in action. New York: McGraw-Hill.

Zuboff, S. (1989). In the age of the smart machine. Oxford: The Perseus Books Group.

Chapter 5.3
Conceptualizing Competences in E–Services Adoption and Assimilation in SMES

Ada Scupola
Roskilde University, Denmark

ABSTRACT

This article investigates the competences deemed necessary both at top managerial and individual levels for the successful adoption and assimilation of business-to-business e-services in small and medium size enterprises. To this end, an in-depth case study of a business-to-business e-service system, a Web-based travel reservation system, was conducted. The results show that three main competences, namely vision, value and control, are important at top management level for the primary adoption of e-services. For secondary adoption and assimilation, three categories of competences were identified as being important either to have or to develop at the individual level, namely technical, interpersonal and conceptual skills.

INTRODUCTION

The aim of this study is to explore the competencies that are needed by small and medium size corporations (SMEs) in order to successfully adopt and assimilate e-services. SMEs are defined here as firms with up to 250 employees (OECD, 2000). An extensive body of literature has argued and investigated the importance of e-commerce technologies and e-services for the competitive advantage of the small and medium size firms (e.g., Grandon & Pearson, 2003; OECD, 2000). In addition, many studies have investigated the barriers to the adoption and diffusion of the Internet, e-commerce and e-business in small and medium size firms, as well as factors affecting the adoption and diffusion of these technologies in this type of firm (e.g., Mirchandani & Motwani, 2001; Scupola, 2003). Some of these studies have focused on competencies as it is thought that they might positively influence the firm's strategic commitment to the adoption and assimilation of technologies such as e-commerce or e-services (Chaston & Mangles, 2002; Eikebrokk & Olsen, 2002; McGowan, Durkin, Allen, Dougan, & Nixon, 2001; Wainwright, Green, Mitchell, & Yarrow, 2005).

In this article, e-services are defined as services that are provided or consumed through the use of Internet-based systems. The consumption or the provision of a service requires the interaction between the service provider and the user. Traditionally, this has been based on personal interactions, most often face-to-face interactions. In e-services, the consumption and the provision take place through the intermediation of an Internet-based system and therefore are separated in time and space (Fuglsang & Sundbo, 2006). E-services can involve a number of different relations: business to consumer, business to business, government services offered on the Internet or e-government. E-services also include the selling of physical goods on the Internet such as an airline ticket that is purchased online, but delivered by surface mail. There are three main characteristics of e-services:

- The service is accessible via the Internet or other electronic networks,
- The service is consumed by a person via the Internet or other electronic networks, and
- There might be a fee that the consumer pays the provider for using the e-service, but that might not always be the case. For example, some e-services offered by the government are free (Scupola, 2008). The purpose of this article is to investigate the competences required for the successful adoption and assimilation of business-to-business e-services in small and medium size enterprises. The basic research question tackled here is: What are the competences required both at the top managerial and individual levels for the successful adoption

and assimilation of business-to-business e-services in small and medium size corporations? To answer the research question, a theoretical model of e-service competencies is developed and a case study of an e-service system is conducted. The results show that three main competences, namely vision, value and control, are important at top management level, while a number of competences are important at the individual level.

The article is structured as follows. This section has presented the main purpose and motivation of the study. The next section discusses adoption and assimilation. This is followed by a literature review relating to the concepts of competence, IT competence, and the development of a model to investigate e-services competencies. It also discusses the methodology employed. The remaining part of the article presents the analysis, the discussion and the conclusions.

Adoption and Assimilation of E-Services

For the purpose of this study, adoption is defined as "the decision to make full use of an innovation as the best course of action available" (Rogers, 1995, p. 21). According to Zaltman, Duncan, and Holbeck (1973) innovation adoption within organizations often occurs in two stages. The first is a firm-level decision to adopt the innovation also called primary adoption; the second is the actual implementation or individual adoption by users also called secondary adoption. At the first level, managers identify objectives to change some aspect of their business and look for innovations that fit their objectives. Then they make the primary adoption decision (Gallivan, 2001). Once the primary adoption decision has been made, the implementation and use of the innovation at the individual level takes place. According to Gallivan (2001), management may proceed by taking three fundamentally different paths to ensure secondary adoption: (1) they can mandate that the innovation be adopted throughout the organization at once; (2) they can provide the necessary infrastructure and support for users to adopt the innovation, while allowing it to diffuse voluntarily; or (3) they may target specific pilot projects within the firm, observe the processes and outcomes that unfold, and decide whether to introduce the innovation more widely later on. This two-stage adoption model has also been defined as a contingent adoption decision, meaning that employees cannot adopt the innovation until primary adoption has occurred at a higher level of authority, often managerial or top management (Zaltman et al., 1973).

Assimilation is defined as the extent to which the use of a technology diffuses across organizational work processes and becomes routinized in the activities associated with those processes (Tornatzky & Klein, 1982). Moreover, it is important to look at assimilation because the adoption of a technology at a company level does not automatically lead to assimilation and use. Fichman and Kemerer (1999), for example, show that most information technologies exhibit an assimilation gap that is their rates of organizational assimilation and use lag behind their rates of organizational adoption.

The Concept of Technology Competence

The concept of competence has been much discussed in different types of research such as management, human resources and information systems and there is much confusion regarding the definition of competence. Furthermore, the concept of competence has been used at different analytical levels: for example, task-specific competences, firm specific competences or industry specific competences (Nordhaug, 1998). Competence has often also been identified with performance. But if performance has been used as a proxy for competence due to the difficulty of measuring competence, the mixing of competence

with performance often implies mixing the outcome with the process. However, a large amount of literature distinguishes between competence and performance, especially in relation to competence as a specific skill. Marcolin, Compeau, Munro, and Huff (2000) define user competence as "the user's potential to apply technology to its fullest possible extent so as to maximize the users' performance on specific job tasks." Competence is also seen as a personality trait, and might include generic knowledge, motivation, social role, or skill of a person linked to superior performance on the job (Haynes, 1979). Competence has also been associated with knowledge, and in this view competence is not only task specific, but embodies the ability to transfer knowledge across tasks, thus becoming interactive and dynamic (Brown, 1994). In human capital theory, the concept of competence has been related to specific firm technologies and to the execution of tasks that are related to the technology and the routines required to use that technology. Furthermore, there are many different typologies of competences found in the literature. For example, Yukl (1989) develops a typology that consists of technical, conceptual and interpersonal competences.

IT COMPETENCE MODELS AND IT COMPETENCE

A number of models have been developed to investigate IT competencies in small firms. Wainwright et al. (2005) develop a competency based model to be used for comparing practice and performance with respect to ICT within small firms. They propose that an ICT competence and capability approach can be a viable research avenue for investigating IT performance in small firms. Chaston and Mangles (2002) propose that the resource-based view of competitive advantage may provide the basis for assessing the ability of an organization to exploit the Internet to enhance market performance. They develop a competency model to define the competencies and capabilities that may influence the execution of an Internet marketing strategy. Their results show that the proposed competencies such as positioning, innovation and so forth, are critical for small firms to achieve market performance.

Finally, as with the concept of technology competence, the concept of competence related to IT has been defined in different ways and has focused on different levels of analysis (Table 1 provides a summary of studies of IT competence).

The stream of literature focusing on the organizational level (e.g., Van der Heijden, 2000) is influenced by parallel studies in the management literature and especially by the resource based view of strategic advantage (e.g., Barney, 1991; Prahalad & Hamel, 1990). The other stream of research focuses on the individual level, for example, Basselier, Reich, and Banbasat (2001) study IT competences in business managers, and identifies a concept of IT knowledge that is decomposed into explicit IT knowledge and tacit IT knowledge. Explicit IT knowledge is knowledge that can be read, taught or explained to others. Tacit IT knowledge is more difficult to explain and to do so Basselier et al. use the constructs of experience and cognition. Experience relates to the managers' know how, while cognition involves more then doing things, and refers to working models of the world that an individual forms, including acumen, beliefs and viewpoints. However, this kind of literature has not focused on other factors related to competences such as communication, social or leadership skills.

Table 1. A summary of studies of IT competences

Author	Definition of Competence	Individual/Organizational Level
Basselier et al. (2001)	IT related explicit and Tacit Knowledge	Individual level (Business Manger)
Lee & Trauth (1995)	Critical Knowledge and Skills	Individual level (IS professionals)
Bharadwaj, Sambamurthy & Zmud (2000)	Critical IT Capabilities	Organizational Level
Van der Heji-den (2000)	IT core capabilities; organization specific routines, skills, resources and processes	Organizational Level and IT management)
Sambamurthy & Zmud (1994)	Capabilities, skills and tacit know-how	Organizational Level and IT management
Chaston & Mangles (2002)	Internet related capabilities; organization specific routines, resources and processes	Organizational Level
Wainwright et al. (2005)	ICT related competence; Organizational ICT performance and practice	Organizational Level

In this study, being interested in the small firm's competencies deemed important for the successful adoption and assimilation of e-services both at primary and secondary levels, the focus is placed on top management and individual level competencies. Top management, through their beliefs and visions can offer guidelines to managers and employees about the opportunities and risks in assimilating technological innovations (Gallivan, 2001; Chatterie, Grewal, & Sambamurthy, 2002). For example, in firms where top managers believe that e-services offer a strategic opportunity, their beliefs serve as powerful signals to the rest of the firm's employees about the importance placed on e-services. This makes the employees and the managers use their time and energy in making sense of e-services or exploring ways in which the technology's functionality could be leveraged to improve the company's efficiency, routines or business value.

In this study, therefore, managerial competences become the basis for the firms' vision, norms, beliefs and strategies in adopting and assimilating e-services (Durkin & McGowan, 2001; Middleton & Long, 1990). Individual competences are relevant in relation to the specific task of adopting and using an e-service system (Brown, 1994; Haynes, 1979).

A MODEL OF COMPETENCY FOR E-SERVICE ADOPTION AND ASSIMILATION

Theoretical Background of the Model

Durkin and McGowan (2001) develop an Internet competency model to investigate which competencies the manager of a small firm must have in order to decide the extent to which the Internet is adopted in marketing activities. They argue that the extent to which the Internet is adopted and offers a fundamental advantage for the marketing activity is contingent upon the development at the managerial level of four main competencies:

vision, value, technical ability and control. These competencies are not independent of each other, but are interrelated. For example, at management level there is sequentiality in the sense that first the company has to develop a vision, then develop the value competency, the technical ability and finally control (Durkin & McGowan, 2001).

Chatterie et al. (2002) describe how the structuration theory of technology assimilation states that firms act as institutions in shaping the behaviours and cognitions of the individuals in the corporation in facilitating or preventing them from assimilating a technology. This can be done in three ways:

1. Structures of signification, where prevailing institutional structures yield meaning and understanding. Individuals apply these structures as guides to understanding how they should behave/act with respect to the assimilation of new technology.
2. Structures of legitimization, where prevailing institutional structures validate specific behaviours as being appropriate in the organization and consistent with the goals and values of the organization. Individuals draw upon these structures as normative templates to reassure themselves about the organizational legitimacy of their assimilation actions.
3. Structures of domination, where institutional structures regulate individual actions and behaviours. Individuals draw upon these structures to ensure that their acts of assimilation do not violate institutional rules and to avoid being the target of organizational sanctions (Chatterie et al., 2002, p. 68).

Finally, Yukl (1989) states that three sets of competences or skills are relevant at the individual level in explicating a specific task or activity: technical, interpersonal and conceptual skills. Technical skills or competences represent knowledge about methods, techniques and processes required to conduct a specific activity and the ability to use the tools and equipment necessary to explicate that activity. Interpersonal skills include knowledge about social skills, the ability to communicate, and the ability to cooperate, as well as empathy. Finally, conceptual skills include creativity, efficiency in problem solving, analytical capability and capacity to understand opportunities and problems.

The Research Model

By drawing on the literature review above and on the work by Durkin and McGowan (2001), Chatterie et al. (2002) and Yukl (1989), a model of competencies for e-service adoption and assimilation is proposed. In accordance with McGowan et al. (2001) it is argued that the faster primary adoption of e-services in the small and medium size firm is contingent upon the development of management level competencies such as vision, value, technical ability, and control. By drawing on Yukl (1989), it is argued that faster secondary e-services adoption and assimilation, by contrast,

is contingent upon the development of individual level competencies related to the specific task that has to be performed (in this case the use of e-services) such as technical, interpersonal and conceptual skills (Figure 1). Finally, after the firm has made the decision for primary adoption, it can enforce secondary adoption by developing structures of signification, legitimization and domination as is asserted by the structuration theory of technology assimilation (Chatterie et al., 2002). This is shown in Figure 1 by the arrow between the two boxes representing the development of competencies. Like Durkin and McGowan (2001) vision is defined as the managerial capability to see what contribution e-services can make to the general business level. The value competency requires that top management clearly understand what the business value of e-services is. Value competency requires more proactivity and implies that the manager goes a step further and contextualizes the initial awareness and general vision of his own company by evaluating appropriateness and receptivity (McGowan et al.,

Figure 1. A model of competencies for e-service adoption and assimilation

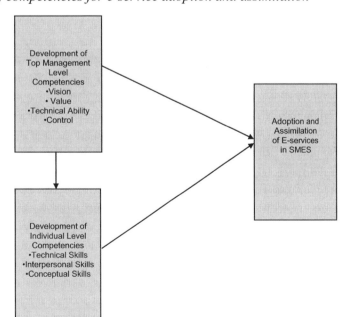

2001). Technical ability implies that the manager is comfortable with new technology and its operation, even though he/she is not a real expert in the technology. It is possible that he/she could attend courses to learn how to use the technology. By developing the "control" competency, the manager enforces rules and policies to ensure that e-services are adopted at the individual level. In fact, as the structuration theory of technology assimilation states, firms act as institutions in shaping the behaviours and cognitions of the individuals in the corporation in facilitating or preventing them from assimilating a technology (Chatterie et al., 2002, p. 68).

By drawing on Yukl (1989), three sets of competence or skills are defined to be relevant at individual level in e-service adoption and assimilation: technical, interpersonal and conceptual skills. Technical skills are mainly identified here with knowledge competency, including the capability to transfer knowledge from one situation to another (Brown, 1994). Following Basselier et al. (2001), e-service knowledge is divided into two components: tacit knowledge and explicit knowledge. Explicit knowledge is formal knowledge that can be acquired through formal training, and can be read or explained. Tacit knowledge by contrast is gained through experience and experiential training. Furthermore, experience increases the memory of how to undertake an activity, which in turn increases competency levels in relation to that experience. The combination and variety of experiences influence the level of tacit knowledge. In this study interpersonal skills include knowledge about social skills, the ability to communicate, the ability to cooperate as well as empathy and judgement. In common with McGowan et al. (2001), it can be argued that judgement is a function of both tacit and explicit knowledge. Finally, conceptual skills include creativity, efficiency in problem solving, analytical capability and the capacity to understand opportunities and problems.

Methodology

To investigate the competences required for the adoption and assimilation of e-services in small and medium size companies, a case study was conducted where the object of analysis was the e-service (Yin, 1989). The e-service was/is a Web-based travel reservation system developed by the travel agency TQ3 which sells business-to-business travel solutions. In the last few years, they have developed a Web-based system, called Web-buster, which can be used by the client companies to make the reservations and buy the travel tickets by themselves, thus bypassing the employees at TQ3. To understand the e-service in question and the competences required for its successful adoption and assimilation in the SMEs, interviews were conducted both with the e-service provider and with the customer companies or adopters of the e-service. Face-to-face qualitative semistructured interviews were used to collect the data. These interviews were complemented by the critical incident technique (see below). The sampling was purposeful. Interviewees were chosen in small firms that had been successful in assimilating e-services. Retrospectively, the study tried to understand the competencies deemed important in both primary and secondary adoption and assimilation. The respondents had to be involved in the adoption process at managerial level or had to be users of the e-services at individual level. Managers and travel bookers at TQ3 were interviewed because they could provide useful information about their customers' competences in the adoption and assimilation of the e-service. A total of 14 interviews were conducted in a total of six companies. The interviews lasted between 60 and 90 minutes, and were tape recorded and fully transcribed by a research assistant. Table 2 provides a brief overview of the companies interviewed.

The semistructured interviews were based on a guide aimed at collecting information both about the managerial level and the individual level

Table 2.Companies interviewed

Company/ Information	Type of Business	Number of Employees
A (TQ3)	Provider of Web-based Travel Solutions	12,000 Worldwide
B	Paint and Varnish Business	No Data
C	Research and Development of Human and Animal Medical Products	140 in Denmark
D	Producer of Cleaning Equipment	No Data
E	Engineering consulting	100
F	Production and service of plastic card products	150 in Denmark

competences. The second part of the interview specifically applied the critical incident technique to elicit critical incidents aimed at highlighting the competences required to successfully adopt and assimilate the e-service in the companies. By relying on Yin (2003), the data were analyzed by following the "general strategy of relying on theoretical orientation" of the case study. Following Miles and Huberman (1994, p. 58), a provisional "start list" of codes based on the conceptual framework was created prior to the field work to guide the analysis. The coding was manual. Specific analytic techniques included making matrixes of categories and placing evidence within such categories (Yin, 2003; Miles & Huberman, 1994) and finding relevant critical incidents (Flanagan, 1954; Fuglsang, 2007).

The Critical Incident Technique (CIT)

The critical incident technique is a research method used to collect data specifically related to competences. This technique was first developed by the U.S. Air Force to select competent pilots (Flanagan, 1954) and has been used in many studies investigating competencies (e.g., Fuglsang & Sundbo, 2006). The critical incident technique gives a detailed description of what happened, why it happened and what specific actions were taken to solve the problem. Here CIT has been

used to collect, organize and structure data about e-services related competences. According to Flanagan (1954):

By critical incident is meant any observable human activity that is sufficiently complete in itself to permit inferences and predictions to be made about the person performing the act. To be critical, an incident must occur in a situation where the purpose or intent of the act seems fairly clear to the observer and where its consequences are sufficiently definite to leave little doubt concerning its effects. (Flanagan, 1954, p. 327)

Following Flanagan, in this study concrete incidents with a positive or negative impact with respect to e-services adoption and assimilation (the aim of the situation) have been identified. The incidents that were found were then analyzed and grouped according to the competency model developed above and reported in the analysis where appropriate to illustrate the point.

Analysis and Results

Top Management Level

The findings mainly support the model of competencies developed in Figure 1. As suggested by the model, vision was the first competency deemed necessary in order for the company to take into consideration the possibility of adopting e-services and making a proactive effort to understand their value (McGowan et al., 2001). In all the companies interviewed, vision involved an understanding of how a Web based travel booking system could add value to the company and contribute to the company's business and strategy. A critical incident illustrating the importance of vision is as follows (TQ3):

Interviewer. What do you think it is important at your customer?
Interviewee. There I believe vision. I am happy when people (top management) say "It is that way we have to go" and then you have to be realistic. ....You need to know if you are geared, but vision, that I like. When people are visionary and can see possibilities, it is nice. I also visit clients that simply work like we did 100 years ago, and they never go forward...

Value competency mainly consisted of finding out what value the Web-based reservation system could bring to the company. This value consisted mainly of decreases in operational expenses, including travelling expenses. In fact, the main idea of TQ3 Web-based reservation system is that it should create value both for the producer and the consumer as it should reduce costs for both. For TQ3, the Web-based system should decrease personnel costs and allow the company to concentrate on the customers with special needs. For the e-service users it should reduce the company's total travel costs as the company can get a discount when they book their travel directly through Webbuster, bypassing TQ3. This was clearly pointed out by the respondents at TQ3, as well as by employees interviewed in the customer companies. A critical incident reported by an employee at TQ3 was as follows:

Interviewee. So many of our things are developed with the purpose of saving money, where we can save money at our company is one of the things, do something new, and where we can save money for our customers is the other thing.

Once the competencies of vision and value have been developed and the decision to adopt an e-service has been made, senior management started developing a new competency to encourage and enforce assimilation at individual level: the "control competency" (Durkin & McGowan, 2001). This competency manifested itself in the development of a company policy to enforce the use of the e-service at the individual level. This included both the person that is in charge of making the travel reservation and the employees that had to travel. The following critical incident illustrates this point (Company D):

Interviewee: But there is a little back and forth sometimes that they prefer one solution, and then you say "Yes, that is possible, but it is so expensive, but ..... we have a travel policy in the company....

In addition, all the respondents that were also users of the e-service in the small companies said that they had to use the Web-based reservation system due to the wishes of top management to reduce travel costs and the company policy of cutting costs. This was also justified by the fact that employees in the companies interviewed were travelling a lot. A critical incident illustrating this point is as follows (company C):

Interviewer. We talked about policy, why has the company introduced that policy?
Interviewee. Simply to save money. Because at TQ3, there you get 5% saving circa per ticket you reserve on the Internet. And if you have a budget of millions crowns, then it is a lot of money that you can save in one year. And then you have a total online solution, so it saves time both for us and TQ3.

The analysis shows that the top management competency "technical ability" was not important for primary adoption. However the study shows that the technical ability and capacity of the whole corporation was important in order to be able to initiate primary adoption. This is shown by the following critical incident (TQ3):

Interviewee. Yes, it is clear, technical they also have to be, and have the right IT equipment and be updated on the IT-side, that they almost must have to be to be able to consider Webbuster.

After the decision to adopt e-services at top management level had been made and the competencies were developed at management level to ensure adoption and assimilation at the individual level, a set of competences at the individual level were deemed necessary to ensure secondary adoption and to make the e-service become an integral part of the company's routines and culture (assimilation). These are presented in the following section and are based on the model of Figure 1.

Individual Level

Technical Skills. The main competence found relevant within this category was knowledge competency both tacit and explicit. The users of the TQ3 e-service system interviewed in this study were all first time users of such an e-service system, and therefore the acquisition of both explicit and tacit knowledge in learning how to use the e-service system was extremely important. Explicit knowledge was acquired through a formal one day training seminar organized by TQ3 after the system was installed at the customer site. Tacit knowledge was acquired through learning by doing, once the user came back to the company and started to use the e-service system. This is shown by the following critical incident (company D):

Interviewee: You do by trying it, when you for ten times have been sitting and writing your user

name, then you become tired of it. Then you ask yourself whether it is possible to make it easier. (Secretary, Company D)

As suggested by Brown (1994), knowledge competency also includes a component relating to the transfer of the skills learned and knowledge acquired in a given context to a new context. For example, in this study this was shown by a transfer of general Internet skills to the specific e-service system in question, the transfer of previous expertise in the travel sector and IT to online travel booking. A critical incident in company B illustrates this:

Interviewer: Are you more used (then your colleagues not willing to use Webbuster) to use this type of technology?
Interviewee: Yes. And it is also that, I believe, that make the difference. I do not believe it is a problem to sit and reserve a flight on the Internet, where others believe that it is difficult....I use also net bank at home and everything, whatever I have to book as ferry tickets or what we do...concert tickets, that I do often on the Internet. All those kind of things...and then I use it also here in all possible contexts (Secretary, Company B).

Interpersonal Skills

The main competencies in this category were communication and empathy. Communication competency manifested itself as the capability to communicate with others. Examples include the ability to understand what other people say and make oneself understood, to negotiate with the travel agency as to what to do with the ticket if the system breaks down during the reservation process, or calling the help desk or the local travel agency for help. A critical incident illustrating this is the following (company D):

Interviewer... I think that they were very good at speaking so that we could understandthat.

Interviewee. So they could understand what your problem was and you could understand, what they said?
Resp. Yes, exactly.

Another example of how it might not be easy to communicate is provided by the following critical incident (company F):

Interviewer. ...That means that you have to communicate with them, that have to   travel, when you go into the system, and say, what possibilities there are.
Interviewee... the best for me is to make them to stay behind the computer monitor, so they can see what possibilities there are....so I have the communication immediately.

Other examples can be calling the help desk or the local travel agency for help as shown by the following critical incident (Company E):

Interviewee Then I call this number (help desk) and say who I am ..in the process of doing something on Webbuster and I cannot go further..... And I can also contact our own travel agency if I have a problem ...

In our study empathy manifested itself as the capability to understand and take into consideration other colleagues' needs and wants with regard to travel and economic restrictions. In fact, the travel booker found herself in the dilemma of accommodating the travel wishes of the colleagues, for example travelling at specific times and dates, have specific seats, minimize travel time, as well as taking into consideration the company's policy with regard to reducing travel expenses. Sometimes this can be difficult. The following critical incident illustrates the capability to take into consideration colleagues' preferences (company F):

Interviewee. It is very different what people believe it is good. I try to find it out   what they prefer. That makes it also easier for me...

Conceptual Skills

In this category two main competencies were found relevant: creativity and judgement.

Creativity manifested itself as the capability to search for new information, to use and understand other sources, the capability to navigate and relate to the IT system, to understand when the information and the knowledge at hand is not enough, and the capability to handle multiple sources at the same time. Clearly this requires a certain degree of reflection, whether conscious or unconscious, about what is known and how to go to get further information or knowledge. An example of looking for more information in the system manual to solve a certain task is given by the following critical incident (company C):

Interviewer: Had you tried, before calling them (help desk), to look at the manual or other sources?
Interviewee. Yes, I had been in the system and looked at what I have printed here (the manual).

The following critical incident (company B) illustrates the capability to look for different solutions:

Interviewee. ...the system could simply not find that out, it comes back and says, that there are some problems with the number, so I try some different ways.

A critical incident illustrating the capability to handle multiple sources simultaneously is as follows (Company C):

Interviewee. So it has also something to do with being able to keep many bolds in the air, certainly.... Because you have so many tickets running at the same time. And you have so many arrangements.

Judgement competency manifested itself as the capability to judge different kinds of situations and make a decision. Examples of this is include knowing when to stop trying to solve a problem by oneself and ask others instead. To judge when it is good to use the online system to book a trip and when it is better to do it manually. To judge when it is the system that has made a mistake or when it is the user making a mistake. To judge the validity of the information the user gets from the system. An example of the capability to question the validity of the information the user gets from the system is provided by the following critical incident (company F):

Interviewee. ....Yes, I believe that they make it look nicer then it is (talking about thehotel information that she can find in the system), some hotels do, for sure..they exaggerate.

DISCUSSION

The analysis has shown that for a successful adoption and assimilation of e-services in small and medium size companies it is important to develop appropriate competencies both at top management and individual levels. In this study three competences were deemed important at top management level: vision, value and control. Through vision and value top management can understand and highlight the strategic importance of e-services and take a proactive approach to creating the condition for its primary adoption. Through control, top management can create the conditions for employees to adopt the e-service (secondary adoption), thus reducing the assimilation gap. In fact according to Chatterije et al. (2002) top management can either encourage or discourage individual adoption by mandating rules and policies about the assimilation of a technology. In all the companies interviewed in this study this was achieved by formulating a company policy to reduce travel expenses. This policy consisted of the following: first the Web-based system had to be used for all the trips as this allowed for a discount in respect to the price charged by the travel agency; second the employees had to travel

as cheaply as possible; third all the travel reservations had to be undertaken by one person. The company travel policy functions as structures of domination by regulating the individual actions and behaviours. The travel booker draws upon this policy to ensure that his/her assimilation actions in using the Web-based travel system do not violate the institutional rules. Contrary to the model described in Figure 1, this study found that the "technical ability" competence was thought unimportant for the adoption of e-services at managerial level. In the companies interviewed top managers were not necessarily acquainted with e-service technology, neither were they interested in or took a proactive approach to learning it. They were mostly interested in the value that it could create for the company and then they delegated the technical tasks to the individuals that had to use it, while developing rules to enforce such use at individual level. However, the analysis shows that the IT capability of the firm is important for primary adoption (Bharadwaj et al., 2000).

In order to use and assimilate the e-service, a number of individual level competences have been identified in this study. These competences can be technical as, for example, knowledge regarding how to use the e-service system, interpersonal such as the capability to communicate, or conceptua! such as judgement and creativity competences.

CONCLUSION AND LIMITATIONS

This study is important because it has shown that both top management and individual level competences are important in e-services adoption and assimilation in small and medium size enterprise. This has been done by developing a competency model and by applying it to a specific e-service system: a Web-based travel reservation system. The empirical findings mainly confirm the validity of the model. Furthermore, this study has identified a number of competences at top management and individual levels that are necessary for the successful adoption of e-services. Competences at top management level are important in order to make the initial decision to adopt the technology and enforce or facilitate its use in the company. Competences at the individual level are important for the successful assimilation of e-services in the company. Some can be acquired through formal training, others have to be acquired by experiential learning.

Finally, this study presents a number of limitations. First of all, the number of interviews is too small to be able to make any generalization regarding competencies in e-services adoption and assimilation in SMEs. Further research could extend this study to a larger sample of companies for the same e-service system or could test the model in other types of e-services. The companies participating in the study were all successful adopters of the Web-based travel system. Further research could focus, for example, on companies that did not succeed in adopting the e-service, to understand major reasons for failure. Finally, there might be other approaches to understanding and conceptualizing competences than the one used in this study. Nevertheless, this study gives some good insights into the competences required at top management and individual levels to adopt and successfully assimilate e-services in small and medium size companies. These results might be of interest to other researchers as well as corporations' managers interested in adopting e-services as a strategic or value adding technology.

REFERENCES

Basselier, G., Reich, B.H., & Benbasat, I. (2001). Information technology competence of business managers: A definition and research model. *Journal of Management Information Systems*, *17*(4), 159-182.

Bharadwaj, A.S., Sambamurthy,V., & Zmud, R.W. (2000). IT capabilities: Theoretical perspectives and empirical operalization. In *Proceedings of the 21ˢᵗ International Conference on Information Systems*, Brisbane, Australia, (pp. 378-385).

Brown, R.B. (1994). Reframing the competency debate. *Management Learning*, *25*(2), 289-299.

Chaston, I., & Mangles, T. (2002). E-commerce in small UK manufacturing firms: A pilot study on internal competencies. Journal of Marketing Management, *18*(3-4), 341-360.

Chatterjee, D., Grewal, R., & Sambamurthy, V. (2002). Shaping up for e-commerce: Institutional enablers of the organizational assimilation of Web technologies. *MIS Quaterly*, *26*(2), 65-90.

Durkin, M.G., & McGowan, P. (2001). "Net Effect"-views from the periphery: Exploring the role and importance of the Internet in marketing activity in entrepreneurial firms. *Irish Marketing Review, 14*, 15-25.

Eikebrokk, T.R., & Olsen, D.H. (2002). Understanding e-business competencies in SMEs. *Seeking success in e-business—multidisciplinary approach* (pp. 575-602). Kluwer Academic Publishers.

Flanagan, J. (1954). The critical incident technique. *Psychological Bulletin*, *51*(4), 327-358.

Fuglsang, L. (2007). Critical incident Teknikken i Teknikker i Samfundsvidenskaberne, In L. Fuglsang, P. Hagedorn-Rasmussen, P. Bitch Olsen (Eds.), *Roskilde universitetsforlag (*pp. 260-277).

Fuglsang, L., & Sundbo, J. (2006). Flow and consumers in e-services self-services: New provider-consumer relations. *The Service Industries Journal, 26*(4), 361-379.

Gallivan, M, J. (2001). Organizational adoption and assimilation of complex technological innovations: Development and application of a new framework. *Database for Advances of Information Systems*, *32*(3), 51-86.

Grandon, E., & Pearson, J.M. (2003). Strategic value and adoption of electronic commerce: An empirical study of Chilean small and medium businesses. *Journal of Global Information Technology Management, 6*(3).

Haynes, J.L. (1979). A new look at managerial performance: The AMA model of worthy performance. *Management Review, 2-3.*

Lee, D.M.S., & Trauth, E.M. (1995). Critical skills and knowledge requirements of IS professionals: A joint academic/industry investigation. MIS Quarterly, *19*(3), 313-340.

Marcolin, B., Compeau, D.R., Munro, M.C., & Huff, S.L. (2000). Assessing user competence: Conceptualization and measurement. *Information Systems Research, 11*(1), 37-60.

McGowan, P., Durkin, M.G., Allen, L., Dougan, C., & Nixon, S. (2001). Developing competencies in the entrepreneurial small firm for use of the Internet in the management of customer relationships. *Journal of Industrial Training, 25*(2-3-4), 126-136.

Middleton, B., & Long, G. (1990). Marketing skills: Critical issues in marketing education and training. *Journal of Marketing Management, 5*(3), 325-43.

Miles, M.B., & Huberman, A.M. (1994). *Qualitative data analysis* (2nd ed.). Sage Publications.

Mirchandani & Motwani. (2001). Understanding small business electronic commerce adoption: An empirical analysis. *Journal of Computer Information Systems, Spring,* 70-73.

Nordhaug, O. (1998). Competence specificity in organizations. *International Studies of Management and Organizations, 28*(1), 8-29.

OECD. (2000). *OECD small and medium size enterprise outlook.* Retrieved November 15, 2007, from http://www.oecd.org

Sambamurthy, V., & Zmud, R.W. (1994). *IT management competency assessment: A tool for creating business value through IT.* Morristown, NJ: Financial Executives Research Foundation.

Scupola, A. (2003). The adoption of Internet commerce by SMEs in the south of Italy: An environmental, technological and organizational perspective. *Journal of Global Information Technology Management, 6*(1), 51-71.

Scupola, A. (Ed.). (2008). *Cases on managing e-service.* Hershey, PA: IGI Publishing (Forthcoming).

Van der Hejiden, H. (2000). Measuring IT core capabilities for electronic commerce: Results from a confirmatory analysis. In *Proceedings of the 21st International Conference on Information Systems,* Brisbane, Australia, (pp. 142-163).

Wainwright, D., Green G., Mitchell, E., & Yarrow, D. (2005). Towards a framework for benchmarking ICT practice, competence and performance in small firms. *Performance Measurement and Metrics, 6*(1), 39-52.

Yin, R.K. (1989). *Case study design.* Newbury, CA.

Yukl, G.A. (1989). *Leadership in organizations* (2nd ed.). Englewood Cliffs, NJ: Prentice Hall.

Zaltman, G., Duncan, R., & Holbeck, J. (1973). *Innovations and organizations.* New York: John Wiley and Sons.

This work was previously published in the Journal of Electronic Commerce in Organizations, Volume 6, Issue 2, edited by M. Khosrow-Pour, pp. 78-91, copyright 2008 by IGI Publishing (an imprint of IGI Global).

Chapter 5.4
Building Local Capacity via Scaleable Web–Based Services

Helen Thompson
University of Ballarat, Australia

INTRODUCTION

Information communications technology (ICT) has been identified as a key enabler in the achievement of regional and rural success, particularly in terms of economic and business development. The potential of achieving equity of service through improved communications infrastructure and enhanced access to government, health, education, and other services has been identified. ICT has also been linked to the aspiration of community empowerment, where dimensions include revitalizing a sense of community, building regional capacity, enhancing democracy, and increasing social capital.

In Australia, there has been a vision for online services to be used to open up regional communities to the rest of the world. Government support has been seen "as enhancing the competence levels of local economies and communities so they become strong enough to deal equitably in an increasingly open marketplace" (McGrath & More, 2002, p. 40). In a regional and rural context, the availability of practical assistance is often limited. Identification of

the most appropriate online services for a particular community is sometimes difficult (Ashford, 1999; Papandrea & Wade, 2000; Pattulock & Albury Wodonga Area Consultative Committee, 2000). Calls, however, continue for regional communities to join the globalized, online world. These are supported by the view that success today is based less and less on natural resource wealth, labor costs, and relative exchange rates, and more and more on individual knowledge, skills, and innovation. But how can regional communities "grab their share of this wealth" and use it to strengthen local communities (Simpson 1999, p. 6)? Should communities be moving, as Porter (2001, p. 18) recommends (for business), away from the rhetoric about "Internet industries," "e-business strategies," and the "new economy," to see the Internet as "an enabling technology—a powerful set of tools that can be used, wisely or unwisely, in almost any industry and as part of almost any strategy?"

Recent Australian literature (particularly government literature) does indeed demonstrate somewhat of a shift in terms of the expectations of ICT and e-commerce (National Office for the Information Economy, 2001; Multimedia Victo-

DOI: 10.4018/978-1-60566-026-4.ch069

ria, 2002; National Office for the Information Economy, 2002). Consistent with reflections on international industry experience, there is now a greater emphasis on identifying locally appropriate initiatives, exploring opportunities for improving existing communication and service quality, and for using the Internet and ICT to support more efficient community processes and relationships (Hunter, 1999; Municipal Association of Victoria and ETC Electronic Trading Concepts Pty Ltd., 2000; National Office for the Information Economy, 2002).

The objective of this article is to explore whether well-developed and well-implemented online services can make a positive contribution to the future of regional and rural communities. This will be achieved by disseminating some of the learning from the implementation of the Main-Street Regional Portal project (www.mainstreet. net.au). To provide a context for this case study, the next section introduces some theory relevant to virtual communities and portals. The concept of *online communities* is introduced and then literature is reviewed to identify factors that have been acknowledged as important in the success of online community and portal initiatives.

BACKGROUND

In regional Australia, many Web-based initiatives have been premised on fear of external electronic commerce ventures adversely affecting local industry (McGrath & More, 2002, p. 50). Media and government reports have reinforced notions that those who ignore the adoption of electronic commerce will do so at their peril (Department of Communications Information Technology and the Arts, 2000). Recent research however identifies a movement beyond the "starry-eyed fascination with, and high expectations of, technology per se," with the focus now more pragmatically on how ICT can enable enhanced business and community processes and more effective organizational relationships (More & McGrath, 2003).

The term *online community* means different things to different people (Preece, 2000). In early definitions, the term described communication facilitated through bulletin boards (Rheingold, 1994, pp. 57-58). More recent definitions reflect the expansion of Web-based technologies and often link online communities with concepts of regional communities and local strengths (Keeble & Loader, 2001).

In Australia the terms *online community, regional portal, Web portal,* and *community portal* are often used more or less interchangeably. Web portals "provide focal points on the Web, places to start, places to go to find things" (Gronlund, 2001, p. 88). They have been identified as one strategy for encouraging regional participation in the information economy. For example, according to the Department of Communications Information Technology and the Arts (2001), a regional portal can achieve the online aggregation of potential and existing regional presence into a comprehensive portal, gateway, or regional Web site. In funding initiatives, preference has been given to projects that offer inclusive regional aggregation of business, government, and community services, and which provide interactive services to clients both in and external to the region.

Some definitions of online communities capture the concepts of both *communities of interest* and *communities of location,* and identify the role of encouraging communication and information sharing among members as important (McGrath & More, 2002). Australia's largest telecommunications provider describes online communities as providing a focal point for the provision of local regional information. In terms of functionality, these community portals generally incorporate local news services, local weather reports, a directory of community organizations, and features such as bulletin boards, discussion forums, a calendar of events, and transaction services (Telstra Country Wide, 2002).

To achieve optimum online collaboration, various issues require consideration. These include notions of community, trust and commitment, processes and structure, knowledge management, learning, and collaboration (More & McGrath, 2003). Some further factors more specific to the success of online community or portal initiatives are considered in the next section.

In forging and managing online collaboration, people issues rather than technological ones have been identified as the most challenging. "Certainly across a broad range of projects, many have come to realize that managing people, relationships, and business processes is harder than managing technology" (McGrath & More, 2002, p. 66). It is easy to underestimate the amount of planning and effort that is needed to build and sustain an online community; therefore care should be taken to avoid miscalculations. In particular, "overlooking the key role of the human facilitator is perhaps the greatest reason that online communities fail to meet the expectations of their designers" (Bernal, 2000, p. 4).

For many projects, collaboration is the key to survival, renewal, and growth, especially in regional areas "where the threat of global competitive dynamics often drove alliances" (McGrath & More, 2002, p. 67). Initiatives, however, with a broad geographical focus, can "encounter difficulties in establishing and maintaining cooperative relationships across multiple communities in their regions" (Simpson, 2002, p. 8).

"Many projects that have adopted a 'build it and they will come' approach have been doomed to early failure" (Simpson, 2002, p. 4). Developers need to work with community members to ensure that the goals of the site owner and the needs of community members are met (Preece, 2000). Good online services provide multiple levels of entry, many-to-many relationships, and rapid movement between the services and content of disparate providers (Local Government Association of Tasmania and Trinitas Pty Ltd., 2001).

Community members also need compelling reasons to use and return to an online community again and again. There will be a need to balance supply-side investment (access, technical platforms) and demand-side investment (content

and services) (Local Government Association of Tasmania and Trinitas Pty Ltd., 2001).

"If you get this right—if you can identify and fill a need in the lives of your community members—you can go a long way on very little technology. If you miss this, no amount of technology is going to make you successful as an online community." (Kim, cited in Bernal, 2000, p. 3)

Engaging and relevant content are vital to increase uptake and sustained use of the Internet. Portal content management strategies should be *bottom-up* in their approach. This can be achieved by providing multiple opportunities for interaction and by providing permission-based access to software that allows members to produce content for their online community (Brumby, 2001; Telstra Country Wide, 2002).

Soft technologies are also essential in building user confidence and comfort with new technology. "Individualized awareness raising…training activities, and learner support are key elements in creating within the community the desire, motivation, and enthusiasm to trial and take up the technology" (Simpson, 2002, p. 7).

This review has highlighted a number of factors which can impact the success or otherwise of portal type initiatives. This background information provides a context for introducing the MainStreet case study in the next section.

MAIN THRUST OF ARTICLE

In May 1999 a collective of regional stakeholder organizations engaged the University of Ballarat to research the requirements and make recommendations on how the Central Highlands and Wimmera regions of Victoria could capture greater advantages from new information and communications technologies.

The research, documented in *Victoria's Golden West Portal Project Business Case* (Thompson, 1999), involved a number of different stages. These included confirming existing regional Web content, examining community portal developments, identifying portal tools, researching potential revenue streams, conducting focus group sessions, and other forms of stakeholder consultation.

The research report described how an environment could be established that would be conducive to the widespread adoption of electronic commerce. Specific recommendations included: establish a membership-based regional association with a specific focus on electronic commerce; establish infrastructure for a manageable and economically sustainable Internet presence in a way that would encourage the enhancement of community service and facilitate communities of interest and trading communities; and through a regional portal, achieve better Web content coordination, provide a valuable information source for residents, and also enhance efforts to promote all the attributes of the region.

The Chamber of Electronic Commerce Western Victoria Inc. (the Chamber) was established to facilitate the advancement of electronic commerce and implement the MainStreet portal project. Funding applications were prepared, and in November 1999 the MainStreet project secured funding of AUD 274,000 through Networking the Nation, with a further AUD 135,000 approved in May 2000. The University's Centre for Electronic Commerce and Communications (CECC) was then contracted to implement the project because it had the specialist skills necessary to develop the portal infrastructure and services.

Research had identified that many portal projects had produced 'static' or 'fixed' solutions. The MainStreet model, with the inclusion of a technical team as a critical element, was different, but the decision to have this team was significant in determining how the MainStreet project would evolve. The technical officer and part-time programmers would develop a portal framework based on the core services identified during the preliminary study. All tools would be selected or developed with non-technical end users

in mind. The initial toolset would include event calendars; news publishing tools; online registration, payment, and product systems; and access to Web wizards and other Web publishing tools. This would be achieved by incorporating a range of in-house developments, with some integration of externally sourced product. The core services would create capacities to link regional Internet information and services, construct searchable directories, dynamically generate content like news and weather, distribute publishing and authoring rights, and promote community news and events.

The MainStreet project was actively promoted in the period leading up to its official launch in July 2000. This promotion was important as it helped to maintain interest in the project while technical developments proceeded behind the scenes.

During the early part of 2002, the MainStreet project attracted its first major client. Success in securing the Ararat Online project (www.ararat. asn.au) was attributed to involving regional stakeholders right from the project's beginning. Ararat's Economic Development Manager had participated in a range of activities, meetings, and focus group sessions. Through these activities he developed a strong understanding of how MainStreet offered Ararat something different that could be applied immediately to benefit his local community.

The Ararat Online project would include a range of elements with more than 80 businesses and community groups to benefit directly from an upgrade of their Web presence. They would also be given the opportunity to undertake training so that each organization would gain the skills to manage their own site. A further opportunity would be available for six businesses through an e-commerce mentoring program. Selected businesses would be assisted in the implementation of electronic commerce initiatives developed to match their particular business needs.

The value derived from the Ararat Online project was substantial. First, although the project did not represent a significant 'bottom-line' contribution in the context of the overall project budget, the investment of AUD 8,000 in a regional electronic commerce context represented a significant buy-in for the MainStreet product. Second, the Ararat Online project provided an opportunity to showcase the full product suite, its technical capabilities, the Web products, and the training and consulting services. Third, the project would help to address one of the early barriers: people in the target region had a very limited understanding of what a portal was. The Ararat Online project would provide a 'real' example, which it was hoped could be used to demonstrate the value and benefits that were associated with the efficient linking of Internet-based information and services in an easily searchable form. In other words, the Ararat Online project would establish the first 'before' and 'after' images. This proved to be a very powerful marketing mechanism for the project.

The project's technical team, however, had their task doubled—they were now expected to build not one, but two portals, and to deliver these within very short periods. They were successful in developing a way to replicate the MainStreet functionality through Ararat Online (www.ararat.asn.au) and later through projects with the Birchip Cropping Group (www.bcg.org.au), Moorabool Shire (www.mconline.com.au), and Pyrenees Shire (www.pyreneesonline.com.au).

The original goal had been to establish Main-Street as the "point of first electronic contact for the region" (Thompson 1999, p. iv). The vision was that people would find MainStreet, and from there be able to search and access information about a particular region or locate services of a particular type. What, however, was now understood was that 'communities' were much more motivated if the functionality of MainStreet could be delivered with local Web addresses and branding. Information could then be filtered up to the MainStreet umbrella so that client communities could be either accessed directly or through MainStreet. While this turned the original concept

upside down, there was a strong indication that communities in the region were prepared to pay to both establish and maintain a service based on the 'replicable portal framework' developed through the MainStreet project.

FUTURE TRENDS

The MainStreet portal infrastructure and tools have since been replicated to suit a range of different clients, with this approach proving to be a very effective way of getting people actively engaged online. Appendix 1 contains a selection of URLs for clients including local governments, town-based communities, membership-based organizations, industry groups, and small and medium enterprises.

While a number of factors have been highlighted, the most successful and distinctive aspect has been the development of the replicable portal framework. It has been this capability that has been leveraged to cause increase in 'buy-in', participation, and ongoing investment in regional Web-based services. Members of 'geographic communities' and 'communities of interest' are able to work with CECC to design and implement sophisticated Web-based services, customized to meet their specific communication, promotional, and/or electronic commerce needs. Through this university/community partnership, initiatives are then sustained by putting community members in charge of the management of their online community. Local ownership and the sustainability of infrastructure and technical support services have been achieved by effectively aggregating regional demand for portal services.

The MainStreet project has made a significant contribution to the advancement of ICT and electronic commerce uptake in the Central Highlands and Wimmera regions of Victoria. Many individuals and communities have been assisted in advancing their uptake of electronic commerce as they update their community sites, publish event information and news items, or show others how to build simple Web sites. The level of functionality and services accessed is high and, because clients have strong ownership of their online activities, maintain their own Web-based information, and are committed to annually investing to maintain the portal infrastructure and services, the services can continue to be delivered after the initial seed funding period.

The MainStreet project has also supported and encouraged a staged uptake of electronic commerce, with a number of organizational clients becoming increasingly confident in both selecting and investing in electronic commerce solutions.

Services have also been customized to meet the needs of small groups such as Birchip Cropping Group, and also larger communities such as Moorabool, Ararat, and the Pyrenees Shire regions. This has overcome a barrier where under most models, the costs to establish (and sustain) a local portal have been substantial, and therefore prohibitive for small towns and community groups.

CONCLUSION

Through the MainStreet project, regional and rural communities have a greater ability to build on local strengths and capitalize on the opportunities that are provided by electronic commerce and ICT. Communities, however, just like businesses, require assistance in identifying the most appropriate online service for their particular circumstances. Policies that encourage communities to enter collaborative partnerships, and which leverage existing infrastructure, knowledge and learning, should thus be seen as preferable to the funding or establishment of discrete or stand-alone initiatives. Well-developed and well-implemented online services can make a positive contribution to the future of regional and rural communities. Case studies such as the one presented in this article

are effective in illustrating the impacts, influences, and challenges that can be experienced in operationalizing and sustaining online communities in a regional and rural context.

ACKNOWLEDGMENT

The author acknowledges Brian West from the University of Ballarat who has been generous in the provision of advice and encouragement that greatly assisted in the preparation of this work.

REFERENCES

Ashford, M. (1999). Online WA: A trickle-up approach to using communications to enhance regional economic and social development. *Proceedings of the Regional Australia Summit,* Canberra, Australia.

Bernal, V. (2000, November). *Building online communities: Transforming assumptions into success.* Retrieved from *benton.org/Practice/ Community/assumptions.html.*

Brumby, H. J. (2001). Connecting communities: A framework for using technology to create and strengthen communities. State Government of Victoria, Melbourne.

Department of Communications Information Technology and the Arts. (2000). Taking the plunge: Sink or swim? Small business attitudes to electronic commerce. Commonwealth of Australia, Canberra.

Department of Communications Information Technology and the Arts. (2001). Funding priorities and principles, networking the nation, the commonwealth government's regional telecommunications infrastructure fund. Commonwealth of Australia, Canberra.

Gronlund, A. (2001). Building an infrastructure to manage electronic services. In S. Dasgupta (Ed.), Managing Internet and intranet technologies in organizations: Challenges and opportunities. Hershey, PA: Idea Group Publishing.

Hunter, A. (1999). Opportunities through communications technology for regional Australia. *Proceedings of the Regional Australia Summit,* Canberra.

Keeble, L., & Loader, B. D. (2001). Challenging the digital divide: A preliminary review of online community support. CIRA, University of Teesside, UK.

Local Government Association of Tasmania and Trinitas Pty Ltd. (2001). Online service delivery strategy paper—gaining the maximum benefit for our communities from the local government fund. Local Government Association of Tasmania, Hobart.

McGrath, M., & More, E. (2002). Forging and managing online collaboration: The ITOL experience. National Office for the Information Economy and Macquarie University, Canberra, Australia.

More, E., & McGrath, M. (2003). Organizational collaboration in an e-commerce context: Australia's ITOL project. *The E-Business Review, III,* 121–123.

Multimedia Victoria. (2002). Connecting Victoria: A progress report 1999-2002. State Government of Victoria, Melbourne.

Municipal Association of Victoria and ETC Electronic Trading Concepts Pty Ltd. (2000). Local government—integrated online service delivery strategy and implementation plan, executive summary—final. Municipal Association of Victoria, Melbourne.

National Office for the Information Economy. (2001). B2B e-commerce: Capturing value online. Commonwealth of Australia, Canberra.

National Office for the Information Economy. (2002). The benefits of doing business electronically—e-business. Commonwealth of Australia, Canberra.

National Office for the Information Economy. (2002). Guide to successful e-business collaboration. Commonwealth of Australia, Canberra.

Papandrea, F., & Wade, M. (2000). E-commerce in rural areas—case studies. Rural Industries Research and Development Corporation, Canberra.

Pattulock, E. & Albury Wodonga Area Consultative Committee. (2000). *Facilitation of e-commerce and Internet use by regional SMEs.* Albury Wodonga, La Trobe University, Australia.

Porter, M. E. (2001). *Strategy after the Net. BOSS,* (April), 17-23.

Preece, J. (2000). Online communities: Designing usability, supporting sociability. Chichester, UK: John Wiley & Sons.

Rheingold, H. (1994). A slice of life in my virtual community. In L.M. Harasim (Ed.), Global networks: Computers and international communication (pp. 57-80). Cambridge, MA: MIT Press.

Simpson, L. (2002). Big questions for community informatics initiatives: A social capital perspective. *Search Conference: Community and Information Technology The Big Questions,* Centre for Community Networking Research, Monash University, Melbourne, Australia.

Simpson, R. (1999). Brave new regions. *Proceedings of the Regional Australia Summit,* Canberra, Australia.

Telstra Country Wide. (2002). Our community online. Letter and brochure distributed to local government conference delegates, 31 October 2002, Telstra Corporation Limited.

Thompson, H. (1999). Victoria's Golden West portal project business case. Centre for Electronic Commerce and Communications, University of Ballarat, Australia.

KEY TERMS AND DEFINITIONS

'Bottom-Up' Approach: Development approach founded upon the principle that communities are better placed to coordinate and integrate efforts at the local level.

Study: The intensive examination of a single instance of a phenomenon or where one or just a few cases are intensively examined using a variety of data-gathering techniques.

Community Informatics: A multidisciplinary field for the investigation of the social and cultural factors shaping the development and diffusion of new ICT and its effects upon community development, regeneration, and sustainability.

Community Portal: Online initiative often developed through participative processes which aims to achieve better coordination of relevant Web-based information and provide communication services for community members.

Regional Development: The act, process, or result of actions to grow, expand, or bring a regional place to a more advanced or effective state.

Web Portal: Focal points on the Web which provide a place to start. Web portals facilitate the location of information by incorporating the strengths of search engines and additionally provide more efficient access to information by categorizing it into easily recognizable subcategories or channels.

APPENDIX 1

University of Ballarat URL University of Ballarat www.ballarat.edu.au

CECC www.cecc.com.au

MainStreet portal URL

Mainstreet.net.au www.mainstreet.net.au

Geographical portal URLs examples

Ararat Online www.ararat.asn.au

Moorabool Online www.mconline.com.au

Pyrenees Online www.pyreneesonline.com.au

Membership based communities URLs examples

Birchip Cropping Group www.bcg.org.au

Young Australian Rural Network www.yarn.gov.au

Rural Regional Research Network www.cecc.com.au/rrrn

Pyrenees Hay Processors www.exporthay.com.au

Comprehensive Web site URLs examples

Ballarat A Learning City www.ballaratlearningcity.com.au

Central Highlands Area Consultative Committee www.chacc.com.au

Pyrenees Shire www.pyrenees.vic.gov.au

Regional Connectivity Project www.regionalconnectivity.org

Chapter 5.5
Electronic Intermediaries Managing and Orchestrating Organizational Networks Using E-Services

Marijn Janssen
Delft University of Technology, The Netherlands

ABSTRACT

Organizations increasingly cooperate in organizational networks. Electronic intermediaries can provide all kinds of e-services to support the creation and management of such networks. While there has been substantial discussion on intermediaries matching demand and supply, there has been little analysis in relation to the management and orchestration of organizational networks. In this article we analyze an intermediary that uses e-services for orchestrating a network in the consumer electronics industry. The empirical results show that the coordination and management of networks requires specific expertise and skills which result in the rise of intermediary specialized in orchestrating such organizational networks. The primary value creation activity of the intermediary is leveraging the products, activities and knowledge of the specialized companies and providing e-services for orchestrating the organizational network to create short lead times, improve customer responsiveness and ensure adaptability.

INTRODUCTION

Organizations increasingly find that they must rely on effective supply chains formed in networks, to successfully compete in the global market and networked economy (Hagel-III, Durchslag, & Brown, 2002). During the past decades, globalization, outsourcing and all kinds of information and communication technology have enabled many organizations to successfully operate solid collaborative networks in which each specialized business partner focuses on only a few key strategic activities.

From a system's point of view, a complex network structure can be decomposed into individual components and firms that have to be coordinated (Fan, Stallaert, & Whinston, 2003). In such a network complimentary resources exist in a number of cooperating and sometimes competing companies. One of the main advantages for companies cooperating in a network is the ability to deliver products by selecting the resources and appropriate companies who are able to deliver these service elements (Provan & Milward, 1995). The aim of networks is to provide a range of products, which a single organization is not able to offer.

Such a network needs to be coordinated that can be done by using of all kinds of e-services. E-services are services that are produced, provided and/or consumed through the use of ICT-networks and also includes e-services for supporting the purchasing and delivery of physical goods (Scupola, 2008). Such e-services are provided and used by various organizations in a network to coordinate their interdependent activities. The larger the number of companies the more complex becomes the management of organizational networks. Furthermore the coordination overhead increases the friction costs. To satisfy and respond quickly to customer demand, effective management is necessary to strengthen the competitiveness of the network.

It is often predicted that by using the Internet the number of traditional intermediaries will be reduced (Gellman, 1996; Malone, Yates, & Benjamin, 1987) and new types of electronic intermediaries will come into existence (Del Aguila-Obra, Padilla-Melendex, & Serarols-Tarres, 2007; Janssen & Verbraeck, 2005; Sarkar, Butler, & Steinfield, 1995). Recently it is suggested that intermediaries have evolved from being merely matchmakers to providers of a set of e-services (Bhargava & Choudhary, 2004; Wise & Morrison, 2000). Bhargava and Choudhary investigated information intermediaries and Wise and Morrison analyzed intermediaries in business exchanges. In

this research we focus on intermediaries providing e-services to manage organizational networks.

Although there is much research in the field of intermediaries operating electronic markets and involved in matching supply and demand there is little work analyzing the range of e-services provided by intermediaries in the management and orchestration of organizational networks. We opted for case study research to analyze how and why e-services are used. Case study research is well-suited for investigating a contemporary phenomenon in its natural setting, especially when boundaries between phenomenon and context are not clearly evident (Yin, 1989) and answering 'how and 'why' questions (Checkland, 1981). This paper explores the concept of orchestrating intermediaries and demonstrates the potential by analyzing a case study in the consumer electronics industry. In the following section an overview of the relevant, state-of-the-art theoretical frameworks around intermediaries is provided. Based on these theories a case study is analyzed and discussed in section. Next, the findings are discussed in the light of these theories. Finally, conclusions and recommendations are drawn.

THEORETICAL BACKGROUND

Intermediaries

The organizational network setting can be described using three main types of players, which can be labeled as intermediary, service provider and service requester. *Service providers* can be all kind specialized organization involved in the delivery of a physical product or service. This implies that also manufacturing and assembling companies are viewed as service providers, as they provide a set of services that result in the production and delivery of a product. *Service requesters* are the consumers who buy the product or services. An intermediary can be defined as an autonomous organization aimed at bringing together demand and supply (Bailey & Bakos, 1997). This definition primarily emphasizes the market role of intermediaries. We consider intermediaries aimed at creating and coordinating networks of competing and cooperating service providers to fulfill the demand of service requesters. Malone and Crowston (1994) define *coordination* as managing the dependencies between activities. Based on coordination theory, we follow Janssen and Verbraeck (2005) and define intermediaries as organizations supporting the coordination of the activities of companies cooperating in a networks to connect to consumers.

In a general sense, there are two possible ways to coordinate between service provider and requesters: bilateral or intermediated contact. This is too simplistic, as in reality an almost infinite number of structures are possible. Figure 1 shows three possibilities. Intermediaries might only facilitate a market transaction and not being involved in the actual transaction or transfer of (physical) products (e.g. Garbade, 1982). Furthermore, even more than one intermediary might be involved in the process, as each intermediary might provide different added value services (e.g. Del Aguila-Obra, Padilla-Melendex, & Serarols-Tarres, 2007).

The literature on electronic intermediaries is related to the *electronic brokerage effect* as mentioned in electronic market theory (Bakos, 1991; Malone, Yates, & Benjamin, 1987). The *electronic brokerage effect* is the prediction that the use of electronic markets would result in the bypassing of intermediaries who previously matched buyers and sellers. This theory has triggered researchers to responses and new theories have been developed which have lead to a shift in focus in thinking about electronic intermediaries.

Institutional theories, especially transaction cost theory, have been used to make predictions about the need for intermediaries (Malone, Yates, & Benjamin, 1987; Sarkar, Butler, & Steinfield, 1995). They are often criticized for not taken into account aspects like, trust, relationships, complexity of product, the need for information collecting and processing resources and specialized knowledge. Aspects that buyers or sellers want to or can manage directly. Moreover, intermediary mechanisms depend on the situational characteristics and circumstances (Janssen & Verbraeck, 2005). As such, there is a need for more explorative and in depth research which takes the situation and circumstances into account.

Figure 1. Levels of intermediation

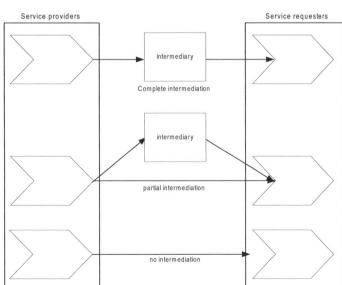

A continuing discussion is going on about the added value of intermediaries and the re- and disintermediation of these intermediaries (Chircu & Kauffman, 1999; Janssen & Sol, 2000; Janssen & Verbraeck, 2005; Malone, Yates, & Benjamin, 1987). Cybermediaries (Sarkar, Butler, & Steinfield, 1995) or electronic intermediaries (Janssen & Verbraeck, 2005) can introduce new complexities to the supply chain. The current status of this discussion is that new roles for electronic intermediaries are coming into existence (e.g. Sarkar, Butler, & Steinfield, 1995). Yet the functions and e-services provided by intermediaries in the future are currently only roughly known, as these kinds of e-services are still in their infancy, and the first type of intermediaries, that provide these services, is now arising (Österle, Fleisch, & Alt, 2000). Therefore, we wanted to investigate intermediaries providing e-services to manage and orchestrate organizational networks.

Holland and Lockett (1997) found that the roles of electronic intermediaries are dependent on organization strategies. Furthermore, intermediation, disintermediation and reintermediation (IDR) are dependent on the life cycle of an industry, and the strategies and the assets of players (Chircu & Kauffman, 1999). It is important to analyze at value chain levels instead of market level (Chircu & Kauffman, 1999). No single variable-based theory, even if intuitively appealing, will successfully predict all events in a phenomenon as complex as the structure of markets (Hess & Kemerer, 1994). Therefore case study research is necessary to investigate one intermediary in detail including the provided e-services.

E-Services

In the preceding parts we argued the rise of intermediaries using e-services to completely or partly intermediate between service requesters and providers. E-services are produced, provided and/or consumed through the use of ICT-networks (Scupola, 2008). An intermediary can play a relatively inactive role by merely providing services, such as secure connections, and leaving the management to others. On the other hand they can play an active role by not only providing facilitating services, but also actively managing the interactions.

E-service definitions emphasize a simultaneous or near-simultaneous exchange of production and consumption, transformation in the experience and value that customers receive from engagement with providers, (Rai & Sambamurthy, 2006). Grönroos (2001) identified three basic characteristics of services 1) services are processed consisting of activities or a series of activities rather than things, 2) services are at least to some extent produced and consumed simultaneously, and 3) the customer participants in the service delivery process. E-services are customer specific and this challenges the standardization of delivery processes and the economies of scale. Additionally, services cannot be inventoried, because the co-production of services requires a high degree of interaction between customers and many service providers.

Spulber (1996) found that intermediaries can provide a whole range of services, including price setting, clearing, matching, searching, inventory management, liquidity, immediacy, quality guarantees and monitoring. Kalakota and Whiston (1996) found that an intermediary can perform the following tasks: (1) processing and retrieving information, (2) searching, filtering, and summarizing large volumes of data, (3) translating or passing on information requests (4) maintaining information directories and (5) monitoring usage patterns and information changes. Bailey and Bakos (1997) analyzed a number of case studies and identified four roles of intermediaries including information aggregating, providing trust, facilitating and matching. Janssen (2005) found that an intermediary or broker can decouple and aggregate supply and demand. The intermediary seeks to balance between optimizing the whole supply chain and taking the self-interest of actors into account. Recently, Del Aguila-Obra, Padilla-Melendex and Serarols-Tarres (2007) investigated infomediaries in the digital, online news industry and found that new Internet intermediaries have appeared aggregating demand and supply in this industry. All these researches take the demand and supply aspect as central to the role of intermediaries. There has been little analysis in relation to the use of e-services for the management and orchestration of organizational networks.

The activities of an intermediary managing and orchestrating organizational networks can systematically be derived by taking a life-cycle view on the service delivery process. In general, an intermediary orchestrating a network performs the following main process phases, in which each phase e-services can be provided.

1. *Service Selection*: the appropriate services provided by service providers need to be determined to fulfill a customer need. Often a service catalogue will be needed. E-services in this phase include searching and browsing products, selecting products based on multiple criteria and product ordering;
2. *Network Configuration*: Number and location of service providers like suppliers, production facilities, distribution centers, warehouses and customers need to be selected. In this phase e-services include asking for availability of products and production capacity, negotiating prices, lead-times and other attributes;
3. *Service delivery strategy*: How the service will be delivered to the consumer. In this phase e-services for finding and ordering transport capacity are used.
4. *Tracking and tracing*: Integrate systems and processes through the supply chain to monitor the status and take appropriate measure if necessary. E-services are necessary for sharing valuable information, including demand signals, forecasts, monitoring, inventory and transportation and prioritizing of orders.

5. *Settlement*. The financial settlement by making use of billing and payment e-services.
6. *After-sales service*. Checking and evaluation of the performance of the network in order to continuously improve and adapt to changing circumstances. This includes e-services for surveying customer satisfaction and the handling of complaints.

There has been little analysis of intermediaries in relation to the management and orchestration of organizational networks and the type of e-services offered by intermediaries are changing. Due to the complexity and dependency among many factors, case study research was chosen to investigate the changing roles of intermediaries.

RESEARCH APPROACH

Different types of theory exist in information systems research that all can potentially be valuable (Gregor, 2006). Gregor (2006) makes a distinction between theories for 1) analysis, 2) explanation, 3) predication, 4) explanation and prediction and 5) design and action. Our aim is to analyze for design and action purposes which is labeled as design science (e.g. Hevner, March, Park, & Ram, 2004). The selection of research instruments depends on the amount of existing theory available, the type and complexity of the problem under study and on the research objective or questions. Although some theory available, the theory concerning e-services and intermediaries orchestrating organizational networks is scarce and there is a need for in-depth investigation of an orchestration intermediary from multiple views. Dunn (1981) provides an overview of the characteristics of well-structured, moderately structured, and ill-structured problems by considering variation in their common elements. Our domain under study is an ill-structured problem as we have to deal with (1) many decision-makers, (2) they might have opposing perspectives, (3) there are many alternatives and (4) the effectiveness and/or the efficiency of the courses of actions cannot be evaluated using only numerical data. According to Yin (1989) case study research is most appropriate in scenarios where the research is exploratory in nature and focuses on contemporary events that occur beyond control of the investigator. Therefore, a qualitative approach based on a case study research was adopted for this research.

Case study research can be characterized as qualitative and observatory, using predefined research questions (Yin, 1989). The case study research methodology is particularly well-suited to information systems (IS) research, since the object of the discipline is the study of IS in organizations (Benbasat, Goldstein, & Mead, 1987). The case study analysis was based on semi-structured interviews with nine representatives representing service requesters, providers and intermediaries. Two interviewees represented the intermediaries and both line managers as administrative staff of the organizations interacting with the intermediaries were interviewed. All the interviews lasted between one and two hours. These interviews were geographically limited to one country, whereas the network is operated on a world scale. In addition five phone interviews were held with interviewees outside the border lasting between 20 and 40 minutes.

Single case study research is often criticized for its limited generalizability, the possibility for researcher bias and its tendency to be open to different interpretations by different researchers (King & Applegate, 1997). The use of multiple research instruments is often encouraged to overcome these limitations (Yin, 1989). Multiple instruments enable a researcher to compare and contrast the analyses derived from using different research instruments. Using a variety of research instruments can cancel the pitfalls and problems encountered with individual instruments and a richer and more objective picture of the research object can be created. Therefore documents relating to the history, the set up and operation of

the intermediary were gathered and examined in order to acquire a good understanding of the operational, technical, management and organizational aspects as well as issues and problems faced during the operation. The researcher was requested to keep the name and products of the company confidential; therefore, the intermediary under study will be denoted as Consumer Electronics Company (CEC).

CASE STUDY: CONSUMER ELECTRONICS COMPANY

Background

CEC is an international company divided into a large number the business units and sells over a thousand different products. This company was founded as a manufacturing company. In the eighties and nineties the production was shifted to countries with low wages and over time more and more of the production units were sold and some were outsourced. In the late nineties it was decided that marketing, research and development and managing the supply chain would become their core business and many of the manufacturing business units were sold.

We investigated only one product line, in which the company solely performed the role of intermediary by orchestrating the demand and supply of products. In this segment the demand for innovation, flexibility, and a shorter time-to-market for new products and the desire to create new revenue sources has led to rethinking the company's activities. CEC played only an intermediary role, as they were not directly involved in the physical production and distribution of the product. CEC's main goal in this product line is defined as the effective management and coordination of the production network by making use of e-services.

Intermediary Position

The intermediary aims at fulfilling customer demand by selecting and evaluating appropriate business partners and creating a customer-driven chain of activities by orchestrating the activities in a particular sequence. This is not simple, as each organization in the network has different expertise, budgets, resources and capabilities. Moreover, most of the organizations are part of more than one chain and other companies claim and make use of their scarce resources. In periods with economic growth, there is a competition for acquiring access to the scarce resources of each company, whereas in economic decline there is a surplus of resources.

Figure 2 provides a schematic overview of the end-to-end supply chain and the position of CEC. The bold arrows depict physical flows, whereas the dotted arrows represent all kinds of information and control flows. This often involves complex interactions in which a number of e-services are used. Dealers sell their products to the customers and place their orders at the intermediary. Moreover, they are periodically involved in demand forecasting and discussions about new product releases. Dealers often have one or more shops and an Internet presence. Some of the dealers only have an internet presence. The dealer orders products at the intermediary who annually creates a product catalogue and can ask wholesalers to deliver products from their stock to the dealers.

CEC also takes care of selecting appropriate manufacturers and assemblers. Periodically the contracts are renegotiated based on the evaluation of their past performance. Several manufacturers produce parts of the products and there are two or three assemblers. A conscious strategy is to have at least 2 organizations in the network, who are able to perform the same type of tasks. In this way these organizations compete with each other to attract a larger amount of orders and are forced to continuously improve. Typically the best performing organization is allocated more than half of the orders and the worst performing organization is allocated a smaller amount. This allocation is dependent on the performance differential, the capacity available at the respective organizations and other circumstances. For example, the intermediary takes care that the worst performing organizations will not get bankrupt due to an abrupt decline in the number of orders, as this would ultimately weaken the position of CEC.

A number of transportation companies are involved as many of the products are manufactured overseas and need to be distributed to many geographically dispersed dealers. For overseas transportation long term contracts are used, whereas inland transportation company have shorter term contracts and are changed more frequently. In the terms introduced in the background part of this paper the service requesters are the dealers, CEC is the intermediary and the service providers are the manufacturing, assembling and transporting

Figure 2. Overview of the network

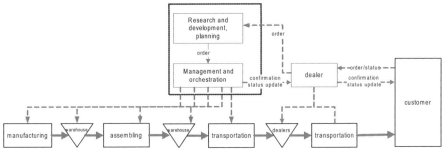

companies. The physical flow is going directly from one organization to another organization and there is no intermediation. Although a number of information flows concerning the operational process flow directly from one-organization to another organization most of the information flows are mediated by CEC. This enabled the intermediary to create an overview of the whole network, take appropriate actions if necessary, continuous evaluate the business partner and create new supply chains. For this purpose a pallet of e-service has been developed and is being used.

E-Services

CEC plays a number of roles and fulfills each role by providing e-services. Unified Modeling Language (UML) is a defacto standard for modeling software systems. UML Sequence Diagrams display the time sequence of the objects participating in the interaction (Fowler, 2000). In Figure 3 the ordering e-service is described in which actors are taken as the objects. This figure shows that a product order results in a quotations process which results in the selection of an assembling party and the ordering of transport. Next the status is tracked. Finally the assembler alerts the intermediary that the goods will be available at a certain date and time. The intermediary sends the detailed transport order instructions to arrange the transport from the assembler to the customer and get informed of status changes. All the interactions and the resulting e-services are well-defined and loosely coupled.

This example clearly shows the complexity of an e-service as many alternative sequences of activities are possible. Typical examples of variations are direct ordering for assembling without a quotation process, the involvement of manufacturers and the use of a quotation process for selecting a transportation company. Moreover, the boundaries of an e-service are not always clear and are dependent on the stakeholder under consideration. As the customer might consider

Figure 3. Interaction diagram for an e-order

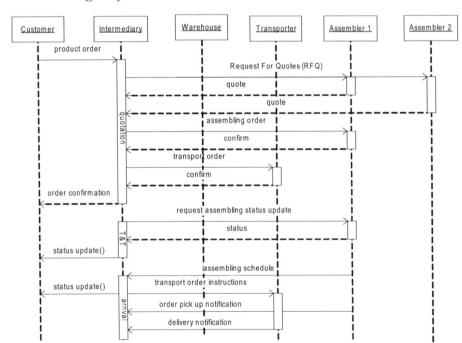

the product ordering process as an e-service, whereas the intermediaries might view this as a combination of several e-services, including quotation, assembling order and transport order services. The customer might consider the ordering e-service ended after the ordering confirmation or after the delivery of the physical products. For the intermediary the delivery notification of the transporter informs the intermediary that the product has been delivered at the customer and the financial settlement can start which requires billing and payment services. In summary, a high-granular e-service might consist of small granular services and what is viewed as an e-service is at least dependent o the stakeholder position.

Apart from the ordering e-services, the intermediary provides a number of e-services at the strategic, tactical and operational level. Table 1 depicts a systematic overview of the e-services as found in our case study. The services are aimed at

supporting the life-cycle phases. In the following paragraphs, we will briefly describe the roles using the facilitation, trusted, information aggregation and matching roles of Bailey and Bakos (1997).

The intermediary performs the *facilitating* role creating a platform supporting the interactions with all their business partners. The shared infrastructure makes it possible to connect to each other and the intermediary provides all kinds of e-services residing on top of this infrastructure to enable effective collaboration. Using this infrastructure the intermediaries supports the close integration with the systems of the business partners, and also provides web-based forms for enabling loosely coupled interactions.

The infrastructure is of vital importance for fulfilling the *trusted* role. The intermediary takes care of securing communication channels and ensures that data will not be lost. Moreover, privacy of companies should be ensured as competing

Table 1. Types of e-services

Level	Type of e-services
Strategic	• Strategic network optimization, including the number of service providers, location, knowledge, quality and reliability • Network evaluation and reporting • Product and service innovation • Development of IT facility and infrastructure, to support the organizational network • Select new network participants, access quality and risks • Align overall network strategy with the strategies of the individual participants • Forecasting of demand and need for new products
Tactical	• Negotiation of contracts, service levels and other decisions • Marketing and advertising • Comparison of prices and quality information • Product and network improvement • Workflow coordination (including tasks, quantity, location, quality, and frequency) • Mid-term forecasting • Evaluating of performance of trading partners and feedback • Billing and payment • Financial reporting • Adapting to changing circumstances
Operational	• Maintain catalogues containing products and their attributes • Maintain catalogues of service providers and their past performance • Daily orchestration of network activities • Sourcing and planning • Tracking and tracing of status • Progress reporting • Taking measure to ensure meeting of service levels required by customers

organizations are often involved in the network and these might benefit from gaining information on the other companies. One of the biggest risks is that information will become available to the wrong party. Moreover, the companies in the network are very afraid that this information might be used to lower prices.

The perceived independent or neutral position of the intermediary is crucial for fulfilling the trusted role. If their business partners get the feeling that the intermediary cannot be trusted or provide information to their competitors they are not likely to continue collaboration. A quote of one of the interviewees underlines this observation *"as soon as we got the feeling that they are biased and more orders go to our competitors without informing us and having clear arguments we will stop our partnership and seek for others".* As such the e-services creating a reliable and secure platform are essential.

A large number of e-services are available for collecting, processing and disseminating information, thus for fulfilling the *information aggregation role*. The intermediary provides e-services for ordering, tracking and tracing of orders, scheduling, and also collects additional data to evaluate the quality and performance of the supplies. This includes client information such as the number of sold products, returned products and the number of repairs necessary. The intermediary uses this system to collect, aggregate, process and disseminate information. The intermediary takes the responsible for overseeing the execution of orders from start to completion and for handling exceptional requests and complaints.

The *matching role* is fulfilled by selecting business partners and creating a unique chain of activities for each order. First, the partners are selected by looking at their past performance and schedule. E-services provide insight into the available resources and the utilization of the manufacturing and assembling capacity of the business partners. Second, the intermediary has the flexibility of invoking various sequences of

loosely coupled web services and in this way can creates a unique chain of activities for each product.

DISCUSSION AND EVALUATION

The Rise of Orchestration Intermediaries

Disintermediation of physical distribution elements in the network has brought about the advent of a new form of electronic intermediary, acting as a manager and orchestrator of the physical activities performed by other organizations using e-services through which delivery and reception of goods is realized. As a former manufacturing organization, the consumer electronic company had the necessary starting point for becoming the orchestrating intermediary of the network. One interviewee stated very strongly *"The reason why we became the spider in the web was that we had the expertise, the funding, knew the business partners and competitors and could even have produced it ourselves".* Later this high-ranked interviewee formulated it in relationship to the competitive environment *"luckily most of the business partners viewed us not as competitors .... they knew that it would be too expensive for us to do it ourselves.... they merely viewed us as a customer or as an additional sales channel".* Although on some aspects they were competing, especially in the field of research and development,

A traditional intermediary is an organization who is in contact with many potential buyers and suppliers and helps to match them (Malone, Yates, & Benjamin, 1987). Such an intermediary substantially reduces the need for buyers and suppliers to contact a large number of alternative partners individually. The electronic brokerage effect predicts that by electronically connecting many different buyers and suppliers an intermediary would not be necessarily anymore. The Internet allows a buyer to search and select suppliers by comparing offerings quickly and inexpensively (Malone, Yates, & Benjamin, 1987). In our case study of the consumer market we did not find this effect at all. The intermediary has expertise in selecting the best service providers and has all kind of tactical knowledge considering their past performance and quality that was used to select the service providers and orchestrate the supply chain. Another reason for not observing this effect might be that the types of products under consideration are not commodity goods but the products are rather difficult to understand and orchestration requires extensive product knowledge. This type of knowledge can also not be easily stored in a system or transferred. Although the electronic brokerage effect might be true for commodity markets, it does not apply to markets for complex, technological products. Therefore we expect that the electronic brokerage effect will not hold for non-commodity markets and we expect the rise of new types of intermediaries aimed at orchestrating and managing networks for producing and delivering non-commodities.

E-Services for Network Orchestration

The basis of the management and orchestration of the chain of activities in the organizational network are the e-services which we briefly described using the facilitation, trusted, information aggregation and matching roles and can be at the strategic, tactical and operational level. We extended the roles of Bailey and Bakos (1997) and found them generic enough to be used to classify a whole range of e-services provided by the intermediary. We did not decide to introduce a new role for describing the management and orchestration aspects, as most elements related to the management and orchestration are already covered by the four roles.

The strength of the four roles, the generality which makes them applicable for various situations, is also their weakness, as inevitably they

remain at an abstract level. The extension of the roles by looking at the strategic, tactical and operational level helps to acquire a better overview by capturing long, mid and short term aspects. Although the roles are suitable for describing all types of intermediaries, in contrast to market intermediaries other e-services were found when using these roles to orchestrating intermediaries. Thus, at a high abstraction level these roles might seem to be similar for intermediaries, whereas at a lower level of abstraction these roles can be completely different fulfilled. This pleas for more in-depth case studies within a certain domain and also for comparative case studies of different types of intermediaries, including market intermediaries, cybermediaries, infomediaries and orchestration intermediaries.

The process of network decomposition and integration is realized through the use of e-services aimed at integrating the efforts of the single business partners. The intermediary in our case study concentrates on performing mere business process management and orchestration activities and has given up performing traditional tasks. The intermediary composes and orchestrates different service providers which are specialized companies in their respective domain. The whole interaction is primarily based on loosely coupled and well-standardized e-services. New business partners can make use of these loosely coupled e-services to connect to the network. In some exceptional cases the systems are tightly integrated. The intermediary has created its own platform and e-services for dealing with these kinds of interaction fitting their own orchestration needs. This platform matches the complex product characteristics and helps to decompose the product into activities which can be performed by the service providers. The case study demonstrates the important role played by componentization and by service orientation in interorganizational networks. Componentization enables a business to operate in a network of partnerships with customers and suppliers supported by real-time information flows and information technology systems. All kinds and types of e-services are necessary to achieve seamless integration of business components.

Many of the activities are related to the orchestration of the organizational network, however, there are also many standalone e-services, for example financial reporting. As a result a differentiation between orchestration services and additional service can be made. The intermediary has a number of basic and specialized e-services. The basic e-services might be provided by other type of intermediaries, whereas, the specialized e-services might be typical for orchestration intermediaries.

Although intuitively it is clear what an e-services is, the formal description of an e-services is much more difficult. E-services are produced and consumed during the interactions among the participants and a pre-defined process flow cannot describe al the possible combinations. The boundaries of an e-service are not always clear and are dependent on the stakeholder under consideration and the outcomes of the interactions. The sequence diagram shown in figure 3 demonstrates that what is viewed as an e-service is at least dependent on the stakeholder position. Furthermore, e-services might be created by deploying other e-services; a high-granular e-service is constructed of small granular e-services.

The Added Value of the Orchestrating Intermediary

The creation of flexible, temporary arrangements results in the creation of business processes that are no longer self-contained within a single organization. The reliability of business processes depends more and more on the performance of external partners. Each organization has different strategic objectives, capabilities and resources available. Moreover, potential partners may have different processes and levels of IT sophistication that need to be synchronized before services can be shared. The dynamic nature of organizational

networks, for example, the changing number and/or types of partners, and the involvement in several networks increases the difficulty and complexity to understand the dependencies in the supply chain. One of the intermediary's main challenges is to understand the relation between demand and the challenges of coordinating the network. One interviewee stated that "*the basic of our added value is not only understanding the need of our customers and innovating products, but consist of understanding what is going on at our business partners, who in fact are also our customers*". Knowledge of the specialties of their business partners and their strengths and weakness are key to selection and creation of a new chain for producing a product. The intermediary's ability to integrate, build, and reconfigure the external resources to address changing needs is their key to success. The e-services help a firm to spot changes and adjust its resource mix and thereby maintaining the sustainability of the network. The intermediary needs knowledge of the companies to create new products and orchestrate the organizational network to create short lead time, improve customer responsiveness and ensure adaptability to changing circumstance. In this way the network profits from specialization (e.g. Clemons & Row, 1992). Each network member specializes in performing certain types of roles and activities. In turn, specialization in a network creates dependencies among participants that need to be orchestrated.

The use of orchestration intermediaries can improve the quality of the network as only the most suitable partners are selected for each service and duplication of efforts can be avoided. The intermediary creates an overview of the total network and ensures that activities are only performed once, at the best suitable service provider. In summary the main benefits of the use of intermediaries as mentioned by the interviewees are

- Creating an overview of the network and reacting to events and changing circumstances

- Knowledge of the business partners
- Continuous improvement of the network
- Reduction of friction costs by making use of specialized e-services
- Avoiding duplication of activities
- Ensuring information quality and availability
- Market and product knowledge

An intrinsic benefit of the intermediary is that it is an intermediary and is not tied to one of the organizations participating in the network. The perceived independent or neutral position of the intermediary is viewed as a condition and not as a benefit by the interviewees. CEC profits also from economies of scale and scope (e.g. Lee & Clark, 1997). Once they are developed CEC faces relatively small incremental costs if new participants make use of their e-services. Furthermore the technological and organizational resources and expertise acquired during the development and operation of in this product line is transferred to other products resulting in economies of scope.

CONCLUSION AND RECOMMENDATIONS

As the process of disintegration and reintegration of organizational networks continues, emerging intermediary players can play a crucial role in managing and orchestrating the network. Our case study demonstrates how a traditional intermediary performing all kinds of physical functions is reborn as an intermediary primarily performing managing and orchestrating activities. For this purposes the intermediary uses a large number of well-defined and loosely coupled e-services. Although transaction cost theory can be used to predict the disappearance of intermediaries, our case study shows that this prediction overlooks the reality that the orchestration of organizational networks requires the solving of complicated issues which needs all kinds of dedicated services. The coordination and management requires specialized expertise and skills which result in the rise of intermediaries orchestrating these networks.

Our in-depth case study shows that the main types of e-services can be described by extending the four roles of Bialy and Bakos (1997). The four roles are generic enough to support the analysis of e-services. The extension of the roles by looking at the strategic, tactical and operational level helps to acquire a better overview by capturing long, mid and short term aspects. Although the roles are suitable for describing intermediaries in general, e-services differ per type of intermediary. More in-depth studies into orchestrating intermediaries and comparative case studies among types of intermediaries are recommendations for further research.

In the case study the primary value creation activities of the intermediary are the leveraging of activities and knowledge of the specialized companies and orchestrating the organizational network to create short lead time, improve customer responsiveness and react to changing circumstances. The type of e-services might be dependent on market characteristics and conditions, product complexity and circumstances. More research is necessary in the type of e-services and the added value provided by intermediaries.

Since we have only looked at one case, albeit extensively, the findings can only be analytically generalized based on the distinguished characteristics (Yin, 1989). Our findings call for additional research in the field of e-services, to further analyze orchestrating intermediaries within different settings and to further statistically generalize the findings.

REFERENCES

Bailey, J. P., & Bakos, J. Y. (1997). An Exploratory Study of the Emerging Role of Electronic Intermediaries. *International Journal of Electronic Commerce, 1*(3), 7-20.

Bakos, J. Y. (1991). A Strategic Analysis of Electronic Marketplaces. *MIS Quarterly, 15*(3), 294-310.

Benbasat, I., Goldstein, D. K., & Mead, M. (1987). The Case Research Strategy in Studies of Information Systems. *MIS Quarterly, 11*(3), 369-386.

Bhargava, H. K., & Choudhary, V. (2004). Economics of an Information Intermediary with Aggregation Benefits. *Information Systems Research, 15*(1), 22-36.

Checkland, P. (1981). *Systems Thinking, Systems Practice.* Chichester: Wiley.

Chircu, A. M., & Kauffman, R. J. (1999). Strategies of Internet Middlemen in the Intermediation/Disintermedation/Reintermediation cycle. *Electronic Markets, 9*(2), 109-117.

Clemons, E. K., & Row, M. C. (1992). Information Technology and Industrial Cooperation: The Changing Economics of Coordination and Ownership. *Journal of Management Information Systems, 9*(2), 9-28.

Del Aguila-Obra, A. R., Padilla-Melendex, A., & Serarols-Tarres, C. (2007). Value creation and new intermediaries on Internet. AN exploratory analysis of the online news industry and the web content aggregators. *International Journal of Information Management, 27*, 187-199.

Dunn, W. N. (1981). *Public Policy Analysis.* Englewood Cliffs, New Jersey: Prentice-Hall.

Fan, M., Stallaert, J., & Whinston, A. B. (2003). Decentralized Mechanism Design for Supply Chain Organizations Using an Auction Market. *Information Systems Research, 14*(1), 1-22.

Fowler, M. (2000). *Distilled: A Brief Guide to the Standard Object Modeling Language*: Addison-Wesley Professional Series.

Garbade, K. (1982). *Securities Markets.* New York: McGraw-Hill.

Gellman, R. (1996). Disintermediation and the Internet. *Government Information Quarterly, 13*(1), 1-8.

Gregor, S. (2006). The nature of theory in information systems. *MIS Quarterly, 30*(3), 611-642.

Grönroos, C. (2001). *Service Management and Marketing: A customer relationship management approach.* Chichester: Wiley.

Hagel-III, J., Durchslag, S., & Brown, J. S. (2002). *Orchestrating Loosely Coupled Business Processes: The secret to successful business collaboration.* Unpublished manuscript.

Hess, C. M., & Kemerer, C. F. (1994). Computerized Loan Originating Systems: An industry case study of the electronic markets hypothesis. *MIS Quarterly, 18*(3), 251-274.

Hevner, A., March, S., Park, J., & Ram, S. (2004). Design scienc in information systems research. *MIS Quarterly, 28*(1), 75-105.

Holland, C. P., & Lockett, A. G. (1997). Mixed Mode Network Structures: The strategic use of electronic communication by organizations. *Organization Science, 8*(5), 475-488.

Janssen, M., & Sol, H. G. (2000). Evaluating the role of intermediaries in the electronic value chain. *Internet Research; Electronic Networking Applications and Policy, 19*(5), 406-417.

Janssen, M., & Verbraeck, A. (2005). Evaluating the Information Architecture of an Electronic Intermediary. *Journal of Organizational Computing and Electronic Commerce, 15*(1), 35-60.

Kalakota, R., & Whinston, A. B. (1996). *Frontiers of Electronic Commerce.* Reading, Massachusetts: Addison-Wesley.

King, J., & Applegate, L. (1997). The Crisis in the Case of Research Crisis. In J. DeGross, A. Lee & J. Lieberman (Eds.), *Information Systems and Qualitative Research.* London: Chapman and Hill.

Lee, H. G., & Clark, T. H. (1997). Market Process Reengineering through Electronic Market Systems: Opportunities and challenges. *Journal of Management Information Systems, 13*(3), 113-136.

Malone, T. W., & Crowston, K. (1994). The interdisciplinary study of coordination. *ACM Computing Surveys, 26*(2), 87-119.

Malone, T. W., Yates, J., & Benjamin, R. I. (1987). Electronic Markets and Electronic Hierarchies. *Communications of the ACM, 30*(6), 484-497.

Österle, H., Fleisch, E., & Alt, R. (2000). *Business Networking. Shaping enterprise relationships on the Internet*: Springer Verlag.

Provan, K. G., & Milward, H. B. (1995). A preliminary theory of network effectiveness: A comparative study of four community mental health systems. *Administrative Science Quarterly, 40*(1), 1-33.

Rai, A., & Sambamurthy, V. (2006). Growth and interest in service management. *Information Systems Research, 17*(4), 327-331.

Sarkar, M. B., Butler, B., & Steinfield, C. (1995). Intermediaries and Cybermediaries: A Continuing Role for Mediating Players in the Electronic Marketplace. *Journal of Computer Mediated Communication, 1*(3).

Scupola, A. (2008). Special Issue on e-services. *Journal of Electronic Commerce in Organizations (JECO)*.

Spulber, D. F. (1996). Market Microstructure and Intermediation. *Journal of Economic Perspectives, 10*(3), 135-152.

Wise, R., & Morrison, D. (2000). Beyond the exchange: the future of B2B. *Harvard Business Review, 78*(6), 86-89.

Yin, R. K. (1989). *Case Study Research: Design and methods*. Newbury Park, CA: Sage publications.

This work was previously published in the International Journal of E-Services and Mobile Applications, Volume 1, Issue 1, edited by A. Scupola, pp. 52-66, copyright 2009 by IGI Publishing (an imprint of IGI Global).

Chapter 5.6
Personalization Services for Online Collaboration and Learning

Christina E. Evangelou
Informatics and Telematics Institute, Greece

Manolis Tzagarakis
Research Academic Computer Technology Institute, Greece

Nikos Karousos
Research Academic Computer Technology Institute, Greece

George Gkotsis
Research Academic Computer Technology Institute, Greece

Dora Nousia
Research Academic Computer Technology Institute, Greece

ABSTRACT

Collaboration tools can be exploited as virtual spaces that satisfy the community members' needs to construct and refine their ideas, opinions, and thoughts in meaningful ways, in order to suc-cessfully assist individual and community learning. More specifically, collaboration tools when properly personalized can aid individuals to articulate their personal standpoints in such a way that can be proven useful for the rest of the community where they belong. Personalization services, when properly integrated to collaboration tools, can be an aide to the development of learning skills, to the interaction with other actors, as well as to the growth of the learners' autonomy and self-direction. This work pre-sents a framework of personalization services that has been developed to address the requirements for efficient and effective collaboration between online communities' members that can act as catalysts for individual and community learning.

DOI: 10.4018/978-1-60566-238-1.ch016

INTRODUCTION

Computer Supported Collaborative Work (CSCW) has long been the subject of interest for various disciplines and research fields. CSCW systems are collaborative environments that support dispersed working groups so as to improve quality and productivity (Eseryel *et al.*, 2002). Varying from stand alone applications to web-based solutions for the provision of communication, cooperation and coordination services, software tools supporting collaborative work -commonly referred to as *groupware*- provide individuals and organizations with support for group cooperation and task orientation, especially in distributed or networked settings (Ackerman *et al.* 2008). Such technologies have enhanced collaboration, affecting peoples' everyday working and learning practices. Furthermore, one of the CSCW discipline core aims has always been to assist individuals and organisations in knowledge sharing, whenever it is required and wherever it is located (Lipnack and Stamps, 1997). Nevertheless, research findings on the usage of collaboration tools show that support of group members in expressing personal ideas and opinions, and the provision with adequate means for the articulation and sharing of their knowledge is an extremely complicated and difficult task (Olson & Olson, 2000). Furthermore, it is generally acknowledged that traditional software approaches supporting collaboration are no longer sufficient to support contemporary communication and collaboration needs (Moor & Aakhus, 2006).

This work concerns the design of personalized web-based tools that enable collaborative work, emphasis given to aspects such as the sharing of knowledge and consequently to learning. We envisage collaboration tools that can promote learning and encourage creative, parallel and lateral thinking during collaboration. Towards this, we argue that personalized services can be of great value as they enable the provision of services tailored according to an individual's (or community's when applicable) skills, needs and preferences. Thus, we first performed a comprehensive literature and practice survey of related issues regarding Communities of Practice, Collaboration and Learning. Then, we developed a generic Learner Profile model to formalize CoP members as human actors in settings where learning takes place. The Learner Profile presented in this chapter contributes to the proper user modelling required for the development of virtual environments for collaboration.

The remainder of this chapter is structured as follows. Section 2 discusses issues related to online collaboration and learning. Section 3 provides an overview of user modelling issues and presents the Learner Profile model of our approach. Section 4 provides information about the acquisition of the data required for the population of the proposed Learner Profile. Section 5 presents the proposed set of personalized collaboration services towards learning and their relation to the proposed Learner Profile. Section 6 concludes with final remarks and future work directions.

ONLINE COLLABORATION AND LEARNING

The Internet is an artefact that emerged from people's need to communicate and share content that enables various kinds of web-based collaboration and virtual teamwork. Early online communities were mostly formed through the use of emailing lists, or bulletin boards. Today, the availability of *social software* applications has resulted in the phenomenal growth of user embodiment in virtual spaces and the constant emergence of online communities (Anderson, 2007). The notion of social software, i.e. software that supports group communications, is perceived as a particular type of software that concerns itself with the augmentation of human social and/or collaborative abilities. As clearly stated in (Boulos & Wheeler, 2007), the increased user contribution leads to the growth of "collective intelligence" and reusable dynamic content. It is a fact that most communities are formulated around some kind of a web-based interface that allows them to exchange their personal ideas, opinions and beliefs, such as blogs or multimedia content sharing applications. In this way, collaboration is facilitated by online communication spaces where individuals can develop a sense of belonging, usually through interacting with other users on topics of common interest. Also, as stated in (Baxter, 2007), in a focused community it is the member-generated content that adds stickiness to a site encouraging people to stay, participate and revisit.

As organizations start to acknowledge the significance of online communities in helping them meet their business needs and objectives, new efforts to better facilitate the processes of collaborative learning in these communities are constantly emerging (Quan-Haase, 2005). In this vein, online communities are considered as "knowledge networks", meaning institutionalized, informal networks of professionals managing domains of knowledge (Ardichvili *et al.*, 2003). Knowledge sharing and exchange is an ongoing process among community members. Knowledge sharing networks, established for the intra- and inter-organizational communities, act as a forum of reciprocal knowledge sharing among knowledge workers. An especially prized type of community, the so called *Community of Practice* (CoP), is formed by groups of people who share an interest in a domain of human endeavour and engage in a process of collective learning (Wenger, 1998). It is this very process of knowledge sharing that results to collective learning and creates bonds between them since such communities are formed by groups of people who are willing to share and elaborate further on their knowledge, in-sights and experiences (Wenger & Snyder, 2000). Being tied to and performed through practice, learning is considered of premium value by practitioners for improving their real working practices (Steeples & Goodyear, 1999).

Above and beyond learning situated in explicitly defined contexts, modern learning theories strongly support the value of communities and collaborative work as effective settings for learning (Hoadley & Kilner, 2005). Thus, collaboration is considered as an essential element for effective learning since it enables learners to better develop their points of view and refine their knowledge. On the other hand, learning is a major part of online communities' activities, one of the most significant roles undertaken by almost all community members is the role of a learner. Much of the work of finding, interpreting and connecting relevant pieces of information, negotiating meanings and eliciting knowledge in conversations with others, creating new ideas and using them to come up with a final product, happens in the head of a knowledge worker or as part of communication or doing work (Efimova 2004). *Situated learning* in particular, *i.e.* learning that normally occurs as the function of an activity, context and culture, is closely related to the social interactions in the community context. To become more specific, situated learning implies the exchange of a series of problem interpretations, interests, objectives, priorities and constraints, which may express alternative, fuzzily defined, or conflicting views. On the other hand, *collaborative learning* work refers to processes, methodologies and environments, where professionals engage in a common task and where individuals depend on and are accountable to each other. When speaking about collaborative learning, we espouse the Wenger's perspective of learning as a social phenomenon in the context of our lived experience of participation in the world (Wenger, 1998). As regards to it, an especially valued activity involves information exchanges in which information is constructed through addition, explanation, evaluation, transformation or summarising (Gray, 2004; Maudet & Moore, 1999).

USER MODELING TOWARDS LEARNING

User Modelling Systems

During the past two decades, various user-adaptive application systems have been developed influenced by the findings of user modelling research. It is a fact though, that in most of these early approaches, user modelling functionality was an integral part of the user-adaptive application. In most recent approaches, several systems were designed to provide personalized content to the users. These systems focused on the design of user profiles, where information about the user's preferences, interests was stored. On the other hand, and due to the rise of the Internet, during the past decade several research studies have conducted user modelling servers. User modelling servers have been developed aiming at operating in a web environment. *Personis* (Kay *et al.*, 2002) for instance, is a user model server focusing on issues like privacy, control and self-exploration. Personis is targeted at adaptive hypermedia applications and is influenced by the *um toolkit*, which follows component-based architecture. Another related approach is *Doppelgänger* (Orwant, 2005), a user modelling system that monitors user actions and detects patterns within these actions. The architecture of the system is based on the server-client paradigm. Client is being implemented through the use of sensors which gather the required information and forward it to the server for further analysis. Following this phase, applications gain access to the information produced from the server. Nevertheless these systems do not adequately model the user, since information system only store the user profile focusing solely on the presentation layer. In order for such systems to be more efficient towards providing personalized support to the users, design should keep in the epicentre of their interest the various user roles, so as to result in a user model which supports user activities and to has the ability of adaptation and self-improve during their lifetime.

Modelling Users as Learners

User models are an essential part of every adaptive system. In the following, we discuss design issues and we present the proposed learner profile model of our approach. The specification of this model is oriented to the development of the personalized services appropriate for learners and/or CoPs. Research findings about learners' modelling prove that due to the complexity of human actors and the diversity regarding the learning context, the development of a commonly accepted learner profile is a highly complex task (Dolog & Schäfer, 2005). For instance, the learner model proposed in (Chen & Mizoguchi, 1999) depicts a learner as a concept hierarchy, but it does not refer to issues such as the learning object, or the learners' interactions with their environment and other people. However, it provides both interesting information about a learner's cognitive characteristics and a representation of knowledge assessment issues. Another related approach, the "PAPI Learner" conceptual model, comprises preferences, performance, portfolio, and other types of information (PAPI, 2000). Yet, this model is too generic as its primary aim is to be portable in order to fit a wide range of applications, and it does not provide any information about a learner's profile dynamic aspects. The IMS Learner Information Package specification (IMS LIP, 2001) is a useful collection of information that addresses the interoperability of internet-based Learner Information Systems with other systems that support the Internet learning environment.

A Proposed Learner's Profile

The primary design aims of our approach in modelling users as learners were to achieve extensibility and adaptability of the user profile as well as the ability to exchange user information between the proposed personalized collaboration services and third party services. In this context, the proposed learner profile comprises both *computational* and *non-computational* information. Computational information comprises information such as the name, contact details, education, training, etc. of users, as well as information about the community they belong to. The non-computational information is calculated after the processing of the users' individual behaviour during their participation in system activities. This type of information comprises fields that can be defined during run-time, whenever a new requirement for a new kind of user information is raised. As regards the source of the information stored in the user model, this may derive from the user, the tool and third party applications. More specifically, fields that can be filled up by users constitute the user derived information (e.g. login name, password, address, etc.). In contrast, fields that are calculated and filled up by the tool are machine derived information (e.g. level of participation, average response time, etc.). Furthermore, some fields can be filled up both from the user and machine (preferences, resources, etc.). In addition, there can be fields that are calculated by external or third party tools (or applications). Although user and machine derived information can be easily gathered, third party tools have to be aware of the user profile and the communication means with the tool in order to interchange data of the user profile. For this purpose, the user profile template is available through an xml schema definition to third party requestors via web services. In the storage layer, user records are stored in a relational database and manipulated through SQL queries.

After the careful consideration of the above, we developed a generic Learner Profile (see Figure 1) that can be employed for the representation of both individuals and communities as learners (Vidou *et al.*, 2006). The proposed model can be employed for developing customized services for both individual and group learners. More specifically, the proposed Learner Profile consists of two types of information, namely static information and dynamic information in compliance with the computational and non-computational data presented in the above. Static information is con-

sidered as domain independent in our approach. The Learner Profile dynamic information elements were chosen to reflect one's individual behaviour during his participation in a specific CoP's collaboration activities. Thus, all four dynamic elements, i.e. *preferences*, *relations*, *competences* and *experience* are to be implicitly or explicitly defined through the learner's interaction with a tool supporting collaboration. *Preferences* regarding the use of resources and services provided by the tool, as well as *relations* among individuals, CoPs and learning items (e.g. argument, URL, or document) can reveal the learners' different personality types and learning styles. *Competences* refer to cognitive characteristics such as the creativity, reciprocity and social skills. *Experience* reflects learners' familiarity and know-how regarding a specific domain. It should be noted that all dynamic elements of the proposed Learner Profile can be of assistance towards learning. Nevertheless, the domain of the issue under consideration is a decisive factor. Thus, dynamic aspects of a learner's profile are treated as domain specific in our approach.

ACQUIRING THE LEARNER PROFILE DATA

In order to enable the operation of personalized collaboration services, the Learner Profile has to be populated with the appropriate data. Such data

Figure 1. The proposed learner profile

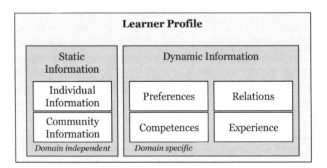

can be acquired in two ways: explicitly from the users' preferences, and implicitly based on the users' behaviour while using the system. Static information of the Learner Profile is explicitly provided by the user, as a required initialization step of the registration procedure. While such information is usually provided when registering to the system, users should be able to edit this set of profile information at any time. Such explicit data acquisition constitutes a subjective way of profiling, since it depends on the statements made by the user (e.g. experience level, competences etc.). Their subjective nature may influence personalization services in an unpredictable way (e.g. suggesting to a novice user a document that requires advanced domain knowledge because the user misjudged his experience or competence level). To cope with such issues, we are currently in the process of designing methods that assess explicitly stated profile data, based on the users' behaviour. We refer to these ways as implicit or behaviour-based data acquisition. In general, the aim of implicit or behaviour-based data acquisition is to assess experience, domains, competences of an individual user based on his behaviour. Implicit data acquisition utilizes the users' actions and interactions and attempts to extract information that can permit assessing or augmenting a user profile data.

A special part of the system's architecture is usually dedicated to support implicit data acquisition and interpretation. It consists of a number of modules, each of which is responsible for a particular task (see Figure 2). More specifically, the User Action and Tracking module is responsible for observing user actions and recording them in a specific repository of the infrastructure called the Action and Event Store. The Action and Event Store only maintains all actions and events that are useful for implicit user action analysis and does not interpret them in any way. Analysis and interpretation of the gathered data as well as triggering of the appropriate computations (i.e. system reactions) is the main responsibility of the Action Interpretation Engine. The Action Interpretation Engine analyses the available information in the Action and Event Store and triggers computations that either update accordingly the user profile or execute a particular action. The rule based interpretation engine can be configured using rules that are also stored within the infrastructure. A rule essentially specifies under which circumstances (i.e. the events and actions of a particular user in the store) an action is triggered. The rule based nature of the interpretation engine makes the engine itself extensible so that even more cases of implicit data acquisition and interpretation are able to be supported.

Based on the explicit or implicit data, explicit or implicit adaptation mechanisms can be supported within the collaboration tool. Explicit adaptation mechanisms refer to approaches where the tool adapts its services based on the explicitly stated characteristics or preferences of the user. Users are

Figure 2. Data acquisition and interpretation structure

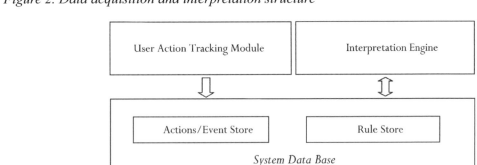

usually aware of explicit adaptations since they themselves triggered the initiation and presence of the respective services. On the other hand, implicit adaptation mechanisms refer to approaches that adapt the system's services to the user, based on his actions within it. Such mechanisms work in the background, thus users are usually unaware of the origin of these services since they did not explicitly initiate their activation and, thus, do not perceive their operation. Implicit personalization mechanisms are automatically triggered by the system utilizing implicit or behaviour-based data in the proposed learner profile.

In order to enable the foreseen functionalities (such as dynamic update of user information, adaptation of the tool according to the user needs, etc.), the most important actions of the entire set of users' actions should be tracked down. As regards the User Action Tracking Mechanism, the recorded data about user actions contain information about who did the action, when, what type of action was executed, and what objects were affected by the action. In this way, it will be possible for the system to give valuable feedback to other mechanisms so as to be able to both examine and calculate dynamic user characteristics. Moreover, a variety of statistical reports that cover both the overall and the specific views of usage of the system should also be produced.

Furthermore, a rule-based approach has been chosen so as to facilitate incorporation of new rules once they are observed or modification of existing ones if they prove to be too restrictive or even harmful. More specifically, we propose the development of a set of rules that deal with resource access, as access to resources are logged and a number of rules operate on the logged data to provide additional information to resources and/or user profiles. These can be based on the frequency of access, as well as the competence and experience levels of users (e.g. a document that is frequently accessed by novice users should augment the documents metadata with elements that mirror this fact, so that this document can

be recommended to any novice user entering a discussion). A second set of rules observing discussion contribution could control how user behaviour in the context of discussions will affect the users' competence and experience (e.g. users that actively and frequently participate can be assigned with a high experience level). Another useful indicator associated to the proposed learner profile is the reasoning about how a competence level of a particular user changes in time. This may provide useful insights about the learning capabilities of the particular user and the usefulness of the system.

THE PROPOSED FRAMEWORK OF PERSONALIZED SERVICES FOR COLLABORATION TOOLS

The establishment of a learner profile gives now the opportunity as the system level to design and implement new services or augment existing ones in collaboration tools with the aim to explicitly support the role of learners that users have during a collaboration. Personalization services are one of the crucial set of services in collaboration environments that can benefit greatly from the existence of the learner profile. In general, such services are important for collaboration environments since users vary greatly in terms of knowledge, training, experience, personality and cognitive style and hence personalization services permit the system to adapt various aspects to the needs of each individual user.

However, currently personalization services in collaboration tools take usually into account only general user defined preferences neglecting aspects related to the role of learner that users of such tools have. In this regard, the learner profile provides the necessary framework to fill this gap in personalization services of collaboration environments. In the following we present a set of services that be employed for enhancing software tools supporting collaboration towards learning.

The proposed set of services has resulted out of a thorough investigation of the related literature, existing case studies that consider diverse aspects of learning within communities, as well as a transversal analysis of a set of interviews with real CoP members engaged in various domains of practice. While the services presented in the next paragraphs can be found in existing collaboration environments and do not introduce a radical new set of functionalities, our emphasis is on how they can be recast and augmented in light of the proposed learner profile.

Awareness Services

According to the findings of our research, CoPs' members consider awareness services as amongst the most valued one for collaboration tools. As defined by Dourish and Belloti (1992) the term awareness denotes "an understanding of the activities of others, which provides a context for one's own activity" and over the years a number of different awareness types have emerged. These include informal awareness, presence awareness, task and social awareness, group, historical and workspace awareness.

Presence and participation awareness provides information about CoP members, on-line members as well as the discourse moves of individual CoP members. Users will be able to see which user is online, how the workspace changed by a particular member, etc. Social awareness provides information on how members are related to other members in the CoP and includes statistics about how and how many times members within a CoP communicate with each other and social networks representing the community. Based on the data populated in the Learner Profile, personalized services can provide the proper set of notification actions for the provision of helpful personalized information about system events to CoP members. For instance, a collaboration tool could alert users about the entrance of another user to the system, or about new content insertion into the system.

In order to enable the personalization of awareness services, terms such as "related" or "interesting" that define a relation between the user and the content should be determined by the user himself or automatically by the system through the manipulation of some characteristics from the user profile. Furthermore, awareness services can play an important role to assist the familiarization on the new learners of the system. By both informing the CoP moderator about the entrance of a new member and proposing some starting guidelines to the incomer, this service can assist the learning of the way of participation within a CoP. On the other hand, the awareness can provide the moderators with the activity monitoring service that helps the moderator to better understand and manage the whole CoPs' procedures. That, in turn, contributes to the process of learning the CoP's moderator role.

Awareness services can also be of use towards the self-evaluation of the participation of a community member, providing her/him with valuable feedback about his overall contribution to the community and assisting her/him in collaborative learning as well as in self reflecting. Using statistic reports populated according to the Learner Profile, such services can measure the level of the member's contribution to the collaboration procedure. More specifically, this kind of services can provide reports about the actual usage of the resources posted by a member, the citations of their resources, or the actual impact of posts to the overall process. In this way, one can be aware of the overall impression that other members have about his participation.

Presentation Services: Ranking, Filtering and Classifying

Presentation is another service that being personalized in collaboration tools can facilitate learning activities, especially for autonomous learners. The aim of personalizing the presentation services is to adapt the way the same set of resources is rendered to the each individual user. While the set of resources may be the same across users, their learning profile will determine how they will be presented to each individual one.

As regards to searching for instance, a Learner's Profile can provide useful information to rank search resources according to a number of factors, such as the learner's preferences, or even his competence and experience level. In this context, the system will be able to adapt to an individual user's needs. Moreover, the information about the user's domains of interest will provide additional information with which a search can be better contextualized, thus leading to more relevant results. Furthermore, reasoning mechanisms could be employed for providing the necessary filtering features for capturing and reusing the knowledge shared in past collaboration activities. Consequently, filtering and recommendation of content services can further support learning. For instance, some of the attached documents of posted positions that contribute to the strengthening of an argument should be suggested for view to the users according to their Learner Profile. Furthermore, a document library could recommend some documents that are related to a specific learner (e.g. experienced learner's recommendations or popular documents). Thus, members will be able to extend their knowledge through explicit learning of associated content.

Services for classifying other learners according to their domain of expertise can also assist learning in the community. Such services enable the community members to request for suggestion, find and communicate with their co-workers in a knowledgeable way. Furthermore, if coinciding with a community's norms and wills, such services could also be used for the assignment of weights regarding the weight of a member's arguments. In addition, services that keep tracking of the members' activity contribute to the procedure of learning by example, in which a member can learn during watching another one's practice in collaborative activities.

Visualization

It has been widely argued that visualization of collaboration conducted by a group of people working collaboratively towards solving a common problem can facilitate the overall process in many ways, such as in explicating and sharing individual representations of the problem, in maintaining focus on the overall process, as well as in maintaining consistency and in increasing plausibility and accuracy (Kirschner *et al.*, 2003; Evangelou *et al.*, 2006). Personalized representation of the associated processes, such as the process of discoursing or knowledge sharing, is an essential feature for tools providing effective environments for learning. Furthermore, personalized visualization of context should provide learners with a working environment that fits to their preferred visualization style. System personalization includes alterations in colours, fonts and text effects, enabling and disabling pieces of information in the working panel, predefinition of system responses in user actions etc. In this direction, taxonomies and classification schemes should be employed wherever possible, as a means for "guiding" users' cognition. In any case, it should be noted that there is no panacea for the design of user-friendly interfaces; the related practices should be interpreted, refined, and exploited according to the needs of the different types of learners involved in the particular environment. Appropriate navigation and help tools should be also provided for users with diverse expertise. Adaptive User Interfaces (AUI) should adapt themselves to the learner by reasoning about the user based on his Learner Profile.

Trust Building Services

Privacy policies and access control services are a critical requirement for the employment of all the above services, as well as for the building of trust between the CoP members and the software application. These should be provided in order to satisfy the learner/users' need to know what information about them is recorded, for what purposes, how long this information will be kept, and if this information is revealed to other people. Furthermore, the security assurance while establishing connections between users and services, or while accessing stored information, should be taken into consideration as well. Towards this end, two major techniques are broadly used to provide denial of access to data, i.e. anonymity and encryption. Anonymity cuts the relation between the particular user and the information about him, while information encryption provides protection of the exchanged personal data. In our approach, we employed the Platform for Privacy Preferences Project (P3P) approach, a W3C recommendation that supports the description of privacy policies in a standardized XML-based form, which can be automatically retrieved and interpreted by the user client (Cranor *et al.*, 2002).

Implementation Issues

According to current trends in developing web-based tools, for reasons such as the reusability of components and agility of services, our approach builds on top of a service oriented environment. In order to exploit advantages enabled by the Service Oriented Architecture (SOA) design paradigm, the proposed set of services should be based on web service architecture so as to enable the reusability of the implemented modules, as well as the integration or the interoperation with other services (from external systems). An overall design for the enhancement of tools supporting collaboration with personalized functionality towards learning is depicted in Figure 3. In this approach, we sketch a generic architecture design in which a Learner Profile Service is the basis for the storage and the provision of each learner's characteristics to a set of proposed services that contribute to the system's personalization. In order to support extensibility, the learning profile service can be dynamically augmented with new learners' characteristics during run-time. Furthermore, targeting to the

openness of the service, the service can provide the learner profile schema in the form of XML Schema Definition (XSD) in the service requestors. Considering the set of proposed services as non-exhaustive, our approach is open for the addition of new personalized services and can use the Simple Object Access Protocol (SOAP) for both internal and external communication.

CONCLUSION

Collaboration is considered as an essential element for effective learning since it enables learners to better develop their points of view and refine their knowledge. Our aim being to facilitate online communities' members as learners, we argue that collaboration tools should provide personalization features and functionalities in order to fit the specific individual and community learning requirements. In this chapter, we investigate collaboration and learning within such communities. Based on our findings, we propose a framework of services supporting personalization that being embedded in collaboration tools, can act as catalyst for individual and community learning. The proposed set of services has derived after the careful consideration of a generic learner profile, developed to formalize human actors in online settings where learning takes place. As a result of our work, we have concluded that personalized collaboration and learning services for online communities should strive for:

1. Transmission services that make tacit or explicit knowledge exploitable.
2. Exploitable storage services for both kind of information.
3. Training, personal support or programs that help in difficult moments such as decision making, handling complex information, designing a workflow, etc.
4. Enhancing the awareness of the collaboration's pattern.

In this chapter we presented a set of services enhancing CoPs interactions and collaborative work based on a generic Learner Profile model. Our approach concerns an alternative form of on-line learning with different forms of interaction, and a new way of promoting community building. Its purpose is to aid researchers and developers in the development of *personalized collaboration systems*, *i.e.* tools that adapt their structure and services to the individual user's characteristics and social behaviour. Our main goal being to support individual and community learning, the proposed set of services is based on personalized features and functionalities. We argue that it can further support learning, as well as the achievement of learning objectives, as it can assist communities' members in the development of learning skills such as the interaction with other actors, growth of their autonomy and self-direction. Nevertheless, in order to be creatively adapted in CoPs' everyday practices, the proposed services must fit into the specific culture, norms and incentive schemes of the community. Moreover, identification of communities' members' individual characteristics, as well as the culture, norms and incentive schemes of the community should be appropriately handled. Our future work directions concern the appropriate handling of these issues as well as the full development of the set of personalization services and its evaluation in diverse online communities.

ACKNOWLEDGMENT

Research carried out in the context of this chapter has been partially funded by the EU PALETTE (Pedagogically Sustained Adaptive Learning through the Exploitation of Tacit and Explicit Knowledge) Integrated Project (IST FP6-2004, Contract Number 028038).

REFERENCES

Ackerman, M. S. Halverson, C.A., Erickson, Th., & Kellogg, W.A. (Eds.) (2008). Resources, co-evolution and artifacts theory in CSCW. Springer Series: Computer Supported Cooperative Work.

Anderson, P. (2007). What is Web 2.0? Ideas, technologies and implications for education. *JISC TechWatch report*. Available at: http://www.jisc.ac.uk/whatwedo/services/services_techwatch/techwatch/techwatch_ic_reports2005_published.aspx (Last accessed on 18th February 2008)

Ardichvili, A., Page, V., & Wentling, T. (2003). Motivation and barriers to participation in online knowledge-sharing communities of practice. *Journal of Knowledge Management*, 7(1), 64–77. doi:10.1108/13673270310463626

Baxter, H. (2007). *An introduction to online communities*. Retrieved on 13/07/2007 from http://www.providersedge.com/docs/km_articles/An_Introduction_to_Online_Communities.pdf.

Boulos, M., & Wheeler, S. (2007). The emerging Web 2.0 social software: An enabling suite of sociable technologies in health and health care education. *Health Information and Libraries Journal*, 24, 2–23. doi:10.1111/j.1471-1842.2007.00701.x

Chen, W., & Mizoguchi, R. (1999). Communication content ontology for learner model agent in multi-agent architecture. In Prof. *AIED99 Workshop on Ontologies for Intelligent educational Systems*. Available on-line: http://www.ei.sanken.osaka-u.ac.jp/aied99/a-papers/W-Chen.pdf.

Cranor, L., Langheinrich, M., Marchiori, M., Presler-Marshall, M., & Reagle, J. (2002). The platform for privacy preferences 1.0 (P3P1.0) Specification. *World WideWeb Consortium (W3C)*. http://www. w3.org/TR/P3P/.

Dolog, P., & Schäfer, M. (2005). Learner modelling on the Semantic Web? *Workshop on Personalisation on the Semantic Web PerSWeb05*, July 24-30, Edinburgh, UK.

Dourish, P., & Bellotti, V. (1992). Awareness and coordination in shared workspaces. In proceedings of the *1992 ACM Conference on Computer-Supported Cooperative Work* (Toronto, Ontario, Canada, November 01 - 04, 1992.

Eseryel, D., Ganesan, R., & Edmonds, G. S. (2002). Review of computer-supported collaborative work systems. *Educational Technology & Society*, 5(2), 130–136.

Evangelou, C. E., Karacapilidis, N., & Tzagarakis, M. (2006). On the development of knowledge management services for collaborative decision making. *Journal of Computers*, 1(6), 19–28.

Gephart, M., Marsick, V., Van Buren, M., & Spiro, M. (1996, December). Learning organizations come alive. *Training & Development*, 50(12), 34–45.

Gray, B. (2004). Informal learning in an online community of practice. *Journal of Distance Education*, 19(1), 20–35.

Hoadley, C. M., & Kilner, P. G. (2005). Using technology to transform communities of practice into knowledge-building communities. *SIGGROUP Bulletin*, 25(1), 31–40.

IMS LIP. (2001). IMS learner information package specification. *The Global Learning Consortium*. Available on line: http://www.imsglobal.org/profiles/index.html

Kay, J., Kummerfeld, B., & Lauder, P. (2002). Personis: A server for user modelling. In Proceedings of the *2nd International Conference on Adaptive Hypermedia and Adaptive Web-Based Systems* (AH'2002), 201–212.

Kirschner, P., Buckingham-Shum, S., & Carr, C. (2003). Visualizing argumentation: Software tools for collaborative and educational sense-making. London: Springer Verlag.

Lipnack, J., & Stamps, J. (1997). Virtual teams. New York: John Wiley and Sons, Inc.

Marsick, V. J., & Watkins, K. E. (1999). Facilitating learning organizations: Making learning count. Aldershot, U.K. and Brookfield, VT: Gower.

Maudet, N., & Moore, D. J. (1999). Dialogue games for computer supported collaborative argumentation. In Proceedings of the *1st Workshop on Computer Supported Collaborative Argumentation* (CSCA99).

Moor, A., & Aakhus, M. (2006, March). Argumentation support: From technologies to tools. *Communications of the ACM, 49*(3), 93–98. doi:10.1145/1118178.1118182

Olson, G. M., & Olson, J. S. (2000). Distance matters. *Human-Computer Interaction, 15*, 139–178. doi:10.1207/S15327051HCI1523_4

Orwant, J. (2005). Heterogeneous learning in the doppelgänger UserModeling System. *User Modeling and User-Adapted Interaction*, 4(2), 107-130, 1995. Available online ftp://ftp.media.mit.edu/pub/orwant/doppelganger/learning. ps.gz, Last access June 21th, 2005).

PAPI. (2000). Draft Standard for Learning Technology —Public and Private Information (PAPI) for Learners (PAPI Learner). IEEE P1484.2/D7, 2000-11-28. Available on-line: http://edutool.com/papi

Quan-Haase, A. (2005). Trends in online learning communities. *SIGGROUP Bulletin*, 25(1), 1–6.

Steeples, C., & Goodyear, P. (1999). Enabling professional learning in distributed communities of practice: Descriptors for multimedia objects. *Journal of Network and Computer Applications*, 22, 133–145. doi:10.1006/jnca.1999.0087

Veerman, A. L., Andriessen, J. E., & Kanselaar, G. (1998). *Learning through computer-mediated collaborative argumentation.* Available on-line: http://eduweb.fsw.ruu.nl/arja/PhD2.html

Vidou, G., Dieng-Kuntz, R., El Ghali, A., Evangelou, C. E., Giboin, A., Jacquemart, S., & Tifous, A. (2006). Towards an ontology for knowledge management in communities of practice. In proceeding of the *6th International Conference on Practical Aspects of Knowledge Management*, (PAKM06), *30* Nov.-1 Dec. 2006, Vienna, Austria

Wenger, E. (1998). Communities of practice: Learning, meaning and identity. Cambridge University Press.

Wenger, E., & Snyder, W. (2000). Communities of practice: The organizational frontier. *Harvard Business Review, 78*, 139–145.

Chapter 5.7

Early User Involvement and Participation in Employee Self-Service Application Deployment:
Theory and Evidence from Four Dutch Governmental Cases

Gerwin Koopman
Syntess Software, The Netherlands

Ronald Batenburg
Utrecht University, The Netherlands

ABSTRACT

This chapter theoretically and empirically addresses the notion that user participation and involvement is one of the important factors for IS success. Different models and studies are reviewed to define and classify types of early end-user involvement and participation. Next, five case studies are presented of Dutch governmental organizations (Ministries) that have recently deployed an employee self-service application. Based on interviews with developers, project managers and users it can be showed that the deployment success of such systems is positively related to the extent of early user involvement and participation. In addition, it was found that expectancy management is important to keep users informed about certain deployment decisions. In this way, employees can truly use the self-service applications without much support from the HR-departments.

INTRODUCTION

In 2007, the Dutch House of Representatives asked the Dutch Government questions about their ICT-expenditures. Concerns were raised about how much money was wasted by governmental ICT projects that resulted in failures. The Dutch Court of Audit was instructed to come up with a report on governmental ICT projects and the possible reasons for failures. When the report (Dutch Court Audit, 2007) was finished, it named several difficulties that can be faced when executing ICT

DOI: 10.4018/978-1-60566-304-3.ch004

projects for governmental organisations. Among this list is the impact of the changes caused by the implementation of the IT-system. Users current way of working may be completely changed by changing work processes when the system is introduced. Users therefore need to be informed an trained to completely benefit from the system. Another cause for problems is the need for clear goals and demands. If the software developer does not receive clear demands and wishes, the actual end-product might not be what the government thought it would receive.

In both of the mentioned problems users play an important role in making the system a success. There is already a lot of agreement on the fact that users should be involved to produce usable software programs. It is recommended in ISO standard 13407 to get better insights in the requirements for a software application. Most attention to user involvement is still on the usability testing of systems, which happens on a later stage in the development process. However, the sooner the end-user is involved, the more efficient it is (Noyes et al, 1996; Chatzoglou & Macaulay, 1996; Blackburn et al, 2000).

One of the challenges in involving users in IT developments is the time factor that plays a very important role in governmental IT projects. Most of the decisions to implement or develop new Information Technology have a political background. This means the project will have to be delivered at the end of the current cabinet's term. This introduces a certain pressure for the project to be delivered as soon as possible. This conflicts with the idea that user involvement will take a serious amount of extra time needed in the development of a new system (Grudin, 1991). The systems that have the specific attention of this research on first sight also seem to conflict with this additional time needed in IT projects when involving users. Main reasons for implementing E-HRM systems and Shared Service Centres (SSC) are increasing efficiency and productivity (Verheijen, 2007; Janssen & Joha, 2006). For the current Dutch cabinet this is very important

because it wants to decrease the number of civil servants with a number of 12,800 to achieve a cost cutback of 630 million Euros in four years (Ministerie van Binnenlandse Zaken en Koninkrijksrelaties, 2007).

Another difficulty in the involvement of users is the selection of the right groups of employees to have participating in the project (Grudin, 1991). This is especially true for most governmental organisations, because they employ a large amount of civil servants. As the applications that are the subject of the research are mainly aimed at self-service these are all potential end-users. This is a very diverse group and it can be considered a challenge to make the right selection of users from this total population.

In this paper we address the question which methods are currently used within the Dutch governmental institutions to involve end-users when deploying employee self-service applications. We also investigate the relationship between end-user participation and involvement and the success of such e-HRM applications. Four Dutch governmental organizations (Ministries) are investigated that have implementing employee self-service applications (i.e. e-HRM), which offers the possibility to compare the different development approaches that are followed. Semi-structured and topic interviews were held with stakeholders within the Ministries to explore which methods are already used to involve users in the process of deployment. Their experiences are described and reflected upon at the closing section of the paper.

THEORY

A Review on the Role of User Participation

DeLone & McLean (2003) evaluated empirical testing and validation of their original D&M IS Success Model (DeLone & McLean, 1992) by other researchers and developed an updated

IS Success Model. An adaptation of this model is depicted in Figure 1. It is based on the three different levels of communication that were already defined by Shannon & Weaver (1949). The *technical* level is concerned with the physical information output of a system, and evaluated on accuracy and efficiency. The *semantic* level deals with the meaning of the output of a system, and specifically with how well the output conveys the intended meaning. The *effectiveness* level or *influence* level (Mason, 1978) concerns the effect of the information on the receiver.

The top layer of the model contains three different quality dimensions. The two dimensions at the left hand side of this layer are similar as in the original D&M model (DeLone & McLean, 1992). Terms to measure *information quality* were accuracy, timeliness, completeness, relevance and consistency. This concept and the terms thus measure success on the semantic level. For *system quality* these terms were ease-of-use, functionality, reliability, flexibility, data quality, portability, integration and performance. These measures are related tot the technical success level. The concept of service quality was added, because of the changing role or IS organisations, they more and more deliver services instead of only products.

The *use* concept in the model measures success on the effectiveness level. It is considered an important indicator for system success, especially

Figure 1. Adapted from D&M (Updated) IS success model (DeLone & McLean, 2003)

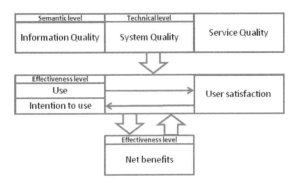

when it is "informed and effective" (DeLone & McLean, 2003). There are however some difficulties in the interpretation of the concept *use*. It has a lot of different aspects, for instance voluntariness and effectiveness. It therefore received critique in research of the original model. One example is that use is not a success variable in the case of mandatory systems. DeLone & McLean (2003) argue however, that no use is "totally mandatory" and that mandatory systems will be discontinued if they do not deliver the expected results. The differences are thus on the different levels: mandatory to use for employees, but voluntarily to terminate for management. Nevertheless, to overcome some of the difficulties, in the updated model a distinction is made between *intention to use* (attitude) and *use* (behaviour).

User satisfaction is considered a useful measure in evaluating the success of information systems (Ives, Olson, & Baroudi, 1983). In most cases this subjective judgment by users is considered to be more user practical, because of the difficulties in measuring the success of IS objectively (Saarinen, 1996; Lin & Shao, 2000). The *net benefits* concept is regarded as a set of IS impact measures, for instance work group impacts and organisational impacts. More specific measures are for instance quality of work, job performance and quality of work environment. To reduce the complexity of the model these are all grouped together, and which impact will be chosen will depend on the information system that is evaluated. These two concepts (user satisfaction and net benefits) measure success on the effectiveness level.

Lin & Shao (2000) investigated the relationship between user participation and system success. They found a significant relationship between both concepts, but warn that the context should be taken into account. Both user participation and system success can be directly and indirectly influenced by other factors. Based on the outcomes of their data analysis they also suggest that "getting users involved in the development process may improve their attitudes toward the system and enhance the importance and relevance users perceive about the system". Other findings were the positive influence of user attitudes on user involvement and the fact that users are asked more to participate when the complexity of systems increases.

In a survey of 200 production managers Baroudi et al, (1986) found positive correlations between user involvement and user information satisfaction and system usage. User involvement in this case was conceptualised as activities during the development that enabled the users to influence the development. Although, this is more towards user participation, it does not completely distinct the behaviour and psychological concepts. Interviewing users and developers from 151 projects, McKeen & Guimaraes (1997) found a positive and significant relationship between user participation and user satisfaction. They also noted that projects concerning systems or tasks with a high complexity called for more user participation.

To positively influence the success of new software applications, developers often turn to user involvement. According to Kujala (2003) user involvement can be seen as a general term and refers to Damodaran (1996) who suggests a continuum from informative to consultative to participative. However, some researchers suggest a difference between user involvement and user participation. User participation will then be the "assignments, activities, and behaviors that users or their representatives perform during the systems development process" (Barki & Hartwick, 1989). User involvement can be regarded as "a subjective psychological state reflecting the importance and personal relevance that a user attaches to a given system" (Barki & Hartwick, 1989). McKeen et al, (1994) in their research on contingency factors also describe the development of the division of these two concepts. The refined model is even further extended, in that user the relationship between user participation and system success is influenced by other moderating variables like the *degree of influence*, *attitude*, *communication* and *type of involvement*. In this study therefore the distinction between the two concepts *user participation* and *user involvement* will also be used.

Several researchers do not only recognize the link between user participation and system success, but even stress the importance of involving end-users in the development of software. Kensing & Blomberg (1998) state the participation of end-users is "seen as one of the preconditions for good design" (see also Shapiro, 2005). The workers have the information about the working environment and organisation, which designers logically do not always possess. Combining the domain knowledge of the workers and the technical knowledge of the designers is considered a foundation for the development of a useful application (Kensing & Blomberg, 1998).Reviewing several studies on user involvement Damodaran (1996) identified a number of benefits of participating end-users:

- **More accurate user requirements:** Numerous problems or defects in software applications can be traced back to poorly capturing requirements at the beginning of the development process (Borland, 2006). Pekkola et al. (2006) also argue one of the reasons for information system development projects to fail are incomplete requirements. In their studies they found user participation useful in gathering "credible, trustworthy and realistic descriptions of requirements". In turn these accurate user requirements result in an improved system quality (Kujala, 2003).
- **Avoidance of unnecessary or unusable costly system features:** Two of the usability guidelines given by Nielsen (1993) are "Designers are not users" and "Less is more". Designers might think of certain features to incorporate in the application without consulting end-users. Functionalities that are completely logical for developers, might be completely

incomprehensible for users. This might result in users having to spent too much time on learning how to use these functionalities or even not using them. Designers might also have the tendency of incorporating too many options to satisfy 'every' end-user. Besides the fact that users might never know of these options and use them, they can also work contra productive by overwhelming to users. A lot of time and effort for developing these features can be saved by participating end-users.

- **Improved levels of system acceptance:** The levels of system acceptance can be in positively influenced by user involvement in several ways. Among the list Ives & Olsen (1984) have found in other literature are for instance the development of development of realistic expectations about the information system (Gibson, 1977). Also decreasing user resistance against the new system and actually creating commitment for it are other results of user participation (Lucas, 1974). Cherry & Macredie (1999) state participatory design as a means to overcome the acceptability problems systems might encounter without the participation of users.
- **Better understanding of the system by the user:** Logically during the participation users will learn about the system by experiencing the development (Lucas, 1974). This familiarisation also leads to the increase in chances users will come up with suggestions during the development, because they will feel more confident (Robey & Farrow, 1982). In the end this greater understanding should lead to a more effective use of the application.
- **Increased participation in decision-making within the organisation:** Clement & Van den Besselaar (1993) point to the fact that participation is not only restricted to the design of an IT-system. The application

will probably change the way tasks are executed, thus affecting the entire organisation and by participating employees have the possibility to influence this (Robey & Farrow, 1982). It might thus not be restricted to the design of the application, but also to other decision-making processes within the organisation.

Although involving users is considered to be useful, it also introduces a number of difficulties. Firstly, a large amount of a user's knowledge about the process or task the software application will have to support has become tacit (Wood, 1997). It might therefore be hard to get information from these users about the way they work. An example of this was also visible at the Ministry of the Interior. Developers built a certain functionality based on the description of how a task was executed by employees without an application. After implementation however, it became clear in the former way of working an extra file was created by users to keep track of the status of the tasks at hand. Since this was not formally part of the process, they forgot to mention this to the developers. It was thus not incorporated in the new application, while this would have been relatively easy to realise. To overcome this kind of problems it is possible to perform field studies, which have the advantage that users do not have to articulate their needs (Kujala, 2003). Other researchers also suggest the use of (paper) prototypes to counter the difficulties users might have in articulating their needs (Pekkol aet al, 2006; Nielsen, 1993).

Users can also be reluctant to have developers observing them while they work (Butler, 1996). They might express concerns about justifying the time they would have to spent with the design team or disturbing their co-workers. Solutions to this problem are getting commitment from management (Grudin, 1991) and having sessions in separate rooms so no colleagues would have to feel bothered. Besides these problems Butler

(1996) mentions the fact that these sessions are considered to consume a lot of time, as well in planning them, as in executing them. Several researchers also point out the fact that involving users most of the time delivers a large amount of raw data that is difficult to analyse and to use in decision making (Brown, 1996; Rowley, 1996). This will make projects where users participate more time-consuming and thus something development teams want to cut back on. Grudin (1991) also noted the judgement of developers that user involvement would take too much time. However, as already stated, allocating more time upfront will result in a faster cycle time for software developers (Blackburn et al, 2000).

Some members of the design team might simply not have the abilities needed to communicate efficiently with users (Grudin, 1991). They might find it difficult to understand the work situations of users or miss the empathy needed when communicating with users that do not possess the computer skills they have themselves. As a solution to the problematic communication between users and developers, mediators could be brought into action (Pekkola, Niina, & Pasi, 2006). They can act as a bridge between both groups, translating the different concepts from one group to the other. Mock-ups and prototypes from the design team are for instance discussed with users, while user input and feedback is given to the design team. Developers can then focus on the design and implementation of the application instead of having to spent time and effort on user participation methods.

A challenge that occurs even before all of these mentioned is the selection of user representatives and obtaining access to them (Grudin, 1991). Even when a application is developed specifically for one organisation, developers might fear the risk of missing a certain user(group) in their selection. A possible solution is to define a few personas based on intended users. A persona is defined as "an archetype of a user that is given a name and a face, and it is carefully described in terms of

needs, goals and tasks" (Blomquist & Arvola, 2002). This can be useful in organisations that have large groups of users, which makes it tricky to randomly take a small selection out of the total group. Subsequently getting hold of the 'selected' end-users might also pose some difficulties. There might be several barriers like information managers acting as user representatives, but who do not resemble the actual end-user. Also the physical distance between developers and users might create problems. One of the solutions is to; if possible, have the development team working on location of the customer. This way easy access to users is possible (planned or ad hoc).

Early Involvement and Participation of Users

The reasons of having user participation are clearly visible, but when should end-users engaged in the development process? Several researchers suggests that users should be involved early in the process. For instance, if users are used as sources in the requirements capturing process, the number of iterations are less than if they are not (Chatzoglou & Macaulay, 1996). Also capturing usability problems early in the process is very rewarding. Mantei & Teorey (1988) estimate that correcting problems early in the development process cost three times less than correcting them later on. Nielsen (1993) also supports the involvement of users just after the start of the design phase. Regular meetings between users and designers could for instance prevent a mismatch the users' actual task and the developers' model of the task.

In comparing software development firms Blackburn et al. (2000) found that the ones that were considered to have a faster cycle time, were the ones that spent more time on for instance getting customer requirements at the early stages of the project. In their follow-up interviews of their quantitative data analysis, managers mentioned that much time in projects is consumed by rework. To reduce this time it is important to capture the needs of the users early in the development, so before the actual programming has started. In the end this will actually improve the speed and productivity of the software developer.

Damodaran (1996) underlines the justification of early user involvement by pointing to one of the principles of a number of social design approaches. That is, organisations will just postpone the detection of problems if there is no effective user involvement. Again, problems that have to be solved later on in the development, or even after implementation, will result in higher costs.

User participation can take on a number of forms in the development of a software product. Kujala (2003) suggests four main approaches are detectible, which are *user-centred design, participatory design, ethnography* and *contextual design*. Since involving end-users from the beginning of the project is considered very beneficiary, the focus will be on those approaches and methods that take place early in the development process.

Gould & Lewis (1985) in their research on *user-centred design* recommend the early focus on users and direct contact between development team and end-users. This implies doing interviews and discussions with end-users, even before any design has been made. Also people should be observed when performing tasks, as well in the present situation as with prototypes that are developed during the project. Also the design should be iterative, this could for instance be realised by using prototypes that can be reviewed by users.

Participatory design is considered to be a design philosophy instead of a methodology (Cherry & Macredie, 1999). It is not prescriptive and therefore the set of techniques that could be used should be considered open-ended. The approach does have some identifiable principles however, firstly it aims at the production of information systems that improve the work environment. Secondly, users should be actively involved at each stage of the development and finally the development should be under constant review (iterative design). Cherry & Macredie (1999) also mention four important techniques, cooperative

prototyping being the main technique. The other techniques are brainstorming, workshops and organisational gaming.

Ethnography consists of observing and describing the activities of a group, in an attempt to understand these activities (Littlejohn, 2002). In the design of information systems it is defined as developing "a thorough understanding of current work practices as a basis for the design of computer support" (Simonsen & Kensing, 1997). The reason for this is the occurrence of differences in what users say they do, and what they actually do (Nielsen, 1993). The approach is descriptive of nature, is from a member's point-of-view, takes place in natural settings and behaviours should be explained from their context (Blomberg et al, 1993). A typical method of ethnography is observing end-users while they perform their daily work. This can be done following them in their work, so designers being present at the office, or recording the tasks on video and then analysing this footage later on.

Similar to ethnography is *contextual design*. It goal is to help a cross-functional team to agree on what users need and design a system for them (Beyer & Holtzblatt, 1999). The approach focuses on the improvement of the current way of working within an organisation. It thus is not only limited to the design of a system, but also incorporates redesigning the work processes. Users are the main source for data to support decisions on what developments should take place. Specific methods to obtain information from users are (paper) prototyping and contextual inquiry. The latter method is a combination of observing users and interviewing them at the same moment (Beyer & Holtzblatt, 1999).

Co-development, ethnographic methods and contextual inquiry are participatory methods that are located early in the development cycle (Muller, 2001). Most of the approaches actually span the entire development. Table 1 summarises this section and lists the techniques that could be used in the early stages of the development.

Table 1. POTENTIAL early participation methods

Method	Approach (Kujala, 2003)
Observation	User-centred Design / Ethnography
Interviews	User-centred Design
Discussion	User-centred Design
Prototyping	User-centred Design / Participatory Design / Contextual Design
Brainstorming	Participatory Design
Workshops	Participatory Design
Organisational gaming	Participatory Design
Video analysis	Ethnography
Contextual Inquiry	Contextual Design

THE CASE: EMPLOYEE SELF-SERVICE APPLICATIONS

As stated in the previous section the type of system and the contextual environment are important factors to keep in mind when measuring IS success. In this paper we focus on Employee Self-Service (ESS) systems that represent one of the fast developing trends in the domain of e-HRM (Strohmeier, 2007; Ruël et al, 2004). This type of systems is specifically relevant for this study as it directly relates to the issue of user participation, as it aims to empower employees within organizations. ESS is defined by Konradt et al. (2006) as "corporate web portal that enables managers and employees to view, create and maintain relevant personnel information". Konradt et al. also identify four different basis channel functions the ESS can support:

- informing employees about rules and regulations
- providing interaction the access to personal information
- supporting transactions, like applications for leave
- delivering for instance payslips or training videos

All of the above tasks are normally done by the organisations' HR departments. Fister Gale (2003), in her study on three successful ESS implementations, describes reducing the workload of these personnel departments is a major reason for implementation. For instance, changing personal information of employees in often several databases normally had to be done by HR employees. This can now be done by employees themselves by filling in web based forms, resulting in (real-time) updates of the databases of the HR systems. The web based nature of the ESS also offer the possibility to significantly decrease the paperwork that needs to be handled. However, the benefits are not only on the organisations' side, employees also profit from the implementation of ESS. They have instant access to information and the effort needed for certain transactions, like expense claims, is reduced. Managers also benefit from the up-to-date information and easy access to for instance reports, resulting in a better overview over their resources.

ESS and User Satisfaction

Konradt et al. (2006) used the well-known Technology Acceptance Model (TAM; Davis, 1989) to describe the influences of a systems' usefulness and ease of use on user satisfaction and system use. The research model they used in their investigation is depicted in Figure 2. Ease of use related positively to user satisfaction, as well as to usefulness. Usefulness in turn positively influenced both system use and user satisfaction. A final relationship was described between user satisfaction and system use.

A number of implications were drawn from these findings to ensure the success of an ESS implementation. The suggestion that system acceptance is mainly determined by the usefulness of the system and its ease of use, implies that enough attention should be paid to these factors. Informing and involving employees during the development is advised to influence the ease of use and usefulness of the application. It should be clear to employees why it is beneficiary to them to use the ESS, to ensure system acceptance. If users do not accept the system, the workload reduction for HR department will not be realised. Instead of the normal workload, HR employees will be flooded with help requests by users who do not understand the system or even are reluctant to work with it.

Data and Methods

To determine in what ways users are involved or enabled to participate in the development of software applications, interviews were held at four Dutch ministries. The cases are described below.

Emplaza at the Ministry of the Interior and Kingdom Relationships

The person interviewed representing the Ministry of the Interior and Kingdom Relationships is the project leader Self-Service / Emplaza. The application is called Emplaza, a combination of the words *Employability* and *Plaza*.

This self-service human resources application is used by approximately 5,500 civil servants within the Ministry of the Interior and Kingdom Relationships. The application is also used by the Ministry of Agriculture, Nature and Food Quality and the Ministry of Economic Affairs, resulting in a total number of about 17,000 users. The software supports up to twenty HR-processes, for instance applying for leave or filing an appraisal conversation. The application is actually a sort of web application and functions as layer over the actual administrative IT-system. It is built and managed by an external party.

At the time of the interview a new release of the application (version 4.3) was under development. This will be the base for this case description. Since the application is not entirely new some of the reactions of the users can be expected based on experiences from the previous releases. These experiences also influenced the way in which new releases or features are developed. This time however, the release has taken more than a year to develop because of some important differences with previous situations. First of all the builders were new to the project and therefore the advantage of having worked together (as with previous releases) was lost. Second, release 4.3 can be considered larger and more extended in words of number of functionalities. As a result testing the application a considerable amount of extra time

Figure 2. User participation and application success

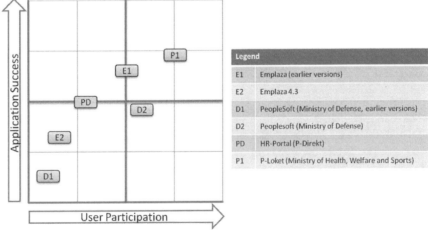

was needed to test this version. Finally, the change in organizational structure with the introduction of P-Direkt (see next section) also took some time to get used to. P-Direkt for instance now takes care of communication between the external builder and the user group of the Ministry.

For the development of the new releases key-users or super-users were selected to participate. These civil servants have a lot of knowledge about the process the application is supposed to support. By interviewing them they current way the process is executed is determined. A next step was to establish which forms should be available to support task within the process. After that the next task was to find out how the forms and workflow should look like in Emplaza. When agreement was found on these issues the Functional Designs were created by the software developer. Before the actual programming started, a number of applications that supported similar HR-processes were investigated. Findings from this analysis formed the starting point of how this should be realized in the Emplaza application.

The key-users are thus very involved in the business rules that need to be implemented in the system. Other aspects they are asked to judge, are the look-and-feel of the user interface and the performance of the application. To do this they have to use test-scripts that will force them through every step and part of the new functionality so they will be able to comment on all the new developments. Members of the HR self-service project team also test the application by looking at it from the viewpoint of a 'new' user. They specifically pay attention to the help texts that are created for the end-users to guide them through certain tasks.

A number of criteria were used in selecting employees to participate in the development of the new release. Participants had to have a lot of knowledge and experience in the field concerning the process at hand. Furthermore, they had to be available to cooperate, i.e. they had to be freed from their normal tasks. Finally, they also had

to be able to think constructively about the new functionality. Most of the time it had become clear in earlier sessions whether or not people met this latter criterion. For testing the application managers are asked to cooperate, they are selected on their position within the organization and thus all have a different role in the HR-process that is going to be implemented in the system. It is tried to have two 'camps': those who are sceptical of ICT and those who feel positive about ICT.

End-users are actually involved just when the new release has gone 'live' i.e. has gone into production. Complaints and issues that come up during the use of the application are gathered and reviewed. These form the foundation for the change proposals that are discussed on a interdepartmental level. During these discussions decisions are taken on which changes really need to be implemented. If end-users are involved earlier after all, most of them come from the central apparatus of the Ministry. The reason for this is that they are located close to the test location. They are chosen as randomly as possible, so no real criteria are used to select participants. This way the development group hopes to get 'fresh' insights about the application.

P-Direkt to be Used Throughout Several Dutch Ministries

In July 2003 the Dutch cabinet chose to start the establishment of a Shared Service Centre (SSC) called P-Direkt. This should be a Human Resource Management SSC for Personnel registration and Salary administration. Although the project had some major problems, it is now still in progress with the same main goal. It should lead to a more efficient HR-column of the government (Ministry of Internal Affairs, 2006). Two identified conditions to reach this goal are joining administrative HR-tasks and the implementation of digital self-service. The latter of these recognised conditions makes P-Direkt an interesting subject to examine and see how user involvement or participation are applied in this project.

The respondent for this interview is the Test manager at P-Direkt and is responsible for the Functional Acceptation Tests and User Acceptation Tests of the HR-Portal that is currently developed. This self-service HR-portal should eventually be used throughout the entire government. In contrast to the Emplaza 4.3 release this is an entirely new application. It is built using mostly standard functionalities of SAP but, if necessary, customization is also applied.

In the process of developing the self-service application users are involved in different ways and at different stages. Right from the start several workgroups are formed. These consist of civil servants from several ministries that in the end will use the application. The members of these groups could be considered end-users, as they will eventually use the application in their normal work. However, they have a lot of knowledge about the HR-processes the application should support. These workgroups are full-time dedicated in the development of the application for a longer period of time. One workgroup for instance has been involved from the start in simplifying and standardizing the HR-processes within the Dutch Government. After twenty-four processes had been defined they formed the basis to build the technical system that should support them. The workgroups were then involved in incorporating the right business rules within this system. An example of such a rule is calculating the maximum compensation that should be granted in different situations.

At the final part of building the application a number of end-users are asked to test the application. This group of end-users do have knowledge about the processes that should be supported, however they were not earlier involved in the development of the application. The involved departments are asked to send one or two employees to take part in the User Acceptation Tests. Per session seven to ten participants are asked to complete the scenarios that are designed to guide them through a certain task. These tasks, for instance filing an expense claim, are subdivided in different steps. This way users cannot only comment on the application in general but also notate findings about specific steps in the process. In this way the scenarios also contribute to being able to easily group comments about certain steps in the process or specific parts from all the different test users. These grouped and summarized comments and findings are then discussed by P-Direkt and the builder of the application. During these discussions it is decided which findings need fixes and those are then built within two to three days. After that a new test session is held to examine whether or not the problems were sufficiently solved.

P-Loket at the Ministry of Health, Welfare and Sport

The Ministry of Health, Welfare and Sport uses an application which is very similar to Emplaza. It is called *P-Loket* and was also developed for the Ministry of Social Affairs & Employment and the General Intelligence & Security Service, because they use the same payroll application. *P-Loket* is a web application, and functions as a layer on top of this payroll application (PersonnelView, or P-View). This situation is thus very comparable to the one at the Ministry of the Interior.

P-Loket is a totally new developed application, which can be used by employees to support them in (personnel) tasks like for instance the filing of a request for leave. In June 2007 around 12 different forms are supported by the application, which can be used by approximately 2,250 civil servants. These numbers should grow to about 18 forms and 5,000 employees by January 2008. The forms and processes that should be supported were chosen based on the outcomes of the standardisation workgroup of the P-Direkt project. The P-Direkt project is also the reason that after the 18 forms are finished no further developments will be done. The P-Direkt application will eventually substitute *P-Loket*.

From the start of the development of the application (in 2006) it was already clear P-Direkt would be the governmental HR self-service application. However, for reasons of more rapidly realisable efficiency benefits and to get used to self-service applications, it was decided to still start the development of *P-Loket*. The first quarter of 2006 was used as preparation and to come up with a plan of how to approach the project. The second quarter of the year was used to prepare for the building, make a process design and setting up authorisations. By the end of June the actual creation of the application could start.

Building the application was done by an external software company that also created the P-View application. *P-Loket* was also a totally new developed application for them. However, P-View and P-Loket are quite similar web applications, which had some advantages. The links for instance that had to be available, were already more or less present and thus had not to be created completely from scratch. They had one developer working full-time on the project.

Employees of the Ministry were involved in several ways during the development. The project group that was formed at the start consisted of hr-employees, members of the audit service and two employees of the Information & Communication department. The latter two were experts on web (applications) and usability. Both these experts had the task to look at the application from a user perspective. The usability expert for instance discussed a number of prototypes (on screen) with the builder. By asking questions like "what will happen if a user clicks this button?" issues could already be addressed before anything was programmed. Apart from the experts the project group members did not attend to the User Interface of the application. Their focal point was on the business rules that should be implemented.

Next to the fact that users were represented in the project group, other civil servants were asked to cooperate in an usability test. This test was carried out by a third party and the main reason was to resolve usability issues the software builder

and the usability expert from the project could not agree on. The test was carried out with one test person and a guide in one room, observers were in another room to take notes and film the session with a camera. In selecting employees to take part in this test, the project group tried to have a balance in computer skills, male/female ratio and office/field staff ratio. To find eight participants, contact persons were asked if they knew employees that fitted the necessary characteristics.

Another way to involve end-users was to have sessions with managers to discuss the functionality that supports performance review conversations with them. Per session the application was demonstrated to three to twelve managers. It took roughly five weeks to complete the sessions with two hundred and fifty managers. Managers could immediately deliver feedback in the form of questions or remarks during the demonstration. Although this way of involving end-users took considerable time and effort, it was considered to be very useful and contributing to the acceptance of the application. One of the strengths of having different sessions was that certain issues came up in numerous occasions. This made it easier to establish the importance of a problem or request. The issues from the different sessions were combined and for each issue the urgency was determined. Subsequently the impact of solutions for these issues was discussed with software developer.

Also the fact that the project group was located in the same offices as end-users that were not in the project group offered the possibility to ask these colleagues for their opinions in an informal ad hoc way. The project group gratefully made use of this opportunity during the development of P-Loket.

PeopleSoft/HR at the Ministry Of Defence

The Ministry of Defence started implementing self-service on HR-processes in 2004, but without involving end-users. As a result the users started having wrong interpretations about the application.

Therefore the Ministry started with improving the self-service parts of the application in 2006. The application is based on the PeopleSoft HR-system and the first processes to be supported were looking into personal data, filing requests for leave and filing requests for foreign official tours. Approximately 80,000 users make use of the software, of which about 65,000 are permanent staff of the Ministry. Besides this large group of users another point of consideration is the sometimes disrupted relationship with the formal superior. This is due to frequent shifts within the organisation, for instance staff being posted abroad for military operations. As a result the application should offer the possibility to delegate certain tasks to other superiors, planners and/or secretaries. It took about one and a half years from the beginning of the project until the improved application went live. As a start it was determined which people and processes should be supported. Subsequently the possibilities of the (then) current application were investigated. There were three important points of departure:

- Outcomes of using should be visible to the user
- Employees use the application in good faith ("the user does nothing wrong")
- No training should be necessary to use the application.

The main idea behind this is that the development should not only be seen as supporting a processes by an application, but also supporting users in their actions when using the application. Usability research was done by someone from outside the Ministry who had no knowledge of HR-processes or PeopleSoft. This person asked the civil servants how the current application was used. Some consultancy was done by external parties, but it felt most of the work was done by the internal organisation to come up with the advises and reports. Besides the usability research, users were also involved in other ways. Employees

with reasonable knowledge and skills about IT were asked to name functional gaps in how the support of certain processes. Next to that case studies were done by randomly asking people in the organisation to perform tasks with the application. They only got a short introduction of the task and the reassurance they could do nothing wrong. So nothing about how the application worked was explained. After this users were observed completing the tasks, while they were invited to think-aloud. The moments when users hesitated or were in doubt, were explained as moments in the process the application should offer help. The outcomes of this test were thus:

- Information on how the application was used
- Whether or not concepts and descriptions were interpreted as intended
- Functional problems

Insights in perceptions on what has happened by performing this task ("what will be the next steps in the organisation?")

These outcomes findings were incorporated in the improved version of the software. It would be valuable to perform such a test again now the build is complete, however at the moment there is no time available to do this.

Demands for support and help options are not the same for every user, for instance because of the mentioned differences in IT-skills. One of the tools for help within the PeopleSoft application is the "See, Try, Know, Do" principle. Users can first look at a demonstration (see) before trying it themselves in a simulation mode (try). A next step is then to take a test to check if they understand everything (know), before finally actually performing the task with the application (do). Users can use one or more of these functions to support them in the use of the software.

In choosing people for the tests information managers were asked if they could point out employees that met certain criteria. One criterion for instance was whether or not they were very skilled in using IT. Although there were some criteria, no standard profiles were used to categorise users in groups. To confront these users with the improved application, during the development, prototypes were used.

Cross-Case Comparison Analysis

The four case studies presented in the preceding sections have several things in common. First of all, they are of course all developments for a governmental organisation. Secondly, they clearly all support self-service on Human Resource processes. Thirdly, they all serve a large number of users, the HR self-service applications have a range from 5,000 to 80,000. The fourth parallel is that in all cases external organisations were hired to assist in the development, although in the case of the Ministry of Defence this was mostly limited to advisory reports.

The previous sections also show that users are involved or are able to participate in the development of IT-systems in the Dutch government. Table 2 depicts the different ways users participated in the different cases that were discussed.

It is clearly visible that users get most attention during the test phase of the development. In all of the discussed applications end-users have participated in one or more tests during the development. Logically, this testing found place in later phases, however in three cases prototypes were used to be able to show users (parts of) the application earlier in the process of development. Non-expert end-users that participated from the start of the projects were visible in two cases (P-Loket at the Ministry Of Health Welfare and Sport and PeopleSoft/HR at the Ministry Of Defence). Most of the users that were engaged from the start had expert knowledge on the processes that were computerised by the implementation of the application. Of particular interest is how the participation of end-users might have influenced the success of the applications in question. Figure 3

Table 2. Used methods to involve end-users

	Prototypes	Testing	Use-research
Emplaza at the Ministry of the Interior And Kingdom Relation-ships		✗	
P-Direkt to be used throughout several Dutch Min-istries		✗	
P-Loket at the Ministry Of Health, Welfare and Sport	✗	✗	
PeopleSoft/ HR at the Ministry Of Defence	✗	✗	✗

has the different applications from the interviews depicted in a diagram that scores them on success (y-axis) and user participation (x-axis). Their position on both axes is based on the interviews, but is of course subjectively determined. It is not meant to imply that any of the applications is 'better' than the others. The concept of 'application success' is seen from the viewpoint of each organisation and is based on:

- Time and effort needed for development (relative to the amount of features)
- Number of problems encountered during tests and implementation
- Satisfaction with the end-product
- Contribution to increase in efficiency of the supported tasks

As a final step to complete the four case studies among the Dutch Ministries, additional information about the (perceived) success of the ESS-applications was collected. This was conducted through one short personal e-mail sent to the interviewees, containing six system quality criteria for which an answer on a 5point scale was requested:

- The number of problems reported by users in the user (acceptation) tests (ranging from 1 being "very few" to 5 being "seriously many")
- The amount of rework needed after testing (ranging from 1 being "very little" to 5 being "very much")
- Current satisfaction with the application by end-users (ranging from 1 being "very dissatisfied" to 5 being "very satisfied")

- The amount of questions that reached the helpdesk shortly after implementation (ranging from 1 being "very few" to 5 being "seriously many")
- Contribution of the application to the increase in satisfaction (ranging from 1 being "very little" to 5 being "very much")
- The overall success of the application (ranging from 1 being "very low" to 5 being "very high")

Table 3 shows the answers of the respondents that were queried for four different Ministries/cases.

Table 3. Scores by respondents to extra questions

	Emplaza at the Ministry of the Interior and Kingdom Relationships	PeopleSoft/HR at the Ministry Of Defence	P-Loket at the Ministry Of Health, Welfare and Sport	P-Direkt to be used throughout several Dutch Ministries
1 Reported problems after test	5	3	2	2
2 Amount of rework needed	5	4	4	1
3 Current satisfaction level	4	4	4	n/a
4 Questions at helpdesk	2	3	4	n/a
5 Contribution to efficiency	4	2	4	n/a
6 Overall success	3	2	4	n/a

Figure 3. User participation and application success

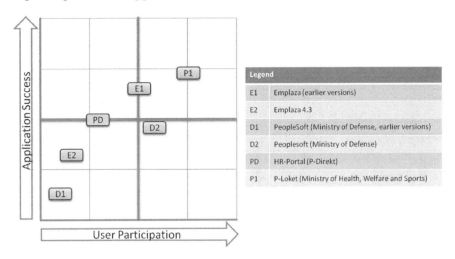

Based on these additional data, the actual relation between early user involvement, satisfaction and application success can be estimated for the four cases under investigation. Before we do so, some remarks beforehand.

First, it should e noted that for Emplaza both the latest version (4.3) and earlier versions were investigated (E1). During the interviews it became clear that in earlier versions a lot more user participation was applied. The short communication lines resulting from the programming team working on the same location as users, made sure users could be frequently consulted. At the deployment of Emplaza 4.3 end-users were involved, but not at all before a working product was developed. A number of problems arose in the development and testing of the 4.3 version. Some functionalities could for instance not be implemented on time, because tests by key users revealed to many hick-ups. User satisfaction with the functionalities that could be implemented on time however, was considered to be reasonable high. Also, it would not be fair to let the low score on participation of end-users to be the only reason for the low score on application success. There were numerous other problems mentioned that contributed to the difficult development of Emplaza 4.3, as described in section 3.2.1. Before these problems are solved however, earlier versions can be considered relatively more successful than the latest one.

Secondly, it needs to be considered that the PeopleSoft/HR application also has earlier versions as ESS within the Ministry of Defence. In the use of the initial version users encountered too many problems. So, the second version was developed to be an improvement of the first version. A lot more attention for usability went hand in hand with the increasing possibilities for users to participate in the development. A lot of problems were therefore found, resulting in quite a lot of rework. Although not all difficulties for users could be solved the second version was considered to be superior to its predecessor. This thus shows in participation, so the second version is placed more to the right

of the graph. However, the success positioning is not as high as might be expected with regard to the amount of user participation. This mainly has to do with the low scores on contribution to efficiency and the overall success rating of the application by the respondent.

Thirdly, it appeared that the P-Direkt application to be used by several Ministries, is hard to compare with regard to its success as Table 3 indicates. For questions 1 and 2, the scores by the respondent were given 2 and 1 respectively. The current application is still only partly implemented and used by two departments, while the goal is to use it at all government departments. Therefore questions 3 to 6 are not applicable in this case.

Fourth and final, we need to clarify how we quantified user participation in order to score the four cases on this dimension and plot it against their application successes. We judged that the Ministry of Health, Welfare and Sports demonstrated relatively the most time and effort spent on user participation. For instance all managers were approached by demo sessions and invited to comment on the application. Although the different approaches used are less than with the Ministry of Defence, the relative amount of time spent is considered to be more, so the P-Loket application is considered to score higher on user participation than the second ESS-version at the Ministry of Defence. Besides the delay in the start of the project, not a lot of problems arose during the development of the application. Also most of the problems users experienced with the application were caught in the different tests during the development. The amount of rework to be done, was therefore considered 'much', but it could be done early in the development. Since the application introduced self-service, it contributed a lot to the efficiency of the organisation. From the interviews it became clear that users participated less in the cases of Emplaza 4.3 and the first version of the Ministry of Defence, therefore the are ordered at the lower end of this dimension.

Given these remarks, the user participation and application scores for the different cases are plotted in Figure 3, recognizing that for two cases actually two measurements in time are included.

Without claiming to have precise measurements and quantifications, Figure 3 clearly confirms that user participation is positively related to (perceived) application success. This is supported by both cross-sectional comparing the four cases, as well as comparing the two Emplaza and People-Soft/HR cases over time. The implications of this hypothesized and convincing result are discussed in next closing section.

CONCLUSION AND DISCUSSION

This paper departed from an analysis of current literature on information system success, user satisfaction and user involvement. A number of researches were found that described what factors influenced the success of information systems. From the DeLone & McLean IS Success Model the concepts of system quality, (intention to) use and user satisfaction were found to be important influential factors. Other findings mentioned the influence of perceived usefulness and perceived ease of use on user satisfaction and intention to use. Subsequently these concepts could be influenced by the involvement of users in the development process of new software applications. Next to this a distinction between the concepts of involvement and participation was suggested. Several findings of positive relationships between user participation, involvement and system success were presented. In the end the literature study was combined into a conceptual model. This model visualised the mentioned links between a number of concepts of the DeLone & McLean's IS Success Model, the Technology Acceptance Model and User Involvement & Participation.

The case studies portrayed are based on interviews with civil servants employed at different governmental organisations. One of the outcomes was a list of currently used user participation methods. In line with the findings from the literature study respondents also argued that users should be involved early, however, not too early because it would delay the development process too much. The challenges faced with involving users also did not deviate from the literature section.

Investigating the cases points also to the positive effect of user participation on the success of an application. Projects that have users participating in the development seem to be more successful than the ones that show less user participation. The only clearly visible exception is the case of the Ministry of Defence. It might be hard to compare the success of the different applications, however the differences between versions of applications are obvious (Emplaza and the Ministry of Defence).Besides this confirmation of the positive results of user participation, also a number of lessons can be learned when studying these cases. A number of hints and points of attention were even explicitly mentioned by the respondents with regard to user participation. A number of important hints are listed below:

- **User participation requires time and a good schedule:** It is important to think about the consequences of participating end-users. Input from users will need gathered and put in order, this takes time. Subsequently the results need to be analysed to for instance decide which requirements should be incorporated in the design or which findings should be solved. Using MOSCOW-lists, it is possible to rank requirements and suggestions in "must have", "should have", "could have" and "would have" items. To ensure the project stays on schedule, it is necessary to set deadlines when decisions need to be made, otherwise endless discussions might arise and requirements will keep changing. Also concerning scheduling is to make sure end-user are brought after some basic ideas are already thought of by the development team.

- **Try to find motivated end-users and have something to show them:** In choosing users to have participating in the project, try to find the ones that will be motivated to constructively think about the application. It might not be an easy task to do this in such large organisations, but the network of the project group or managers could be asked to produce a list of possible participators. To enable this set of end-users to come up with useful suggestions, it is wise to visualise parts of the application already. People will find it difficult to supply ideas without something they can see, even a simple mock-up will be fine to start a discussion.

- **Keep in mind the overall process that needs to be supported or automated:** The development of the self-service application itself is not the main goal of the project. There is a process or task that needs to be automated or supported. When designing, developing and testing always keep in mind this process or task. For instance observe users when executing a task to find out what other processes might be linked to this task. Or, when testing, ask the test person about his or her perceptions on what has happened and what the next step in the process will be.

- **Development team on location:** Having the development team close to end-users, for instance on location, shortens the communication lines. This enables more frequent consultation between end-users and programmers concerning for instance uncertainties about requirements or just asking user's opinions on what has been developed thus far. Being able to follow the progress more easily will also positively influence the involvement of end-users.

- **Expectancy management:** Make sure to tell participating users what will be done with their input and why. Not all of their suggestions and problems might be implemented or solved. In ensuring they maintain willing to cooperate it is important to communicate why certain decisions have been made and why some of their input is not visible in the developed application.

A number of additional lessons were mentioned by the respondents. It was mentioned to keep in mind employees should be able to use the self-service applications without too much support from the HR-departments. Otherwise it would only be a shift of the workload for the HR-department from HR-tasks to supporting users with the use of the application. In that case the organisations would not show the targeted improvements in efficiency. A third important aspect to take into account is the distinct decision process organisations like the Ministry have. This was a confirmation of one of the points in the report of The Netherlands Court of Audit. The decision process includes fairly a lot of people, takes considerable time and can be politically oriented.

REFERENCES

Barki, H., & Hartwick, J. (1989). Rethinking the concept of user involvement. *Rethinking the Concept of User Involvement*, *13*(1), 53–63.

Baroudi, J. J., Olson, M. H., & Ives, B. (1986). An empirical study of the. *Communications of the ACM*, *29*(3), 232–238. doi:10.1145/5666.5669

Beyer, H., & Holtzblatt, K. (1999). Contextual design. *Interaction*, *6*(1), 32–42. doi:10.1145/291224.291229

Blackburn, J., Scudder, G., & Van Wassenhove, L. N. (2000). Concurrent software development. *Communications of the ACM, 43*(11), 200–214. doi:10.1145/352515.352519

Blomberg, J., Giacomi, J., Mosher, A., & Swenton-Hall, P. (1993). Ethnographic field methods and their relation to design. In D. Schuler, & A. Namioka (Eds.), Participatory Design: Principles and Practices (pp. 123-155). Hillsdale: Lawrence Erlbaum.

Blomquist, Å., & Arvola, M. (2002). Personas in action: ethnography in an interaction design team. *Proceedings of the second Nordic conference on Human-computer interaction* (pp. 197 - 200). ACM.

Borland. (2006). Retrieved April 25, 2007, from http://www.borland.com/resources/en/pdf/solutions/rdm_whitepaper.pdf

Brown, D. (1996). The challenges of user-based design in a medical equipment market. In D. Wixon, & J. Ramey (Ed.), Field Methods Casebook for Software Design (pp. 157-176). New York: Wiley.

Butler, M. B. (1996). Getting to know your users: usability roundtables at lotus development. *Interaction, 3*(1), 23–30. doi:10.1145/223500.223507

Chatzoglou, P. D., & Macaulay, L. A. (1996). Requirements capture and analysis: a survey of current practice. *Requirements Engineering*, (2): 75–87. doi:10.1007/BF01235903

Chatzoglou, P. D., & Macaulay, L. A. (1996). Requirements capture and analysis: a survey of current practice. *Requirements Engineering, 1*(2), 75–87. doi:10.1007/BF01235903

Cherry, C., & Macredie, R. D. (1999). The importance of context in information system design: an assesment of participatory design. *Requirements Engineering, 4*(2), 103–114. doi:10.1007/s007660050017

Clement, A., & Van den Besselaar, P. (1993). A retrospective look at PD projects. *Communications of the ACM, 36*(6), 29–37. doi:10.1145/153571.163264

Damodaran, L. (1996). User involvement in the systems design process-a practical guide for users. *Behaviour & Information Technology, 15*(6), 363–377. doi:10.1080/014492996120049

Davis, F. D. (1989). Perceived usefulness, perceived ease of use, and user acceptance of information technology. *MIS Quarterly, 13*(3), 319–340. doi:10.2307/249008

DeLone, W. H., & McLean, E. R. (1992). Information system success: The quest for the independent variable. *Information Systems Research, 3*(1), 60–95. doi:10.1287/isre.3.1.60

DeLone, W. H., & McLean, E. R. (2003). The DeLone and McLean model of information success: a ten-year update. *Journal of Management Information Systems, 19*(4), 9–30.

Dutch Court of Audit. (2007). Lessons from IT-projects at the government [*Lessen uit ICT-projecten bij de overheid*] Retrieved from http://www.rekenkamer.nl/9282000/d/p425_rapport1.pdf.

Fister Gale, S. (2003). Three stories of self-service success. *Workforce, 82*(1), 60–63.

Gibson, H. (1977). Determining User Involvement. *Journal of System Management*, 20-22.

Gould, J. D., & Lewis, C. (1985). Designing for usability: key principles and what designers think. *Communications of the ACM, 28*(3), 300–311. doi:10.1145/3166.3170

Grudin, J. (1991). Systematic sources of suboptimal interface design in large product development organization. *Human-Computer Interaction, 6*(2), 147–196. doi:10.1207/s15327051hci0602_3

Ives, B., & Olson, M. H. (1984). User involvement and mis success: a review of research. *Management Science*, *30*(5), 586–603. doi:10.1287/mnsc.30.5.586

Ives, B., Olson, M. H., & Baroudi, J. J. (1983). The measurement of user information satisfaction. *Communications of the ACM*, *26*(10), 785–793. doi:10.1145/358413.358430

Janssen, M., & Joha, A. (2006). Motives for establishing shared service centers in public administrations. *International Journal of Information Management*, *26*(2), 102–115. doi:10.1016/j.ijinfomgt.2005.11.006

Kensing, F., & Blomberg, J. (1998). Participatory Design: Issues and Concerns. *Computer Supported Cooperative Work*, *7*(3/4), 167–185. doi:10.1023/A:1008689307411

Konradt, U., Christophersen, T., & Schaeffer-Kuelz, U. (2006). Predicting user satisfaction, strain and system usage of employee self-services. *International Journal of Human-Computer Studies*, *64*(11), 1141–1153. doi:10.1016/j.ijhcs.2006.07.001

Kujala, S. (2003). User involvement: a review of the benefits and challenges. *Behaviour & Information Technology*, *22*(1), 1–16. doi:10.1080/01449290301782

Lin, W. T., & Shao, B. B. (2000). The relationship between user participation and system success: a simultaneous contingency approach. *Information & Management*, *37*(6), 283–295. doi:10.1016/S0378-7206(99)00055-5

Littlejohn, S. W. (2002). Theories of Human Communication. Belmont: Wadsworth/Thomson Learning.

Lucas, H. J. (1974). Systems quality, user reactions, and the use of information systems. *Management Informatics*, *3*(4), 207–212.

Mantei, M. M., & Teorey, T. J. (1988). Cost/benefit analysis for incorporating human factors in the software lifecycle. *Communications of the ACM*, *31*(4), 428–439. doi:10.1145/42404.42408

Mason, R. O. (1978). Measuring information output: A communication systems approach. *Information & Management*, *1*(4), 219–234. doi:10.1016/0378-7206(78)90028-9

McKeen, J. D., & Guimaraes, T. (1997). Successful strategies for user participation in systems development. *Journal of Management Information Systems*, *14*(2), 133–150.

McKeen, J. D., Guimaraes, T., & Wetherbe, J. C. (1994). The Relationship between user participation and user satisfaction: an investigation of four contingency factors. *MIS Quarterly*, *18*(4), 427–451. doi:10.2307/249523

Ministerie van Binnenlandse Zaken en Koninkrijksrelaties. (2007). *Nota Vernieuwing Rijksdienst.* Retrieved Februari 08, 2008, from http://www.minbzk.nl/aspx/download.aspx?file=/contents/pages/89897/notavernieuwingrijksdienst.pdf

Ministry of Internal Affairs. (2006). Press statement Retrieved July 21, 2007, from P-Direkt: http://www.p-direkt.nl/index.cfm?action=dsp_actueelitem&itemid=QKNGJL8E.

Muller, M. (2001). A participatory poster of participatory methods. *Conference on Human Factors in Computing Systems, CHI '01 extended abstracts on Human factors in computing systems*, (pp. 99 - 100).

Nielsen, J. (1993). Usability Engineering. San Diego: Academic Press.

Noyes, P. M., Starr, A. F., & Frankish, C. R. (1996). User involvement in the early stages of an aircraft warning system. *Behaviour & Information Technology*, *15*(2), 67–75. doi:10.1080/014492996120274

Pekkola, S., Niina, K., & Pasi, P. (2006). Towards Formalised End-User Participation in Information Systems Development Process: Bridging the Gap between Participatory Design and ISD Methodologies. *Proceedings of the ninth Participatory Design Conference 2006*, 21-30.

Robey, D., & Farrow, D. (1982). User Involvement in Information System Development: A Conflict Model and Empirical Test. *Management Science*, *28*(1), 73–85. doi:10.1287/mnsc.28.1.73

Rowley, D. E. (1996). Organizational considerations in field-oriented product development: Experiences of a cross-functional team. In D. Wixon, & J. Ramey (Eds.), Methods Casebook for Software Design (pp. 125 - 144). New York: Wiley.

Ruël, H., Bondarouk, T., & Looise, J. K. (2004). E-HRM: innovation or irritation. an explorative empirical study in five large companies on Web-based HRM. *Management Review*, *15*(3), 364–380.

Saarinen, T. (1996). SOS An expanded instrument for evaluating information system success. *Information & Management*, *31*(2), 103–118. doi:10.1016/S0378-7206(96)01075-0

Shannon, C. E., & Weaver, W. (1949). The mathematical theory of communication. Urbana: University of Illinois Press.

Shapiro, D. (2005). Participatory design: the will to succeed. *Proceedings of the 4th decennial conference on Critical computing: between sense and sensibility*, (pp. 29-38). Aarhus, Denmark.

Simonsen, J., & Kensing, F. (1997). Using ethnography in contextural design. *Communications of the ACM*, *40*(7), 82–88. doi:10.1145/256175.256190

Strohmeier, S. (2007). Research in e-HRM: Review and implications. *Human Resource Management Review*, *17*(1), 19–37. doi:10.1016/j.hrmr.2006.11.002

Verheijen, T. (2007). Gestrikt: E-HRM komt er uiteindelijk toch. *Personeelsbeleid*, *43*(11), 20–23.

Wood, L. E. (1997). Semi-structured interviewing for user-centered design. *Interaction*, *4*(2), 48–61. doi:10.1145/245129.245134

KEY TERMS

Application Deployment: The adoption, implementation and usage of an information system or IT application within the context of a organization

Employee Self-Service: Corporate web portal that enables managers and employees to view, create and maintain relevant personnel information

Shared Service Centres (SSC): Newly created organization units, mostly implemented in large organizations to centralize supportive activities as administration, facilities, HR and IT-services

Semi-Structured (topic) Interviews: Case study method to collect qualitative and/or intangible data by questioning pre-selected respondents in a non-conditional, informal setting.

User Participation: Assignments, activities, and behaviors that users or their representatives perform during the systems development process

User Involvement: A subjective psychological state reflecting the importance and personal relevance that a user attaches to a given system

User Satisfaction: Subjective judgment of the information system by the user. Used as a measure for the success of an information system

Index

Symbols

3D model 1283, 1287, 1288, 1289, 1294
3D modeling system 1282, 1287
3D modeling tools 1288
3D production systems 1287

A

ability 846
acceptable sacrifice 496
acceptance behavior 1265
access control 678, 679, 684, 686, 698-704
accessibility 332, 336
accounting practices 1027
Acousto-Optic Tunable Filters (AOTFs) 2023
active information 1957
Active Server Pages (ASP) 1869
activity diagrams 680
Activity-Based Costing (ABC) 1985
Actor Network Theory (ANT) 1266, 1668-1673,
        1677, 1683, 1684, 1686, 1687
adaptive execution 527, 535, 537, 538
additive 711
Adjusted Goodness of Fit Index (AGFI) 1792
Administration on Aging (AoA) 1647, 1649
ADvanced Object Modeling Environment (ADOME)
        216, 220, 240
Agence d'Évaluation des Technologies et des Modes
        d'Intervention en Santé (AETMIS) 1925
agent-based modeling 202
agents 653, 655, 658
Agglomeration schedule 338
Aging and Disability Resource Center (ADRC)
        1647-1662, 1665-1667
agricultural products 723

Akaike Information Criterion (AIC) 207
ALDUS project 1620, 1627
algorithm 885, 888-893, 897, 903, 904, 906
aligning ontologies 652
alignment 94, 95, 99, 100, 101, 103, 105
ambient intelligence (AmI) 394, 395, 397
American Institute of Certified Public Accountants
        (AICPA) 1042
amin scenario 313-317, 321, 322
analysis 490, 721
Analytic Periodical Statement (APS) 1041, 1054
angle of arrival (AOA) 762
application front end 75
Application Infrastructure Provider (AIP) 47, 49
application portfolio 561
Application Programming Interface (API) 75, 151,
        156, 157, 159, 162, 164, 165, 607, 608, 626,
        920, 1209, 1218
Application Service Provider (ASP) 44-49, 86, 92,
        498, 1096
application services 583, 584, 585, 587-592, 594,
        595, 596, 597
architecture 913, 916-922, 925-932, 935, 936
ARchitecture of Integrated Information Systems
        (ARIS) 287, 288, 298, 299, 305, 307
Artificial Intelligence (AI) 110, 115, 125, 132, 529
aspect-oriented security modeling 678
Aspect-Oriented Software Development (AOSD) 67,
        69
assignment 1643, 1644
Assisted GPS (A-GPS) 762, 764
assistive technology 1661, 1951, 1952, 1957
Asymmetric Digital Subscriber Line (ADSL) 1051,
        1059
Asynchronous Transfer Mode (ATM) 1804

F